Copyright © 2018 John Lobell

Copyright © 2001 Mimi Lobell

Published in the United States

All rights reserved. This book may not be reproduced in whole or in part, stored in a retrieval system, or transmitted in any form or by any means electronic, mechanical, or other without written permission from the publisher, except by a reviewer, who may quote brief passages in a review.

Published by
JXJ Publications
A Division of JXJ Productions, Inc.
JXJPublications@gmail.com
ISBN-13: 978-1986180030
ISBN-10: 1986180034
Also available on Kindle
Information at MimiLobell.com

Printed in the United States of America

1. Architecture. 2. Feminism.
3. Archeology. 4. Spirituality.

Book design by Anthony Iatridis

BRIEF CONTENTS

PREFACE BY JOHN LOBELL i
PREFACE BY CRISTINA BIAGGI ix
INTRODUCTION 1
THE SENSITIVE CHAOS 17
THE GREAT ROUND 67
THE FOUR QUARTERS 133
THE PYRAMID 201
THE RADIANT AXES 281
THE GRID 325
THE DISSOLUTION 393
CONCLUSION BY JOHN LOBELL 397

APPENDICES 399
ENDNOTES 463
BIBLIOGRAPHY 493
DETAILED CONTENTS 537
ACKNOWLEDGMENTS 543
ABOUT MIMI LOBELL 547

Mimi Lobell

PREFACE

By John Lobell

A Remarkable Book

I wish to introduce you to a remarkable book by a remarkable person. Mimi Lobell, my late wife, was a force of the cosmos, someone who took up the space around her and and pulled the currents of cosmic energy through her. She read, studied, traveled, designed, experienced. She was an architect, a scholar, a professor, a mentor, a spiritual being, and much more. And she approached all that she did with a powerful mind and an appetite for life.

This is a book about cultures, about how cultures move through archetypes over their histories, but it is unlike other books that attempt to cover such material. It absorbs Oswald Spengler's morphological patterns, Joseph Campbell's mythological insights, Carl Jung's depth psychology, and the Goddess scholarship to which Mimi made major contributions. And then with access to the remarkable advances in archeological scholarship of the latter half of the twentieth century, plus a deep awareness that architecture is the crystallization of a culture into form, Mimi's work goes further than any previous study in understanding the patterns of human development. Cultures are symbolic entities, a notion not understood in current materialist approaches to culture but presented in *Mimi Lobell's Spatial Archetypes: The Hidden Patterns of Psyche and Civilization*. It is a book rich with insights that gives us a deeper understanding of cultures and ourselves.

Mimi's Approach

Oswald Spengler published his *Decline of the West* between 1918 and 1923. It was immensely popular and widely discussed, as it seemed to describe the decline of Western civilization experienced after the Great War. But much of the book is actually about something else, about the nature of cultures. Spengler rejects the Eurocentric model of history that sees a progression from primitive to ancient to Greece and Rome to the Middle Ages to the Renaissance to the modern world, with some non-Western cultures as footnotes. Instead he says that there have been nine major high cultures: Babylonian, Egyptian, Chinese, Indian, Meso-American, Greek and Roman, Arabian, Russian, and Western.

For Spengler, each culture is an independent entity with its own "psychology," which Spengler calls its "Prime Symbol." And each culture goes through "stages" which he describes with seasonal analogies (spring, summer, autumn, winter) and with organic analogies (from youth to old age and death). Spengler begins each of his descriptions with the emergence of the high civilization but is unable to describe what comes before, saying that cultures "bloom with the randomness of the wild flowers of the field." Mimi completes what Spengler could not, going back before the emergences of each of the high civilizations.

The mythologist Joseph Campbell, who was influenced by Spengler, began his career by identifying the archetype of the Hero Journey that we see in fairy tales, mythology, literature, and religion: separation from ordinary reality, a journey to a realm of fabulous forces, the winning of a decisive victory, and a return to enrich the world. The Hero Journey is an archetype. The manifestation comes in thousands of stories from that of Odysseus to that of Luke Skywalker. Campbell went on to look at the differences between cultures, for example the identification with transcendent oneness in the East and the emphasis on the individual in the West. But Campbell was struggling to bring into focus the morphology of cultural stages in his unfinished last work, a morphology that Mimi resolves with her seven Spatial Archetypes.

We also find this notion of archetype and manifestation in the work of Carl Jung, who was influential on both Campbell and Mimi. But just as important to Mimi was Jung's notions of individuation and of the collective unconscious. Individuation is the process whereby a fully integrated Self emerges out the components of the immature psyche. Mimi shows how this process is different in different historical periods (her Spatial Archetypes); thus she develops a historical psychology. Jung's collective unconscious is a complex and often misunderstood notion, but it has to do with the relationship between archetypes and their manifestations, notions well developed by Mimi in this book.

Finally, as a woman, Mimi brought a totally new perspective to this material. In the 1960s and 1970s work was being done that demonstrated a male bias in academia, psychology, and spirituality, and that entire histories of female-centered cultures and historical goddesses were being suppressed, and Mimi's approach was in the context of that work.

Spiritual Feminism

The 1960s saw the emergence of what is now called second-wave feminism. (What is now called first-wave feminism was associated with the women's suffrage movement.) Second-wave feminism was focused on gender roles, sexuality, family, the workplace, reproductive rights, and inequalities between men and women. When Mimi got out of school, the help wanted sections of newspapers were divided into male and female. You can imagine which section advertised for architects. Faculty members in architecture schools might occasionally say to a woman student something like, "I am not going to waste my time with you, you are just going to get married and have babies." Although Mimi never experienced anything like that at the University of Pennsylvania where she studied architecture, she did have some difficult experiences as a woman in some architectural offices where she worked and as a faculty member in the School of Architecture at Pratt Institute.

Mimi became involved in the women's movement in architecture. She was one of the originators of an exhibit at the Brooklyn Museum in 1977 titled "Women in American Architecture." She co-founded the Alliance of Women in Architecture and The Archive of Women in Architecture and briefly explored, with several colleagues, creating an office of women architects. These efforts lead to some interesting questions. Should women be brought into more prominent roles in architectural offices and schools because they are just as good as men? And if so, what is to be gained by the offices and schools? Or should women be brought into more prominent roles because they have something different to offer? And if so, what might that be, and if it is kitchens, is that not perpetuating a discriminatory stereotype? Advocates for enhancing the role of women in architecture took both sides, but Mimi came to approach the issues of women in general and women in architecture from a different perspective. To see from this perspective, we have to back up for a moment.

In the 1960s Mimi began various spiritual studies including Tai Chi with Professor Cheng Man-ch'ing, Buddhism with Chogyam Trungpa and others, and shamanism with Michael Harner. She attended lectures on mythology by Joseph Campbell, read the works of Carl Jung, and attended lectures at the New York Jung Foundation and the New York Open Center. And she later regularly lectured on the material you see in this book at the Jung Foundation and the Open Center. While she found all of this enriching, she also found all of it male-centered. She had become friends with Jan Clanton, a Jungian analyst, and together they began to explore feminine spiritual perspectives.

Around the time Mimi began to have these interests, scholarship began to appear about goddesses in ancient cultures. In 1974 Marija Gimbutas, a well respected scholar, published *The Gods and Goddesses of Old Europe* (only later did her publisher allow her to change the title to what she originally intended, *The Goddesses and Gods of Old Europe*). Gimbutas's thesis is that Eurasia was filled with Neolithic egalitarian goddess-worshiping cultures. These cultures were overrun by Indo-Europeans who worshiped gods and brought war and a male-dominated hierarchical culture wherever they went. (You will find extensive references to this in Mimi's book.) Gimbutas had few written records to work from, so she did her work from fragmentary artifacts, ruins, folktales, myths, languages, and other material that she would piece together, an approach that Mimi also used. In 1976 Merlin Stone published *When God Was a Woman*. Mimi began working with psychologists interested in "the feminine principle," and with scholars interested in "the Goddess" and female-centered cultures.

At the same time there was a growing interest in all kinds of spirituality, including in Buddhism and Shamanism, and as I mentioned earlier, Mimi became involved with leading teachers and spiritual leaders in various disciplines. Many people were lumping all of this together into a generalized spiritual interest. One of Mimi's contributions was to sort it out. Shamanism, she realized, is a Paleolithic Sensitive Chaos discipline. The Goddess belongs to the Neolithic Great Round. And Buddhism belongs to the periods of the Four Quarters and Pyramid archetypes. (All of which is explained in great detail in this book.)

So part of the uniqueness of Mimi's approach was the incredible breadth of her background, her scholarship, and her experiences. She brought together architecture, art, history, archeology, archaeo-astronomy, anthropology, mythology, cultural studies, spirituality, and more.

For Whom is this Book?

For whom is this book; how should you read it; how might you even enter into it? It is hard to say. It is so broad and its underlying premises are so far from current materialistic thought. Many of us read to find confirmation of what we already believe, while Mimi's book presents new material in new ways. How many of us were educated to understand that history has a "psychology," and that psychology has a "history?" That there are spiritual feminisms as well as political feminisms? That cultures are symbolic entities and they unfold through archetypal forms? That the world's mythological traditions are rich with insights? So let's just say that this book is meant for those who are willing to open up to a new vision of our cultures, of our histories, of our notions of the arts, and of themselves.

About Mimi Lobell

There is a brief biography of Mimi Lobell (1942-2001) at the end of this book, and you can visit the Architectural Archives of the University of Pennsylvania, where you will find a hundred boxes of her work. But for here, a few thoughts about how she was uniquely positioned to write this book. First, Mimi was brilliant—she had a quick mind and was well educated. Besides a strong undergraduate education in the liberal arts, she had one of the best architectural educations of the 20th century at the University of Pennsylvania. There architecture was presented in its fullness, as form, as history, as construction, and most importantly, as a manifestation of culture. Then she read thousands of books on every aspect of every culture. Today one could do some of the research for a book like this online—certainly check the dates for monuments, people, and publications. But the Web did not exist when Mimi began this book and Wikipedia was only a couple of months old when she died. She did all of her research from books, and not books from libraries, but books that she bought. Thousands and thousands of books.

And she had the good fortune to teach at Pratt Institute. Pratt had and has its limitations, but one of its advantages was that it left its faculty alone to pursue their (sometimes radically) creative ideas. Here is just one example: Mimi, in this book, is able to show the strong parallels between Egyptian and Mayan pyramids and their underlying cultures. Not just with a cursory glance, but with a mastery of the key scholarship on each, and with the advantage of having visited the Mayan pyramids. Pratt allowed this. At other institutions, and academia in general today, this might be difficult, as an Egyptologist might not work on the Maya and vice versa. Pratt let Mimi follow her broad interests, which were fundamental to her doing this book.

Mimi was not only immersed in the scholarship of numerous cultures, but she went beyond scholarship to experience. She studied not only Buddhist architecture, but Buddhism with various Buddhist masters; not only Chinese architecture, but the *Tao Te Ching* and Tai Chi with Tai Chi masters; not only the lives of hunter-gatherers, but shamanism with shamans; etc. And she studied Modern Architecture with major modern architects: Louis Kahn, Robert Venturi, Denise Scott Brown, and Edmund Bacon all taught at Penn when she was there, and she worked for Marcel Breuer who had been a key figure at the Bauhaus.

So Mimi could do things that other scholars could not do, both because of her brilliance and also because she worked outside the centers of academia. Outside the centers, but not outside. Once, while she was at a conference in Malta on ancient Mediterranean religions to present a paper, she was having cocktails with a group that included Colin Renfrew, the "dean" of European archaeology. In conversation Mimi remarked that a particular motif "appears everywhere." Renfrew challenged her: "Everywhere?" Mimi conceded, "Well, only where there were people," and then rattled off a dozen cultures, identifying the specific periods with the dates during which the motif appeared, and for good measure identified the key scholars who had done work pertinent to the motif in each culture. Renfrew was quiet for a moment and then invited her to present a paper at a group he was organizing at the 1986 World Archaeological Congress in England.

Preface by John Lobell vii

About This Manuscript

Mimi worked on this book for twenty-five years, from 1976 until her death in 2001, so some references to the "contemporary" world will refer not to "today," but to the time during which she was writing. The book expanded and seldom contracted. It had commitments from publishers, and then it didn't. It went through computer crashes. She wrote it with word processing software that no longer exists—the version here comes from a printed copy that was scanned and then cleaned up. Mimi was meticulous in her work, so the errors that I am sure you will find are my fault and the fault of the scanning process, not hers. (If you do find errors, please contact me and I will attempt to fix them.)

You will notice that there are a lot of quotes in the manuscript. Some of them are from original texts, and these she would have kept. Others are to expand examples. Central to the thesis of the book is the universality of the Spatial Archetypes. Pyramids appear not just in Egypt, but in dozens of cultures during their Pyramid stages. Many of the quotes show how widespread the archetypes are and she would have kept these as well. Other quotes she would have removed, and she would have integrated the material into her text. At the time Mimi died, she was about to do one more edit, deal with the quotes, and finish several sections (for example, "Dissolution"). Rather than attempt to remove quotes and complete the incomplete sections, I am leaving the manuscript as is—otherwise it could be another decade before it gets out. And Mimi had intended the book to have hundreds of illustrations. Again, by leaving them out, I am able to get the book published. If I were to gather them, it would also take a decade, but today we have images online and you can look them up.

So here is Spatial Archetypes, not finished, but rich with brilliant insights, overflowing with material, and presenting a new way of seeing ourselves and our cultures.

John Lobell, 2018

JohnLobell.com
JohnLobell@mac.com

PREFACE

By Cristina Biaggi

This extraordinary book was twenty-five years in the making and the world and I have been waiting for another seventeen years since Mimi's death for its publication. Finally, here it is in its entirety. This is a Magnum Opus, an elegantly written, sweeping compendium not just of architecture but of all aspects of civilization, comparable to the work of Oswald Spengler, Henry Adams, and Joseph Campbell. But because Mimi was a woman and a feminist, it employs a feminist lens. It is the epitome of an archaeomythological work, in the Marija Gimbutas sense, because it merges together disparate disciplines of knowledge into a harmonious, entirely new confluence of ideas.

The reception of this book will start with its enthusiastic adherents, and as it gets to be known, its popularity will mushroom to the stratospheric heights it deserves.

I feel so humbled in trying to express my enthusiasm about the originality of this work that instead of going on with heartfelt superlatives, which are bubbling out of me pell-mell, I will speak about how I met Mimi, our friendship and our collaboration.

I first met Mimi at a Goddess group gathering at Buffie Johnson's house in New York City. Buffie was a fine artist and wrote her own book about the Goddess, The Lady of the Beasts. *This was the second incarnation of the "Goddess Group" that had grown out of the magazine HERESIES: (A Feminist Publication on Art and Politics) published by the Heresies Collective, which had produced a special edition called* The Great Goddess, *now considered a classic. The group consisted of Buffie, Mimi, Grace Shenell, Donna Henes, Gail Dunlap, Mary Beth Edelson, Rosemary Dudley, Donna Wilshire, and myself. Most of these women had been part of the Heresies Collective and had contributed to the publication of the Goddess issue. Every one of these women was in the process of writing about the Goddess and a number of their works were being published. It was a heady time. I was drawn to each of these women for different reasons, and especially to Mimi. I was instantly impressed by Mimi's brilliant mind and taken by her down-to-earth quality and her crystalline laugh.*

Mimi and I started seeing each other socially and, as they say, hanging out. I attended her brilliant lectures and even presented talks and papers with her at various conferences and women spirituality events. She came to my gallery exhibitions and was interested in my artistic ideas.

One of the most interesting things we did as a collective was to go on a field trip to Malta in 1985 to attend the first International Conference on Archæology and Fertility Cult in the Ancient Mediterranean conference where Mimi, Buffie and I presented papers. It was there that we met the great archaeologist Marija Gimbutas and the dean of British archaeology Colin Renfrew. And it was there that I organized a two-hour ritual in the Hypogeum, attended only by women: our Goddess Group and Marija Gimbutas, and her two students/attendants. We got to know Marija well on that trip, and we all had wonderful meals together al fresco under the Maltese stars, having animated conversations and eating splendid food.

Subsequently, in 1986, Mimi was invited by Colin Renfrew to present a paper at the World Archaeological Congress in Southampton, England. Her paper, "Male-Biased Paradigms in Archaeology," caused quite a stir. Much to her dismay, she was heavily criticized by not only the male "elite" scholars at the conference, but by some women scholars (who were toeing the "party line") as well. I too presented a paper at that conference which was published by Ian Hodder in his book The Meaning of Things. Even though Mimi's paper was far superior to mine in its originality and approach, it was not published because it was considered too radical and not "worthy." But she had made her point brilliantly and forcefully. She had proved that she was a forward-thinking pioneer and an innovator.

As a part of my PhD dissertation I conceived and built what I called the Great Goddess Sculpture, a reclining female figure in the form of a negative shape which I covered over with a large amorphous-looking rock shape. All of this was built out of wood, chicken wire and papier-mâché, and measured 24' x 14' x 8.5'. Based on the idea of depicting a female figure as a negative space to be entered like a temple, I went on to create a maquette of a female figure in a birth-giving position. The piece was to be covered by an earth mound (see CristinaBiaggi.com). Mimi was very excited about my idea and created spectacular architectural drawings depicting my vision. In addition, she wrote a brilliant architectural description of the proposed piece, computing all its solstices, equinoxes, and alignments, as well as its lunar metaphors. She carefully calculated the siting, the outward dimensions of the mound itself and the inside dimensions of the female figure in birth-giving position, to reflect the sunrises and sunsets at different times of the year, just as was the case with its prehistoric precedents. As Mimi elegantly put it, "The Mound's astronomical metaphors are of two types: those involving proportional dimensions and those involving numerical motifs. Through these the Mound and Sanctuary honor two heavenly bodies traditionally associated with the Goddess: the moon and Venus."

I was amazed and thrilled at Mimi's taking my idea and making it so much richer with her archaeoastronomical calculations and lunar and stellar metaphors.

The Goddess Mound still has to be built somewhere, somehow. I am still actively trying to interest those who might help its realization. It will be a tribute to our inspired collaboration in the spirit of the Goddess.

Let me state in conclusion that I am very grateful to John Lobell for all his diligent and hard work in bringing this "ovarian" book to life at long last.

Cristina Biaggi, 2018
amandla72@optonline.net

INTRODUCTION

> *I have, in my place, books about English history. I like the bloodiness of it. I have one set of eight volumes. I read only the first volume, and of that only the first chapter, in which each time I see something else. But really, I am interested only in reading Volume Zero, which has not been written. And then Volume Minus One. History could not have started in the places they speak of. History preceded this; it just is not recorded. The beauty of architecture is that it deals with the recessions of the mind, from which comes that which is not yet said and not yet made.*
> ~ Louis Kahn[1]

Volume Zero

The recessions of mind of which Kahn spoke—the pre-formers of civilization in history's unwritten "Volume Zero"—are very much like the psychological territory C. G. Jung called the collective unconscious—the repository of instincts and archetypes that pre-form human behavior. An archetype is a psychological center "from which comes that which is not yet said and not yet made." According to Jung, archetypes are buried so deeply in the collective unconscious they cannot be known directly by the conscious mind, but they do shape our ideas and forms of expression—art, architecture, music, literature, relationships, social structures, cosmologies, worldviews. Through these, archetypes become known indirectly. Since archetypes are part of the collective unconscious, like it, they are shared by all human beings. Some are active, while others are latent. A latent archetype does not strongly affect daily life, but an active one shapes every detail of existence and every aspect of a culture. We can easily see the universality of archetypes by looking at world mythology. Mythological archetypes, such as the Great Mother, the Dragon-Slayer, or the Dying-and-Resurrecting God, appear in various disguises throughout the world. The Dying-and-Resurrecting God, for example, appears as Quetzalcoatl in pre-Columbian

Mesoamerica, as Viracocha in South America, as Tammuz or Dumuzi in the ancient Near East, as Osiris in pharaonic Egypt, as Dionysus in classical Greece, as Jesus in the Christian world, and as Buddhas and Bodhisattvas in Asia. Comparative mythologist Joseph Campbell pointed out that the underlying *structure* of an archetypal myth is universal; its particulars—its details, character traits, and local colorations—vary to reflect specific cultures and geographical regions.

This gives a useful model for distinguishing between the universal and the particular in architecture. The pyramid is one example of a universal form in architecture. Clearly, the Pyramid[2] is an *archetype*: a sky-reaching, human-made World Mountain that signifies the sacred place where high priests negotiate the relation of Heaven to Earth. Heaven—the numinous, immortal, eternal realm. Earth—the mundane, mortal, temporal realm. Civilizations all over the world have embodied variants of this archetype: the Egyptian pyramid, used as a tomb; the temple-topped ziggurat of Mesopotamia and temple-topped stepped pyramid of Mesoamerica; the hemispherical *stupa*, *chôrten*, or *dagoha* of Buddhist Asia, used neither as tomb nor temple but as a ritually circumambulated reliquary. Even Solomon's temple, the Athenian Acropolis, and the Gothic cathedral were *"pyramids."* They (or the hills they were built upon) towered above their surroundings, and they each precisely modeled the underlying structure of the Pyramid archetype in their respective cultures.

Archetypes help us to understand our innermost selves. And, paradoxically, they connect us in a profound way with ancient civilizations and with people in other cultures. The path of archetypal self-knowledge leads not into isolating self-centeredness, but into union with the whole of human civilization. For instance, Jungian analysts explore their clients' dream images by comparing them to motifs in world mythology. World travelers sometimes awaken heart-and-soul affinities with foreign people and places. New Consciousness centers abound in cross-cultural course offerings from Ashanti fertility rituals to Zen calligraphy.[3]

Spatial archetypes are especially intriguing because our minds can translate almost anything into spatial terms: time can be seen as a line, a circle, or a spiral. Managerial systems can be egalitarian, implying that everyone is on the same level, or they can be hierarchical, implying that everyone is ranked in a pyramidal chain of command. A person can be straight or square. A bad job or relationship makes us feel cramped or low, but good ones make us feel elated or high. Beyond these personal "spatializations," socio-cultural sensitivities affect our daily use of space: the way desks are arranged in a classroom or office; the shape of a dining table and who sits where; the personal distance we maintain in a face-to-face conversation; what we consider "private" and "public" space; the way we visually convey information in a chart or graph; the mental map we construct to find an address. Beyond these socio-cultural "spatializations"[4] are the grand concepts of space that attempt to explain how the universe is shaped and what its origins are. Imagine the spatial differences between the "Big Bang" and the "Steady State" universes, between one that expands and contracts and one that does not, between one with two or three dimensions and one with four, five, seven, eleven, or fifteen.

We even build spatial models of how our minds work around such structures as ego, unconscious, id, or whatever seems verifiable by our experience. Our mythic and religious ideals are often symbolized as places: the Garden of Eden, the New Jerusalem, Mount Meru, the Elysian Fields, the Lunar Mansions, Shangri-La, the Kingdom of Shambhala, King Arthur's Roundtable, Atlantis, and so on. Certain mythic places also symbolize our fears: Hades, the Cretan Labyrinth, Dante's Inferno.

Because our minds so eagerly spatialize everything we encounter,[5] spatial archetypes offer profound insight into the psyche and civilization of humanity. Spatial archetypes are expressed most directly through architecture—the art form that engages society in its entirety and marshals the most extravagant resources to build, when it is at its best, a mediator between the self, society, and the cosmos. This is architecture's highest function. It has been the function of every monument of world architecture from Stonehenge to the Egyptian and Mayan pyramids, from Greek and Indian temples to Gothic cathedrals and Persian mosques, from Pueblo kivas to the lines and figures in Peru's Nazca desert. Civilizations have left these exemplary works of architecture— their supreme achievements—to carry on their worldviews. As the modern architect Mies van der Rohe said, "Architecture is the will of the age conceived in spatial terms."[6]

The "high civilizations" of the ancient world are justly famous for their impressive cities and their monumental pyramids, temples, and ceremonial centers. But these civilizations did not spring full blown into their Classic Periods. Long periods of gestation, struggle, innovation, and cultural infusion built up to their "Golden Ages," and centuries, sometimes millennia, of decadence, stagnation, and decline followed before dissolution.

All civilizations have had much longer life cycles than we normally realize. Vico, Hegel, Spengler, Neumann, and others have argued that civilizations go through essentially the same developmental stages as individuals: birth, childhood, adolescence, young adulthood, middle age, old age, and death. Though this cultural version of "phylogeny recapitulates ontogeny" generally holds true, the analogy risks oversimplifying the great complexity of human culture. (Especially dangerous is the idea that cultures naturally or inexorably "evolve" through a progression of stages toward the Western model of the modern, industrialized nation. The problems with this idea will become clear when we look at each spatial archetype.)

In *The Origins and History of Consciousness*, psychoanalyst Erich Neumann presented his theoretical and clinical findings on the psychological orientations individuals display at the different stages of life: oceanic, embryonic oneness in the womb (the Uroboros); birth and dependence on the mother (the Great Mother); separating from the mother and establishing one's place in the world (the Hero); assuming adult responsibility in the male-dominated world of the fathers (the Slaying of the Mother); and finding one's mature place in the world (the Slaying of the Father). These orientations parallel the worldviews revealed by the spatial archetypes. Without insisting that cultures go through the same developmental stages as individuals, we can still appreciate insights gained from these parallels.

Two or more cultures oriented to the same worldview will produce similar buildings, towns, social structures, values, mythologies, and the like, even though the cultures are widely separated by time and space. For instance, when the Mayan and Egyptian civilizations were each manifesting the Pyramid archetype—even though they were separated by half the globe and three thousand years—they shared pyramid-building, class-structured society, hieroglyphic writing, rule by theocratic god-kings from dynastic families, elaborate funeral rites, astronomy, the keeping of records and histories, the maintenance of a standing army and a governmental bureaucracy, similar myths about the deities of heaven and the underworld, and an obsession with dualism and reintegration. There is nothing mysterious about these similarities: they are simply common features of theocratic nations and city-states. Few of these traits would be found in cultures expressive of another archetype. The hunter-gatherers of the Sensitive Chaos,[7] for instance, share a completely different set of similarities. Although there are many spatial archetypes, there are only a few prime archetypes that represent basic worldviews and types of cultures. I have identified seven. Each symbolizes and generates a worldview, which coheres all the qualities, characteristics, belief structures, actions, and forms of expression of a culture or individual. (In the *American Heritage Dictionary*, cohere means "to cause to form a united, orderly, and aesthetically consistent whole." This is the action of a worldview.)

The seven archetypes—the Sensitive Chaos, the Great Round, the Four Quarters, the Pyramid, the Radiant Axes, the Grid, and Dissolution—are inclusive of all of human civilization from the earliest evolution of our hominid ancestors to the present, including all of the world's historical periods and cultures. Each archetype represents a way of life, a way of knowing, and a way of being in the world that is complete in itself. Earlier archetypes are not backward or less developed "stages" on the way to more advanced or developed "stages."

Here are brief profiles of the archetypes, which are more fully explored in the succeeding chapters.

The Sensitive Chaos

The Sensitive Chaos is the archetype of nomadic hunter-gatherers living in small egalitarian bands like our prehistoric ancestors from the beginning of human evolution through the Upper

Paleolithic era. As they live absorbed in nature, not removed from it like city-dwellers, they interact with the world directly rather than through abstract concepts, numbers, and geometries. "Chaos" is not meant negatively. It simply indicates that there are no obvious, organizing, Euclidean geometries in the spatial archetype. "Sensitive" recognizes that cultures of this archetype, like the raw nature that surrounds them, beat to a subtle, intricate intelligence that may escape over-technologized people of the Grid.[7]

The people of the Sensitive Chaos sense nature as a living organism: a roiling sea of energy whose power courses through the landscape, the sky, and all living things. It supercharges some places with palpable force fields. These become sacred places. The spirals and meanders of the archetype symbolize the continuum of nature and human life, animated by an overwhelming sense of spirit in everything, to which people sensitize themselves through dances, rituals, psychoactive plants, shamanic trances, and sympathetic magic. Within this spiritual continuum, one life form can change into another—a human can become an eagle or a deer. This "sympathetic identification"[8] is critical to the hunter-gatherers' survival and constitutes a psychoerotic (psyche + eros) way of knowing as sophisticated in its way as modern Western civilization's technelogos (techne + logos) way of knowing. The intuitive, organismic sensibilities of psychoerotic knowledge are another aspect of the meandering spiral.

The Sensitive Chaos corresponds with Neumann's psychological stage of the Uroboros: the child's state of mind in the womb and shortly after birth before it separates from its mother and begins to develop an individual identity and ego.[9] The symbol of the archetype illustrates the corresponding spatial configuration of the psyche, without the ego to fix a central reference point. Similarly, there are no permanent towns or buildings in the Sensitive Chaos. Such edifices obstruct the free flow of nature's life forces, as well as the nomadic way of life, and hunter-gatherers have no use for them. The buildings that nomads do make—huts, windbreaks, igloos, tents, blinds, shelters—are constructed of simple, readily available, natural materials: mud, thatch, ice, hides, bones, leaves, bark. Like the people, they leave no permanent marks on the landscape.

The Great Round

This archetype marks a distinct break from the Sensitive Chaos. It is the realm of the Neolithic and Early Bronze Age farmers, settled permanently on the land and grouped into egalitarian clans. The circle or sphere symbolizing the Great Round[10] illustrates the farmers' worldview, centered in a stable, intimate relationship to the land. It is echoed in the arcs of the sun, moon and stars in the great circle of sky, now observable from a fixed location. Time revolves in cycles, following the rhythms of the heavenly bodies, especially the moon. The round of life turns with the agricultural seasons, accented by planting and fertility rituals, harvest feasts, and propitiations of the deaths of winter.

The analogous psychological orientation is centered on the archetype of the Great Mother, when the young child begins to separate from its mother and comes into conscious relationship with her.[11] Since most ancient Great Round cultures were prehistoric and left no written records, it is difficult to discern their social structures. But their art and burial patterns often suggest they were matrilineal, tracing inheritance and descent through the mother's line like the Pueblo Indians, a contemporary Great Round culture.

Spiritually, the Great Round worldview is similarly focused on the Great Goddess. She is not the lesser half of a dualistic Godhead as seen in male-dominated cultures—the compliant fertility goddess; the barefoot-and-pregnant Earth Mother; the submissive yin principle; or the medieval Christians' corrupting power of flesh, matter, and nature. As an archetype, the Great Goddess is the whole—not just earth, matter, nature, body, birth, nurture, being, and space; but earth and heaven, matter and spirit, nature and culture, body and mind, birth and death, nurture and torture, creation and destruction, being and non-being, space and time. She is the entire matrix of the cosmos. The elemental characteristic of the "feminine" principle represented by the Great Goddess is not fertility, pregnancy, nurture, or submission—it is the principle of non-duality.

The Great Goddess is the first anthropomorphization of the spiritual continuum that animated the Sensitive Chaos. She weaves the mysteries of human fate and confides in sibyls and oracles. Her rites bring the knowledge of immortality and the mastery of physical, sexual, and earthly energies. Above all, she teaches her initiates how to transcend duality, reintegrating the fragments into the holistic wisdom of the feminine archetype—symbolized, too, by the circle of the Great Round.

Great Round cultures have embodied the archetype in countless monuments all over the world: goddess-shaped megalithic temples in Malta; vulviform passage mounds in Brittany, Great Britain, and Ireland; womb-like kivas in the American southwest; circular earthworks and communal burial mounds in the United States, Western Europe, and India; uterine beehive houses, pit-houses, and tholoi throughout the Neolithic Mediterranean, Middle East, and Asia.

Roundness of architectural form, however, is not the defining feature of the archetype. An extremely inventive period, the Great Round saw the rise of urban cultures like Çatal Hüyük, Minoan Crete, the Indus Valley civilization, and the Anasazi. These cultures more often built rectilinear rather than round buildings, yet they displayed another, more important aspect of the Great Round's holism: peacefulness. War is almost completely absent from the Great Round (which means that war is not always inherent in human nature). This archetype prevailed for thousands of years in comparative peace, yet its civilizations were highly innovative, the source of not only agriculture and animal domestication but also astronomy, metallurgy, writing, textiles, pottery, irrigation, plumbing, stone and mud brick architecture, and cities.

The Four Quarters

Symbolized by the cross within a square, the Four Quarters[14] draws and quarters the Great Round. Territoriality and war invade human affairs for the first time, and the warrior ethic dominates social values, just as the heroic epic dominates literature. As the ego emerges in the psyche, the chieftain emerges in society as the central authority figure. The ego becomes the central reference point that quarters the mind into distinctions of "self" versus "other," "mine" versus "thine." Similarly, society gets quartered into a hierarchical caste system headed by a military or priestly aristocracy. The chieftain is paralleled mythically by the archetypal Lord of the Four Quarters—Zeus, Indra, Thor, Horus, Brahma, Jehovah, Quetzalcoatl—who reigns supreme over the Four Quarters of the universe. He often lives in a heavenly palace or temple, walled and divided into quadrants by crossroads, four rivers, or the cardinal axes. Gates and guardians at the cardinal points in the wall protect the Lord's territories and possessions, just as the ego sets up psychological defenses to protect its position.

Coinciding historically with the Late Bronze Age and the Iron Age,[12] Four Quarters cultures perfect and revere metallurgy, crafting superior weapons and war chariots. The blacksmith, mirrored in mythology by the thunderbolt-wielding storm and war god, is as powerful as the chieftain.

Psychologically, the Four Quarters is analogous to the ego's pulling away from the mother, seeking to identify with the archetype of the Hero to become master of its own will and destiny.[13] We often see in Four Quarters cultures a great struggle over the balance of power between men and women. Matrilineal descent and the worship of certain goddesses may continue, but an increasing masculinization of culture begins in the Four Quarters that continues throughout the succeeding archetypes. The final dualistic separation from the Great Mother archetype is acted out in the mythic themes of the Separation of the World Parents and the Slaying of the Dragon (the Dragon being the demonized aspect of the mother that is holding back the Hero/ego).

The architecture of the Four Quarters perfectly models the archetype. Typical features include forts, walled cities, centralized temples, rectilinear ceremonial terraces, and cruciform or cross-axial layouts such as quartered town plans with gates at the cardinal axes. Variants of these appear in every Four Quarters culture. From China's Bronze and Iron Age dynasties—the Hsia, Shang, and Zhou—comes the legendary Ming T'ang, the model for all Chinese capital cities including Beijing. Similarly, India's Iron Age Vedic culture established canons for architecture and city planning that influenced temple cities such as Shrirangam and Madurai as late as the 17th century. Hierakonpolis, a predynastic Egyptian capital, was a walled temple city built over an earlier circular shrine of the Great Round period (such overlays are common as each succeeding culture seeks to impose itself on the earlier one). The Vikings' round, earthen forts of Trelleborg and Fyrkat were divided cross-axially, as were the Plains Indians' Medicine Lodges. In the first millennium B.C., Peru's Four Quarters Chavin culture built in the heart of their capital a cross-axial configuration of passageways, at the center of which was the intricately carved, phallic Lanzon Stele.

The Pyramid

The Pyramid archetype rises from the base of the Four Quarters. The archetype's symbol represents the dominant mythic image: the World Mountain. The World Mountain is a sacred place where Heaven and Earth meet, where human and divine communicate. The Mountain's levels stand for the different classes of the pyramidal social system. Its faces retain the quadrated symbol system inherited from the Four Quarters, each face having a designated direction, color, season, guardian spirit, and so on.

The Pyramid's overall form, especially the double pyramid or octahedron, expresses the dualism of the worldview resulting from the ego's divisive effect on the psyche. In this archetype, the entire world is divided into two opposing realms: the upward, sky-reaching, positive, "masculine," light-seeking, eternal, conscious, solar realm, and the downward, earthbound, negative, "feminine," dark, temporal, unconscious, lunar realm. Thus logos opposes eros and techne opposes psyche in a violent cleaving of the formerly holistic Great Round.[15] This increasing logos orientation can be seen in the growing emphasis on the Word, the Law, special names, written records and historical accounts, sacred numbers and geometry, and standardized systems of measurement.

Socially, in the Pyramid archetype, the nation or city-state emerges, militarily uniting several former chieftainships and petty kingships under a dynastic, theocratic God-King. This Divine Ruler is the son or incarnation of the Father-God. Psychologically, in this archetype the Hero of the Four Quarters—the newly independent and willful ego—becomes inducted into masculine society,[16] identifies with the father, and assumes adult responsibilities.

The psychology of the Pyramid and Four Quarters archetypes has mainly concerned the male psyche. Presumably, the struggle to separate from the mother is less acute in the female psyche, since girls grow up to be women like their mothers, but boys do not. To come into their own, it seems that boys must at some point define themselves in opposition to femaleness. Historically, it was in Four Quarters and Pyramid cultures that once independent women and powerful goddesses were transmogrified into dutiful wives and mothers or into demons and monsters—the gorgons, dragons, harpies, and witches whom the Heroes killed, appropriating their quarry's powers and sacred sites.

Naturally, the prominent architectural works of the Pyramid archetype are the various pyramids and temple mountains described earlier.

The Radiant Axes

The Radiant Axes is the archetype of the empire, which subsumes nations and city-states in its vast net of power. The goal of the empire and the emperor is to have unbounded power like the sun, thus the sun is the dominant symbol of the archetype. Most empires have identified themselves with the sun: the Aztecs sacrificed thousands to their bloodthirsty sun-god Tonatiuh; the Incas reckoned their descent from the sun-god Inti; Egypt's expansionist Ramessides empire glorified the sun-god Amen-Ra at the monumental temples of Karnak and Luxor; the brutal Assyrians assumed the name of their war-god Asshur, whose emblem was the winged-disk of the sun; Louis XIV was known as the Sun-King in imitation of the sun-god Apollo; even the English, not given to mythological thought, were fond of boasting that "the sun never sets on the British Empire."

The psychological parallel of the Radiant Axes is the inflated ego, which knows no bounds.[17] It believes it is God. This conceit is impossible to maintain—after all, the ego belongs only to a fallible human being, not to a god—so the ego goes to the other extreme: deflation. Icarus's flight too close to the sun that caused him to drown in the ocean mythologizes the ego's frenzied swing from inflation to deflation. Radiant Axes empires also overreach themselves. Ordinary gods cannot compete with a despotic emperor who assumes unnatural divine rights. Mercifully, most Radiant Axes empires are short-lived, drowning ignominiously in social revolution, invasion, or internal collapse.

Architecturally, the rays of the archetype appear as avenues radiating from imperial palaces and capital cities such as Versailles, New Delhi, and Washington, D.C. Also, networks of imperial highways radiate throughout empires to carry messengers, troops, provincial governors, tax collectors, census takers, and other government agents. The Roman, Incan, Mongolian, and British empires were all famous for their road systems. Other features of the Radiant Axes include colossal sculptures showing the ego-inflation of the emperor (Abu Simbel), intimidating propagandistic murals or bas reliefs (Persepolis), and obelisks. Obelisks were fashionable in the Radiant Axes New Kingdom in Egypt, where they symbolized a ray of the sun; in the Roman Empire (Trajan's column); and in Europe's imperialistic Baroque era. In India, Asoka's edict columns were a variant of the obelisk, as were the "Mandate of Heaven" columns of China.

The Grid

The Grid archetype becomes apparent in the international commercial-industrial networks that survive the collapse of Radiant Axes empires. The Grid marks the decline of a civilization, characterized by deflation, anonymity, mechanization, commercialism, crushing bureaucratization, secularism to the point of despiritualization, and paralysis of the creative will. Technelogos steamrolls psychoeros, eliminating the intuitive, holistic, organismic wisdom needed to counterbalance the cold rationalism of the Grid.

The Grid *has no center.* Thus, it separates everything into identical units, becoming the champion of statistical uniformity, quality control, measurement, and census-taking. The Grid is the handmaiden of any operation seeking to reduce something—products, people, information, land—into predictable, manageable units. Hence it is favored by industry, the military, bureaucracies, and colonial governments. Rewards are given for the techne skills of making things, figuring things out, and "getting the job done." The marketplace governs human affairs.

The Grid, a beneficiary of the Radiant Axes empires, builds its technocracy upon the imperial infrastructure of roads and shipping lanes, trade alliances, international currency systems, and vast governmental bureaucracies. Thus, within one civilization, it is nearly impossible for the Grid to precede the Radiant Axes. However, Radiant Axes cultures often use the Grid pattern as an expedient layout for military camps, as seen in the Roman camp, and slaves' or workers' quarters, as seen in the sun-god-king Akhnaten's capital at Tel el Amarna. Four Quarters and Pyramid cultures are fascinated by the Grid's logos properties, shown for instance in the mathematical "magic squares" revered in Vedic India, ancient China, and elsewhere.

Psychologically, the Grid represents the existential malaise of the deflated ego, with no centering inner Self to turn to and no sense of power in the world. The deflated personality is adrift on the Grid's endless alienating sameness. This state, however, can be the precursor to the *death of ego*, an experience shown in mythology and religion as a painful but necessary step toward enlightenment. Similarly, the Grid can help to break down the centralized and often corrupt hold of organized religion, freeing us to see how we contain the archetypes within ourselves. We realize that the Animal Spirit, Goddess, Hero, God-King, and Emperor are part of us. Instead of projecting these archetypes into exterior beings to whom we look for deliverance, we can take the Inner Path and see ourselves as our own spiritual liberators.

The Grid became the banner of revolutionaries fighting corrupt autocracies. It symbolizes the political systems designed to redistribute power from the few to the many—democracy, socialism, communism, republicanism—which usually follow the dissolution of empires.

Naturally, the Grid archetype produces grid forms in architecture: street grids, modular building facades, rectilinear rooms, right-angled surfaces, grids of chair and desk layouts, and so on. The Grid has also organized military barracks, workers' housing, colonial cities, industrial plants, factory towns, and land divisions in the West since the Industrial Revolution, as well as in the Grid periods of Hellenistic Greece and Ptolemaic Egypt, and the late or declining empires of the Romans, Aztecs, Incas, Chinese, and Japanese.

In Western culture, we can witness the archetype in the Cartesian coordinates and the scientific method, the isotropic universe (uniform in all directions, that is, made up of stuff more or less evenly distributed throughout space, rather than being centered on the earth, the sun, or our galaxy), modern social mobility, the nuclear family and suburban sprawl, the move toward metrification, the spread of democracy, and many other phenomena.

Dissolution

[Dissolution refers to the ultimate disintegration and death of a culture. Mimi did not write this section, but below are some of her notes for it. JL]

Civilization: Breakdown of social structures and institutions, ad hoc groupings and cults, experimental communities and families, decadence, terrorism, anarchy.

Psyche: Death, survivalism, nihilism, opportunistic worldview, scavenging, recycling, sampling, eclecticism. Multidimensional time. The Inner Path.

Space: The Wasteland—charnel ground, apocalypse, chaos, shantytowns, urban decay, homelessness, refugee camps, battlegrounds, virtual space, Home as Sacred Place.

Examples: Egypt ca. 100-700 CE, post-Hellenistic Greece, fall of the Roman Empire, any country at war, natural disasters, USA since....

Bits of Colored Glass

Since spatial archetypes reside in the elusive recesses of our unconscious minds, we cannot see them directly, but we can see them indirectly through their manifestations in space, civilization, and the psyche. Space, or rather, conceptions of space, appear in numerous tangible forms: art, architecture, town planning, mythic images, and cosmological models, to name a few. Civilization memorializes itself in artifacts, written records, archaeological remains, technological inventions, and theories of history and culture. Psyche—the individual mind and the collective unconscious—can be approached through meditation, dreams, myths, psychoanalysis, the arts, and various philosophies, psychologies, and religions.

We can think of space, civilization, and the psyche as the three sides of the triangular mirror in a kaleidoscope. Alone, each mirror reflects only what we can already see with our naked eyes. But put the three mirrors together, give them some bits of colored glass to reflect, and they create miraculous patterns. Each turn of the kaleidoscope organizes and reflects the assorted fragments into glorious but accidentally structured images. The bits of colored glass are fragments of space, psyche, and civilization: art, architecture, town planning, myths, cosmology, artifacts, written records, archaeological remains, theories of history, dreams, philosophies, psychologies, religions. With this device, perhaps we can glimpse what would otherwise be invisible: the spatial archetypes themselves.

Each chapter in this book is a turning of the kaleidoscope to reveal each spatial archetype. In a kaleidoscope, we see bits of colored glass forming patterns reflected in the three mirrors. We are aware of the patterns but not of the bits of glass. Some are hidden from view; the overlapping of others changes their colors; and all appear transformed in their myriad symmetrical reflections. Similarly, when we examine all the pieces of information that form an image of a spatial archetype, we see that some of their individual characteristics are occluded, colored, or transformed. This does not make the image invalid. It is to some degree inevitable in any conscious effort to make the world meaningful.

At the end of the book, Appendix 1 "Bits of Colored Glass" collects the nuances, exceptions, permutations, hidden dynamics, general observations, opinions, recommendations, and caveats that apply to all the archetypes. All of these are in the nature of hypotheses—tentative statements ready to yield to future discoveries and insights.

1. The archetypes are not meant to be used in a reductive manner to diminish the actual complexity of cultures.
2. Each spatial archetype imprints all forms of cultural expression and represents a complete worldview and way of life.

3. Always evaluate archetypal motifs in light of the entire cultural context. A society might use an archetypal motif in minor ways without being "in that archetype."
4. All archetypes are and always have been present in every culture and individual, but some are latent and others are dominant.
5. The archetype that appears to dominate complex societies may represent only the worldview of the ruling elite.
6. On the whole, there is no "natural evolution" from one archetype to the next. The impetus to change nearly always comes from external forces.
7. Precise divisions between one archetype and another rarely exist.
8. A culture may live predominantly in one archetype throughout its lifetime.
9. The sequence of archetypes is rarely reversible.
10. Some cultures appear to skip archetypes.
11. Every archetype has positive and negative aspects.
12. An archetype usually follows a life cycle from incipience to realization to decline (apparent especially in the four archetypes from the Four Quarters through the Grid).
13. The timespan of each succeeding archetype tends to be shorter than the previous one.
14. As the archetypal periods shorten in time, they expand in space.
15. Each succeeding archetype domesticates or demonizes the driving spirit of the former archetype.
16. All archetypes are culturally represented in the world today.
17. All archetypes are alive in each of our psyches.
18. Through understanding archetypes we can achieve a sense of unity with all other human beings while at the same time preserving and enjoying cultural diversity.

THE SENSITIVE CHAOS

World of the Animal Powers

1a. Swirling Clouds. Sensitive Chaos cultures are close to nature, feeling directly the swirling currents of air, water, and earth energies. Sensitive Chaos people directly experience things that Grid cultures are just beginning to be able to detect only through advanced scientific instruments.

1b. Study of water. By Leonardo da Vinci, c. 1508-9. Leonardo is representative of the rationality of the Renaissance, but his work here, observing the workings of nature, exemplifies the Sensitive Chaos.

1c. A Yanomami Shabano, a village structure for from 50 to 400 people. The Yanomami live in the Amazon rainforest on the border between Venezuela and Brazil. The Yanomami are not fully nomadic hunter-gatherers, but are foraging horticulturalists: they gather fruit, hunt, and fish, but also do slash-and-burn planting. They move on when they have exhausted the nearby soil.

1d. Ancient Chinese Neolithic Pottery. 3500 BC. The spiral is characteristic of the Sensitive Chaos, but remains into the Neolithic Great Round. If you put a pole in the ground and mark the ground where the shadow of the tip falls each day at the same time for a year, you get a double spiral.

The Sensitive Chaos 19

1a

1b

1c

1d

THE SENSITIVE CHAOS

WORLD OF THE ANIMAL POWERS

> *People experienced the fluid element to be the universal element, not yet solidified but remaining open to outside influences, the unformed, indeterminate element, ready to receive definite form; they knew it as the "sensitive chaos."*
> ~ Theodor Schwenk[1]

Origins

The Sensitive Chaos, symbolized by the serpentine spiral, is usually regarded as the most "primitive"[2] kind of consciousness—that of Stone Age hunter-gatherers. The archetype permeated life in the Pleistocene epoch for millions of years from the earliest phases of hominid evolution up to the agricultural revolution beginning about 15,000 years ago. It still potentiates the lives of the few remaining hunter-gatherers who have managed to keep their traditions intact: some Mbuti Pygmies and !Kung (Bushmen) of Africa, a few Eskimos and Australian aborigines, isolated pockets of Amazonian Indians, and a handful of others.

The Sensitive Chaos is about origins: the origin of the universe, of the solar system; the origin of time and space; of life; of perception, consciousness, language, and order; the origin of art, architecture, and culture. The Sensitive Chaos is the immeasurable out of which comes the measurable, the Sea of Chaos out of which comes the Cosmic Egg. It guards the inchoate structures of the shamanic psyche that high civilizations later build into monumental architecture, and it gestates the seeds of the world religions.

Psychologically, the Sensitive Chaos is the state of mind of the child in the womb and shortly after birth before it begins to separate from the mother. To the hunter-gatherer, the whole feeling of the archetype is of being enfolded in the womb of nature. This generates one of the defining characteristics of the Sensitive Chaos: an apparent absence of ego.[3] Like all human beings, hunter-gatherers have egos, but, for reasons we will see later, they develop the skill of transcending ego. The term "ego" denotes that central reference point bounded within a portion of the psyche, giving what is inside a unique and immutable identity forever separate from what is outside. The primary quality of ego is the distinction of center and boundary. The center is the ego itself—the new point of reference from which everything is interpreted. The boundary defines and protects the ego's territories. Without the ego's boundaries, the self becomes Self, the great transpersonal Self, which expands infinitely into oneness with the universe. In the Sensitive Chaos there are no fixed boundaries, no extreme centralizations of space, no walls and fences, no immutable distinctions between the "I" and the "not I," and no axial geometries to organize the world according to human will. (The absence of these spatial configurations in the Sensitive Chaos will become clearer when we see, by contrast, how they enter into and influence later archetypes.)

Like all spatial archetypes, the Sensitive Chaos generates a worldview that coordinates every facet of daily life: the ways of getting food; the way daily chores are apportioned; what people wear; how they make homes and house wares; how they have fun; what they believe in and what they fear; how they measure status; what rites of passage they go through; how they behave as men and women, parents and children, friends or enemies, and so on. On the one hand, it is not possible to understand any one of these facets without grasping the essence of the entire culture. On the other, when we grasp this essence, the pattern underlying all the facets of the culture becomes so clear that we can often predict unknown elements from the elements we know.[4]

In the worldview of the Sensitive Chaos, the cosmos is a fluctuating continuum. All of its components—the animals, fishes, plants, people, rocks, waters, mountains, earth, and heavens—are one great, living, conscious being. The varied appearances of things arise when this being coalesces its infinite, ever-flowing energy and spirit into distinct entities. But always underneath these transitory appearances, all things are mutable.

> Life is not divided into classes and subclasses. It is felt
> as an unbroken continuous whole which does not admit
> of any clean cut and trenchant distinctions. The limits

between the different spheres are not insurmountable barriers; they are fluent and fluctuating. There is no specific difference between the various realms of life. Nothing has a definite, invariable, static shape. By a sudden metamorphosis everything may be turned into everything.
~ Ernst Cassirer [5]

This worldview is so different from our Grid mentality that we find it hard to imagine how the universe would appear from this perspective. We can get hints of it from remembering the magical world we experienced in childhood, or in our dreams, or perhaps when we attained a vividly altered state of consciousness through meditation, mind-expanding drugs, a high fever, sexual ecstasy, childbirth, or a near-death experience.

As a state of mind, the Sensitive Chaos can have a compelling attraction simply because it is the opposite of our everyday, working view of the world. It is important to realize, though, that hunter-gatherers consciously construct and maintain their worldview. It is not a matter of their lacking ego or social hierarchy or material acquisitiveness, but rather of their consciously arresting these tendencies because they are so destructive to the hunting-gathering way of life. Though the Sensitive Chaos may conjure the innocence and primordial harmony that we lose in our psychological expulsion from the Garden of Eden, to the Paleolithic gatherer or hunter it is simply a natural, practical, and inevitable way of life under the circumstances in which they live. The original Stone Age hunters-gatherers—roaming amidst untouched nature, dependent wholly on the bounty of its fruits for sustenance with no means of forcing more out of nature than it gave of its own accord—knew nothing of the technological world that would lead their twentieth century descendants to muse nostalgically about their seemingly simpler way of life. And yet, in the underlayers of our making, we are more hunter-gatherer than anything else. In his book *Humankind*, Peter Farb writes that ninety per cent of the total number of humans (about 180 billion) who have ever lived on the earth since the earliest hominids appeared several million years ago have been hunter-gatherers.

Other ways of life—farming and city-dwelling, for instance—have come into being only in the last few thousand years.

Farb further points out the sad fact that whereas the ten million or so people who lived on the planet prior to 12,000 years ago were all gatherers and hunters, today, out of the world's approximately four billion people, only .005 per cent are able to maintain this way of life. Other sources cite even lower figures.

> The 12,000 years since the earliest agriculture represent only about five hundred human generations, surely too few to allow for overwhelming genetic changes. Therefore the origins of the intellect, physique, emotions, and social life that are universal to human beings must be traced to preagricultural times. Humans are the evolutionary product of the success of the hunting adaptation, even though almost all of Homo sapiens alive today have abandoned that way of life.
>
> ~ Peter Farb[6]

The Animal World

Since hunter-gatherers do not domesticate animals, all their animal food is won from the wild at great personal risk. Naturally, in ancient times, hunters had no devices such as guns and safari jeeps and were highly vulnerable to attacks from wounded or predatory animals. Wild animals reign over life in the Sensitive Chaos, and the hunter-gatherer's relationship to them is far more complex than mere survival factors suggest. In all but the most extreme climates, gatherer-hunters rely on the food gathered by women for the majority of their diet,[7] reserving animal food mainly for ceremonial feasts. The Sensitive Chaos reaches back at least two million years ago into the evolution of our Pleistocene ancestors. Thus, it is in this archetype that the boundaries between human and animal worlds are most elusive.

Animals predominate in the earliest known art produced by homo sapiens: the Upper Paleolithic murals and carvings in the caves of Europe.[8] The beautiful, naturalistic paintings of bison, horses, and other animals from caves such as those at Lascaux in

France are justly famous, and there are similarly exquisite prehistoric paintings and rock carvings on every continent: in the caves of Tassili n-Ajjer in the Sahara and the Drakensberg Range in South Africa, for example, and throughout Australia where aboriginal peoples made rock carvings and paintings possibly as early as 30,000 years ago.[9] Veneration of animals continued even in some non-Sensitive Chaos state societies. For instance, throughout the 3000 year history of pharaonic Egypt, and continuing into the Roman Empire, cats, bulls, rams, and other animals were worshipped as deities in their own temples. In *The Eternal Present: The Beginnings of Architecture*, Sigfried Giedion describes the changing relationship to animals revealed in the art of ancient Egypt and Mesopotamia. He says that the Egyptians' "attitude toward the animal is their strongest link with the prehistoric conception of the oneness of all life." Throughout Egypt's Predynastic period, Giedion observes, animals continued to play a far greater role than humans. However, a shift from sacred animals to an "anthropomorphic world of gods" occurred with the rise of nation states.

Concurrently, human beauty entered art in such works as the Fourth Dynasty triad sculpture of King Mycerinus with the cow-goddess Hathor. Giedion writes:

> The religious structure of the first high civilizations was
> founded upon the discovery of the human form and the
> human face. Without this, its entire edifice could not
> have been built up, Only after man had begun to consider
> himself beautiful could his own image be used as a
> model for the object of his worship .... For this to occur,
> the primeval conception of man as inferior to the animal
> had first to be overcome.[11]

The fate of Imdugud, a lioness-headed eagle revered by the Sumerians, reveals a more violent conquest of the animal world of the Sensitive Chaos by a Pyramid civilization. When powerful city-states formed in Mesopotamia, the rulers and priests changed Imdugud from an independent hybrid with awesome powers, including the control of human fate, to a domesticated heraldic emblem of the storm-war-and-city-god Ningirsu. In the

Vulture Stele in the Louvre, Ningirsu brutally clutches Imdugud in his hand as it closes around the top of a net full of captured enemies.[12] Siegfried Giedion writes, "This vulture stele, from the second half of the third millennium, is a highly meaningful historical document. It shows the subservience of the ancient bird of fate and the rise to dominant power of the god."[13]

All veneration of animals, whether in their own right or as incarnations or emblems of gods, was eventually repressed with varying success by the Biblical religions—Judaism, Christianity, and Islam. Motivated by an entirely different worldview, with their doctrine of human superiority over animals, these faiths led ultimately to the modern Grid's complete de-*human*-ization of the animal world. Fortunately, this destructive and alienating doctrine is being challenged as industrialized people begin to listen to the wisdom of their indigenous sisters and brothers.

Though the ideas of non-literate[14] people will always remain a mystery, we might glimpse something of them by looking at the ideas and animal art of contemporary gatherer-hunters. Leading scholars have found that contemporary practices stem from beliefs that are far more sophisticated than the simple notion of "hunting magic" formerly put forth as an explanation for Paleolithic cave-painting. Some Australian aboriginal societies, for instance, still maintain their rock-paintings of sacred animal ancestors. As we will see in more detail later, the aborigines believe that if they neglect the paintings, life itself will wane, for the paintings are vehicles for the flow of life from the spirit world of the Dreamtime into the human world. The paintings both preserve cultural identity and generate psychological meaning. Different tribes are responsible for different paintings, so their upkeep also cements social relationships and obligations, helping to maintain community harmony in the absence of formal legal codes.

It may be that hunter-gatherers do not see themselves as inferior to animals, as Giedion suggested, but rather as undifferentiated from them. Some of the earliest art portrays animal-human composites, suggesting blurred distinctions between the animal and human realms in the Paleolithic mind.

The dancing, bearded Sorcerer in the Les Trois Frères cave in the Pyrenees is a wonderful example. He has enormous antlers, stag's ears, transfixed owl's eyes, a horse's tail, the sexual organs of a big cat or lion, and animal paws. He may be the first animal-human figure in art, and he illustrates a practice that has become one of the longest lived and most universal: the animal-mimicking dance. In evidence as early as the Old Stone Age and no doubt of shamanic origin, the animal dance is still practiced by such performers as the Morris dancers of England and the Pueblo dancers of the American Southwest. It reaches the height of virtuosity, however, among Sensitive Chaos hunters— the natural masters of animal mimicry.

In *Animals and the Origins of Dance*, Steven Lonsdale suggests that animal dancing may be one way that humans seek to return spiritually to their animal origins:

> [The animal dancer's] sense of mime and powers of imagination combine in a complex and seemingly endless array of patterns to serve, honour and reflect the infinite mystery that is the dumb beast. His quest is ultimately a spiritual one for instinctive origins. And if the dance returns the performer to his earliest rhythm, the danced animal image confirms the link to his animal brethren ineradicably residing within him in the form of animal instinct.[15]

Animal Dancing

Lonsdale proposes that in addition to recalling humanity's animal origins, imitative animal dancing helps hunter-gatherers to:

- Simulate an animal's strength, perception, or other powers
- Gain control over an animal or attract it for hunting purposes
- Give a sense of unity and shared experience to the hunting party
- Communicate with animals for divination or magical purposes
- Learn animal language to gain access to privileged information
- Enact myths of origin involving the animal world
- Provide amusement and play
- Teach the young, especially future hunters, about animal behavior

The !Kung are gatherer-hunters who live in Africa's Kalahari Desert and exemplify the Sensitive Chaos worldview. They are dependent upon the whole antelope family, and springboks and gemsboks figure prominently in their art, myths, and dances. The !Kung are also expert animal mimickers. In a paper titled "!Kung Knowledge of Animal Behavior," the authors, an anthropologist and an ethologist, write, "...the !Kung appear to know a good deal more about many subjects than do scientists .... Some !Kung observations [of animal behavior] which we refused to believe were later proved correct when subsequently checked with ethologists who have worked in Africa."[16]

Among the more than 8000 rock paintings by the ancestors of the !Kung in the Drakensberg Range in southern Africa is a spectacular fresco in the Sebaayene Cave in the Ndedema Gorge showing a procession of "antelope men" These dignified mythical figures, painted nearly three times as large as the ordinary humans in the frescos, parade majestically above action scenes of earthly life as if they belonged to a wholly other realm of being.

According to various accounts, the !Kung believe that the figures show the spirits of the dead, and that living humans, too, were springboks before Mantis, the creator, turned them into humans. They believe also that in the beginning all animals were people. Magical time, "when all these personages were present in the same world and vitally connected with one another," ended when animals became animals and people became people.[17] Alternatively, the figures may represent men in states of altered consciousness attained through a type of dance that raises n/um, the !Kung version of Kundalini energy.[18] In any case, the principle of mutability within the unity of being prevails.

Sympathetic Identification

The key to Sensitive Chaos culture is sympathetic identification. Generated by an animistic worldview and reinforced by shamanism, totemism, sympathetic magic, and the regular attainment by some or all of the population of transcendent states of consciousness, sympathetic identification gives hunter-gatherers the elaborate, intimate knowledge of their natural habitat that they need to survive. It proves vital to every facet of their existence from identifying edible and medicinal plants, to tracking prey, to locating water sources and good campsites, to protecting themselves from predators and the vagaries of nature. Since they have neither the ability nor the desire to "conquer" nature, sympathetic identification allows them to work with nature, indeed, to be part of it and to know its patterns and energies from the inside.

Through sympathetic identification, Sensitive Chaos people become the elements of their environment. For instance, a hunter of antelope does not merely study the antelope and devise theories about its behavior from a subject-object duality like a modern Western scientist. Through animal-dances, rituals, and trance states, he temporarily becomes an antelope and thereby gains knowledge of the animal's thoughts, habits, smells, travels, and hiding places. For the hunt, he takes pains to camouflage his human smells and colors and disguise himself as an antelope, hoping that the animal will mistake him for one of its own kind and unwittingly let him get close enough for the kill. In social gatherings the hunter shares his knowledge with others, and entertains them as well, by precisely mimicking the antelope's every sound, gesture, and mannerism. Taking pride in this art, he competes with other antelope hunters and learns from the performances of other animal mimickers.

The !Kung hunter's identification with the antelope is only a small part of the vast belief system of his culture, which continuously dissolves the boundaries between the human and animal worlds. One who lives in the Sensitive Chaos may be identified through myths, secret names, tribal ancestry, and transformative initiation rituals with one or more totemic spirits that serve as guides and guardians in the ever-fluctuating unity of being. Sensitive Chaos children learn that the most basic skills of their people were taught by animals and nature spirits: weaving by spiders, fire-making by lightning spirits, root-finding by boars, shelter-building by birds and insects, etc. It is no wonder that in the Sensitive Chaos nature spirits are venerated as the first deities, ancestors, teachers, and spiritual guides of humankind.

This cultural immersion in the world of animals is psychologically reinforced by a suppression of ego that overcomes the normal boundaries between self and other, making complete sympathetic identification possible.

Psychoerotic Extensions

Animals—and apparently even plants—have an astounding array of sensory capacities unmatched by human capabilities and modern technology. Trees warn each other to prepare for insect invasions. Various species of animals can predict earthquakes and weather changes; orient themselves by the polarized light of the sun; perceive infrared light and other wavebands invisible to the human eye; generate phosphorescence; navigate thousands of miles; use inbuilt sonar; and detect minute thermal differences, magnetic fields, and electrical charges—to name a few abilities that humans generally lack.

Through sympathetic identification with wildlife, Sensitive Chaos people probably extend their human senses by vicariously assuming those of the animals, birds, insects, and even plants to which they are attuned. The entire collection of seemingly magical extra-human perceptions that Sensitive Chaos people have acquired, refined, and passed on generation after generation for thousands of years can be considered their psychoerotic extensions. These are equivalent to what Marshall McLuhan called technological extensions:[19] the tools, machines, electronics, and other inventions of technelogos that extend the sensorimotor capacities and even mental processes of industrialized people. Where we depend on radio telescopes and electron microscopes to tell us about the universe, Sensitive Chaos people depend on the specialized sensors of birds, fish, insects, and animals. Gatherer-hunters extend the abilities of their limbs and senses through sympathetic identification with nature. Sometimes this gives them what we might call "extrasensory perception."

These psychoerotic extensions are by no means inferior to technological extensions. They represent an extremely developed and useful way of knowing the world that draws on a great variety of extended receptors, a way of knowing that is at least as sophisticated as any other.

The Cosmic Continuum

We glimpse the fluctuating, mutable, physical world of the Sensitive Chaos every time we see smoke curling up from a cigarette, or watch wave interference patterns in water, or note how water spirals down a drain, or see the rhythmic markings that wind and water leave on sand, or observe the undulating folds in sedimentary rocks.[20] These are everyday evidence of the laws of form in the cosmic continuum, evidence of the subtle intelligence suggested by the word "Sensitive" in Sensitive Chaos. "Chaos," whether in nature or culture, is a form of order governed by laws so subtle that they are beyond the limited grasp of the rational mind.

For the most part, our technological way of life cuts us off from the direct perception of the cosmic continuum of which we are a part. Influenced by static nineteenth century science, we tend to see everything fragmented into discrete categories governed by regular mechanical, mathematical, and natural laws. But recent discoveries confirm that we do, in fact, live in a world where the only certainty is flux itself. For example, scientists no longer see the earth's land masses as permanently fixed on continental rocks, but as moving, folding, and shifting radically over geological time. They know that the sun, once the pinnacle of constancy, is actually a lively stellar organism that was born, lives an unstable existence, and one day will die, just as the universe itself appears periodically to come into being and disappear through rhythmic expansions and contractions over numberless eons. Particle physicists and theoretical mathematicians are discovering ever subtler realms of the material universe. Seemingly erratic, unpredictable mathematical laws governing natural phenomena that previously eluded our sense of order are just beginning to be understood in catastrophe theory, fractal simulation, and chaos science. In scientific laboratories, even the assumption that the scientific method is "objective" is being challenged as scientists recognize the subjectivity of the observer and its impact on whatever is observed. "Fuzzy logic" is becoming an attractive alternative to Cartesian rationalism.

The roiling, unpredictable, asymmetrical currents of electromagnetic energy; the explosive, transformative power of nuclear

32 Spatial Archetypes

energy; and the newly discovered "weak force" have joined steady gravitational force as the four prime energies of the universe. The web of magnetic currents may well have been felt intuitively by ancient and primitive peoples.[21] These magnetic fields are now thought to be generated by the earth's molten core as it churns with the rotation of the planet, forming swirling eddies and lines of force that emanate to the surface. From the north and south poles, a strong field sweeps out into space, circling the planet in the shape of a gigantic teardrop, flattened on one side by solar winds streaming from the sun at close to a million miles per hour.

Einstein's space-time continuum and his lifelong search for a unified field theory created a new paradigm that inspired a generation of physicists to seek the basic nature of the cosmic continuum. Biologists and chemists are studying the subtle forces emanating from the sun, moon, stars, and planets that pervade all living organisms and influence their rhythmic cycles, moods, and biological clocks. What is emerging from these new scientific efforts is an image of the cosmos as a universal field-in-flux composed of an infinite number of finely interacting, continuously changing forces.

> [Adrien] Douody and [John] Hubbard used a brilliant chain of new mathematics to prove that every floating molecule does indeed hang on a filigree that binds it to all the rest, a delicate web springing from tiny outcroppings on the main set, a "devil's polymer," in Mandelbrot's phrase. The mathematicians proved that any segment—no matter where, and no matter how small—would, when blown up by the computer microscope, reveal new molecules, each resembling the main set and yet not quite the same. Every new molecule would be surrounded by its own spirals and flamelike projections, and those, inevitably, would reveal molecules tinier still, always similar, never identical, fulfilling some mandate of inner variety, a miracle of miniaturization in which every new detail was sure to be a universe of its own, diverse and entire.
> ~ James Gleick[22]

To the native of the Sensitive Chaos, the interconnectedness of matter, energy, and spirit in the cosmic continuum is the background assumption in every daily action and thought. For instance, Sensitive Chaos people do not see illness as resulting from physiological factors—from intrusive foreign microbes acting on a body weakened by internal chemical imbalances and breakdowns in its mechanical processes. Instead, they see illness as the result of someone or something acting maliciously from a distance, usually through witchcraft or sorcery, to manipulate the energies of the cosmic continuum. This results in a loss of life force or a displacement of soul that is only superficially indicated by the physiological symptoms of dis-ease. Treatment—whether by shaman, herbalist, sand-painter, curandero, or root doctor—consists not of dealing with the symptoms but of fundamentally restoring the balance of energy in the microcosm of the person and in the extended macrocosm of the cosmic continuum.

In the Sensitive Chaos, human consciousness is not bounded by the envelope of skin around the body, nor by the differentiating ego, nor by conventional time and space. It can see all parts of the universe at once and move freely as an active agent in the universal field-in-flux. Thus, the inner being of every person is inextricably woven into the cosmos and is responsible for its harmony.

Ego and Transcendence

> Being fiercely egalitarian, the lKung do not allow n/um to be monopolized or hoarded by a few religious specialists...
> ~ Richard Katz[24]

Everything about Sensitive Chaos culture focuses on the goal of transmuting life forms within the unity of being. We have seen why it was crucial for hunters to "change" temporarily from humans to animals. This ability to maintain a fluidity of being informs every facet of the culture. For example, although gatherer-hunters avoid accumulating wealth, property, and permanent buildings for practical reasons—such burdens would hinder nomadic mobility—they avoid them for spiritual reasons as well.

Possessions constitute a coagulation and fixation of matter that would obstruct the flow of energy in the Sensitive Chaos.

Similarly, gatherer-hunters minimize social distinctions that create competition, strife, or imbalances of power within or among bands. Not only would these inequities undermine the tight cooperation on which the band depends, but they would also deny the essential unity of all parts of the One Great Being. In the ethos of the Sensitive Chaos, anything that contributes to the ego is divisive, undermines- sympathetic identification, and threatens the harmony of the cosmos.

There is little evidence that contemporary gatherers and hunters simply lack ego, but there is strong evidence that they intentionally suppress or transcend ego. The !Kung spend one or two nights a week from dusk to dawn in intense dance sessions to raise n/um or Kundalini energy. These sessions, cadenced to the singing and clapping of women, bring on the dramatic trance state called !kia, in which the !Kung see the energies of the cosmic continuum. In his essay, "Education for Transcendence: !Kia-healing with the Kalahari !Kung," anthropologist Richard Katz describes !Kia as a deeply emotional "state of transcendence," intensely painful and difficult to attain, in which "a !Kung experiences himself as existing beyond his ordinary level of existence." While in this extraordinary state, "he performs cures, handles and walks on fire, claims x-ray vision, and at times says he sees over great distances."[24]

The sight gained by the !Kung in !kia is clearly non-ordinary, a gift from the mythic dimension. Tsau, a blind n/um master, says that God plucked out his eyeballs and now keeps them with him in heaven in a little cloth bag tied to his belt. When Tsau dances and the singing rises to heaven, God comes down and puts his eyeballs back in their sockets. He can then heal. When the women stop singing, God takes the eyeballs back up to heaven. Tsau feels he is only truly and fully himself when he is in !kia.

Tsau describes the action of n/um as it rises, tingling, up his spine like a "pointed something" which "makes your thoughts nothing in your head." This transformative energy seems to suppress the logos principle, removing concepts that might block psychoerotic perception. Bo, another n/um master, brings this transformation to life:

You dance, dance, dance, dance. Then n/um lifts you in your belly and lifts you in your back, and then you start to shiver. N! um makes you tremble; it's hot. Your eyes are open but you don't look around; you hold your eyes still and look straight ahead. But when you get into !kia, you're looking around because you see everything, because you see what's troubling everybody...Rapid shallow breathing that's what draws n/ um up...then n/ um enters every part of your body, right to the tip of your feet and even your hair.[23]

!Kia is not reserved for an elite. Katz states that about half of the older adult males and one-third of the adult women learn to !kia. N/um and !kia, he says, are their most important allies against illness, adversity, and death. "Being fiercely egalitarian, the !Kung do not allow n/um to be monopolized or hoarded by a few religious specialists; rather they want to spread the teachings and n/um widely within the group."[24] This gives people a way to help others and fosters social cohesion. It also provides a cathartic release of emotional tension and fear, and then opens the doors to the sacred.

When Tsau, Bo, and other !Kung are in *!kia*, they can heal others because they can see, enter, and act in the dangerous, supernatural realm where the ghosts of dead ancestors live. They cannot do this in ordinary reality where they are separate, ego-based, limited individuals. The ghosts cause sickness and death by carrying off the "chosen ones." Fighting the ghosts to effect healing is the main reason that large numbers of !Kung undertake this difficult transformation.

The ghosts are strong but not invincible Masters of n/um may struggle with the ghosts and may often win. While in !kia, a n/um master argues and contends with these ghosts. He carries on a sometimes heated dialogue: "Don't take this person yet, he's not ready to go." In his ordinary state, a !Kung is in awe of the supernatural and avoids talking about it; certainly he does not deal directly with it lfa person's n/um is strong, the ghosts will retreat; and the sick one will live. This struggle is at the heart of the n/um master's art, skill, and power.[24]

Many other indigenous peoples, particularly in the Americas, achieve similar states through sessions with hallucinogenic plants and mushrooms. Australian aborigines have strong shamanic traditions, and the men undergo powerful initiation rites in which they experience the mythic dimension called the Dreamtime through chants, long periods of seclusion, and blood rituals. Ecstasy—whether achieved through Kundalini energy, painful rituals, or hallucinogens—is an authentic religious experience, marshaling not only the powers of the mind but also the visceral energies of the total organism to effect a revelation of the unity of being.

Mythical Time

One indication that the ego-transcendent state is not the normal waking consciousness even of contemporary hunter-gatherers is that they themselves have a nostalgia for a long lost mythical paradise when the boundaries between animals, humans, and deities, and the limits of time and death, did not exist. In *Shamanism: Archaic Techniques of Ecstasy*, Mircea Eliade writes that in the ecstatic state, the shaman "abolishes the present human condition and, for the time being, recovers the situation as it was at the beginning. Friendship with animals, knowledge of their language, transformation into an animal are so many signs that the shaman has re-established the 'paradisal' situation lost at the dawn of time."[25] The shaman, in other words, restores a state that in mythical time was the natural condition of every human being.

> In numerous traditions friendship with animals and understanding their language represent paradisal syndromes. In the beginning, that is, in mythical times, man lived at peace with the animals and understood their speech. It was not until after a primordial catastrophe, comparable to the 'Fall' of Biblical tradition,

that man became what he is today—mortal, sexed, obliged to work to feed himself, and at enmity with the animals.
~ Mircea Eliade[25]

Perhaps mythical time represents for the contemporary hunter-gatherer, just as it may for us, a dim ancestral memory of our ancient past when we emerged from the animal world through millions of years of evolution. If this is the case, then our proto-hominid ancestors would have been the legendary race that could still converse with animals, since they were evolutionarily closer to animal existence. Perhaps, they lived always in the ecstatic mind-frame that we find so difficult to regain.

But the mythical time in the land of paradise is also present within us at every moment. The Dreamtime of the aborigines, Tir na Nog of the Celts, the Elysian Fields of the Orphics, and the Garden of Eden in the Bible are not historical places, but different names for an archetypal place in the mind: the pure psychoerotic world where synchronistic, eternal time unfolds when we transcend ego and our linear sense of time. Children live also in mythical time before schooling and conditioning replace their natural psychoerotic powers with the socialized constructs of technelogos. The Balinese believe that infants—newly emerged as they are from the spiritual dimension—are still gods until they are six months old. At that age, amidst much ceremony, babies touch their feet to the earth for the first time. In some parts of the world, India and the Himalayas for example, people believe that the paradisal realm can be entered only by mastering subtle physio-spiritual energies and endocrine processes. And some people such as Teilhard de Chardin believe that this perfect world lies in a future consummate stage of evolution and that our memories presage the glory that is to come.

Serpent Energy

In his book *Kundalini, The Evolutionary Energy in Man*, Gopi Krishna conveys the torture and terror he endured for decades after his body's Kundalini energy spontaneously came alive. He felt the mysterious, fiery, intelligent energy darting around his body, working on all of his organs and cells. At times he almost perished from the inner heat,[26] which the !Kung describe also as a property of n/um. Slowly, Gopi Krishna was able to master the wildly erratic, dangerous force, which eventually brought on enlightenment. His description of this energy, with its intersecting streams and whorled eddies and vortexes, could well be a description of the Sensitive Chaos itself.

> ... it is utterly impossible to picture or to depict even hazily the colossal world of Prana, or life energy, as described by seers, its unbounded extent traversed by streams and cross-streams, currents and cross-currents, radiating from innumerable stars and planets with motionless spots and storm centres, vortexes and eddies, all throbbing with activity everywhere, the animate worlds rising out of this marvelously intelligent but subtle ocean of vital activity as foam appears on the surface of the perennially moving oceanic currents.
> ~ Gopi Krishana[28]

The great serpents, dragons, and water creatures of world mythology teem with meaning and personify the swirling currents of air, water, and subtle energy. Examples include the Hindu serpent goddess Kundalini, the Rainbow Serpent of the Australian aborigines, the Dogon's Nummo ancestors, the Delphic Python, the caduceus of Mercury, the Norse Midgard Serpent, the Egyptians sun-devourer Apophis, the Plumed Serpent Quetzalcoatl of Mesoamerica, and the great Asian dragons and nagas.

The serpent as a symbol of undifferentiated chaos, raw cosmic or Telluric energy, uroboric oneness, and the primordial waters reasserts itself in later civilizations as a primal force that must repeatedly be confronted. To the extent that a culture acknowledges its roots in the Sensitive Chaos, it honors the serpent. Conversely, the more it is alienated from the Sensitive Chaos, from nature, and from psychoerotic perception, the more it seeks to destroy the serpent.

Order and Chaos

One of the major themes in world mythology concerns how order is brought out of chaos. One way of looking at this is to explore how human concepts and language arise to differentiate the original oneness into its multiple mundane parts. In other words, how do we go from the "Tao" to the "ten thousand things?" We perceive this transformation, which is ongoing as well as historical, both as a fall from the grace of pure consciousness and as an opportunity to act humanly in the world made manifest. We can gain some perspective from societies that have moved beyond the Sensitive Chaos but still retain vivid memories of their emergence from it.

One such culture is the Dogon, subsistence farmers who live in Mali near the Upper Volta border in West Africa. Today, the Dogon mostly display Four Quarters characteristics, but their mythology is full of the Sensitive Chaos, as well as other archetypes. They trace their ancestry from the mythical Nummo, who were created when water entered the womb of the earth. The Nummo, synonymous with water—the life-force in that arid region—are male and female, half-human and half-serpent, green, and completely flexible, having limbs with no joints. How the mythic mind personifies the first emergence of order is beautifully captured in the Dogon myth of how the Nummo taught the earth her first language.

The Nummo's First Word

The Nummo, looking down from Heaven, saw their mother, the earth, naked and speechless. It was necessary to put an end to this slate of disorder. The Nummo accordingly came down to myth, bringing with them fibres pulled from plants already created in the heavenly regions. They took ten bunches of these fibres, corresponding to the number of their ten fingers, and made two strands of them, one for the front and one for behind. To this day masked men still wear these appendages hanging down to their feet in thick tendrils.

40 *Spatial Archetypes*

But the purpose of this garment was not merely modesty. It manifested on earth the first act in the ordering of the universe and the revelation of the helicoid sign in the form of an undulating broken line.

For the fibres fell in coils, symbol of tornadoes, of the winding of torrents, of eddies and whirlwinds, of the undulating movement of reptiles. They recall also the eight-fold spirals of the sun, which sucks up moisture. They were themselves a channel of moisture, impregnated as they were with the freshness of the celestial plants. They were full of the essence of Nummo: they were Nummo in motion, as shown in the undulating line, which can be prolonged to infinity.

When Nummo speaks, what comes from his mouth is a warm vapour which conveys, and itself constitutes, speech. This vapour, like all water, has sound, dies away in a helicoid line. The coiled fringes of the skirt were therefore the chosen vehicle for the words which the Spirit desired to reveal to the earth. He endued his hands with magic power by raising them to this lips while he plaited the skirt, so that the moisture of his words was imparted to the damp plaits, and the spiritual revelation was embodied in the technical instruction.

In these fibres full of water and words, placed over his mother's genitalia, Nurnrno is thus always present.

Thus clothed the earth had a language, the first language of this world and the most primitive of all time. Its syntax was elementary, its verbs few, and its vocabulary without elegance. The words were breathed sounds scarcely differentiated frown one another, but nevertheless vehicles. Such as it was, this ill-defined speech sufficed for the great works of the beginning of all things.

~ Marcel Griaule[28]

Clothing the earth with the intelligence of the Sensitive Chaos, the Nummo brought her to the brink between order and chaos. They did this through language, a language of nature reminiscent of the Celtic tree alphabet Beth-Luis-Nion (Birch-Rowan-Ash), which surely had pre-Celtic roots in Europe's own Sensitive Chaos era. Both the tree alphabet and the Nummo's first language hover in that liminal realm where the logical mind is not yet fully born and tendrils of magic and mystery still envelop the psyche. The Chinese *Tao Te Ching* begins in the same spirit and also speaks of language or "the named" as the "beginning of all things."

> The Tao that can be told is not the eternal Tao.
> The name that can be named is not the eternal name.
> The nameless is the beginning of heaven and earth.
> The named is the mother of ten thousand things.
> Ever desireless, one can see the mystery.
> Ever desiring, one can see the manifestations.
> These two spring from the same source but differ in name; this appears as darkness.
> Darkness within darkness
> The gate to all mystery.
> ~ Lao Tsu[29]

Language

> In the beginning was the Word, and the Word was with God, and the Word was God
> ~ John 1:1

We have seen that language takes part both in the fall from paradise (losing fluency in the language of animals) and in the creation and ordering of the manifest world (the Dogon's first language, the "named" as the "mother of ten thousand things"). Language is an organizing filter that orders the perceptual field into conceptual categories while it obscures holistic vision. How language changes consciousness was dramatically portrayed in the film *The Miracle Worker* when the deaf-blind-mute Helen Keller grasped the significance of her first spoken word, "water." Suddenly an entirely new world opened before her, no longer a random accumulation of sense impressions, but a world that could be rationally known. Every child learning to speak repeats this potent moment of cognition,[30] echoing the ancient belief in the magical power of names, especially strong in Egypt and the Near East, and in divine creation through the Word.

If language is such an active agent in bringing order out of chaos, the purest form of the Sensitive Chaos must have existed before language developed. It follows that it is recapitulated in infants who have not yet learned to speak. To attain this language-transcendent state on a more advanced, conscious level, certain religious adepts practice silent meditation or take vows of silence. People who take psychotropic drugs chemically similar to those used by gatherer-hunters often temporarily lose the ability to speak coherently. Some also experience speech as a flow of breath and vapor, much like the Nummo's, which intelligibly carries the meaning of their thoughts without having been consciously formed into words and sentences.[31] There is also the mysterious display known as "speaking in tongues"—if not the virtually extinct universal language stored in the collective unconscious, as some claim, then at least a language anomaly triggered by religious ecstasy. In 1874, the Congolese demanded that the explorer H. M. Stanley burn his notes, believing that his written records of them would bring sterility and death. Considering how European/American colonialism and economic exploitation have nearly annihilated life in the Sensitive Chaos in Africa as elsewhere, they were right. Like Sensitive Chaos people everywhere, the Congolese must have sensed the same connections that McLuhan observed among literacy, linear thinking, and technological excess. (Stanley appeased the Congolese by burning his copy of Shakespeare, which he led them to believe was his log.)

Hallucinogens, Shamanism, and Psychoerotic Perception

> The chief spoke in a low, pleasant tone, "Visions begin."
> He had completely captured my attention with two

words of magic. I instantly felt a melting away of any
barrier between us; we were as one.
~ Manuel Córdova-Rios

A sympathetic encounter with primitive people is recounted in the curious story of Manuel Córdova-Rios, told by Bruce Lamb in *Wizard of the Upper Amazon*. Córdova-Rios was a healer who claimed to have gained his powers around the turn of the century when, as a young man fresh out of school seeking a career in the rubber industry, he was kidnapped by hunting-gathering Amahuaca Indians in the Amazon forest.

After his harrowing capture and imprisonment, Córdova-Rios proved unaggressive, and his captors eventually trusted him. They inducted him into their way of life and initiated him in the art of seeing with the aid of *honi xumu* (or *ayahuasca*), an hallucinogenic herbal concoction. Several days of preparation preceded the *hani xumu* sessions. Different tribal members collected and carefully brewed the "vision vine," prepared certain foods and purgatives, and built a special shelter to isolate Córdova-Rios for his purifying fast.

During the sessions, Córdova-Rios underwent classic mind-expansion: time ceased, luminous intricate detail emerged in everything, spectacular visual patterns spontaneously appeared, and intense erotic sensations enveloped him. He also saw the inner nature of various birds and animals who were evoked, one by one, by the chants of the chief. After his first session, Córdova-Rios noticed that he understood the language of his captors much better. It was as if their language had been born from the sounds of the jungle, made comprehensible by *honi xumu*. The chief's preparatory chant, sung before the honi xumu was ingested, invoked animal spirits for their aid as psychoerotic extensions:

> Spirits of the forest
> revealed to us by honi xuma
> bring us knowledge of the realm
> assist in the guidance of our people
> give us the stealth of the boa
> penetrating sight of the hawk and the owl

acute hearing of the deer
brute endurance of the tapir
grace and strength of the jaguar
knowledge and tranquility of the moon
kindred spirits, guide our way[32]

Once the spirits had been invoked and the magic brew ingested, Córdova-Rios recalls:

> We both lay back in our hammocks. Imperceptibly a feeling of euphoria entered my consciousness. I heard a brief pulsating hum in one ear, which seemed to float off, up into the treetops. My eyes tried to follow it, and as my glance wandered in the treetops I became aware of undreamed beauty in the details of the textures of leaves, stems and branches. Every leaf, as my attention settled on it, seemed to glow with a greenish golden light. Unimaginable detail of structure showed. A nearby bird song—the irregular arpeggios of the siete cantos (seven songs)—floated down. Time seemed suspended; there was only now and now was infinite ....
>
> The chief spoke in a low, pleasant tone, "Visions begin" He had completely captured my attention with two words of magic. I instantly felt a melting away of any barrier between us; we were as one. The mere glance of an eye had infinite meaning. The slightest change of expression conveyed full intent. We had complete rapport at all levels of understanding. I knew his thought as he knew mine. Did this telepathic facility come from some primitive recess of mind used before ancestral man communicated in formal language?[33]

Córdova-Rios came to see the *honi xuma* sessions as an essential and practical part of Amahuaca life. Among other things, they were an integral part of the men's continuous efforts to hone their hunting skills, for they opened the barriers between humanity and nature, giving access to the pre-verbal sensate world in which the animals themselves lived. Before he gained some of these skills himself, Córdova-Rios was amazed by the Indians' detailed knowledge of the forest and its denizens; by their finely tuned muscular coordination as they moved quickly, quietly, through tangled undergrowth; by their sensitivity to the faintest sounds and scents; and by their instant absorption of all environmental signals that contributed to the success of the hunt. Córdova-Rios chose to use the skills he learned from the Indians to become not a hunter but a healer.

Córdova-Rios's story is still steeped in mystery. Some anthropologists question its authenticity but find it consistent with innumerable accounts in the scholarly literature of similar encounters with South American tribespeople, which feature hallucinogenic rituals, transcendental and transformative experiences, excursions outside the normal bounds of time and space, the acquiring of extra-human perception, entering into special relationships with animals, and so on. In *Hallucinogens and Shamanism*, anthropologist Kenneth M. Kensinger describes the use of ayahuasca (banisteriopsis) among the Cashinahua, a small Peruvian tribe. In a footnote, he reports some ensuing non-ordinary perceptual abilities:

> Hallucinations generally involve scenes which are a part of the Cashinahua's daily experience. However, informants have described hallucinations about places far removed both geographically and from their own experience. Several informants who have never been to or seen pictures of Pucallpa, the large town at the Ucayali River terminus of the Central Highway, have described their visits under the influence of ayahuasca to the town with sufficient detail for me to be able to recognize specific shops and sights. On the day following one ayahuasca party six of nine men informed me of seeing the death of my chai, "my mother's father." This occurred two days before l was informed by radio of his death.[34]

In the following passage from *Hallucinogens and Shamanism*, anthropologist Michael Harner describes a Jivaro shaman from the Ecuadorian Amazon who takes banisteriopsis to help him heal a sick man.

He had drunk, and now he softly sang. Gradually, faint lines and forms began to appear in the darkness, and the shrill music of the tsenlsak, the spirit helpers, arose around him. The power of the drink fed them. He called, and they came. First, pangi, the anaconda, coiled about his head, transmuted into a crown of gold. Then wampang, the giant butterfly, hovered above his shoulder and sang to him with its wings. Snakes, spiders, birds and bats danced in the air above him. On his arms appeared a thousand eyes as his demon helpers emerged to search the night for enemies.

The sound of rushing water filled his ears, and listening to its roar, he knew he possessed the power of Tsungi, the first shaman. Now he could see. Now he could find the truth. He stared at the stomach of the sick man. Slowly, it became transparent like a shallow mountain stream, and he saw within it, coiling and uncoiling, makanchi, the poisonous serpent, who had been sent by the enemy shaman. The real cause of the illness had been found.[35]

Note the Sensitive Chaos elements in the Jivaro shaman's craft. First, he alters his own consciousness by drinking the banisteriopsis brew, then he focuses his mind by singing.[36] He assembles various spirit and animal helpers—his psychoerotic extensions, which greatly expand his perception. And finally, transcending his own limited ego-self to open to the greater Self, personified by the first shaman Tsungi, he attains psychoerotic perception: "Now he could see." Now he could find the truth behind the veil of ordinary reality.

Harrier writes, "The normal waking life, for the Jivaro, is simply a 'lie,' or illusion, while the true forces that determine daily events are supernatural and can only be seen and manipulated with the aid of hallucinogenic drugs." *Seeing* in this case means seeing through the body of the sick man to the cause of his illness: the poisonous serpent that an enemy shaman had placed in his stomach.[37] Whether the offending serpent is considered real, as it is to the Jivaro, or symbolic, as it may be to us, it localizes the cause of the illness and gives it a form that can be dealt with on a shamanic or psychological level. Giving the illness a comprehensible image renders it workable. The shaman can extract the serpent, and, whether this is understood to happen physically or psychologically, the goal is the same: to relieve the patient and give him faith that he will now be better.[38]

Spirit Centers: "The Point Existing Here and Everywhere, Now and Always"

Induction into the spirit world of the Sensitive Chaos can bestow wondrous gifts. Gopi Krishna says that his enlightenment inspired him to write poetry in several foreign languages that he had never read or heard spoken, much less learned. Of these experiences he writes,

> On every such occasion I am made to feel as if the observer in me, or speaking more precisely, my lustrous conscious self, is floating, with but an extremely dim idea of the corporeal frame in a vividly bright conscious plane, every fragment of which represents a boundless world of knowledge, embracing the present, past, and future, commanding all the sciences, philosophies, and arts ever known or that will be known in the ages to come, all concentrated and contained in a point existing here and everywhere, now and always, a formless, measureless ocean of wisdom from which, drop by drop, knowledge had filtered and will continue to filter into the human brain.[39]

The "point existing here and everywhere, now and always" is a commonly perceived nexus in the Sensitive Chaos. Like a "wormhole" in space, it permits passage from one space-time continuum to another, or, better yet, it leads beyond space and time altogether. Like the nierika in a Huichol painting, it is the paradoxically non-dimensional bridge, gate, or perilous passage described by Eliade that connects the two universes of the psyche: the eternal, infinite, paradisal world of pure consciousness, and the temporal, bounded, mundane world of manifest reality.[40] This point is the path to the soul. It can even be the mirror of the soul itself. When projected onto the landscape, especially onto a spot that already has strong geophysical powers, this point becomes a sacred place.

As we saw earlier, the psychic space of the Sensitive Chaos is not concerned with the fortification of ego territories or with the political extensions of human will. It is an open, flowing, immediate space with landmarks of potent nodes of energy, It is a space of spirit centers that fuse past, present, and future; humanity and nature; and the heavenly, earthly, and underworld planes of the shaman. They are like the fibers of the corpus callosum in the cerebral cortex that connect the left hemisphere with the right. As totemic places they lead to the collective unconscious, bringing alive the ancestors in oneself, fostering the mutability of life forms, and storing the power of the inner Self.

Worldviews in which the ego is more dominant produce radically different conceptions of space. Instead of spirit centers, personal and political power centers become the landmarks, serving as points of identity for the individual and collective ego. As these points are fortified by walls defending the ego's territories, the earth is accordingly divided into parcels of private property and governmental provinces. Such concepts are an anathema to the flowing Sensitive Chaos, which admits no property lines, legal boundaries, deeds of ownership, walls, or fences. Since everything, including the landscape, is sacred and imbued with the spirit of the unity of being, it would be inconceivable for any part of it to be claimed under private ownership. This does not mean that space is homogeneously "owned" by everyone. Tribal and personal territories are strongly delineated and defended, as they must be if every gathering-hunting band is to have enough rangeland to meet its needs, but the boundaries are defined not by laws and fences but by myths.

The entire mental and physical landscape of the Australian aborigines is laced with mythological paths and spirit-centers. The paths and centers map the travels and deeds of Dreamtime figures—men, women, animals, and birds—whose lives and legends engendered social institutions, codes of conduct, totemic relationships, tribal territories, and the general order of things. The spirit-centers may be marked by standing or piled stones, rock-paintings, a tree or waterhole, or other natural feature. The paths are generally unmarked.

As well as being sites of important mythical events, the spirit-centers are places where the Dreamtime figures leave the spirits of unborn children and animals. They are also places where the soul returns after death to await reincarnation. To the aborigines, conception is not related to fertilization by male sperm, but to the activation of the spirit-centers, which release the unborn spirits that reincarnate as living beings. This process depends on human action. As we noted earlier, the spirit-centers and paths must be regularly attended (the same as any church altar). Their paintings must be refreshed, and the young must be initiated into the knowledge of their whereabouts and sacred meaning. If there is any discontinuity in these traditions and humans fail to do their part, then the entire system breaks down and life stops flowing. The paths important to different tribes often overlap, which ensures social cohesion—each group must depend on the others to maintain their part of the total mythological system.

The paths and centers of the Dreamtime do more than ensure the continuance of fertility and social order. They are also channels of psychoerotic perception that transcend the ordinary bounds of time and space. Attending to the landscape of the Dreamtime, like any spiritual devotion, is a twofold act. Beyond appearing to appease a spiritual force in the outer world—a deity, mythical event, or sacred place—it enlivens the psyche's inner communication with the collective unconscious and the Self. The intensity of the aborigines' communication with the Self over thousands of years has given them, in addition to a highly spiritual culture, a wealth of psychic skills that baffle the whites. In *The Australian Aborigines*, A. P. Elkin describes an instance.

> A man may be away with his employer on a big stock
> trip, and will suddenly announce one day that his father
> is dead, that his wife has given birth to a child, or that
> there is some trouble in his own country. He is so sure
> of his facts that he would return at once if he could, and

the strange thing is, as these employers ascertained the aborigine was quite correct; but how he could have known, they do not understand, for there was no means of communication whatever, and he had been away from his own people for weeks and even months."[41]

Halfway around the world, a similar knowledge of spirit-centers flourishes in Peru. After publishing his popular *Stonehenge Decoded* in 1965, archraeoastronomer Gerald Hawkins went on to study other ancient sites that showed promise of astronomical alignments. One was the work of an early Andean proto-Pyramid culture, the Nazca, who spanned from about 400 B.C. to 600 A.D. Their capital city, Cahuachi, is now buried in sand dunes, but their highly pictorial pottery and textiles still tell their stories. Most importantly, they left an immense, enigmatic network of lines and figures in the Nazca desert. Recognizable among the figures are a monkey, a spider, a lizard, condors, other birds and animals, and several labyrinths, spirals, and concentric rings, including some made with astounding geometric precision.

Inspired by decades of research by the legendary Maria Reiche.[42] Hawkins tried to find astronomical alignments in the Nazca configurations, but his computer analyses produced few significant findings. Coincidentally, he learned about "waca" or spirit centers from a wizened old huaquero, a pilferer of precious objects from sacred sites.

> We talked about the Peruvian "waca," that place inhabited by a spirit. The waca might be a tree, a spring, a mountain—any spot selected by folklore or same happening in the past to be a spirit place. The Spanish took the word from the Incas and transliterated it huaca. The spirit had malignant influence an any passer-by who did not leave an offering. Icons, jewels, and ceremonial vessels were placed at these spots and became part of the spiritual component of the place. Hence the name huaquero, a thief of spirits.
> ~ Gerald Hawkins[43]

Hawkins eventually concluded that the huge Nazca drawings probably were intended to honor huacas or spirits, and Evan Hadingham thoroughly pursues this thesis in *Lines to the Mountain Gods: Nazca and the Mysteries of Peru.* He links the Nazca phenomenon to the use of powerful hallucinogens and to shamanistic beliefs and practices still current in remote Andean villages.[44]

The knowledge of huacas surely stems from the Sensitive Chaos, which is both a prehistoric era in South America and a current, though endangered, mode of life for thousands of Amazonian tribespeople. The most sophisticated Andean version of huaca veneration appeared in the Radiant Axes empire of the Incas, which flourished in the 15th and early 16th centuries A.D. Reflecting the image of their archetypal worldview, the Incas organized 328 spirit centers in a radial pattern of forty-one lines or ceques centering on the Temple of the Sun and extending into the landscape surrounding the Inca capital at Cuzco.[45] We will look at this remarkable system in the Radiant Axes chapter.

Jung's Stone

> Am I the one who is sitting on the stone, or am I the stone on which he is sitting?
> ~ Carl Gustav Jung

Children know about spirit-centers. They live in a world much like the psychoerotic, animistic world of the gatherer-hunter where the boundaries between self and other are blurred and time is eternal. In his autobiography *Memories, Dreams, Reflections*, Jung describes his own boyhood as being filled with secrets and special places and what might be called totemic relationships. For a while he faithfully tended a sacred fire in a "cave" he found in the interstices in the stone wall of his family's garden.

> In front of this wall was a slope in which was embedded a stone that jutted out—my stone, Often, when I was alone, I sat down on this stone, and then began an imaginary

52 Spatial Archetypes

game that went something like this: "I am sitting on top of this stone and it is underneath." But the stone also could say "I" and think: "I am lying here on this slope and he is sitting on top of me." The question then arose: "Am I the one who is sitting on the stone, or am I the stone on which he is sitting?" This question always perplexed me, and I would stand up, wondering who was what now. The answer remained totally unclear, and my uncertainty was accompanied by a feeling of curious and fascinating darkness. But there was no doubt whatsoever that this stone stood in some secret relationship to me. I could sit on it for hours, fascinated by the puzzle it set me.

Eric Holm observed from the petroglyphs of South Africa, "In the primitive state .... a man can be a stone .... everything can take place in heaven as well as on earth."[47] Jung continues:

Thirty years later I again stood on that slope. I was a married man, had children, a house, a place in the world, and a head full of ideas and plans, and suddenly I was again the child who had kindled a fire full of secret significance and sat down on a stone without knowing whether it was I or I was it. I thought suddenly of my life in Zurich, and it seemed alien to me, like news from some world and time. This was frightening, for the world of my childhood in which I had just become absorbed was eternal, and I had been wrenched away from it and had fallen into a time that continued to roll onward, moving farther and farther away. The pull of that other world was so strong that I had to tear myself violently from the spot in order not to lose hold of my future.
    I have never forgotten that moment, for it illuminated in a flash of lightning the quality of eternity in my childhood.[44]

In that moment, Jung's childhood sacred place caught him up again in the magical, everpresent eternity of his early life in the Sensitive Chaos. Thrust into the realm of the psyche where time is eternal and synchronistic, he rediscovered psychoerotic time. But he found it terrifying to be yanked out of the kind of time to which he had become accustomed: the linear time that rolls onward toward the future.

A Place of Predilection

> "This is the site of your last stand," he said. "You will die here no matter where you are."
> ~ Carlos Castaneda[50]

Had Jung lived in a culture that valued spirit-centers and knew how to use their power, he might not have been so frightened. Anthropologist Carlos Castaneda's "don Juan" series tells of a teacher and a culture for whom spirit-centers are part of a well-structured belief system.[48] His accounts of his trials in the Sonora desert with don Juan, a Yaqui Indian[49] shaman and teacher, are full of references to "places of power" special "spots" and "centers" in the landscape, and to "lines" or "strings" of power coursing through the air—the subtle, familiar landmarks of the Sensitive Chaos. In the whole series, one particular "place of power" stands out as being of vital importance to the course of Castaneda's life.

Castaneda found the place, described in *Journey to Ixtlan*, on the other side of a hill he saw through while looking for a healing plant to soothe his legs after an exhausting run through magical time. Don Juan navigated the run to find Castaneda's "place of predilection." Once Castaneda found the place, it took him hours to consecrate it, a task called "suspending the spot." Afterward he slept there. When he awoke, he felt a strange new sense of quiet ebullience and wanted to stay in that spot forever. "'Fix all this in your memory,' don Juan whispered.... 'This spot is yours. This morning you saw and that was the omen. You found this spot by seeing. The omen was unexpected, but it happened. You are going to hunt power whether you like it or not. It is not a human decision, not yours or mine.'"[50]

The omen, Castaneda's seeing the healing bush (the means to wholeness) through the mass of the hill (the ego), indicated that he was capable of suspending ordinary reality and perception, He was capable of transcending his separateness and reentering the world of psychoerotic oneness in the Sensitive Chaos. A sign from the setting sun heralded agreement from the natural universe. Once this world is entered, there is no denying it, no turning back; the promise of our original wholeness is irresistible. Castaneda would hunt its power whether he liked it or not. It was not a "human" decision, not one that fell under the jurisdiction of the discriminating ego.

Castaneda's "place of predilection" like Jung's stone, was an exterior counterpart of an interior place in the psyche—the still center, the "point existing here and everywhere, now and always." These two places—the exterior and the interior—are really one place and this place is the instrument through which the Self continuously works to reintegrate all the dualistic distinctions and conceptions that fragment its original wholeness.

Does the place actually belong to Castaneda? After some joking, don Juan makes it clear that although the place is real and can be visited, its primary importance is spiritual.

> "This is the site of your last stand," he said. "You will die here no matter where you are. Every warrior has a place to die. A place of his predilection which is soaked with unforgettable memories, where powerful events left their mark, a place where he has witnessed marvels, where secrets have been revealed to him, a place where he has stored his personal power.
>
> "A warrior has the obligation to go back to that place of his predilection every time he taps power in order to store it there. He either goes there by means of walking or by means of dreaming.
>
> "And finally, one day when his time on earth is up and he feels the tap of death on his left shoulder, his spirit, which is always ready, flies to the place of his predilection and there the warrior dances his death ....
>
> "And thus you will dance to your death here, on this hilltop, at the end of the day. And in your last dance you will tell of your struggle ... And your death will sit here and watch you.

"The dying sun will glow on you without burning, as it has done today. The wind will be soft and mellow and your hilltop will tremble. As you reach the end of your dance you will look at the sun, for you will never see it again in waking or in *dreaming*, and then your death will point to the south. To the vastness!"[50]

The Architecture of the Sensitive Chaos

Formal works of architecture—monuments, palaces, forts, tombs, and temples—are significant in this archetype only by their absence. In other types of cultures, architecture permanently marks sacred places and symbolically mediates between the self, society, and the cosmos. In the Sensitive Chaos such architecture would obstruct the direct experience of energy and spirit, not to mention impeding the nomadic lifestyle. Thus, nothing is constructed except for immediate use. Huts, tents, and other shelters are always made of readily available natural materials—leaves and vines in the tropics, mud in arid zones, ice in the arctic, animal hides and bones on the steppes. When the inhabitants leave, these ephemeral structures dissolve back into the earth with no traces.

Dwellings in the Sensitive Chaos are the spiritual doubles of the people who live in them. People build new huts built to signal rites of passage into puberty or marriage, and when someone dies, the person's hut crumbles into dust like the mortal body, which often is buried inside. Sometimes huts are burned during funerals, cremating the dead inside, or other measures are taken to ensure that the spirit abiding in the hut will not wander out to bother the living. In some societies, a death means that the entire band must move from the stricken camp and build anew.

One characteristic example of Sensitive Chaos architecture is the typical forest camp of the Mbuti pygmies in Africa. It has no fixed plan, follows no particular principle of orientation such as toward sunrise or sunset, and uses no axial alignments or abstract geometric forms other than the roundness of the huts and some awareness of the importance of the center of the camp. Colin Turnbull noted that a man speaking from his own doorway speaks only as an individual, but one speaking from mid-camp is speaking for the band.[51]

Women build the huts of bent withes and broad leaves, and their placement of the huts, especially the entrances, is revealing. Summarizing Colin Turnbull's observations, Douglas Fraser writes,

> The placement of the entrance, simply a gap in the withes, is perhaps the most telling decision the woman has to make. If she wishes to express her esteem for some group or individual, she will arrange the entrance so that it faces the other person's hut, the exact orientation depending on the warmth of her regard. But if she is irritated by the behavior of someone in the camp, she will build her door pointing away from that person's house. Should her feelings change once the house is erected, the Mbuti woman may reorient her doorway as many times as she wishes. In extreme cases she may move to another site, or she and her family may go and live for a while in a village. As a rule though, members of the camp will attempt quickly to heal the social breach that is obvious to all. In this way the Mbuti camp plan is capable of contributing to social harmony and group cohesion.[52]

The camp changes from day to day to accommodate visitors and the comings and goings of members of the band. Thus, the Mbuti camp does not depend on the permanence and rigidity found in settlements characteristic of other archetypes—the permanence of the villages of the Great Round, the axial walled rigidity of the Four Quarters, the monumentality of the Pyramid, the ceremonial pomposity of the Radiant Axes, or the relentless regularity of the Grid. Rather, the Mbuti camp exhibits a relaxed fluidity and a sensitivity to minute fluctuations in the group's emotional attachments and social relationships.

Archaeologist John E. Yellen writes that !Kung camps are basically of two types: small work camps for the rainy and post-rainy season and larger dry-season base camps, which may be lived in for up to six months, unless a death or a bug infestation forces relocation to a nearby site. In one of Yellen's studies, which spanned a six and a half month period mostly coinciding with the rainy season, a !Kung group moved thirty-seven times and used twenty-seven different camps for an average of three days each. During these nomadic periods, each !Kung group hunts and gathers in a particular area large enough to meet its needs. Yellen cautions:

While it is convenient to describe such areas as 'territories' this term can be misleading. The boundaries of these regions are not clearly defined, and, in fact, !Kung have no single term in their own language to describe them. To some extent areas overlap; they are not defended, and in some instances more than one group will move within a single area. They may be described best as an informal and highly flexible method for arranging the population in a workable relation to available resources.[53]

The camps, which are usually circular and built by the women, consist of nuclear family huts arranged in extended family groupings. Reflecting the impermanence of Sensitive Chaos architecture, !Kung huts can be built in half an hour and usually last less than a year, though they may be used more than once within a season. The typical hut is made of grass tied over branches arranged in a circle to form a domed shape a little over six feet in diameter and six feet high. Sometimes just a few branches thrust into the ground serve as a temporary shelter, similar to the windbreaks of Australian aborigines. (Foundation stones from a similar windbreak were found in Olduvai Gorge dating 2,000,000 years ago—thus far, the world's oldest remains of architecture by our proto-hominid ancestors.) Whenever possible, the !Kung build rainy season camps around small trees and bushes to reduce construction, and these camps are not always circular.[54] A 1968 plan shows a strong east-west axis linking a camp with dance circles and a boys' initiation camp.[55]

The !Kung: A Sensitive Chaos Culture

These are some of the characteristics of the !Kung that exemplify the Sensitive Chaos.

- Strong ethic of sharing, gift-giving, and cooperation so that no one becomes wealthier than anyone else and everyone is provided for
- Egalitarian social structures and an avoidance of authoritarianism in any form
- Non-acquisitive attitudes toward material things
- Emphasis on generosity and humility
- Little need for privacy
- Teaching the young through experience at parents' sides
- Respect for knowledge gained from transcendent states of consciousness (achieved by the !Kung through dancing)
- Healing while in trance states, using a direct knowledge of subtle bodily, and spiritual energies (*n/um, !kia*)
- Strong heritage of rock-painting
- Animal mimicry and storytelling
- Reverence for animals as teachers, creators, ancestors Mythos centered on magical human/animal interactions and transmutations

In one of the principle Kung fables...Manlis [the Creator] is transformed into a cow antelope, who feigns death because it wants man to dismember it and deliver it from life. But soon the severed limbs slip from the hands of the terror-stricken men, and with the first rays of the sun are joined together once again. And now this being soars up to heaven in its true essence and circles the earth with a dancing step. It is now no longer animal, insect or man, although still recognizable as such, but a being comprehending the Universe, representing totality and the source of life, the very daystar.[58]

The Invisible Architecture of Shamanism

Even though Sensitive Chaos people are only marginally engaged in building, their culture and the archetype itself is extremely important to architecture. On the one hand, the people of this archetype are the first to identify sacred place. All later architecture, in one way or another, taps into the numinous spirit-centers of the Sensitive Chaos and builds around them the phantasmaoric structures that proliferate in the human mind as it molds the primal energy into its changing image of the cosmos.

The recurring form motifs of world architecture originate in the invisible architecture of shamanism: the archetypal structure and geography of the non-ordinary reality that shamans are uniquely equipped to enter. The shaman's Three Worlds (Upper, Middle, and Lower) become the clerestories, naves, and crypts of great cathedrals, His Celestial Ceiling—the starry dome overhead in the night sky—becomes the fabulously painted, tiled, and coffered domes of Baroque cathedrals, Chinese temples, Islamic mosques, and neo-classical pantheons. The axis mundi—the vertical axis that the shaman uses to travel between the worlds—becomes the Egyptian and Roman obelisks, Ashoka's and Trajan's columns, the Chinese Mandate of Heaven pillar, the Empire State Building, and the latest space probe rocket. The Tree of Life, a variant of the axis mundi, can be seen in Chinese and Japanese pagodas, the throne pillar in Fatehpur Sikri's Diwan-i-Khas, and the central pole of the Plains Indian's tipi. The shaman's Cosmic or World Mountain, from which she travels to the Upper World, materializes in nation states as the pyramids of Egypt and Mexico, the ziggurats of Sumer and Akkad, and the Buddhist stupas of Asia.

The Navel of the World—that point existing here and everywhere, now and always—can grow through the accretions of the centuries to become a world religious center such as St. Peter's in the Vatican, the Ka'aba in Mecca, the Temple Mount in Jerusalem, and Benares in India. In the next chapters, we will see how succeeding cultures build these archetypes into monumental architecture. (See Appendix 6, "The World of the Shaman," for more on Shamanism.)

SYNOPSIS OF EACH ARCHETYPE

The synopses at the end of each chapter on an archetype list the most representative cultural characteristics of the archetype. Naturally, not all characteristics will be found in every culture. The synopses are best used for orientation and prediction rather than for description. In other words, they can help us to understand the essence of the archetype and to predict what cultural characteristic we can expect to find, but they cannot accurately tell us what we will find in a culture. Since every culture is unique, we cannot use the synopses to describe a given culture without further research. The rainforest dwellers of South America, for example, usually raise a few crops in addition to hunting and gathering. Since farming is not a characteristic of the Sensitive Chaos, we could not predict this from the synopsis.

SYNOPSIS OF THE SENSITIVE CHAOS

World of the Animal Powers

SYMBOL

Meandering spiral

SOCIETY

Era
Paleolithic (Old Stone Age)

Society
Nomadic hunter-gatherers in egalitarian bands, ethic of sharing and cooperation with little occupational specialization. No accumulation of personal wealth or sense of private property beyond personal tools and huts.

Examples
All Paleolithic hunter-gatherers—living examples include (to the extent that they have maintained their traditional way of life) the !Kung San or "Bushmen" and Mbuti Pygmies of Africa, Australian aborigines, Eskimos, and many Amazonian cultures.

Technology
Stone Age technology—hunting and gathering tools and techniques. No agriculture, animal domestication, metallurgy, pottery, textiles, written language, or developed mathematics. Technelogos is weak; psychoeros, strong.

Gender Relations
Equality of the sexes, sexual division of labor (women generally do more gathering and men, more hunting), dwellings usually built and "owned" by women, matrilineal descent or equal matri-patrilineal descent.

PSYCHE

Psychology
Prenatal uroboric oneness, suppression and transcendence of ego, participation mystique, magical thinking, altered states of consciousness (clairvoyance, ecstatic trance states, dream realities).

Stagnation
Psychological stagnation in the Sensitive Chaos can produce a desire to "return to the womb," to regress into uroboric unconsciousness, to drown in the Sea of Chaos through psychosis, alcoholism, drug addiction, and the like.[59]

Breakthrough
Cure the "loss of soul" (displacement of Self from ego) through psychological/shamanic means (analysis or a vision quest, for example), which realign the Self and ego, allowing the seeker to find his or her unique soul and life-purpose (quest) within oceanic oneness.

Liberation
Psychological liberation in the Sensitive Chaos can lead to transcending (not losing) the ego and healing the primal Self/other duality. Enlightenment then arises from knowing oneself to be in union with all being, while at the same time committing

one's life in an individually unique way toward maintaining the harmony of the living cosmos.

SPIRIT

Worldview
The cosmos as an all-encompassing, sacred unity of being, in which everything is alive, conscious, mutable, interactive, and capable of volition.

Spiritual Focus
Shamanism, animism, sympathetic identification, sympathetic magic, oneness with nature and veneration of nature spirits, oracles and divination.

Mythic Themes
Shamanic journeys, symbols and imagery of Shamanic reality, initiation rites, secret maps of spirit paths and centers in the mythic landscape, totemic animals, serpents, uroburus, hallucinogenic plants, natural and shamanic healing.

CULTURE

Prime Symbol
A Sensitive Chaos animated by spirits, power animals, the forces of nature, lines and nodes of subtle energy, synchronistic linkages, and magical events that transcend our laws of space and time.

Art
Psychoerotic art forms—ritualistic music, arts, dance, magical paraphernalia, masks, drums, spears, costumes, ritual settings, rock art and other paintings (often as residual traces of the transformative experience),[60] oral traditions, storytelling, animal mimicry.

66 *Spatial Archetypes*

Astronomy
Animistic heavens, recording of lunar cycles.[61]

Time
Mythical time—non-linear, synchronistic, eternal, timeless.[61]

Space
A flowing, immediate, topological continuum with little geometric order.

Landscape
An alive, conscious, sacred organism with lines and nodes of energy that depend for their vitality on ritual human participation prescribed in tribal myths and loosely timed to a ceremonial cycle. Territories defined mythologically.

Architecture
Impermanent, undifferentiated huts, windbreaks, igloos, tents, caves, rock shelters, and so on. Dwellings as spiritual doubles of their inhabitants. The invisible architecture of shamanism.

THE GREAT ROUND

World of the Great Goddess

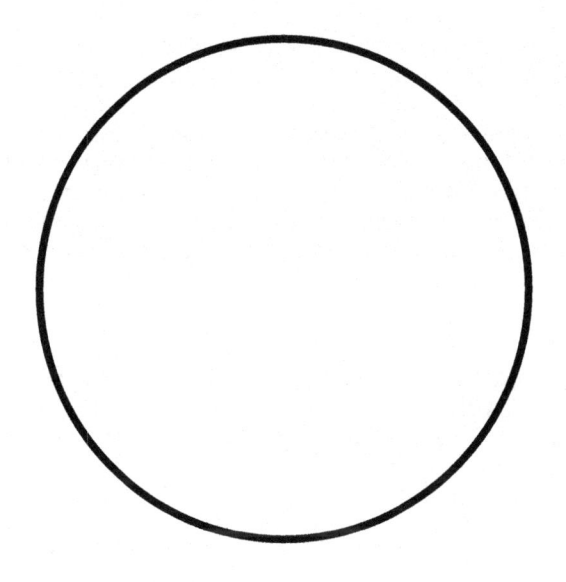

2a. Temples of Malta. Built by a female center Neolithic culture between 3600 BC and 700 BC, thus predating the Egyptian pyramids. Parts of the complex display sophisticated stone carving. The temples are in the form of the body of the Goddess, so that entering a temple is entering the body of the Goddess.

2b. Newgrange Passage Mound. Aerial view. Built in Ireland around 3200 BC, making it older than the Egyptian pyramids. The complex is rich with symbolism, including a ring of kerbstones surrounding it that may mark the phases of the moon. The mound might have been used for burials with bodies left there for a period of time, and then removed.

2c. Newgrange Passage Mound. Plan showing cross shaped passage which is predictive of the plans of Christian churches, including Gothic cathedrals that were to come over 4000 years later. Thus we might see European culture of the Gothic period rooting itself in ancient Europe as well as Christian Middle East. On the Winter solstice the sun comes through a light box over the entrance and strikes spirals on the back of the apse.

2d. Pueblo Bonito. Built between 850 AD and 1150 AD in what is today New Mexico. The square forms were residences while the round forms were kivas, ceremonial spaces. It was a center of the Chaco Culture whose descendants live in Pueblo communities today. This was and is a Great Round culture, different from the Four Quarters culture of the Plains Cultures.

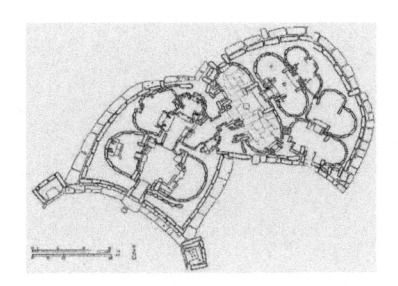

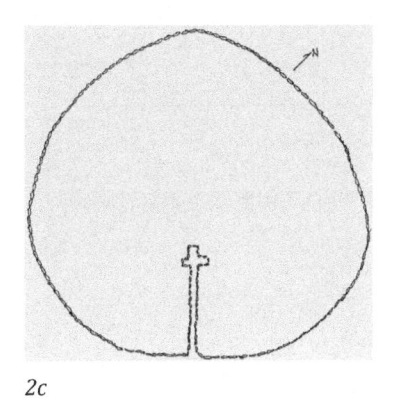

The Great Round 69

2a

2b

2c

2d

THE GREAT ROUND

World of the Great Goddess

> *In its entire phenomenology, the elementary character of the Feminine appears as the Great Round, which is and contains the universe.*
> ~ Erich Neumann[1]

Origins of the Great Round

The Great Round condenses out of the Sensitive Chaos as a solar system condenses out of interstellar dust—swirling, concentrating, centralizing, densifying, rounding out, solidifying. The center of this new cosmos is the Great Goddess. Just as the child's first human relationship when it emerges from uroboric oneness is with its human mother, humanity's first archetypal relationship when it emerges from the Sensitive Chaos is with the archetypal Mother. She is the first deified personification of the One Great Being.

Identification with the Great Goddess unites the whole of creation into one organism. She is the creator and matrix of the universe. All things living and inanimate are at once her children and cells in her body. As her children, all beings enjoy the love and acceptance that a mother bestows unconditionally on her offspring regardless of their qualities or shortcomings. Thus the Great Goddess embraces the totality of life, continually working to unify its emerging oppositions of body and spirit, light and darkness, male and female, consciousness and unconsciousness, birth and death, heaven and earth, nature and culture. As cells in her body, all beings have unique functions and personalities, and can act independently, but the health of the mother organism depends upon the cells working in harmony and balance with one another. War is inconceivable for it would mean tearing self from self. More than any literal spherical shape, it is this holism that generates the imagery of the Great Round.

The moment our Paleolithic ancestors began to express

themselves through art some 30,000 years ago, they portrayed the Great Goddess. Her image appears in cave art and sculpture from France to Siberia toward the end of the Sensitive Chaos. The last twenty to thirty thousand years of the Paleolithic era saw rapid changes that distinguished it from the preceding millions of years of slow evolution. True homo sapiens such as the Cro-Magnons of Europe mysteriously appeared and replaced the earlier Neanderthals. These first modem humans apparently enjoyed a much richer spiritual life than their predecessors, or at least they left more evidence of their beliefs. As we saw in the last chapter, they held certain animals such as the bull and the bison to be sacred, and they practiced shamanism. Their art shows also that they venerated the female, revered the cave as a sanctuary, may have used a lunar calendar, and believed in an afterlife. These beliefs endured into the Great Round era as the bedrock of its civilization.[2]

The transition from the Sensitive Chaos to the Great Round accelerated around 10,000 years ago when the end of the last Ice Age brought drastic climatic changes. Rising temperatures melted glaciers and caused the sea level to rise. The increased heat dried up formerly lush areas, and many species of wild game became extinct. In harder hit areas, these changes slowly put an end to the hunting-gathering way of life. Unable to rely on the dwindling resources they could reap from the wild, people found it necessary to produce food and keep domesticated animals. The gradual change from hunting and gathering to agriculture and animal husbandry was probably not so much a "great leap forward" in human ingenuity as a reluctant compromise with a deteriorating environment.[3] Although academics debate whether agriculture came before village life or vice versa, it is clear that both usually went hand in hand with an increasingly settled way of life, growing trade networks, and more complex societies.

> Implicit in the domestication of plants was the domestication of man himself.[4]

Life in the Great Round

Imagine that we have a bird's eye view of a region, say in the Near East, in the eighth millennium B.C. early in the Neolithic era. We see no evidence of national boundaries, capital cities, imperial highways, military installations, or land divisions. Instead, we see a still-undifferentiated landscape dotted with self-sufficient farming communities centered on small market villages. Around the farming communities, arable land has been cleared for fields, and cattle and sheep graze in the more rugged areas. The villages are connected by well-traveled, far-ranging trade routes.

A typical village is a cluster of about two hundred round, closely-packed, semi-subterranean, one-room houses made of stone and clay, with storage bins packed between them. Later we see that the village has grown and differentiated; retaining its round ovens, granaries, graves, shrines, and other vital facilities from before, while adding new rectilinear, multi-roomed houses, built confidently on the surface rather than half-underground. Throughout the whole Neolithic era, for millennia after millennia, people have placed thousands of little clay goddess figures in strategic locations: in burials to midwife the great passage from life to death and perhaps back again; in granaries and fields to bring bountiful crops; in pastures and cattle byres to ensure the fertility of the herds; in households and shrines to bless daily life.

This picture is based on actual villages described by the archaeologist James Mellaart in his book *The Neolithic of the Near East*. The scene is essentially the same during the Neolithic era in most parts of the world where village life and agriculture are just beginning. This bucolic life lasts several millennia. But unlike the Sensitive Chaos, which could favor stasis over change for thousands or even millions of years, the Great Round embraces a lively period of about ten to fifteen thousand years of accelerating change—from the Upper Paleolithic, when people were still living in caves and huts, to the early Bronze Age (in the Old World), which gave birth to the first great cities. Besides agriculture and animal domestication, other hallmarks of civilization developed during this period include weaving and textiles, pottery, irrigation and plumbing, metallurgy, mathematics, measurement systems, astronomy, writing, permanent mud-brick and stone architecture, megalithic monuments, and villages and towns.

Settled farming life affords a degree of luxury and material comfort inaccessible to the nomadic hunter-gatherer. By 5500 B.C., the residents of Çatal Hüyük in Anatolia (Turkey) lived in a dense, multi-storied town resembling a large New Mexican pueblo adorned with colorful frescoes. By the end of the Great Round, from the third to the mid-second millennia, two transitional, goddess-oriented, Bronze Age, urban cultures emerged. The Indus Valley (or Harappan) civilization in present-day Pakistan with its capital city of Mohenjo-Daro, and the urbane culture of Crete with its palatial megastructures such as Knossos and Phaistos. These pleasurable urban centers featured comfortable, multi-storied, courtyard houses surrounded by lush gardens. They had pools and sophisticated plumbing and drainage systems such as the Romans would not contrive for another two thousand years.

Luxury-loving women in ancient Great Round cultures adorned themselves with imported beads and jewelry, used exquisite toiletry utensils, and applied a range of cosmetics (which not only enhanced their appearance but also protected against infections[5]). They must have loved to shop—their taste for the exotic generated extensive networks of trade in obsidian, amber, shells, spices, quartz, and other prized goods.

For all of their inventiveness and luxury, the cultures of the Great Round appear remarkably egalitarian. Most villages and towns show few signs of status differences in homes, public buildings, and burials. People are typically buried in collective family or community graves under earthen mounds, rather than in the kind of status-oriented individual tombs that hold later chieftains and kings. Dense centers like Mohenjo-Daro and Knossos, as well as simple clan compounds, have communal storehouses where food is collected and redistributed.

Great Round cultures appear also to be remarkably peaceful. The most outstanding feature of Great Round sites all over the world is the relative absence of signs of war. They rarely contain weaponry and are seldom fortified. Scenes of battle are refreshingly absent in art. Warriors and heroes do not appear in mythology. Battle-mutilated bodies do not haunt grave sites. It seems that the people of the Great Round know how to build a sophisticated civilization that can live in unbroken peace for thousands of years, contradicting the common assumption that war and territorial aggression are inherent in human nature.

Female-Centered Civilizations

The fact that the cultures of the Great Round see the universe as the Great Goddess, the Mother of All, means that they are *female-animated* in the sense that everyone, male and female, is attuned more to the female spirit in human nature than to the male. To the extent that a culture meets the criteria listed below, we could say that it is female-centered, gynocentric, or matrifocal (less misleading terms than "matriarchal," "gynaearchical," "gynocratic" and so on, which imply a simple reversal of patriarchy).[6] Here are some characteristics of a Great Round female-centered culture:

1. Its worldview and institutions are molded by the values and sensibilities of the female psyche personified by the Great Goddess (or by multiple goddesses and venerated female forces), just as male-dominated societies are molded by the values and sensibilities of the masculine psyche personified by God (or by multiple gods and venerated male forces
2. Its art, architecture, and other forms of cultural expression display a preponderance of female imagery (though the absence of dominant male figures in society, art, and mythology might itself be evidence of a matrifocal culture).
3. Women in the culture enjoy equality, independence, and respect, though not necessarily in the same roles as men nor in positions of superiority over men.
4. Inheritance and descent are traced through the mother's line instead of the father's, implying very different family structures, institutional models, and codes of sexual conduct.

If we sincerely search for matrifocal cultures with these criteria in mind, we do not simply seek societies based on the patrifocal model where the roles happen to be reversed. Rather, we are open to discovering societies that display fundamentally different structures and values. To identify a culture as matrifocal does not imply that males in that culture have no place or are oppressed. It means that the female voices and forces for which the Goddess is a vehicle have a decisive influence on social values, customs, and institutions; in contrast to patrifocal cultures in which the female voices and forces have been muted or stilled.

Some cultures, sites, and periods that exemplify matrifocality, based on available evidence, include: Jōmon culture in Japan and China's Yang Shao culture; the Indus Valley civilization; Mesopotamia to the pre-Sumerian Ubaid period; Egypt to the predynastic Gerzean period, Neolithic Great Zimbabwe; the pre-Hellenic Aegean world including Minoan Crete; the Neolithic and Copper Age cultures of Old Europe, the pre-Indo-European megalith builders in Western Europe and Malta; North America's Neolithic Mogollan, Hohokam, and Anasazi cultures and the contemporary Hopi, Zuni, and Pueblo Indians in the Southwest, and the Neolithic Adena-Hopewell culture in the Eastern Woodlands; the Neolithic Tehuacan Valley civilization, the Valdivia culture of Ecuador.

"Minoan" Crete and the Indus Valley Civilization, with its cities of Mohenjo-Daro and Harappa are included as Great Round Cultures, even though they date from the Bronze Age, because they display mostly Great Round characteristics: goddess-centered religion, peacefulness, extensive trade,[7] a love of luxury, a predominance of women in art, relatively egalitarian societies with women enjoying respect and autonomy, sacred baths (Indus Valley), cave sanctuaries and labyrinths (Crete), sacred bulls, and so forth. Naturally, the criteria for matrifocal cultures raise the question of whether there are basic differences between the male and female psyches. An in-depth consideration of this exceedingly complex question would warrant a separate book. For now, we can encapsulate the issue by reading Joseph Campbell's observations of the differences between the effect on the psyche of the male, as father and god, and of the female, as mother and goddess.

> Psychologically and sociologically, the problem is of enormous interest; for, as all schools of psychology

agree, the image of the mother and the female affects the psyche differently from that of the father and the male. Sentiments of identity are associated most immediately with the mother; those of dissociation, with the father. Hence, where the mother image preponderates, even the dualism of life and death dissolves in the rapture of her solace; the worlds of nature and the spirit are not separated; the plastic arts flourish eloquently of themselves, without need of discursive elucidation, allegory, or moral tag; and there prevails an implicit confidence in the spontaneity of nature, both in its negative, killing, sacrificial aspect (lion and double ax), and in its productive and reproductive (bull and tree).[8]

Note that the sentiments of identity and the dissolving of dualism are associated with the female psyche; the sentiments of dissociation and separation with the male. These differences have enormous impact, tending to generate egalitarian social structures, peace, and holistic modes of thought in matrifocal societies; and hierarchical sociahstructures, war, and dualistic modes of thought in patrifocal societies.[9]

The Great Goddess

The Great Goddess, as the collective projection of the feminine archetype, imprints powerful female imagery on the myths, art, and architecture of the Great Round. Images of the womb, birth, suckling, nurturance, and fertility abound, as do metaphorical symbols such as springs, caves, grottoes, rivers, earth mounds, ovens, cauldrons, blood, the moon, and the all-seeing eyes of holistic wisdom. Time does not follow the linear trajectory it traces in masculine societies. It pulses to the periodicities of nature to which women's bodies are attuned.

Through their identity with the Great Goddess, women enjoy authority, autonomy, and respect. They are shown in art, myth, and literature not only in the mainstream of society, but at its very center of power as mothers, priestesses, healers, teachers, seers and oracles, advisors, spinners and weavers, potters, gardeners, grain-keepers, bakers of sacred breads and cakes, and a diversity of other roles. They are revered as clan ancestors in a system of matrilineal inheritance that makes all children legitimate whether the father is known or not.

Male-oriented societies, where descent and inheritance are traced through the father, limit female sexuality through stringent "moral" codes, which punish or execute women for pre-marital sex, adultery, and promiscuity. In the Great Round, female sexuality is celebrated as a sacred, creative, and procreative force emanating from the Goddess for the good and enjoyment of all. Phallic symbols are common, indicating the relish with which women receive their male consorts.

No civilization is without hardships. The most pervasive in the Great Round is the vulnerability to natural disasters that destroy settlements and crops. This generates ambivalence about the Great Mother, who, like the human mother, seems at times loving and nurturing, at other times, callous and rejecting. These frustrations forge a complex relationship with the archetypal Mother, expressed in the variety of guises in which she is portrayed: Great Mother, Goddess of Fate, Wise Woman, Priestess-Initiator, Devouring Mother, Queen of Heaven, Virgin, Sorceress, Lady of the Beasts. To sort out the manifold appearances of the Goddess, it is useful to make a basic distinction between primary and secondary goddesses.

Primary and Secondary Goddesses

For many reasons, it is important to clarify the differences between primary and secondary goddess-worship. A kind of proto-primary goddess-worship appears as early as the Upper Paleolithic Era of the Sensitive Chaos as seen in the evidence of the Venus figurines. Primary goddess-worship fully emerges in the female-centered context of Great Round, where cultures are egalitarian, cooperative, peaceful, matrifocal and matrilineal, and their art and architecture primarily feature female imagery. Secondary goddesses are found in the male-oriented contexts characteristic of the remaining archetypes, where cultures are hierarchical, competitive, warlike and expansionist, patrilocal and patrilineal, and their art and architecture primarily feature male imagery. Men appear especially in connection with power, although female figures such as goddesses and queens are also common.

The objects of primary goddess-worship tend to be elemental and transformative, both physically and spiritually. They are usually represented in small, personal, hand-held figurines, but in photographs in texts where their size is not apparent, they look monumental, larger than life, and even impersonal. Whether in the form of the ample-breasted, red ochre-covered, birth-giving Great Mother or the small-breasted, white, Death Goddess, they tend to emit a benevolent, kindly, uncomplicated aura. The ferocious sides of the Goddess sometimes appear in animal form, such as in the Vulture Murals at Çatal Hüyük. The ubiquitous Eye Goddess, the seer and soul transformer, can appear enigmatic, owl-like, and awestruck. Primary goddesses are complete in themselves, or in the case of the Mother Goddesses, complete in the great mother-child round of being. They are usually prehistoric, so they have no history, no genealogy. They are the beginning and the end of the universe. They are the universe. Thus, unlike secondary goddesses, they have no need for temples or abode. Nonetheless, people place the goddess's image in locations where she can protect them and their household: rock shelters, graves, granaries, homes, cattle byres. Examples of primary goddesses include the Venuses of Laussel and Willendorf from the Sensitive Chaos, and from Great Round cultures: the Great Mothers of Çatal Hüyük, the large Neolithic Maltese goddesses, the Eye Goddesses of the Near East and Europe, the Jomon figurines of Japan, and the little Neolithic goddess figurines from all over the world.[10]

The objects of secondary goddess-worship are more human and complicated. They have histories and genealogies. Stories are written about them. They are nearly always the wife or daughter or mother of some hero or god, and they can only be fully understood in relationships. They have specific protectorates: love, war, wisdom, childbirth, sovereignty, the crops, the hunt, the dawn, the night sky, fire, earth, and so on. Their temples and sculptures are often large and imposing, just like those of the male gods. Secondary goddesses include Athena in Classical Greece, Isis in pharaonic Egypt, Innana in Sumer, Ix Chel among the Maya, Am-

80 *Spatial Archetypes*

aterasu in Imperial Japan, Kali in Hindu India, the Taras of Buddhism, and the Virgin Mary in Medieval Europe. All are defined and revered in male-centered, post-Great Round cultures.

Some secondary goddesses deteriorate into little more than male anima projections, be they positive or negative (the Babylonian Ishtar, the classical Aphrodite, Kali, Eve, the Virgin Mary). Others are domesticated Great Goddesses who originated in the Great Round but were stripped of their powers and married off to the supreme new gods (Isis to Osiris, Hera to Zeus). Still others are demonized Great Goddesses (Lilith, the Gorgons, dragons, harpies). Some secondary goddesses (Inanna, Hathor) can lead back to the primary goddess, but, on the whole, the distinction helps to prevent confusion between the Goddess in her pure form and the Goddess in a form that has been tinkered with.[11]

To gain insight into the Great Round civilization, imagine living—like the Neolithic farmers—inside the cosmic body of the primary Goddess.[12] Here we can discover the secrets of her inner geography and find the source of the creative energy that her people channel into agriculture, geomancy, architecture, prophecy, and initiation.

Telluric Currents

> A vast concept took the form of the universe as a living being in the likeness of a great mother, within whose womb all the worlds, both of life and of death, had their existence.
> ~ Joseph Campbell[13]

As the people of the Great Round stabilize around permanent settlements, their relationship to the old spirit-centers of the Sensitive Chaos changes. Their growing need for granaries, animal pens, toolsheds, and permanent homes eventually eclipses the dematerialized ethos of the hunter-gatherers. Farming itself requires that forests be cleared and land be cultivated.

In the absence of legal boundaries and property deeds—these do not appear until the triumph of ego in the Four Quarters—farmers need some way of establishing occupancy rights to the land they work so hard to clear, cultivate, and perhaps irrigate. Anthropologist Kent Flannery asserts that in ancient times they did this by improving their land with "investments" such as permanent facilities for storage, water-control, and food processing. They reinforced their occupancy rights with "an ideology of descent which stressed maintenance of land ownership through many generations, with continued participation of the deceased ancestors in the affairs of the descent groups."[14]

Among the most impressive monuments of the ancient Great Round are the collective graves—megalithic dolmens, passage graves, and cemeteries—that hold the ancestors and serve as centers of worship for the living. The tomb-shrines and the rites enacted within them maintain the continuous participation of the ancestors in the daily life of the community. This is both practical: it demonstrates a clan's right to occupy the land; and spiritual: it fuses the realms of life and death in an integration of opposites characteristic of the Great Round.

Building permanent architecture requires the farmers to enter into a new relationship with the land. Now that the Earth's energy currents, so vital to the fertility of the soil, can no longer flow unimpeded by human-made obstructions, the problem arises of how to design every building, tomb, barrier, and trade route to harmonize with these subtle forces. In the Great Round as in the Sensitive Chaos, the planet is an alive, conscious being. But now, rather than being an amorphous primordial world of spiritual energy continuously constellating into mutable entities, it is a divine cosmic body: the body of the Great Goddess.

The old spirit lines and sacred places of the Sensitive Chaos are now lines and nodes of energy in the planetary body of the Great Mother, just as in Asian medicine and martial arts the human body is laced with a network of meridians and nodes of subtle energy—*ch'i* or *qi* in China, *prana* in India, *ki* in japan. Just as subtle energy in the human body can be manipulated through yoga or acupuncture, subtle energy in the planetary body can be manipulated, as we will see in the next chapter, through *geomancy* or "earth divination."

Earth energies are known by many names throughout the

world: fairy paths, ley lines, dragon's breath, dragon's veins, serpent energy, and Telluric currents (in honor of Roman earth goddess Tellus). Throughout the ages, people have linked Telluric currents with serpents, women, mythical events, healing, sacred architecture, and religious pilgrimages. Today they are still palpable to some dowsers, shamans, healers, peasants, farmers, and hunter-gatherers, but for most of us civilization's hard technologies have blocked any residual sensitivity we might have had to these subliminal, natural forces. Over the centuries our mechanistic worldview has steeled us to them conceptually, forging an ignorance only recently broken by the scientific discoveries of the cosmic continuum discussed in the last chapter.[15]

The combined mythic image of the planet as Mother, divine body, and network of energy captures both the familiarity and the mystery of the maternal matrix. Like a mother, the earth can be fertilized and bring forth life, yet exactly how she does this is a great wonder. Just as a child knows the taste, feel, and scent of its mother's breast, the people of the Great Round are intimately familiar with their homelands within the Great Mother's planetary body. They know that some places are beneficial to life; others, malevolent. Malevolent places have a fetid, stagnant, or malignant atmosphere that saps energy and causes psychic turmoil, accidents, decay, and even death. In benevolent places life flourishes, healing springs gush forth, groves of trees stand proud, crops and livestock thrive, people enjoy a sense of well-being, and joyous things happen. Some places abound in curative plants and healing waters. Others are favored by wild birds and animals or by domesticated herds. Still others are revealed in dreams and visions, or are the sites of magical events, omens, and divinations.

As in the Sensitive Chaos, these special places become sacred centers where rites and festivals are held. Some accumulate offerings as people leave little votive plaques and effigies, tie bits of clothing to trees, or sacrifice animals to gamer healing energies for themselves or their relatives. Eventually people mark these places with massive earthworks and megaliths—monumental rough-hewn stones, standing alone or in circles or alignments.

The spirits animating the Earth's subtle body are personified in myth and folklore as sirens, mermaids, sprites, nymphs, elves, goblins, gnomes, trolls, fairies, winged serpents, *nagas* and *nagarajas* (protective water deities), dragons, and the like. These *genii loci* sometimes materialize to people who are in altered states of consciousness. The personalities of these apparitions, and their degree of friendliness or hostility, are generated by the energy of the site they inhabited, by the mental state of the observer (receptive or fearful), and by the nature of the hallucinogen that had made them visible, if one was used. In South America, the most common apparitions under ayahuasca are serpents and jaguars, which may explain the prevalence of these creatures in pre-Columbian art.[17]

The powers of the *genii loci* and their associated spirit-centers are consciously courted also in hierarchical chieftainships, states, and empires to win the blessings of the life-renewing Great Goddess. In China, for example, the Bronze Age kings consorted with beautiful rain nymphs:

> From fragmentary literature of later times it appears that the ancient kings were believed to be able to renew their heaven-derived power from liaisons with rain-goddesses—lovely nymphs, clothed in swirling mists, who haunted sacred mounds and mountains, cloudy peaks and healing springs. Chinese myths that preserve faded remembrances of early religion abound with references to the ritual matings of these goddesses with the king in the role of shaman—the medium between man and the spirit world. In such rituals the king became the temporary embodiment of Heaven and sought the love of a divine woman who could hardly be distinguished from the ancestress of his own clan. Indeed, the authority of the earliest Chinese kings appears to have derived as much from their intimacy with lovely female rain-spirits as from their kinship to revered kings of the past.[18]

The ritual mating, "sacred marriage" or *hieros gamos* in which the chieftain or king acquired power through sexual union with the Goddess, or with a priestess in whom the Goddess was incarnated, was historically one of the favorite means of tapping into the vital forces of the Great Round. It also initiated the male into the mysteries of the feminine. Through this sacred rite, the male consort identified with the Great Goddess, united with her, and participated in her energy, wisdom, and glory. In Jungian psychology, the *hieros gamos* symbolizes the male's integration with his anima or female self in the union of opposites that culminates the Hero's journey toward wholeness, bringing the prize of self-fertilizing creativity.[19] Later we will see more of the *hieros gamos* in the Great Round, and the way it was transmogrified under other archetypal worldviews.

Geomancy

In time the knowledge of how to discern and manipulate Telluric currents became a specialty now known as geomancy (*geo* = earth, *mancy* = divination). In the Sensitive Chaos, everyone was probably a geomancer since every aspect of daily life pulsed to the subtle currents of the cosmic continuum. In the Great Round, surely most farmers had some direct knowledge of the Telluric currents, as they still do insofar as farmers are able to predict weather changes and land fertility with keener accuracy than city-dwellers. (Despite the mechanization of the modern agriculture, farmers still tend to be closer than their urban relatives to the land and to animals.) The more finely-tuned divinations were most likely the prerogative of priestesses and shamans who knew how to read a multitude of natural signs, topographical configurations, omens, dreams, and trance revelations to determine precise Telluric conditions at any given site. After the Great Round, the art became a science, and specialized geomancers developed instruments, such as the wands and rods used by Western dowsers and the elaborate compasses used in China, to enhance and codify their empirical observations of nature.

Although geomancy appears to have been practiced in all parts of the world at one time or another, it is best preserved in Taiwan, where the tradition has been kept alive after Mao Tse-tung outlawed it in mainland China. In his definitive book *An Anthropological Analysis of Chinese Geomancy*, Stephan Feuchtwang writes: "In popular Chinese thought the landscape teemed with demons and spirits of mountains, of streams, of trees, of localities, all of which could receive offerings at one time or another. The natural physical environment had a numinous quality to the Chinese. It was worshipped by the unlettered and was a subject for the fine art and the seclusion of the literati."[20] Who among us has not admired the subtlety of Chinese landscape painting or the curve of a dragon-protected Chinese roof, both inspired (literally "breathed into") by the noble spirit of nature perceived through Chinese geomancy?

In China the Telluric currents are known as "feng-shui." Feuchtwang writes:

> Feng-shui (Feng = wind, shui = water) as a single term stands for the power of the natural environment, the wind and the airs of the mountains and hills; the streams and the rain; and much more than that: the composite influence of the natural processes. Behind it is a whole cosmology of metaphysical concepts and symbols. By placing oneself well in the environment feng-shui will bring good fortune. Conversely, an analysis of the site of any building or grave with knowledge of the metaphysics of feng-shui will tell the fortune of the site-owners.[21]
>
> Until the Maoist revolution, geomancy determined nearly every detail in Chinese life: the auspicious siting, design, and dates of ground-breaking of houses, pavilions, gardens, and every other kind of construction; the sale of property and the founding of new homesteads or villages; the routes taken by travelers; the manner in which the dead were to be buried and cared for; the path to and plan of a house; the orientation of a bed or dining table in a room.

From its origins in prehistory, when everyone had an intuitive knowledge of feng-shui and the eternal Tao of nature, Chinese geomancy degenerated under patriarchal Confucianism into an exceedingly rational science reserved only for specialists.[22] The earliest written records of the practice stem from this decadent period, but we can still discern in them some of the original inspiration.

Legends trace the first revelation of geomantic knowledge

86 *Spatial Archetypes*

to different sources. In one, a turtle of the River Lo revealed the secrets to the legendary emperor Yu as a reward for having controlled the river with hydraulic engineering. In another, a heroic archer learned geomancy from the female spirit of the River Lo whom he had raped. Another credits a legendary woman who "first arranged the Former Heaven Sequence of the Eight Trigrams [of the *I Ching*] in accordance with the eight winds, the eight directions and the eight parts of the human body." One legend recounts how *Hsu Nu* (*the Dark Girl*), who was sent from heaven to aid the Yellow Emperor in a battle, became a mythical patron of the art of geomancy. Another heaven-sent woman "who determined the directions by the movement of the sun by day and by the stars and the 28 asterisms by night" is credited in the fabulously titled *Nine-Heaven Mysterious Girl's Universe and Ocean Corner Manual* of feng-shui.[23] As varied as these sources of geomancy are—a turtle, a female river spirit, a legendary woman, the Dark Girl, and another "heaven-sent" women—they clearly recall the totemic animals and nature spirits of the Sensitive Chaos and the goddesses of the Great Round whose powers were appropriated by the emperors and heroes of a later age.

Europe appears also to have had a strong tradition of geomancy, which is being vigorously researched and revived today, particularly in England.[24] Western Europe has thousands of megalithic constructions: dolmens, mounds, stone circles, standing stones, banks, ditches, terraces, avenues. Before plows and bulldozers leveled great numbers of these works, they dotted landscapes throughout the British Isles, Western France, Scandinavia, the Iberian Peninsula, and the Mediterranean. Frequently they appear to have been built in alignments or at the intersection of two or more lines so that a succession of perfectly aligned megalithic sites may stretch for dozens of miles, criss-crossing other alignments, forming a dense network of paths and nodes similar to the systems known to the Australian aborigines and the ancient Peruvians. Researchers often find these lines still delineated by animal paths, as well as by Roman roads and old parish boundaries, which presumably were laid out when respect for the ancient system still obtained.

The Fairies and Langton House
Lift one, lift a',
Baith at back and fore wa'—
Up and away wi' Langton House,
And set it down in Dogden Moss.

The fairies had a grudge against Langton and its inmates, and determined to carry it away to Dogden Mass, several miles to the west in the parish of Greenhaw. On a moonlight night at the end of autumn, they set to work to loosen the foundation, singing the song given above, and had just begun to lift the house, when one of the inmates woke up, felt something like an earthquake, heard the singing, and ran to the window. He saw what the fairies were doing, and cried out, "Lord, keep me and the house together, what's this o't?" At the prayer the fairies dispersed, and fled away through the air, leaving the house safe.
~ Katherine Briggs[25]

Many folktales recount how the "little people" and "magical agents" (the *genii loci*) would move in at night and relocate or destroy structures made by humans during the day.[26] They seem to have been particularly hostile to cathedral builders, and the feeling was mutual. Christians were as intent on exorcising the pesky spirits from the countryside—by ringing bells, waving crosses, and generally nullifying the Telluric serpent—as they were on stamping out the old, nature-based religion that communicated with the invisible beings. Thus it is said of St. Patrick, who successfully converted Ireland to Christianity in the 5th century A.D., that he rid the country of serpents forever.

Spirals

Ley-hunters who search for starkly straight ley lines, tracing them from site to site across miles of landscape until it becomes an abstract exercise in linear point connection, miss another kind of pattern far more common in the Great Round: the spiral. It is as if the straight line symbolizes emerging technelogos, while the spiral is the backcloth of psychoeros. The holism of the Great Round holds the two modes in delicate balance. To see the straight line and not the spiral is to miss the metaphorical essence of the archetype.[27]

A profusion of spirals animates Neolithic pottery the world over. So important is the invention of pottery that archaeologists use it it to define one of the most important chronological divisions of prehistory: ceramic versus *aceramic*, denoting whether a culture has or has not yet invented pottery. Pots are the most common type of artifact studied by scholars to identify cultures and to determine their spread of influence. Virtually everywhere in the world where Neolithic pottery appears, the spiral is a common motif, and is found also in jewelry, houses, tombs, frescoes, carvings, cosmetic utensils, and other artifacts.

The spiral, or its labyrinthine, meandering, serpentine, and concentrically-ringed variants, adorned natural and megalithic stones everywhere. They were meticulously pecked out, sometimes as the small labyrinths found from India to Cornwall to Arizona, and sometimes at a scale that covered yards and yards of stonework such as the walls of the passage grave at Gavr'inis, France, the kerbstones of the Boyne Valley mounds in Ireland, the monumental Goddess temple at Tarxien in Malta, and the sacred caves of the Canary Islands. Often the markings were combined with *oculi*, abstract representations of the Eye Goddess, perhaps indicating the importance of seeing the invisible powers traced by the markings.

We do not know what these spirals meant to the people who delineated them in such abundance. They may have been simply ornamental—an easy way to decorate a pot. This might explain spiral motifs on pottery, but it does not explain the profusion of spirals in such sacred settings as the Boyne Valley passage mounds or the Tarxien temple. So many spirals occupy places of majesty and sacredness as to rule out their being solely decorative. What, then, do they mean? We may never know for sure, but we have clues. The Telluric currents seem to be closely related to the Earth's geomagnetic field. Like it, they are said to be strongly affected by metal, underground water, and the movements of the sun, moon, stars, and planets. The terms scientists use to describe phenomena such as magnetic storms and aurorze parallel the images used in the art and lore of the Great Round and the Sensitive Chaos: lines of force, threads, centers or nodes, alternating polarities, eddies, swirls, meanders, and especially spirals. For instance, note the terms used by Sydney Chapman of the High Altitude Observatory in Boulder to describe some of the history of research on the aurorae in the book *Magnetism and the Cosmos*:

> Alfvén introduced a very important method of treating paths with many spirals, he represented the motion by a combination of Larmorian circular movement around a field line, relative to a centre that moves to and fro approximately along the line. For this moving centre I suggest the name Alfvén centre, instead of his term the guiding centre.[28]

The ancient megalith builders may have seen their structures as interacting with the variations in the Earth's electromagnetic field. There is evidence that humans can sense these variations enough to navigate by them to some extent, and experiments with many animals have shown that they attune their biological rhythms to very low level magnetic forces.[29] Our developing portrait of the Earth's magnetic anomalie[30] shows a "middle-ground" between the macrocosmic forces generating magnetic storms and aurora and the microcosmic forces of the cosmic continuum. Possibly it is this middle ground that figured in the ancient art-science of geomancy.

Dowsers and ley hunters have begun to use rods and gaussmeters to survey low level magnetic fields at megalithic sites where they are discovering spiraling and undulating patterns similar to those found in Neolithic art. Underground springs appear to generate beautifully intricate spiral fields. Many more people need to be doing this research, and with increasing rigor, before there will be conclusive and reliable results. For now, we can only speculate that the similarities of form and pattern between Neolithic artifacts and geomagnetism are not coincidences, and that as geomagnetic research progresses we will find a more solid, scientific basis for the Neolithic farmers' predilection for spiraling forms. It is as if the numinous but inchoate spiraling patterns of the Sensitive Chaos, seldom explicitly drawn by gatherer-hunters, become ornamental motifs to the farmers whose entire way of life depends on the domestication of the Earth's Telluric energies. This ornamental use of the prime symbols of a former archetype is not unusual (see "Bits of Colored Glass," number 15).

Springs

The spring, especially the underground spring, is a powerful metaphor for the internal sacred place, the "point existing here and everywhere, now and always" that connects us to the ever-flowing font of creativity and wisdom. The route to it is not the celestial path of logos but the spiraling, labyrinthine, underworld birth-passage of the unconscious. There we confront the shadows and demons guarding the spring—not to kill them and flee heavenward like the Hero, but to neutralize their danger, reclaim their power, and pass onward into the secret depths.

In the Great Round, where the Goddess is the entire universe, water is one of her most elemental attributes. Water recalls birth-waters and milk, its tidal harmony with the moon and the menses is close to women's rhythms, and, like the Goddess herself, it is the basis of all life. Springs are sanctuaries where life sustaining waters issue from deep womb-caverns in the earth, and then flow into rivers and oceans, eddying and swirling with the motions of the cosmos, evaporating and condensing as fertilizing rain. Mircea Eliade writes, "The sacred rivers of Mesopotamia were supposed to have their source in the generative organ of the Great Goddess. The source of rivers was indeed considered as the vagina of the earth. In Babylonia the term *pu* signifies both 'source of a river' and 'vagina.' The Sumerian buru means both 'vagina' and 'river.' The Babylonian *nagbu*, 'stream,' is related to the Hebrew neqeba, 'female.'"[31]

Goddess-worship is intense in areas with copious springs and underground water systems, and most bodies of water are named for goddesses. The River Ganges in India, the Boyne in Ireland, and the Danube in Europe, for instance, are named for the goddesses Ganga, Boann, and Danu, respectively. Oshun is the goddess of all waters in Yorubaland, and in Mesopotamia, Tiamat represented the primeval ocean,[32] to name a few.

Naturally, people have always established their settlements near springs, rivers, and other good sources of water. One of the most densely populated areas in the Old Stone Age, the Dordogne region in southwestern France, is a beautiful, forested, limestone shelf riddled with protective caves and rock shelters and liberally watered with rivers and streams. Jericho, the earliest known city, flourished at the site of an abundant spring. The ill-fated "walls of Jericho" were probably built to limit access to this lone spring in that arid region, one of the rare instances of a fortified Great Round town. The holy city of Jerusalem was founded some 5000 years ago around the Gihon spring by the Canaanites, a Bronze Age culture that preserved many aspects of the old goddess-based religion, which outraged the Hebrew patriarchs. Jerusalem's system of underground passages and shafts was elaborated during Herodian times into a network of reservoirs and aqueducts that is densest under the temple mount. Sacred baths and lakes were built in cities such as Mohenjo-Daro and at later temples such as the great Temple of Hathor in Dendura, built during Egypt's Grid period under Ptolemaic rule.

One of the earliest Great Round civilizations blossomed in eastern Europe,[33] where even today people flock to the famous healing springs and spas in the Carpathian mountains. The holy wells of Cornwall were sacred first to the cairn-and-quoit building Neolithic peoples, then to the Christians. The magnificent Pyramid city of Teotihuacan in the Valley of Mexico was founded on volcanic land riddled with subterranean caves. The Pyramid of the Sun was built on top of a system of caves that most likely was sacred to an earlier Great Round population. Another Pyramid culture, the Mayan civilization (which might have been matriarchal in origin[34]) drew its water and much of its *imago mundi* from the limestone caves, underground streams, and sinkholes or cenotes lacing the riverless Yucatan lowlands. The Colorado plateau area of the American southwest—home of the Great Round Anasazi culture and the matrilineal Pueblo and Navaho Indians—is richly supplied with underground aquifers that belie the arid surface of the land.

The Colorado Plateau

> The lightning field is the Kundalini of the planet.
> ~ Joan Price

The spectacular Colorado Plateau spans much of the Four Corners region of the American Southwest, where Colorado, New Mexico, Arizona, and Utah come together. A high desert drained by the Colorado River, and varying from 2000 to 12,000 feet in elevation, the Plateau contains the nation's largest concentration of National Parks and Monuments, including the red spired architecture of Bryce Canyon; Zion's sheer, stratified palisades; the sandstone needles, mazes, and arches of Canyonlands; the Petrified Forest, eerily frozen in time; Mesa Verde and Canyon de Chelly, with their abandoned, sun-facing cliff dwellings; Chaco Canyon, heart of the ancient Anasazi civilization; and the vast, multi-hued gorge of the Grand Canyon, which slashes through two billion years of geological history, cutting the Earth's crust to its quick.[35] The Colorado Plateau nurtured some of North America's earliest Great Round farming cultures: the Anasazi, Mogollan, Hohckam, and Sinagua. Today the area hosts their descendents—the Hopi, Zuni, Tiwa, and other Pueblo tribes—as well as Navajo, Apache, Ute, and Havasupai.

For several years, Joan Price, an artist-turned-environmentalist based in Santa Fe, New Mexico, has been studying the area with the Hopi (who have selected her as an honored spokesperson) and other Native Americans to interpret their knowledge of the Earth in light of recent scientific findings from the National Center for Atmospheric Research in Boulder and other research centers. Of the Plateau, she writes:

> At least seven native American Sacred Breathing Mountains' have cave systems associated with volcanic mountains, a significant factor in the ionization cycles on the Plateau. Dr. Doyne Sartor of the National Center for Atmospheric Research investigated Wupatki National Monument at the base of the San Francisco Peaks,

one of these Sacred Breathing Mountains. Within the ruins are a number of surface 'blowholes' into which air rushes at the rate of up to thirty miles an hour for approximately six hours; then it rushes out again for six hours, in constantly repeating cycles. Sartor deposited fluorescent particles in one blowhole and collected them from another one located twenty-four miles away. He estimates that seven billion cubic feet of underground waterways and caverns exist in that area.

Evidently, the [positive ion] count of the dry desert air is reversed as it rushes into the cool cavern system and is blended with foaming underground streams where it is recharged with [negative ions]. Then the air surges to the surface and vitalizes the life of the area. Connected to this network of caves is an enormous caldera (underground basin) of water located in the middle of the Colorado Plateau called the Black Mesa Aquifer. At the far eastern side of the Plateau, at the base of the volcanic San Juan and Sangre de Cristos mountain ranges, is the underground caldera called the San Juan Aquifer, which is so deep that drilling has not reached the bottom. These two known subsurface water collections and the underground river system have a profound influence on the ion balance crucial for healthy bioelectric states in the biosphere.[36]

"Electrical fields commonly have an overall positive or negative charge, which in turn has strong physiological and related emotional effects," Price says.[37] One of the most effective negative ion generators is the moving water found in the rivers, fountains, springs, waterfalls, and surf so common to sacred places the world over. Moving water absorbs positive ions and releases negative ions in its spray.[38] High proportions of negative ions are induced in mountainous areas, and in areas with clean air, lots of sunshine and lightning activity, radioactive subsurface minerals, and rushing water. The Colorado Plateau is one of the few places on Earth where all of these features combine to generate massive amounts of negative ions, which are strongly related to the lightning field, "The lightning field moves from the Colorado Plateau south to the Amazon Basin and back to the Four Quarters area over the course of a year, replenishing the ozone in the ionosphere." Price continues. "The lightning field is the Kundalini of the planet. The Amazon is the oxygen source for the planet and the Colorado plateau is its ozone source."[39]

Through her work with the Hopi, Joan Price rediscovered the old understanding of the Earth as an alive, breathing organism, delicately poised in a chain of life forces, depending for its health and vitality on sites that have intensely salubrious combinations of atmospheric, geological, and climatic patterns.[40] The people of the Great Round surely sensed this, too, when they deemed certain places sacred: mountains, springs, spas, rivers, oceans, deserts, forests, caves. Like the Hopi, a contemporary Great Round culture, these people did not need to be scientists to know the Earth. They sensed the interconnectedness of Earth's ecological cycles from direct experience.

Silbury Hill

> ... even the dualism of life and death dissolves in the rapture of her solace ...
> ~ Joseph Campbell[41]

Until recently most scholars thought that stone circles had been built by Druidic priests, that earth mounds concealed the rich burials of Bronze Age kings and chieftains, or that the entire megalithic system was the product of cultural diffusion from the Near East, and few seriously considered that these impressive monuments might have been built by a local, peaceful, bucolic, female-centered, Stone Age civilization. Now that the monuments have been shown by more accurate dating methods to have preceded the Celtic Druids, the Iron Age, and the high civilizations of the Near East, this idea is rapidly gaining currency. One reason they were probably built was to honor the Goddess in her various forms. For example, Silbury Hill—one of the earliest mounds in England, erected nearly 5000 years ago—is suffused with female imagery.

Michael Dames's studies of Silbury Hill and Avebury, the largest mound and stone circle, respectively, in Europe, help to unravel the mystery of how megalithic monuments figured in the lives of the early farmers. Much to the consternation of the "chieftain's burial" enthusiasts, Silbury Hill renders no skeletons or burial treasures whatsoever no matter how much it is tunneled into, bored, mined, excavated, x-rayed and probed with state-of-the-art electronic sensors.

Rather that being a rich king's tomb (although it was mistakenly named for one King Sil), Silbury was, according to Dames, the site of an annual First Fruits Festival that initiated the harvest in August. He believes that the hill, which is 522 feet high and 130 feet in diameter, and its surrounding moat were designed as an effigy of the Great Goddess that accentuated her womb and eye, symbols of her dual nature as the source of physical life and spiritual vision. Especially important is the siting of the structure where the Swallowhead and Kennett springs issue from the mouths of underground water sources at the beginning of the River Kennett.

The Swallowhead, a vagina-like gash in the pastures surrounding Silbury, is called the "Cunnit" by local country people. Dames found that the words Cunnit, Kennett, and the now-derogatory Anglo-Saxon term "cunt" are etymologically linked to the Celtic word *kuno* meaning "the exalted holy river." He found related words meaning "cradle, earliest abode, the place where everything is nurtured in its beginning" (cunabula); "a hole or passage underground" (cunicle); "to know, skilful, expert ... possessing magical knowledge or skill" (cunning); "range of sight or vision, to generate, mental perception, to give birth to" (ken); and a Welsh word for a "posset to hold milk" (cunnog).[42]

Dames saw in this symbolism a hint of what the purpose of the hill might have been. From further research on goddess-worship in ancient times and the residues of it in contemporary folklore, place names, and country festivals; he concluded that on Lammas Eve, at the full moon nearest the midpoint between the summer solstice and the vernal equinox, the people of the region gathered at Silbury Hill to witness a spectacle of cosmic theatre: the Great Goddess giving birth to the Divine Child. In the Great Round, the Divine Child, among its other associations, symbolizes the grain implanted in the body of the Goddess. The cycle by which the grain grows, is reaped and replanted is governed by the cycles of the moon, as any Farmer's Almanac shows. Also, like the grain, the waxing and waning moon seems to die and be reborn. In the universal symbolism of the Vegetation Mysteries, the Divine Child who becomes the Dying and Resurrecting God as Son/Lover of the Goddess is symbolized as the bull. With its crescent-shaped horns, the bull is the quintessential lunar power animal and male fertility symbol in one. This manifold bucolic symbolism reveals that the grain born of the Goddess matures to become the seed that refertilizes her in an eternal round of life, death, and rebirth, ever emanating from and folding back into the Great Mother.

The mystical birth at Silbury is revealed by the full moon (whose beams were long thought to impregnate women) as it traverses the springs and is reflected from the moat into the eyes of the beholders gathered on top of the hill. The shape of the moat and hill as an effigy of the Goddess oriented to the moon enables all the stages of birth to be acted out: the child emerging from the vagina, the umbilical cord being cut as the moon's reflection is interrupted by causeways in the moat, and the infant suckling as the moon's milky reflection moves to the Goddess' breasts.[43]

At Silbury, death accompanies birth just as the eye accompanies the womb. In a compensating integration of opposites characteristic of the Great Round, spiritual rebirth into the world of psychoerotic vision parallels physical death to this world. Dames writes:

> The ancient Silbury goddess, who paid such obvious regard to the terrestrial and celestial environment, was built to help propagate and perpetuate the totality....
>   The Silbury birth, the Silbury treasure, is completed by death, the cutting of the umbilical lifeline between mother and child, the *execution* of crops. All authorities agree on the profound sense of apology which pervades the first acts of harvesting in coherent rural cultures. Indeed the honest recognition of death is one of the mainsprings of first fruits ceremonial....
>   So Silbury was a lamb, after all, from where the

dead earth, coming to life, died as it was born, and was devoured once again. But when death was formed as a mother, deprivation was replaced by security at every stage, because everything was both dead and alive.[44]

"... even the dualism of life and death dissolves in the rapture of her solace ..."
        ~ Joseph Campbell[44a]

Cyclical Time

In the Great Round, time itself moves in majestic cycles. The year turns with the seasons, highlighted by the times when seed and soil are ripe for planting and harvesting. In the cycles of life and death, the spirits of beloved elders are reborn in the young. The heavens circle above cultivated fields in regular patterns that can now be observed from the same spot year in and year out, generation after generation.

    Neolithic farmers had as much interest in the rhythms of the sky as in the currents of the Earth. Now from fixed positions, they could systematically observe how the moon careens wildly through the night sky from month to month, setting sometimes far to the south, sometimes far to the north, waxing and waning all the time, and disappearing altogether for a few days each month. By contrast, the sun readily reveals its predictable itinerary. Like clockwork, it journeys annually through the Tropic of Cancer and the Tropic of Capricorn between its solstitial reversals.

    The agricultural year of the prehistoric European calendar is timed by four solar events: the winter and summer solstices, when the sun's extreme points of rising and setting appear to "stand still" on the horizon for a few days and then reverse course (*sol-stice* means "solar standstill"); and the spring and autumn equinoxes, those elusive midpoints between the solstices when the sun crosses the equator dividing the day equally between light and dark (*equi-nox* means "equal night"). The four cross-quarter points between the solstices and equinoxes became great feast days, later given Celtic and Christian names: Imbolc or Candlemas, the purifying Fire Festival (beginning of February); Beltane or May Eve, the Fertility Festival (beginning of May); Lammas or Lughnasadh, the First Fruits Festival (mid-August); and Samhain, All Hallow's Eve, or Halloween, the end-of-harvest Festival of the Spirits (end of October, beginning of November).

The people of the prehistoric Great Round often aligned megalithic monuments and other sacred structures to important risings and settings of the sun, moon, stars, and planets. Certainly they were interested in establishing the calendar, but that was not all. The heavenly bodies personified mythic archetypes in the human imagination, as we saw in Silbury Hill. While the moon's phases spin out the lunar calendar, they also reveal the Great Goddess, the Divine Child, the Dying-and-Resurrecting-God, the bull or celestial cow with its Horns of Consecration, and a lunar force that impregnates women. In the mythic mind, such seemingly disparate identities merge into one another without conflict. Indeed, meshing of various meanings is one of the main functions of a symbol. In symbolism, the whole always exceeds the sum of the parts by several orders of magnitude.[45]

The Neolithic farmers needed to ensure that their lives, their crops and livestock, and their ancestors would resonate sympathetically with the movements of the Great Goddess's sky-body. Astronomically aligned structures were probably not computers for an elite group of priests or proto-scientists, as archaeologists like to suggest. Such specialization is a defining feature of later, more hierarchical societies and is not characteristic of the Great Round. To the people of the Great Round, these human-made loci in the planetary body of the Goddess were ritual centers where the population could attune itself to the cosmos for practical as well as spiritual reasons.

Stonehenge

The most famous astronomically aligned megalithic monument is, of course, Stonehenge. Standing on the stark Salisbury Plain in southern England, Stonehenge was begun as early as 3100 B. C. and completed as late as 1100 B. C. In *Stonehenge Complete*, archaeologist Christopher Chippendale describes the situation before Stonehenge was built.

From the 4th millennium, evidence of human occupation by farming communities proliferates. A dozen major monuments—ten long barrows for collective burials, a long "mortuary enclosure" on Normanton Down, and a "causewayed camp" (circular enclosure) at Robin Hood's Ball... pre-date even the first phase of Stonehenge. Causewayed camps with their attendant flocks of long barrows, are spaced across the Wessex chalklands; they may show territorial divisions between different social groups, each owing allegiance to the land belonging with their particular causewayed camp.

The Cursus, and the Lesser Cursus to its west, probably were built during the period of long barrow construction and therefore belong with, or even pre-date, activity at Stonehenge.

The first Stonehenge, then, was constructed among other, broadly contemporary monuments, in a landscape already partly grassland. It was part of a complex of ceremonial structures, already several hundred years old when its site was chosen, with a causewayed camp as its central territorial focus.[46]

There are three important things to realize about Stonehenge. The first is that it didn't spring out of nowhere, as if inspired by visitors from outer space. Its original context is entirely consistent with the Great Round: egalitarian farming communities building earthworks and megaliths as territorial "investments" in the land they worked so hard to cultivate. The land surrounding Stonehenge is littered with such investments. The second is that over 2000 years many different cultures contributed to the Stonehenge that we know today. Only the early phases fall well within the Great Round archetype. The third thing to remember is that Stonehenge is a true mystery, and we will never fully discover its original purpose and meaning. Like all true mysteries, it is an enigma on which we project our own imagination and desires. We will always learn more about ourselves in what we see in Stonehenge than about Stonehenge itself.[47]

The first phase, called Stonehenge I, was built in the late Neolithic on the well-established plan of the "causewayed camp." It consisted of the outer circular ditch and bank, 106 feet in diameter; two gateway stones; the Heel Stone aligned with sunrise on the summer solstice; and the ring of fifty-six Aubrey holes, which held cremation burials and Neolithic pottery. Gerald Hawkins asserts that the Aubrey holes served as a computer for predicting the 18.61-year cycle of lunar eclipses. Some postholes possibly formed additional alignments to key positions of the moon. The four Station Stones may have been placed during this phase. They form a large rectangle in the outer bank, like a loom frame on which is woven an intricate web of lunar and solar alignments.

The next phase, Stonehenge II, was erected at the end of the Neolithic by a somewhat different type of people who used distinctive pottery beakers. They abandoned the Aubrey holes, changed the entrance, and began the Avenue. In the center, they raised double crescents (in plan) made of over eighty bluestones quarried from the distant Prescelly Mountains in Wales.

In Stonehenge III, yet another group dismantled the bluestone crescents and erected the elements that make Stonehenge famous: the great sarsen circle and the impressive horseshoe of five freestanding trilithons. Later a bluestone circle and horseshoe were re-erected inside the sarsen circle and trilithons.[48]

There is some dispute about whether the last building phase at Stonehenge coincided with the coming of the Wessex chieftains, which would fall within the archetypal Four Quarters era in Britain. Colin Renfrew, the dean of British archaeology, has argued that the sheer monumentality of the Stonehenge III undertaking is evidence that it could not have been erected by an egalitarian society but had to have been the product of an organized chieftainship.[49] Whatever the outcome of this debate, it is clear that the progressively more formal, centralized, and monumental additions to Stonehenge point to a society whose ceremonial life was becoming more formal and hierarchical. Since neither Stonehenge II nor Stonehenge III seem to have appreciably enhanced the monuments astronomical significance, we could say that the earlier Great Round culture that built Stonehenge I was more concerned with astronomy, calendrics, and attunement to the heavens; while the later cultures that built Stonehenge II and III were increasingly concerned with accommodating hieratic ceremonies typical of the Four Quarters archetype. This is probably when a priesthood entered the pictures.[50]

Newgrange and the Boyne Valley Calendar

Newgrange, built in 3200 B.C., is a huge passage mound that was once covered entirely with white quartz. Under its 280-foot diameter earthen mound, Newgrange contains a megalithic, corbel-vaulted chamber, twenty feet high. The sixty-five foot passageway and the chamber's cross-shaped plan form the primordial prototype of the Gothic cathedrals built 4000 years later. The vault is also the oldest known architectural expression, albeit crude, of what becomes the "Dome of Heaven" in the Radiant Axes.

Certain kerbstones surrounding the mound and the exquisite "hymen stone" partially blocking the entrance are covered with spirals and other symbols. Inside the mound, there are two engravings of Newgrange's signature: the triple spiral (perhaps an early aniconic version of the Triple Goddess—Maiden, Mother, and Crone—later worshipped on the same soil by the Celts).

The mound and passageway are precisely oriented and carefully constructed so that on the winter solstice the rays of the rising sun penetrate the chamber, architecturally enacting the birth of the Divine Child—the sun—from its winter nadir. (This version of the Divine Child is recalled today in the birth of the Christ child near the Winter Solstice.) The ray of dawning sun snakes down the long passageway into the womb chamber, fertilizing the Great Goddess. Again, the Divine Child is the Dying-and-Resurrecting Son and Lover of the Goddess.

Newgrange is cradled, along with her sister mounds Knowth, and Dowth, in the Valley of the River Boyne, named after the Goddess Boann. The three mounds form a vast Triple Goddess. Martin Brennan, an Irish-American artist and writer from Brooklyn, spent twelve years researching the art and astronomical alignments of Ireland's megalithic structures. After developing theories, Brennan field-tested them with amateur astronomer Jack Roberts. Brennan shares their discoveries in *The Stars and the*

Stones, Ancient Art and Astronomy in Ireland[51] which he also superbly illustrated.

Brennan and Roberts found that the Boyne Valley—with its three major mounds and several other earthworks and megaliths oriented to the risings and settings of the sun on the solstices, equinoxes, or cross-quarter days—is an extensive megalithic calendar.[52] Unlike Stonehenge, which has no art to speak of, Newgrange and its neighbors have many stones engraved with a rich symbolic language of spirals, meanders, zig-zags, lozenges, oculi or eye goddesses, solar disks, lunar crescents, astronomical and calendrical notations, and signs that Brennan believes are an early form of writing.

The Anasazi Sun Dagger

The astronomically aligned structures in British Isles and Western Europe are the best documented, but thousands of others still stand throughout the world. As in Europe, the earliest were built by Great Round cultures. Most sites in Africa, Asia, and Oceania still await decipherment, but research is well underway in the Americas. Among Native American sites are the stone Medicine Wheels in the northwestern United States and southwestern Canada. The best known, Big Horn Medicine Wheel in Montana, has cairns aligned to summer solstice sunrise and sunset and to key rising positions of the stars Aldebaran and Rigel.[53] These circular stone Wheels resemble the stone circles of Western Europe. Other astronomically aligned structures include the earth lodges of the matrilineal Mandan Indians; the "American Woodhenge" of the hierarchical, proto-pyramid, Mississippian culture at their capital city of Cahokia near St. Louis; some Plains Indians' council circles in Kansas; several controversial stone structures in New England; and the great kivas of Chaco Canyon in New Mexico, which we will look at later.[54]

The Anasazi, an early Native American Great Round farming culture centered in Chaco Canyon, were as concerned with the calendrical round as the megalith builders of Neolithic Europe had been four thousand years earlier. Like their European counterparts, the Anasazi needed to predict the solstices and equinoxes both for agricultural purposes and to prepare for their elaborate, annual, ceremonial dance cycle, the mytho-ritual armature of their whole civilization. The Anasazi's descendents, the Pueblo Indians, are among the few Great Round cultures surviving in the world today. They continue their ancestors' dry farming methods and their ceremonial dances, which are divided by the solstices into sacred kachina dances for half the year from the Summer to the Winter Solstice and non-kachina dances for the other half from the Winter to the Summer Solstice.

The Anasazi's villages and kivas are often astronomically aligned, and they left a number of astronomically significant petroglyphs on the canyon walls nearby. Atop the majestic Fajada Butte in Chaco Canyon, is a seemingly accidental arrangement of three stone slabs leaning against a cliff wall. Behind them, the cliff is inscribed with two spiral petroglyphs, one large and one small. In 1977, Anna Sofaer, an artist from Washington, D.C., discovered that the slabs had been carefully sculpted and placed to shape and direct the sun's rays as they fall on the spirals at midday during the solstices and equinoxes.

On the summer solstice, a dagger-shaped ray slices between the slabs, piercing the exact center of the larger spiral. On the winter solstice, two dagger-rays inscribe the outer circumference of the larger spiral leaving no sun in the center, since the winter solstice is the shortest day of the year and has the least sun. On the equinoxes, rays pierce both spirals: the smaller one, in the center; and the larger one, halfway between the center and the outer edge, as if the larger spiral served also as a calendar marking the halfway point between the two solstices. According to Sofaer, the arrangement functions as a lunar observatory as well, directing the moon's rays against the edges of the slabs and casting shadows on the petroglyph when the moon is in key positions of its 18.61-year cycle. The number of rings in the spiral comes into play as a counting device.[55]

Lunar Eclipses

In most cultures, lunar calendars preceded solar calendars, just as lunar mythology preceded solar mythology.[56] The power of the moon over water, ocean tides, menstrual blood, the emotions, plant growth, and birth are traditional women's mysteries. The moon's waxing and waning are tied to the archetype of the Triple Goddess: Maiden (new moon), Mother (full moon), and Crone (waning moon). Although the Goddess is associated as much with the sun as with the moon, it was her lunar mysteries that motivated humanity's first systematic studies of astronomy and calendrics.[57]

Among lunar observations, none is more complex than the eclipse cycle. As we saw at Stonehenge, the fifty-six Aubrey holes may have been used to determine the 18.61-year lunar standstill cycle from which eclipses can be predicted.[56] Alexander Thom found the prediction of lunar eclipses the only plausible explanation for the major megaliths at Carnac in Brittany, including both the famous Le Menec alignments, consisting of 1600 stones splayed in rows over a half mile long, and the Grand Menhir Brise, which once stood sixty feet high and was the largest megalith known.[59]

Of Native American astronomy, Anthony F. Aveni writes, "Eclipse prediction was a great challenge for the ancient astronomers. The fear engendered by the departure from the regularity of nature epitomized in the eclipse was as real then as is our present fear of nuclear war."[60] He quotes Bernardino de Sahagun's eyewitness account of the fear of lunar eclipses among Mexican women: "When the moon was eclipsed, his face grew dark and sooty; blackness and darkness spread. When this came to pass, women with child feared evil; they thought it portentous; they were terrified [lest], perchance, their [unborn] children might be changed into mice; each of their children might turn into a mouse."[61] To protect their children from being born "monstrous or imperfect" the women placed obsidian in their mouths or at their breasts.

It is difficult for us to understand why eclipses were so feared, and why such efforts were expended to predict them. True, they are awesome events, but they occur with enough regularity and frequency that they might not be considered catastrophic. Eclipses do, however, cause demonstrable disturbances in the Earth's magnetic field. Extreme disturbances in the Earth's field—such as when the North and South Poles periodically reverse their negative and positive charges—have caused the extinction of masses of small species due to the influx of cosmic and ultraviolet radiation. Strong magnetic fields have been found to cause cancer in humans,[62] and we have already looked at the geomantic importance of magnetic fields in the Goddess's earth-body.

The Mexican women's fears seem to have been exaggerated but not entirely without foundation, inasmuch as there appears to be a relationship between eclipses and birth, through the medium of the Earth's magnetic field.[63] Perhaps Neolithic farmers are psychoerotically sensitive to disturbances in the field, especially to those caused by eclipses, just as they appear to be psychoerotically sensitive to low level magnetic fields affecting geomancy. To these people, cyclical time means more than attending to the regular round of solstices and equinoxes. It means being attuned to the entire spectrum of cyclic rhythms and pulsating currents in the cosmic body of the Great Goddess, perhaps reaching a subtlety that we can hardly imagine.

The Queen of Heaven

The most common misconception about the Great Goddess is that she was purely an Earth Mother or a Moon Goddess, embedded in nature and the unconscious, revered for giving birth like a brood mare, and worshipped mainly in nocturnal, orgiastic, fertility rites. This notion is a projection of the "keep her barefoot and pregnant" mentality that has so circumscribed woman's range of action the world over.

In the female-centered Great Round, the Goddess is the whole. She is worshipped as the *universe itself*. In male-centered cultures she gets divided up, as Tiamat was torn to pieces by Marduk. Dualistic symbolic systems arise—China's *yin/yang*, India's *Siva/Shakti*, Europe's alchemical marriage—which strip the Goddess, and by extension the female, of half of her natural whole. These systems are putatively complementary, but in practice, whether in China, India, or Europe, the Goddess/female becomes "inferior" helpmate to the "superior" ruling God/male. We will see the full implications of this in the Four Quarters chapter.

Residues of Great Goddess's original totality—avatars that transcend her Earth Mother/Good Wife/Love Goddess/Fertility Symbol aspects— sometimes persist in secondary goddess-worship in post-Great Round civilizations,[64] where the Goddess as universe becomes the Sky Goddess, the Sun Goddess, or the Queen of Heaven. In ancient Egypt, the Sky Goddess Nut and the celestial Cow Goddess Hathor were the sources of the Milky Way, which gushed from their breasts. The Hittites, a Four Quarters culture, worshipped the Sun Goddess of Arinna, the deity of the Hattian people they had conquered. For over 1500 years, Japanese emperors have claimed descent from the Sun Goddess Amaterasu, who still emblazons the Japanese flag. Her temple at Ise is the most important shrine in Japan. In order to revivify its indwelling spirit, Ise has been reverently dismantled and rebuilt on alternating sites every twenty years from A.D. 685 to today, and it is not known how far back the original temple dates.[65]

> The mother of our songs, the mother of all our seed, bore
> us in the beginning of things and so she is the mother
> of all types of men, the mother of all nations... She is the
> mother of our dance paraphernalia, of all our temples
> and she is the only mother we possess... She alone is the
> mother of the fire and the sun and the Milky Way.
> ~ Kagawa chant, Columbia[66]

The Sumerian Pyramid culture worshipped the Goddess Inanna, among other gods and goddesses. One of her most important myths concerns her Descent into the Nether World, which Inanna braved because she wanted to be the Queen of the Great Below as well as the Queen of the Great Above, implying that she wanted to become whole again, in the case, by regaining the severed underworld half of her natural totality. To make the descent, she abandoned heaven, Earth, and seven of her major temples, and fastened to her side the *seven me*—"the divine rules and regulations that keep the universe operating as planned."[67] Inanna (later called Ishtar by the Babylonians) was named also on cuneiform tablets as "Queen of all the me," a position similar to that of Maat in Egypt. Inanna's seven temples and her mastery of the seven me suggest her power over the seven visible heavenly bodies: Mercury, Venus, the Moon, Mars, Jupiter, Saturn, and the Sun. The belief that these revered bodies regulated the cosmos and controlled human life was orthodoxy until the Renaissance, and it survives today in astrology. Inanna's seven temples most likely symbolized the solar system and, and by extension, the order of the universe.

The Queen of Heaven not only inspired the science of astronomy and the determination of the calendar, but more broadly, reigned over the intellect as well as the senses. In *When God Was a Woman*, Merlin Stone summarizes Rivkah Harris's research on a group of Sumerian women known as the naditu who "were engaged in the business activities of the temple, held real estate in their own names, lent money and generally engaged in various economic activities. [Harris] also found accounts at this same period of many women scribes." Stone observes, "In the Sumerian hymns the female precedes the male. The epic of Gilgamesh reveals that the official scribe of the Sumerian heaven was a woman, while the initial invention of writing was credited to a Goddess." She concludes, "it may well have been the priestesses, possibly the *naditu* who kept the temple business accounts, who first developed the art of writing. The earliest examples of writing (from about 3200 B.C.), discovered in the temple of the Goddess Inanna of Erech, where many of the *naditu* women lived, turned out to be the temple's accounts of payment for land rental."[68]

As a Pyramid culture, the Sumerians were hierarchically organized into powerful, male-dominated city-states, but clearly women made significant intellectual contributions to the culture. They created, or at least shared in creating, some of the main indices of civilization including writing, record-keeping, and temple administration.

In the Great Round, knowledge is not the unbalanced rational technelogos that we find in Radiant Axes and Grid cultures, but it is also not the relatively pure psychoeros of the Sensitive Chaos. In the Great Round, rational thought and intuition are equally important, and it is in the balance of these ways of knowing that social institutions, temples, and towns are built. The Queen of Heaven, then, represents the duality-transcendent intellectual aspect of the feminine, balanced between technelogos and psychoeros, which flowed naturally and abundantly into the matrifocal cultures of the Great Round. This modal agility is what enabled the Goddess's people to be so inventive and dynamic, while at the same time preserving peace and equality among people and between the sexes.

> Into the Womb-Cavern
> The Valley spirit never dies;
> It is the woman, primal mother.
> Her gateway is the root of heaven and earth.
> It is like a veil barely seen.
> Use it; it will fail.
>   ~ Lao Tsu[69]

Great Round cultures built important institutions and architecture around the gifts of prophecy and initiation. Evidence of the ancient world's enduring esteem for these gifts can be seen in the importance of the Delphic Oracle, the Sibyls, the Eleusinian Mysteries, the Mysteries at Samothrace and those of the goddess Cybele, the hieros gamos, yogic initiations into the energy fields of Kundalini and other serpent goddesses, European and Near Eastern Eye-Goddesses, Sardinian vision springs, the muses, the Goddesses of Fate and the Amerindian's Spider Woman, Cerridwen's Cauldron of Wisdom, and the classical goddesses of wisdom like Athene and Sophia.

Like those who knew the secrets of the spirit-centers of the Sensitive Chaos, all oracular vehicles—whether legendary figures, Goddesses, Mysteries, initiations, power objects, or sacred places—share the ability to negotiate the passage between the worlds of the psyche. In the Great Round as in the Sensitive Chaos, this passage is the path to wisdom. Here, time stops and the Self senses immortality as it expands infinitely into oneness with the universe. In our journey through the Great Goddess's cosmic topography, we saw how her energy currents spiral and interlace, how the water of life flows from her, how her milk sprays across the sky as the Milky Way, and how her intelligence regulates the order of the universe. Now we penetrate her secret depths and enter her ultimate generative source: the *Womb-Cavern*.

The Womb-Cavern

In the same way that the womb's amniotic fluid recalls the ocean— individual life having been born of the one as all life was born of the other—the Womb-Cavern recalls the cave as primordial sanctuary; the one shelters the gestating fetus as the other sheltered evolving humanity. The infamous desire to "return to the womb" can be more than a desire for prenatal oblivion. There are in effect two wombs: one, the physical or exoteric womb, gives biological birth; the other, the metaphysical or esoteric womb, gives spiritual birth. The esoteric womb is the inner numinous source from which we give birth to our Selves. This is the meaning of the *Virgin Birth*.

The esoteric womb is the Holy Grail sought by the Hero in his quest for original wholeness. The Grail Seekers female counterpart is the Virgin, not the trophy virgin won by the Dragon-Slayer—a creation of Four Quarters masculine mythology—but the Self-creating "Virgin" of primary goddess-centered cultures. She may give birth to babies through her biological womb, but her inner life revolves around giving birth to her Self through her esoteric womb.[70]

The esoteric womb, like the Eternal Spring, is the point *"existing here and everywhere, new and always"* from which we give birth to the universe, creating and destroying through the rhythmic pulses of consciousness. In the Womb-Cavern we enter what Lao Tsu called "darkness within darkness, the gate to all mystery."[71] We descend into the underworld of the mind, the chthonic depths, twisting through its labyrinthine passages into moist darkness and seeming chaos until we come out on the other side of the unconscious into the clear, luminous world of psychoerotic vision. It is in the Womb-Cavern that we reverse the alchemical work of evolution, dissolving its stars, sun, moon, Earth, life, cells, molecules, and atoms until matter becomes pure energy and spirit. This realm lies beyond time and space.

Throughout the ages, the urge to reunite with the primal mystery has drawn countless seekers, pilgrims, heroes, ascetics, mystics, prophets, and sages into the Womb-Cavern. The world's mythologies and religions abound with such tales. Those who failed the encounter came out mad. Those who succeeded emerged with the holy books, oracles, visions, and sacred gifts that inspire the human spirit and empower the world's religions.

The sainted Tibetan poet Milarepa lived in a cave most of his life. He slowly turned green from subsisting on nettles, but he received (in the West, we would say "produced") some of Buddhism's most treasured songs and literature. Zeus was born in the Dictaean Cave on Crete, where his mother Rhea hid him to save him from his father Cronos. Early Christian ascetics gestated the new religion in desert caves, while Roman devotees took refuge in the catacombs.

Muhammad received the Koran from the Angel Gabriel during his customary retreat in a cave on Mount Hira near Mecca. The initial experience was sudden and frightening, nearly compelling him to commit suicide so as not to be taken as an ecstatic seer. Once reassured by the Angel, a Messenger of God, Muhammad braved the nearly shamanic crisis of his revelation.

> Sometimes Muhammad would wrap himself in a cloak [Sura[74]], possibly an inducement for the reception of revelation, but he was not in control or able to predict when revelations would come to him. When they did come, Muhammad would undergo physical changes apparent to those around him, such as shaking and profuse sweating, even on cold days. This led his detractors to charge that he had fits or epilepsy, a charge which persisted among Western writers for many centuries.[72]

Because the journey into the cavern of the underworld is the central human quest, the Womb-Cavern is the archetype of the holy-of-holies in nearly all religions. It is the apse and crypt of the Gothic cathedral, the kiva of the Pueblo Indians, the *garbha-griha* or "womb-house" of the Hindu temple, the *anda* or "cosmic womb" of the Buddhist stupa, the "Great Womb Store" of the Japanese Shingon Buddhist sect, and the dome of the Islamic mosque.

The Great Round civilization has thousands of caves and grottos sacred to the Goddess that are connected with vision and prophecy: the cave-sanctuaries of Crete; the great megalithic temples of Malta shaped like the ample body of the Goddess whom one enters to be reborn; the shrines of Çatal Hüyük with images of the Goddess giving birth to the sacred bull; the vaginal corridors and womb-like crypts of the western European megalithic passage graves linked with the Eye-Goddess; the caves that preceded and now lie buried under the Pyramid of the Sun at Teotihuacan in Mexico; and the sacred caves of the Upper Paleolithic era such as the famous "Hall of Bulls" at Lascaux.

Caves and springs of initiation and divination abound in the classical Mediterranean world. Like the vapor-emitting cleft in the earth and the Kastalian spring at the Oracle of Delphi, natural sites were sacred since the Great Round era, and architectural "Womb-Caverns" were probably based on earlier precedents. In the Eleusinian Mysteries, Persephone emerged from the underworld through the "Ploutonion Cave" at Eleusis to rejoin her mother Demeter. Other examples include the apse of the Hieron where the Samothracean Mysteries were held; the sacred caves of the Etruscans; the cave of the Cumaean Sibyl in southern Italy; and the subterranean spring temples of Sardinia, said to "cure eye problems," that is, to give the gift of *seeing*.

In the most elementary Great Round cultures, there is no distinction between sacred and secular structures. The home is everything: shelter, place of production, shrine, and grave. Simple homes—the *tholoi* or beehive houses at Arpachiyah in Mesopotamia and Khirokitia in Cyprus; and the semi-subterranean pit-houses found in Banpo, China, in Neolithic Japan, and in the American Southwest—model the birth passage and uterus of the Great Goddess.

The granary, too, is a Womb-Cavern because of its all-important function of protecting the seed.[73] So is the oven because it magically, alchemically transforms the seed into bread, the symbol of flesh and life. Ovens are still made in womb-like shapes among the Pueblo Indians as seen, for example, in Taos Pueblo, New Mexico,[74] Shrines often center on ovens, hearths, and egg—shaped charcoal mounds having mystical significance. One of the earliest, a shrine from Sabatinovka, Moldavia in Old Europe dating from about 4500 B.C., featured a large oven, presumably for baking sacred bread. The shrine had other images commonly found in Great Round cultures: goddess figures, serpents, bulls, and the Horns of Consecration.[75] Soon we will investigate the meaning of the fire in the Womb-Cavern.

The Kiva

The architecture of the Great Round is manifestly maternal. Sometimes it even gives birth, as we saw in Michael Dame's analysis of Silbury Hill. Often we can see the Great Round gestating and giving birth to the Divine Child, who eventually grows up to become the Hero of the next archetype. The Divine Child often appears as a small cross, a fetal Four Quarters secreted away in the uterine folds of the Great Round. We see this, for example, in the Hopi labyrinth, which symbolizes the womb of the Earth Mother and the Emergence of the Hopi people from previous worlds of existence. According to Frank Waters, the straight line in the square type of labyrinth "represents spiritual rebirth from one world to the succeeding one, as symbolized by the Emergence itself."

> Its two ends symbolize the two stages of life—the unborn child within the womb of Mother Earth and the child after it is born, the line symbolizing the umbilical cord and the path of Emergence. Turning the drawing so that the line stands vertical, at the top of the page, you will see that the lower end is embraced by the U-shaped arm of the maze. The inside lines represent the fetal membranes which enfold the child within the womb, and the outside lines the mother's arms which hold it later.
>
> Of the circular type, he writes:
>
> The center line at the entrance is directly connected with the maze, the center of the cross it forms symbolized the Sun Father, the giver of life. Within the maze, lines end at four points. All the lines and passages within the maze form the universal plan of the Creator which man must follow on his Road of Life; and the four points represent the cardinal or directional points embraced within this universal plan of life. 'Double

security' or rebirth to one who follows the plan is guaranteed, as shown by the same enfoldment of the child by the mother.[76]

This striking example of the birth from the Great Round of the Divine Child, and eventually of the Four Quarters archetype, is further illustrated in the history of Pueblo architecture. The kiva, the sacred structure of the Pueblo Indians, is a round underground structure which, like the labyrinth, symbolizes the womb of Mother Earth and the Place of Emergence. It evolved from the pithouse, which in turn evolved from the cave.

The caves pitting the steep sides of Colorado Plateau mesas (such as Mesa Verde) sheltered the ancestors of the Pueblo Indians when they began to turn from nomadic hunting and gathering to farming in the first few centuries A.D. Farming the fertile mesa tops and drawing river water from the valleys, these cave-dwellers soon became typical Neolithic agriculturists. By the time they invented pottery and adobe, they were building the most common type of dwelling in early Great Round cultures, the semi-subterranean pit-house. This allowed them to leave the caves and move to the tops of the mesas nearer their fields.

The cave, universal symbol of the womb, had given birth to the pit-house. With its dark, round, underground chamber, the pit-house closely resembled the cave, but it had an aboveground roof as well, which rose from a circular base to a square platform punctured by a square hole in the center through which light and people entered and smoke exited. Thus freed from the cave, the people had fashioned a new dwelling in which the Four Quarters was visibly emerging, like the cross in the labyrinth. It was as if the protruding pregnant belly of the Earth Mother were molding a square, showing the shape of the new form gestating within.

The pit-house, like all early Great Round dwellings, was undifferentiated, serving both as residence and as sacred place. House and shrine were not separate because sacred and profane were not separate. But in time the sacred and profane divided, and accordingly the pit-house split in two, the round, underground part becoming the sacred kiva, the square above-ground part, the secular dwelling. The kiva gained a flat roof that served both as an open plaza and as a dance platform for sacred ceremonies. The breach between the sacred kiva and the secular houses severed the umbilical cord, letting the Divine Child leave its mother to venture into the mundane world.

Many sources say that the kiva became the exclusive domain of the men's secret societies. If this were true, then it would indicate that the splitting of the pit-house into kiva and pueblo was symptomatic of a growing status division between the sexes, less typical of the Great Round than of the Four Quarters. Banishing women from the kiva would not only deprive them of kiva's warmth and comfort, especially in winter, but would also banish them from the realm of the sacred, since the kiva was Mother Earth. This is hard to imagine in the matrifocal society of the Pueblos.

Whether women are now or were ever excluded from the kivas—this is most likely a fiction perpetuated by white observers—it is certainly true that the ceremonial cycles of the men's secret societies then as now dominated the life of the kiva, reflecting the influence of a budding Four Quarters archetype contained within a predominantly Great Round context.

The development of male secret societies (a complex subject in itself) appears in some cultures to be an important step in the psychological formation of the Four Quarters, leading to a male establishment that eventually takes over. In other cultures, it appears to be merely a compensatory form of male-bonding among men living in overwhelmingly female-centered contexts. The latter seems true of the Pueblo Indians because, to this day, their culture displays a preponderance of Great Round characteristics. In fact, the Hopis, Zunis, and other Pueblo peoples of the American Southwest are among the last vestiges of Great Round civilization on earth.

The Pueblo Indians: A Great Round Culture

- These are some characteristics of the Pueblo Indians that exemplify the Great Round.
- Matrilineal descent patterns centered on clan structures and village life

- Cooperative, egalitarian social structures
- Consensus decision-making processes that include women
- Agrarian way of life
- Strong traditions of honoring Mother Earth and a humble veneration of nature
- Emphasis on prophecy
- Powerful womb-symbolism of the sacred space—the kiva
- Cyclical view of time as seen in the ceremonial cycle, the Fajada Butte observatory, and various naked-eye horizon astronomy techniques
- Spiral-ornamented pottery and other Neolithic types of crafts
- General peacefulness and gentleness (the name Hopi means "the peaceful people")

The traditional kivas such as those found in the ruins of Mesa Verde and Chaco Canyon, with their round shapes and deep, dark, hearth-centered, earth-penetrating voids of space, are quintessential Womb-Caverns of the Great Round. Like all wombs, they represent a place of primordial transformation: in this case, the place where the people were born into the Fourth World, the World of the Sun, after three previous worlds had been destroyed. The last world was destroyed by flood, and the chosen people who remembered to sing the songs of the Creator survived by floating in a reed. A little hole in the floor of the kiva called the *sipapu* represents the open end of the reed, the Place of Emergence into this world. It symbolizes also the *kopavi*, the top chakra located at the fontanelle in the head (the chakra system is known to the Pueblo Indians). During the destruction of the previous worlds, the Creator advised the chosen people to follow this place of wisdom in themselves, the place where the spirit leaves the body at death.

The kiva is also the place where ceremonial dancers undergo a ritual transformation from their ordinary human persona into kachinas: the many spirits who come into visible manifestation in the Pueblo dances. When the kachina dancers emerge from the small opening in the kiva's roof, they are being reborn in a transformed state.

In the brilliant colorful light of the Southwest, the Earth Mother displays her glorious natural womb caverns and places of emergence. Of course, the most majestic of all is the Grand Canyon, sacred to all Native Americans in the region. Its one mile deep vaginal gash cuts through more than 600 million years of Earth history to early geological stratum. As the greatest of all natural cathedrals, the Grand Canyon is the ultimate sipapu, the archetypal sweat lodge, the place of emergence par excellence, the Holy of Holies of the Earth herself. It is the best place for initiations, for gathering powerful medicines, for seeking visions, and for leaving prayer bundles. As Frank Waters,[77] Jamake Highwater, and others have observed, Native American sacred places—whether Grand Canyon, kiva, sipapu, or sweat lodge—do not soar into the sky like pyramids, temples, and churches. Instead, they reach downward into the earth, back to the Mother.

The Grand Canyon, which became a national park in 1919, has assumed an ironic function in the white world. It has become a repository of names and places in world mythology. Alongside formations with Indian names stand Wotan's Throne, the Freya Castle, the Siegfried Pyre, Valhalla Overlook, the Tower of Ra, Cheop's Pyramid, Rama's Shrine, Angel's Gate, Dragon Head, the Devil's Corkscrew, and the Temples of Jupiter, Venus, Vishnu, Zoroaster, Osiris, Isis, Horus, Buddha, Confucius, Manu, Solomon, and Sheba. In effect, the Canyon, the womb of the Great Mother, protects the seeds of our collective unconscious—of our *soul*—that we forgot in the fervor of the Industrial Revolution and the "Taming of the West."

Soma, Ambrosia, and the Witch's Brew

The Womb-Cavern exemplified the desired visionary state, but, other than being reborn through the Great Mother, it gave no practical clues as to how to attain that state. Several means were used, singly and in combination. Although the Delphic Oracle was said to have had its own naturally rising narcotic gases, it is more likely that the pythoness attained her insights from inhaling the smoke of hemp, laurel, and barley. According to Robert Graves, these were burnt over an egg-shaped mound of charcoal on a tripod painted red, white, and black, the colors of the moon.[78]

The prevalence of serpent imagery and snake pits in Greece,

Crete and the Near East led Merlin Stone to speculate that the serpent may have aided prophecy. She cites a study showing that people who have been immunized by gradual exposure to snakebite do not die when bitten by a venomous serpent, but instead have prophetic visions.[79]

Dream incubation—a purposeful way of having, recalling, and interpreting dreams for their prophetic or revelatory content—may have been another means, as suggested by the figurines of sleeping women found on Malta and in Çatal Hüyük.

The Eleusinian Mysteries, which enlightened the ancient Greeks for nearly two millennia from the prehistory of the Great Round all the way through the Classical era, have remained a mystery to this day due to the strict secrecy that protected them. The first insights into the rites that come anywhere near to explaining both their power and their secrecy are put forward by R. Gordon Wasson, Carl A. P. Ruck, and Albert Hoffman (the chemist who discovered LSD) in their book *The Road to Eleusis*. Although they agree with most experts that something *seen* seems to have been at the heart of the mystery, they believe that the Greeks were much too sophisticated about drama to have been in such awe over a theatrical performance reenacting the myth of Demeter and Persephone, no matter how deep its symbolism. Ruck writes:

> There were physical symptoms, moreover, that accompanied the vision: fear and a trembling in the limbs, vertigo, nausea, and a cold sweat. Then there came the vision, a sight amidst an aura of brilliant light that suddenly flickered through the darkened chamber. Eyes had never before seen the like, and apart from the formal prohibition against telling of what had happened, the experience itself was incommunicable, for there are no words adequate to the task. Even a poet could only say that he had seen the beginning and the end of life and known that they were one, something given by god. The division between earth and sky melted into a pillar of light.
>
> These are symptomatic reactions not to a drama or ceremony, but to a mystical vision; and since the sight could be offered to thousands of initiates each year

dependably upon schedule, it seems obvious that an hallucinogen must have induced it.[80]

The authors conclude that the vision of the secret of immortality, for which the Mysteries were famous, lay in the sacred barley-water served to the initiates. As bland as barley-water may sound, it was made from grain grown on the Rarian Plain adjacent to Eleusis that was then and still is infested with ergot, a parasitic fungus containing water-soluble psychoactive alkaloids and lycergic acid amide (similar to LSD). Referring to a paper by C. Watkins, Ruck identifies the Eleusinian potion with the Vedic Soma ritual and shows both to be identified with women.

> Watkins has shown that the procedures and ingredients for the preparation of such magical or ritual potions in Greek show exact formulaic correspondences with the Vedic Soma ritual and he concludes that these correspondences cannot be coincidental but must instead indicate that the Greek pattern reflects the ritual drink of the Indo-Iranian religion. That drink is hallucinogenic, a mixed potion that is always prepared by a woman or marked as female by the inclusion of milk and always placed in a special vessel to be drunk by participants who are seated. In terms of these correspondences in formulae, it is interesting to note that priestesses performed the ceremony of mixing the sacred potion and that the initiation hall at Eleusis provides seating space for the initiates on the tiers of steps that line the interior walls.[81]

According to the authors of *The Road to Eleusis*, the rites of Demeter constituted initiation into the highest mysteries of the Great Goddess. They suggest that initiates attained an ecstatic state that revealed the enacted birth of the Divine Child—the central theatrical event of the rites in Classical times—to be not merely the birth of a son (though the birth of male from female was still imbued with an aura of the miraculous), not merely the birth of a stalk of barley (though Vegetation Mysteries were still extremely important to agrarian culture), but the birth of the Self, the eternal, all-knowing, all-seeing, great, transcendent Self. Demeter's coveted secret of immortality lay in the revelation of the Self, the essential return to wholeness in the Great Round.

The pharmacopoeia of the Great Round was well-stocked with psychoactive agents—ergot, narcissus, crocus, hyacinth, laurel, hemp, hellebore, henbane, belladonna, amanita mascara. The names Mykonos and Mycenae stem from the Green *mykes*, a word for mushroom related to mycology, the study of mushrooms. In Europe, women's knowledge and use of these agents for visionary experiences and healing continued well into the 18th century when it finally died out after centuries of fanatical witch-hunting.[82]

In the Great Round, there was yet another means of attaining mystical vision, one which instead of being outlawed, became the source of religious imagery throughout the world—the *Fire of Immortality*.

The Fire of Immortality

The Egyptian Goddess Isis and the Greek Goddess Demeter are similar in many ways due to the Egyptian influence on classical Greek mythology. Both goddesses lose, mourn, and then partially restore loved ones. Isis, the Goddess of Sovereignty, had a twin brother and consort Osiris, a Dying-and-Resurrecting God of fertility who represented the dead pharaohs (the living pharaohs were represented by the Solar Hawk Horus, son of Isis and Osiris). Osiris was murdered and dismembered by his brother Seth, who scattered the parts of Osiris's body over the land. Demeter, the Grain Goddess, had a daughter Persephone (or Kore, originally), who was abducted into the underworld by Hades while she was in a field with the daughters of Ocean gathering crocus, hyacinth, narcissus, and other flowers.

Both Osiris and Persephone have come to represent the grain central to the life of agricultural communities. Persephone's disappearance underground marks the time when the grain is gestating in the earth; Osiris's dismemberment, the reaping and sowing of grain. Both myths also represent transformations of consciousness. Osiris's dismemberment probably refers to the well-known shamanic experience of shedding the flesh prior to ecstasy. In the pre-classical Great Round version of Persephone's myth, her underworld journey was likely prompted not by the rape of Hades, who is a later god, but by the psychoactive flowers she was picking at the time.[83] In *The Lost Goddesses of Early Greece*, Charlene Spretnak gives the myth a shamanic interpretation, saying that Persephone wished to enter the Underworld and become its Queen so that she could renew the souls of the dead. She succeeds in this work throughout the winter before rejoining Demeter in the spring to see the fruits of her efforts. Spretnak's version gives Persephone a more active, transformative role than that of the passive, hapless rape victim in the classical myth, and thus is much truer to the spirit of the Great Round.[84]

While they were mourning and searching for their loved ones, both Isis and Demeter hid for a time in royal households where, disguised as nurses, they were entrusted with the care of newborn princes. Both were expelled from the palaces when the Queen Mothers discovered that, rather than suckling their babies, the nurses were putting them into fires at night to burn away their bodily parts and make them immortal. Isis revealed her identity and enlisted the Queen's aid in restoring Osiris's body. Demeter reacted differently. Outraged that the "witless mortals" refused her offer of immortality, she commanded that they build her a great temple at Eleusis where she could teach her rites. Many other goddesses are associated with the Fire of Immortality.

To the Irish, Brigid (the "exalted one") was a triune goddess of fire, counterpart of Britain's Brigantia. Under Christianity Brigid was assimilated into the historical Saint Brigid who, with nine nuns at her great sanctuary at Kildare, kept a perpetual fire that was surrounded by a hedge which no male could cross. The rich lore of the cauldron pervades Celtic mythology. Immersion in the Irish Cauldron of Immortality brought dead warriors back to life. Three drops from the Welsh Goddess Cerridwen's Cauldron of Wisdom made her son at once understand the nature and meaning of all things past, present, and future.[85] Hestia, the Olympian goddess of the hearth, became the Roman's Vesta whose priestesses, the Vestal Virgins, kept a perpetual fire burning in her circular temple. According to Graves, the Great Goddess was abstractly represented throughout the eastern Mediterranean as a heap of glowing charcoal covered with ash that kept it from smoking. This smoldering fire formed the center of family and clan gatherings, and was also the charcoal mound at Delphi, the famous *omphalos* or "Center of the World," inscribed with the name of Mother Earth.[86] In "Fire, the Feminine, and the Sun" in the Pyramid chapter, we will take a close look at Egyptian fire goddesses, Pele, the great Polynesian fire goddess, is as revered and honored today as she is volcanically active. And let us not forget that Amaterasu and all her sister Sun Goddesses throughout the world are Fire Goddesses of the first order.

What was this Fire of Immortality? Why would the Great Goddesses Isis and Demeter hold infants in a flame to make them immortal? There was more to St. Brigid's and the Vestal Virgins' faithfully tended fires than a sentimental symbol of life-everlasting. All these mythic images are possibly metaphors for something much more powerful, an inexpressible fiery force widely tapped by the people of the Great Round.

Serpent Energy Revisited

Gopi Krishna's firsthand experience of enlightenment offers one clue about this force. Throughout the decades in which the spontaneously aroused Kundalini energy worked on his system, he repeatedly suffered a sensation of consuming internal heat:

> ... *a fiery stream of energy shot into my head, and I felt myself lifted up and up, expanding awfully with unbearable terror clutching at me from every side. I felt a reeling sensation while my hands and feet grew cold as ice, as if all the heat had escaped from them to feed the fiery vapour in the head which had risen through the cord like the ruddy blast from a furnace and now, acting like a poison on the brain, struck me numb.... The whole delicate organism was hunting, withering away completely under the fiery blast racing through its interior. I knew I was dying ....*[87]

122 Spatial Archetypes

Although Gopi Krishna had meditated for many years prior to the onset of his ordeal, he was not schooled in Kundalini yoga. In his desperation, he recalled books he had read years earlier, and they helped him to understand what was happening.

> It stated that Kundalini represents the cosmic vital energy lying dormant in the human body which is coiled round the base of the spine, a little below the sexual organ, like a serpent, fast asleep and closing with her mouth the aperture of the Sushumna, the hair-like duct rising through the spinal cord to the conscious centre at the top of the head. When roused, Kundalini, they said, rises through the Sushumna like a streak of lightning carrying with her the vital energy of the body, which for the time being becomes cold and lifeless, with complete or partial cessation of vital functions, to join her divine spouse Shiva in the last or seventh centre in the brain. In the course of this process, the embodied self, freed from the bondage of flesh, passes into a condition of ecstasy known as Samadhi, realizing itself as deathless, full of bliss, and one with the all-pervading supreme consciousness.[88]

Here are all the elements of Demeter's and Isis's fearsome initiation: the submersion in fire, the burning off of the mortal parts of the body, and the promise of immortality and bliss. The Fire of Immortality in whose flames Isis and Demeter held their infant charges, the Virgin's everlasting flame, and Kundalini energy were undoubtedly the same. Obviously, the initiation was dangerous. Gopi Krishna learned that others before him had literally been burned to death by excessive internal heat.[89] He could have been spared some of his pain had he been initiated by an experienced teacher, but he was unable to find one.

The image of Kundalini—shooting up from the base of the spine, bursting open the seven chakras in her path, exploding the final "Thousand-Petalled Lotus" at the top of the head initiating enlightenment—is an archetype that appears worldwide in various guises. The serpent associated with a female energy that opens the mind to higher consciousness can be seen also in the Uraeus serpent (the Cobra Goddess Buto) emerging from the sixth or "Third Eye" chakra in the crown of Egyptian pharaohs. The seven-headed serpent aureole surrounding the Buddha in radiance illustrates the protective *nagus*, serpent wisdom deities who guard Buddhist scriptures in their sea palaces until humans are ready to receive them. Long serpent avenues once extended from the great earthworks and stone circles at Avebury. A related image is the well-preserved Serpent Mound in Ohio, and both sites are the work of Great Round cultures. The monumental, serpent-adorned, stone temples at Angkor Wat and Angkor Thom in Cambodia, which we will explore in the Pyramid chapter, architecturally model the myth of the Churning of the Sea of Milk in which the gods and demons collaborate to use the giant serpent Vasuki to produce the Elixir of Immortality.

Double serpents appeared in numerous Mesopotamian pottery seals. A 6000-year-old seal from Susa shows ibex-headed figures holding vertically rising snakes in each hand. One figure is surrounded by double lozenges resembling eyes, which may represent the popular Near Eastern Eye Goddess who initiates visionary sight, in this case through the mastery of serpent power. Intertwined serpents appear in a remarkable 4500-year-old textile fragment from Huaca Prieta in Peru, in the *caduceus* of the Greeks, on Sumerian cylinder seals, in an Aztec codex, on a prehistoric European menhir, on a Celtic cross in Ireland, and, of course, in the art of India from the remote past to the present. Widespread variants of serpent energy symbols include single or paired serpents ascending or descending multiple levels or stages of consciousness. Such symbols can be found on the roof of a Benin palace in Africa, on the great Buddhist stupa of Borobudur in java, on Thai temples, and on Mayan and Aztec pyramids. Stages of consciousness were symbolized also as a series of levels or tiers in Mesopotamia's stepped ziggurats and in royal crowns made of several tiers of bulls' horns.

The Hopi hold that there are several vibratory centers in the human body, just as there are along the Earth's axis. In the body, the highest center is the *kopavi* at the crown of the head, a spot recognized also in India, Tibet, and ancient Egypt as the site of the soul's exit from the body after death. The Hopi and many other Amerindian groups trace their origins to seven mythical Caves of Emergence, which, as Frank Waters suggests in *Pumpkin Seed Point*, may symbolize the seven chakras. In this they may be similar to the seven houses of the Egyptian underworld, the seven me that Inanna fastened to her side and the seven gates of the underworld through which she led her consort Dumuzi. Also related are the seven levels of initiation in Mithraism, the seven heavens of Islam, the seven-branched Jewish *menorah* and the *Seven Pillars of Wisdom*, and the seven sacred cities of India collectively called the *Nagara* after the serpent wisdom deities. Similar symbolism is probably hidden somewhere among the seven-fold seals, angels, churches, plagues, spirits, stars, trumpets, and vials in the *Book of Revelation*, although the most overt Kundalini images were degraded by Christianity into the Satanic seven-headed red dragon and the Whore of Babylon astride her seven-headed beast. The seven chakras are gruesomely suggested also in the seven serpents that spurt from the necks of decapitated players in Ball Court bas reliefs in the Radiant Axes, Post-Classic, Mayan city of Chichen Itza.

One of the oldest representations of archetypal serpent energy comes from China, found among the earliest pottery from a Yang-Shao settlement in the birthplace of Asian agriculture. It is a clay figure of a horned, densely tattooed, awestruck head rising from a "Thousand-Petaled Lotus" base ornamented with fiery radiating lines.[91] The tattoo around the mouth on this and a similar figure from the same site somewhat resembles that worn today by the indigenous Ainu women of Japan and is identical to a chin tattoo shown by the Cape Dorset Eskimo artist Kenojuak in her 1960 print "The Woman Who Lives in The Sun."[92]

Independent researcher Grace Shinell has studied recent scientific findings that an extraordinary amount of electrical energy courses through women's brains and wombs. She seeks to verify the abundant historical and mythological evidence that the earliest initiations into transcendent consciousness were everywhere conducted by women through the Goddess. "The greater ability of women to raise Kundalini energy from their uteruses," Shinell writes, "accounts in a most practical way for the intense sacrality accorded women in ancient civilizations. This gynec capacity also explains the long and awesome association of women with snakes, the spiraling zoomorphic representation of Kundalini energy."[93] She maintains that Kundalini initiation was widely practiced by trained priestesses, and that this explains the essence of the *hieros gamos*, which is usually taken to be a purely sexual fertility rite, just as the whole complexity of Great Round religion is so often perfunctorily summed up as a "fertility cult."[94]

Shinell's view is corroborated by an observation made by Mircea Eliade in *The Forge and the Crucible*.

> According to the myths of certain primitive peoples, the aged women of the tribe naturally possessed fire in their genital organs and made use of it to do their cooking but kept it hidden from men, who were able to get possession of it only by trickery. These myths reflect the ideology of a matriarchal society and remind us, also, of the fact that fire, being produced by the friction of two pieces ol wood (that is, by their "sexual union"), was regarded as existing naturally in the piece which represented the female. In this sort of culture woman symbolizes the natural sorceress. But men finally achieved "mastery" over fire and in the end the sorcerers became more powerful and more numerous than their female counterparts.[95]

The Great Round's Fire of Immortality—forged in the crucible of the Womb-Cavern, Cerridwen's Cauldron of Wisdom, the Holy Grail—ultimately inspired the imagery of enlightenment in the world's major religions. It is behind all the impossible-to-articulate ecstatic references to illumination, radiance, halos, auras, light, holy spirit, emanation, vision, glory, life-everlasting, and purification by fire, In *The Feminine: Spacious as the Sky*, Miriam and José Argüelles append passages from the sacred texts of many cultures attributing wisdom and enlightenment to the Goddess, including this from the *Bible*:

She is a breath of the power of God,
Pure emanation of the glory of the Almighty ....
She is indeed more splendid than the sun.
She outshines all the constellations:
Compared with light she takes first place,
For light must yield to night, but over Wisdom darkness can never triumph.[96]

SYNOPSIS OF THE GREAT ROUND

World of the Great Goddess

SYMBOL

Circle or sphere

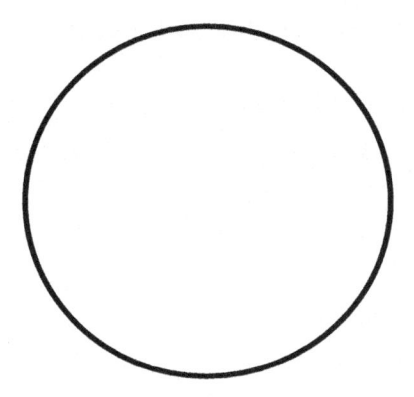

SOCIETY

Era
- Neolithic (New Stone Age), also Chalcolithic (Copper Age) and occasionally Bronze Age.

Society
- Self-sufficient farming communities, villages, and towns. Egalitarian social structures indicated by collective burials, homogenous dwelling types, and the absence of royal tombs and palaces.
- Some occupational specialization.
- Sustained peace indicated by the absence of war, weaponry and fortifications; the lack of battle images and warriors in art and mythology; and the absence of battle-mutilated bodies in grave sites.

128 *Spatial Archetypes*

Examples
- Jōmon culture in Japan and China's Yang Shao culture; the Indus Valley civilization; Mesopotamia to the pre-Sumerian Ubaid period; Egypt to the predynastic Gerzean period, Neolithic Great Zimbabwe; the pre-Hellenic Aegean world including Minoan Crete; the Neolithic and Copper Age cultures of Old Europe, the pre-Indo-European megalith builders in Western Europe and Malta; North America's Neolithic Mogollan, Hohokam, and Anasazi cultures and the contemporary Hopi, Zuni, and Pueblo Indians in the Southwest, and the Neolithic Adena-Hopewell culture in the Eastern Woodlands; the Neolithic Tehuacan Valley civilization, the Valdivia culture of Ecuador.

Technology
- Agriculture and animal domestication.
- Pottery, spinning and weaving.
- Naked-eye astronomy.
- Permanent architecture including megalithic structures. and Toward the end of the Great Round—writing, metallurgy, irrigation, plumbing, and cities.
- Balance of psychoeros and technelogos with psychoeros maintaining a slight edge.

Gender Relations
- Matrilineal families or clans (descent and inheritance traced through the mother's line). High status and autonomy of women in actual and mythic roles as creators and mothers, spinners and weavers, potters, priestesses, healers, prophets and oracles, decision-makers, ancestors, and clan leaders. Liberal sexual codes that do not restrict women to monogamous marriage. Sexuality celebrated as a sacred, life-giving energy.
- *Hieros gamos* or Sacred Marriage as female initiation of the male occurring informally or in goddess temples or natural sanctuaries.

PSYCHE

Psychology
- In childhood, separation from the mother in which the child consciously perceives the mother as the center and source of life, but also as the first "other" with whom it has a relationship.
- At any age, identifying with the feminine principle.
- Psychoerotic ways of knowing through dreams, intuition, omens, ecstatic trances continue.
- Technelogos begins to emerge (as seen in the technological inventiveness of Great Round civilizations). Integration of opposites to achieve holistic vision.

Stagnation
- Psychological stagnation in the Great Round can cause a paralyzing centripetal retreat into the private sphere and the unconscious, resulting in prolonged passivity, vegetative states, and infantile dependency. Self-sacrificial nurturing and smother-mothering are also a danger.

Breakthrough
- Distinguish between the material physical womb and the transcendent spiritual womb. Transmute the quest for regression into the physical womb into a quest for the wisdom of the spiritual womb, which leads to giving birth to one's Self.

Liberation
- Enlightenment through the feminine principle as personified by the Great Goddess.
- Psychological liberation in the Great Round generates the perception of the Self as Mother, which brings both a nurturing sense of responsibility for the health and vitality of all life and the spiritually enlightening experience of psychologically giving birth to the phenomenal world, This leads to the form of enlightenment the Buddhists call sunyata or "emptiness."[88]

SPIRIT

Worldview
- Perceiving the world as a "Great Round," cyclical in its rhythms, embracing nature and culture as one, encircling one's being in a nurturing matrix, and centered in the Great Mother. The cosmos is the body or Womb-Cavern of the Great Goddess.

Spiritual Focus
- Religions, rites, and initiations offering direct, personal participation in the Goddess and her mysteries (rather than an indirect relationship to a pantheon of gods mediated by a hieratic priesthood, as in patriarchal cultures). In traditional Great Round cultures, enlightenment consists of knowing oneself to be the child or incarnation of the Great Mother.

Mythic Themes
- The Great Goddess, especially in her elemental and abstract forms.
- Traditional women's activities: spinning, weaving, grinding grain, baking, giving birth and so on.
- The Womb-Cavern: caves, sacred vessels (cauldrons, *kernos*, libation vessels, the Holy Grail), semi-subterranean houses, granaries, ovens, interior spaces, vulva symbols.
- All waters, the ocean, rivers, sacred springs and wells, rain, baths of purification, water flowing in the desert or the Wasteland, baptismal and holy waters.
- Spirals and labyrinths, meanders, concentric circles, cup-and-ring marks.
- Sacred cows and bulls, the Horns of Consecration (linked with the bull, moon, and vulva), the bull as moon and consort of the Goddess.
- The Divine Child as grain, daughter, bull, or son/lover of the goddess, Moon God, Dying-and-Resurrecting vegetation god.
- The Sacred Serpent as Kundalini and Telluric energy.
- The Eye Goddess, mystical or holistic vision, sibyls and ora-

- cles, prophecy and divination.
  - Healing through dreams, herbs, foods, and cooked medicines.
  - The phallus as fertility icon. The hieros gamos or sacred marriage as female initiation of the male.
  - Farming festivals, first fruits festivals, harvest feasts, planting rituals, vegetation mysteries.
  - Solstices and equinoxes: celebrations of the quarter-points and cross-quarter-points of the agricultural year.
  - Goddess sanctuaries and pilgrimage sites in nature (see Landscape below).

CULTURE

Prime Symbol

  - The Womb-Cavern (the physical or exoteric womb giving biological birth; the metaphysical or esoteric womb giving spiritual birth).

Art

  - Art as ornament and as spiritual expression. Megalithic art, petroglyphs, pictograms, frescoes, pottery, textiles, jewelry, ornamented utilitarian objects, ceremonial items, and sculpture (in stone, clay, wood, and so on, with a predominance of small goddesses and female figurines, although a few monumental sculptures are known such as the Seated Goddess of Tarxien, Malta).
  - Artistic motifs include spirals, meanders, astronomical signs, lozenges, vulva symbols, serpents and other reptiles, animals (especially cows and bulls), birds, trees, and plants.

Astronomy

  - Calendrical naked-eye astronomy focusing on alignments to the sun's risings, zeniths, and settings on the solstices, equinoxes, and cross-quarter days, plus some systematic observations and markings of the moon's cycles, including its 18.6-year cycle of eclipses. Megalithic architecture frequently involved in astronomical observations.

Time
- Cyclical time based on the agricultural cycle, the solstices and equinoxes, and the phases of the moon, with lunar calendars more common than solar calendars.

Space
- Space centered in the Womb-Cavern, a still center that extends to encompass the "Great Round" of the cosmos.

Landscape
- Land as the body of the Goddess whose nodes and meridians of subtle energy ("Telluric currents," later personified as serpents, dragons, nymphs, faeries, elves, goblins, and the like) can be partially manipulated through geomancy. Reverence for sacred places in the Goddess's earth-body such as springs and rivers, caves, grottoes, groves, trees, forests, hillocks, mountains, and any natural sanctuary associated with healing, fertility, revelatory visions, and spiritual rebirth.
- Territoriality expressed as the right to occupy farmlands, defined not by property laws but by the accumulation of generations of ancestors ("ancestor worship") in collective, usually megalithic, grave-shrines, which display the clans' longstanding occupation of and investment in the land.

Architecture
- The Womb-Cavern as the most important structure, whether natural cave, passage grave, beehive house, tholos/kiva, or temple sanctuary.
- Emerging centrality and permanence in architecture, growing out of the settled agricultural way of life—granaries and other storage facilities, permanent homesteads, villages, towns, and the earliest cities.
- Megalithic construction frequently used for the most sacred structures (tombs, temples, geomantic and astronomical structures). Tendency to shift over time from undifferentiated round structures (tholai, beehive houses, and semi-subterranean pit-houses) to more differentiated rectilinear structures, with sacred buildings sometimes remaining round.

THE FOUR QUARTERS

World of the Hero

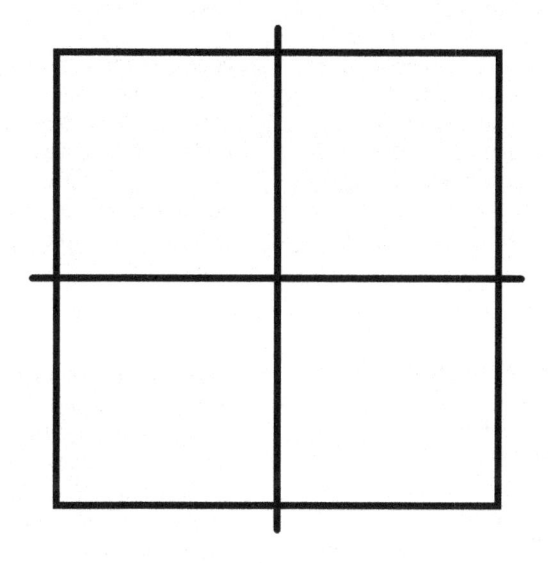

3a. Combat of Achilles and Hector. From a red-figured volute-krater (bowl for mixing wine and water). The Greeks of this Mycenaean period (c. 1600–1100 BC) were the invaders of Troy about whom we read in The Iliad and The Odyssey. Homer's depictions present their character, one shared with other Bronze Age warrior societies.

3b. St. George and the Dragon. By Raphael, 1504-06. Many Four Quarter heroes are dragon slayers. The Dragon is symbolic of the earth energies of the Great Goddess, who once ruled the universe, but is overthrown by her adolescent son and now becomes the helpless maiden in need of rescue.

3c. The Great Medicine Wheel. Bighorn National Forest, Wyoming, US. Before the arrival of Europeans, Native Americans were of the Sensitive Chaos, Great Round, Four Quarters, and even Pyramid cultures. Four Quarters cultures, characteristic of the Plains nations, constructed medicine wheels, typically with spokes radiating to the cardinal directions.

3d. Indo-European migrations. Eurasia was covered with Great Round Neolithic villages. Their culture was female centered and peaceful. Beginning around 4000 BC the Proto Indo-Europeans moved out of the steppes of what is now Russia and spread down into India, into Greece, and up into Scandinavia. They brought with them epic poems and a pantheon of male gods. The Greek pantheon headed by Zeus is parallel by one in India headed by Indra and one in Scandinavia headed by Odin.

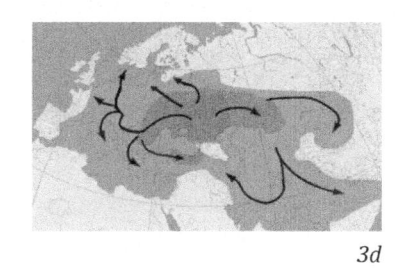

The Four Quarters 135

3a

3b

3c

3d

THE FOUR QUARTERS

WORLD OF THE HERO

Typically, in the symbolic cosmos, the locus or the most supreme and intense powerfulness was the axial center, and any figure or object occupying this position became thereby highly numinous and evoked feelings of awe and reverence.[1]

The Divine Child

In the last chapter we saw how the Great Round crystallized out of the Sensitive Chaos, just as the Goddess grew out of the One Great Being as personified deity, and the mother emerges in the child's world as the first person with whom it has a relationship. In the Four Quarters, the child, in turn, crystallizes out of the maternal matrix, gains its own ego and identity, and asserts itself against the mother in its struggle to separate from her. In this archetype, the Divine Child—who had issued from the womb of the Great Goddess with every waxing moon, winter solstice sunrise, harvest, physical birth and spiritual rebirth—grows up to become the Hero.

In the Great Round, the Divine Child figured more as an abstract symbol of vegetal growth and natural renewal than as a central character with a human personality. Even when it appears as a human infant in Neolithic "madonna" figurines, it is rarely possible to make out the baby's sex. In later mythology, however, the Divine Child is usually a male. Representing a part of the Goddess that she gives birth to, which in turn refertilizes her, he becomes her son/lover. In the Great Round, masculinity is part of the totality of the Great Goddess. The androgynous models of later male-oriented religions (yin/yang, Shiva/Shakti, etc.) define the universe as turned by the opposing forces of maleness (positive, solar, aggressive, light, warm) and femaleness (negative, lunar, receptive, dark, cool), a dualism entirely alien to the holistic Great Round. Neumann writes:

In the matriarchal world the woman as vessel is not made by man or out of man or used for his procreative purposes; rather, the reverse is true: it is this vessel with its mysterious creative character that brings forth the male in itself from out of itself ....

The Great Vessel engenders its own seed in itself; it is parthenogenetic and requires the man only as opener, plower, and spreader of the seed that originates in the female earth. But this seed is born of the earth; it is at once ear of grain and child, in Africa as in the Eleusinian mysteries. (Later the patriarchate postulates the reverse just as one-sidedly; namely, that the male seed is the creative element while the woman as vessel is only its temporary abode and feeding place.)[2]

In the Four Quarters, the Son/Lover of the Goddess matures into the central figure of the psychological dramas Neumann described as the Separation of the World Parents, the Birth of the Hero, and the Slaying of the Mother.[3]

Thus in the Four Quarters the son separates from the mother, the masculine principle forms in the collective unconscious, and the patriarchate emerges in society. These four phenomena are interrelated—all grow out of the formation of the central reference point in the psyche known as the ego. The emergence of the ego in the individual and collective psyche profoundly and irreversibly alters how the entire world appears to present itself. Within the mind, the ego is the principle that separates Self from other, distinguishing between the "I" and the "Not-I."[4] Within society, it is personified by the chieftain who rises to a position of power over the rest of the community. The chieftain is mirrored in the mythic Lord of the Four Quarters, be he Buddha, Brahma, Jehovah, Quetzalcoatl, the Chinese Son of Heaven, Zeus, Thor, Indra, or innumerable other gods. The Lord of the Four Quarters reigns over the universe from his celestial citadel where his center is the world's center. In civilization, the Four Quarters culture is the hierarchical chieftainship with a caste-stratified social structure, which is reified in a stratified pantheon of gods and goddesses.

In the Four Quarters symbol, the cardinal axes extend North/South and East/West (or occasionally along the diagonals Northeast/Southwest and Southeast/Northwest). Their crossing forms the central reference point. The cardinal axes overlay the Great Round, drawing and quartering it, and distorting its shape into a square enclosure. Where the circular symbol of the Great Round represented the cosmos in its diffuse entirety, the axial co-ordinates of the Four Quarters fix a locus about which everything else revolves. This locus—the domain of the Lord of the Four Quarters—is symbolic of the ego's organizing action on space and perception. It divides the cosmos according to its own body references: front and back, left and right, up and down, which correlate to the cardinal directions, heaven and earth. All of the qualities of the known universe move into position along one or another of the cardinal axes. North, South, East, and West each accrue associations with particular colors, elements, seasons, animals, castes or tribes, personality traits, deities, historical epochs, stages of life, continents or mountains, seas and rivers, and so forth. The quartered cosmos replaces the Great Round. The circumambulation of the cardinal points becomes an important Four Quarters ritual, used both to establish territorial sovereignty (to master the Four Quarters of the universe) and to effect a spiritual reintegration of that which has been fragmented (to master the Four Quarters of the psyche and return to the center.)

As it distinguishes between "mine" and "thine" the ego gives rise to the concept of private property. It generates around itself a territory that must be defended. Now something can be owned. A young child whose ego has just emerged will say over and over, "That's mine!" Figuratively speaking, the ego builds a wall around its territory, a defensive fortress that protects its dominions and property. It sends out guardians to protect the gates in the wall, and it ritually circumambulates the quarters of its realms to ensure that everything is secure. The four guardians at the cardinal axes are personified mythically by innumerable quartets of celestial guardians and world-supporters. The Maya have several such quartets including four chacs, bacabs, and Itzam Nas. The Navajo have the deities of the four sacred mountains; Buddhism, the five Dhyani Buddhas; Hinduism, the four Lokapalas; China, the Masters of the Four Directions; ancient Egypt, the four sons of Horus. In Christianity, the four Evangelists surrounding Christ canonically represent the Four Quarters and fulfill the same functions as the other figures.

The Lord of the Four Quarters, reigning at the center of an axially divided universe surrounded by a wall with guardians at the cardinal points, is a perfect spatial symbol of the ego. Furthermore, the architecture of the Four Quarters directly reflects this symbolic image, and the extensive building of fortified towns and cities by Four Quarters cultures testifies to the warlike nature of the archetype.

The typical town is rectilinear, surrounded by walls with gates at the cardinal points, and divided by two major avenues. At the central crossing of the avenues stands the residence of the Lord in the form of a temple, mansion, palace, castle, fort, or citadel. This scheme and its variations took over the town planning of the Sumerians, Babylonians, Egyptians, Hittites, and Israelites in the Middle East; the Greeks and Romans in the Mediterranean; the Chinese, Japanese, Indians, and Khmers in Asia; to some extent the Celts and Vikings in Europe; as well as and many other cultures, including African, American, during their respective Four Quarters periods. This seminal plan often endures throughout succeeding archetypal eras. In India, the ancient Vedic Four Quarters mandalas underlay town planning and temple design even today. The Romans favored the Four Quarters as a layout for their military camps and colonial cities for over five hundred years—through the height of their Radiant Axes empire and into their decline, to which the grid inherent in the plan was well suited, if not prophetic.[5]

Many Four Quarters cities are stratified into different quarters for different castes. The most common plan arranges precincts in concentric squares around the central complex, like nesting Chinese boxes, with the highest ranks closest to the center and the lowest at the outer edges. This social stratification is usually mirrored in a syncretic religious hierarchy that enthrones the tribal god of the chieftain at the sacred center and arranges the deities of lower castes and conquered peoples toward the periphery, as is the case in Hinduism's caste system, city-planning, and religion.

The goddesses of the Great Round may remain quite strong in Four Quarters cultures, but they are usually displaced from the center of power by being made into the wives or consorts of the central god: Zeus and Hera, etc. Often former Great Goddesses, like Maeve in Ireland and Isis in Egypt, retain the sole power to bestow sovereignty. But goddesses can also be demonized into gorgons, harpies, dragons, and witches who test the valor and virtue of the Hero.

The Separation of the World Parents

It is impossible to overestimate the importance of the mythic theme of the Separation of the World Parents in the Four Quarters worldview and civilization. Although in Egypt the sky was portrayed as a female, the Goddess Nut, and the earth as a male, the God Geb, the roles are usually reversed in the Four Quarters conception so that the earth is feminine and the sky masculine. In the Mesopotamian Great Round civilization, the Goddess Nammu is credited with creating Heaven and Earth, and, as we saw earlier, Inanna was revered as the Queen of Heaven. But as Mesopotamia shifted to the Four Quarters frame of mind at the end of the Ubaid period and the beginning of Sumerian culture in the fourth millennium B.C., it developed a syncretic religion in which Heaven became the God An and Earth, the Goddess Ki. The separation of these World Parents by the Air-God Enlil is recorded in an ancient text:

> The lord whose decisions are unalterable,
> Enlil, who brings up the seed of the land from the earth,
> Took care to move away Heaven from Earth,
> Took care to move away Earth from Heaven.[6]

The creation myth of the Maori, a New Zealand culture that had developed into Four Quarters hierarchical chieftainships before European colonization, exemplifies the drama of the Separation of the World Parents. In the myth, Ragni and Papa, Father Heaven and Mother Earth, clung together, and there was only darkness. Wishing to end the oppression of darkness, their

142 *Spatial Archetypes*

children conspired to slay their parents. But one of the sons, the forest god Tane-mahuta argued, "It is better to rend them apart, and to let Rangi stand far above us, and Papa lie beneath our feet. Let Rangi become as a stranger to us, but the earth remain close to us as a nursing mother." Several siblings failed in their attempts to separate Rangi and Papa. Finally, Tane-mahuta, acting with great physical heroism on behalf of his siblings, raised his father into the sky and pressed his mother down to earth. The Maori say, "It was the fiercest thrusting of Tane which tore the heaven from the earth, so that they were rent apart, and darkness was made manifest, and light was made manifest also."[7]

This myth, like all of the separation myths involving a Sky Father and an Earth Mother, dramatizes a process central to the establishment both of the ego in the psyche and of the male-centered worldview of civilization: the splitting of the Great Round into two opposed camps with the masculine principle usually elevated to the sky and the feminine confined to the earth (as in the East's yin and yang principles, for instance). By this means, the masculine principle became identified with the glorious, infinite reaches of the heavens, the spirit, consciousness, and the purity of abstract thought; and the feminine, with the dark, nether regions of the earth, the body, the unconscious, and the turbid maelstrom of emotions. Consequently, the original totality of the Great Round and the Great Goddess was divided into two halves with a higher value placed on the "male" half.[8]

The Great Round civilization of pre-Hellenic Greece attributed creation to the Goddess of All Things, Eurynome, who emerged from Chaos and danced on the waves of the sea, whipping up a wind around her which she fashioned into the great serpent Ophion. Impregnated by the wind, she changed into a dove and laid the Universal Egg, around which she made Ophion coil seven times until the Egg hatched out everything in heaven and earth. The Indo-European Greeks greatly altered this myth in their syncretic Olympian mythology. The Great Goddess became the Earth Mother who gave birth not to the serpent but to the Sky God Uranus, who then fathered the Titans by her. According to Graves, Uranus was identified with the Aryan god Varuna of India, but his name was a masculine form of Ur-ana, Greek for "queen of the mountains, summer, winds, and wild oxen."[9] This may further indicate a usurpation of the Goddess's powers. The Sky Father Uranus and the Earth Mother Gaia were separated by their son Cronos, who castrated his father with a flint sickle because Uranus refused to let the Titans be born, forcing them back into Gaia, which caused her excruciating pain.

There are several telling elements in this Olympian myth. The castration of the father by the son, for instance, is a fairly common theme in Four Quarters mythology. It dramatizes the inborn jealousy between father and son—Freud's "Oedipal complex"—which is indicative of the competitive male relationships that dominate the Four Quarters. Secondly, the pain that Uranus caused Gaia by preventing her from giving birth is symbolic of how the superimposition of the patriarchal Four Quarters did in fact close off the creative energies of the matriarchal Great Round. As Graves and others have pointed out, the dramatic tension of this struggle drives countless Greek myths and plays. A third element is the symbolic meaning of Uranus's castration, which has been interpreted as a severing of the creative, paradisal, mythic mind, leaving only the literal mind of ordinary consciousness.[10] In support of this interpretation, it is important to recall that Cronos, from whom we derive the term "chronology" and similar words relating to time, was known among the Greeks as Father Time for the old Titan lived a long time fathering or grandfathering all twelve of the official Olympian deities. The Separation of the World Parents, then, is the first dualistic breach of the universe that creates time, the linear time that "rolls onward" from which there is no return to the eternal paradise that existed before the "beginning of time." In the Great Round, time is cyclical; in the Pyramid, it is linear. Usually in the Four Quarters, time falls between these two—it is linear within great cycles such as India's *yugas* or the "Great Year" in ancient Mediterranean cultures.[11]

The beginning of time—coinciding with the rise of the ego—marks the Expulsion from the Garden of Eden, from the realm of immortality and innocence before the discriminating ego ate of the fruit of the Tree of Knowledge of Good and Evil, bringing the dualistic perception that exiled us from our original wholeness in the Great Round. This is the archetypal "cross to bear" symbol of the dark side of the Four Quarters, the existential burden of *self-consciousness* that is possible only when the ego castrates the holistic self, flinging it, like Uranus's genitals, back into the primeval Sea of Chaos.

A major theme in the Four Quarters is divisiveness: warrior against enemy, father against son, male against female, Hero against Dragon, men against nature. Gone is the participation mystique of the Great Round and the Sensitive Chaos when the boundaries between things were faint or nonexistent. Now the dominant force is the ego, which, according to Erich Neumann, "classifies and arranges the world in a continuous series of opposites."

> Not only do day and night, back and front, upper and lower, inside and outside, I and You, male and female, grow out of this development of opposites and differentiate themselves from the original promiscuity, but opposites like "sacred" and "profane," "good" and "evil," are now assigned their place in the world .... The experience of "being different," which is the primary fact of nascent ego consciousness and which occurs in the dawnlight of discrimination, divides the world into subject and object; orientation in time and space succeeds man's vague existence in the dim mists of prehistory and constitutes his early history.[12]

This divisiveness, Neumann writes, is accomplished on several levels.

> Besides disentangling itself—its fusion with nature and the group, the ego, having now opposed itself to the nonego as another datum of experience, begins simultaneously to constellate its independence of nature as independence of body.... The ego, having its seat, as it were, in the head, in the cerebral cortex, and experiencing the nether regions of the body as something strange to it, an alien reality, gradually begins to recognize that essential portions of this nether

corporeal world are subject to its will and volition. It discovers that the "sovereign power of though" is a real and actual fact: the hand in front of my face, and the foot lower down, do what I will .... If technics are an extension of the "tool" as a means of dominating the world around us, then the tool in turn is nothing but an extension of the voluntary musculature. Man's will to dominate nature is but an extension and projection of that fundamental experience of the ego's potential power over the body, discovered in the voluntariness of muscular movement.[13]

This brings to mind the muscular, heroic imagery of the Four Quarters: Greek vase paintings of sparring warriors, ferocious Celtic warriors fighting naked, war games in Nuba compounds and New Guinea villages, Olympian competitive sports. But even more importantly, it shows the ego's infatuation with its capacity to dominate nature and the body through will, *logos*, and *techne*. Predictably, then, it is in the Four Quarters that we see the beginning of an ever-increasing emphasis on technelogos to the detriment of psychoeros.

Even the Bible begins, "In the beginning God created the heaven and the earth," and proceeds to describe how God separated the waters above from the waters below, distinguished light from darkness, created everything in the world, made male and female in his own image, and gave them dominion over nature. Significantly, the uncompromising patriarchs who wrote the Old Testament would not acknowledge the existence of any previous deities, least of all the Great Goddess. Rather than casting the story of God's Separation of the World Parents with pre-existing gods and goddesses, they opted for a euphemism: the separation of the "waters above" from the "waters below."

It is also consistent with the Biblical patriarchs destruction of the more goddess-centered civilization of the Canaanites that the sole creator of the universe is envisioned not simply as a male, but as the wrathful, authoritarian Father God, Yahweh.[5] Like Zeus, he was given to wielding lightning bolts to enforce his idea of order. Both deities are archetypal, egocentric Storm-and-Thunder Gods of the Four Quarters who concede to no other force in the universe.

146 *Spatial Archetypes*

The Separation of the World Parents, then, is a multivalent mythological theme that interweaves the most basic qualities of the Four Quarters: the linear time that rolls onward, the Expulsion from Paradise and the alienation from the Self, the polarization of opposites and the rise of dualistic thinking, the beginnings of male dominance, the mythic image of heroically willful deeds, the power struggles inherent in syncretic religions, the Oedipal animosity between fathers and sons, and so on. But most of all, it portrays the spatial impact of the emergence of ego. When the child psychologically rends apart the archetypal Mother and Father—Heaven and Earth—it wrests a place for itself in the cosmic scheme of things, winning an independent existence that is verified by the fundamental divisions of space.[16]

Ego and War

Out of the hurly-burly Four Quarters, warfare arises at the same time that the archetype generates ego and the primacy of the masculine principle, just as the ego fixes in the image of the Lord of the Four Quarters and the Hero, society pivots about the male figures of the chieftain, the blacksmith, the shaman, and the warrior. The gifts of the storyteller turn to epic tales of the heroes like the Celtic Cuchulainn and the Greek Heracles. And the enlightening moments of truth are no longer played out in the secret folds of the Earth Mother and the Great Goddess, but, as in Greece's *Iliad*, India's *Bhagavad-gita*, and Ireland's *Tain Bo Cuailnge*, on the battlefield, Historically, the psychological violence attending the Separation of the World Parents was not an inner experience, safely waged in the psyche. It was vividly acted out in the innumerable battles, raids, and massacres that bloody the chronicles of the Heroic Age. War is the great preoccupation of the Four Quarters. It is as if the peaceful, agrarian Great Round civilization was suddenly exploded and fragmented by a new order of society, one that had collectively discovered its ego and now saw enemies everywhere.

Not surprisingly, the most common form of the Lord of the Four Quarters is the aggressive Storm God, who may also be the God of War and Blacksmiths: Zeus of the Greeks, the Vedic god Indra, the Norse Thor, Finnish Ukko, early Russian Perun, Prussian Perkuno, and the Lapps' Tiermes. Near Eastern Storm Gods include the Canaanite Baal, the Babylonian Marduk, and the Semitic Yahweh. Among African Storm and Thunder Gods are the Egyptian Seth, the Yoruban vishu Shango, and the Gods So of the Ewe and Gus of the Ga. The Chinese have Lei Kung; and the Japanese, Raiden. Many Four Quarters Amerindians venerate the Thunderbird whose eyes flash lightning, and like many storm gods, the Iroquois' Hino is also a serpent-slayer. In Mesoamerica, there are the rain god Tlaloc and the Mayan Chacs; and in Peru, Illyap'a was petitioned to bring rain with offerings of starving black dogs. These Storm Gods—arising, as far as we know their origins, during the Four Quarters eras of their respective cultures—mold the perfect mythic image of ego and war. They have absolute power over human life, since they control the life-giving rains as well as the death-dealing hurricanes, hailstorms, and lightning. They hold in their grip the elemental forces of fire and water, and, because they are sky-dwellers, they seemed to have power over earthbound nature. Like warriors and many heroes, they are noisy, violent, and demanding of attention, and their strikes against their enemies are decisive and effective.

Although the perceptions of "danger," "enemy," and "threat" that animate so much of Four Quarters culture operate on the instinctual animal level, they do not inspire epic poetry without the illumination of the ego, which carries the discrimination between "friend" and "enemy" to archetypal proportions.

The drama of ego emergence is more a masculine than a feminine drama, since sons cannot grow up to become women like their mothers, whereas daughters can. Sons must break from their mothers and define identities in opposition to femaleness. In traditional societies, it is at this point that the male secret societies tear sons away from their mothers, usually in a rather frightening manner through abduction, ordeals that test manhood, and grueling initiation rites. From then on the son's life is no longer embedded in the female sphere. It revolves around the masculine mysteries of the hunter and warrior.

From the Four Quarters point of view, the glory of war is that it tests men against the ultimate enemy—death. Through war, men prove their bravery, strength, and character. Their sphere of raw, courageous action is alien to the Great Round's feminine mysteries of life, childbirth, fertility, sacred sexuality, planting and harvesting, prophecy, spiritual transformation, and death. The warlike epic literature of the Four Quarters reveals the tension between these two worlds. Underlying the dramatic battle scene is a backcloth of warfare between the sexes in which women struggle to maintain their former power and autonomy. All of these themes can be seen in the Irish epic *Tain Bo Cuailnge*, the Cattle Raid of Cuailnge.[17]

Cuchulainn's Battle Frenzy

The *Tain* opens with the strong-willed and lusty Queen Medb (or Maeve), Queen of Connacht and embodiment of Celtic sovereignty, engaging in pillow talk with Ailill, one of her string of husbands. "It struck me," Ailill says, "how much better off you are today than the day I married you." "I was well enough off without you," Medb retorts, trying to curb Ailill's self-importance. Ailill responds that Medb's wealth when he married her consisted mainly of "women's things." Offended, Medb proudly reminds Ailill that her royal genealogy and her feats as a warrior leading tens of thousands of soldiers had won her a huge estate more extensive than his. Ailill challenges her claim, and they each proceed to take painstaking inventories of their possessions, including clothing and jewelry, household furnishings, and herds of pigs, sheep, and cattle. They find that their estates are equal except for one white bull, Finnbennach, the White-Horned. Though he had been born to one of Medb's cows, Finnbennach had refused to be led by a woman and had joined Ailill's herd. Deeply hurt in the face of her inequality, Medb plans a raid on the neighboring province of Ulster to obtain the prized Brown Bull of Cuailnge to restore her parity and pride.

The men of Ulster are unable to fight Medb and her army because they are suffering under the curse of Macha. Macha's husband had boasted at a fair that his wife could outrun the king's chariot and horses, even though she was pregnant and in labor. Macha bravely saved her husband's pride by running the race and giving birth at the end to twins (from which derives the name of the legendary site in Ulster: Emain Macha—the Twins of Macha). But because of the cruel demands made on her, Macha screamed out in labor that all the men who heard her would suffer the same pains for five days and four nights whenever they faced great difficulty, and so would their descendants for nine generations.

The hero Cúchulainn was not under the curse, so he volunteers to fight for Ulster in place of the disabled men. After he kills Medb's soldiers thirty at a time, she agrees to let him fight them one by one in single combat at a ford on the Cronn River. She spurred her soldiers to fight, despite the tremendous odds, by offering various prizes including land, kingships, her daughter in marriage, or her own thighs. So ferociously does Cúchulainn win at single combat that the whole affair escalates until armies from the four provinces of Ireland are camped on the Murtheimne Plain waiting to do battle with him. At this sight, Cúchulainn gives his blood-curdling warrior's scream, and in the resulting panic, one hundred of his enemies die of fright.

Cúchulainn's battles do take their toll on the hero, however. Running on thin reserves from his habit of not sleeping for months, he was now also heavily wounded. While a warrior from the mythical side and a boy-troop a hundred-and-fifty strong from Ulster stave off Medb's men, he sleeps for three days and nights to let his wounds heal. He awakes so revivified that, after he and his charioteer don battle gear, he begins to go into full battle frenzy.

> The first warp-spasm seized Cúchulainn, and made him into a monstrous thing, hideous and shapeless, unheard of. His shanks and his joints, every knuckle and ankle and organ from head to foot, shook like a tree in the flood or a reed in the steam. His body made a furious twist inside his skin, so that his feet and shins and knees switched to the rear and his heels and calves switched to the front .... On his head the temple-sinews stretched to the nape of his neck, each mighty, immense, measureless knob as big as the head of a month-old child. His face and features became a red bowl: he sucked one eye so deep into his

head that a wild crane couldn't probe it onto his cheek
out of the depths of his skull; the other eye fell out along
his cheek. His mouth weirdly distorted: his cheek peeled
back from his jaws until the gullet appeared, his lungs
and liver flapped in his mouth and throat, his lower jaw
struck the upper a lion-killing blow, and fiery flakes large
as a ram's fleece reached his mouth from his throat.
His heart boomed loud in his breast like the baying of a
watch-dog at its feed or the sound of a lion among bears.
Malignant mists and spurts of fire—the torches of the
Badb—flickered red in the vaporous clouds that rose
boiling above his head, so fierce was his fury .... Then, tall
and thick, steady and strong, high as the mast of a noble
ship, rose up from the dead centre of his skull a straight
spout of black blood darkly and magically smoking like
the smoke from a royal hostel when a king is coming to
be cared for at the close of a winter day.[18]

After the spasm passes, Cúchulainn steps into his sickle war-chariot, which bristles with blades, hooks, prongs, spikes, tearing nails, and ripping instruments and is driven by two "wild and wicked, neat-headed and narrow-bodied" steeds.

In that style, then, he drove out to find his enemies and
did his thunder-feat and killed a hundred, then two
hundred, then three hundred, then four hundred, then
five hundred, where he stopped—he didn't think it too
many to kill in that first attack, his first full battle with
the provinces of Ireland.[19]

The battle rages on. The Ulster men join in when their pangs abate. Medb herself fights fiercely, though Cúchulainn has the advantage. Finally, the two bulls fight each other, circling all of Ireland. In time, Ulster's Brown Bull is sighted with "the mangled remains of Finnbennach hanging from his horns." As he wanders, he leaves the loins, shoulder blade, liver, and other pieces of the White Bull in various places, which give them their names. At last, the exhausted Brown Bull falls dead. In the end, "Ailill and Medb made peace with Ulster and Cúchulainn. For seven years afterward none of their people was killed in Ireland."[20]

Though Cúchulainn bests Medb in battle, she regains her equality when the two bulls kill each other. In fact, Celtic women did enjoy a high degree of equality and autonomy, and goddesses were prominent in the Celtic mythos. However, this equilibrium was not to last, and Medb's state of balance was precarious. The coming of Christianity tipped the scales. Cúchulainn is a quintessential Four Quarters Hero: completely action-oriented, unreflective, superhuman. Joseph Campbell noted that heroes are more brawn than brain, prototypes of today's jocks and hunks. Of course, the masculine archetype of the Lord of the Four Quarters also has other dimensions: the Culture-Bringer (Quetzalcoat, the Dogon's Smith nummu), the Trickster (Coyote, Loki, Eshu, Krishna, Pan), the agent of enlightenment (Christ, Buddha).

The general pattern, however, is that ego, the masculine principle, competitiveness, and warfare arise simultaneously, along with an exaggeration of the age-old male role of protector, which occurs during the transition between the Great Round and the Four Quarters worldviews. What is it about the rise of male power that brings about this particular constellation of effects?

Why Males Exist

In *Why Males Exist*, a delightfully written book on the evolution of sexual (in contrast to asexual) reproduction in the animal world, Fred Hapgood writes: "When one looks at females in nature one sees industry, progenitiveness, and efficiency; when one looks at males one sees the most amazingly elaborate forms of wastefulness."[21] Hapgood examines the whole spectrum of life from simple, asexual bacteria where the "females" reproduce parthenogenetically and there are no males at all, through species that can switch between single-sexed and dual-sexed reproduction at will, all the way up to the sexually reproducing higher primates. Throughout he asks at what point in this spectrum do the females decide to make males and why, especially since males usually have very little to do except impregnate females, make noise, fight with each other, and threaten social stability.

He concludes that males exist when there is competition for resources and it becomes advantageous for the female "to cover her bets, produce a mix of specialists, and so position herself to profit from opportunities arising anywhere on the vocational spectrum."[22] Although the hymenoptera (bees, ants) can parthenogenetically produce males, usually the female by herself can only clone herself. It is the alien genes of the male partner that randomize the genetic dice game and form distinctly different individuals. "Competition forces specialization," Hapgood writes. Specialization is impossible without gene-mixing, and gene-mixing is impossible without males. So, in the long chain of evolution, males, it seems, came into being precisely to contend with competitive situations.

Contrary to the stereotype of the all-powerful dominant male carrying off the female of his choice, the males of the vast majority of animal species delicately cater to female preferences and reserve their displays of domination for their male competitors. Males, Hapgood contends, "have a problem with competition. What a female does to reproduce: build up eggs and superintend their development, takes time; what a male does—find fertile females and fertilize them—can take next to no time at all (depending on the social situation). This means that males will usually find themselves reentering the breeding pool much faster than females, and that a population of competing males will arise."[23]

While it is often inappropriate to imply direct relationships between biological and human situations, it is sometimes useful to make metaphorical comparisons. Ultimately, the image that arises—and that translates best to the human species—is of males competing with each other for the right, given by females, to increase and defend their own gene pools. The female is highly selective. She has one offspring or litter or nest of eggs per mating season. It is in her interest to choose the "dominant male" as a partner for he will bring her the best, most tested set of genes. The male is highly promiscuous. It is in his interest to impregnate as many females as possible to spread his assets. It is in his interest also, as protector of his gene pool, to restrict the females' access to other males, protect his own offspring, and, if possible, kill the offspring of competing males. This happens frequently in the human as well as in the animal world. Witness the killing of the first born children of the Israelites by the Egyptians and vice versa, and of the Trojans by the Greeks.[24]

The question remains: Why did the competitive, protective role of the male come to the fore in history when it did? Sometime between about 4000 and 1000 B.C., most of the Great Round cultures that flourished in every corner of the world gave way to the Four Quarters, leaving only small pockets of matrifocal society surviving to the present. How did this happen? What conditions and forces in the ancient world sparked this transition?

From the Great Round to the Four Quarters: The Social Scientist's View

When there is a transition from egalitarian farming villages to stratified, warlike chieftainships, the prevailing view among social scientists is that the change can be attributed to rising specialization and competition for resources (precisely the same factors that we saw above gave rise to the male gender in the first place). While this materialist view takes no account of psychological impetuses, it does neatly correlate social and technological changes.

Compared to the Sensitive Chaos, the Great Round saw rapid social change and technological change as innovations abounded. Improved farming methods meant, on the one hand, that more people could be fed from the same amount of land, and, on the other, that some people could be released from farming chores to learn crafts and trades. Thus, populations increased, villages grew into cities, and a new class of specialists arose. The need to oversee the growing complexities of food storage and distribution, trade relations, and irrigation maintenance created the world's first managers. Also, as some families fared better than others over the generations, inequities in private wealth developed and competition heightened. Finally, the increasing complexity of society usually spurred a centralization of authority. The more complicated life became, the more a leader was apparently needed to keep everything organized and under control. Thus the rise of the chieftain.

Working in combination, these changes eventually led ancient cultures across an invisible boundary from the Great Round to the Four Quarters. Unlike egalitarian societies, hierarchical societies headed by a chieftain or king display marked caste and class distinctions. Archaeologists know that a society has become hierarchical when they find burials and dwellings reflecting status and rank. In the egalitarian Great Round, people lived in essentially the same kinds of houses and were buried, often collectively, in graves where everyone was treated more or less equally. The degree to which a culture has shifted away from the Great Round can be measured in part by the degree to which its settlements have houses for the poor with few rooms, poor drainage, and humble construction, and houses for the rich with many rooms, multiple floors, costly construction, lush gardens or courtyards, and excellent plumbing and drainage. In hierarchical societies, burials perpetuate status differences into the afterlife by providing elite individuals (especially chieftains and kings) with more elaborate tombs and richer burial goods. Related to these status distinctions is the appearance of seals, boundary markers, and other indications of private property. In the Near East, for instance, there was little social stratification before 6000 B.C. Setting aside the more developed trading center at Çatal Hüyük, Robert Wenke observes, "Elsewhere in the Zagros, northern Mesopotamia, and the Iranian Plateau, communities established between 8000 and 6000 B.C. were undeviatingly simple, undifferentiated farming villages, with little public architecture, elaborate mortuary cults, or obvious occupational specialization." He states that, "no evidence exists of differential access to wealth, power, or prestige."[25]

The Formative Era between 6000 and 3500 B.C. witnessed a slow transformation of society, seen first in the wide distribution of uniform Samarran and Halafian pottery styles, indicating the rise of at least one type of specialized artisan: the potter. Prior to 4500 B.C., there is little to suggest that Near Eastern civilization had moved beyond the Great Round, but after 4500, the transitional Ubaid culture spread throughout the Mesopotamian Alluvium, bringing "full-fledged cities, massive public buildings, and all of the other characteristics we associate with early complex societies."[26] Most telling were the temples typically found in

Ubaid settlements: mud-brick structures, sometimes two stories high, raised on clay or stone platforms. They presaged the ziggurats of Mesopotamia's Pyramid cultures, and suggest the emergence of a ruling class. By 3500 B.C., a number of urban centers sprung up with populations sometimes reaching into the tens of thousands, as at Uruk. Most of these cities were fortified, rectilinear strongholds, clearly following the prototypical Four Quarters plan. Large numbers of people left their rural farms to live in fortified cities, presumably for protection during the frequent wars. At about the same time, stamp and cylinder seals came into use to identify private property.

By about 3000 B.C., the fortified cities had so increased their administrative control and military might that they became true city-states. In Mesopotamia, they constituted the Sumerian civilization, a fully developed, stratified society with classes of business people, artisans, farmers, and slaves, all headed by a god-king. This social hierarchy was reflected in dwellings—Uruk had lavish two-story houses for the rich and humble one-story houses for the poor—and in burials, especially in the sixteen royal burials found at Ur. The most famous was the tomb of a queen (who may have been sacrificed when her husband died), which contained masses of gold and jeweled artifacts, chariots, and an entire court of sacrificed women, soldiers, and grooms.

This kind of "retinue burial" was common in developed Four Quarters cultures, and was practiced by the warlike Scythians in Eurasia, the Shang dynasty rules in China, the Mississippian culture in North America, and the first Egyptian dynasts. It showed that even human beings were considered the private property of their sovereign. With no reason for living after their king or queen died, they were sacrificed to serve the royal household in the afterlife. In Pyramid cultures, retinue burial was replaced by a symbolic version, which must have been devised by desperate court nobles seeking an alternative to their own sacrifice. The universal solution was to substitute effigy statues of the court members, which not only saved their lives but turned out to be a boon to us as well. The practice has given us the wonderful little *shabti* of Egypt, the elegant *haniwa* sculptures of Japan, and the early terracottas of China, including the enormous army of the first Emperor of Qin, consisting of thousands of life-sized warriors and horses.

Social scientists continually debate the causes of social complexity as they analyze the interactive influences of various systems, both social (political, economic, religious) and natural (climatic, ecological). As social systems get larger, they naturally get more complex. The simple hunting-gathering band of fifty people or so need only a few older adults to supervise things. But large social systems—kingships, nations, and empires—break into multiple ranks of supervisors, managers, and leaders. Thus, the larger the social system, the more differentiation, hierarchy, and centralization of power we would expect.[27]

Why societies "evolve" to more complex levels is another question. Basically, social scientists approach the question from a materialistic point of view, attributing these changes to a society's response to sources of stress-population increases, dwindling resources, a changing or deteriorating environment, interaction with other cultures through warfare or trade, and so on. These stresses force societies to adapt to new conditions, generally pressuring them to become more centralized and hierarchical.

From the Great Round to the Four Quarters: Other Theories

The social scientist's explanation for the transition from the egalitarian, Neolithic, farming communities to complex stratified Bronze and Iron Age cultures may be enlightening as far as it goes, but it does not attempt to deal with the transformation in human consciousness that accompanies the transition, or that could be part of its cause. Jungians, by contrast, see consciousness as the prime mover of human affairs. One theory put forth by Neumann and other Jungians holds that the masculine principle eventually asserted itself to carry civilization toward consciousness, individuality, moral law, and social order. In this view, the Goddess-centered Neolithic era was mostly unconscious, oppressive to the individual, amoral, and socially disordered—a biased view not based on evidence since, as we have seen, none of this was true of the Great Round. On the contrary, historical hindsight shows the Four Quarters to have been far more destructive since it generated alienation from nature, social inequity, authoritarianism, competitiveness, violence, and war.

Another possibility might be that the change from female-centered to male-centered values and institutions reflects what researchers currently see as a difference in the functioning of the male and female brains, the female's being less divided between the left and right hemispheres and, therefore, more "holistic;" the male's being more divided and, therefore, more "dualistic."[28]

Part of this shift was reflected in the change of spiritual allegiance from goddesses to gods. An unorthodox but intriguing explanation of this change was advanced by Hugh Fox in *The Gods of the Cataclysm*. Fox believes that the ancient female-centered civilizations grew disillusioned with their goddesses after a cataclysm of unprecedented proportions hit the earth, such as when, as Velikovsky claims, Venus came careening into the solar system causing floods, earthquakes, volcanic eruptions, and general geocosmic chaos. When things settled down again, the men, who had already begun to gain political power, claimed responsibility for putting the world in order through their gods who resided in the mountains that emerged from the Sea of Chaos after the floods subsided. The Goddesses lost the trust of the people and were transformed into devouring, treacherously unpredictable demons: the Furies, Harpies, Gorgons, Tiamat, Kali, Hecate. Meanwhile, the masculine principle was impressed forever in the human brain as the champion of order.

This theory is worth noting because whether or not one subscribes to Velikovsky's theories—some have been confirmed but most remain speculative—there is evidence of active flooding in the Near East from 4000 to 2500 B.C., the period that marked the end of the Great Round in that area. There was also a massive volcanic eruption on the island of Thera around 1500 B.C. that obliterated the great female-centered Minoan civilization on nearby Crete. Looking at what is left of Thera today, we see that it was a huge volcanic eruption, one that was followed by major earthquakes collapsing mud brick and stone buildings, and that would have lead to tsunamis that would have leveled costal towns throughout the region. It was devastating. Moreover, every civilization has legendary and historical evidence of having suffered cataclysmic events. The mythic images of these events—floods, the battle between Order and Chaos, the Mountain Arising from the Sea of Chaos, Storm Gods, Volcano Gods, and fire-breathing Dragons—are powerful presences in Four Quarters mythology.

Indo-Europeans on the Move

A final theory, based on history and advanced by Marija Gimbutas, Joseph Campbell, Robert Graves, Merlin Stone, and others, holds that the change from the matriarchal Great Round to the patriarchal Four Quarters (in much of the "Old World" at least) was due to the diffusion of semi-nomadic, warlike tribes of Indo-European pastoralists. Originally a barbaric lot, they left few cultural remains of their own, so their origin is unclear. They appear to have originated in the Caucasus Mountains and the area around the Black Sea, and in a series of aggressive migrations beginning by the third millennium B.C. or earlier, they eventually spread as far west as the British Isles and as far east as Chinese Turkestan. Although backward in the arts of culture, they excelled in the arts of war and were master metallurgists. They forged superior weapons, invented the war-chariot, and escorted in the Iron Age wherever they went.

Most of the Eurasian peoples we would associate with warlike aggression were of Indo-European origin: the Aryans of India; the Persians of Iran; the Hittites, Phrygians, Amorites, and others in the Near East; the Corded-Ware Battle-Axe, Wessex, Urnfield, Hallstat, Scythian, Celtic, Viking, Anglo-Saxon, and Teutonic cultures of Europe; the Aeolians, Ionians, Achaeans, and Dorians who became the Greeks, and the Etruscans and Romans in Italy.

The term "Indo-European" refers more to a language group than to a culture. One measure of the vigor of the Indo-European expansion is the fact that today about half the people in the world speak Indo-European languages including English, Russian and other Slavonic languages, Persian, Greek, Gaelic, the Germanic and Scandinavian languages, the Indian languages derived from Sanskrit, and the Romance languages (French, Spanish, Italian and others).

Since they were pastoralists rather than farmers, the Indo-Europeans did not have the same organic relationship to the earth that sustained the Neolithic culture of the Great Round. As Joseph Campbell has pointed out, the Indo-European's relationship was to the sky. It was their referential constant as they moved from rangeland to rangeland with their herds. Wherever they went, they carried a reverence for their sky gods: gods of storms, thunder, and war; violent gods like Zeus, Indra, and Thor who were fond of hurling thunderbolts at their enemies. Second only to the sky in the herder's world is the mountain—landmark on the horizon, highest point on earth, meeting place of earth and sky, defensive lookout, and sanctuary against raiders. The mountain—especially the phallic, fire-spouting, volcanic mountain—overlays and often replaces the womb-cavern as the object of veneration in the landscape. Thus we have the origins of the archetypal World Mountain that is to be recreated on earth in the Pyramid archetype. Intimately bound up with the gods of the sky, storms, thunder and lightning, mountains, volcanoes, and fire is the whole mystique of metallurgy that dominates the Four Quarters era.

Sometimes the Indo-Europeans assimilated the beliefs of the Great Round cultures into a new syncretic religion, as in India where a 3000 year old overlay of official Aryan gods sits lightly on a deeper popular adoration of the pre-Aryan Dravidian Mother Goddess. In Ireland, a remote land never reached by the Romans, worship of the pre-Celtic goddesses still shines through layers of Celtic and Christian influence in the Irish adoration of the Virgin Mary. Sometimes, however, the Indo-Europeans forcefully imposed their religion and social order as was the case in the Aegean during the Bronze Age. The Indo-Europeans repeatedly invaded the Aegean, especially after 1500 B.C. when the volcanic eruption on Thera destroyed the idyllic Great Round civilization of Minoan Crete and Thera.[29] They eventually forged the Greek civilization familiar to us today, with its Olympian mythology dominated by Zeus, its ceaseless warfare, and its view of women as chattel with about the same rights as slaves.

Early Greek mythology was concerned primarily with the battle between the indigenous matriarchy and the superimposed patriarchy. This can be seen in the Greek's contrivance to domesticate the formerly autonomous goddesses by marrying them off to Zeus and other gods, a device used everywhere in the world at the juncture between the Great Round and the Four Quarters. They even co-opted Athena, who could not be married to Zeus without destroying her essential nature as a Virgin (self-creating) Goddess. They solved the problem by bizarrely rewriting her birth scenario so that she springs from the head of Zeus, a classic male *anima* projection.

Through devices such as these, the Great Goddess who had created and inspired Neolithic and early Bronze Age civilization, and possibly the Upper Paleolithic world before that, eventually loses the battle for cosmic hegemony. In her various forms, she is conquered, domesticated, exploited, demonized, raped, and killed by the gods of the Four Quarters. What happens to the Goddess happens to women. When the Goddess loses power, women lose authority. The priest usurps the power of the priestess; the chieftain governs human affairs; the warrior replaces the prophetess as the repository of human hopes.

Just as the Goddess is domesticated by becoming the wife of the tribal god, women are domesticated by becoming the wives and property of men. As women face more danger and violence under the advance of the Four Quarters, they undoubtedly often decide to exchange some autonomy for the protection of a husband. The new creator-gods foster the doctrine of divine birth through the father, and people begin to trace their own descent through their fathers instead of their mothers. To insure patrilineal inheritance, strict codes of sexual morality are imposed on women to guarantee that they cannot beget children by anyone other than their husbands. Children born outside of marriage are "illegitimate." The term "virginity" comes to mean "chaste" and becomes a prerequisite to marriage. The concepts of monogamy and adultery emerge, monogamy being absolutely required; adultery, punishable by death. A family's honor depends on the sexual control and obedience of its women.

It is clear that, despite the social scientist's scenario of smooth and continuous evolution, the shift from the Great Round to the Four Quarters causes sweeping changes in every condition of life.

Of course, some cultures combine important elements of both the Great Round and the Four Quarters. The dynastic civilization of ancient Egypt, for instance, retained at least nominal matrilineal inheritance throughout most of its history, and the goddesses of the Great Round continued to be worshipped both in Egypt and in Mesopotamia, albeit in demoted roles as wives and daughters of the gods. The early civilizations of the Americas developed along the same lines even without metallurgy, horses, or chariots.[30]

Minoan Crete displayed many Great Round characteristics although it appears to have been somewhat socially stratified, and it flourished in the Bronze Age rather than the Neolithic. The advent of cities cannot be said to be solidly in the Four Quarters since the Indus Valley civilization developed one of the most advanced cities of the ancient world, Mohenjo-Daro, while remaining egalitarian and worshipping the Goddess. And finally, there is the telling disparity between how two manifestly masculine, warlike, tribal societies of nomadic herders—the Celts and the Israelites—saw women and the Great Goddess. Among the Celts, women retained their high status as queens and warriors, and the ancient goddesses were often stronger than the Celtic gods. The Israelites, in contrast, massacred the goddess-worshipping Canaanites, imposed rigid patriarchal laws on women, and tried to eradicate all evidence of female divinity. Through Christianization, the Celts, too, unfortunately embraced the misogynistic Old Testament principles in the early centuries of this era. These variations and exceptions aside, the preponderance of evidence in the first few millennia B.C. in most parts of the world points to the simultaneous rise of stratified societies, warfare, heroism, bronze and iron technology, private property, the subjugation of women, and the worship of male deities.

The Birth of the Hero from the Burial Mound

The Four Quarters archetype often gestates in the Great Round in the form of the Divine Child, as we saw in the last chapter in the examples of the pit-house and Hopi labyrinth. European burial mounds display a similar evolution. The earliest known megalithic tombs were built in Brittany in the mid-fifth millen-

162 *Spatial Archetypes*

nium B.C., and by 4000 B.C. Breton tombs boasted the first drystone, corbelled vaults, built over 1000 years before stone was used in Egyptian architecture, and predating by more than 2500 years the vaulted tholoi used for Mycenaean tombs such as the so-called "Treasury of Atreus."

During the Neolithic era, megalithic tombs were built throughout Western Europe for collective burial. Through some ingenious detective work on the distribution pattern of the tombs and the population patterns of Neolithic society, archaeologist Colin Renfrew concluded that the tombs were built by small communities of 25 to 50 people, one tomb per community. In *Before Civilization* he writes:

> ... we cannot possibly think in terms of groups with a very large number of different ranks or statuses, or of territorial chiefs. Each territory must surely have been occupied by an extended family or lineage, all its inhabitants tracing their descent, or that of their spouse, back to a common ancestor... We are led to think, then, in terms of a straightforward and fairly egalitarian tribal organization; and the extreme paucity of finds in these tombs certainly does not contradict this view.[31]

In general, the tombs of the Great Round evolved from simple to more complex forms. Some of the major later tombs contained transepted chambers in the plan of a cross—the cathedral plan in its archetypal origins. Newgrange in Ireland and Maeshowe in the Orkney Islands both contain fine transepted chambers, the Four Quarters cross secretly gestating in the architectural womb of the Great Round.

After about 2500 B.C., the nature of finds changes dramatically, as Renfrew notes:

> The dagger makes its appearance over much of Europe ..., and it is now that bronze metallurgy develops, in place of the unalloyed copper of previous centuries. It is now too that burials, over much of central and northern Europe, are accompanied, for the first time, by rich grave

goods. In Poland, north Germany and Brittany, as well as in Britain, there are graves with rich finds warranting the term "princely burial"; in south Germany and Czechoslovakia, the territory of the Unetice culture, there are likewise rich burials; and similar customs are seen in southern France.[32]

Renfrew and many of his colleagues find an explanation for these changes in the rise of hierarchical chieftainships. For instance, R. J. C. Atkinson comments on the Wessex culture in southern England:

Now in the rich and martially furnished Wessex graves we can admittedly see evidence for chieftainship, and the grouping of graves in cemeteries may imply whole dynasties of chiefs. Yet the pattern of society which they represent is surely that of so many other heroic societies, in which clan wars with clan, and rival dynasties carry on a perpetual struggle for power.[33]

We witness here a clear transition in Europe from the Great Round to the Four Quarters: from small, egalitarian communities of farmers building megalithic tombs for collective burial to the simultaneous rise of bronze metallurgy, weaponry, warfare, hierarchical chieftainships, heroic society, and princely individual burials. Unlike their Neolithic predecessors, the people who wrought these changes were of Indo-European descent. In the succeeding centuries, they vigorously expanded in Europe and elsewhere, developing iron, building hill-forts, evolving into highly stratified caste societies, and devising the myths and legends that have come down to us through Celtic, Norse, Slavic, Greek, Latin, Persian, and Sanskrit traditions.

The tomb of a Celtic prince dating from 550 B.C., recently discovered at Hochdorf near Stuttgart, Germany, shows how drastically the burial mound changed under the Four Quarters. This grave was an important discovery because, unlike hundreds of others that had been plundered before archaeologists could excavate them, this one was found with all of its contents intact. Under a twenty-five foot high earthen tumulus, archaeologist Jorg Biel discovered a rectangular chamber built not of impressive megaliths like the Neolithic tombs, but of rustic oak beams and stone boulders. The roof had collapsed, filling the room with fifty tons of stones that fortunately had discouraged potential looters. The chamber held a lone individual, a man about 40 years old and six feet tall, who, Biel points out, would have been a head taller than his average contemporaries, and had lived ten years longer. If the construction of this prince's crypt was primitive, his burial goods were not. Among opulent gold, bronze, and textile treasures were several items traded from far-off lands. A huge 104-gallon bronze cauldron made in Greece still contained the dried remains of mead. Various wall hangings, as well as the prince's own robe, were embroidered with Chinese silk. The tomb contained a full-sized iron-plated wagon stocked with butchering tools and tableware, but the most stunning find was the prince's funeral bed. A ten-foot long bronze bier with back and side arms, it rested on eight statues of women, which, in turn, were balanced on bronze and iron wheels so that the whole bier could be wheeled about. On the back, embossed warriors performed a funeral dance and horses pulled a four-wheeled chariot.

Of the evidence amassed from his discovery and previous ones, Biel writes, "Beyond the uncovering of ordinary graveyards, excavations have revealed proof of a stratified society, including an aristocratic class, that dwelt in hilltop fortresses. Rulers were buried in large tumuli, sometimes more than a hundred meters [330 feet] in diameter and ten meters [33 feet] high.[34]

Similar graves have been found in many other parts of the world—China, Korea, Japan, the Middle East, the steppes of Eurasia, the British Isles, Mexico, South America—for princely burials were typical of the Four Quarters. Wherever they appear, they are an infallible indication that the archetype has taken hold. Ironically, such transformations in the dwellings of the dead provide one of the clearest ways to see the Birth of the Hero.

Metallurgy and the Violation of the Earth Mother

It is impossible to overestimate the importance of metallurgy in the Four Quarters. It is to this worldview what the mystique of the Telluric currents and Kundalini energy was to the Great Round. The art of extracting ores from the earth and transforming them into bronze or iron (or even gold, as some tried to do) was not the matter-of-fact, industrial process it is today. It was a sacred, secret art surrounded with ritual and taboo. Behind it lay the old Sensitive Chaos belief in the unity of matter, which lingered in the minds of alchemists until a few centuries ago. In *Alchemy: The Philosopher's Stone*, Allison Coudert describes the Aristotelian version of this view:

> Substances were constantly changing; they appear, grow, decay, diminish and finally disappear. Aristotle explained this by saying that the elements within substances were in constant flux, changing from one to another—earth to water, water to air, air to fire and back again. In this Aristotelian fairyland the practiced alchemist had only to do intentionally what everywhere happened naturally. By varying the proportions of the four constituent elements in a substance, he should have been able to change one thing into another.[35]

The beginnings of metallurgy actually reach back into the Great Round. Copper was smelted at Çatal Hüyük in Turkey before 6000 B.C., and the late Neolithic era saw similar developments in the Balkans, Iberia, the Aegean, and Western Europe. The furnace, which was to become a devastating instrument of war by forging the bronze and iron used to make weapons and chariots, evolved peaceably enough from women's baking ovens and pottery kilns. Not interested in war, the people of the Great Round used whatever metals they made for jewelry, ceremonial paraphernalia, and farming tools. Thus, in its origins, metallurgy fitted sympathetically into the peaceful, agrarian, Great

166 *Spatial Archetypes*

Round way of life. But this equilibrium did not last.

Bronze metallurgy demanded higher technology than the forging of soft copper. It required the alloying of copper with tin or arsenic, much higher furnace temperatures, and precise casting techniques. The forging of iron was even more difficult. It is not surprising, then, that the development of these techniques (by about 3000 B.C. for bronze and 1500 B.C. for iron) brought a new reverence for the blacksmith. He was the one who knew the secrets of forcing an artificial transmutation of matter from one state into another. Because people believed in the unity of matter, they thought that the blacksmith's skill was open-ended, that he had knowledge of the ultimate secrets of creation. This knowledge burdened metallurgists with profound awe and guilt as they comprehended the extent to which they were violating —and even replacing—the Earth Mother. In The Forge and the Crucible, Mircea Eliade describes this anxiety:

> It has been established that among miners, rites calling for a state of cleanliness, fasting, meditation, prayers and acts of worship were strictly observed. All these things were ordained by the very nature of the operation to be conducted because the area to be entered is sacred and inviolable; subterranean life and the spirits reigning there are about to be disturbed; contact is to be made with something sacred which has no part in the usual religious sphere—a sacredness more profound and more dangerous. There is the feeling of venturing into a domain which by rights does not belong to man— the subterranean world with its mysteries of mineral gestation which has been slowly taking its course in the bowels of the Earth-Mother. There is above all the feeling that one is meddling with the natural order of things ruled by some higher law and intervening in a secret and sacred process. Consequently every precaution is taken that is considered indispensable to the "rites of passage." There is the obscure feeling that some mystery is at stake involving human existence, for the discovery of metals has indeed left its mark on man. Mining and

metallurgy have altered his entire mode of existence. All
the myths surrounding mines and mountains, all those
innumerable fairies, elves, genies, phantoms and spirits,
are the multiple manifestations of the sacred presence
which is affronted by those who penetrate into the
geological strata of life.

Still charged with this dread holiness the ores are
conveyed to the furnace. It is then that the most difficult
and hazardous operations begin. The artisan takes the
place of the Earth-Mother and it is his task to accelerate
and perfect the growth of the ore. The furnaces are, as
it were, a new matrix, an artificial uterus where the ore
completes its gestation. Hence the infinite number of
precautions, taboos and ritual acts which accompany the
smelting.[36]

Ores were thought to grow in the womb of the earth like embryos, and in some cultures people believed that given enough time the Earth Mother would eventually ripen all matter into gold. But the princes and warriors of the Four Quarters could not wait the eons they thought this would take. Better to abort the ores and hasten the process artificially. The ideal substance was the meteorite. Falling miraculously from heaven and often already formed into iron, it was a gift of the gods that spared men the messy and frightening encounter with the Earth Mother. Even today several hundred million Muslims venerate the meteorite encased in the Kaaba in Mecca.

Meteorites have been crashing into the Earth since the Earth was born, and there is some evidence that the people of the Great Round associated them with goddesses.[37] With the rise of dualistic thinking, however, the meteorites heavenly origin placed it squarely in the masculine realm. Eliade writes:

But the heavenly, and hence masculine, essence of the
meteorites is none the less beyond dispute, for certain
silex and neolithic tools were subsequently given names
like "thunderstorms," "thunderbolt teeth" or "God's axes."
The sites where they were found were thought to have

been struck by a thunderbolt, which is the weapon of the God of Heaven.[38]

Note the close ties between metallurgy and the Storm Gods of the Four Quarters. In fact, the thunderbolt-wielding god of the Four Quarters was often a smith (as in the cases of Donar, Thor, Ogun, and Gua), and both as god and as smith, he was essential to war. On the ambivalence with which ancient peoples regarded iron—although it was revered for its technological properties, it was also feared and hated, especially by people who had been conquered by iron-wielding invaders—Eliade writes: "The Iron Age was characterized by an uninterrupted succession of wars and massacres, by mass slavery and by almost universal impoverishment. In India, as elsewhere, a whole mythology classes iron-workers among the various categories of giants and demons. All are enemies of the gods [and goddesses] who represent other ages and other traditions."[39]

Thus, with the development of bronze and iron metallurgy, the protective spirits of the Telluric currents were violated and the sacred Womb-Caverns of the earth raped. The symbolic generative functions of the earth Goddess were stolen by the blacksmith, and, for the first time, a male-dominated technology began to conquer nature.

The Dragon-Slayer

A hundred snake heads grew from the shoulders of
this terrible dragon, with black tongues flickering and
fire flashing from the eyes under the brows of those
prodigious heads. And in each of those terrible heads
there were voices beyond description: they uttered every
kind of sound; sometimes they spoke the language of
the gods; sometimes they made the bellowing noise of
a proud and raging bull, or the noise of a lion relentless
and strong, or strange noises like dogs; sometimes there
was a hiss, and the high mountains re-echoed. The day
of his birth would have seen the disaster of his becoming

the ruler of men and gods, if their great father had not been quick to perceive the danger. He thundered hard and strong, so that Earth and broad Sky above, Sea and Ocean-streams, and the Tartarus region below the earth, all rumbled with the awful sound. Great Olympus quaked under the divine feet of its royal master as he rose up, and the earth groaned also. The heat from both sides, from the thunder and lightning of Zeus and from the fiery monster, penetrated the violet deep and made the whole earth and sky and sea boil.
~ Hesiod, The Theogomy

Thus does Hesiod describe the destruction of Typhon, the great Dragon that Hera bore in anger against Zeus for creating Athene without her. The voices of Typhon resound with the terrors of Dragons everywhere. No other creature so clearly captures the raw power of nature. In its various guises, the Dragon is the raging ocean and the flood; the North Wind, the "ill wind," the hurricane and tornado; the killing freeze of winter and the cold-bloodedness of fish and reptiles; the cause of earthquakes and volcanic eruptions and the waster of the land; the bringer of plagues and famines and the devourer of youth; the guardian of the Tree of Life and the Womb-Cavern's Golden Hoard; the earth-encircler and the horror of Chaos. But above all, the Dragon is the maker of Heroes.

The Dragon represents the ferocious, demonized aspect of the Great Round, combining the chthonic Telluric serpent, the fiery serpent Kundalini at the base chakra, and the feathered bird-serpent Kundalini risen to the top chakra in enlightenment. The Hero's conquest of the Dragon symbolizes the domination by the Four Quarters of these powerful female-based energies. With his conquest, the Hero makes substantial gains for the Four Quarters world: he usurps the sacred place, wins the Golden Hoard, saves the chaste Virgin or the King's dutiful daughter (symbols of the new domesticated womanhood) and erects his temple or palace on the spot where he slew the Dragon.

Psychologically, the victory of Hero over Dragon establishes the ego's preeminence in the psyche, without which none of the other attributes of the Four Quarters—whether psychological, social, historical, or mythological—could ensue. According to Erich Neumann, the slaying of the Dragon represents, at its root, the slaying of the archetypal Mother. This psychological act allows the ego to come into its own. Through the Dragon-Slaying metaphor, the developing ego conquers the obstacles to its emergence—the unconscious, the body, nature, and most of all, the maternal matrix. The good, nurturing mother of childhood is demonized in the adolescent, would-be Hero's psyche into the clinging, "devouring" mother who must be "slain" if he is to gain the independence required to win his adulthood.

The forces that threaten the developing ego are also internalized, constituting the shadow, Jung's term for the repressed facets of the psyche. As the ego sculpts the *persona* or "mask" that it presents to the world, it simultaneously and unconsciously creates the shadow. Jung writes, "The shadow personifies everything that the subject refuses to acknowledge about himself and yet [it] is always thrusting itself upon him directly or indirectly..."[40]

Neither the ego (or persona) nor the shadow is all good or all bad. In fact, taken together, they contribute to the completeness of the person. Overcoming the duality between ego and shadow is an important part of the psychoanalytical journey toward wholeness and integration called individuation, which means becoming "indivisible" or "undivided." But since the shadow accrues all the things that the ego is not, the ego cannot accept the shadow as part of itself. The two principles can be reconciled only in the great, transpersonal Self, but by definition the ego is separated from the Self. Therefore the ego projects its shadow onto beings in the outside world whom it sees as its enemies.[42] A classic example of the monstrous proportions that unconscious shadow-projection can assume was the mass projection by Nazi Germany of its collective shadow on the Jews. We might also say that during the Cold War Russia and the United States were dangerously projecting their respective shadows on each other, keeping the two superpowers on the brink of nuclear holocaust.

In the archetypal Hero myth, the Dragon is the shadow of the Hero. Both are formed together as worthy adversaries, each defining the other. The Hero's confrontation with the Dragon brings him face to face with his own death, that is, with the death of his ego. "The hero ... must realize that the shadow exists and that he can draw strength from it. He must come to terms with its destructive powers if he is to become sufficiently terrible to overcome the dragon, i.e., before the ego can triumph, it must master and assimilate the shadow."[41] In this formulation, killing the Dragon symbolizes the successful assimilation of the shadow's powers. Unsuccessful relationships to the shadow/Dragon include not confronting it, in which case it maintains its destructive power over the personality (just as the Dragon continues to terrorize the community, hoarding treasures and devouring virgins), or killing it egocentrically without learning from it and transforming its dark powers.

Most civilizations at the juncture between the Great Round and the Four Quarters develop Dragon-Slayer myths. The Greek myths that evolved following the Indo-European invasions abound in them. Apollo kills Python to wrest control of the Delphic Oracle from the Earth Goddess Gaia. Zeus slays Typhon after a protracted battle that ended, in one version, when the god smashed the monster with Mount Etna, mythically explaining why the volcano continues to spout fire to this day. Heracles' numerous monster-slaying feats included his conquest of the Hydra, with its multiple serpent heads. Perseus beheaded the serpent-haired Gorgon Medusa, an act similar to Bellerophon's killing of the Chimaera, the serpent-tailed she-goat. Robert Graves notes: "Both feats record the usurpation by Hellenic invaders of the Moon-goddess, whose calendar-symbol was the Chimaera; and the Gorgon-head is a prophylactic mask, worn by her priestesses to scare away the uninitiated, which the Hellenes stripped from them."[43] After killing the Medusa, Perseus went on to kill the female sea-monster who was about to devour Andromeda, a story related to Marduk's slaying of the sea-serpent. Tiamat in the Babylonian creation epic, which inspired the Biblical accounts of Jehovah splitting the heads of several primordial sea-monsters including the Wild Sea Beast, Rahab, and Leviathan. As a rule, the Biblical religions (Judaism, Christianity, and Islam) abhor and persecute everything they associate with the "Satanic" serpent.

The Indo-European "pagan" traditions that flourished in the

Four Quarters abound in Dragon and Serpent-Slaying myths. The Hittite Weather God Inar slew the Great Serpent just as the Norse Thunder God Thor vanquished the Great Serpent of Midgard whose multiple coils (like the Telluric currents) encircled the earth numerous times. Also, the Norse Hero Sigurd slew Fafnir, the giant who had transformed into a Dragon and was guarding the Golden Hoard and ring of the Nibelungs in his cave. That the Dragon secretes psychoerotic wisdom became clear when Sigurd tasted drops of Fafnir's blood—he gained the power to understand the language of birds. The Anglo-Saxon hero Beowulf first slew the sea-monster Grendel, then the monster's mother, and finally lost his own life slaying the Dragon who, like Fafnir and so many others, hoarded the Golden Treasure of the land in his cave.

The treasure-hoarding Dragon in the cave can be likened to the first *chakra*, where Kundalini energy lies coiled ready for action but has not yet been rendered usable. Joseph Campbell often remarked that the Dragon hoards the Golden Treasure but does not know what to do with it. Just as the Dragon itself is the shadow, the Dragon's hoarding habit is the shadow side of the ego's possessiveness. As the guardian of the hoard, the Dragon mirrors the guardians of the cardinal axes that the ego posts to defend its territories. The Golden Hoard hidden away in the Dragon's cave is the great transpersonal Self, hidden away in the Womb-Cavern of the collective unconscious. The treasure appears in many forms: "... the water of life, the healing herb, the elixir of immortality, the philosopher's stone, miracle rings and wishing rings, magic hoods and winged cloaks, are all symbols of the treasure."[45]

The enmity between Dragon and Hero prevents the treasure from being rescued to re-infuse the land with wealth and fertility. In other words, the dualism between ego and shadow prevents the creative bounty of the Self from being released. Specifically, the Treasure is the life-energy that would flow from the creative wellspring of the Self if access to the Self were not blocked by the ego and shadow being locked in combat. Typically, the warlike Four Quarters resolves the duality through violence: the Hero kills the Dragon.

Assimilating the Dragon's energy, the Hero emerges victorious. His reward often includes not only the Golden Treasure, but also the maiden who then becomes his wife. Neumann sees the maiden or virgin as the *anima* or female soul of the Hero with whom he needs to unite to find the Self. By slaying the Dragon, the Hero slays the Mother aspect of the feminine principle and releases the domesticated wife/anima aspect. Whereas in the Great Round, the male was archetypically the son and lover of the Mother, this is not possible in the Four Quarters. The feminine principle is cleaved into "Mother" and "Wife." The rejection (slaying) of the "Mother" allows the Hero to transfer his love and affection to the "Wife." The marriage of the Hero and the virgin is the Four Quarters version of the old *hieros gamos*. Neumann writes:

> In this marriage, which in the oldest mythologies was consummated at the New Year festival immediately after the defeat of the dragon, the hero is the embodiment of the 'heaven' and father archetype, just as the fruitful side of the mother archetype is embodied in the rejuvenated and humanized figure of the rescued virgin. The liberation of the captive has the effect of releasing the virgin wife, the young mother and partner, from her fusion with the uroboric mother, in whom dragon and virgin-mother were still one; but now they are finally differentiated from one another through the activated masculine consciousness of the hero.[46]

Neumann further observes, "With the freeing of the captive and the founding of a new kingdom, the patriarchal age comes into force."[47]

The Dragon-Slayer myth flourished throughout Europe's protracted Four Quarters era into the Middle Ages. The Medieval Heroes were the numerous saints and martyrs—George, Patrick, Michael, Margaret, Silvester, Martha, Philip—whose energetic exorcism of paganism culminated in Dragon-conquering feats. Yet another example of how the Dragon-Slaying myth helps to establish a new social order by projecting the shadow onto a pre-existing society or religion. By the time of the Medieval Christians, the remnants of the Great Round were represented in pagan beliefs in Dragons, the little people, and the witch, all of whom were destroyed.

Despite its dominance in the annals of World mythology, the Dragon-Slaying myth is not quite universal. In the Americas, it is almost nonexistent even though the Four Quarters developed there as elsewhere. In fact, the serpent is a strong cult focus in many Amerindian traditions, possibly because native hallucinogenic plants and fungi induce visions of serpents, bathing them with psychoerotic affinity and awe. Compared with Near Eastern, Greek, and European traditions, the Dragon-Slaying theme is only weakly developed in Hinduism and Buddhism, both of which are Indo-European in origin. And, although China has several folk takes of Dragon-Slayers and Japan has the national myth of Susanoo versus the eight-headed Dragon, the Far East has as more positive images of serpents and Dragons than negative. The serpent deities called nagas are revered as beneficent spirits throughout all of Asia, and China is renowned for its veneration of Dragons.

Navel of the World

The death blow dealt the Dragon by the Hero's sword—a magic weapon—epitomizes the nullifying effect that ferrous metals have on the Telluric currents. We have already seen how miners, metallurgists, and blacksmiths thought of themselves as violating Mother Earth. Clearly, iron distorts magnetic fields, as any schoolchild can attest who has seen iron filings dance on a plate held over a magnet. Folklore encodes the effects of iron in its tales of the "little people" being banished by iron crosses and bells. And the Iron Age did sound the death knell of the Neolithic era.

When the Hero pierces the Dragon with his sword, he achieves a geophysical transformation: the fixing of the Telluric currents. Rather than flowing with these energies like the people of the Sensitive Chaos and the Great Round, the gods and heroes of the Four Quarters attempt to fix them at a central point—the *omphalos* or "navel of the world." This reifies in the external world the centrality of the ego in the psyche.

> This point acted as a center, a pivot about which
> everything else revolved. It remained fixed when all else

moved, stable in both the whirling of the heavens in its cycles of days and years, and during earthquakes.

The fixation to a central place of the hitherto free energies of the earth, which were formerly able to wander almost at random, represents the change from the diffuse, worldwide shrine of the Earth Mother to the centralized, geomantically defined temple of the solar god ....

In mythology, the fixing of this energy was depicted as a mortal struggle, not lightly undertaken, whose outcome was uncertain, puny man pitted against the massive forces of the earth .... Symbolically, the solar hero transfixes the dragon with his arrow, spear or lance. The sword of St. Michael, the lance of St. George or the arrows of giants like the Herfordshire dragon-killer Piers Shonkes, all represent the peg or hole which pierced the dragon's head, immovably fixing it at the omphalos. Thus the powers of the sun and earth were fused at a specific place and time, potently defining the site.[48]

In this way Susanoo builds his palace and Apollo his temple at sites they consecrated to themselves by pinning, with arrow and lance, the dragons that guarded the holy places. Even the staffs of Moses and Aaron could change into serpents, suggesting the power of the Semitic heroes to fix the Telluric currents at will. Although every Four Quarters village and kingdom had its own omphalos, believing itself to be the center of the universe and its chief or god to be the only true Lord of the Four Quarters, the term *omphalos* originally referred to the charcoal mound at Delphi that symbolized the Great Goddess. When Apollo usurped the Oracle, the meaning and origin of the omphalos was revised to conform to the character of its new owner. In the Indo—European myth, "the site was divined by Zeus, who sent out two eagles (or swans) in order to determine the Earth's true center. One bird was released to the west, the other to the east. Where their paths crossed, at Delphi, the omphalos was defined."[50]

The claim of being the center of the universe is entirely alien to the all-encompassing circle of the Great Round. It is pure Four

Quarters imagery, which has little to do with the original meaning of the omphalos at Delphi. In a way, we could say that war arose when the worldview shifted from one of encirclement to one of central points. Since points can be only in one place at a time, arguments and wars erupted among groups jealously trying to eliminate the competition so that their point could lay claim to being the center of the universe. Whatever else may be the reason for war, its psychological background is egocentricity and the accompanying belief that one's own central point in the universe is the only true one.

The Mandala of Reintegration

Because the Four Quarters generates the ego, it generates also the need to transcend the ego. This is the great problem facing humanity in the Four Quarters and all succeeding archetypes. It is something quite new that did not exist, at least not as intensely, in the Sensitive Chaos and the Great Round, since both were based on unity. The psyche senses its expulsion from paradise, and, discovering too late that paradise once existed, longs to return to it. The mind suffers the severing of its creative, psychoerotic half and yearns to regain access to that lost magical realm. When the Hero realizes his mortality and the limitations of the temporal world with its enticing illusions of power, he becomes the seeker wandering in the wilderness, longing to return to the eternal world of light and radiance, the home of his immortal spirit.

The obstacle is *duality*: duality versus unity, ego versus Self, paradise versus the mundane world, technelogos versus psychoeros, mortality versus immortality, eternity and infinity versus the world of time and space. In the *Bhagavad Gita*, the Lord Krishna advises the seeker Arjuna: "... be free from the dualities [the pairs of opposites]; be firmly fixed in purity, not caring for acquisition and preservation; and be possessed of the Self."[51]

The philosophical conundrums surrounding the problem of transcending duality are worthy of the Mad Hatter. How can you achieve unity when you know that unity exists? To know that unity exists is to be observing unity from a state of disunity. If you desire unity, you will never achieve it. To desire unity is to have a subject-object relationship with it, that is to say, a dualistic relationship. Dualism is the obstacle to unity. Opposing unity to duality makes unity itself a co-producer of duality. And on it goes.

The problem of reintegration arises in the social as well as the psychological realm. Joseph Campbell noted that the mandala—the concentric image of order and harmony—appears in art only after society becomes fragmented. It does not appear in the art of the hunter-gatherer. He writes:

> For, whereas in the camps of the hunters the community was constituted of a group of practically equivalent individuals, each in adequate control of the whole inheritance, in the larger, more greatly differentiated communities that developed when agriculture and stock breeding had made for a settled, more richly articulated social structure, adulthood consisted in acquiring, first, a certain special art or skill, and then, the ability to support or sustain the resultant tension—a psychological and sociological tension—between oneself (as merely a fraction of a larger whole) and others of totally different training, powers, and ideas, who constituted the other necessary organs of the body social.[52]

The image of the Four Quarters, then, is not simply an image of the divisive action of ego but also of the orderly balance of the resultant paris into a workable whole. Similarly, the Lord of the Four Quarters at the center is not simply the symbol of the heroic ego, but also of the unity that results from transcending ego. In this sense he is Brahma or the Buddha as Supreme Being beyond opposites. Just as in the Great Round there were two wombs—the biological and the spiritual—there are two Lords of the Four Quarters: the ego-centered and the ego-transcendent. In the social sphere, the ego-centered Lord is the chieftain who organizes society politically, and the ego-transcendent Lord is the supreme deity who organizes society spiritually. The chieftain acts in the field of time and space; the supreme deity, in the field that transcends time and space, that is, in the realm of the sacred.

The Granary of the Master of Pure Earth

With some difficulty, the Dogon's supreme god Amma initially created ancestors with the Earth Mother. When he tried to enter her vagina (an anthill), a termite hill rose up and blocked the way. This was the Earth Mother's clitoris, considered to be her masculine element. So that he could mate with her, Amma cut it out, (which is why Dogon girls, like so many African and Middle Eastern women, suffer the mutilation of clitoris-excision).[53] This violation of the Earth Mother resulted in incest and menstruation, both considered serious breaches of the natural order. In a classic example of the "second birth through the Father" so common in patriarchal mythology, Amma turned his back in disgust on his first creation and molded a new Primal Pair out of clay without the participation of the Earth Mother. They in turn begat the eight *Nummo* ancestors from whom most Dogon mythology, rituals, and social customs derive.

In time, the eight Nummo, who had once come down to earth, found it too difficult to meet the standard of perfection required for living in heaven, and decided to return to earth. The first ancestor, a blacksmith, prepared a basketwork structure to contain everything that the Nummo or the humans on earth might need. For a model he took a woven basket with a circular opening and a square base and turned it upside down (incidentally making it resemble both a Neolithic pit-house and a truncated pyramid). He made the circular part twenty cubits in diameter and the square part, which became the roof, he made eight cubits on a side and ten cubits high. In addition to containing things, the structure became a standard of measure.

When he had completed the basketwork, the Promethean smith stole a piece of the sun to fire his smithy, and quickly flung the structure to earth along a rainbow. He jumped onto its roof carrying his hammer and anvil, and, fighting off the angry Primal Pair who besieged him with thunderbolts and lightning, descended to earth with his creation. The French anthropologist Marcel Griaule describes the structure based on his celebrated thirty-three days of conversations in 1946 with the venerable, old, blind, Dogon wise man Ogotemmeli.[54]

This framework he covered with puddled clay made of the earth from heaven, and in the thickness of the clay, starting from the centre of each side of the square, he made stairways of ten steps each facing towards one of the cardinal points. At the sixth step of the north staircase he put a door giving access to the interior in which were eight chambers arranged on two floors.[55]

The symbolic significance of this structure was as follows:
- The circular base represented the sun.
- The square roof represented the sky.
- A circle in the centre of the roof represented the moon.
- The tread of each step being female and the rise of each step male, the four stairways of ten steps together prefigured the eight tens of families, offspring of the eight ancestors.
- Each stairway held one kind of creature, and was associated with a constellation, as follows:
- The north stairway, associated with the Pleiades, was for men and fishes;
- The south stairway, associated with Orion's belt, was for domestic animals.
- The east stairway, associated with Venus, was for birds.
- The west stairway, associated with the so-called 'Long-tailed Star' was for wild animals, vegetables, and insects.[56]

As Ogotemmeli described in great detail all the specific animals, birds, trees, fish, and so forth on each step,[56] it became apparent that the wondrous structure was an entire world system.

"The whole thing," he said, "with its stairways is called the 'Granary' of the Master of Pure Earth. It is divided into eight compartments, four below and four above. The door opens to the north on the sixth stair. It is as it were the mouth, and the granary is the belly, that is the interior, of the world."[57]

Wishing to see a real granary, but not wishing to invade the villagers' privacy by inspecting any of the half-dozen or so granaries surrounding them in the courtyard, Griaule had Ogotemmeli take him to an abandoned one in good condition After using hoes to pry open a door "fastened as if in the jaws of a vice," amidst the odor of old grain, the men compared the compartments and structure of the real granary to those of the celestial granary.

Two stories with four divisions each made eight compartments within the granary. In the celestial granary, these housed the eight different seeds that God gave to each of the eight ancestors, and also represented the eight principal organs of the Spirit of water (the same as those of humans plus a gizzard, for the Spirit has the speed of a bird).

Because of its form—a balanced, harmonious, circular design that resolves itself in the center—and because of the cosmological and organic totality it represents, The Granary of the Master of Pure Earth is a mandala. Made of the *prima materia*, puddled clay from heaven, with all the creatures and plants of creation arrayed on its steps, and all the grains needed for human sustenance contained within, it is a complete world system. Even more: its seeds and symbolic organs encode the complex social system and genealogy of the Dogon people.

But what is in the center of the Granary? After all, the center is the most important place in any mandala, the place where the unending multiplicity of nature, society, kinship patterns, language, thoughts, and the cosmos paradoxically become unified into one dimensionless dot—the Great Mystery—like the universe just before the Big Bang. Griaule writes:

> The four lower compartments in a Dogon granary are separated by two intersecting partitions, the junction of which forms a cup-like depression in the earth big enough to hold a round jar. This jar, containing grain or valuable objects, is the centre of the whole building ....
>
> A round jar in the centre symbolized the womb; a second smaller jar closed the first; it contained oil of *lannea acida*, and represented the foetus. On top of it again was a still smaller jar containing perfume, and on the top of this last was a double cup.

Now the Granary can be seen in a different light. Griaule continues:

All the eight organs were held in place by the outer walls and the inner partitions which symbolized the skeleton. The four uprights ending in the corners of the square roof were the arms and legs. Thus the granary was like a woman, lying on her back (representing the sun) with her arms and legs raised and supporting the roof (representing the sky). The two legs were on the north side, and the door at the sixth step marked the sexual parts.

The world system of the granary processed and absorbed symbolic nourishment in the same way that our internal organs process and absorb food, through the stomach and the intestines, into the blood, liver, and gall-bladder, and finally through the breath, which is a vaporous form of water, the principle of life:

As Ogotemmeli spoke, the deserted granary came to life, and the setting sun lighting up the west beyond the gorges heightened the illusion. The walls of the building became tinged with rose color, and cast gleams of light on the sandstone surfaces and the straw of the dung-heap. On the roof a bunch of purple sorrel stood out like fire. The moment was near when all the western walls of Upper and Lower Ogol would be aflame. All the visible surface of the granary shared in this prodigal display of light, while in the dark interior the wonders of the past came to life again.

Ogotemmeli, his head bowed and his hands on the nape of his neck, was lost in the past history of the heavens. At last he arrived at the final stratum of symbols which showed the universe compressed within the walls of the primal granary, as a body filled with life and absorbing food.

"What is eaten," he said, "is the sunlight. What is excreted is the dark night. The breath of life is the clouds, and the blood is the rain that falls on the world."[58]

The Hindu Temple and the Union of Opposites

After the coming of the Aryans in about 1500 B.C., Indian society fragmented into a racially-based caste system. At the lower end of the social hierarchy were the workers (*shudras*), the dark-skinned native Dravidians. At the upper end as the powerful priests (*brahmins*) were the light-skinned Aryan conquerors. In between were two other major castes, although there came to be several thousand hereditary occupational castes as the system differentiated over time.

The mythical origin of the caste system is recorded in the hymns of the *Rig Veda*, the oldest body of Indo-European literature. Thought to have been written down at least by 1000 B.C., the Vedic hymns were based on Aryan oral traditions going back several centuries. They describe the origins of the caste system in terms of the body parts of the *Purusha*, the supreme essence residing three-fourths in heaven and one fourth on earth, from whose sacrificed body the phenomenal world is born.

> When they divided the purusa, into how many parts did they arrange him? What was his mouth? What his two arms? What are his thighs and feet called?
>
> The brahmin was his mouth, his two arms were made the rajanya (warrior), his two thighs the vaisya (trader and agriculturist), from his feet the sudra (servile class) was born.
>
> The moon was born from his spirit (manas), from his eye was born the sun, from his mouth Indra and Agni, from his breath Vayu (wind) was born.
>
> From his navel arose the middle sky, from his head the heaven originated, from his feet the earth, the quarters from his ear. Thus did they fashion the worlds.
>
> Seven were his sticks that enclose (the fire), thrice seven were made the faggots. When the Gods spread out the sacrifice, they bound the Purusa as a victim.
>
> With the sacrifice the Gods sacrificed the sacrifice. These were the first ordinances. These great powers

reached to the firmament, where are the ancient Sadhyas, the Gods.[59]

This hymn asserts that the social order of the caste system was created simultaneously with the cosmos itself. Sun, moon, and heaven were associated with the head, and thus with the brahmins. The earth was associated with the feet, and thus with the shudrus. At the same time, the gods of the Vedic pantheon came into being. Note also the linking of the number seven with the generation of fire. Possibly, this is the fire of Kundalini energy and the seven sticks and thrice seven faggots may in some way be metaphors for the chakras. In the end, with the establishment of the first ordinances, the *purushu* himself is sacrificed.

This cosmological story of how the gods brought the world into being and put it in order is recapitulated in the plan of the classical Hindu temple. The temple's plan and site are regulated by a square ritual diagram, which is drawn on the ground prior to construction and may also be drawn on the temple's altar. In her definitive study, The Hindu Temple, Stella Kramrisch describes it as follows:

> The square is Vastupurushamandala. Purusa is the universal Essence, the Principle of all things, the Prime Person whence all originates. Vastu is the site; in it Vastu, bodily existence, abides and from it Vastu derives its name. In bodily existence, Purusa, the Essence, becomes the Form. The temple building is the substantial, and the "plan" (mandala) is the ritual, diagrammatic form of the Purusa. Purusa himself has no substance. He gives it his impress. The substance is of wood, brick or stone in the temple.
>
> The form of the temple, all that it is and signifies, stands upon the diagram of the Vastupurusa. It is a "forecast" of the temple and is drawn on the levelled ground: it is the fundament from which the building arises. Whatever its actual surroundings, forest glade, seashore, hill or town, the place where the temple is built is occupied by the Vastupurusa in his diagram,

184 *Spatial Archetypes*

> the Vastupurusa mandala. That it is surrounded by the streets of a town, walls of a fort, ravines or fields, becomes of secondary importance, for its particular topography is but the hinge by which a changeable panorama is linked with the structure of the universe. The site is ritually levelled each time a temple is built; the ground from which the temple is to rise is regarded as being throughout on an equal intellectual plane. It is at the same time terrestrial and extra-territorial. It is the place for the meeting and marriage of heaven and earth, where the whole world is present in terms of measure, and is accessible to man.[60]

By means of the *vastu purusha mandala*, the unformed universe is pressed and bound into an orderly square (the Four Quarters) representing the manifested universe. Thus, "In their activity as builders men order their environment in the same way as once in the past Brahma forced the undefined purusha into a geometric form."[61] This act of bringing order—of bringing the manifest out of the unmanifest—is not something that was done only in the past by Brahma. It is also something that each of us does every waking moment.

The *vastu purusha mandala* is an image of the hierarchical Vedic pantheon, which in turn is reflected socially in the caste system. It may be drawn in over thirty different ways containing from one to 1024 squares or *padas*. The meaning and appropriate use of each type of mandala is spelled out in the sacred texts on *Vastuvidya*, the science of architecture. Each pada within the mundala is governed by a different deity or principle. The center is the realm of Brahma, the supreme principle. In the sacred precinct as a whole, this square is the temple; in the temple, it is the inner sanctuary; and in the sanctuary, it is the altar. The padas surrounding Brahma in the mandala are occupied by successively lower ranking deities. The outermost padas have zodiacal significance and are called the "lunar mansions." The cardinal axes are among the most important spatial differentiations within the mandala. In the 81 square mandala, for instance, "Each 'lunar mansion' coincides with one of the 32 gods of the outer ring. Eight of these gods—those in the corners and those in the middle of each side of the square—are considered to be guardians of the cardinal paints, and determine the spatial orientation of the magic square."[62]

The struggle to use form and symbolism to achieve a union of opposites shapes the Hindu temple. The inner sanctuary is called the *garbha-griha* or "womb-house." Like the Pueblo kiva, it is symbolic of the primordial Womb-Caven. Small, dark, and usually devoid of ornamentation, it is not designed for large congregations, but rather to help the individual priest or devotee transcend the illusory world of material manifestation. It is, in fact, an architectural representation of the eternal, infinite realm of consciousness, which in Hindu philosophy is our natural habitat, despite our persistent rebirths into the world of flesh, time, and space.

The *garbha-griha's* prototype was the burial chamber hidden inside India's megalithic dolmens. These chambers are also called *garbha-grihas*. Under Vedic influence, the stark, megalithic Womb-Cavern came to be surmounted and suffused with masculine symbolism. In North Indian temples, a tower in the shape of a lingam or phallus rises above and contains the *garbha-griha*. (In South Indian temples, the tower is more pyramidal.) Furthermore, the most common object of veneration on the altar within the *garbha-griha* is the Shiva-lingam. The *garbha-griha* or "womb and house of the Embryo"[63] is at the same time contained within the phallus as the latter's anima or fecund female element, and *contains* the phallus at its own animus or fecundating male element.

The *vastu purusha mandala* determined the plans of whole cities as well as temples. It dictated where the four castes were to live, using the colors, tastes, and sounds of four types of soil, and other criteria.

> The custom of reserving particular quarters of the town
> for certain castes is justified in manuals of architecture
> by reference to the image of the earth and the sky
> as "Mount Meru": out of the infinite cosmic sea the
> phenomenal world rises up like a pyramid. The four

triangles which form the pyramid are of different colors. The white triangle is the residence of Brahmins, the red one that of Kshatriyas, the yellow one that of Vaishyas, and the black one that of Shudras."[64]

This symbolism presages the Pyramid archetype's central image—the World Mountain, which we will see in the next chapter. Unlike the distinct breaks, reversals, and oppositions that occur between the Four Quarters and the Great Round, the relationship between the Four Quarters and the Pyramid archetype is continuous. In many parts of the world, the Four Quarters is the prelude to the Pyramid archetype's high civilizations. The mythic division of the cosmos into quarters that align colors, social classes, and deities with the cardinal directions forms the foundation upon which the Pyramid is built, symbolically and literally. For example, this essential quartering occurs just before the rise of the Toltec and Mayan civilizations in Mesoamerica; the Hsia, Shang, and Chou dynasties in China; the Yayoi and Yamato in Japan; the Ubaid and Sumerian periods in Mesopotamia; the first dynasties in Egypt's Old Kingdom; and the Hindu dynasties of India. Even the late temples and cities discussed in this section were based on the earlier Vedic precepts of India's Four Quarters era.

Vedic city planning deemed certain city *mandalas* appropriate to only one caste. Some texts considered the perfect square fit only for *brahmins* and relegated other castes to less perfect forms and rectangles. For example, one type of town for the *shudras* (workers) was a half octagon called the *"khet."* This plan's lack both of symmetry and of a true center was considered an appropriate reflection of the *shudras'* own spiritual imperfection. The texts also prescribe the exact sizes and proportions of houses for each caste, predictably giving the *brahmins* rights to the grandest residences.

A classical Hindu city based on the vastu purusha mandala was laid out as a perfect rectangle, or, if the topography permitted, as a square. A hierarchy of streets running north/south and east/west marked off the padas of the mandala. They consisted of a wide "royal way" marking the cross-axes of the town for princely processions and marching troops. The royal way continued outside the four gateways or gopura located at the cardinal points, connecting with other cities and regions. Next came the "large carriage ways" and the "simple carriage ways" with footpaths on either side. Running around the wall enclosing the city was the "processional way" equal in width to the royal way. The layout of the city had ritual as well as practical significance:

> It is laid out on a grand scale, not only in order to facilitate deployment of troops in the case of an attack but also in keeping with an ancient Aryan tradition: during the sacrificial rite the Vedic altar was venerated by being carried around clockwise in procession. Such sacred circumambulations were common in early Hinduism, whether the god being worshipped was originally a Vedic or a Dravidian one. The chief object of veneration was at first the sacrificial altar, and later the image or symbol of the god. Finally, in planned settlements, it was the invisible Brahma-sthana of the vastu-purusha mandala.[65]

The sacred act of founding a Hindu city requires a ritual that is among the most beautiful in the annals of architecture. After the site is selected, the priest-architect first determines the cardinal points by erecting a large sundial. As it traverses the sky, the sun casts a shadow of the gnomon on the circle, first to the west in the morning and then to the east in the afternoon. Upon this east-west axis, the priest-architect geometrically constructs the north-south axis, thereby establishing the Four Quarters. He then marks out the entire mandala and workers level the site. After making sacrificial offerings and cleansing and purifying himself, the priest-architect ritually plows the east-west axis of the city—the axis of the sun's path. Workers then cultivate the rest of the site and plant varieties of corn. When the corn is ripe, the future residents of the city bring their cattle and other livestock to eat the harvest. "'After two nights,' we are told, 'the terrain is cleansed by the grazing of the livestock, consecrated by the breathing of the cows and the lowing of the oxen, sanctified by the saliva from the mouths of calves, washed by their urine, smeared with their mire and chewed fodder, and marked by their hooves.' On the ground so cleansed and sanctified the vastu-purusha mandala with all its padas can now be drawn."[66]

In temple-cities, the whole ritual is repeated in the central precinct to doubly consecrate it. The priest-architect then proceeds to determine the size, proportion, date of commencement, zodiacal sign, and lifespan of the temple according to a series of sacred formulas, which coordinate with the cardinal directions, the days of the week, the planets in the solar system, the star under which the temple must be built, the signs of the zodiac, the lunar cycle, and the caste of the donor. The key in these calculations is the remainder left after the appropriate multiplications and divisions are completed. In general, it is not desirable for the formulas to come out even and leave no remainder as this would indicate perfection, and perfection is not attainable in the mundane world, even in temple building. Certain remainders are considered more auspicious than others, such as four (the Four Quarters). If, after completing all these calculations, the priest-architect comes up with an inauspicious remainder in any of the formulas, he has to "go back to the drawing board" and start all over.

The Medicine Wheel: Journey to the Self

These are some of the ways Hindus attempt, through their architecture and city planning, to integrate human life with the order of the cosmos. They use the Four Quarters mandala, a hierarchy of deities and spiritual principles, ritual circumambulation, and a *hieros gamos* or sacred marriage of the masculine and feminine principles, in this case, expressed architecturally. These are common elements in Four Quarters cultures. The Plains Indians, for instance, envision life as the Medicine Wheel, a quartered round image both of the cosmos and of the whole person. In *Seven Arrows*, a beautiful book of Plains Indian teaching stories, it is described as follows:

> To the North on the Medicine Wheel is found Wisdom. The Color of the Wisdom of the North is White, and its

Medicine Animal is the Buffalo. The South is represented by the Sign of the Mouse, and its Medicine Color is Green. The South is the place of Innocence and Trust, and for perceiving closely our nature of heart. In the West is the Sign of the Bear. The West is the Looks-Within-Place, which speaks of the introspective nature of man. The Color of this Place is Black. The East is marked by the Sign of the Eagle. It is the Place of illumination, where we can see things clearly far and wide. Its color is the Gold of the Morning Star.

At birth, each of us is given a particular Beginning Place within these Four Great Directions on the Medicine Wheel. This Starting Place gives us our first way of perceiving things, which will then be our easiest and most natural way throughout our lives.[67]

The Medicine Wheel aids in "Growing and Seeking" the goal of which is to become a whole person by acquiring the gifts of the directions in the Medicine Wheel beyond one's own Starting Place.[68]

One of the teaching stories in *Seven Arrows* concerns a Vision Quest undertaken by Youngman (or Youngwoman) to find the Singing Stone. The young seeker is first advised by his Grandfather to search for the stone in the North. After a four day journey, in which Youngman encounters numerous symbolic animal helpers, songs, foods, Medicine lodges, and natural sacred places, he reaches the North only to be told by his Grandfather, whom he meets there, that the stone in not in the North but in the South. Another four days' journey with more spiritual encounters brings him finally to the South. There, a beautiful Dragonfly tells him the stone is not to be found in the South but in the West. Discouraged but still determined, Youngman sets out for the West, again meeting magical creatures and natural wonders. After four days he reaches the West. A mouse in a Cave tells him not to seek the stone in the West but in the East. During another four days' walk, Youngman crosses a wide and difficult river, bringing him finally to the East where he rests upon a hill overlooking a strange camp.

"The Closer he Came to the Lodges, the more he Felt the Bow of Tension Pulled within him: But he was Determined to Go On. He Stepped into the Circle of Lodges. Then his Sisters, Mothers, Brothers, Fathers, Grandmothers, Grandfathers, Uncles, Aunts, and all his Relatives Came Out to Greet him, saying 'Welcome to our Counsel Fire, Singing Stone.'"[69]

Each of Youngman's journeys to the North, South, West, and East helped him absorb the spiritual principles of those directions, represented by the animals, songs, foods, lodges, and sacred places he had encountered. Each of his journeys had filled out a quarter of his psyche so that by the time he reached the East he was a whole person. When he reached the East, the Place of Illumination, he found that he himself was "Singing Stone." He was recognized, welcomed, and named as such by his whole family. As Singing Stone, Youngman had reintegrated the Four Quarters of his being so that he himself was the object of his Quest: the *Self*. He had crossed the Great River.

Under the Bodhi Tree

Youngman's story is strikingly similar to one that long ago grew out of another Four Quarters culture half a world away: the story of the enlightenment of Prince Siddhartha Gautama, who then became the historical Buddha, also known as Sakyamuni. Gautama attained enlightenment while meditating under the Bodhi tree (*bodhi* = "awakening"). Throughout the world, the tree is an ancient symbol for the World Axis connecting heaven and earth, which effects the union of opposites that leads to passage beyond the portals of time and space into the realm of the sacred. The Buddha-to-be, however, had some difficulty in determining the right spot on which to sit under the tree:

> ... coming to the Bodhi tree, the one who was about to become the Buddha stood on the southern side and faced north. Instantly the southern half of the world sank until it seemed to touch the lowest hell, while the northern rose to the highest heaven.
>
> "Methinks," then said the Buddha-to-be, "this cannot

be the place for the attainment of supreme wisdom"; and walking around the tree with his right side toward it, he came to the western side and faced east. Thereupon, the western half of the world sank until it seemed to touch the lowest hell, while the eastern half rose to the highest heaven. Indeed, wherever the Blessed One stood, the broad earth rose and fell, as though it were a huge cartwheel lying on its hub and someone were treading on the rim.

"Methinks," said the Buddha-to-be, "this also cannot be the place for the attainment of supreme wisdom"; and walking further, with his right side toward the tree, he came to the northern side and faced south. Then the northern half of the world sank until it seemed to touch the lowest hell, while the southern half rose to the highest heaven.

"Methinks," said the Buddha-to-be, "this also cannot be the place for the attainment of supreme wisdom"; and walking around the tree with his right side toward it, he came to the eastern side and faced west.

Now it is on the eastern side of their Bodhi trees that all the Buddhas have sat down, cross-legged, and that side neither trembles nor quakes.

Then the Great Being saying to himself, "This is the immovable Spot on which all the Buddhas have established themselves: this is the place for destroying passion's net."[70]

Like Youngman, who had to circumambulate the Four Quarters before achieving the goal of his Vision Quest, the Buddha-to-be had to try out each of the cardinal points around the Bodhi tree. Until he completed the circle in the East, the entire world tilted wildly. In other words, he was not centered. He had not brought the Four Quarters into balance. He had not found the still center, the *"point of existing here and everywhere, now and always."* Once he reached this point, he eventually attained enlightenment. As Campbell makes clear, the immovable Spot is not a physical place; it is psychological. It is "the still-standing point of disengagement around which all things turn ... an all-supporting midpoint, a hub where the opposites come together, like the spokes of a wheel, in emptiness."[71]

Neither of these stories is intended as a history of something that happened long ago to someone else, either to Youngman or to the Buddha. Both are about us, now. They are about our own quest for something to stop our constant reeling back and forth, to and fro, from pleasure to pain and back again, from jealousy to desire to ambition to disappointment. They are about our timeless human need to find the Self, which offers sanctuary from the baffling, frustrating, multiplicities of life. The varied means of reintegration are the gifts of the Four Quarters, the blossoms on its cacti.

# SYNOPSIS OF THE FOUR QUARTERS

WORLD OF THE HERO

SPATIAL SYMBOL

Cross within a square

(Also mandalas with crosses inside of circles or inside of circles and squares combined.)

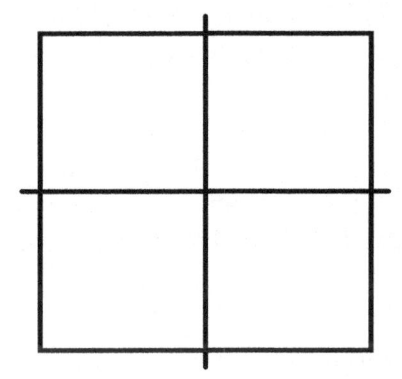

SOCIETY

Era

- Bronze and Iron Ages; the "Archaic," "Formative," "Proto-," Late Pre-Dynastic, or Early Dynastic periods of a civilization.

Society

- Hierarchical chieftainships with authority centralized in a chieftain, petty king, or powerful blacksmith. Societies include gangs of raiders; tribes of nomadic pastoralists; and feudal kingdoms with lords, knights, peasants, and

194 *Spatial Archetypes*

so forth. Caste systems headed by warrior aristocracies or elite priesthoods.
- Warfare, territorial tension, rape, plunder, bloodlust. Kinship system of honor and shame maintains social order. Concept of private property seen in emerging money economy, use of seals to denote ownership, princely or "retinue" burials containing sacrificed people considered the private property of the chieftain or king.

Examples
- Bronze and Iron Age Indo-Europeans (such as the Wessex, Scythian, Celtic, and Viking cultures of Europe; the Aryans of India; the Persians, Hittites, and Phrygians of the Middle East; and the Etruscans, Aeolians, Ionians, Achaeans, and Dorians of the Mediterranean); the Hsia, Shang, and Chou dynasties in China, and the Yayoi and Yamato periods in Japan; the Ubaid culture of Mesopotamia, and the Gerzean and Early Dynastic periods of Egypt; the nomadic Bedouin, Kirghiz, and Qashqai pastoralists of the Near East; the Israelites before King David's bringing of the Ark of the Covenant to Jerusalem; the Plains and Northwest Coast Indians of North America; the pre-pyramid phases of Mexico's Olmec culture and Peru's Chavin culture; the Dogon, Yoruba, Masai, Nuba, and many other traditional cultures in Africa.

Technology
- Bronze and iron metallurgy, perfection of weapons and war-chariots.
- Domestication of the horse.
- Fortified camps and towns.
- Technelogos begins to dominate psychoeros.

Gender Roles
- Emerging patriarchy in descent patterns, family structures, and values. Secret male societies or male elders become important decision-making groups. Myths and legends of the appropriation of female powers by males. Goddesses killed and torn apart (Tiamat) or made into

the wives of the new gods (Isis, Hera). Heroes slaying the Goddess or her protective serpents, Dragons, and demons (Perseus, Apollo, Theseus, Heracles). Men's theft of women's magical instruments, which are then forbidden to women. Metallurgist as obstetrician extracting embryonic ores from the womb of the earth.[72]
- Second (spiritual) birth through the father through doctrine, baptism, initiation.
- Hieros gamos (Sacred Marriage) as sovereignty-bestowing ritual (as for example among the Celts), which usually occurred in the castle or stronghold of the chieftain or king, in a goddess temple, or in the Lord of the Four Quarters' temple.

PSYCHE

Psychology
- Emergence of ego as the central reference point in the psyche mirroring the Lord of the Four Quarters in mythology and the chieftain or king in society.
- Self-versus-other duality, generated by the rise of ego, poses the problem of how to transcend ego to achieve the Union of Opposites that brings enlightenment.
- Adolescence and the establishment of personal autonomy and territory, tests of will and valor, identity quests, proving oneself, Identification with the Warrior-Hero archetype, leading to the symbolic "Slaying of the Mother" to permit the emergence of ego, modeled in Dragon-Slayer myths.[73]
- Territorial preoccupations, paralleling the rise of ego, which generates the concept of private property.

Stagnation
- Psychological stagnation in the Four Quarters generates excessive machismo, violence, aggression, paranoia, and destructive competitiveness; racism, bigotry and intolerance; jealousy and possessiveness; misogyny and con-

196 *Spatial Archetypes*

tempt for the feminine principle; and a militant obsession with the role of protector.

Breakthrough
- Distinguish between the ego and the Self, harness the energy of the ego, use it to drive the chariot, and let the Self become the charioteer.

Liberation
- Psychological liberation in the Four Quarters forges individual character and will, which, when the ego is integrated with the Self (the mandala), fosters enlightened action in the world.

SPIRIT

Worldview
- Cosmos as a quartered universe organized around the central Lord of the Four Quarters

Spiritual Focus
- Lord of the Four Quarters, a mythic analog or projection of the centralized authority of the chieftain in society, the father in the family, and the ego in the psyche. Can be a Storm God or Jealous God such as Indra, Jehovah, Thor, or Zeus; a legendary hero or ancestor; a powerful "official" such as a patriarch, chieftain, king, blacksmith, or shaman; groups such as elders, the highest caste, or men's secret societies; or a savior, messiah, or culture-bringer, who has mastered and can teach the Union of Opposites, such as Buddha, Brahma, Vishnu, Christ, or Quetzalcoatl.
- Syncretic religion assimilating the deities and beliefs of diverse groups.
- Shamanism flourishes in the Four Quarters.

Mythic Themes
- The Separation of the World Parents
- Birth of the Hero

- Lord of the Four Quarters
- Dragon-Slayers and other gods and heroes such as Storm and thunder gods, volcanic mountain gods, father gods, jealous gods, culture-bringers, initiatory gods, gods of fire and metal.

Male Roles, Rituals, and Concerns

- Roles: warrior, blacksmith, hero, father, son, rebel, protector, chieftain or king (including tribal forms of divine kingship).
- Rituals: initiation rites, induction into secret societies, rites of coronation and sovereignty, ritual regicide,
- Concerns: honor, loyalty, bravery, chivalry, technical skill, personal power, competitiveness, displays of rank and status (pageantry, heraldry, "colors," uniforms, status possessions).
- Metallurgy, the mystique of metals, mining rituals and superstitions; veneration of meteorites, fire, and metal from the gods or the sky; miraculous swords, weapons, and war chariots; veneration of the blacksmith.
- Warfare, epic battles (the *Mahabharata*, the *Iliad*), gifted warriors, battle frenzy (Cuchulainn), the glory of war as the ultimate initiation (for instance, to prove bravery or to overcome fear of death), war games and training sagas, military camaraderie (esprit de corps, battlefield buddies), twins (one a warrior, one a priest, shaman, poet, scholar, philosopher, etc.).
- Warring dualities: light versus darkness, gods vs., titans, heroes vs. demons, order vs. chaos.
- Horses, magical steeds, ritual races, Horse Goddesses, the Horse Sacrifice.
- The Cardinal Axes: crossroads, the "urban mark," four Sacred Mountains at the cardinal points, circumambulation of the Four Quarters, lifting a sacred pipe or other ritual paraphernalia to the Four Quarters or the Six Directions.
- The Quartered Cosmos: four directional groups of castes or tribes, colors, elements, seasons, ages, heavens, deities, animals, attributes, sacred mountains, and so on. The

center often forms a fifth group at the top of the hierarchy.
- The Center: the Omphalos, Navel of the World, Center of the Universe, the crossing or center of the cardinal axes, palace or temple of the Lord of the Four Quarters, capital or seat of kingship, place of origin.
- The Heavenly Mansion of the Lord of the Four Quarters surrounded by a wall with gates and guardians at the cardinal points
- Hierarchy in the family, society, and the spirit world, which often has many levels or ranks of heavens and hells.

CULTURE

Prime Symbol
- The Quartered Cosmos

The Arts
- Metalwork—fine bronze, iron, silver, and gold work made into swords, shields, helmets, and other weaponry; scepters, staffs, and various symbols of sovereignty; ceremonial vessels and grave goods; coins and status-jewelry.
- Literature—Heroic epics and oral traditions; genealogies, king-lists, magic squares and other alpha-numeric records; calligraphy and illuminated manuscripts (in feudal and monastic cultures).
- Sculpture—bas-reliefs of battle scenes and heroic feats, commemorative stelae and cairns, sculptures of deities and heroes, divinatory and ritualistic paraphernalia
- Textiles—carpets, woven goods, and needlework (especially in pastoral cultures).

Astronomy
- The solstices and equinoxes, which divide the year into Four Quarters.

Time
- Linear time within great cycles (recurring ages, yugas, or "Great Years"), The past as a legendary time of heroic deeds, battles, migrations, and lineage ancestry.

Space
- The Four Quarters, the Quartered Cosmos, the Center, and so on (see Mythic Themes above).

Landscape
- Strong Territoriality: land as a source of power, honor, and sovereignty; also as currency in trade and booty in warfare. Territoriality symbolized by the Lord of the Four Quarters' domain surrounded by a wall, which divides sacred from profane, friend from enemy, "mine" from "thine."

Architecture
- Forts, fortified encampments, castles, walled towns and temples: architecture models the archetype with square or rectilinear enclosures surrounding the residence, temple, or stronghold of the Lord of the Four Quarters, which occupies the center, and avenues stretching to the north, south, east, and west guarded by gates at the cardinal axes.
- Raised terraces, ceremonial platforms, and tentative pyramids show the axis mundi beginning to appear weakly.
- Princely burials, rich grave goods, tumuli (earther mounds or cairns with rich individual burials, not to be confused with the Great Round's egalitarian collective burials in megalithic passage mounds and dolmen). Retinue burials with sacrificed horses and humans (wives, warriors, retainers, servants, and the like).

THE PYRAMID

WORLD OF THE GOD-KING

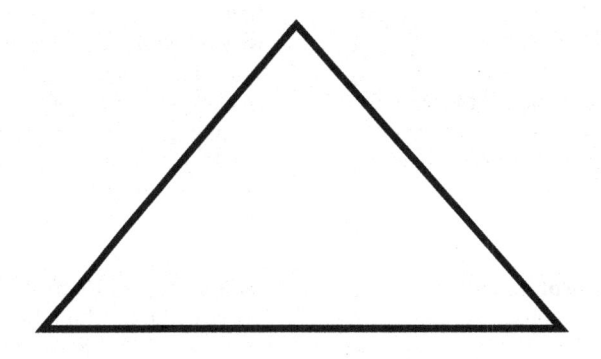

4a. The Great Pyramid. Giza, Egypt. Finished around 2560 BC. While we associate pyramids with Egypt, they were built in various forms in many cultures. They model the universe, represent hierarchical societies, and bring transcendent energies into this world.

4b. El Castillo. (Also known as the Temple of Kukulcan.) Built by the Mayan civilization in the Yucatán Peninsula between the 9th and 12th centuries. The ancient Mayans paralleled the ancient Egyptians not only in building pyramids, but in theocratic nation or city state, stratified societies, dynastic succession of rulers, spiritual and political power of the state theocracy vested in a God-King, syncretic state religions with pyramidal pantheons reflecting the social structure, and cosmoses as World Mountains. But technological they were far apart. The Mayans had no bronze and did not use the wheel.

4c. Borobudur. A Mahayana Buddhist stupa built in the 9th century in Central Java, Indonesia. It is a three dimensional mandala, which is a model of the world, a model of the mind, and a means of putting the two in harmony. One climbs to each level and walks around before climbing to the next level. The sculpted relief panels on the walls depict the life of the Buddha and scenes from his past lives.

4d. Chartres Cathedral. Chartres, France, built between 1194 and 1220. Chartres is as much a manifestation of a native European spirituality as it is of a Christian spirituality. It shows how transcendence can come into this world, and symbolizes the sky aspirations of Europeans. Is it also a "pyramid?" The answer to that question comes not only from the form of the building, but also the nature of the culture that built it.

The Pyramid 203

4a

4b

4c

4d

THE PYRAMID

WORLD OF THE GOD-KING

> O Atum-Kheprer, thou wast on high on the primeval hill;
> thou didst arise as the ben-bird of the ben-stone in the
> Ben-House in Heliopolis ...
> O Atum, put thou thy arms about King Nefer-ka-Re,
> about this construction work, about this pyramid, as
> the arms of a ka. For the ka of King Nefer-ka-Re is in it,
> enduring for the course of eternity.[1]

From the Four Quarters to the Pyramid

The most famous pyramids are those of the Egyptians in the Old World and the Maya and Toltecs in the New, but there are many others throughout the world. When French masons were building Gothic cathedrals, Khmer kings of Cambodia were erecting great temple-mountains in Angkor; and when Europe was still in the Dark Ages, the kings of the Java's Sailendra Dynasty were building Borobudur, an elaborately carved stone model of the Buddhist World Mountain.

Less familiar pyramids include those built by the pre-Incan Chavin, Mochica, and Tiahuanacan cultures in Peru; a pyramidal royal tomb in Apia, the capital of Western Samoa; and the now nearly destroyed Marae Mahaiatea, originally an eleven-step fifty foot high pyramid built in the 18th century in Tahiti by the female Chieftain Purea. Nearly vanished, too, are all the mud-brick ziggurats built some 4000 years ago in Mesopotamia.

One of the largest pyramids in the world is in the United States, in St. Louis, where Cohokia, the capital city of the Mississippian culture, flourished between about A.D. 900 and 1600.[2]

Some structures such as the legendary Temple of Solomon, the Acropolis in Athens, and the Gothic cathedrals, are not perceived as pyramids; nonetheless they are, in a cultural and symbolic sense if not in actual form. The Temple of Solomon, planned by King David and built on Mount Moriah by his son Solomon, gave the nomadic Israelite tribes a permanent capital, a "Navel of the World," which unified them into a nation state. The temple housed the Ark of the Covenant, symbol of the fixed, centralized power of the new state and of the special relationship between the people and their Father God.

Even though not in true pyramid form, the Acropolis in Athens was nonetheless the "pyramid" of classical Greece—the culminating architectural achievement of Greece's Pyramid era, its "Golden Age." Financed by wealthy dynastic Athenian families, it expressed an Indo-European religion that revered sacred mountains (Mount Olympus, Mount Parnassus) and their resident deities. The Acropolis's major temple, the Parthenon, was dedicated to the goddess of wisdom, Athena, a logos-oriented virgin warrior. Though not itself a pyramid, the Parthenon was built on the highest hill in the area, making it similar to the temples surmounting the artificial mountains of Sumer and Mesoamerica.

The Gothic cathedrals, too, do not overtly resemble pyramids, but they serve the same symbolic role in Western culture that true pyramids did in other cultures. Cross-shaped in plan, sky-reaching in form, and built during Europe's theocratic Middle Ages, they rose above their medieval surroundings just as the Sumerian ziggurats had risen loftily above their surroundings to express the newly emerging hierarchy of church and state. Medieval Europe's aspiration to the pyramid-mountain form is especially apparent in structures such as Mont St. Michel, begun in A.D. 708.

Pyramids were built for different functions in different cultures, serving variously as tombs, temples, reliquaries, geodetic markers, astronomical observatories, sites of rituals and initiations, and models of consciousness and the cosmos. It is impossible to explore each variation fully, but there are enough parallels among them to warrant general conclusions about the social circumstances and mythic impulses that led to pyramid-building. Also, by focusing on the similarities rather than the differences among pyramid-building civilizations, we come closer to the archetype. From this perspective, many of the differences turn out to be variations on a central theme.

As a physical form, the Pyramid is built directly on a Four Quarters base. Similarly, the psychological and cultural manifestations of the Pyramid archetype grow out of the Four Quarters. The Pyramid is essentially the Four Quarters with the addition of a vertical axis called the axis mundi or "World Axis." Whereas the Four Quarters had two axes and four directions—North/South and East/West—the Pyramid has three axes and six directions—North/South, East/West, and Heaven/Earth. Connecting the points of these axes and directions makes the true form of the Pyramid archetype—a double pyramid or octahedron, with one pyramid pointing up and the other down. The two opposed pyramids embody a dualistic worldview: the upward-pointing one symbolizes the now "positive," skyward realm; the downward-pointing one, the now "negative" earthward realm. Paradoxically, the pyramid encloses an infinity of realities, conceptually extending upward through heaven and whatever may lie beyond, downward to the core of the earth, and horizontally throughout all of space to the North, South, East, and West.

The World Axis is implicit in the Four Quarters spatial archetype and appears in the mythology and rituals of many Four Quarters cultures, as we saw in the symbolism of the Bodhi tree, for instance. The axis mundi and the World Mountain are venerated by the Navaho, the Plains Indians, and other Amerindian cultures and by all cultures influenced by Siberian shamanism. The difference is that people who adhere primarily to the Four Quarters worldview do not build massive, permanent, architectural pyramids as do people who adhere to the Pyramid worldview. They may worship the corollary of the Pyramid in nature: the Sacred Mountain. They may consider the central pole of their hut or tent or the tree in the center of their village to be the World Axis, and they may, like the shaman, seek to travel along that axis spiritually. But they do not build pyramids. Thus, it is easy to identify a Pyramid culture simply because the architectural form is so outstanding. If the culture has not produced large stone or brick (or occasionally earthen) pyramids, temple-mountains, monumental temples on top of mountains, or soaring religious structures, then it probably is not a Pyramid culture.

The Rise of the Pyramid in the Nation State

Pyramid-building nearly always accompanies and heralds the rise of the nation state. Like the complex termite societies that build great pyramidal towers on the savannahs of Africa, human beings almost compulsively build pyramids when they organize themselves into socially complex nations or city-states. Unlike termite colonies, however, pyramids are purely symbolic structures. Few human-made structures are more useless in terms of biological survival or of meeting the daily needs of ordinary people.

The form of the architectural pyramid, the coordinated effort required to build it, and the hierarchical priesthood associated with it may provide a symbolic model of the centrality needed to maintain cohesion in a society that is becoming more fragmented and complex. Some anthropologists argue that the massive amount of human labor needed to build a pyramid could not be marshaled without the centralization of power characteristic of the state. Others assert that the activity of pyramid-building itself organizes the state by siphoning surplus wealth into public works. Whether the pyramid is the cause or the effect of the highly organized, class-structured society characteristic of the nation state, it is certainly the symbol of it and the pinnacle of its material achievements.

In most cultures, the earliest signs of future pyramid-building can be seen in the erection of ceremonial platforms, temples on low terraces, or individual burial mounds called tumuli. This formative stage typically occurs at the end of the Four Quarters when chieftainships have become large and powerful. At first these formative structures may be quite modest, but over the centuries they are enlarged into sophisticated pyramids, reflecting society's transformation into a nation state.

This type of development happened in Mesopotamia, the Americas, Southeast Asia, and Oceania. The Egyptian pyramids followed an accelerated version of the sequence, evolving rapidly from the rectangular, mud-brick mastaba tomb. Before the Buddhist stupa brought pyramid-building to the Far East, the early proto-nation states of China (during the Chou dynasty), Korea (under the Silla dynasty), and Japan (in the Yamato period) had already devised stepped ceremonial platforms or impressive tumuli or both. Though the pre-Buddhist East seems to have preferred the worship of natural sacred mountains to the building of pyramids, there is the example of Mount Li, the pyramidal tomb of the first "Emperor" of China, with its nearby terra cotta army of thousands of life-sized warriors and horses. Built by the man who first unified China into a true nation and erected the Great Wall of China, Mount Li is a perfect image of the Pyramid form sited in a Four Quarters enclosure symbolizing the cardinal directions of the universe. With Buddhism came the numerous artificial Mount Merus called stupas, chortens, dagobas, and pagodas, culminating in the perfection of Borobudur on Java.

The key feature in the evolution of pyramid-building in most cultures is the increasing emphasis on height, which expresses the growing complexity and size of the state. Once inspired by the Pyramid archetype, people build as high as their engineering skills allow. It is as if they have an overwhelming urge to escape the earth and reach for the sky. This is not surprising, since the Pyramid worldview is built upon the Four Quarters, and the entire ethos and mythos of the Four Quarters is already sky-oriented. The Indo-European sky gods dominate people's idea of divinity. The desert-based religions of the Indo-Europeans and Semites turn away from the hostile, arid earth in favor of the heavens that bless human life with rain and with stars by which nomadic herders can navigate their migrations.

The nation state is like a big fish swallowing little fish. It brings a multitude of formerly independent tribes, farming communities, and chieftainships under the aegis of a powerful, theocratic dynasty. Typically this happens when an unusually strong chieftain conquers one neighboring community after another, conscripting troops along the way, until he has subdued a vast region. Certainly some of the conquered resist, but some probably concede in order to gain protection from other invaders.

The nation state not only offers its people a standing army to protect them from invasion, but also public works that provide both employment and vital facilities such as irrigation systems and roads. It also offers centralized food stores that can be doled out in case of famine. And it awes and entertains with a spell-binding array of stately ceremonies designed to induce national pride. To reciprocate, citizens send their youths to join the army, labor on the public works projects, pay taxes (usually in the form of food and other goods), pledge allegiance to the state, and worship the gods of the state religion. In so doing, they gave up their self-sufficiency and many of their own religious beliefs, although native beliefs may continue as folk religions, which influence the state religion.

The Social Pyramid

The hierarchical chieftainship of the Four Quarters is organized along kinship lines, that is, along the blood lines of hereditary castes. Although a chieftainship can be several thousand members strong, it is small enough for its members to know each other, at least indirectly. The dealings of ordinary life runs through brothers, sisters, aunts, uncles, cousins, distant cousins, in-laws, and across lines of friendship or marriage into other families, other tribes.

With the formation of nations, people find they are now expected to identify not only with a comprehensible community of relatives and friends, but also with that vast abstract collectivity of strangers called the state. The cultural shock of being dependent upon and controlled by a remote central authority must have far-reaching effects. This is the first time in history that people's lives are ruled by distant beings whom they have never seen. And for the first time there is a group that can be called the "common masses." The need to organize and govern the anonymous masses, together with the growing urbanity and complexity of life, generates a new kind of hierarchical social structure—not based on kin and caste but on occupational classes. Thus society itself forms a Pyramid. At the bottom are prisoners of war or slaves or both. Next come peasants; then merchants, artisans, and trades people; then various strata of state employees—supervisors, soldiers, tax collectors, census-takers, government representatives, magistrates, advisors, scribes, and, at the top of this class, the state priests. Finally, the ruling family occupies the top of the Pyramid with the king at the apex.

For the first time in history, the ruling family constitutes a dynasty. In earlier cultures, if kings existed at all, either they were not very powerful, or, through ritual regicide, they were periodically sacrificed to keep them from gaining too much power. Eventually human, and then animal, substitutes were sacrificed in place of the king, and by these means the term of office gradually was extended.[4] The rise of the Pyramid archetype in any civilization is heralded by the establishment of the first dynasty of hereditary rulers, which passes kingship from generation to generation. With few exceptions, the ruler is a male, but he is not simply a man. He is god and man at the same time. The Pyramid archetype parallels the Hero's complete separation from the Mother when he becomes fully identified with the Father and with masculine society.[5] The Father in this case is not so much the biological human father as the archetypal spiritual Father: the Father God.

In the Pyramid archetype, the state is theocratic, and the king is divine. His political authority is based on his spiritual authority, and his spiritual authority is based on his claim of being the son or representative of the Father God. The divine ordination of the institution of kingship, a characteristic of theocratic society, is spelled out in an ancient Sumerian text. Toward the beginning of the text, the god or gods "directed the [building] of the temenos, perfected the rites and the exalted divine ordinances." On earth they then brought the "black-headed people," vegetation, and animals into existence. After a gap of thirty-seven obliterated lines, the text continues:

> After... kingship had been lowered from heaven, After the exalted tiara and the throne of kingship had been lowered from heaven.
> He perfected the rites and the exalted divine ordinances...,
> Founded the five cities in pure places,
> Called their names, apportioned them as cult centers,
> The first of these cities, Eridu, he gave to Nudimmud, the leader [the water-god Enki][6]

The implied sequence of creation, then, begins with the gods establishing divine order in heaven through designing the *temenos* (the sacred enclosure built around holy places in ancient times), and perfecting the divine rites and ordinances. Then, after bringing human, vegetable, and animal life to earth, they channeled divine order to earth by lowering kingship from heaven. Finally, by calling their names, they founded the first five antediluvian cities as holy places dedicated to specific gods and goddesses.

The Spiritual Pyramid

Just as religion in Four Quarters cultures mirrors Four Quarters society, so religion in Pyramid cultures mirrors Pyramidal society. In fact, the religious and social structures of the two archetypes have much in common: both are hierarchically stratified, both focus on male gods, both are sky and logos-oriented, both are devised by a priestly class or caste, and both are syncretic, absorbing the indigenous deities of conquered peoples.

Whether in China, India, Egypt, Mesopotamia, Peru, or Mexico, the religion of the Pyramid era was usually contrived by an elite class of priests who worked closely with the founding ruler. Together they wove synthetic state religions by threading new gods and principles into the warp of old beliefs. Almost invariably they placed the ancestral deity of the ruling family at the apex of the Pyramid.

In the Pyramid form, the *axis mundi* and the apex (called the "pyramidion" by Egyptologists) are the centers of attention, but they are not the physical bulk of the pyramid; that is fleshed out by the widely splaying base that predictably symbolizes the lower social classes and life's more worldly aspects. In designing the spiritual Pyramid, the priests artfully array the deities of the conquered peoples beneath the apex in a rigidly descending hierarchy that reflects the social status of their adherents, depending on how much political or economic power they continue to wield, how effectively they court the governing elite, or how much they still constitute a military threat. Some particularly threatening groups find their patron deities turned into demons, just as the people of the Great Round witnessed, to their horror, the blasphemous demonization of the Great Goddess by the agents of the Lord of the Four Quarters. Such was the fate, for instance, of Seth in early dynastic Egypt, the Canaanite goddess Ashtoreth and god Baal in Israel, the Dravidian deities in Khmer-ruled Cambodia, and the pagan nature god Pan, who by medieval times had been transformed by the Christians into the Devil.

Through the spiritual Pyramid, the priests of the past established the primacy of the dynasty and pacified the conquered. Their sophisticated manipulation of the spiritual as well as the political needs of the governed even surpassed the efforts of our contemporary politicians to contrive persuasive platforms and winning coalitions. The spiritual Pyramids were not mere platforms for political gain but three-dimensional metaphysical scaffolds on which were built the high civilizations of the ancient world.

The spiritual Pyramid stratified not only deities, but also the metaphysical landscape, dividing it into heaven, earth, and underworld like the shaman's Three Worlds. Heaven and the underworld were often further subdivided into different realms. For instance, the Maya (and later the Aztec) saw heaven as having thirteen layers and the underworld as having nine. At death, people went to specific heavens or hells depending on their station in life. Different deities presided over each stratum in the supramundane world and over corresponding occupations in the mundane world. Thus warriors were allotted one cycle of festivals, patron deity, and realm of heaven; farmers, another; sorcerers, yet another, and so on.

A similar stratified vision from Europe's "Pyramid Age" can be seen in Dante's medieval vision of Paradise, Purgatory, and Hell. Here, however, access depends not only on one's occupation but on one's moral behavior during life. Many Pyramidal civilizations share Dante's view, that is, that one's assignment to the various strata of heaven or hell, or the various ranks of afterlife or reincarnation, depend on one's virtue. Like the occupational stratifications, these moral judgments are fully in keeping with the spirit of the Pyramid archetype. One is an outright reflection of class society; the other, of the logos-oriented moral laws devised by the priesthood.

Morality and Individual Will

Much has been written about the origin of laws and moral codes. Written laws and codified morals are not vitally necessary before the advent of the nation state. It is as if the very size and complexity of the state breaks the back of the time-honored ways of ensuring social order through an innate sense of responsibility to the whole (in the Sensitive Chaos and the Great Round) and the kinship-based system of honor and shame (in the Four Quarters). Formal moral and legal codes are born out of the breakdown of the old, intuitive and familial ways of maintaining good behavior. The *Tao te Ching* puts it this way:

> When the great Tao is forgotten,
> Kindness and morality arise.
> When wisdom and intelligence are born,
> The great pretense begins.
> When there is no peace within the family,
> Filial piety and devotion arise,
> When the country is confused and in chaos,
> Loyal ministers appear.[7]

The mounting influence of individual virtue in determining one's place in heaven is illustrated in this passage about India:

> The relationship between gods and men in early Vedic times was collective rather than individual. A sacrifice offered to Indra or to Agni was essentially an offering to all the gods, for it was only by their concerted efforts that the world was sustained .... Supplications were thus made for the tribe or people and not primarily for the individual .... At that stage of cultural development the ancestors (pitrs), rather than the deceased individual father, were the objects of reverence. The notion of individual immortality and of a particular place (*loka*) in the celestial world were a later priestly device, a further incentive for the performance of individual sacrifice.[8]
>
> The kind of individual sacrifice described here was probably

the earliest form of taxation. Naturally, it was in the priesthood's interest to encourage individual pilgrimages and sacrifices to their temples. The economic benefits they must have derived from the practice are suggested by the fact that later threats to the same type of system caused by Mohammed's monotheism resulted in his *hegira* or flight to Medina to escape the wrath of Meccan priests deprived of their lucrative polytheistic business. Martin Luther was similarly persecuted for speaking out against the sale by the Roman Catholic Church of indulgences to people wishing to insure their place in heaven.

However, this is not the only evidence of the increasing emphasis on individual action. Individual salvation is consistent also with the steady progress of the Hero. The Hero is above all the champion of individual will. The Four Quarters mythological Hero is concerned primarily with conquering the psychological "enemies" that inhibited his progress—the Shadow, the Dragon, the Mother—just as the historical hero is occupied mainly with conquering enemies on the battlefield. With these battles out of the way, his will is unrestrained. He is now able to achieve his destiny: becoming God-King. As absolute ruler of the land, he has the ultimate responsibility for the shape and fate of human society.

The moral imperative of the Hero suffuses the God-King with divine authority that filters down to and is implemented by ordinary human souls through the doctrine of individual responsibility for one's place in heaven. The archetype, the law, and the nature of the afterlife evolve in concert with one another, mirroring one another endlessly through developing social institutions and religious precepts. Spiritual life, too, becomes regulated by the concept of Divine Law, as in the Dharma of Hinduism and Buddhism, the Torah in Judaism, and the Ten Commandments in Judaism and Christianity.

The Emergence of Technelogos

The development of legal and moral codes is but a small part of an overall trend toward the logos principle in Pyramid civilizations. We can see this in how the God-King (or his priests) chronicle history, keep records, establish standards of measurement and canons of sacred geometry, and systemize astronomy and mathematics. These activities move society toward technelogos, with its emphasis on "doing" and "making," and away from psychoeros, where "knowing" and "seeing" are the goals. This shift begins in the Four Quarters but accelerates in the Pyramid to become a key feature of its worldview.

It was in the spirit of technelogos that Babylon's King Hammurabi compiled his famed Code of Laws, and that Ashoka, the first great king and unifier of India, erected inscribed edict columns throughout the land. In the same spirit, the Mayan, Egyptian, and Babylonian priests studied the stars and gained hermetic knowledge of astronomy that gave them extraordinary authority.

The Pyramid archetype spawns the beginning of recorded history and the proliferation, if not the invention, of the written word. Writing, the recording of information in a linear, rationalized system of abstract symbolic conventions; and history, the enumeration and description of events in a linear chronology, are both logos phenomena. The earliest known *dated* (that is, historical) monument of the Maya is a stele in the city of Tikal with the deciphered date of A.D. 292. The Leyden Plate from the same city dated twenty-nine years later shows a "richly bedecked Maya lord, trampling underfoot a sorry-looking captive,"[9] evidently commemorating the victory of an early king. The glyphic recording of these and other events in Mayan history—including the names, portraits, and detailed achievements of individual kings—coincided with the rise of the Classic Mayan theocratic city-states such as Tikal, Copan, and Palenque, all of which also boasted impressive pyramidal temples and tombs.

Similarly, in Egypt the first king of the First Dynasty was commemorated on the Narmer Palette, which, like the Leyden Plate, shows the king conquering his enemies in his rise to power. And, like the Maya, the Egyptians began recording more historical data about their kings, even to the point of compiling chronological "king-lists." The earliest of these known so far is the Palermo Stone dating from the Fifth Dynasty (around 2400 B.C.), which falls within the Old Kingdom when Egypt was dominated by the Pyramid archetype. The development of recorded history can similarly be traced in other Pyramidal cultures. This focus on the king in both the Old World and the New implies that the king is seen, like the Lord of the Four Quarters, as the ego of humanity. There is a difference, however: since the king in Pyramid cultures is usually a God-King, he also represents the Self. Thus the God/King ego/self apex of the pyramid symbolically compresses all of humanity into one representative individual through whom the human race gains access to the immortal and the divine.

The advent of recorded history and king-lists, as well as the increasing preoccupation with the immortality and afterlife of the God-King, points to a growing emphasis on *linear* time—on the left brain's time that rolls onward, separating us from the non-linear synchronistic time of our childhood in the Sensitive Chaos and the cyclical time of the Great Round. Despite its tragic consequences—the loss both of "Paradise" and of a kind of natural "immortality"—this perception of time gives us some of the world's most celebrated monumental architecture—the Sakkara and Giza pyramids in Egypt, the pyramid-tomb at Palenque in Mexico, and others.

Unlike synchronistic and cyclical time, linear time gives a one-directional lifeline in which there can be no return to the beginning, neither to an inner sense of primal origin, nor to a prehistoric beginning in time. Whereas the dweller in the Sensitive Chaos returns upon death to the clan-pool of spirits, and the inhabitant of the Great Round can depend on the ever-renewing continuity of the Great Goddess's cycles, the Pyramid archetype's God-King apprehends for the first time the great dilemma of human mortality. More tragic than mere physical mortality, this is a mortality of the spirit, destined the moment the ego is born.

In his anxiety over the finality of his own death, the king commissions priests to rework mythology, incorporating complicated notions of a second birth of the soul. He has embalmers preserve his flesh and scribes record his deeds. But most importantly, he commissions architects to entomb him in a structure that will protect his mortal remains and earthly treasures throughout eternity, while channeling his spirit skyward. And what better to accomplish this than a Pyramid—a form that begins massively rooted in the earth and ends vanishing into heaven.

All of these new preoccupations—systems of measurement, geometric canons, codes of law, written history, linear time—involve linear/logical thinking, enumerating, and verbal skills. This is another aspect of the *axis mundi*. In this sense, the axis mundi is not only the axis between heaven and earth, but also between the head and the body. It is the inner axis that the dualistic mind thinks exists between consciousness and the unconscious, between the spirit and the body, between logos and eros. The ascent away from the body and the unconscious and toward the rational mind and a disembodied notion of spirit leads eventually to the linear, logical, rationalism of the Grid archetype, which dominates the modern world.

But the Pyramid archetype is not the Grid. And the Divine Ruler is the *ego-Self*, not merely the ego. To the Pyramid's hierophant, logos is not a synonym for a computer—like intellect, as it often is for us. Logos is a numinous, spiritual power that reveals the secret order of the universe through the magic of the Word, the power of number, and the knowledge of the true names of things. Through the power of logos, kings and priests are admitted to the mind of God. They know the hidden geometric, numeric, and calendrical order behind the apparent chaos of the phenomenal world. In temples and hermetic rituals, they identify with the gods to bring order out of chaos for human benefit. Only kings and priests can petition the gods to attend to human needs because the gods of the Pyramid archetype are psychological projections of the ruling elite, not of ordinary people. The theocracy sanctions the rule of the gods as much as vice versa. In the Sensitive Chaos and the Great Round, everyone has access to the sacred. In the Four Quarters and the Pyramid, the centralization of access to divinity parallels the centralization of political power.

The Hermetization of the Sacred

The centralization of power is reflected not only in the building of pyramids but also in the increasing exclusivity of the sacred places within temples. In Sensitive Chaos and early Great Round cultures, sacred places are not markedly separate from nature or dwelling. Four Quarters and Pyramid cultures, however, display an increasing differentiation of sacred versus profane space, reflecting a similar dualism in the psyche. Not only are temples set apart from dwellings, but even within temples there are hierarchical degrees of access to the sacred.

In Mesopotamia, for instance, one of the earliest temples was built in the fifth millennium B.C. in Eridu—the first cult center established by the gods when they lowered kingship from heaven. The temple was a simple, small rectangular room measuring twelve by fifteen feet, with an altar in a little apse at one end. ty. The later, more elaborate temples included antechambers and courts that filtered out ordinary people, denying their access to the sacred. Giedion writes:

> In the pre-Sargonid period, before the middle of the third millennium, a growing severance between the deity and the faithful became apparent. Instead of many entrances there was only one, placed toward the far end of the cella [shrine]. Then an antecella was inserted before the cella. An inner court further helped to accentuate the distance.[10]

As we might expect, this transformation in temple design concurred with the growth in Mesopotamia both of city-states and of the ziggurat. As well as becoming more elaborate, the temple rose ever higher off the ground. The tiny Eridu temple was on flat earth; the lofty White Temple at Uruk, built in the third millennium B.C., was placed on a high platform reached by steps; and the enormous Ziggurat of Urnammu, built at the peak of Sumerian civilization in 2100 B.C., had several terraces reaching a total height of seventy feet.

In Egypt, as in other Pyramid civilizations, the life-force of the nation was conceived as channeling from heaven through the apex of the pyramid to the ruler, and through the ruler to the people. In contrast to the Sensitive Chaos where everyone is united within the Great Spirit, the God-King and only the God-King has direct access to Supreme Being. He is the mediator between heaven and earth on behalf of all his subjects.

The God-King's most crucial functions are connected with the axis mundi, which is much more pronounced in the Pyramid archetype than in the Four Quarters. In the nation state, most of the duties of the Four Quarters chieftain—waging war, acquiring territory, settling disputes, storing and redistributing food—are no longer carried out directly by the ruler, but instead are delegated to standing armies and government bureaucracies. This frees the king for the higher work of maintaining the spiritual life of the state. Although he certainly is concerned with normal political affairs, his most potent activities—the ones that give him mystical power and authority—all have to do with negotiating the axis mundi, the world axis between heaven and earth, between the divine and the human. Henri Frankfort writes:

> ... if we refer to kingship as a political institution, we assume a point of view which would have been incomprehensible to the ancients. We imply that the human polity can be considered by itself. The ancients, however, experienced human life as part of a widely spreading network of connections which reached beyond the local and the national communities into the hidden depths of nature and the powers that rule nature. The purely secular—in so far as it could be granted to exist at all—was the purely trivial. Whatever was significant was imbedded in the life of the cosmos, and it was precisely the king's function to maintain the harmony of that integration.[11]

The God-King conducts his most important rituals in, around, or on top of pyramids. It is here, at these places where heaven and earth meet, that he communicates directly with the gods and goddesses to preserve the order of the cosmos, the sovereignty of kingship, and the symbolic fertility of the land. Later, we will see this in the coronation rites of King Zoser's Heb Sed festival in ancient Egypt and in the sacred marriage between kings and priestesses atop the ziggurats of Mesopotamia and the temple-mountains of Angkor.

The Mountain Arising from the Sea of Chaos

Nearly every Pyramid civilization has a myth about a Mountain Arising from the Sea of Chaos: Mount Ararat in Judeo-Christian tradition; the Primeval Hill in Egypt, modeled by ancient pyramids; Mount Sumeru of the Sumerians; Marduk's tower Esaglia in Akkadian and Babylonian belief; Mount Meru in India; the Mayan cosmic mountain of the Popul Vuh, and so forth.

The myth is quasi-historical in that nearly every Pyramid civilization actually suffered a flood in its early history, and, as in the Biblical story of Noah, the mountain peak was the first dry land to offer refuge to survivors. But, like the Flood myth itself, the Mountain Arising from the Sea of Chaos is also a psychological metaphor. The Flood is the universal experience of dissolution in the unconscious, which occurs when we sleep, when we are "out of our minds" for whatever reason, when we die, and when we are not yet born.

Similarly, the Sea of Chaos is the unconscious. The Mountain is its opposite: consciousness, the rational mind, the ego. The Mountain Arising from the Sea of Chaos is a dualistic mythic image opposing the Mountain—hard, firm, reliable, to the Sea of Chaos—swirling, dangerous, uncontrollable. The Mountain arises from the Sea of Chaos as the ego arises from the Self. The Mountain is rock and not sea. The ego is unique and not of the collective Self. Both are in immutable opposition to each other, as figure and ground. "Chaos," as we have seen in the Sensitive Chaos and the Great Round, is not really chaotic at all, but its swirling round of transpersonal forces is perceived as chaotic by the rationally structured ego. Chaos is the realm predating the ego, the realm the ego has to "rise above" if it is to come into its own like the immovable Mountain.

In *Ego and Archetype*, the Jungian analyst Edward Edinger presents a diagram of the "ego-Self axis" showing four progressive stages of the ego's emergence from the Self. With elegant simplicity, the diagram captures all the relationships between the ego and the Self that we have seen thus far in the sequence of archetypes. The first diagram shows the ego completely absorbed in the Self—the condition in the uroboric Sensitive Chaos. In the second diagram, the ego is beginning to emerge but is still mostly embedded in the Self-the relationship in the Great Round when the Divine Child has been born but is not yet the Hero. In the third diagram, the ego has emerged mostly, but not completely, from the Self, just as in the Four Quarters the Hero still struggles to separate from the Mother. Finally, the fourth diagram shows the ego completely emerged and separate from the Self, defining the polarizing "ego-Self axis." This is the situation in the Pyramid archetype when the Mountain Arises from the Sea of Chaos. The "ego-Self axis" is the all-important axis mundi, which exists in the psyche as well as in mythology and architecture.

The final separation between the ego and the Self accentuates the longing for a return to the Self that we saw beginning in the Four Quarters' quest for reintegration. This means that the God-King does not really represent the integrated ego-Self, but rather the ego-Self in opposition. The longing quest for re-integration preoccupies the God-King as he incessantly negotiates the axis mundi on behalf of humanity. Edinger lists mythic images that proliferate from this longing, including wholeness, totality, the union of opposites, the central generative point, the world navel, the axis of the universe, the creative point where God and man meet, the point where transpersonal energies flow into personal life, eternity as opposed to the temporal flux, incorruptibility, the inorganic—united paradoxically with the organic protective structures capable of bringing order out of chaos, the transformation of energy, the elixir of life—all refer to the Self, the eternal source of life energy, the fountain of our being which is most simply described as God.[13]

The Mountain arising from the Sea of Chaos is the social as well as the spiritual Pyramid. As we have seen, the two are inseparable. The Mountain is the mythical abode of the gods, and the Divine Ruler's identification with the gods makes the Mountain at once the center of the kingdom and the celestial throne of the God-King. The powers and laws he gains on the Mountain are, in the eyes of the theocracy, what bring society out of turmoil into a condition of heavenly ordained law and order. The nomadic hunters of the Sensitive Chaos, the self-sufficient farming villages of the Great Round, and the fiercely independent warlike tribes of the Four

Quarters are seen by the theocracy as cruder types of society, the social equivalent of the Sea of Chaos. The state, in contrast, is the Mountain Arising out of the Sea of Chaos. As Frankfort writes, "The Ancient Near East considered kingship the very basis of civilization. Only savages could live without a king. Security, peace, and justice could not prevail without a ruler to champion them."[14]

Thus the Mountain Arising from the Sea of Chaos is at once the ego arising from the Self; logos arising from eros; consciousness arising from unconsciousness; the state arising from pre-state society; the God-King rising above the common masses; the Pyramid archetype arising from previous archetypes; and the architectural pyramid rising above the plains, jungles, deserts, and cities of the world.

The World Mountain of the Shaman

> For in the view of the old Sumerian astronomical observers, the universe was neither flat nor a sphere, but in the form of a great mountain rising in stages from an infinite sea; and it was this glorious world mountain, marked in its stages by the orbits of the circling spheres—the moon, Mercury, Venus and the sun, Mars, Jupiter, and Saturn—that the imposing temple towers were designed to reproduce in local, visible form.[15]

We looked at shamanism in some detail in our discussions of the Sensitive Chaos, the Great Round, and the Four Quarters, and described shamanism as a source of many of the themes of later religions. Now we will look at how shamanism is a source of the theme of the World Mountain, and in seeing its source we will be able to delve deeper into its meaning.

The World Mountain is the prime symbol of the Pyramid archetype, just as the Womb-Cavern was the prime symbol of the Great Round. It is an older mythic image than the Mountain that Arises from the Sea of Chaos, but it is really the same mountain. Its origins reach far back into shamanism, that "archaic technique of ecstasy" as Eliade calls it.

As we saw in the primal cultures of the Sensitive Chaos, a shaman is a man or woman who has achieved mythical powers through an initiatory crisis. Eliade writes, "like any other religious vocation, the shamanic vocation is manifested by a crisis, a temporary derangement of the future shaman's spiritual equilibrium...[causing a] 'dialectic of hierophanies'—the radical separation between profane and sacred and the resultant splitting of the world."[16]

Shamans emerge from their temporary madness with several gifts including "special relations with spirits, ecstatic capacities permitting of magical flight, ascents to the sky, descents to the underworld, mastery over fire, etc."[17] These abilities harken back to themes we saw in earlier chapter: the hunter-gatherers' special relation with spirits, the out-of-body magical flights of the witches, Inanna's descent into the underworld, Isis's and Demeter's initiation by fire, and the mastery over fire sought in Kundalini yoga. According to Eliade, "The mythical origin of fire from the vagina of an old woman ... seems to indicate that the feminine magic is earlier than the masculine sorcery."[18] In Japanese mythology, the goddess Izanami dies giving birth to fire. It may be that most religious ideas have their origins in shamanism, since it seems to be the oldest form of spiritual expression. Some researchers report that during initiation (especially when hallucinogenic plants are ingested), many shamans have horrifying visions and sensations of being flayed and dismembered, and of having their flesh eaten away until they are skeletons. In *Shamanic Voices*, Joan Halifax writes:

> For hunting and gathering peoples, bone, like seed, represents the very source of life. To divest oneself of flesh and be reduced to a skeleton is a process of reentering what Mircea Eliade has called the 'womb of primordial life' in order to be born anew into a mystical condition. Furthermore, bone, like a quartz crystal or seed, is the enduring source from which light and life spring anew, Shamans, like other religious ascetics, divest themselves of flesh reduce their bodies to that mysterious yet durable matter which, like the liquid

crystal of semen, is the fertile source, ever capable of reproducing itself, and, like the sacred quartz crystal, is the clear body, the diamond body, the bone of emanant light.[19]

The divestment of flesh is a divestment of the *persona*—the social personality—and the ego. The death-and-resurrection theme indicates that in the shaman the limited, mortal, individual has died and the great, transpersonal Self has been reborn. In Eliade's view, "It is only this initiatory death and resurrection that consecrates a shaman."[20] The secret of the shamans' mystical powers is that shamans communicate directly with the fabulously rich world of the collective unconscious. Its archetypes come alive in their dreams, visions, and trances. In ecstatic trances, their minds and spirits are said to "leave their bodies" and travel freely beyond space and time through the vast, mysterious realms of the psyche. They thus become the seers, healers, and spiritual guides of their communities.

In shamanic symbolism, the journey to the Self is a journey to the Center of the World where shamans can travel the cosmic axis between the sky, the earth, and the underworld; that is, they can reintegrate pure consciousness (the sky) with the deepest recesses of the collective unconscious (the underworld), and bring the fruits of both back to enrich daily life (the earth). This reintegration is the Union of Opposites through which the Self is reborn. In terms of the creative process, the three planes represent the conscious mind where ideas are formulated (the sky); the deep creative wellspring of archetypes within the Self where meaning is intuitively conceived, (the underworld); and the everyday world where meaningful ideas can be brought to realization (the earth). Like the shaman, the artist must be adept at traveling between these three realms to bring the contents of the collective unconscious into manifestation in the world. Works produced through a dialogue solely between the conscious mind and the everyday world, without confirmation from the Self, tend to be dry, overly rational and pragmatic. They lack that numinous quality of archetypal meaning found both in great art and in shamanistic ritual. They do not produce "esthetic arrest."[21] They are

226 *Spatial Archetypes*

products of the Wasteland—that desiccated existence in which there is no flow of life-giving, fertilizing waters from the wellsprings of the creative unconscious.

The Center of the World—where the connection between the earth, the underworld, and the sky becomes possible—is the Center of the Psyche, the *point existing here and everywhere now and always*. One of the most common shamanic symbols of the Center of the World is the World Tree representing the axis mundi. Eliade describes another: the Cosmic Mountain:

> Another mythical image of the "Center of the World" that makes connection between earth and sky possible is that of the Cosmic Mountain. The Tatars of the Altai imagine [the god] Bai Ulgian in the middle of the sky, seated on a golden mountain. The Abakan Tatars call it "the Iron Mountain"; the Mongols, the Buryat, and the Kalmyk know it under the names of Sumbur, Sumur, or Sumer, which clearly show Indian influence (= Mount Meru). The Mongols and the Kalmyk picture it with three or four stories; the Siberian Tatars, with seven; in his mystical journey the Yakut shaman, too, climbs a mountain with seven stories. Its summit is in the Pole Star, in the "Navel of the Sky." The Buryat say that the Pole Star is fastened to its summit.
>
> In Indian cosmology Mount Meru rises at the "Center of the World" and above it shines the Pole Star. Just as the Indian gods grasped this Cosmic Mountain (= World Axis) and stirred the primordial ocean with it, thus giving birth to the universe, so a Kalmyk myth relates that the gods used Sumer as a stick to stir the ocean, thus creating the sun, moon, and stars. Another Central Asian myth shows the penetration achieved by Indian elements: the Mongolian god Ochirvani (= Indra), taking the form of the eagle Garide (= Garuda), attacked the snake Losun in the primordial ocean, wound it three times around Mount Sumeru, and finally crushed its head.[22]

The World Mountain of the Priest

The shamanic scaling of the Cosmic or World Mountain at the Center of the World to communicate with the Pole Star in the sky—that fixed Center about which all of heaven appears to revolve—is the mythic image that inspired ancient civilizations to build great pyramids. The pyramids manifested the World Mountain in material form, just as the rituals of the God-King and his priests manifested the spiritual flight of the shaman in codified, ceremonial form. This transferred both the World Mountain and the shaman from the realm of the sacred to the realm of human artifice. This "secularization of the sacred" will concern us more as we progress through the remaining archetypes, but according to Joseph Campbell, one of the major turning points occurred during the shift from hunting to agriculture. Using the Indians of North America as examples, Campbell writes:

> Contrasting patterns appear in North America according to whether tribes are hunters or planters. The hunters emphasize in their religious life the individual fast, for the gaining of visions. The boy of twelve or thirteen is left by his father in some lonesome place, with a little fire to keep the beasts away, and there he fasts and prays, four days or more, until some spiritual visitant comes in dream, in human or animal form, to speak to him and give him power. His later career will be determined by this vision; for his familiar may confer the power to cure people, as a shaman, to attract and slaughter animals, or to become a warrior....
>
> Whereas among the planting tribes—the Hopi, Zuni, and other pueblo dwellers—life is organized around the rich and complex ceremonies of their Masked Gods. These are elaborate rites in which the entire community participates, scheduled according to a religious calendar, and conducted by societies of trained priests.[23]

Campbell contrasts the priest and the shaman, saying that the priest is an initiated representative of an organized religion,

228 *Spatial Archetypes*

while the shaman is one who has had a personal crisis that has lead to their own powers. Illuminating the actual historical tension between shamans and priests, Campbell retells a myth of how the Hactcin, the Apache equivalent of the pueblo-dwellers' Masked Gods, managed to bring the unruly, individualistic shamans into conformance with their social order by upstaging the shaman's magic and building the World Mountain. The same tension, he says, occurred in other parts of the world and was dramatized in the mythic theme of the gods against the titans:

> The situation in Arizona and New Mexico at the period of the discovery of America was, culturally, much like that which must have prevailed in the Near and Middle East and in Europe from the fourth to the second millennium B.C., when the rigid patterns proper to an orderly settlement were being imposed on peoples used to the freedom and vicissitudes of the hunt. And if we turn our eyes to the mythologies of the Hindus, Persians, Greeks, Celts, and Germans, we immediately recognize, in the well-known, oft-recited tales of the conquest of the titans by the gods, analogies to this legend of the subjugation of the shamans by the Hactcin. The titans, dwarfs, and giants are represented as the powers of an earlier mythological age—crude and loutish, egoistic and lawless, in contrast to the comely gods, whose reign of heavenly order harmoniously governs the worlds of nature and man. The giants were overthrown, pinned beneath mountains, exiled to the rugged regions at the bounds of the earth, and as long as the power of the gods can keep them there the people, the animals, the birds, and all living things will know the blessings of a world ruled by law.[24]

In Europe, the period citied by Campbell—the fourth to the second millennium B.C.—witnessed the transition from the Neolithic farming communities of the Great Round to the earliest heroic Four Quarters cultures. In the Near East, the same era saw the rise of theocratic nation and city-states, the laying down of the first laws, and the building of the pyramids of Egypt and the *ziggurats* of Mesopotamia.

Thus, what had been the mystical experience of a few individuals the earlier archetypes, became institutionalized as priests replaced shamans under the Pyramid archetype. Through co-opting the authentic, individual, spiritual vision of the shaman, the theocracy tapped the great wellspring of wisdom, which had originated in the Sensitive Chaos, coursed through the Great Round, and branched into the tributaries of the Four Quarters like the four rivers of Eden.

However, the king and his priests saw the waters of wisdom originating not from underground springs, that is, from the unconscious, but from the top of the World Mountain. Pure consciousness is the source of the logos principle, just as actual mountains are the source of the great drainage systems that begin as snow and ice and turn into mountain streams producing rivers to the sea. The flow runs not from bottom up, but from the top down—from mountain peak to valley below.

This mythical feat of hydraulic engineering rechanneled the source of wisdom from the core of the earth, by then defined as the limited realm of the feminine, to the peak of the heaven-reaching mountain, by then considered the infinite realm of the masculine. In so doing, it furthered the transformation of the mythical World Mountain, once the province of the Great Goddess and the shaman, into the Pyramidal model of the state.

The World Mountain as Pyramid retains the all-important spiritual axis between sky, earth, and underworld. However, this axis is now traveled not by the shaman but by the king, and not by spiritual inspiration but by right of status. Whereas the World Mountain was primarily a symbol of the Self to the shaman, to the God-King the Pyramid is a symbol of social and cosmic order. As an image of the World Mountain, the Pyramid is a three-dimensional *mandala* in which the horizontal coordinates of the Four Quarters are fleshed out by the vertical hierarchy of state, priesthood, and God-King.

Mount Meru and the Mayan *Imago Mundi*

The World Mountain best described in ancient literature—in the Brahmanas, Puranas, and the *Mahabharata* of India—is Mount Meru. It is sacred to Hindus, Jains, and Buddhists, and, as Mount Sumeru, was revered by numerous Four Quarters and Pyramid cultures in the Near East including the Sumerians, who are named for the mountain. Mount Sumeru is said to be located in the highlands of the Himalayas (Tibet's Mount Kailash is one candidate), but its significance is not its geographical reality but its fabulous mythic image.

The mythic Mount Meru is the Indian Mount Olympus. It rises from the Center of the World, conceived of as an island continent called Jumbu-dvipa (jambu = "rose apple tree," dvipa = "island"). Symbolically, jambu-dvipa is India, and, like King Arthur's Avalon, it is the Island of the Golden Apples. This island of immortality, on which Mount Meru rises, is the central continent of seven concentrically ringed continents separated by seven seas made of salt-water, sugar-cane juice, wine, clarified butter, curds, milk, and fresh water—all symbols of fertility.[25] The enormous Rose Apple tree, from which *Jumbu-dvipu* derives its name, rises from Mount Meru as the Tree of Life, the axis mundi "visible like a standard to the whole continent." Monier-Williams describes Mount Meru in his *Sanskrit-English Dictionary*:

> ... all the planets revolve around it and it is compared to the cup or seed-vessel of a lotus, the leaves of which are formed by the different Dvipas [continents]; the river Ganges falls from heaven on its summit, and flows thence to the surrounding world in four streams; the regents of the four quarters of the compass occupy the corresponding faces of the mountain, the whole of which consists of gold and gems; its summit is the residence of Brahma, and a place of meeting for the gods...[26]

Mount Meru was sometimes identified with the human body. Campbell describes the Jain image:

> ... a colossal human form, usually female, with the earth plane at the level of the waist; seven halls beneath, in the pelvic cavity, legs and feet, stratified as in Dante's vision; fourteen celestial stories above, in the chest cavity and shoulders, neck and head; while soaring above in the shape of an umbrella of luminous white gold 14,230,250 yoganas in circumference, 8 yoganas thick at the center and tapering to the tenuity of a gnat's wing at the edge, is a place of unalloyed perfection called 'Slightly Tilted' (*isat-praghbara*), to which the released soul ascends when the last least taint of a trace even of heavenly attachment has been burned away through the practice of yoga.[27]

At the waist of this cosmic being are arrayed the seven continents and seas surrounding Mount Meru. In Tantric tradition, the axis of Mount Meru is the "Merudanda" or the *susumana* in the body, the channel in the spinal column in which Kundalini rises through the *chakras*. Philip Rawson notes that "the possible Universe each man knows is a flat 'circle' radiating from his own axial center."[28]

Hindu and Jain temples symbolize Mount Meru as well as the human body (as do Buddhist stupas, as we will see later). The axis rises from the center of the temple's mandala plan, through the lingum in the sanctuary and the lingum tower, becoming visible in the spire.

> The spire above the main icon, through both of which the axis passes, represents Mount Meru; around its lower slopes the 'heaven hands' filled with sculpture are slung like garlands. Away from its plinth stretches the earth, with its continents, rivers and seas—which are in this case "actual" and convincing instead of purely notational...[29]

Indian civilization has perhaps the most articulated vision of the World Mountain, but the essential symbolic meanings of Mount Meru—Center of the World, place of immortality, root of the axis mundi and the Tree of Life, focal point of the celestial and social hierarchy, meeting place of the gods, and still center of the whirling universe—have been attributed to other World Mountains in other cultures.

At the opposite side of the world, the Mayan *imago mundi* (World Image) pictured heaven as having thirteen layers called *taz*, which also means layers of blankets, connecting the concept of heaven to weaving.[30] These layers "were arranged as six steps ascending from the eastern horizon to the seventh, the zenith, whence six more steps led down to the western horizon."[31] Similarly, the nine layers of the underworld were arranged in five steps: four descending, the bottom, and four ascending. Thus, in keeping with the true image of the Pyramid archetype, the heavens formed an upward-pointing pyramid; the underworld, a downward-pointing one.

An eternal war raged between the *Bolon ti Ku*, the nine Lords of the Underworld, and the *Oxlahun ti Ku*, the Thirteen Gods of Heaven. The *Bolon ti Ku*, as the Lords of Death, were darkness and evil incarnate. Curiously, the most common number of levels in a Mayan pyramid is nine, not thirteen, suggesting that the Maya wished their pyramids to represent the underworld rather than the heavens.[32]

Through the whole of the layered Mayan cosmos from the nadir of the underworld to the zenith in heaven ran a giant *ceiba*, the sacred tree of the Maya. The spirits of the dead traveled up its roots, trunk, and branches from the underworld to the heavens. The Center of the World Mountain— the World Axis embodied in the *ceiba* tree—was considered the fifth direction and given the color green. Deriving from an earlier Four Quarters worldview in Mayan history, the schema also assigned to each of the four cardinal directions a ceiba tree, deity, rain god called *chac*, sky-supporter called *bacab*, previous world age, season, and color.[33]

The physical representation of this cosmology can still be seen in Maya ruins. For instance, all the major buildings at Uxmal and other Puuc sites in the Yucatan have tiers of *chac* masks at each of their four corners, once painted the colors of the four directions. The *chacs* gaze out over the flat, Yucatan horizon to the infinite reaches of the Four Quarters. As rain deities, the *chacs* had the same power as the Indo-European Storm and Thunder Gods. Anyone who has suffered a wet season thunderstorm in the tropics, with its sudden, ear-splitting thunder, violent lightning, and torrential rains, knows the power these spirits wielded.

To many Maya today, the mountains, and particularly mountain caves and springs, are the homes of the gods and goddesses. The Dresden Codex (the finest of the four remaining pre-Conquest Mayan books) shows, in addition to the four directional *chacs*, a fifth *chac* "seated in a sort of cave or underground chamber with the glyphic label *yolcab*, 'in the heart of the earth.'"[34] One of the deities who played a major role in the Maya creation myth recorded in the post-Conquest *Chilam Balam of Chumayel* is "Heart of Heaven."[35] It may be that at the Center of the World a transcendent equilibrium is reached: Heart of Earth and Heart of Heaven bring the dualistic poles of existence into balance.[36] Although the Maya worldview was extremely dualistic, it displayed a great desire to transcend dualism. For instance, all the major Mayan deities were both animal and human, male and female, good and evil, and each had aspects of all four World Directions.[37]

Of course, the Maya most clearly manifested their vision of the cosmos in the temple pyramids rising majestically above their cities and ceremonial centers, where the priests and kings conducted hierophantic rituals at certain times of the year. Some, like the Toltec-influenced Pyramid of Kukulcan (the so-called "Castillo") at Chichen Itza, reached highly refined degrees of calendric and astronomical design. Its terraces, niches, and steps encode calendrical information. For example, the 365 steps (91 on each of four sides plus the platform at the top) represent the 365 days of the solar year, and the 52 niches on each side correlate with the 52 year Mesoamerican century when the 365 day agricultural calendar and the 260 day sacred calendar coincided.

Kukulcan, to whom the pyramid is dedicated, is the Mayan Quetzalcoatl, the Feathered-Serpent revered throughout Mesoamerica. Originally a heroic, dying-and-resurrecting, culture-bringing, bearded, white Lord of the Four Quarters, Quetzalcoatl/Kukulcan was born of a virgin and was associated with a cross. As the priest-king of legendary Tollan, he lived in a "marvelous temple-palace comprised of four radiant apartments:

that at the East was yellow with gold; the South, white with shell and pearls; the West, blue with turquoise and jade; and the North, red with bloodstone. Moreover, the building was set above a majestic river that passed directly through Tollan, so that the godly king might descend at midnight to bathe in its pure waters...."[38]

Quetzalcoatl/Kukulcan came to represent kingship in Mesoamerica, and the Toltec kings, among others, used his name as their title. As the Feathered-Bird-Serpent, he personifies the dual nature of the God-King as ego-Self. The serpent embodies the primal energies of the earth and the subtle energies of the body; the bird connotes the transmutation of those energies into spirit. The most widespread symbol of Kundalini energy is a pair of intertwined serpents surmounted by a bird, as shown in the caduceus of Mercury. Quetzalcoatl/Kukulcan is also the planet Venus, and in this role he embodies another dualism characteristic of the Four Quarters and the Pyramid archetypes: as the Morning Star, he is the Lord of Life; as the Evening Star, the Lord of Death. During the periods when Venus is invisible, Quetzalcoatl descends into the Underworld to engage in ordeals and negotiations on behalf of life above.[39]

The Pyramid of Kukulcan at Chichen Itza does more than model the Mesoamerican calendars, as remarkable as this is. The whole pyramid is sited and designed to produce a cosmic hierophany. At the equinoxes, the setting sun casts a shadow from the nine terraces adjacent to the northern stairway, forming a line with seven angular undulations. This pattern resembles both a serpent descending the stair and the skin pattern of the diamond-backed rattlesnake, the most common indigenous serpent in pre-Columbian art and a symbol of time.[40] The northern stairway, and only the northern stairway, has a base ornamented with the huge Feathered-Serpent heads of Kukulcan. Thus, at the equinoxes, Kukulcan descends the pyramid and enters the land, and heads toward the cenote not far from the pyramid.

The *cenote*, a natural limestone sinkhole about sixty-five feet across and smoothly rounded out by Mayan hands, is the negative model of the pyramid's positive form. Conversely, the pyramid is the positive inversion of cenote's negative form. This is consistent with the fact that the major Mayan pyramids, including the Pyramid of Kukulcan, have the same number of levels as the underworld. There are two cenotes at Chichen Itza. One, in the old part of the city, was used for drinking water. The cenate near Kukulcan's pyramid was reserved as a sacred well of sacrifice into which the Maya threw humans as well as gold and precious objects.

The *cenote* was the local home of *chac*, the rain god who, like Kukulcan, had serpentine features. The Maya believed that chac draws water from the *cenote* up into the heavens where it evaporates, becomes clouds, and eventually falls as rain. They thought also that humans thrown into the well did not die, but instead were able to enter *chac's* world and communicate with him as an advocate of the human community.

The hierophany of Kukulcan's descent from the pyramid is especially important at the spring equinox in late March when it announces the beginning of the agricultural year—time for farmers to burn their fields and prepare for the year's planting; time for Kukulcan to ask chac to prepare the rains that by May end the dry season. Thus the pyramid invokes and dramatizes the yearly return to the land of chac's fertilizing rains and Kukulcan's serpentine Telluric currents. At the height of Mayan civilization, this important rite was controlled by the theocracy, who took credit for the workings of nature. Today, thousands of Mayan farmers, who still use the old slash-and-burn agricultural techniques, come to the pyramid to witness the equinoctial spectacle, now no longer staged by a theocratic elite but by the collaboration of nature and architecture.

On the other side of the world, in Tibet near the home of Mount Meru, an ancient pre-Buddhist Bon myth of creation pictures heaven as having thirteen layers, just as in the Mayan vision. The myth is rich with archetypal Pyramid imagery, which puts in context many of the motifs we have been exploring.

In the beginning the great god Cha, The All-Knowing One, created the universe out of the five elements. He created the heaven with its thirteen ascending layers and the earth with its thirteen descending layers. Inside the domes of heaven and earth there emerged light and darkness, representing positive and negative principles. From the interaction between the two emerged golden and turquoise flowers. From the union of the two was born a son, The Immaculate Lord of the Universe, and a daughter, The Excellent Life. These were the heavenly ancestors of the gods who were believed to be the protectors of the four continents and also of the first king, Nyatre Tsanpc, the protector of the "Land of the Snowy Mountains."[41]

The Ben-Stone: The Primeval Hillock Arises

The pyramid inscription at the beginning of this chapter captures the meaning of all Egyptian pyramids. Carved inside the pyramids of Mer-ne-Re and Pepi II (Nefer-ka-Re) in the 24th century B.C. during Egypt's Sixth Dynasty, the text served "... in the dedication ritual of a royal pyramid by recalling the first creation, when the god Atum of Heliopolis was on a primeval hillock arising out of the waters of chaos and there brought the first gods into being. In like manner, the god is now asked to bless the rising pyramid, an analogue of the hillock."[41]

Perhaps more clearly than any other Pyramid civilization, early dynastic Egypt illustrates the equation: Mountain = ego = logos = consciousness = state = God-King = Pyramid. All arise virtually simultaneously (that is, within two or three hundred years of each other) in ancient Egypt during and shortly after the founding of the First Dynasty. The "Primeval Hillock" is the archetypal Mountain Arising from the Sea of Chaos, symbolized by a sacred rock called the ben-stone and its ben-bird, the creator god Atum. The ego is personified by the "King" half of the God-King or Pharaoh (the title means "Great House"). From the first Pharaoh Menes on, the king is commonly rendered much larger than ordinary humans in commemorative art.

The patron god of the First Dynasty, Ptah, "conceives the elements of the universe with his mind ('heart') and brings them into being by his commanding speech ('tongue'). Thus at the beginning of Egyptian history, there was an approach to the Logos Doctrine."[43] The rise of consciousness is symbolized by the rising of the Primeval Hillock, the bringing into existence of the first theistic gods, Ptah's creation by the *word*, and a series of Unions of Opposites that we will learn more of later. The formation of the state and the office of divine kingship (Pharaoh) coincided with the founding of the First Dynasty, and the building of pyramids began not long afterwards in the Third Dynasty.

The pyramid of Nefer-ka-Re and all the major Egyptian pyramids were built during what is known as Egypt's Old Kingdom, which spanned dynasties III through VI and lasted from about 2665 to 2155 B.C.[44] The period immediately preceding the Old Kingdom (called the Archaic, Thinite, Predynastic, or Early Dynastic Period, which encompassed the first two dynasties) saw the unification of Egypt into a state, the establishment of dynastic succession, the founding of the capital at Memphis, and the development of proto-pyramidal tumuli and *mastaba* tombs. Compared with other ancient civilizations, Egypt moved relatively quickly from the Great Round, through the Four Quarters, to the Pyramid archetype.

In the Nile Valley, people had lived by hunting and gathering for countless millennia until between 6000 and 4000 B.C. By that time, farmers were growing wheat and barley, making pottery, burying their dead in the kind of egalitarian grave sites typical of the Neolithic era, making effigies of the Goddess, and living in villages like Merimbe in the Nile Delta, which had a cluster of oval semi-subterranean pit-houses with mud and stick roofs. Thus by about 4000 B.C., the ancient Egyptians had developed essentially the same way of life under the Great Round archetype that the pit-house-dwelling ancestors of the Anasazi in the American Southwest enjoyed about 5000 years later.

By 3400 B.C. a predynastic culture known as the Gerzean developed, which had copper metallurgy, budding social classes, cylinder seals, mud-brick architecture, large towns with ceremonial public buildings, tombs displaying status and rank, the beginnings of hieroglyphic writing, and independent land divisions or chieftainships. Gerzean culture, in other words, displayed the typical features of the Four Quarter's hierarchical chieftainships.

Although scholars debate whether Pharaonic Egypt was a native development or the result of foreign influences from the Near East, the Eastern Mediterranean, or other parts of Africa, there is agreement that the unification of Upper and Lower Egypt[45] into a nation state under a Divine Ruler occurred by about 3100

238 Spatial Archetypes

B.C. under King Narmer, who was probably the legendary first Pharaoh Menes.

The Narmer Palette and The Egyptian Union of Opposites

The unification of Upper and Lower Egypt provides an illuminating example of the process by which a powerful chieftain forms a nation by conquering and welding together the chieftainships of the Four Quarters. In Kingship and the Gods, Henri Frankfort likens predynastic Egypt to parts of modern Africa where several villages are united by a common chief into a loose confederation that can act as a single community.[46] According to Frankfort, Menes had become a "strong man" who had organized just such an alliance in Upper Egypt. After extended fighting by Menes and his predecessors, Menes ultimately won over "Scorpion," the opposing Upper Egyptian leader. Presumably Menes had by then built up enough military strength to conquer Lower Egypt as well.

The famous Narmer Palette dating from the First Dynasty shows his victory. On one side of the palette, Narmer (Menes),[47] wearing the crown of Upper Egypt, is clubbing his fallen adversary "Scorpion" whom he has seized by the hair. The other side features two mythical beasts with necks entwined symbolizing the unification of Upper and Lower Egypt, and a scene in which Narmer, wearing the crown of Lower Egypt, reviews the piled-up, beheaded corpses of his enemies. On both sides of the Palette, Narmer is shown substantially larger than all the other figures; even his prime adversary is smaller. Thus Narmer is a personification of the emerging ego. Also, both sides are crowned by heads of the predynastic cow-goddess Hathor, as if she were being invoked to witness and sanction the new social order commemorated by the Palette.

Mene's victory marked a turning point in Egyptian history. The conquest and unification of Upper and Lower Egypt was seen not as the act of a chieftain who happened to be more successful than others, but, in Frankfort's words, "as the revelation of a predestined order." Realizing that the foundation both of dynastic rule and of the nation state required a new mythos if the new institutions were to endure, Menes articulated a transcendent ideal of kingship that was to last for nearly three thousand years. At its core was the concept of the dual monarchy—the kingships of Upper and Lower Egypt united in one ruler. In one stroke, this brought into equilibrium the longstanding dualism in Egyptian thought that divided the Nile Valley into "the two lands," the earth into "north and south," and the universe into "heaven and earth." Menes's kingship was glorified not so much because Menes had united two pre-existing nation states—as we have seen, Upper and Lower Egypt were not nations but loose confederacies—but because, as all Divine Rulers in the Pyramid Age would claim to do, *he had united heaven und earth*. This archetypal Union of Opposites transcended mere military conquest and political ingenuity, making Menes and all kings after him not only the central, most powerful force in the nation, but also masters of the *axis mundi*.

So central was the concept of dual monarchy to Egyptian cohesion that "Whenever in later times the central power collapsed and local centers assumed autonomy, this return to predynastic conditions was viewed not as a departure from a political norm but as a fall from grace."[48] Mene's concept of kingship healed and reunited Egypt during the major crises in its long history, such as the anarchic period preceding the Twelfth Dynasty and the Hyksos and Ethiopian invasions in the Eighteenth and Twenty-Fifth Dynasties.[49]

Mythology Rewritten: The Memphite Theology

Inspired, we might say, by the Pyramid archetype, Menes and his priests consciously defined the new spiritual entities of kingship, dynasty, and state in the Memphite Theology. Among its multiple functions, the Theology reworked the predynastic tribal goddesses and gods, turning them into aspects or creations of the Memphite god Ptah. Ptah was credited, for instance, with creating Atum, the formerly autonomous creator god of Lower Egypt. Moreover, the Theology brought Horus, as the god of kingship, into a pivotal position that subtly altered the relationships among the nine gods of Lower Egypt's Heliopolitan Ennead, including Isis and Osiris.[50]

Identifying the ruler with Horus rendered him divine, and, although the Theology at first apportioned the two lands equally to Horus and Seth, it soon gave Horus dominion over both saying "the two Great Sorceresses grew upon his head."[51] This referred to two important predynastic goddesses: the vulture goddess Nekhbet of Upper Egypt and the cobra goddess Wadjet (or Buto) of Lower Egypt. They "grew upon his head" in the form of the Red and White crowns of the two lands, and as the vulture and *uraeus* serpent that empowered the Pharaonic crown throughout Egyptian history. The *Theology* thus absorbed the goddesses of the Great Round as symbols of the highest spiritual and sovereign powers of the king.

By complicated, ingenious means that drew on the logos principle's reverence for names, the *Theology* also managed to shift the "Navel of the World" to the newly founded capital at Memphis at the base of the Nile Delta. The city's name means "White Wall," a transference of color symbolism from Menes's home in Upper Egypt. The *Theology* further named Memphis as the "House of Ptah" where Horus and Seth were united, making it the "'Balance of the Two Lands,' in which Upper and Lower Egypt have been weighed."[52] Moreover, the reference to a balance scale and the measurement of weight poetically evoked an equilibrium achieved through the logos principle.

The authors of the *Theology* named Memphis also as the burial place of Osiris, a pure mythic invention but an effective one. Whereas the living king embodied the youthful sun-god Horus, the deceased kings became his father Osiris, the Dying-and-Resurrecting God of the Underworld. But Osiris was also the old vegetation god whose death, dismemberment, and resurrection, and his consequent fertilization of Isis (who bore Horus from the union) was symbolic of the life cycle of the seed so vital to agrarian peoples. By naming Memphis as his burial place, the *Theology* cleverly exploited the dual aspects of Osiris: the city was both the seat of the dynasty—since kingship was passed from Osiris to Horus, that is, from deceased rulers to their offspring—and the "granary" of the land, the storehouse of the seed, "the center from which the vitalizing forces radiated."[53]

These mythic devices are typical of how the early theocracy of the Pyramid Age cements its rule in every high civilization. We can trace the same process in Mesopotamia, India, China, Japan, Peru, Mexico, Greece, and Europe.

The Egyptian Pyramid

As might be expected, the first Egyptian pyramid arose near Memphis at Sakkara, a ceremonial and mortuary complex built to emulate the "white walls" of the capital. The stepped pyramid at Sakkara was built by King Zoser, the first Pharaoh of the Third Dynasty. By the Third Dynasty, the dust had settled enough from the work of establishing the nation state that monumental architecture could begin to be built. Zoser's architect, Imhotep, the first named individual architect in history, was later revered as a god of medicine, suggesting that at one time architecture and healing were intimately related.[54]

At Sakkara, Zoser's stepped pyramid appeared suddenly without prototypes and with little experimentation. Within one hundred years Egyptian builders had gone from making mud-brick mastaba tombs to erecting giant pyramids using thirty-ton boulders. Zoser's pyramid was part of a thirty-five acre complex housing facilities for his Heb Sed Festival as well as his mortuary structures. The Heb Sed Festival was a periodic event much like a twenty-five year Royal jubilee, during which the Pharaoh demonstrated his physical fitness by running a symbolically-charged race. A successful ruler was rewarded with re-coronation by the goddesses of Upper and Lower Egypt.[55] Concern with vitality both in life and in the afterlife fused at Sakkara to make an eloquent statement of the nature of Egyptian kingship, setting the pattern for all the pyramids in the remaining few centuries of the Old Kingdom.

From Zoser's pyramid to those of Sneferu, and finally to the Great Pyramid of Cheops at Giza, the main discernible development was the increasing abstraction and height of the pyramid's form. Zoser's was stepped and contained earlier experimental structures modeled on the mastaba. Sneferu's first one was bent, and near it he later built the first true planar pyramid. Of Sneferu's pyramids, Sigfried Giedion writes:

> Here in the desert the earth appears as though seen from astronomical heights: intangible, immaterial. Here there is nothing else. The two pyramids resting upon an endless plain confront only the cosmos. The heavens arch over them like the figure of the goddess Nut. Everything earthly has fallen away and man grasps what it means to stand before eternity.[56]

Rising to a height of over 480 feet, the Great Pyramid of Cheops at Giza was taller and steeper than either Zoser's or Sneferu's, expressing greater attenuation along the *axis mundi*. Its external form was conceived whole without change or experimentation, and some researchers assert that it embodies an astounding synthesis of mathematical, geodetic, and astronomical measurements. The only changes during the building process occurred on the inside, in the location of the mortuary chamber, and these may be of some significance. The first design placed the chamber deep in the earth under the center of the pyramid. This pit seems never to have been used. A second design extended the entrance passage up and then horizontally to the so-called "Queen's Chamber" located higher in the heart of the pyramid. The final chamber, the so-called "King's Chamber" in which the empty sarcophagus of Cheops was found, was located higher still, 130 feet off the ground at the end of the Grand Gallery.

Though they may not have been intended as such, the three chambers record a kind of passage from the Womb Cavern of the Great Round (the pit deep in the earth) to the Pyramid archetype, (the geometrically precise, elevated chamber). If we assume that these spaces were not designed for different functions, but represent changes of mind as to the appropriate location for the same function (for instance, the king's burial or the housing of a sacred standard of measure, as has been suggested), then we can draw an interesting conclusion: the movement upward of the "holy of holies"—the mortuary chamber—vividly shows an increasing urge toward the sky and away from the earth. This architecturally illustrates the ego separating from the Self. The metaphysical center of gravity was shifting away from the body toward the macrocosmic head, toward the logos principle. In most cultures the logos principle is associated with the Sky Father, but in Egypt the sky was the goddess Nut. However, the heavenly principle to which the pyramid aspired was not so much Nut as the sun god Re, an aspiration we will later see in detail.

The Ka

The Egyptian pyramid was, above all, the burial place of the immortal king. This seems contradictory: if the king is dead and buried, how can he be immortal? Here the dualistic Egyptian mind again comes into play. What was buried was the king's mortal body, but he possessed also a vital force called the "*ka*." As the apex of the social and spiritual Pyramid, the king received his *ka* directly from the gods and goddesses. The *ka* of his subjects, if indeed they had *ka*, was channeled through the king—another facet of the king's role as negotiator of the axis mundi and the reason that proof of his vitality was so important. The health and vitality of his subjects, the land, the livestock, and the entire nation depended upon the vigor of his *ka*. (This was generally true in all Pyramid civilizations, although the "vital force" of the God-King was symbolized in different ways.)

After the mortal death of the king's body, elaborate mortuary rituals insured the preservation and proper treatment of the *ka*, which lived on in the pyramid complex, its home in perpetuity. The *ka* had free roam, and, as at Sakkara, could wander in and out through specially designed, always-open *ka* doors. At rest, the *ka* resided not in the mummy, but in the stone *ka* statue of the king. Since the *ka* could reside only in stone, this material was reserved exclusively for sacred structures.[57]

The concept of the ka has been traced at least as far back as the First Dynasty, though it must certainly have developed from an earlier animistic sensibility. But the *ka* in dynastic Egypt was an inspired theocratic tool that made every subject dependent upon the king for his or her very life force. Through the *ka*, the king became the divine Father whose power to bestow spiritual life superseded the powers of the earth and the mother to bestow life itself. The alleged need for a second spiritual birth is central to masculine initiations, religions, and cultures. In the Pyramid Age, the "real" birth—the one claimed to make people fully human—is through the Father, the mediator between Heaven and Earth. In Egypt, the *ka* was the medium through which the second birth was effected, even after the king's death! It was the *ka*, and not the living or the dead, that the Egyptian pyramids immortalized.

Fire, the Feminine, and the Sun

Egypt retained matrilineal inheritance throughout most or all of its period of high civilization, sometimes in combination with patrilineal descent in a complicated dual system that divided various ranks and privileges between the two lineages. As we have seen, Egypt also kept goddesses in highly visible and powerful positions in its pantheon. Possibly the longevity of ancient Egyptian civilization, as well as its subtlety and greatness, owed something to its relatively open acceptance—for a Pyramid culture—of the feminine principle. Certainly Egypt offers enough mystical lore about geometry, numerology, measurement, and astronomy to delight enthusiasts of the masculine principle's crystalline logos sensibility. But to focus solely on that aspect of Egyptian thought—as most Egyptophiles do—is to miss the rich, fertilizing, female infusion in Egyptian civilization.

Even Narmer's successful consolidation of Upper and Lower Egypt depended on a woman named Neith-hotep, shown on the Narmer "wedding" Macehead found among the rich tomb treasures at Hierakonpolis. Referring to Walter B. Emery's book *Archaic Egypt*, Michael Hoffman describes Neith-hotep's image on the macehead: "This artifact depicts an important personage, apparently from the north, being received by Narmer, who wears the crown of Lower Egypt. Emery thinks that the figure is a woman, that the woman is Neith-hotep, and 'that the conqueror of the North attempted to legitimize his position by taking the Northern princess as his consort.'"[58]

This "wedding" may be simply another example of using marriage as a strategy of statecraft to cement an advantageous political alliance, as Hoffman asserts, comparing Neith-hotep to Isabella of Castile and Leon. However, in view of the cultural and historical context of the marriage—at the critical transition from the Great Round and brief Four Quarters periods in Egypt to the period expressive of the Pyramid—it is likely that Neith-hotep was much more powerful in her own right than Isabella and similar European princesses.

Many of the most enduring forces in Egypt's spiritual life are derived from its Goddess-centered Great Round culture. For instance, the same predynastic cow-goddess Hathor who reigns over the Narmer Palette made around 3100 B.C., reigns over her own grand temple at Dendura. Hathor's horns are Egypt's version of the archetypal Horns of Consecration, whose meaning we will explore. The persistence throughout Egyptian civilization of the Pharaoh's Coronation by the Goddesses of the Two Lands testifies to the continuing importance of feminine sanction, whether human or divine.

In predynastic times, before Menes founded Memphis, the spiritual capital of Lower Egypt was the city of Pe, or Buto, the Greek name by which it is more commonly known. The tutelary deity of Pe-Buto was the cobra goddess Wadjet (called also Ua Zit and Buto, among other names). Her holy city of Pe was one of those sacred places suffused with extraordinary forces of nature where life flourishes with special abundance and power. A pyramid text says that a Pharaoh, King Teti, will even survive death because he is buried at Pe. The opening lines cite Pe as a source of the ka's:

> Ka's are in Pe; Ka's were always in Pe; Ka's will be in Pe;
> and Tetrs ka is in Pe.
> Red like a flame, alive like the beetle-gods.[59]

The comparison of Teti's ka with the red flame and with the beetle-god (Scarab) of the rising sun invokes the two most intensely alive phenomena in the hot, desert country of Egypt: fire and the sun. Both of these, says Frankfort, were aspects of Pe and Wadjet. Pe was the city of the Red Crown symbolizing flame and sunrise, and flame was a common epithet for the goddess Wadjet,

246 *Spatial Archetypes*

who was also called the "eye of the sun."

Another text, enumerating the various forces that protect the Pharaoh Unas, refers to Wadjet as the uraeus serpent in the Pharaonic crown:

> The Ka's of Unas are behind him;
> His Hemsut [female ka's] are under his feet;
> His Gods are over him;
> His uraeus-serpents are over his head.
> The leading snake of Unas is at his forehead, she
> Who perceives the soul ...
> She who excells in force of fire.[60]

The cobra goddess Wadjet as "She who excels in force of fire" is none other than the Egyptian equivalent of Kundalini. Attributed to her are fire, the color red, the perception of the soul, the all-knowing "eye of the sun," and the sacred place Pe wherein both the vital force *ka* and immortality are obtained. Her presence as the *ureaus* serpent in the Pharaonic crown signifies that the Pharaoh's Kundalini energy has risen to the *ajna* chakra in the forehead, that is, to the "third eye" that transcends duality. As the "eye of the sun," the eye-goddess Wadjet is also the original "Eye of Horus" (recalling the Great Goddess's mystical vision and the subsequent masculinization of her powers). Horus and the reigning Pharoah are one, the king being the bodily incarnation of the god. "*Inu*," the Red Crown of Lower Egypt with its uraeus serpent, is not just a symbol of kingship or of the goddess, *it is the goddess*. Like Nekhbet, the vulture goddess in the White Crown of Upper Egypt, and Isis as the royal throne, she personifies sovereignty.

Like all other goddesses, Wadjet was seen mythically as the king's mother; he issued forth from her. In the Pharaoh's Coronation ritual, the two crowns were placed in the dual shrines to Nekhbet and Wadjet. Pyramid texts describe the king's assumption of the crown of Lower Egypt, which constituted both a rebirth of kingly power and a rebirth of the goddess. In this rite, the king recited a hymn invoking the power of the crown:

O Red Crown, O Inu, O Great One,
O Magician, O Fiery Snake!
Let there be terror of me like the terror of thee.
Let there be fear of me like the fear of thee.
Let there be awe of me like the awe of thee.
Let there be love of me like the love of thee.
Let me rule, a leader of the living.
Let me be powerful, a leader of spirits.
Let my blade be firm against my enemies.[61]

The terrible fiery power that the king seeks from the Snake Magician Wadjet is the same terrible fiery power that nearly consumed Gopi Krishna and the infant boys nursed by Isis and Demeter. It is the fiery breath of the Dragon, the raw energy of the Goddess, the force channeled into enlightenment in the original *hieros gamos*. Now, under the Pyramid archetype, that force supports and defines kingship. We can see in this an example of how the potent energy of a former archetypal era can be transformed and rechanneled to nourish the Zeitgeist of a later era. Diverting this awesome energy from its original course undoubtedly diminishes its power, but some flows nonetheless into the altered purpose. The pyramids of Egypt grew out of barren desert, watered by the underground streams of the Great Round. They nursed the monuments on the rich archetypal symbolism of the ka, the sun, Kundalini, the Horns of Consecration, the World Mountain, and the Goddess.

The Horns of Consecration: Gateway to the Great Mystery

The Egyptian hieroglyph for "*ka*" is a pair of upraised arms, which is also how the *ka* is most commonly shown in sculptures and paintings. The raised arms signify the life-bestowing power of the *ka* as "vital force," like the force that emanates from healers' hands. An early prototype of the upraised arms of the *ka* appears in a predynastic Egyptian goddess who lifts her arms in a joyful, lyrical gesture. Later, Minoan goddesses (or priestesses) make exactly the same gesture, which is echoed in miniature

Horns of Consecration upon their heads. These Horns, in turn, frame a small model of a mountain in the headdress, just as the Horns of Consecration at Knossos on Crete frame distant horned mountains containing cave sanctuaries of the Goddess.[62]

The Horns of Consecration is an archetypal motif found in all eras. The idea of Horns of Power goes all the way back to the Paleolithic "Hall of Bulls" at Lascaux in France. As a symbol of the bull as son/lover of the Goddess, they appear in Çatal Hüyük in Anatolia as early as the sixth millennium B.C. The sacred bull or cow with its Horns of Consecration animates Malta's Tarxien temple, sanctuaries in Beycesultan in Anatolia, prehistoric cave paintings in Tassili N-Ajjer in Algeria, Neolithic sculpture from Great Zimbabwe, and Mesopotamian and Indus Valley seals. The Indus Valley seals are the earliest sign of the reverence for cows and bulls that flourishes in India to this day. Few regions lacked the Horns of Consecration symbol, the most notable being the New World, which had no cattle until the arrival of the Spaniards.

In *The Gate of Horn*, Gertrude Rachel Levy analyzes the ties between the mysteries of the Great Goddess and the cave-sanctuary, the bull, and the Horns of Consecration. Throughout the book, she demonstrates the essential meaning of the Horns as the Gate to that ineffable mystery that is only reduced by such terms as "supreme consciousness," "Paradise," "bliss," and "immortality." In a similar vein, Joseph Campbell sees the Horns as symbols of the eternal dualities that must be transcended—literally passed through—to achieve wholeness and enlightenment. They are like Scylla and Charybdis in the Odyssey, the Clashing Rocks that threaten Jason, the outer prongs of Shiva's and Poseidon's tridents, the *ida* and *pingala* channels flanking the sushumna in the subtle body, the dual guardians at the entrances to Buddhist temples, the columns Jachin and Boaz that stood before the Temple of Solomon, the two towers flanking the doors of Gothic cathedrals, and the two doors flanking a cathedral's central portal.

All of these represent the last and most demanding test in the quest for enlightenment: the Union of Opposites that opens the final gates in the rite of passage to the ineffable mystery. Hence one must pass between the Horns of Consecration, like a Minoan bull-leaper, to achieve the transformation that reveals original unity. It follows that whatever is framed by the Horns is the prime symbol of that unity or of the final path to it. Between the Horns of Crete are the revered mountains containing the sacred caves of the Great Goddess. Between Jachin and Boaz in the Temple of Solomon is the Ark of the Covenant. Beyond the entrance towers of the Gothic cathedral is the altar. And beyond the Buddhist Guardians is the statue of the Buddha, symbol of enlightenment.

Like the Horns of Consecration, the upraised arms of the *ka* hieroglyph and of the Cretan and pre-dynastic Egyptian goddesses are similar to the pincers of the sacred Scarab. In Egyptian iconography, the Scarab pushes the rising sun Khepri into the sky just as the actual beetle rolls along the precious ball of dung in which she has laid her eggs—the ball of dung will nourish her grubs as the sun nourishes life, even in the scorching desert. Because the Scarab raises the sun each day, and because her shell resembles a human skull and a baby's head emerging from the womb, she is a symbol of renewal, resurrection, and immortality. A necklace of Hathor found in a tomb at Deir el Medineh was fastened by a Scarab counterweight,[63] and the sacred Scarab seems to have been associated with the Cow-Goddess, in part because the beetle's pincers and Hathor's horns are similar in shape, but also both deities brought forth the sun. Hathor's name means "House of Horus." She was the mother of Horus, the falcon, Lord of Heaven, the sun-god, the King-God. (Horus was also the son of Isis, but in a slightly different aspect). In Egyptian art, the Hathor's headdress became an attribute of Isis and frequently featured the sun resting between its lunar crescent-shaped horns.

As we have seen, the Egyptian pyramid represented the Primeval Hill, the Egyptian World Mountain on which stood the creator-god Atum and on which the Pharaohs resided symbolically, especially once buried in their pyramids. From Mexico to Crete to Japan, the World Mountain is an outgrowth not only of the shamanic Center of the World but also of the mountain containing the cave-sanctuaries of the Goddess. The ancient Egyptians expressed this by painting goddesses on the lids of the sarcophagi in which the Pharaohs' mummies were buried deep within the pyramids. The goddesses received the deceased king into the underworld, the realm of Osiris, where they initiated the

250 *Spatial Archetypes*

rebirthing that immortalized the God-King.

A predynastic ceramic dish from Egypt shows the sun traversing two mountains in its daily journey from dawn to dusk.[64] These two mountains are the Mountains of the East and the West: the two ranges of hills flanking the Nile. They make Egypt itself a natural, topographical embodiment of the Horns of Consecration. Between them runs the Nile, the real source of life in the desert and the earthly counterpart of the heavenly river traversed by stately deities in their celestial barges. In 1884 an Italian scholar, E. Schiaparelli, interpreting amulets from tombs in the days before the pyramid texts had been deciphered, discovered a connection between the pyramid and the sun.

> Upon one amulet he saw pyramid emerging from between two mountains, which looked like the hieroglyph of the "sun in its horizon ...."
>
> From inscriptions, Schiaparelli proved "the simultaneity of the cult of the soul of the dead Pharaoh buried in the pyramid with the cult of the sun represented by the god Ra and other divinities with essentially solar character, above all the goddess Hathor," who was simultaneously known as "Daughter of Ra" and "Mother of Ra:" self-procreating, parthenogenetic, the ancient ever-recurring symbol of life and of the self-renewing sun.[65]

Thus, in Egypt, that which is framed by the Horns of Consecration—the pincers of the Scarab beetle, the horns of Hathor and Isis, and the Mountains of the East and the West—is the sun. And, by accruing transformative affinities with several mythic images, the architectural pyramid is also the sun. But the World Mountain in the Pyramid Age is also the Mountain Arising from the Sea of Chaos. Hence, the pyramid represents the essence of enlightenment in the rise from the everlasting maternal matrix of the crystalline, masculine consciousness ultimately symbolized by the sun. We have moved from the Birth of the Hero, which began in the Great Round and heralded the coming of the Four Quarters, to the Birth of the Sun-God, which begins in the Pyramid and heralds the coming of the next archetype, the Radiant Axes.

The Buddhist Stupa

Buddhism is based on the teachings of Siddhartha Gautama, who was born in northern India in 563 B.C. and named the Buddha, the "awakened one," after he became enlightened at the age of thirty-five. But, like Hinduism, Buddhism has roots in earlier shamanistic and Aryan traditions. These origins typically foster reverence for the god residing in the World Mountain who is a champion of light over the demons of darkness. In Buddhism, darkness is equated with embeddedness in the ego, which keeps our minds so busy solidifying its position that we cannot see our true eternal nature. The wrathful deities forcefully portrayed in Tibetan *thangka* paintings usually personify some aspect of the ego's tenacity and greed. Greatly concerned with the problem of how to transcend ego, Buddhism presents a path toward that end, which is modeled in its sacred structure: the *stupa*. Centuries of convoluted solutions to the problem of ego-transcendence have gone into the stupa mound's sculpturally simple but symbolically complex form.

The stupa derives from India's megalithic burial mounds or "cist graves," which modeled the Womb Cavern of the Great Round. Referring to these mounds, the Buddha instructed his disciples to erect similar cairns at the four crossroads to the King of Kings and the Awakened Ones. These monuments were to serve as reliquaries to hold bits of bone, hair, teeth, and other relics of great teachers and disciples, who would serve as inspirations to the living in their struggle for enlightenment. The stupa acquired more elaborate symbolic meanings as it evolved, but functionally, it has essentially remained a reliquary.

In the *Psycho-Cosmic Symbolism of the Buddhist Stupa*, Lama Govinda describes the stupa as consisting of a stone fence (*vedika*), separating the sacred from the profane, in which four gates (*torana*) mark the cardinal axes oriented to the "sunrise, zenith, sunset, and nadir." The gates symbolize four stages in the enlightenment and life of the Buddha. Within the fence is a circular ter-

252 Spatial Archetypes

race (*medhi*) "for ritualistic circumambulation in the direction of the sun's course." The terrace is surmounted by a hemispherical mound or cupola (*anda*), which "imitates the infinite dome of the all-embracing sky which includes both destruction and creation, death and rebirth." (The dome-shaped *anda* represents also the Cosmic Egg, and thus retains a residue of Great Round symbolism.) An "altar-like structure (*harmika*) which rose on the summit of the cupola, symbolized the sanctuary enthroned above the world, beyond death and rebirth." Penetrating the altar was a spire representing the World Axis, crowned by an honorific umbrella (*hti*).

Of the whole stupa, Govinda writes:

> The entrances were built in such as way that they appear in groundplan as the four arms of a swastika, which has its center in the relic shrine on top of the hemisphere. In other words, in place of the cosmic center, which according to ancient Indian ideas, was Mount Meru with the tree of divine life and knowledge (in Buddhism, the Bodhi tree), there stood the Buddha, the Fully Enlightened One, who realized that knowledge in his own life.[66]

The stupa, then, is a hemispherical version of the World Mountain (with a spire representing the World Axis) set within an image of the Four Quarters, complete with surrounding fence and gates at the cardinal axes. In addition, Lama Govinda notes, "some of the old stupas were covered from top to bottom with small triangular recesses for oil lamps, so that the whole monument could be illuminated and appeared as one huge, radiating dome of light."[67] When the whole stupa was thus illuminated, it became the "sacred quartz crystal, the clear body, the diamond body, the bone of emanant light" that we saw in the shamanic ideal. Shamanism's ancient symbolic imagery filtered down over the millennia into organized religions, thus, all of these shamanic images are equally important in Buddhism as symbols of the incorruptible, eternal Self revealed in enlightenment.

The path to enlightenment involves a reunification of the

Four Quarters, which is expressed in how the stupa is used. It is not a temple and usually does not have an inner shrine (except sometimes in the Himalayas). Buddhists generally do not go into stupas as one would go into a temple or church. Rather, they walk around them in a meditative reenactment of the Buddha-to-bes circumambulation of the Bodhi tree and the sun's apparent course around the earth.

Like the Plains Indians' circumambulation of the Medicine Wheel, this is a ritual reintegration of the Four Quarters. The Cardinal Axes are laden with meaning in Buddhism. In the stupa, among other meanings, East represents the birth of the Buddha; South, his enlightenment; West, his beginning to teach (his first turning of the Wheel of the Law); and North, his *parinirvana* or final release from the sorrowful, delusionary cycle of birth, death, and rebirth. One who circumambulates a stupa, therefore, reenacts the Buddha's life, repeating the stages that the Great Teacher went through to be awakened.

In the centuries following the Buddha's death, Buddhism spread throughout Asia, reaching China in about A.D. 65 and Japan in about A.D. 538. Wherever Buddhism went, the stupa soon followed. It became the *dagoba* in Sri Lanka, the *chorten* in the Himalayas, and was built as the massive Borobudur in Java and the dazzling golden Swee Dagon in Rangoon. It even influenced Angkor Wat in Cambodia. Stupas are featured in Himilayan thangka paintings and altar icons; and they appear in the form of gold, jewel-encrusted tombs for Lamas buried in the Potala in Lhasa. The stupa influenced the shape of all sorts of other items: Balinese ceremonial cakes, Thai dancers' headdresses, incense burners, cremation platforms. In China and Japan, the stupa evolved into the high-rise pagoda, just as in Egypt the pyramid evolved into the towering obelisk. Unlike the pyramids, however, the stupa is still in use in many parts of Asia and is, therefore, an alive form.

The classic symbolic elements of the stupa took shape in the third century B.C. under the reign of Ashoka, the beloved king of India who converted to Buddhism, became its first royal patron, and is said to have sponsored the greatest surge of stupa building in history. One legend claims he raised 84,000 stupas in a single night. His life sheds light on the historical context in which the

254 *Spatial Archetypes*

stupa, the preeminent Asian pyramid, arose.

Ashoka was the grandson of Chandragupta Maurya, who, after helping to expel the Macedonians from India and observing the strategies of Alexander the Great, established the first state by conquering most of northern India and founding the Mauryan dynasty. Chandragupta is somewhat the Indian equivalent of King Narmer in Egypt, while Akoka, like King Zoser, gained fame as the great builder. Chandragupta laid down the typical institutions of statehood: elaborate standing armies, systems of taxation, a harsh legal code, a secret police, and various social and economic systems. Following the example of his warlike grandfather, Ashoka became a prodigious conqueror and added most of the Deccan to the state, thereby unifying the greater part of present-day India under one rule.[68]

It is Ashoka, however, rather than Chandragupta, who is admired as the greatest king in Indian history. This is due not only to his military conquests but also to his turn of heart after his victories. Haunted by his bloodthirsty past as a warrior, he turned to the teachings of the Buddha and became a monk while remaining king. Among his acts was the raising throughout the country of edict columns inscribed with laws that were not merely secular but also incorporated the dharma, the sacred Law of Buddhism. In Buddhist teachings, it is the turning of the Wheel of the Law, the *Dharmachakra* (*dharma* = law, *chakra* = wheel) that offers deliverance from the Wheel of Life, the continuous round of reincarnation into the painful limitations of flesh and ego. In the spirit of the Pyramid Age, the law (the logos principle, the *Dharmachakra*) churns away the Great Round's messy cycle of life, death, and rebirth in preference for an eternity of pure, disembodied consciousness.

An intimate relationship connects the Buddha, the dharma, circumambulation, and the sun, as the Buddha's life came to be seen not just as the story of a great teacher but as an heroic myth personifying cosmic phenomena:

> ... the Buddha's birth is likened to the rising of another sun; on his Enlightenment, like the sacrificial fire of Agni, the Buddha mounts transfigured to the highest heavens

of the gods; in his turning of the Wheel of the Law he assumes the power of the world-ruler or Chakravartin to send the wheel of his dominion, the sun, turning over all the worlds in token of his universal power.[69]

The circumambulator of the stupa identifies with the Buddha as Chakravartin and "turns" the stupa, itself a symbol of the *Dharmachakra*.

The stupa, then, took form at the founding of India's first dynastic nation state, which had theocratic overtones and promoted a spiritual path based on Divine Law as a means of transcending ego. The symbolism accruing to the stupa vividly reveal the growing logos-orientation of this age. In the earliest stupas modeled on burial mounds, the relic was placed in the center of the earth under the mound. During the Mauryan dynasty, the stupa changed to become a model of the cosmos. This involved a telling shift in the location of the reliquary—the stupa's holy of holies.

A shift of the ritual centre only became possible after the stupa had lost its original significance as a burial mound, during the reign of Ashoka, and had become an interminably repeated symbol of the teaching and cosmology of the Buddha. The cubic chamber of a Megalithic tomb (the Womb-Cavern), which incidentally may also be interpreted as a prototype of the Hindu cella, was replaced in the stupa by the reliquary, which was moved from the centre of the arida (the Cosmic Egg) to the summit; the rounded form of the anda became the image of the infinite cosmos. The Aryan symbol of the axis of the universe, the tree in the middle of the village under which the elders took counsel, reappears in the stupa as a vertical wooden axis.[70]

The stupa underwent anthropomorphization more clearly than any other architectural form as it came to model both the macrocosm and the human body as microcosm. Each of its forms symbolized both a chakra in the subtle body and an anatomical part of the gross body. Volwahsen summarizes the latter.

> In the stupa the medhi is the abdomen, the anda is the upper part of the body, and the honorary umbrella surrounded by the railing, or the urn containing the

256 *Spatial Archetypes*

relic, is the head. Thus it is also understandable the eyes should have been painted on the harmika of a stupa at Katrnandu, the core of which dates from as early as Ashoka's reign.[71]

Again, we see in the development of the Buddhist stupa a movement toward the sky, the logos principle, and the head. In the classic Buddhist stupa, the urn containing the relic—the holy of holies—is the head. Despite their obvious differences, the Egyptian pyramid and the Buddhist stupa have much in common. Both arose during and are expressive of the Pyramid archetype in their respective cultures. Both model World Mountains. Both had negligible interior spaces. Both had their holy of holies shifted ever higher toward the sky, pointing the way to eternal life, and in time, both evolved vertically (into obelisk and pagoda). And both stood in close relationship to the sun.

Borobudur

[One of the sections of this book that Mimi Lobell did not finish was on Borobudur, a magnificent stupa in Indonesia. Mimi visited Borobudur and taught about it extensively. Rather than attempt to write what she might have written, I am including here the introductory section of the Wikipedia article on Borobudur. ~ JL]

Borobudur, or Barabudur (Indonesian: Candi Borobudur) is a 9th century Mahayana Buddhist temple in Magelang, Central Java, Indonesia, as well as the world's largest Buddhist temple, and also one of the greatest Buddhist monument in the world. The temple consists of nine stacked platforms, six square and three circular, topped by a central dome. The temple is decorated with 2,672 relief panels and 504 Buddha statues. The central dome is surrounded by 72 Buddha statues, each seated inside a perforated stupa.

Built in the 9th century during the reign of the Sailendra Dynasty, the temple was designed in Javanese Buddhist architecture, which blends the Indonesian indigenous cult of ancestor worship and the Buddhist concept of attaining Nirvana. The temple also demonstrates the influences of Gupta art that reflects India's influence on the region, yet there are enough indigenous scenes and elements incorporated to make Borobudur uniquely Indonesian. The monument is both a shrine to the Lord Buddha and a place for Buddhist pilgrimage. The journey for pilgrims begins at the base of the monument and follows a path around the monument and ascends to the top through three levels symbolic of Buddhist cosmology: Kāmadhātu (the world of desire), Rupadhatu (the world of forms) and Arupadhatu (the world of formlessness). The monument guides pilgrims through an extensive system of stairways and corridors with 1,460 narrative relief panels on the walls and the balustrades. Borobudur has the largest and most complete ensemble of Buddhist reliefs in the world.

Evidence suggests Borobudur was constructed in the 9th century and abandoned following the 14th century decline of Hindu kingdoms in Java and the Javanese conversion to Islam. Worldwide knowledge of its existence was sparked in 1814 by Sir Thomas Stamford Raffles, then the British ruler of Java, who was advised of its location by native Indonesians. Borobudur has since been preserved through several restorations. The largest restoration project was undertaken between 1975 and 1982 by the Indonesian government and UNESCO, following which the monument was listed as a UNESCO World Heritage Site.

Borobudur is still used for pilgrimage; once a year, Buddhists in Indonesia celebrate Vesak at the monument, and Borobudur is Indonesia's single most visited tourist attraction.

~ Wikipedia contributors. "Borobudur." Wikipedia, The Free Encyclopedia. Wikipedia, The Free Encyclopedia, 22 Dec. 2016. Web. 22 Dec. 2016.

258 *Spatial Archetypes*

The Potala in Lhasa

Lhasa, the capital of Tibet, is one of the most romantically spiritual places on earth. Because of its otherworldly Himalayan setting at an altitude of 11,830 feet and because it was sealed off from Westerners for centuries by mountains and by order of the Tibetan rulers, it has secured a place of mythic proportions in the Western imagination. Tibet itself seems to be the spiritual capital of the world: the World Mountain incarnate.

The most renowned structure in Lhasa is the imposing, mysterious Potala, named for Mount Potala, home of the Bodhisattva of Compassion Avalokiteshvara, who is called Chenrezi in Tibet. Before the brutal Chinese takeover in 1959 and the Cultural Revolution's atrocities between 1966 and 1976, Tibet was a classic theocracy. Thousands of huge, well-organized monasteries were the equivalents of our Harvards, Yales, and Oxfords, and Tibet was ruled by holy reincarnated Dalai Lamas, who even today are often identified as "God-Kings." The fourteenth in succession is the current, innovative, warmly inspiring Dalai Lama, Tenzin Gyatso, the 1989 Nobel Peace Prize Laureate who has energetically rebuilt Tibetan culture in exile in Dharamsala, India.

Though the spiritual center of Tibet was the Jokhang Temple in Lhasa, the Potala had great spiritual significance also. As Tibet's governmental center, it perfectly expressed the theocratic combination of temporal and divine rule typical of Pyramid cultures. Built on a natural rise called Red Hill, the Potala towers 1000 feet above the Lhasa River valley below. The Potala itself is thirteen stories high. Its various levels give a compete cross-section of the Tibetan social pyramid from the dungeons of the Cave of Scorpions at the bottom, to service spaces like granaries and storerooms on the next levels, to warrens of monks' cells, to ceremonial rooms, and finally to the chapels and apartments of the Dalai Lamas on the roof. In other words, the Potala is a pyramid!

Buddhism was brought to Tibet in the 7th century A.D. by two wives of King Songtsen Gampo, the warrior King who made Lhasa his capital after unifying Tibet. His activities reflect a logos-orientation typical of kings in Pyramid cultures. He is responsible for adapting Sanskrit to give Tibet a system of writing; he wrote the first code of laws; and his reign marks the beginning of Tibet's recorded history. The powerful king had three Tibetan wives, and he acquired two foreign wives, both princesses, through alliances with China and Nepal. They converted him to Buddhism, though he continued to practice some aspects of the Bon faith as well, which contributed shamanic elements to the unique character of Buddhism in Tibet. Songtsen Gampo's Chinese wife, Wencheng, brought with her from Chang-an a gold statue of the Buddha, now considered the most sacred object in Tibet. The statue survived the Cultural Revolution and is still housed in the Jokhang, one of two temples Songtsen Gampo built for his foreign wives. The king also built the first Potala fortress on Red Hill.

After Songtsen Gampo, Tibet's kings were variously engaged in military campaigns and in the growing centrality in Tibetan life of Buddhism and its sects. Kings had texts inscribed, founded monasteries, vied with and disbanded rival sects, imported and exported Buddhist scholars, held debates, clarified doctrine, initiated reform movements, and so on. In short, they acted much the same as rulers in other Pyramid cultures, attending to the secular concerns of the state while aggressively shaping its spiritual life.

Songtsen Gampo's seventh century Potala is now mostly gone, except for the Saint's Chapel and the Dharma Cave. The present Potala is largely the work of the Great Fifth Dalai Lama, who reigned between 1617 and 1682. Famous for reunifying Tibet by making the austere Yellow Hat sect supreme over the Red and Black Hat sects, he proclaimed all Yellow Hat abbots called Dalai Lamas to be reincarnations of Chenrezi (Avalokiteshvara). He thus gave all Dalai Lamas the status of God-Kings and wisely included King Songtsen Gampo in his declaration. The powerful, centralized form of theocracy that the Great Fifth Dalai Lama founded flourished almost without change until the Chinese invasion in 1951. Its center was the enormous Palace that the Great Fifth built in Lhasa on the ruins of King Songtsen Gampo's Potala. The Great Fifth's naming of the Dalai Lamas as incarnations of Chenrezi in a way also crystallized the relationship between the sexes. Songsten Gampo's Chinese and Nepalese wives are symbolized by the White and Green Taras, respectively. In what appears to be a typical patriarchal reworking of a prepatriarchal goddess,

Tara is said to have originated as a tear in the eye of the compassionate Avalokiteshvara. The White Tara represents the motherly, merciful, compassionate aspects; and the Green, the active, energetic aspects. Thus, portrayals of Songsten Gampo flanked by his two wives, of which there are many in the Potala and throughout Tibet, can be read on several levels: as historical images (the actual king and his wives), as deities (Avalokiteshvara/Chenrezi, whom the king incarnates, White Tara, and Green Tara), as personifications of compassion, and as models of the appropriate relationship between the sexes in the Pyramid archetype with the male as the dominant central character and the females as his wives or even his own bodily issue (as Avalokiteshvara's tears, much as Eve sprung from Adam's rib or Athena from Zeus's headache). Tibet's origin myth displays a similarly biased view of the sexes:

> Long ago ... the Bodhisattva of Compassion, Chenrezi, sent his disciple, a holy monkey, to be a hermit in the mountains. Meditating in his cave, the monkey heard an ogress crying among the crags and took pity on her loneliness. (Some say she threatened to marry a demon and people the world with their offspring.) In either case, the monkey got Chenrezi's permission to marry the ogress. In due time they had six children who grew up to be human beings with noble traits from their father such as generosity, bravery and piety, and base ones from their mother like greed, envy and lust. They multiplied and became the Tibetan people whose first kings descended from the sky.[72]

It should be noted that despite this bias, Tibet has had many women scholars and mystics,[73] and Tara is one of the most widely esteemed deities. In hymns, she is praised as a virtually autonomous goddess. In her various aspects she is a self-liberated goddess of wisdom and action, mercy and compassion, music and dance, perfect rhythmic timing, the full moon, the Forest (of Khadira) and its animals, and the Eye of transcendent vision.[74]

As the center of a Pyramidal culture spiritually focused on Sacred Mountains (Mount Meru, Mount Kailash, Mount Potala) and set within the world's highest mountains, the Potala is a superb materialization of the Pyramid archetype. It has over 1000 rooms and consists basically of a sacred Red Palace surrounded by a secular White Palace. The Red Palace was built during ten years in which the death of the Great Fifth was kept secret. The White Palace was built by the Great Fifth and extended in the early twentieth century by the Thirteenth Dalai Lama.

The Red Palace houses the Great West Hall and its adjoining tour large chapels, which commemorate the Fifth Dalai Lama. The North Chapel is especially revealing; within it are statues of the Buddha on the left and the Fifth Dalai Lama on the right. The facts that the two figures are the same height and both are crowned and seated on fabulous gold thrones testifies to their equal status.[75] The East Chapel honors the founder of the Yellow Hat Sect, Tsong Khapa, and the South Chapel is dedicated to the highly revered eighth century Indian mystic Padmasambhava. The West Chapel houses the mummified Fifth Dalai Lama in a magnificent jeweled sandalwood stupa, which stands more than three stories tall and is encased in 8,200 pounds of gold! Surrounding the Great Fifth's stupa are four other stupas, which contain scriptures and two other Dalai Lamas. Above the Great West Hall are three levels of mural-painted galleries with windows that give light to the Hall and chapels below.

West of the Great West Hall[76] is the tomb of the Thirteenth Dalai Lama, considered the greatest Dalai Lama since the Fifth. It contains a forty-six foot high jeweled stupa containing a ton of gold, which was built in 1933. This indicates how atemporal the archetypes are: the same archetype that inspired the building of the Egyptian pyramids 4500 years ago also produced additions to the Potala and the Thirteenth Dalai Lama's funereal stupa in the 20th century.

The Gothic Cathedral: Pyramid of the West

Toward the end of the Dark Ages in Europe, a series of powerful Christian kings arose: Clovis, Charlemagne, and Ottos I and II in continental Europe; Henry II in England; and Brian Boru in Ireland. Sanctified by a "divine mission," they unified sections of

Europe into states, Charlemagne and other kings forcibly converted their subjects, and, with the quelling of the non-Christian Viking, Saracen, and Magyar invaders, Europe became almost completely Christianized by the 11th century.

The establishment of the church, nation states, and divinely empowered kings—typical characteristics of the Pyramid archetype—catapulted Europe out of its protracted pagan Four Quarters era into the Christian Pyramid age. The Four Quarters lingered both in feudalism with its fortified castles, heroic knights, and chieftain-like lords of the manor, and in ongoing monasticism. But overarching both were the Pyramidal hierarchies of church and state, two superpowers often at odds with each other.

Finally, in the Gothic era, the church prevailed and Europe's Pyramid age came to full realization. Worked into a frenzy by the call of the Crusades to win back the holy city of Jerusalem from the "infidel" Muslims, Europe balanced the explosive energy of the Crusades with an implosive "Cathedral Crusade" at home. The pioneering French Gothic cathedrals, in particular, were astonishing in their vision of light and height, their structural brilliance, and their mobilization of all the guilds of medieval artisans: stonemasons, carpenters, glaziers, and sculptors. Wherever they were built, the cathedrals became towering magnets of secular discourse and the latest in technology, as well as centers of spirituality. A cathedral could house a bishop's seat, a high mass, and holy relics, certainly, but imagine stepping inside one on a late afternoon. We see also a rousing guild meeting; a smattering of chatting friends; families of pilgrims and their animals sheltering for the night; circles of needleworkers tatting market items to sell for the church; free-lance vendors hawking their wares, chary of being evicted; and a sort of "homeless program" hosting a hodge-podge of the ailing, widowed, orphaned, elderly, and addled. Chickens and hounds peck and patrol the straw-strewn granite floor, oblivious to the doves flitting among the vaults above. The late sun streams through kaleidoscopic stained-glass clerestory windows, raying chromatically through dust and incense to dapple color on grey stone walls.

Often built upon pre-Christian sacred sites, the cathedrals echoed a silent continuity with the ancient, now-forbidden, religions that still reverberated in the marrow of newly-converted descendants of pagan generations who pilgrimaged to these same healing centers. Indeed, the cathedrals were as much the creation of the pagan spirit as of the Christian. In many Pyramid cultures, the state religion is for the elite and others are allowed to keep their practices and beliefs in the form of "folk religion." In the Pyramid culture of Europe, however, Christianity stamped out the folk religions. Forced into subliminality like the "little people" in mythology, they survived in hidden forms apparent only to the trusted. Resonating through the proportions, plans, geometric rose windows, sculpture, and stonework of the cathedrals were the visions of pre-Christian sages. They secreted the Green Man among sculptured Old Testament patriarchs. They alluded to the subtle geometries that had ordered the megalithic structures and monuments of long ago. They invoked ancient deities to make the sacred place more sacred still.

Each cathedral had an unmistakable sign of its pre-Christian origins built in plain sight on the floor of its nave: a paved stone labyrinth. Today, the only survivor is in Notre-Dame de Chartres. Tragically, but perhaps predictably, the others were removed during the Age of Reason when Europe was intent upon exorcising all traces of the irrational and the feminine.

Although Christianity certainly has had one of the most brutal records of misogyny of any religion in history, the Gothic Age was comparatively receptive to the feminine principle. This, according to Henry Adams, was one of the reasons for its greatness. Adams points out in *Mont-Saint Michel and Chartres* that the Gothic cathedrals were built at a time when French Queens were powerful, when women participated quite fully in medieval society (there are records of payments to female quarry owners and to women laborers who took part in building the cathedrals), and when European culture was being fertilized by passionate pagan legends dressed up as the literature of courtly love and the traditions of chivalry, which were sympathetic to women. But most of all, he attributes the building of the French cathedrals to the blossoming of the "Cult of the Virgin." Recall that most were named "Notre Dame de..." ("Our Lady of...") followed by the name of the town in which they were built: Notre Dame de Chartres,

Notre Dame de Paris, Notre Dame d'Amiens, and so on. Unlike the authoritarian God, dour fathers, and abstract theological principles of the official church, Mary was warm, human, and compassionate. Her adoration was not dictated by Rome; it was a spontaneous outburst, possibly a desire to return to the worship of the Great Goddess who had flourished in Western Europe until the coming of Christianity. Even the lowliest person considered it a personal duty and a spiritual privilege to carry a cartload of building materials for the Virgin's glorious cathedrals.

Angkor

Deep in the jungles of Cambodia, the awesome ruins of Angkor rise above the treetops like a phantasmagorical dream metropolis, its buildings writhing with sculpted serpents preternaturally predictive of the giant jungle vines that grip the city today. Discovered for modern Europeans more than a century ago by Henri Mouhot, a French botanist, the ruins long remained a mystery. Various theories attributed Angkor to angels, to giants, to a lost race, or to the Leper King. Some locals told Mouhot it built itself. Decades of careful scholarship, particularly by the French, finally penetrated the Cambodian mystery. Angkor was not attributable to any of these fantastic builders, but to local dynastic Khmer rulers. Nor was it thousands of years old as some thought, but only a few hundred. Built between the ninth and fifteenth centuries A.D.—when Europe was building Romanesque, Gothic, and early Renaissance cathedrals—it is roughly contemporary also with Mesoamerica's Late Classic and Post Classic Mayan civilization.[79]

The Khmers traditionally traced their royal line back to the Funan kingdom, founded in the first century A.D., which embraced Cambodia, southern Thailand, and part of China. According to a Chinese legend, this kingdom came into being when Kaundinya, a Brahmin, followed a spiritual message to set sail eastward, arriving at the shores of Cambodia where he was met by a hostile ruler, Queen Willow Leaf, whom he later placated and married. Queen Willow Leaf was a *nagini*—a half-human, half-serpent spirit of the waters. The legend implies that the Funan kingdom was founded when seafarers from a western land, probably India, invaded and conquered the native Cambodians, who, because they were ruled by a Serpent-Queen Spirit-of-the-Waters, may still have been living in the Great Round. Kaundinya's conquest of and marriage to Queen Willow Leaf suggests that he, like most Four Quarters heroes, subdued the Telluric serpent and domesticated the Goddess—both represented by Queen Willow Leaf. However, as we will see, the serpent and the Goddess continued to be powerful mythic forces in Cambodia right through to the end of the Khmer empire.

The development of architectural styles from the Funan through the Khmer kingdoms reveals a typical transition from the Four Quarters to the Pyramid. The major surviving Funan buildings were brick shrines housing *linga*, the phallic cult images of the royal ancestors. These shrines were square or rectangular in plan, surrounded by a walled enclosure, with smaller cells grouped around a larger central shrine. The square plans, walled enclosure, and large central shrine celebrating the royal lingam make these Funan structures perfect images of the Four Quarters with its "Lord" at the center.

Assailed from many sides between the sixth and eighth centuries, the Funan kingdom finally collapsed in warfare. Among the rival claimants to the Funan royal line were contestants from Laos, invaders from Java, and Cambodian Khmers from northern Indochina. The Khmers prevailed and established a royal line that was to last over six hundred years, producing out of its stability and prosperity some of the most magnificent monumental architecture in the world. Everything about the Khmer rulers—their temples, cities, history, government, and mythic vision—indicates that they were Pyramid Age God-Kings *par excellence*. Perhaps the most revealing is their glorification of the old Funan and Indian temple image of the World Mountain as Center of the World and home of the God-King.

> In the beginning of the Classic Period of Khmer art, we notice the appearance in architecture of other completely new types of building methods and ornamentation. Most important and typical is the elevation of the cells of the pre-Khmer type to the summit of a stepped pyramid.

The form of this type of sanctuary and its lofty stepped base are the result of the cult of the temple-mountain and of the Devaraja or "God-king." The temple-mountain, simulating the imagined shape of either Mount Meru or Mount Kailasa, is, of course, the importation of the old Indian concept of pratibimba, the making of either sacred mountains or unseen celestial regions in architectural constructions.

With regard to the cult of the Devaraja, it must be explained that the Khmer kings, even in their lifetimes, were regarded as incarnations of a deity like Siva, Vishnu, or Lokesvara, to whom the well-being of the realm was confided. The ritual and cult of the Devaraja centered around a sacred lingam which was imbued with the essence of divine kingship and installed in a temple-mountain, described in many inscriptions as being located in the centre of the capital and Empire—and magically in the centre of the Universe.[80]

Three centuries after the establishment of the Khmer state, this conception was perfected in the capital city of Angkor Wat. Initially founded by Jayavarman II, the first great Khmer king (*jaya* = "victory," *varman* = "protector" thus the king was the "Protector of Victory"), the capital was completed under Suryavarman ("Protector of the Sun"), who reigned from A.D. 1112 to 1152.

Angkor Wat was not really a city—commoners usually lived in the jungle outside the walls of Khmer royal cities—but a temple, tomb, and perhaps palace of the God-King. Oriented west, the direction of the setting sun, death, and the spiritual quest in Eastern thought, Angkor Wat is basically a pyramid encased in layers of rectilinear galleries and moats several miles long. As is so often the case in the structures of all Pyramid civilizations, the Four Quarters is as obvious in the plan as the Pyramid is in the elevation.

A tour through Angkor Watt begins on an entrance avenue over a causeway, which is lined with balustrades shaped like gigantic seven-headed serpents flaring their enormous hoods. Beyond is a monumental cruciform portico leading to the first platform and gallery, which was meant to be circumambulated in a counterclockwise direction (the direction of death, against the sun's course). Some 2500 feet of relief sculptures in the gallery tell the story of Vishnu, the supreme Hindu deity whom the God-King incarnated, in the Land of Yama, the Lord of Death. Back along the main western axis, the gallery then leads to a square divided by colonnades into four courtyards, like an evocation of the Four Quarters in preparation for the central pyramid.

From the courtyards, a stair rises through another gallery to a second platform on which stands the precipitous pyramid structure, the center of the entire complex, supporting the innermost sanctuary. It has stairs on all four sides, their steep angles exaggerating the illusion of height. The platform at the summit of the pyramid is again divided into four courts and is surrounded by a gallery, which, like the second gallery, has towers at its corners and gates at the cardinal axes. The four corner spires frame the central tower in imitation of the four holy mountains surrounding Mount Meru.

Angkor is profusely covered with sculptures and bas reliefs showing a multitude of motifs: stories from the Hindu classics the Rumuyumz and the Muhubhuratu, historical events in the king's life, the myth of the Churning of the Sea of Milk (including one 160 foot long bas relief), scenes of heavens and hells, dancing apsurns,[82] idealized portraits of royal patrons, floral motifs, niches with deities and Buddhas, and so on. Originally the whole was dramatically surmounted by a golden lotus crowning the central tower and rising more than two hundred feet above the ground.

The Churning of the Sea of Milk

With all its emphasis on pyramidal height, perhaps the most surprising feature of Angkor Wat was something discovered under its central tower, that is, under "Mount Meru."

> Under this central tower which contained the image of the Devaraja was discovered a well, more than one hundred and twenty feet deep, in which a deposit of gold objects was found. It is likely that this shaft symbolized the world pivot that was the pestle employed by the gods and giants in the churning of the Sea of Milk.[83]

This is one of the most stunning examples of myth-modeling in the history of architecture: Angkor Wat, the Khmer Navel of the World, symbolizing the churnstick used by the gods and demons to extract amrita, the Elixir of Immortality, from the Sea of Milk. The entire myth is a fabulous allegory of the inner quest to transcend ego, bring order out of chaos, effect a Union of Opposites, find the still center, and release the font of eternal wisdom in the inner Self.[84]

The myth opens with the god Indra, a Hindu Lord of the Four Quarters who often personifies the ego, complaining that a curse has robbed him and the world of energy and strength. Vishnu, the Teacher of Opposites, advises Indra to seek the Elixir of Immortality, which lies at the bottom of the Sea of Milk, the undifferentiated Waters of Chaos where Vishnu himself dwells. To do this Indra must forge an alliance between the Gods and the Demons (the duality of good and evil within himself), since all of their combined energy will be needed to churn the Sea of Milk. Vishnu says the Gods and Demons must use Mount Mandara, a mythical white mountain similar to the golden Mount Meru, as a churning stick. In other words, the World Mountain is to be the psychological axis mundi within Indra, within the person. The turning rope is to be Vasuki (or Ananta in the Khmer version), the Great Serpent who lies coiled about the World Mountain.

After a dispute about who is to pull the head of Vasuki, the Gods concede to the Demons and take the less honorable tail. They proceed to pull Vasuki to and fro, turning the World Mountain, but, lacking a pivot, it keeps slipping back into the waters. Seeing that the Gods and Demons are not firmly centered, Vishnu shows them how to find the still point within the illusions of life by becoming a sea-tortoise and offering his own back as a pivot under the Mountain.

The work begins again, and, after a time (eons by some accounts), flames and poison begin to erupt from the serpent. Vasuki's flaming breath—the untamed fire of Kundalini—threatens to scorch the Demons at his head, but clouds and rain generated by the Gods at the opposite end blow the flames away. The poison—inner sickness and neuroses—threatens to destroy the world as it rises in Vasuki's throat. Seeing the danger, the god Siva steps in and swallows the poisonous vomit, suspending it in his throat through powerful yoga, which gives him the blue burn worn today by Siva worshippers.

These negative energies neutralized, the Gods and Demons continue their churning. In time, fabulous beings and gifts begin to emerge from the Sea of Milk; the magical white elephant of Indra; Parijata, the perfumed, wish-fulfilling Tree of Paradise; Kamadhenu, the Cow Goddess of abundance; the entrancing, dancing *apsaras*; and a thousand other treasures. Then, seated upon a golden lotus, the radiant goddess Lakshmi rises, and the sight of her charms the world. Finally, Dhanwantari, the youthful black god of healing, emerges bearing the prized cup of *amrita*. Out of jealousy for Lakshrni's preference for Vishnu, the Demons attempt to seize the Elixir, but Vishnu, turning himself into an alluring woman, distracts them and gives the potion to the Gods. It is said that "Whoso hears this story of the birth of Lakshmi from the Milky Sea, whosoever reads it, that goddess of good fortune shall never leave his house for generations three; strife or misfortune may never enter where the hymn of Lakshmi is sun."[85]

The myth recalls many familiar themes: the Buddha-to-be's circumambulation of the Bodhi tree in search of the still point where the universe remains stable, the enlightenment engendered by the Kundalini serpent's ascent up the *sushumna*, the Mountain Arising from the Sea of Chaos, and so on. Angkor represents the World Mountain that churned the Sea of Milk both in overall form, with its 200 ft. high tower and its 120 ft. deep well under the Devuraja lirigum, and in ornament, with its 160 ft. long bas-relief of the myth. While the Khmers designed their capital to be the center of the universe, we can see in it also a model of the center of the Self. A later Khmer capital, Angkor Thom, expresses the myth even more literally. The avenue to its central pyramid is lined on one side with the Gods, who bear the Aryan faces of the Khmers, and on the other with the Demons, who resemble the conquered natives. Both are pulling the gigantic serpent that turns the World Mountain, which is Angkor Thom itself.

270 Spatial Archetypes

The Hieros Gamos

Another aspect of the Churning of the Sea of Milk as the Union of Opposites is apparent in the Khmer capitals. Heavily influenced by India, the Khmer civilization alternated between Hinduism and Buddhism throughout its history. This myth is of Hindu origin, and much Hindu symbolism delightfully fuses the spiritual with the erotic—witness the orgiastic scenes on the temples at Khajurajo and Konarak, where sexuality and fertility are metaphors for the Union of Opposites. The lovers represent not only women and men in sexual union, but also the dualities of the psyche uniting in ego-transcendence. The myth of the Churning of the Sea of Milk is alive with these sensuous spiritual undercurrents. They can be seen also in the mystical "Island of Jewels" in the center of the ocean of universal consciousness—"the vast sea of infinite life-energy, the ocean of nectar, the elixir of immortality"—described by Heinrich Zimmer from a Rajput miniature:

> The ocean represents the "Alogical Immense." It is an expanse, dormant in itself, and full of all potentialities. It contains the germs of all conflicting opposites, all the energies and features of all the pairs of co-operating antagonisms. And these energies concentrate and evolve here at the center, in the Island. Out of the dormant, quiescent state they move here to creation.
>
> ... The Island ... regarded as the metaphysical Point of Power .... is called "The Drop" (*bindu*) the first drop, which spreads, unfolds, expands, and becomes transmuted into the tangible realm of our limited consciousness and the universe. The Island is represented as a golden, circular figure. The shores are made of powdered gems (*mani*)—hence the name of the Island, Mani-dvipa. It is forested with blooming, fragrant trees, and in the center stands a palace made of the precious stone that grants all desires (*cintamani*), a kind of *lapis philosophorum* [Philosophers Stone]. Within the palace is a jeweled awning (*mandapa*), under which,

on a jeweled and golden throne, is seated the Universal Mother (*jagad-amba, matar*), "The Fairest One of the Three Worlds or Towns" (*tripura-sundari*). She is the deity, the energy of the Bindu, which in turn was the first, concentrated Drop of the dynamic force of universal divine substance. Out of the Goddess, there come into being the three world-spheres of the heavens, the earth, and the space between.[86]

Red in color, the Goddess is the creative, active, primordial energy that plans, produces, and measures out the evolution of the universe. She is Maya, from *ma*, to measure out or plan, as a carpenter might measure to build a house. Zimmer likens her to the experience of the first "This" or "Other," the first pure object of divine Self-experience, out of which she emerges. In other words, in the initial breakdown of the "all-containing Divine Essence" of the Self, into the duality of Self versus other, she is the principle of "otherness." Later this duality evolves further into the distinction between mind and matter, and she becomes simply "matter" the *prima materia* from which all things arise, the "Mother of the ten-thousand things" in Taoism.

Although these dualisms arise in all of us during the natural childhood process of differentiating ourselves from Uroboric Oneness, they become metaphysical principles only in the religions of the Four Quarters and Pyramid archetypes. These religions, formulated by male prophets, teachers, rulers, and priests, present the experience of the masculine psyche as the experience of all humankind: both male and female. Thus, the primal "other"—which in universal experience is an impersonal, ungendered principle—becomes in the male mind, the female. This objectification of the female reinforces the idea of a "male" society in opposition to a "female" society.

But it generates also an intense, often unconscious, desire for union with the female, a "genderized" expression of the primal desire to heal the breach between "Self" and "other" This, then, is the meaning behind the *hieros gamos* in masculine society. The sacred marriage, which began as an initiation of the male by the female, becomes in the Four Quarters and the Pyramid archetypes the male's attempt to reabsorb his objectified other half to become whole again. If the experience is successful, sexually and psychologically, then wondrous things happen: life-giving waters flow abundantly into the Wasteland, the Holy Grail is recovered, the king's sovereignty is reaffirmed, the land becomes bountiful, crops and livestock reproduce with luxuriant fertility, and the nation prospers. All these bounties flow from the renewed virility, vitality, and psychological wholeness of the king (as a stand-in for Everyman), obtained through his reunion with the Goddess, that is, with his inner feminine principle. This may be one reason that female figures continue to play such a prominent part in the myths, rituals, and legends of many Pyramid civilizations. They appear not in their own right so much as in their roles as personifications of the king's estranged anima.

The more dualistic and logos-oriented the culture, the more crucial the *hieros gamos*. The Radiant Axes archetype extends the breach beyond repair and degrades the *hieros gamos* into the cynical exploitation of royal concubines sequestered in palace seraglios. But in the Four Quarters and Pyramid archetypes, the *hieros gamos* is known to have been a highly sacred rite practiced between chieftains or kings and the Goddess's priestesses at the Celtic stronghold of Tara in Ireland, in Greek and Indian temples, on the summits of Mesopotamian ziggurats, in certain New Kingdom Egyptian temples, in sacred royal compounds in ancient China and Japan, and in temples crowning Khmer pyramids. It is significant that the sacred marriage takes place on the pyramids, the highest, most sacred places in the nation. In these special locations, the king joins Heaven and Earth with his own penis, which becomes the axis mundi. Perhaps nowhere is this more evident than in the Khmer capitals where the Devarujas enshrined their penises symbolically in the royal *linga* in the centers of their magnificent pyramid-temples. It was also in these temples, according to Chou Ta-kuan, a Chinese historian who visited Cambodia in 1296, that the sacred marriage took place. He writes:

> The king sleeps in the summit of the palace's golden tower. All the people believe that the tower is also inhabited by the Lord of the Sun who is a nine-headed

serpent. Every night the serpent appears in the form of a woman with whom the king sleeps during the first watch. The king leaves at the second watch to go to his wives and concubines. If the naga spirit does not appear one night, it is a sign that the king's death is imminent. Should the king fail to visit the naga for a single night, the welfare of the kingdom will suffer dire consequences.[87]

The masculinization of the Goddess as "Lord of the Sun" is probably a late development. In essence, though, Chou Ta-kuan has described a classic *hieros gamos* where the well-being both of the king and of the nation depends upon the king's ritual mating with a High Priestess, through whom flows the vital force of the cosmos. We are reminded of Herodotus's suggestion of a similar rite in the Babylonian ziggurats, and of much earlier cuneiform texts voluptuously describing the Sumerian *hieros gamos* so beautifully translated in Samuel Noah Kramer's *The Sacred Marriage Rite*.[89]

The Churning of the Sea of Milk, then, conjures the image of the *Devaraja lingam*, as World Axis, sexually churning the Primordial Sea, the Womb-Cavern in its elemental, unmanifested state. The searing hot vortex created by the churning is expressed in the fire erupting from the serpent like fiery lava erupting from a volcano. Eliade writes, "In Vedic India the sacrificial altar (*vedi*) was looked upon as female and the ritual fire (agni) as male and 'their union brought forth offspring.'" The altar was the navel of the earth, Center of the World, and womb of the Great Goddess. "... fire itself was the result (progeny) of sexual union: it was born as a result of the to-and-fro motion (as in copulation) of a stick (representing the male organ), in a notch made in a piece of wood (female organ)."[87]

The sexual terms, says Eliade, link cosmological conception with the *hieros gamos*. Starting from the center (navel), the ritual fire engendered magically in the vagina of the Priestess reproduces the birth of the world. In alchemy, too, the crucible is seen as a woman and the production of the Philosopher's Stone or the Elixir of Immortality is compared to the birth of a child. Eliade cites numerous examples, for instance, Western alchemical writings state that "the fire under the receptacle or container must burn continuously for forty weeks—the period necessary for the gestation of the human embryo."[90]

The ultimate natural symbol of the Pyramid is, of course, the volcanic mountain. The worship of such mountains intensified all over the world wherever the Pyramid archetype dominated civilization. More than a mere mountain, the volcano churns fire up from deep within the earth. Like a penis pumping semen, it erupts flaming magma into the sky. A long, urethra-like pipe carries magma from the earth's molten core to the volcano's mouth. Both the penile urethra and the volcanic pipe are physical analogs of the axis mundi, representing the active, procreative aspect of the masculine principle. But the symbolic equation of penis and volcano captures also the destructive power of the masculine principle. When it is severed from the Self and unleashed like the violently erupting volcano, it cuts down everything in its path, humanity and nature alike.

Patterning Energy

The Pyramid archetype outlined a new vision of human society, one which could organize unheard of numbers of people to achieve undreamed of wonders and heights of power. Perhaps this was the first totalitarian vision in history, but it was also the first revelation of what humanity is capable of, for better or worse, when it organizes itself on a massive scale. Unlike the pyramidally-structured secular organizations of today (corporations, the military, any large hierarchical system), the Pyramid Age's theocracy knew that motivating people required addressing their spiritual needs at least as much as manipulating their political aspirations.

In each of the archetypes we have discussed, we have seen the psyche, society, religion, government, art and architecture, mythology, cosmology, and technology all changing shape according to the precepts of the prevalent archetype. This produces great changes in the way life is lived and the world is seen, but the impersonal, animating energy driving these changes is itself a constant. It is the way it is shaped and channeled and patterned that changes. The Great Round brought the spiraling energies of the Sensitive Chaos into conformance with the spherical cosmos of the Great Goddess. The Four Quarters split the Great Round along the cardinal directions and aligned the energy accordingly to reinforce the new ego's command of its territories. In this chapter, we have seen how the Pyramid archetype has stretched that same energy vertically to create the Pyramid form, the World Mountain, and the axis mundi. In the next chapter, we will see yet another redirection of this energy in the Radiant Axes, the *archetype of the Sun*.

SYNOPSIS OF THE PYRAMID

World of the God-King

SPATIAL SYMBOL

Pyramid or octahedron

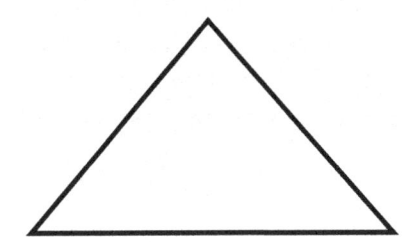

SOCIETY

Era
Dynastic Era, Classic Period, "Golden Age," "High" Civilization

Society
Theocratic nation or city-state
    Class-stratified society reflected in class-differentiated residences and burials
    Dynastic God-King or Divine-Ruler at the apex of the social pyramid, followed by an elite priesthood or an aristocratic ruling class or both

Examples
Old Kingdom Egypt; Sumerian, Akkadian, and First Babylonian civilizations in Mesopotamia; India under Ashoka and the Buddhist and Hindu dynasties; Qin through Song dynasties

278 Spatial Archetypes

in China; Teotihuacan and Mayan cultures in Mesoamerica; Moche, Nazca, and Tiahuananacan civilizations in Peru; Classical Greece; Medieval (Gothic) Europe

Technology

Statecraft: standing armies, public works programs, law codes, administrative bureaucracies, written records and histories, taxation or tribute systems, census-taking, food storage and redistribution systems, state religious ceremonies, urban centers and capital cities.

Logos principle dominates, seen in creation myths based on the Word; order and enlightenment through the Law; belief in the sacredness of rational forms including numbers, geometry, names, mathematics, standards of measurement, and canonical proportions; interest in the sky and the mind as opposed to the earth and the body. Technelogos increasingly dominates psychoeros.

Gender Roles

Patriarchal family structures and social systems (although a residue of older matrilineal traditions may persist as in pharaonic Egypt).

Hieros gamos as a sovereignty-fertility-bestowing ritual and as a coronation rite, usually occurring at the tops of pyramids, as for example in Sumer and Angkor.

PSYCHE

Psychology

In young adulthood, identification with the father to complete the separation from the mother, establish the ego, and assume adult responsibilities. At any age, identification with the logos principle.

Perceiving the world as a Pyramid: pyramidal social classes and power structures, the chronological stratification of time, and so on; ambition to move up the pyramid to reach the apex of power and wisdom, Increasing dualistic thought, symbolized by the upward and downward pointing pyramids.

Stagnation
Psychological stagnation in the pyramid can produce a rigid adherence to conventional codes of behavior and dogmatic religious doctrines, and an excessive identification with the masculine principle as highly authoritarian father figure

Liberation
Psychological liberation in the pyramid generates the perception of the Self as the incarnation of transcendent being, which, having negotiated the *axis mundi* to master the three planes of existence—heaven (pure consciousness), earth (ordinary waking consciousness), and the underworld (the unconscious)—sees the order of the universe.

SPIRIT

Worldview
Cosmos as the World Mountain, the creation and kingdom of the Father-God.

Spiritual Focus
Spiritual and political power of the state theocratically vested in the God-King, his priesthood, and the state religion. A syncretic state religion with a pyramidal pantheon reflecting the social structure.

An elite priesthood with a secret knowledge of science, astronomy, and spiritual matters.

Mythic Themes
Mythic images and rites concerning the World Mountain, the Mountain Arising from the Sea of Chaos, the nightly or annual *hieros gamos* on the World Mountain to restore the king's vitality or sovereignty; the Separation of the World Parents and their reunion (through the *hieros gamos*); shamanic journeys on the axis mundi (mastery of heaven, earth, and underworld); immortality, mortuary rituals, embalming; the second birth through the Father; ritualized tests of the king's fitness to rule (e.g., the Heb Sed Festival in Egypt).

CULTURE

Prime Symbol
The World Mountain

Art
Substitution of ceramic effigies of members of the king's retinue who formerly would have been buried with him (may be related to the secure establishment of the nation state)

Astronomy
The fixed and moving stars (planets) indicate the order to be recreated in the earthly realm.

Time
Linear sense of time, preoccupation with immortality and the transcendence of temporal reality, use of a solar calendar

Space
Space as the World Mountain, whose layers and faces symbolize the realms of existence, the heavens and hells, and the social structure. Great emphasis on the axis mundi—the vertical axis between heaven and earth—mediated by the God-King (seen as the Son of Heaven, as in China, or the son, agent, or incarnation of the Father God, as in Egypt and the pre-Columbian civilizations).

Landscape
Four quartered landscapes and gardens.

Architecture
Architectural representations of the World Mountain—pyramids, ziggurats, stupas—as the most important structures, which may serve as temples, royal tombs, reliquaries, or astronomical observatories.

THE RADIANT AXES
World of the Emperor as Sun-God

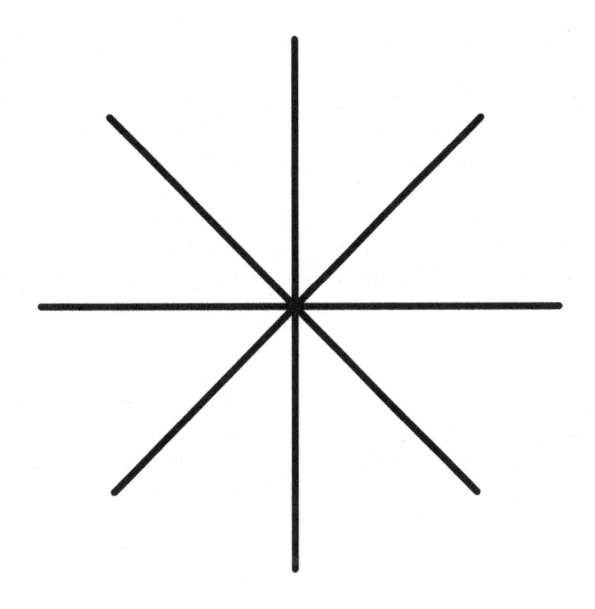

5a. Gardens and Palace of Versailles. Versailles, France. Louis XIV began expanding an existing lodge in 1661. Seen here is the 1700 Plan of Nicolas de Fer. The radiating paths of the gardens (by André Le Nôtre) symbolize the extension to infinity of the absolute power of the monarch. Louis XIV was the Sun King, but so were most emperors. Versailles became a model for other European palaces and numerous imperial capitals.

5b. The McMillan Plan. For the Mall in Washington DC. Pierre L'Enfant did the original plan for Washington in 1791, but the monumental core we know in Washington today is the result of the McMillan Plan done in 1902. As a result of the Spanish–American War of 1898 the United States became a global power, and a monumental capital seemed appropriate.

5c. Ceque system. Cusco, the capital of the Incan empire, was at the center of a series of roads, as was Rome and many other capitals of empires, but it was also at the center of a series of ritual pathways that radiated out over the empire. In a sense, the Ceque system was a conceptual network of radiating boulevards organizing the empire.

5d. New Delhi. National Capital Territory of Delhi. Designed by British architects Sir Edwin Lutyens and Sir Herbert Baker, New Delhi's status as an empire capital was secured when George V, Emperor of India, laid its foundation stone in 1911.

The Radiant Axes 283

5a

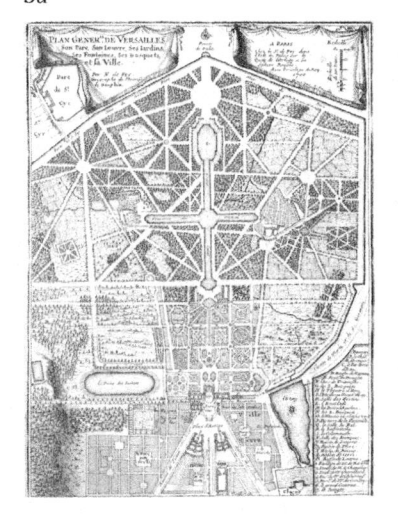

5b

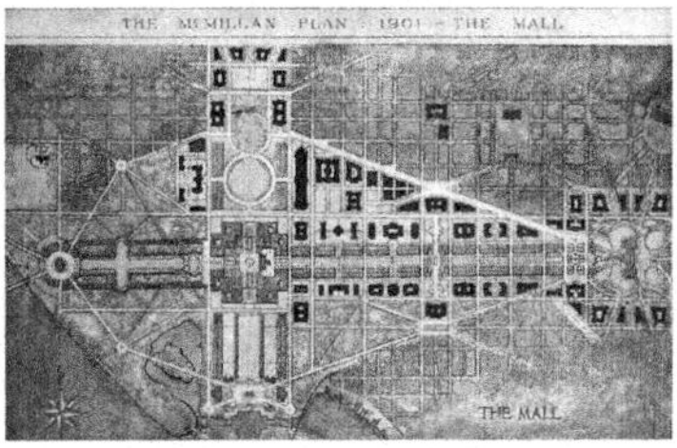

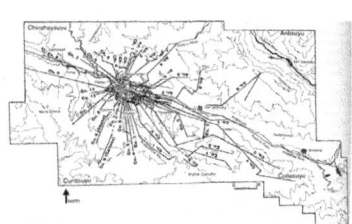

5c

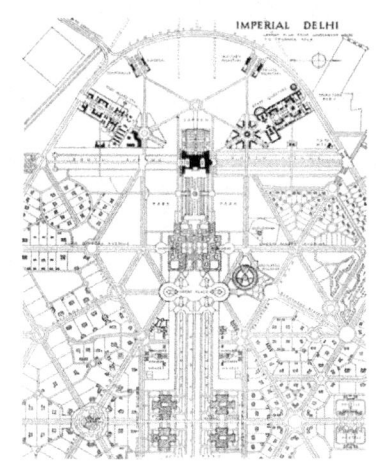

5d

THE RADIANT AXES

World of the Emperor as Sun-God

> One climbs the Aha, the lonesome place of the majestic soul, the high room of the intelligence which moves across the sky; one now opens the door of the horizon building of the primordial god of the two countries in order to see the mystery of Horus shining.
> ~ Egyptian inscription, 840 B.C.[1]

The Empire and the Inflated Ego

In the last chapter we saw that the Pyramid is often associated with the sun: the Egyptian pyramid was equated with the sun rising between the Horns of Consecration; the Buddhist stupa is circumambulated in imitation of the sun's apparent course around the earth; and the golden towers of the Khmer pyramids were nightly visited by a female "Lord of the Sun." But pyramids are predominantly symbols of the World Mountain. In the Radiant Axes archetype the sun itself becomes the prime symbol. The rays of the Radiant Axes diagram are the sun's rays, radiating their light infinitely through the cosmos. Now there are no boundaries. The old walls around the Four Quarters have crumbled, and the earthbound base of the pyramid has evaporated. Only that singular point of blazing energy and its infinite radiation of power remain. This is the age of the empire.

An empire results when one nation state undertakes military expansion on an unprecedented scale, swallowing other nations whole just as at dawn the sun swallows the stars in its brilliant light. The ruler of an empire is an exponentially more powerful being than the king of a nation state. He is Emperor, absolute monarch, King of Kings. More often than not he fancies himself an incarnation of the Sun-God. No mere nature spirit, tribal deity, or national god can compete with the sun. The sun blazes around the world, the mightiest heavenly being of them all. It is the constant in a world of flux, and the highest conceivable champion of light and consciousness.

This is the age both of the visionary and of the inflated ego. Like the Empire and the Emperor—indeed, like the infinite rays of the Radiant Axes—the inflated ego knows no bounds. It no longer looks for guidance to the mothers and fathers, heroes and chieftains, priestesses and priests, goddesses and gods; it believes it is god, invincible, omnipotent, eternal.[2] Sometimes ego-inflated people are revered as visionaries and prophets, and a few do achieve a deep identification with the Self and a total extinguishment of ego. In many others, however, it is at best a source of ego-centrism, and at worst a source of psychosis, sociopathic behavior, despotism, and even brutal fascism.

Any of us may experience mild ego-inflation at various points in our lives, carrying us to manic exhilaration and the temporary feeling that we are omnipotent. A strong religious background may color the episode with the conscious illusion that we are God, or Christ, or the Virgin Mary, or Isis, or Buddha, or whomever is our central religious figure. Usually we cannot maintain this exaltation. The more we try, the more it slips away. We may fall into depression and feel we have failed. We may even spin ever deeper into a vortex of despair, into the antithesis of the inflated ego: *deflation*.

In the schema of the Buddhist Wheel of Life, deflation is represented as a fall from the God Realm to the Realms of the jealous Gods, Hungry Ghosts, and ultimately to the Hell Realm. In Greek myth, inflation and deflation are represented by the flight of Icarus. In order to escape from Crete after Minos had imprisoned him in the Labyrinth, Daedalus fashioned wings out of feathers and wax for himself and his son Icarus. As they flew heavenward, Daedalus warned his son not to fly too close to the sun lest the wax melt, but Icarus could not resist the sun's attraction. He flew too close (inflation); the wax melted, his wings disintegrated, and he fell into the ocean and drowned (deflation). Hindu writings liken the experience to that of the moth, seeking illumination, flying into a flame, which incinerates it.[3] In this chapter, we will be dealing only with the inflated half of the experience, since it is one of the most crucial aspects of the Radiant Axes. Its consequences—deflation—will become clear in the following chapter on the Grid.

Decadence

In tracing the spatial archetypes, we have seen analogies between the development of the individual psyche and the development of civilization. In this chapter we see the inflated ego expressed in civilization through the empire and the Emperor. The God-King of the pyramid archetype represents the mature development of the psyche to the point of assuming responsibility for the welfare of society; the Emperor of the Radiant Axes represents, more often than not, the decay of that sense of responsibility into an ego-inflated craving for personal gratification. Of course there are despotic God-Kings and benevolent Emperors, but, despite any beneficent aspects, the Radiant Axes empire would not exist without an insatiable lust for power.

Empires usually have extremely exploitive relationships with their colonies. Subjects are likely to be burdened with high taxes or tributes, which not only support the necessary machinery of the state but also fill the coffers of the imperial palace and support its luxuries. Among his luxuries an Emperor usually has a formal, institutionalized royal harem composed of hundreds or even thousands of women—prisoners of war, slaves, and innocent daughters offered as tribute by ambitious fathers hoping to win some petty colonial appointment, privilege, or favor from the Emperor. Such harems are a telling sign that the Radiant Axes archetype has overtaken a civilization. Moreover, they indicates the decreasing status of women—now women can be collected and traded like a commodity. The harem is also the final degradation of the *hieros gamos*, especially when the royal concubines serve as in-house, readily available "priestesses" or "temple prostitutes." One common variant is the sequestering of a select group of highborn virgins such as the Vestal Virgins of Rome and the Incan Empire's "chosen women." In effect, this practice takes the most eligible women from the most influential families "off the market" reducing the threat that the emperor's rivals will gain power through strategic marriages.

Other Radiant Axes palace luxuries include royal zoos, botanical gardens, seasonal villas, and feasts of extremely rare and exotic foodstuffs (peacocks' eyes, for instance). All of these express the conquest of nature in this acceleratingly logos-oriented era. Emperors take pride in their collections of unusual animals, plants, women, culinary delicacies, and even indigenous peoples from remote territories. The more exotic the species, the more it demonstrates the Emperors ability to collect rarities from the ends of the earth—in other words, the more it proves that the Empire's territories and powers are inconceivably vast. Like most "dominant males" in the animal world, Radiant Axes Emperors intimidate rivals by making elaborate displays of their territorial command.

Secularism and the State Religion

When ego-inflated people believe they are divine, they see gods and goddesses are mere pretenders to the spiritual throne. They are on an equal footing with the deities, know their secrets, and see their frailties. This is expressed in the general hollowness of the religious institutions of the Radiant Axes. Even the God-King of the Pyramid archetype understood that he was not God but his son or incarnation or representative on earth. Not so with the Emperor. Like the God-King, the Emperor rewrites history and myth to shape the state religion, but his purpose is somewhat different. The God-King usually elevates his tribal deity to supremacy; the Emperor elevates himself.

Often the Emperor's view of himself as divine is unconscious, just as people with inflated egos may have no insight into their problem. The empire fronts an imperial Sun-God or supreme deity, but the Emperor outshines this god, as at Abu Simbel, where the statues of Ramses II are far more monumental and numerous than those of the deities; or at Versailles, where the radiant presence of the Sun-King Louis XIV everywhere outshines the decorative Apollo motifs.

Whether conscious of his assumed divinity or not, the Emperor uses the state religion to aggrandize his image through pompous, imperial ceremonies and rigid hierarchies devoid of authentic spiritual inspiration. At worst, the state religion grotesquely projects a kind of collective imperial neurosis, as when Aztec rulers sacrificed thousands of people and offered their beating hearts to slake the unquenchable thirst of the Sun-God—a personification of the rulers' own insatiability. At best, empires recognize that the state religion's purpose is mainly political and permit their subjects a fair amount of religious freedom, provided the imperial deities are duly respected. The Incan and the pre-Christian Roman Empires exemplified this tolerant eclecticism.

The Radiant Axes symbol hints at this growing secularism. It is a point from which lines radiate in all directions. The point—the sun, the Emperor, the empire, the capital city—is the center of the universe. This is very unlike the Pyramid symbol, with its vertical axis as the vital link between heaven and earth, human and divine. No such link exists in the Radiant Axes. Heaven and earth, human and divine are fused in the central point, but when that point is the inflated ego, heaven and the divine lose their power.

The corruption of religion in the Radiant Axes further diminishes the power of spirituality in human affairs, a trend that runs through the successive archetypes from the Sensitive Chaos (the most spiritual) to the Grid (the most secular). Two larger trends produce this effect: the growing dominance of technelogos (with its dualistic, linear, rational, left-brain thinking) and the ever-decreasing status both of women and of female-centered spirituality.

The Radiant Axes archetype follows directly from the Pyramid, but it represents a turning point as well. The Pyramid archetype was still infused with a sense of the divine. Even its laws and logos-oriented sciences were like luminous new filaments in a collective psyche still overwhelmingly imbued with awe and mystery. We can group the six archetypes into pairs. The Sensitive Chaos and the Great Round form a natural pair as the psychoerotic wellspring of all spiritual experience. The Four Quarters and the Pyramid solidify the dominance of the masculine principle in civilization and begin the shift toward technelogos. The Radiant Axes and the Grid actualize technelogos and generate the despirited, materialistic ethos rampant today.

Palaces and Radiating Roads

The architecture of the Radiant Axes empires expresses the archetype perfectly. The palace is the solar center of the empire:

the home of the Sun-King in Louis XIV's France, the Son of Heaven in China, and the descendent of the sun in imperial Japan, Incan Peru, Aztec Mexico, and the New Kingdom in Egypt. The Radiant Axes palace, which had inherited importance as the "Center of the World" from the Four Quarters and as the axis mundi from the Pyramid, accrues the grandiose symbolism of the sun. It is the focal point of the radiating rays of power, which take concrete form in axial streets and avenues tanning out from the palace through the capital city, and from the capital to the remote frontiers of the empire.

These road systems most purely embody the Radiant Axes image, especially in the Versailles-influenced Baroque capitals built during the Western Age of Imperialism. These include not only European cities but also Washington, D.C. and New Delhi in India. The centers of these cities have clearly delineated networks of radiating roads, but nearly every empire in history has laced the landscape with its Royal Roads and King's Highways.

Perhaps the most familiar is the road system of the Roman Empire, which reached as far as the British Isles. However, the empires of the Persians, Alexander the Great, Kublai Khan, and others also had thousands of miles of imperial highways. Even the Incan rulers built roads over 2000 miles long, and they had no wheeled vehicles.

Roads and sea lanes are the vital arteries and nervous systems of empires. Along them move goods, intelligence, military troops, governors, and imperial progresses. From Incan Peru to Kublai Khan's China, imperial highways were outfitted with way-stations for the convenience of official travelers and for changing shifts of twenty-four hour relay messengers, who carried information back and forth from the capital to the colonies. This highly effective pre-electronic communications system is another manifestation of the Radiant Axes.

Obelisks and Colossi

The Radiant Axes archetype expresses itself in three other prevalent art forms: obelisks, colossal statues, and panoramic propagandistic murals. The obelisk is the axis mundi freed of its pyramidal base. In the three-dimensional energy field of the Radiant Axes, the axis mundi is simply another ray of power, but an important one due to its past associations. Theoretically, an obelisk marks a point in space that acts as an energizing center, just as the sun does in the sky. Unless there is some mathematical symbolism at work, the linear dimension of the obelisk is important only as an embodiment of radiant axiality and as a giver of presence.

The Egyptian obelisk, which was seen as a ray of the sun and served as a sundial in astronomical measurements, evolved out of the pyramids of the Old Kingdom. Pyramid building declined after the Fourth Dynasty (after 2473 B.C.).[4] One transitional structure was the Fifth Dynasty sun-temple of Ne-user-ra, a squat cross between a pyramid and an obelisk. As a sun-temple (which figured in Schiaparelli's equation of the sun and the pyramid), it presaged the New Kingdom's obsession with the sun.[5]

The first obelisk was built during the Middle Kingdom, at the temple of Sesostris I in Heliopolis, the city of Helios, the sun. But nearly all of the other Egyptian obelisks were built during the imperialistically expansive New Kingdom period in Egyptian history (about 1570 to 1080 B.C.). This was the era when the Hebrews were held in captivity, when much of the Near East fell under Egyptian domination, and when worship of the sun god, Amen-Ra, was at its height. The most striking Egyptian obelisks were erected at the temples of Amen-Ra at Karnak and Luxor, which we will see later in this chapter.[6]

In Europe, the use of obelisks as focal points of radiating avenues in capital cities followed soon after the rise of Western imperialism. By the early fifteenth century, Europeans had "discovered" much of the world. By the end of the fifteenth century, this expansive thrust found expression in Pope Sixtus V's new plan for Rome. Long interested in bringing order to the design of the city to make it a fitting capital for Christendom, Sixtus V initiated his plan in 1585, the first year of his five-year reign. In *Design of Cities*, Edmund Bacon describes how Sixtus V erected four Egyptian obelisks at strategic points in the city: near the Porta del Popolo, at the west end of Santa Maria Maggiore, in front of San Giovanni in Laterano, and, of course, in front of Saint Peter's. Rather than contributing a park here, a plaza there, Sixtus V drew the entire city into his design field. Bacon shows how the obelisk-points and their connecting lines of force generated tensions, thrusts and counterthrusts that energized great distances of space and centuries of time. Thus was created the Rome of today, with its generous network of piazzas and interconnecting vias. Sixtus V's plan influenced not only later Roman architects, but also the designers of nearly every Western capital that followed.[7]

Many other obelisk-like structures accompanied the rise of empires. Asoka's edict columns in India resemble the obelisk, both in form and meaning, and Asoka was the closest to an empire-builder that India had before Moghul, Rajput, and finally the British rule. The Roman Empire had Trajan's column, and China similarly had Mandate of Heaven columns signifying the heavenly ancestry of the ruler. In China, the Buddhist stupa evolved into the vertical pagoda, which japan also adopted—somewhat uncomfortably. The Islamic minaret, too, echoes the obelisk. It functions as the place where the muezzin calls the faithful to prayer, and, in that extremely expansionistic civilization that grows by winning or forcing converts, calling the faithful to prayer is a most important activity. The other two art forms prevalent in the Radiant Axes are colossal statues, such as those of Ramses II at Abu Simbel; and panoramic murals, such as those lining the Persian capital at Persepolis. These huge works of art, expressive of the inflated ego, are designed mainly to intimidate the viewer. The murals at Persepolis, for instance, consist primarily of ranks upon ranks of identical soldiers, hundreds in all, forming a formidable array of power. Their display of military might was designed to awe visiting dignitaries into submission. The statues at Abu Simbel, and the temple surrounding them, give us one of the clearest portraits of the Radiant Axes Emperor in world art and architecture.

Abu Simbel

Abu Simbel is the renowned Egyptian rock-cut temple that was painstakingly moved, with United States help, when the area was flooded by the High Dam at Aswan.[8] The temple was carved out of the living rock by the architects, laborers, and slaves of Ramses

II, the greatest builder of the New Kingdom. Ancient inscriptions name the temple's original cliff site as a Holy Mountain, suggesting a lingering or fabricated association with a sacred site of the Pyramid Age.

Imposingly presiding over the temple's exterior are four colossal statues of Ramses II over sixty-five feet high, which flank the entrance in pairs. Ramses II is thus the only presence on the outside of the temple, having completely replaced the gods and goddesses in the external world. Eight somewhat smaller statues of Ramses line the temple's inside passage, which leads deep within the cliff to the holy-of-holies, where four still smaller statues show Ramses alongside the gods Amen, Ptah, and Re-Harakhty.[9]

This temple, a study in hubris, is oriented so dawn sunlight illuminates the four rear statues twice a year, on about October 20th and February 20th. As far as anyone knows, these days have no cosmic import—they have not been correlated with any major celestial event such as the rising or setting of an important star or a key marking in the phases or eclipses of the moon. Apparently Abu Simbel's peculiar solar hierophany celebrates dates that were notable only in the life of Ramses II. Egyptologist Louis Cristophe believes that the temple was designed to celebrate Ramses' thirty-year jubilee (a descendent of the Heb Sed Festival) in 1260 B.C.[10] If so, Ramses II sanctioned his continued reign with solar rays, in keeping with the inflated quality of the Radiant Axes. This monumental work of architecture—one of the most admired in the world—leads nowhere but to the ego of its builder. It has virtually no transcendent significance.

On one of his exterior colossal statues, Ramses had his "favorite wife" Nefertari, who had a small temple of her own several hundred yards upstream on the Nile, sculpted as a tiny figure at his feet. This is a revealing measure of the diminished role of the queen and of women in Egypt's Radiant Axes era. The choice of Abu Simbel for immediate rescue through an unprecedented effort by the United States government, the United Nations, and the Egyptian government is telling. This temple, perhaps more than any other ancient monument, glorifies the brute force of unrestrained, imperialistic egoism. Meanwhile, the much older and far more sacred healing center of Isis on the nearby island of Philae was flooded and neglected. Although its beautiful Ptolemaic temple to Isis was eventually moved to dry land, the sacred place itself, with its thousands of years of accumulated power, was allowed to disappear beneath Lake Nasser.[11] Similarly, the rich living culture of the Nubian people, for whom the Aswan Dam region had been ancestral homeland for thousands of years, was wiped out under the unnatural deluge.

The Solar Temples of the New Kingdom

The temples of Amen-Ra at Karnak and Luxor, the largest ever built in Egypt, embody the gigantism of the Radiant Axes. At Karnak, the Great Hypostyle Hall completed by Ramses II is large enough to contain Paris's Notre Dame Cathedral. Before the New Kingdom, Karnak's site was sacred to Amen, then a local god of the ambitious Theban princes who vied for power with the established Pharaohs to the North. In those days, Amen was honored only by a small brick and stone temple on the east bank of the Nile. The Theban kings rose to power during the Middle Kingdom, but it was not until they had succeeded in ending centuries of foreign domination by the Hyksos, around 1560 B.C., that the prosperous New Kingdom began, with Thebes as its capital. Amen became the national god and assimilated the properties of the sun god Ra, as befits the royal deity of a Radiant Axes empire, and thus came to be known as Amen-Ra. All succeeding generations of New Kingdom Pharaohs competed to honor this vigorous, solar deity by building ever bigger pylons, obelisks, halls, temples, and avenues at Karnak. They often even dismantled the works of their predecessors and reused the materials in their own constructions. Like a temple on steroids, Karnak grew more bloated with each successive Pharaoh's architectural muscle-flexing.

While the capital city at Thebes long ago dissolved, the great temples at Karnak and Luxor survived, and indeed, were built to last. The capital was probably made of mud brick, the most common building material in the Near East, but the temples were made of stone, Egypt's material of choice to confront eternity. The temples, more than the capital, formed the political center of the kingdom. They accommodated the vast bureaucracy of the state priesthood, surrounding its activities with an aura of mystery and import. Their layers of walls, pylons, entrance courts, and halls filtered out the lower classes, allowing only the elite into the inner temple.

Most forbidding were the rows of massive pylons punctuated with obelisks that flanked the entrances. Along their major axes, Karnak had five pairs of pylons, and Luxor three. These huge, canted, double piers are late stylizations of the mountains flanking the Nile. They are the Radiant Axes New Kingdom version of the Horns of Consecration, and, as such, it is what is between them that is significant. At first it looks as if the pylons simply frame a seemingly endless, axial, sequence of spaces: entrance courts, colonnaded halls, forecourts, antechambers, and sanctuaries. But taken together these spaces make up a path, a progression, a sacred way that leads ultimately to the sacred barge of the Amen-Ra in the revered inner temple. The barge is the Sun-God's abode on earth, the place where he touches down to send his rays of power into human life.

Only the highest elite have access to this power source, identified foremost with the Pharaoh. What is important in the New Kingdom temples—what is framed by the Horns of Consecration and animates the entire culture—is the sun, the cosmic source of the Radiant Axes.

Karnak, Luxor, and other New Kingdom temples were connected less with the spiritual meaning of the sun (as a symbol of the Self, for instance) than with its political radiance. On state occasions, the Pharaoh and the high priests carried the barge of Amen-Ra out of its temple through the land in great royal processions, which moved along two axes. Along the east/west axis of death and resurrection, funerary processions traversed between the temples on the Nile's eastern bank (the direction of sunrise and life) and the tombs in the Valley of the Kings on the west bank (the direction of sunset and death.) Along the north-south axis of life and fertility, the sacred marriage pageants moved between the temple of the Goddess Mut and Karnak to the north and Luxor to the south. Though the voyage to Mut's temple was sometimes made by land, the north/south processional route, like the east/

west route, also used the Nile as a means of conveyance. Amen-Ra in his solar barge, traversing the earthly Nile, mirrored Egypt's time-honored vision of the deities in their sacred barges majestically traversing the celestial Nile.

The New Kingdom's spectacular processions were nominally spiritual, but mostly they provided an impressive opportunity for a multitude of political activities: solidifying loyalties, collecting offerings, hearing petitions, cementing allegiances, making pronouncements, bestowing favors, showing off the state regalia. Elizabeth I, an acute politician, used her processions for the same purposes. Our presidential and congressional campaigns, which get the candidates and incumbents out to "press the flesh" every few years, are our nearest equivalent.

Since the Nile River served Egypt as a natural transportation system, the New Kingdom never developed the radiating network of roads typical of other empires. However, it did have a type of processional way worth noting: the sphinx-lined avenue. The grandest example is the one built by Ramses II at Karnak, approaching the Temple of Amen-Ra on the east bank of the Nile. Originally it was lined with 124 ram-headed, lion-bodied sphinxes, each protecting a small figure of Ramses II between its paws. Both the ram and the lion are solar animals: the lion, because of its power, its golden color, and the sun-like mane of the male lion; the ram, because of its long mythic associations with masculinity, procreation, and creativity. The ram is the icon of male-oriented cultures that favor the abstract constancy of what they view as the "masculine" sun over the irregular cycles of the "feminine" moon.

Throughout the "Old World", the displacement in art and religion of the bull by the ram signals the displacement of the Great Round's peaceful, agrarian, goddess-centered civilization by the Four Quarters' warlike worshippers of the storm and sky gods. Since cattle were the prime economic assets of the people of the Great Round, it is natural that they revered the bull and cow as religious symbols. Similarly, the economy of the original Four Quarters cultures depended on sheepherding, hence their reverence for the ram. Thus it was fitting that in the solar-identified Radiant Axes' New Kingdom in Egypt, when Amen became

Amen-Ra the sun-god, he adopted the ram as his animal emblem and the lion as his celestial throne.[13]

The High Room of the Sun

The most unusual solar reference in Amen-Ra's temples is described by astronomer Gerald Hawkins in *Beyond Stonehenge*. After conducting a computerized search for celestial alignments among the axes at Karnak, he concluded, simply, that the great temple was oriented eastward, away from the Nile toward sunrise on the Winter Solstice. Inside the temple he noted a mural, which dates from the reigns of Hatshepsut and Thutmose III.

> It showed the sun-god in his yearly journey, carried around the sky on a boat. Ra, Horus, Sokaris, Kepri, the sun-god in all his names was, apparently, born each year at a special location in the temple. An inscription dating to 840 B.C. said*: One climbs the Aha, the lonesome place of the majestic soul, the high room of the intelligence which moves across the sky; one now opens the door of the horizon building of the primordial god of the two countries in order to see the mystery of Horus shining!*[14]

How poignantly this inscription captures the existential malaise of the solar-identified ego: *the mystery of Horus shining*—the mystery of the solar hawk, of Horus as the living Pharaoh; *the horizon building of the primordial god of the two countries*—the place of witness to the primordial schism, represented here as the two Egypts, Upper and Lower; *the high room of the intelligence which moves across the sky*—the inner sanctuary of the temple of the sun, both on earth and in the psyche; the *Aha, the lonesome place of the majestic soul*—that place where no mortal or divine can offer comfort or counsel, where one stands alone before eternity.

Hawkins found that the Aha is not only a mythical or psychological place described in an Egyptian inscription but also an actual place in the temple of Amen-Ra at Karnak, He writes:

> We climbed a stairway—steep, narrow, without sides—
> into a small open-to-the-sky chamber, the so-called High
> Room of the Sun. There was a square altar of alabaster
> in front of a rectangular aperture in the wall. This roof
> temple was dedicated to Ra-Hor-Akhty, the sun-god rising
> on the horizon. The wall carried a picture of the pharaoh,
> facing the aperture, one knee to the ground, making a
> gesture of greeting to the rising sun: Make acclamation to
> your beautiful face, master of the gods, Aman-Ra ...[15]

This room high up in the temple away from the main axis was, like the temple itself, aligned to Midwinter Sunrise. Both inscription and painting confirmed that this was the place where the Pharaoh celebrated, or even thought he *caused*, the birth of the sun from its annual nadir.

If we understand temples as models of the psyche, with intricacies and elaborations reflective of the psyche's complexity, then we can learn a lot from Karnak's dual sacred places—the inner temple and the High Room of the Sun. The barge of Amen-Ra in the inner temple is part of the persona of the temple, Despite layers of architectural barriers—pylons and obelisks, hypostyle hall, and so on, which are also part of the *persona*—the barge is meant for public display. The barriers are but stage-fronts designed for theatrical and political effect, their obscuration of the inner mystery serving to enhance its attraction. The High Room of the Sun, however, is the secret place—the one never revealed to the public, off the main axis/access route, accessible only to the Pharaoh. It is the soul-room of the Pharaoh, the holy-of-holies of his inner being. Here, he confronts the ultimate mystery that guided psyche, empire, and history. Here beats the solar heart of the Radiant Axes.

The Forbidden City

Building a huge empire upon the conquests of his grandfather Genghis Khan and other predecessors, Kublai Khan overcame the Southern Song Dynasty in China[16] and founded the Yuan Dynasty. As the Great Khan, leader of all the Mongols, he was Emperor of a realm that extended far beyond China to include Korea, Manchuria, Mongolia, most of Tibet, Mesopotamia, Persia, and southern Russia. In 1264 Kublai moved his capital from the Mongol stronghold of Karakorum south to Khanbaligh, "City of the Khan" later to become Beijing. He laid out the city on a grid eight miles on a side based on the traditional Chinese square. Three telescoping enclosures, now called the Inner City, the Imperial City, and the Forbidden City, were cut by a strong north-south axis running through the entire capital and blending with the grid in the outer precincts. Sibyl Moholy-Nagy observes that "there is no monumental termination of the central axis .... space asserts its infinity toward the endless horizon."[17] In the center of this infinite axis was the Imperial Palace, set symbolically above its surroundings on three platforms in the heart of the Forbidden City.

Here the Emperor enjoyed exotic excesses and presided over spectacular festivities. Among his "possessions" were hundreds of beautiful young women who served as concubines in the royal harem. The Khan's estate boasted other luxuries characteristics of Radiant Axes empires—rare botanical gardens; an animal park with an extraordinary collection of lynxes, leopards, and predatory birds used in elaborate hunting outings; a bountiful stock of deer and goats on which the carnivorous collection fed; and Shang-tu,[18] a northern Summer Palace. A significant portion of the palace housed the Emperor's military supplies and huge ceremonial wardrobe. Marco Polo reported that during annual New Year's celebrations and on the Khan's Birthday, the Emperor's subjects presented him with lavish tributes including a hundred thousand white horses—only the royal family was allowed to drink the milk of white mares.[19]

Marco Polo also describes an extensive public road system that stretched from Beijing to the outlying colonies, which permitted "ambassadors to the court and royal messengers [to] go and return through every province and kingdom of the empire with the greatest convenience and speed." Every twenty-five or thirty miles, posthouses were furnished with apartments and a stock of two hundred horses (supplied by or extorted from the local residents) for the use of diplomatic couriers. All the roads were clearly marked with trees or stones placed at six-foot intervals, and special runners with lights were provided for night travel.

> In between the post houses there are small villages, at a distance of every three miles, which may contain about forty cottages. In these are stationed the foot messengers in the service of his Majesty. They wear girdles round their waists, to which several small bells are attached, and as they run only three miles from one station to the next, the ringing gives notice of their approach and preparation is accordingly made by a fresh courier to continue with the packet. It is thus carried so swiftly that in the course of two days and nights his Majesty receives news that normally could not be obtained in less than ten days. It often happens that in the fruit season fruit gathered in the morning at Khan-balik is conveyed to the Great Khan at Shangtu by the evening of the following day, although the distance is generally considered as ten days' journey.[20]

Kublai Khan's Beijing was anything but a barbarous Mongol outpost. As the capital of the whole Mongol empire, it was the mercantile center of Eurasia and saw a continuous flow of people, goods, and ideas. Kublai Khan was known for his religious tolerance, but he ruled China autocratically, dividing the land into twelve bureaucratic provinces and the people into four classes. Topping the social ladder were the Mongols, who were given tax-exempt land. Next came foreigners chosen to serve the empire as administrators or traders. The Northern Chinese had given the least resistance to the Mongols in battle and were considered the lower middle class. Lastly, the conquered Song Chinese were treated as barbarians without rights, property, or permission to trade despite the fact that before the Mongolian conquest they had built the world's highest civilization at that time. Kublai Khan's class system spurred the national Chinese resentment and resistance that overthrew the Yuan Dynasty less than one hundred years after its founding.

The major features of Kublai Khan's empire are typical of the Radiant Axes: a vast cosmopolitan empire won through vigorous military expansionism, an absolute central authority whose power is aristocratic rather than theocratic, a lavish axially-planned capital and central palace, an extensive supporting bureaucracy, a spatial and temporal unification of the empire through a system of radiating roads, and an aristocratic social system that exploited the poor and the conquered to the point of generating a revolution.

After the fall of the Yuan Dynasty, Beijing continued to be China's capital through the succeeding centuries of the Ming and Qing (Manchu) Dynasties, the turbulent first half of the twentieth century, and the communist second half. Beijing has frequently been expanded, renovated, remodeled, and rebuilt since Kublai Khan's time, but his original layout of grids and axes still survives.

Versailles: Palace of the Sun-King

Before Louis XIV ascended to power, Europe had been weakened by the decline of Spain, the Papacy, and the Holy Roman Empire. It lacked identity and focus. Louis, the epitome of the Radiant Axes divine-right monarch, transformed France into a cultural and political axis around which all Europe revolved. The Age of Louis XIV consummated absolutism in Europe, spurring Voltaire to deem it one of the four great eras of Europe comparable to the civilization of fifth century Athens.

Coronated king at age five in 1643, Louis reached maturity at ease in his power. In 1661 he was invited to a reception at the splendid new chateau of the enormously rich and ambitious Marquis de Belle-Isle. Louis, still only twenty-three years old, was so jealous of the chateau's grandeur that within a month of the reception he arrested and imprisoned the Marquis on charges of treason and misappropriation of funds; confiscated the chateau's furnishings, ornaments, and trees; and retained the Marquis's prestigious design team—architect Louis Le Vau, interior designer Charles Le Brun, and landscape architect Andre Le Notre—to plan a palace around his father's old hunting lodge at Versailles.

From the beginning, Louis's intention in building Versailles was to create a court so unprecedented in glamour, fashion, and prestige that it would lure all self-respecting (and therefore potentially threatening) nobles away from their country estates to become courtiers at the palace. Here, Louis could favor them with court appointments, diffusing their ambitions while keeping them under close watch. Versailles became the key that turned the lock on Louis XIV's ever-increasing centralization of power.

Exploiting academic art's penchant for historical and mythological allusion, Louis shrewdly commissioned works that linked him with Alexander the Great and other heroes and with the sun-god Apollo. These potent associations proclaimed his unlimited ambitions, carved out a central place for him in myth and history, and announced that his reign would be a turning point in Europe's destiny, which indeed it was.

The Academic art itself was a product of the Radiant Axes, as we can see in these excerpts from Jose Argüelles's *The Transformative Vision*:

> The academization of art made a social institution of the one-point perspective system and the entire "backward"-looking school of humanism in general, thus inaugurating a profoundly conservative and authoritarian attitude within the arts and the creative process as a whole .... The doctrine of art for art's sake arose in the court and academy of Louis XIV ... Not only was art rational but in the art of history painting, the noblest visual art conceivable, lay the basis for the creed of progress: history, the unique propulsion of human events .... The consequences are enormous for they ultimately imply a denial of divine intervention; a negation of archetypes, replaced by the inalienable uniqueness of the individual ego ... reason and history triumphant in the arts was tantamount to a decapitation of the senses and a banishment of the right-hemisphere functions of the psyche.[21]

The cutting off of the senses and the right brain that Argüelles mentions unhinged humanity's whole relationship with nature.

The Age of Reason, which we will look at more closely in the next chapter, was a complete reversal of the Great Round. Under that archetype, people enjoyed their full sensual and psychoerotic capacities and perceived little division between humanity and nature. The people of the Great Round wove a civilization around their desire to live in utmost harmony with nature's seasonal vicissitudes and to find a graceful participation in its semi-erratic energies.

Several archetypal eras removed from the Great Round, the Age of Reason culminated three thousand years of worsening schisms between mind and body, humanity and nature, male and female. By the time of Louis XIV, the break was complete. The negated half was severed. In the worldview of the Age of Reason, human intellect governed the cosmos. Nature was a dangerously irrational force to be conquered and subdued. The vast formal gardens at Versailles exemplify rationalism's ideal relationship to nature.

> To the enlightened seventeenth-century mind formal gardens like those at Versailles—hedged, trimmed, and carefully laid out in precise geometrical patterns—represented the triumph of man over nature, of civilization over barbarism. A carelessly meandering branch or twig or blade of grass was immediately seized upon and snipped, clipped, pressed, or mowed back into its assigned place.[22]

In Apollo, Louis chose the most apt academic mythological figure to convey his identification with the sun. The Greek god emblazoned Versailles's buildings, pavilions, and theatrical events. The dramatic fountains of Apollo and his mother Latona (Leto) "occupy the place of honor in the gardens of Versailles, along the axis of the chateau's main promenade. Apollo, god of the sun, the symbol of Louis XIV, is shown in his chariot being drawn into the depth of the sea by his four charges, that he may illuminate the heavens!"[23] The implication was, of course, that Louis XIV would similarly illuminate the world.

Like Apollo in the garden, the palace at Versailles itself occupies a strategic point. It is the focal point, to the west of the

304 *Spatial Archetypes*

Palace, of the elaborate system of radiant axes in the garden, and, to the East of the Palace, of the three grand avenues leading to Paris. The axes of the eastern avenues, separated by the sweep of two semicircular stables, converge in the very center of the palace, in the king's bedroom. This arrangement turns Versailles into Apollo's chariot "drawn" by the twin arcs of the stables, the "equine palaces" housing the king's horses. In silent testimony to the potency of the Sun King, the major axial avenues—the architectural solar rays of the empire's manifest destiny—radiated from the king's bed.[25]

After his death in 1715, Louis XlV's style of absolute monarchy lasted in France only seventy-four years. The internal unrest and social injustices caused by such an extreme centralization of power set off the French Revolution in 1789, just six years after the American Revolution had won recognition of the new nation at the Treaty of Paris. The Radiant Axes archetype in Western civilization still had some time to run—the British Empire did not reach its peak until Queen Victoria's reign, and the newborn United States had yet even to conceive of joining the club of imperialistic powers.

Copernicus, Kepler and the Baroque Radiant Axes

Louis XIV ascended to the throne exactly one hundred years after the death of Copernicus and one year after the death of Galileo and the birth of Newton. The king's solar metaphor mirrored the sun's new importance to the scientists of the time who showed that the sun, not the earth, was the center of the universe. The heliocentric theory, European imperialism, the centralization of power in France in an absolute divine-right monarch, and Louis XIV as that monarch with the epithet the *Sun-King* all reflect Radiant Axes solar imagery.

The plan at Versailles perfected a radically new approach to city design, one that had begun with Pope Sixtus V's proposal to bring order to the chaos of medieval Rome by imposing a system of axial avenues that converged on focal obelisks. This concept grew out of the perspective techniques of Renaissance painting and architecture. After Versailles, it burst into capital city planning all over Europe as an axial force smashing through the old walled, fragmented, medieval towns.[23] It became the model also for the radial avenues of Washington, D.C., designed in the late 18th century by the Frenchman Charles L'Enfant. Consistent with the boundlessness of the Radiant Axes archetype, Versailles and the later axial capitals were designed without walls or fortifications.

> All in all, the Radiant Axes was as brief in Europe as in other cultures, compared with the lifespans of earlier archetypes. The politically simple Sensitive Chaos cultures could survive through the millennia with little change or disruption. Not so the high-tension Radiant Axes empires. Like Icarus soaring for the sun, they could not sustain themselves. Their unnatural inflation eventually caused their downfall. The same pattern prevailed in the New World as in the Old, as we will see in the Incan Empire. (For a timeline of Europe's Radiant Axes, see Appendix 9.)

The Radiant Axes in the Americas

Before the European conquest of the Americas, two indigenous cultures achieved full Radiant Axes empires: the Aztecs in Mexico and the Incas in South America. Despite their differences, the two empires had much in common. Both were founded by tribes rising out of obscurity through military might. The Aztecs grew out of the Mexica, one of seven tribes that traced their origin to Chicomoztoc (seven caves) in Aztlan to the northwest of the Valley of Mexico. Migrating and raiding their way into the Valley, they conquered it in A.D. 1428 and proceeded to amass an empire covering most of Mexico, using as a cultural model the warlike Toltecs who had gone before them.

The Incas grew out of a minor kingdom that ruled the little city-state of Cuzco and was constantly engaged in petty warfare with its neighbors. After an important defensive victory in 1438, the Incas added more and more territory to their rapidly growing empire until, at its height just before the Spanish Conquest, it

306 *Spatial Archetypes*

contained over six million people and extended more than 2600 miles along the coast and highlands of western South America.

Both empires built massive machines of statecraft, well-organized, and fueled by an imperialistic adoration of the sun—the bloodthirsty Tonatiuh to the Aztecs and the divine royal ancestor Inti to the Incas. Another deity also played a critical role in the destiny of the two cultures: the bearded, white culture-bearer called Quetzalcoatl in Mexico and Viracocha in South America. Like King Arthur in British lore, Quetzalcoatl and Viracocha were semi-legendary rulers who had brought civilization to a golden age, and then disappeared with the promise that they would one day return. Believing Cortes to be the bearded, white god Quetzalcoatl, whose return had been foretold almost to the day, the Aztecs welcomed the Spaniards with open arms, a mistake that destroyed their civilization. The Incas welcomed Pizarro as the returning Viracocha, with similar tragic consequences. Both empires enjoyed less than a century of glory before they fell to the brutal *Conquistadores*—the Aztecs in 1519, and the Incas in 1532. It would be illuminating to explore both empires in depth as examples of the Radiant Axes, but space permits only one. Thus, we will look at the Incan—on the whole one of the more benevolent and enlightened empires.

South America Before the Incas

Before the Incan empire, western South America had progressed through the archetypes in the typical manner. Like Egypt, it had gone through alternating periods of unification and decentralization, with certain motifs continuing from one period to the next. An indeterminably long Sensitive Chaos period, when people lived exclusively by hunting, gathering, and fishing, was followed by Great Round cultures that began to build villages and develop agriculture. Between 2500 and 1800 B.C., typical egalitarian Great Round villages such as Huaca Prieta on the coast left their mark on the archaeological record. These Neolithic people invented that greatest of South American arts: weaving. A swatch from Huaca Prieta shows a stunning intertwined double serpent motif—possibly a very early example of Kundalini in the New World.

Shortly after 2000 B.C., some communities such as Kotosh and El Paraiso boasted large, complex, rectilinear stone and masonry temples on artificial ceremonial platforms as high as twenty-six feet. By 1000 B.C., the inland site of Cerro Sechin had a massive platform mound rising to about 100 feet and spanning nearly 1800 by 1300 feet at the base (three by two football fields). Adorning the stones around the Cerro Sechin complex were gruesome carvings of priests wielding axes and of their dismembered victims oozing gore. Clearly by this time Peruvian civilization was well into the Four Quarters archetype and on its way to establishing the Pyramid.

One proto-Pyramid culture that was almost a nation state due to its widespread cultural influence was the Chavin, centered in the ceremonial city of Chavin de Huantar with its platform pyramid. Bearing many uncanny artistic similarities to the contemporaneous Shang and Chou dynasties in China, the Chavin culture revolved spiritually around two deities: an older jaguar-serpent "Smiling God," who may have been an archaic god of eros and the underworld, and a more official "Staff God" a sky-god who became the prototype for later Andean deities. The transition at Chavin de Huantar from the Smiling God to the Staff God may parallel the Old World transition from the worship of serpents and Pan-like nature gods as consorts of the Great Goddess during the Great Round to the worship of the authoritarian sky and storm gods of the Indo-Europeans who brought the patriarchal Four Quarters.

The Chavin culture flourished between about 1000 and 300 B.C. Its fall was followed by a period of regionalism in which emerged several national states such as the pyramid-building cultures of the Mochica and the Nazca (creators of the mysterious lines and figures in the Nazca desert). From 200 B.C. to A.D. 1000 (called the Classic Period by archaeologists), the typical features of the pyramid archetype spread throughout Peru: the rise of nation states, stratified social structures, bureaucratization, large cities with monumental architecture, state-maintained irrigation and food-distribution systems, conquering armies that amassed huge territories, etc.

Of all the pre-Incan states, the one that proved most influential was the Tiahuanacan, based in the city of Tiahuanaco near Lake Titicaca, the "Birthplace of the Sun." This culture was to the Incas what the Toltecs were to the Aztecs: part legendary ancestor, part borrowed mythological treasury, and part cultural inspiration. Significantly, one of the most outstanding surviving structures in Tiahuanaco is the "Gateway of the Sun" a ten by twelve foot solid grey andesite portal with Viracocha, descendent of the Chavin Staff God, carved over the door. The Gateway seems mysteriously to announce the solar-oriented Incan empire to come.

The Tiahuanacans were a relatively peaceful people who preferred to disseminate their culture through missionizing and trade, leaving the more violent means of spreading the faith to their militaristic brother culture, the Huari. Together, the Huari and the Tiahuanacans were responsible for the second great period of unification in western South America, which ended inexplicably around A.D. 1000.

Predictably, another phase of regionalism then set in, with at least seven different states vying for supremacy. The most powerful was the Chimu whose capital city of Chan Chan had not one but nine enormous palace compounds.[26] The Chimu had formed a proto-Radiant Axes empire, which the Incas had to conquer if they were to become the full-fledged imperialistic power they aspired to be. If the cultural ancestors of the Incas were the Tiahuanacans, then the Chimu were their worthy adversaries, whom they finally conquered in 1465, adding their prized fertile coastland to the empire.

The Incas: Children of the Sun

Despite their humble origins, the Incas proved to be masterful rulers. Their reign brought order, security, and prosperity to millions. They excelled in administration, engineering, and agriculture, so that once a territory had been conquered, it was soon brought under the same well-organized, productive system that benefited the rest of the empire. This was based socially on the *ayllu* or clan, economically on *mita* or labor taxes, and administratively on a hierarchy of officials who oversaw everything from the public works projects in Cuzco, to each individuals fulfillment of the labor tax, to the clipping of every stray blade of grass encroaching on the extensive system of imperial highways. Like Kublai Khan, the Incan rulers were religiously tolerant. In newly acquired territory, they would build a Sun Temple and require their subjects to acknowledge the Sun-God Inti, but as long as the people did that, they were free to continue their own religious traditions. Confident and patient, the Incas assumed that future generations would naturally see the superiority of Incan ways and beliefs and want to adopt them as their own.

Properly speaking, the term "Inca" referred only to the ruling elite, and even more specifically to the Emperor himself. This class of "Incas-by-blood" was supplemented by the Quechua-speaking tribes around Cuzco who served in the government and were designated "Incas-by-privilege." Virtually all others were merely non-Incan peasants. By the time of the Spanish Conquest, the Incas were so obsessive about organizing everyone into tidily numbered hierarchical groups of 100, 500, 1000, 5000, 10,000, and 40,000 that they seem to have been on the verge of the Grid archetype with its bureaucratic mentality. They would even move people about or conscript them into the labor force just to keep their groups numbered to desired multiples.

Unique among Radiant Axes empires, the Incas had no written language. Instead they used intricately knotted cords called *quipu* to keep detailed, precise records of absolutely everything of even minute concern to the empire: births, deaths, marriages, and relocations within every family; business transactions, military operations, imports and exports, inventories and labor projects; histories, ancestral legends, astronomical observations, calendrical information; etc. Among the most important government officials were the keepers of the *quipu*. Unfortunately, even though there are Andean natives who still use *quipus* today, the Incan *quipus* have not yet been deciphered.

One of the most vivid ways in which the Incas expressed the Radiant Axes archetype was through their road system. A coast road and a highland road ran the length of the empire—over 2000 miles. Transverse roads and paths connected these two arteries, forming a network that linked Cuzco with every administrative outpost in the empire. To the sixteenth century Spaniard

Pedro de Cieza de Leon, the Incan roads seemed the longest and finest in the world, and were all the more astounding because they cut through living rock over sheer, barren sierras and precipitous mountains, bridging seemingly bottomless valleys, and paving a smooth way through drifted snow and thick forest. As with the Chinese roads, these were built solely to facilitate managing the empire and were used only for official business. Cieza de Leon describes the theatrical spectacle of an Incan Emperor on a progress through his land:

> When the Incas set out to visit their kingdom, it is told that they traveled with great pomp, riding in rich litters set upon smooth, long poles of the finest wood and adored with gold and silver. Over the litter rose two high arches of gold set with precious stones and long curtains hung from all sides of the litter in such a way as to cover it all .... Everything about these litters was luxurious and on some the sun and moon were carved, and on others great serpents intertwined about a kind of staff—this was their insigne or coat of arms.[27]

As the emperor rode on his fabulous jeweled litter—carried on the shoulders of high-born lords and surrounded by an elaborate retinue of guards, archers, halberdiers, lancers, captains, and runners—the hills would be thick with people coming to watch him pass and calling out: "Most great and mighty lord, son of the sun, thou alone art our lord, may the entire world hearken unto you." Cieza de Leon noted that the Inca traveled about four leagues a day (the Spanish league was about 2.63 miles), stopping wherever he wished to inquire into the state of his kingdom, listen to complaints, right wrongs, and punish those guilty of injustices. Throughout these progresses, the local residents served the Inca and his retinue, supplying their every need.

As we might expect, the roads were fully outfitted every few miles with lodgings, storehouses, administrative centers, temples to the sun, and post-houses for relay messengers. As was the case in China, the relay messengers could to carry information with amazing speed; by some accounts they could run the length of the empire in less than a week. The Imperial roadways in South America served as the same kind of efficient communication system as the Mongol, Roman, and Persian roads did in their respective empires.

As the capital city and predynastic home of the Incas, Cuzco was, of course, the focal point of the road system. From it, four main roads branched out, dividing the land into four quarters, which gave the empire its Incan name: *Tahuantinsuyu*, "Land of the Four Quarters." (As we have seen, Pyramid and Radiant Axes cultures often retain strong Four Quarters imagery in their architecture, city planning, and mythology since they are built, in a very real way, upon Four Quarters foundations.) The four quarters of *Tahuantinsuyu* were the *Collasuyu*, encompassing the fertile highlands around Lake Titicaca and the Bolivian ultiplano to the south of Cuzco; the *Chinchaysuyu*, covering the rich coastal plain to the north, the *Cuntisuyu* to the west; and the *Antisuyu* to the east.

As is typical of Radiant Axes civilizations, the Incas linked their racial origins, as well as the founding of their capital, to the sun. Lake Titicaca, the "Birthplace of the Sun," was their legendary place of origin (possibly indicating that they had migrated from there). In one version of the Incan creation myth, the father-god Viracocha fashioned the earth, sky, and people, but there was no sun, and the people lived in darkness. He eventually flooded this world because the people disobeyed him. A surviving man and woman landed in Tiahuanaco, the home of Viracocha, and from them he made new people out of clay and also formed nations, giving each a language, songs, and seeds to sow. "Then he breathed life and soul into the clay and ordered each nation to pass under the earth and to emerge in the place he directed. Some came out of caves, others from hills, others from fountains, others from the trunks of trees. Each nation made a shrine of the place from which it had issued."[28]

There was still no sun, however, nor moon, nor stars. After making each of these, Viracocha ordered them to go to the island of Titicaca and rise to heaven. As the sun rose to heaven in human form, he called out to the Incas and their chief Manco Capac saying: "'Thou and thy descendents are to be Lords, and are to subjugate many nations. Look upon me as thy father, and thou shalt be my children, and thou shalt worship me as thy father.'"[29] So saying, the sun-god Inti empowered Manco Capac by giving him a headdress and a battle-axe, whereupon the chief and his brothers and sisters descended under the earth and emerged from the cave of Pacaritampo (the "camp of origin"), where the sun rose on the first day after Viracocha had divided night from day.

Using many powerful motifs spanning from the Sensitive Chaos to the Radiant Axes archetypes, this myth ingeniously ties the origin of the Incan rulers to the origin of the sun itself. Not only were they the "Children of the Sun," but they emerged from the cave of Pacaritampo (Womb-Cavern of the Great Round) on the same day that the sun (consciousness, the Radiant Axes) first arose after Viracocha (the Creator-God and Father of the Sun) had divided night from day (Separation of the World Parents). Also, upon its birth from the waters of Lake Titicaca (the Sea of Chaos), the sun empowered Manco Capac (the Hero) to found a new society (to establish a new world order) and become its ruler (God-King and Emperor in one).

The myth explains other important Incan concepts such as the belief in the power of *huacas*, the spirit-centers in the landscape from which the people of the several nations emerged (much as they did in the myths of the Australian aborigines.) The idea that the world is filled with *huacas*, which may be people or things as well as places, and that these special entities have supernatural powers, animates the whole of Andean thought—before, during, and after Incan rule. It surely stems from the animistic Sensitive Chaos, which has been kept alive in South America because of the surviving rainforest, hunter-gatherers, hallucinogenic plants, and shamanism.

The myth is also credited with establishing the brother-sister pattern of royal marriage followed by the Incas (as by the Egyptians) since Manco Capac and his brothers were the husbands of their sisters. Such marriages greatly eased the problem of keeping the dynasty in the family. Among the Incas, the most competent son of the Emperors sister-wife was named heir to the throne, although the Emperor also had countless wives and concubines in a large harem typical of the Radiant Axes. Moreover, the Incas sequestered certain highborn, beautiful women, in effect taking them off the marriage market and making them inaccessible to potential rivals, just as the Romans did with the Vestal Virgins. These *acclacuna* or "Chosen Women" lived chaste, temple-bound existences, weaving special ceremonial cloth and brewing maize beer for honored festival celebrants and government workers. The remote mountain sanctuary of Machu Picchu appears to have been built for a group of Chosen Women because nearly all of the burials were of females.

The version of the creation myth recounted above was probably to some extent fabricated to justify Incan rule. In another, probably older, version recalled by the 16th century Peruvian writer Huaman Poma, Manco Capac married not his sister, but his mother. According to Huaman Poma, Manco and his mother belonged to the "caste of the Serpents," which suggests a mythic origin in the most primitive stratum of Native American psychotropic experience.

Manco's mother, Mama Huaco, was a powerful shaman who "was able to talk to sticks and stones, and even mountains and lakes" through the voices of spirits. The people regarded her powers as miraculous and "were content to obey and serve her." A strikingly beautiful, dark-skinned, lusty woman fond of wearing pink clothes and large ornamental silver pins, Mama Huaco must have been an impressive figure. Discovering that she was pregnant with a son, she acted on the advice of her spirits and concealed her pregnancy. Once her child was born, she hid him in one of the caves of Tampu Toco for two years with a nurse to care for him.[29] Meanwhile, she let the people know that a great king named Manco Capac Inca would come to rule the country. Huaman Poma writes:

> In the course of time the mother became the wife of her son and assumed the title of Queen of Cuzco ... She was friendly with the most important nobles, and indeed with a wide range of people, and thus wielded more power than her husband Manco Capac. As well as being uncommonly wise, she was known for her charity to the poor of Cuzco and the rest of the country. She survived

her husband and died at Cuzco during the reign of her son by him, Sinchi Roca Inca.[31]

This version shows Manco Capac to be a far less heroic figure. In fact, here he is more like the son-lover of the Great Goddess that we ought expect to find in the Great Round. He is completely overshadowed by his beautiful, charismatic mother. Huaman Poma even points out that Manco Capac claimed to be the son of the Sun and Moon because his father was unknown. In the discrepancies between these two version, we may be witnessing the new imperial dynasty reworking the myths of origin to suppress a preceding matriarchal era and inflate the heroic nature of the founding ruler.

In the more imperialistic versions of the myth, after leaving the cave, Manco Capac and his people were ordered by Inti, the sun-god and their father, to found a capital city at a place where a golden rod would disappear into the ground, indicating good soil for farming. Accounts vary slightly as to what happened during the search, but they all involve rivalry among the brothers—in one Manco Capac murders his brothers to become chief, in another he and one brother imprison the third in a cave. In the end, Manco Capac finds that the rod disappears into the ground at Cuzco and founds the capital there. The capital, therefore, is chosen under the orders and divine guidance of the sun itself. Its Incan name is Aca Mama, which according to Huaman Poma, means "mother of the fermented maize" but also "navel." Thus, in the Incan mind, Cuzco is the archetypal "Navel of the World," the *omphalos*, the hub of the universe.

The Ceque System of Cuzco

The Incas embodied the concept of Cuzco as the Navel of the World in a pattern of forty-one lines called *ceqaes*, which radiated from the city and linked 328 huacas or spirit places in the surrounding landscape. In effect, the *ceque* system was like a gigantic *quipu* thrown over the Valley of Cuzco, recording and coordinating all aspects of Incan life: social, astronomical, calendrical, ceremonial, religious, governmental, architectural, and geographic.

The Radiant Axes 315

The concept was common throughout the Andes. Every village had its own little *ceque* system, and many survive today. A *huaca* could be a number of things: a temple, standing stone, well or spring, Incan fortress, notch on the horizon aligned to solsticial or equinoctal sunrises, and so on. Some *huacas* were *intihuatanas*—"hitching posts of the sun" like the famous one at Machu Picchu. The Spaniards destroyed all the *intihuatanas* they found, believing them to be works of the Devil, but the one at Machu Picchu remained unrediscovered until the early 20th century.

The *ceque* system embraced the Incan social structure in that each of the twelve clans of Cuzco was responsible for a number of *ceques*. Each clan maintained the *huacus*, or sacred sites, along their designated *ceques* and held the proper ceremonies at appropriate times of the year for each site. The *ceques* managed by a clan were not adjacent to one another, but alternated with the *ceques* tended by other clans. This created the effect of weaving the various clans into an interdependent, tightly knit, social fabric. In indigenous civilizations throughout the Americas, weaving is a sacred art.

According to R. T. Zuidema, an anthropologist and the leading authority on the *ceque* system, the entire system was also a calendar. Each *huaca* represented one day; each *ceque*, one month; and each clan took care of one month's portion of the radial pattern. Furthermore, the system coordinated three different calendars—those of the sun, the moon, and Venus—but it primarily embodied a 328 day lunar calendar,[32] "an exclusively female calendar," says Zuidema. The year consisted of forty-one weeks of eight days each, which Zuidema correlates with one emperor's practice of spending one week with each of his 41 wives. He had forty secondary wives and one principal wife; correspondingly, there were forty regular *ceques* and one "royal" one.

Like everything else about Incan civilization, the *ceque* system was a marvel of intricate subtlety and sophistication. Also, like all things Incan, it showed an obsession with bringing everything into conformance with an orderly, integrated plan, as if only the empire could bring the world into the glorious sun-tinged harmony of heaven on earth. The grand radial pattern of the *ceque* system, and the majestic confidence it emitted throughout the empire, could have been conceived only by a Radiant Axes civilization with a grand imperial vision of being at the center of space and time.

The Temple of the Sun

To the Incas, the *ceques* must have represented the rays of the sun, since the center of the whole system—the point at which all the czques converged in Cuzco—was the *Coricancha*, the building the Spaniards called the "Temple of the Sun" but whose name in Quechua meant "golden enclosure." Said to have been built by Manco Capac when he founded Cuzco, the *Coricancha* was unquestionably the most spectacular building in all of pre-Hispanic America. Made of huge stones, cut and fitted in the Incan manner without mortar, the temple was lavishly gilded in pure gold. According to Cieza de Leon,[32] the temple was over 400 feet in circumference with many gold gateways, and it contained four heavily gilded, thatched roofed buildings. Against one wall were two benches on which shone the rising sun. Set with precious stones and emeralds, these benches were reserved for the Lord Incas. "If anyone else sat there" reported de Leon, "he was sentenced to death." The temple was the home of the heavily-guarded Virgins of the Sun. The richest of the temple's houses held an image of the sun "of great size, made of gold beautifully wrought and set with many precious stones." In the same house were great treasures and statues of the former Incan rulers. By other accounts,[34] these "statues" were actually the mummies of Inca emperors, elaborately dressed and seated on golden thrones to preside over the empire as if they were alive.

The *Coricancha* of Cuzco completes the Radiant Axes image of Incan civilization. Politically and spiritually, it was the solar power source of an empire that had reached a high degree of perfection in a very short time. Nonetheless, like all empires, the Incan empire was destined to be short-lived. It collapsed not because of internal revolution, although a long dispute over who was the rightful heir to the throne had weakened the government, but because it was the loser in a head-on collision with another Radiant Axes civilization: that of Europe in general and

Spain in particular.

Soon after the Conquest, the Spaniards looted the *Coricancha* for its gold and jewels, then razed it and erected a Dominican church on its ruins. As we have seen, most conquering cultures usurp the sacred places of the vanquished and superimpose their own temples.[34] The gold that the *Coricancha* rendered up in Spanish melting pots inflamed the gold fever that drew ever greater numbers of Europeans to America's shores in search of El Dorado. Tragically, they directed their lust for gold outward, in a literal, materialistic interpretation of the same metaphor that the Alchemists of the time were wisely seeking within. In the fanatical zeal of their religious fundamentalism, the *Conquistadores* destroyed thousands of artifacts, buildings, books (in Mesoamerica), and human beings, wiping out whole cultures. These are the actions of a people already grossly alienated from wisdom and spirit, a tragic flaw that becomes the central problem of the Grid archetype we will see in the next chapter.

SYNOPSIS OF THE RADIANT AXES

World of the Sun-God

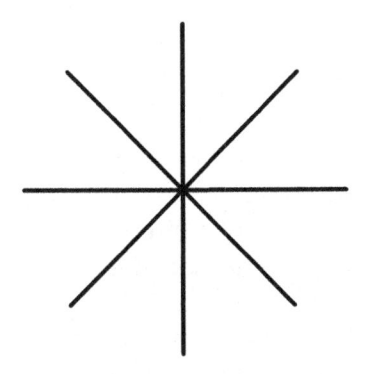

SPATIAL SYMBOL

Rays radiating from a central point (like the rays of the sun).

SOCIETY

Era
- Age of Imperialism, "Late" or "Post-" Classic Period.

Society
- Military expansionism.
- Rule by a solar-identified absolute monarch.
- Complex class-stratified social structure with colonialism, economic exploitation, and great extremes of wealth and poverty leading to social unrest.
- Slavery. (Slavery may exist in the Pyramid or Four Quarters archetypes, but it is more widespread in the Radiant Axes).
- Layering of archetypes as the empire subsumes Sensitive Chaos, Great Round, Four Quarters, and Pyramid cultures. Often the aristocracy and the educated upper classes

share the Radiant Axes worldview, while the colonized maintain their own beliefs and customs as best they can.
- Social revolutions or barbaric invasions overturn empires, which often are already weakened by overextension and internal strife. Radiant Axes empires are comparatively short-lived.

Examples

- Africa: New Kingdom Egypt; Roman, Islamic, and European colonialism.
- Near East: Babylonian, Assyrian, and Persian Empires; Ottomon and other Islamic empires.
- Asia: Moghul Dynasties in India, Mongol Empire and the Yuan through Qing dynasties in China, Late Khmer Kingdoms in Cambodia.
- Mediterranean: Alexander the Great; Roman Empire The Americas: Aztec and Incan empires, United States Europe: Imperial Age of Europe-Louis XIV and Versailles; Spanish, Portuguese, and British empires, etc.

Technology

Technelogos eclipses psychoeros.

- Engineering eclipses art.
- Communications systems consisting (in non-electronic empires) of vast networks of roads equipped with post-houses at regular intervals for twenty-four hour relays of messengers, as well as for the convenience of government representatives and the military.
- Other imperial infrastructure: roads, shipping, imperial administrative machinery, systems for the collection and redistribution of resources, and so on.
- Enumerative logos activities—census taking, record-keeping, inventories, and the like—as in the Pyramid but on a bigger scale and without the spiritual logos mystique so central to Pyramid cultures.
- Gender Roles Vast royal harems attest to the sexual colonization of women, and the hieros gamos is degraded into the practice of keeping "temple prostitutes" or

palace concubines.
- Women are the property of men, sequestered at home with few rights.
- Repression of the feminine principle in the culture leads to militarism, brutality, excessive rationalism, and other imbalances.

PSYCHE

Psychology

- Inflated or boundless ego (the opposite of having no ego or of transcending ego): having an unrealistic sense of one's personal power; believing that one is omnipotent and omniscient, that one is God or has the power of the sun. The Slaying of the Father, symbolically, to liberate individual power and will (paralleled in society by the secularized state religion supporting the monarchy) Sociopathic or psychopathic personality where the lack of ego boundaries can lead to brutality and the ruthless exploitation of others.
- Messianic delusions: perceiving the world as extending to infinity and eternity from one's own being, place, and time. Obsessed with the delusion that one is destined to bring about the apocalyptic apotheosis of humanity or of the chosen few.

Enlightenment
- The total extinquishment of ego in a blaze of light characteristic of the "true" messiah.

Stagnation
- Psychological stagnation in the Radiant Axes can produce an insatiable craving for power, wealth, and material goods; an extreme existential aloneness; and an obsession with various drives and addictions.

Liberation
- Psychological liberation in the Radiant Axes can trans-

322 Spatial Archetypes

mute the inflated ego's unbounded territoriality into a transcendent spaciousness in which the ego is dissolved in complete enlightenment and bliss.

SPIRIT

Worldview
- Cosmos centered on the sun.

Spiritual Focus
- Worship of the sun or Sun-God and identification with the solar principle.
- Decadent state religion politically controlled by the monarchy and devoid of authentic spiritual inspiration. Religious eclecticism and tolerance in some empires (such as the Roman, Incan, and Kublai Khan's Mongol Empire).

Mythic Themes
- The Sun: solar deities and rites, sacrifices to perpetuate the sun's cycles.
- Light: enlightenment, radiance, the victory of light over darkness.
- Elaborate state ceremonies such as imperial processions, celebrations of the King's birthday, formal rites concerning the payment of tribute, passive entertainments (theatrical performances, dancers, musicians).

CULTURE

Prime Symbol
- The Sun

Art
- Gigantism and pomposity in state rituals, art, and architecture.

Astronomy
- Cycles of the sun and stars, heliocentric universe.

Time
- Linear time, sometimes with a sense of imminent realization through the empire (or the Self) of the full glory and expression of human will; also, calendars using an event in the life of an enlightened being or culture hero as year zero (as in the Christian and Moslem calendars)

Space
- Unbounded space as an infinite field of energy radiating from a central source—sun, monarch, capital, empire.

Landscape
- An exploitable resource and territorial proof of the empire's power and extent.
- Vast formal gardens with axial walks, manicured trees, topiaries and clipped hedges, geometric flower beds, elaborate fountains, classical sculpture, and so on (as at Tivoli, Isfahan, and Versailles).

Architecture
- Elaborate palaces as the most important structure, with large harems, exotic royal zoos, deer parks, botanical gardens, royal collections of high-born virgins or "chosen women," and "specimens" of foreign or "primitive" races—all of which attest to the emperor's colonization and mastery of women, animals, nature, and other races. Spectacular summer palaces and royal villas
- Radiating roads. Roads, avenues, and imperial highways radiate from the palace throughout the capital and empire, imitating the sun's rays.
- Obelisks as a vertical component of the Radiant Axes, sometimes serving as the focal point of a system of radiating roads, or symbolizing a ray of the sun. Often inscribed with the edicts or accomplishments of the monarch.

- Colossal statues and murals pompously proclaim the mightiness of the emperor and the invincibility of the empire (as at Abu Simbel and Persepolis).

THE GRID

WORLD OF THE BUREAUCRAT

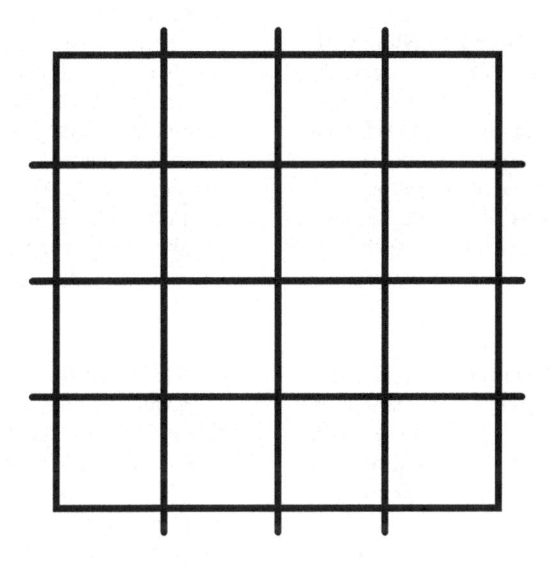

6a. Artist Drawing a Nude with Perspective Device. By Albrecht Dürer. Woodcut done ca. 1600. Dürer's artist is looking between his model's legs, but misses the eroticism of the situation as he is fascinated by his perspective generating device and the grid that it lays over nature.

6b. The Land Ordinance of 1785. The Ordinance established a system for rationally dividing up the country down to the scale of a single lot with little regard to features of the land. The system eventually pertained to over three-quarters of the area of the continental US. To this day we can see the effects when flying over the country by plane.

6c. Commissioners' Plan of 1811. For the street grid of Manhattan (New York City). It was described as combining "beauty, order and convenience" by the Commission, but most characteristically of The Grid, it shows a distrust of nature, ignoring hills and streams. Fortunately it was later violated by the placing of Central Park in the center. Other US cities were given similar grids.

6d. The Seagram Building. By Mies van der Rohe. Opened in 1958, the building is on Park Avenue in New York. While not the first "glass skyscraper," the Seagram Building is regarded as the prime representative of the style. The anonymous grid of the facade symbolizes the work style of the period presented in William H. Whyte's book, *The Organization Man.*

The Grid 327

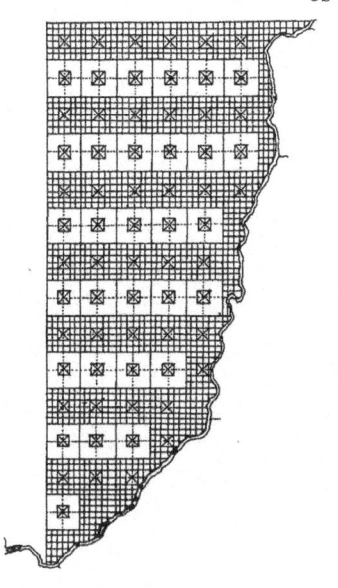

6b

6a

6c

6d

THE GRID

World of the Bureaucrat

Turning and turning in the widening gyre
The falcon cannot hear the falconer;
Things fall apart; the center cannot hold;
Mere anarchy is loosed upon the world.
  ~ W. B. Yeats[1]

Much of modern cosmology is based upon the assumption that the universe will look very much the same from whatever position it is inspected. In other words, there is no center and no boundary.
  ~ Edwin P. Hubble[2]

The Rise of the Grid

The Grid, the opposite of the Sensitive Chaos, culminates shifts and reversals that have been growing throughout the sequence. In the Sensitive Chaos, people are enveloped in uroboric oneness with the cosmos; in the Grid, they are exiled from spiritual wholeness by a denial of the spirit. In the Sensitive Chaos, all nature is magically in kinship with humankind, singing its secrets in the realm beyond space and time. In the Grid nature is alien, silent, inert. The Sensitive Chaos knows how to free itself of ego. The Grid seeks ego, finding it not inflated and invested in one solar being as in the Radiant Axes, but deflated, fragmented, and dispersed throughout the anonymous mass of humanity. The mythopoeic, synchronistic, non-ordinary reality of the Sensitive Chaos is denied in the rational, linear, ordinary reality of the Grid, where technelogos finally wins its protracted battle with psychoeros.

As the archetype of the ordinary person or the so-called "common man" the Grid represents the despirited individual as isolated ego, deflated by the anonymity imposed by the archetype and having no still center of the Self within. Similarly, as the archetype of the "common masses" the Grid represents mass society without a world organizing center—neither a shared ethos, nor a common god, nor a dictatorial ruler.

The Grid seeks to classify people as separate, equal units without identity or focus. Statistical uniformity is one of the archetype's most powerful attributes, making it the organizational model for management systems that need to mold personnel or products into standardized, predictable, quality-controlled units. This model pervades the military, industry, colonial governments, bureaucracies, and many "scientistic"[3] endeavors.

Historically, the Grid emerges in three different though sometimes related ways. In the first, it serves earlier archetypal eras (namely, the Radiant Axes, the Pyramid, and the Four Quarters) as a "handmaiden" that organizes the infrastructure for handling the masses: workers' housing, military camps, bureaucratic land divisions, colonial settlements—workers, soldiers, peasants, and colonials being seen as agglomerations of more or less identical human units. Some examples are the homes of ancient Egypt, the workers' quarters in Akhenaton and Nefertiti's capital at Amarna, Roman camps (Ostia), feudal European fiefdoms, Kublai Khan's provinces and his Beijing grid, 19th century American factory towns (Gary, Indiana); and colonial cities all over the world. In these cases, the Grid is not necessarily the predominant archetype. In ancient Egypt and Kublai Khan's China, for instance, the Grid functioned as a static substructure for the lower classes, while the ruling class enjoyed the richer symbolism of the symmetrical, axial, energetic thrust of the Radiant Axes.

The second way in which the Grid arises is, ironically, as an ideological model for mass revolts against the Radiant Axes aristocracy. We can see this in social revolutions that overthrow despotic empires. Witness those occurring in our own time: the twentieth century's communist revolutions in Russia, China, and Cuba; the overthrows of the Shah in Iran and the Marcos regime in the Philippines; and the many revolts against Latin American dictatorships. Revolutions are waged by those who dream of having their own "place in the sun"—of winning the bounties of life formerly available only to Radiant Axes aristocrats. Regardless of their actual outcomes, which too often simply replace one despotic regime with another, the initial aim of social revolutions is to disperse power from the few to the many. In terms of the archetypes, this is a desire to end the ever-increasing centralization of power that begins in the Four Quarters and gains momentum in the Pyramid and Radiant Axes archetypes. No matter in what "-ism" that is touted—republicanism, socialism, communism, capitalism—the Grid promises an end to this trend. After all, the Grid has no center and all of its parts are equal.[4]

The physical transformation of the Radiant Axes *symbol* into the Grid *symbol* provides a metaphor for the tumultuous social transformation of the Radiant Axes *archetype* into the Grid *archetype*. Visualize the extreme centralization of power in the Radiant Axes and imagine how it saps and weakens the extended rays. When a sun dies, it first becomes a red giant, bloated but weak in radiance. The Radiant Axes empires become inflated and overextend their reach. The center fails to send sufficient "energy" in the form of food, services, resources, and governance to the "rays," that is, to the empire's socially alienated—the enslaved and exploited, the poor and the disenfranchised, the dissident and the radical—as well as to its geographical hinterlands. Soon the empire's entire political, economic, diplomatic, ideological, and mythological armature begins to collapse.

As the rays weaken, they "cross back" on themselves in mounting turmoil. Eventually they bring chaos to the center and neutralize its power. Citizens of the French Revolution storm the Bastille; Iranian Moslems oust the Shah and take over the American Embassy; Mao-Tse Tung's Long March to Shensi rallies the peasants to the Communist cause that would eventually win the country; aggrieved rural Mexican Indians innocently join Cortez's march on the Aztec imperial capital, Tenochtitlan; and exploited American colonists rise up against the British. The weakened rays of the Radiant Axes, crossing back on themselves in apparent anarchical abandon (from the perspective of besieged emperors and dictators), form the incipient Grid archetype, which draws the waning power of the declining Radiant Axes into its own robust new form.

Whether in retrospect the outcome justifies the cause is not the issue here. The fundamental motivation of mass social revolutions is the desire to spread power from the few to the many. In terms of the archetypes, this is a desire to end the ever-increasing centralization of power that began with the Four Quarters some five thousand years ago and gained momentum under the Pyramid and Radiant Axes archetypes. Ideologically and symbolically, the Grid promises an end to this trend. No matter what the "-ism" in which it is touted, the Grid promises to disperse centralized power to the masses. Because of the very nature of its spatial image, it has no center. All of its parts are equal. Seductively, it promises a place in the sun to everyone. That it often fails to do so has less to do with the Grid itself than with human frailty and with the natural life-cycle of archetypes. What an archetype promises in the beginning inevitably sours as it become realized, institutionalized, and corrupted. When this happens, a new archetype comes to the fore, offering deliverance but ultimately destined to follow the same pattern of promise, realization, and dissolution.

The third way in which the Grid arises is as an archetype. In this aspect, it is every bit as powerful as it is in the guise of a management system for centralized authority or a social program for revolutionaries. Like all archetypes, the Grid initially wells up in the interstices of thought and eventually floods out the preceding archetype. In Western civilization, the Grid began to take hold with the rise of Renaissance humanism, which constituted the first assault on the fortress of medieval theocracy. It gained momentum during the Age of Reason, and finally burst forth in the Industrial Revolution and the Machine Age.

The Grid in Western Civilization

The West is now fully immersed in the Grid archetype. We live in towns and cities laid out as grids: work in offices with grid glass facades, grids of desks inside, and grid patterned floors and ceilings; from airplane windows we see the countryside from coast to coast laid out in grids of fields and farms (especially in the United States). We also immediately recognize the Grid in our culture's infatuation with measurement, statistics, mathematics, computers, technology, product uniformity, bureaucracy, specialization, and so on. We map everything on grids; archaeologists stretch grids of string across sites to measure the location of finds; space photographs come back with little cross marks regularly spaced on them; air and ocean navigators refer to the grid of latitudes and longitudes lacing the terrestrial and celestial globes; scientists use the Cartesian "xyz" coordinates in their measurements and charts; architects and engineers use the coordinates of orthographic projection to make plans, sections, and elevations of their designs.

We are so used to the Grid and it so thoroughly pervades our existence that we might be tempted to think that the West invented it, or that this archetype has been manifested only in modem Western civilization. But this is not true; every mature civilization experiences the Grid. China, which began to shift to the Grid during the Qing dynasty with its bloated bureaucracy, is fully realizing the archetype under communism. Egypt experienced the Grid during its long decline after the New Kingdom when it continually reiterated old cultural forms, inventing no new ones, and was eventually colonized by Greece and then Rome. Post-Alexandrian Hellenistic Greece exhibited the main features of the Grid archetype, and in Rome, the Grid coincided with the decline and fall of the empire. The Incas with their bureaucratic passion for organizing everything in multiples of ten were verging on the Grid before the Conquest. And contemporary Japan has surpassed the West in actualizing the highly organized, high-technology aspects of the Grid. However, because the Grid of Western civilization is the most powerful archetype at work in the world today, both in our lives and in international affairs, we will concentrate on how it arose. If we understand its origins, we can better understand how and why it now affects us as it does.

First, we need to define what we mean by "Western Civilization." This term has more than one meaning. For instance, we use it in its broadest sense to refer to the vast reticulum of industrialization emanating from the West that is now spreading over the globe. Thus we identify modern airports, hotels, housing projects, superhighways, and industrial installations as being "Western" even when we encounter them in Nairobi, Bangkok, or Ulaanbaatar. In a more limited sense, we use the term "Western

Civilization" to mean that textbook culture centered in Europe, which intellectually crystallized in Classical Greece, reached an early political apogee in the Roman Empire, fell into the Dark Ages, roused a bit in the medieval Gothic era, fully renewed itself in the Renaissance, and went on to colonize much of the world, attaining a degree of wealth and technological inventiveness unprecedented in human history.

Although both views of Western civilization are very common, both are relatively recent constructs. The first or "global" view would have been inconceivable before the spread of Western imperialism beginning in the 15th century, and it has really only reached the popular mind with the 20th century's growth of multinational corporations. The second or "historical" view is a product of the Renaissance. It was only then that intellectuals, in defiance of Church dogma, began tracing the descent of Western civilization to pagan Greece and Rome. But there is yet another interpretation of the term "Western Civilization," which may be more useful than the other two. It splits the "West" into three overlapping spheres, separating and clarifying the major cultural influences on Western thought as it evolved over the centuries.

The Celtic Sphere

The first could be nicknamed the "Celtic" sphere. Geographically centered in continental Europe and the British Isles, it also includes Scandinavia. The term "Celtic" serves as shorthand for all the European cultures—the Celts, Angles, Saxons, Goths, Vikings, etc., and their Neolithic and Bronze Age predecessors—that have in common the fact that they are not primarily Mediterranean in origin and so constitute a cultural sphere distinct from that of Greece and Rome. Although the term "Celtic" may seem inaccurate when used to encompass such a wide variety of peoples, it is more suitable than the common but biased terms favored by Christian scholars: "Tribal" or "Barbaric" Europe. At least "Celtic" evokes in its full dignity one of the largest representative cultures, and the widespread Celtic underpinnings of modern Europe have indeed had an influence that has not been adequately recognized. After the Neolithic Great Round era in Europe, the Celts and other Indo-European peoples brought Europe into a prolonged Four Quarters era that finally ended with the theocratic rule of Christianity, culminating in the building of Europe's closest equivalent to the pyramid: the Gothic cathedral.

The Celtic Individual

The Celtic sphere instilled in Europe a raw heroic warrior ethic of individual will more powerful than anything coming out of ancient Greece. The Celtic impress of this ethic was rooted in the very soil of Europe, unlike the Greek version, which initially entered Europe through the Romans, whom the European tribes despised, and, two thousand years later, through the rose-colored lenses of nostalgic Italian Renaissance intellectuals. In addition, the European tribes waged a longstanding battle against the Christianization that also emanated from Rome. They preferred their mythologically rich nature spirits, wizards, goddesses, and legendary heroes to the systematized monotheistic religion of the East that was to spread from Rome.[5]

The Graeco-Roman Sphere

The second sphere, then, is the Graeco-Roman. From the point of view of the Celtic sphere, the Graeco-Roman was the alien culture. The Roman Empire fiercely subjugated the Europeans, imposing its language, religion, currency, taxation, customs, and centralized government. This was intolerable to the fiercely independent Europeans, but it was the usual clash between a Radiant Axes civilization intent upon cementing its empire and a loosely tribal Four Quarters culture. Of course, is was in the destiny of the archetypes that the more "advanced" culture would prevail, but to see "Western Civilization" as originally stemming from Greece and Rome ignores about two thousand years of Western history.

The Eastern or Christian Sphere

The third sphere is the Eastern or Christian. With its emphasis on submission, monotheism, martyrdom, piety, the doctrine of salvation, and faith in the hereafter, Christianity was alien to both the Celtic and the Graeco-Roman spheres, which at least shared a vigorous polytheism, appetite for life, and sense of individualism. Christianity was a desert religion, a product of nomadic Semitic herdsmen, of desert ascetics and hermits, and influenced by a multitude of Middle Eastern sects. Christianity's birthplace could hardly have differed more from the temperate, forested, individualistic homeland of Celtic Europe. It was only because of the doctrine of intolerance (the idea that non-believers were destined to spend eternity in hell, a notion totally absent in Celtic and Graeco-Roman religions), and the missionary zeal of Paul and his successors that Christianity got a foothold in Europe at all.

Working its way up from the common folk in the early centuries after Christ's death, the new religion finally succeeded in converting key Roman emperors such as Constantine I and Theodosius I in the 4th century. Constantine made both the Western and Eastern Roman Empires tolerant to Christians, and Theodosius terrorized the non-Christian world, smashing its "idols" and closing its temples or converting them to churches. In the next centuries a series of powerful Christian kings—Clovis, Charlemagne, and Ottos I and II in continental Europe; Henry II in England; and Brian Boru in Ireland—sanctified by a "divine mission," unified sections of Europe into states. Charlemagne and other kings forcibly converted their subjects, and, with the quelling of the non-Christian Viking, Saracen, and Magyar invaders, Europe became almost completely Christianized by the 11th century.

The establishment of the church, the nation states, and the divinely empowered kings—typical characteristics of the Pyramid archetype—brought Europe out of the Celtic Four Quarters into the Christian Pyramid age. The Four Quarters continued to exist in a supportive role in feudalism, which, with its fortified castles, heroic knights, and chieftain-like lords of the manor, resembled the Four Quarters archetype in any civilization. Paralleling this secular Four Quarters structure was the monasticism of the church, forming the hieratic priesthood that always accompanies the rise of the Pyramid. Interestingly, the monasteries had their own explicit Four Quarters image: the cloister, which the monks circumambulated. But overarching both feudalism and monasticism were the Pyramidal hierarchies of church and state. These two superpowers were often at odds with each other: the Roman papacy continued to be a thorn in the side of Christian Celtic Europe just as the Roman Empire had been a thorn in the side of pagan Celtic Europe

Finally, in the Gothic era, the church prevailed and Europe's Pyramid age came to full realization. Worked into a frenzy by the call of the Crusades to win back the holy city of Jerusalem from the "infidel" Muslims, Europe balanced the explosive energy of the Crusades with an implosive "Cathedral Crusade" at home. The pioneering French Gothic cathedrals, in particular, were astonishing in their vision of light and height, their structural innovation, and their mobilization and integration of the efforts of all the guilds of medieval artisans: stonemasons, carpenters, glaziers, sculptors. Wherever they were built, the cathedrals became the technological, economic, political, and spiritual centers of their regions. In addition to being churches for religious services, they served as meeting places for the guilds, as temporary shelters for pilgrims and their animals, as refuges for the sick and abandoned, as social centers for the whole community, and even on occasion as marketplaces. Often built upon pre-Christian sacred sites, they echoed a silent continuity with ancient, now-forbidden, religions that still reverberated in the marrow of the descendents of generations of "pagans" who had made pilgrimages to these same healing centers.

Indeed, the cathedrals were as much the creation of the Celtic spirit as of the Christian. In many Pyramid cultures, the state religion is for the elite and others are allowed to keep their practices and beliefs in the form of "folk religion"; in the Pyramid culture of Europe, however, Christianity stamped out the folk religion. Forced into subliminality like the "little people" in mythology, they survived in hidden forms apparent only to the trusted. Resonating through the proportions, plans, geometric rose windows, sculpture, and stonework of the cathedrals was the voice of the pre-Christian sages who secreted the Green Man among the sculptured Old Testament patriarchs, who alluded to the subtle geometries that had ordered the megalithic structures and monuments of an earlier age, who invoked the older deities to make the sacred place more sacred still. Each cathedral had an unmistakable sign of its pre-Christian origins built in plain sight on the floor of its nave: a paving pattern in the form of a labyrinth. Today, the only surviving one is in Notre-Dame de Chartres. The others were tragically, but perhaps predictably, removed during the Age of Reason when Europe was intent upon exorcising all traces of the irrational and the feminine.

Although Christianity certainly has had one of the most brutal records of misogyny of any religion in history, the Gothic Age was comparatively receptive to the feminine principle. This, according to Henry Adams, was one of the reasons for its greatness. Adams points out in *Mont-Saint Michel and Chartres* that the Gothic cathedrals were built at a time when French Queens were powerful, when women participated in medieval society (there are records of payments to female quarry owners and to women laborers who took part in building the cathedrals), and when European culture was being fertilized by passionate pagan legends sympathetic to women, which were dressed up as the literature of courtly love and the traditions of chivalry. But most of all, he attributes the building of the French cathedrals to the burgeoning "Cult of the Virgin." Recall that most were named "Notre Dame de..." ("Our Lady of...") followed by the name of the town in which they were built. Unlike the authoritarian God, dour fathers, and abstract theological principles of the official church, Mary was warm, human, and compassionate. Her adoration was not dictated by Rome; it was a spontaneous outburst, possibly a desire to return to the worship of the Great Goddess who had flourished in the Celtic sphere until the coming of Christianity. Even the lowliest person considered it a personal duty and a spiritual privilege to carry a cartload of building materials for the Virgin's glorious cathedrals.

Oswald Spengler saw the Gothic era as Western culture's equivalent of the Pyramid Age of ancient Egypt and the Classical Age of Greece, periods in which each culture found the full flowering of its creativity, laying down its basic forms and worldview, particularly through the perfection of its temple type. The Pyramid age of any civilization is commonly considered its Golden Age.

In Greece, the Pyramid age reached its peak in Periclean Athens with the building of the Acropolis, the temple complex of the self-creating virgin goddess Athena Parthenos. Classical Greece is a Pyramid civilization, as can be seen from the rise of the city-states, the dynastic-like rule of important Athenian families, the worship of the pantheon of deities residing on Mount Olympus, the reverence for natural mountains, and the building of the Acropolis on the highest hill in the heart of Athens. After its classical Pyramid age, Greece briefly manifested the Radiant Axes under Alexander the Great, and the Grid in its decadent Hellenistic period. It was the Romans, however, who truly mined the gold of Greece's Golden Age. The Romans derived much of their cultural and spiritual ideas from Greece. Their great achievement was the mastery of empire management.

Clarifying the relationships between the Celtic, Graeco-Roman, and Christian spheres of Western Civilization helps us to see how the Grid arose in Europe. By distinguishing between Celtic Europe and the Mediterranean Graeco-Roman world, we avoid confusing the archetypal eras of each sphere. To recapitulate the full sequence of archetypes, Western (or Celtic) Europe had a long Sensitive Chaos phase up through the time of the Neanderthal hunters. The period between the coming of the Cro-Magnons about 30,000 years ago, with their images of venerated females, to the invention of farming some 8000 years ago, was a slow transition from the Sensitive Chaos to the Great Round. The Neolithic era of agricultural communities, Goddess worship, and megalithic structures was Europe's Great Round era.[6] The Indo-European tribes that fanned out over Europe and reached Britain by about 2000 B.C.—building forts, fashioning princely graves, living in more hierarchically structured communities, waging war, and glorifying male gods and chieftains—brought the Four Quarters. Beginning with the Hallstat, Urnfield, Wessex, and other prehistoric tribes, the Indo-European complex of cultures eventually generated more sophisticated peoples such as the Celtic and Germanic tribes previously mentioned. They perpetuated the Four Quarters era in Western Europe through the Dark Ages to the Gothic age.

Meanwhile, Graeco-Roman civilization was going through

its own Four Quarters, Pyramid, and Radiant Axes phases at a much more accelerated pace. Long before Europe's Gothic era, Greece had enjoyed its Golden Age and Rome had built its empire, subjugating most of Europe and the Mediterranean in the process. The influx of Christianity via Rome eventually jarred Celtic Europe out of its protracted Four Quarters era into its own golden Pyramid age with the theocratic rule of the Church, the building of the Gothic cathedrals, and the efflorescence of many pre-Christian traditions. As we have seen in the example of Versailles and Louis XIV, Europe expressed the Radiant Axes archetype during its Baroque Period, which saw the imperialistic expansion that made most of Africa, the Americas, and parts of Asia into European colonies. Finally, the wealth and technological inventiveness resulting from its Radiant Axes phase catapulted Europe into the Grid, but the character of the Grid archetype in Western civilization had its roots in humanism and the Age of Reason.

Humanism

Although the Gothic age may have been Europe's Golden Age, like any archetypal era, it had inherent dynamics and limitations that eventually caused it to give way to a new archetypal era. After the Crusades, the growth of urban centers, the middle class, and a money economy all contributed to an increasing secularism that threatened both church and state. Moreover, the tension between church and state mounted as the two centers of power vied for control of one another. The strangleholds that the feudal system had on individual liberty and that church dogma had on freedom of inquiry became increasingly intolerable. What had once been a unifying body of received wisdom—the Bible, Aristotelian science, Scholasticism—in time became unbearable constraints on courageous individuals who wished to explore the human and natural worlds beyond the doctrines of the church. From the church's point of view, there was no need to study or observe the natural world since everything to be known about it was already stated in orthodox doctrines and texts. The stultifying effect that this had on medieval science is well known. Similarly, people wishing to improve their lot found themselves bound to static social positions dictated by the hierarchies of state and fiefdom.

In the long run, the most effective ideological assault on these limitations was the philosophy of humanism, which crystallized in the latter half of the 14th century in Italy and then moved into other European countries, bringing the Renaissance that ended the medieval age. In retrospect, we can see that humanism provided one of the underlying matrices of thought on which the West eventually built the worldview of the Grid still in effect today.

The humanists were inspired by what they learned, especially through Arab contact, of the classical world of Greece and Rome. While the early Christians were burning the books and libraries of ancient civilization (including the great library at Alexandria in Egypt—Theodosius is reputed to have had its female director, Hypatia, flayed alive), the Arabs, unencumbered by Christian dogma, were preserving as many of the texts and ideas of classical science as they could obtain. They thus performed an incalculable service to the history of human thought. Fragments slowly filtered into Europe through the Moorish occupation of Spain, the Saracen advances on southern Europe, and the Crusades.

The humanists looked to Graeco-Roman antiquity as an historical, mythic, and intellectual source of ideas that synchronized perfectly with the needs of their own time. And, being centered in Italy, the movement also evoked the past glory of the Roman Empire, thus shifting the balance once again from the Celtic to the Graeco-Roman sphere. From classical culture, the humanists drew two main tenets that virtually made the Grid inevitable: the idea of the autonomy and freedom of the individual, and the imperative of reviving empirical science.

The renewed belief in the autonomy, value, dignity, and freedom of the individual flew in the face of church doctrine, but it reflected the increasing pressures of social mobility in the late medieval age. The conflict took explicit form in the design of Renaissance churches. In the cross-shaped Gothic cathedrals, the altar—the holy of holies—was removed from the public by a long, axial nave and by various combinations of gates and screens.

These devices perfectly mirrored the elaborate hierarchy of the church, which denied parishioners immediate access to the divine, allowing them only to witness the priests' celebration of the mass. God could be reached only with the intercession of priests, bishops, cardinals, popes, etc. In contrast, the Renaissance architects built circular churches with beautiful mandala-like plans, which placed the worshipper in the presence of the altar immediately upon entry. The hottest argument among Renaissance architects, perceptively described by Rudolf Wittkower in *Architectural Principles in the Age of Humanism*, was whether the altar should be placed at the center of the church or against one of its walls. It is significant that Bramante's centralized, mandalic plan for St. Peter's in Rome[7] (altered and completed by Michelangelo) was later changed by the papacy by tacking on a traditional nave, with all of its hierarchical implications.[8]

What the humanists and the Renaissance architects were saying, in effect, was that all people are equal in the presence of the divine and that no individual—neither king nor pope—has any privileged or pre-ordained relationship to the sacred. In its thrust toward the equalization of all human beings, humanism comes close to the heart of the Grid, and, indeed, this radical concept ultimately undermined the hegemonies of both church and state in Europe. While Martin Luther's apostasy was prompted by his protest against the sale of indulgences, it was like a match to a religious and social tinder. Where the flame spread, peasants burned churches and marched with pitchforks against their landlords.

The imperative of reviving empirical science was a reaction against the church's suppression of scientific knowledge gained through the direct observation of nature rather than through religious faith (the same suppression later led to the trial of Galileo and, after a controversial colleague had been executed, intimidated Copernicus into waiting until he was near death to publish his unorthodox heliocentric theory of the solar system).[9] The humanists discovered the advances in thought made in the classical world by Archimedes, Hippocrates, Plato, Pythagoras, and others, and they wanted the same freedom of inquiry for their own civilization.

Still another by-product of humanism had far-reaching effects: the development of historical and optical perspective. The backward-looking infatuation with the classical world had the effect of extending the time sense of the humanists from the present to the seemingly distant past, giving them historical perspective. Because this was systematized in the elite intellectual centers of Europe (for instance, the humanists succeeded in getting classical studies added to the Liberal Arts curricula of universities), it constituted a change in consciousness far more influential than the usual sort of folkloric sense of history held by the common folk. By the Age of Reason, the backward-reaching timeline of historical perspective had generated a forward-reaching line: the idea of progress on which the confidence of modem Western civilization was built.

Along with the change in time perception came an equivalent change in space perception. Renaissance artists and architects began using linear perspective in which receding parallel lines converge at a vanishing point on the horizon, generating the three-dimensional perspective grid in paintings. Medieval paintings showed distant objects above objects in the foreground but not smaller in size, and the scene did not converge on a vanishing point. It was, in effect, a God's eye view—a view seen from a being who is everywhere at once and from whom all objects are equidistant. This lent a kind of simultaneity and immediacy to medieval painting, just as the medieval town was a jumble of crooked streets and houses. The medieval artist was concerned more with rendering a story than a moment in time, more with depicting transcendent soul than corporeal reality, more with depicting God's viewpoint than that of any human observer.

Related to this is the relative insignificance of portraiture in medieval art—the result of a worldview that sees human beings as hierarchical entities rather than as individuals. The Renaissance portraits of the 15th and 16th centuries such as Jan van Eyck's *Giovanni Arnolfini and His Bride*, Domenico Ghirlandaio's *An Old Man and His Grandson*, and Leonardo da Vinci's *Mona Lisa* would have been unthinkable except in an environment strongly infused with humanism. Even Donatello's and Michelangelo's sculptures of David are portraits in the most generic sense—portrayals of human being as seen not by God but by a human being.

In contrast to medieval painting, Renaissance painting is

constructed from the specific vantage point of the individual viewer—the artist or the observer of the picture. This implies that the observer generates the frame of reference, that everything is organized from that observer's perspective, and that the scene captures a single moment of time. The Great Renaissance architect Leone Battista Alberti, one of the developers of linear perspective, is said to have exclaimed, "At last! I can see the world as God sees it." In other words, Alberti was putting himself in the place of God, an attitude that earlier might have been a heresy in the eyes of the church. How could an ordinary person presume to see the world as God sees it? But this is the humanist vision.

One further idea of the humanists bears mentioning because of its contribution, along with empirical observation, to the foundations of modern science. This is the notion, inherited from Plato, Pythagoras, and other Greeks, that the "book of nature" is written in the language of mathematics. To the rational intellectuals of Greece, the secrets of the universe were revealed through numerical relationships: harmonics, proportions, geometry, the intervals of the "music of the spheres." If the language of mathematics could be deciphered fully, they believed, the universe would render up its last mysteries. So firmly has this notion taken hold of us that vast transfers of wealth are effected by digital manipulations on computers, and computers speak, write, translate—all by converting input into number systems and retransforming those systems into sound or graphics. And, of course, the pursuit of measurable phenomena continues to be the central activity of scientists today.

The Dark Side of the Renaissance

We usually see the Renaissance in a positive light. The very name means "rebirth" in French, implying the rebirth of Europe from the Dark Ages. However, modem scholars no longer equate the entire medieval period between the Fall of Rome and the Renaissance (about 500 to 1400 A.D.) with the Dark Ages. That term is now confined to the period between 500 and 1100, and some scholars compress it even further to between the Fall of Rome and the reign of Charlemagne beginning in 800 A.D. The later Middle Ages from

1100 to 1400, and especially the Gothic period between 1200 and 1300, are now recognized as an age of the flowering of trade, the arts, poetry, and architecture. Marco Polo's descriptions (albeit at second hand) of his journeys indicate that the vast territories between Europe and the East were also alive with trade, travel, and industry.[10] As we have noted in our discussion of Gothic architecture, this period saw the building of some of the largest and most structurally sophisticated buildings in human history. Some critics such as William Morris, John Ruskin, Frank Lloyd Wright, and Victor Hugo saw the medieval period as a model for modernism far superior to that of the Renaissance. Frank Lloyd Wright liked to quote Victor Hugo reference to the Renaissance as the setting sun all Europe mistook for dawn.

While the Renaissance brought many humanistic advances, it had a dark side. The brilliant flourishing of the arts, literature, commerce, universities, and sciences is only half of the picture. In the underbelly of the Renaissance were the horrors of the Inquisitions and witch-burnings, surface symptoms of even deeper diseases festering in the soul of Europe. Leonardo da Vinci, the exemplary "Renaissance man" renowned for his prophetic mechanical inventions as well as for his art, was himself troubled by dark forebodings of destruction—perhaps by a future technology—seen as a monster running amuck and vanquishing humankind.

> Alas, how many attacks were made upon this raging fiend; to him every onslaught was as nothing. O wretched folk, for you there availed not the impregnable fortresses, nor the lofty walls of your cities, nor the being together in great numbers, nor your houses or palaces! There remained not any place unless it were the tiny holes and subterranean caves where after the manner of crabs and crickets and creatures like these you might find safety and a means of escape. Oh, how many wretched mothers and fathers were deprived of their children!
>
> How many unhappy women were deprived of their companions. In truth ... I do not believe that ever since the world was created there has been witnessed such

lamentation and wailing of people accompanied by so great terror. In truth the human species in such a plight has need to envy every other race of creatures ... for us wretched mortals there avails not any flight, since this monster when advancing slowly far exceeds the speed of the swiftest courser.

I know not what to say or do, for everywhere I seem to find myself swimming with bent head within the mighty throat and remaining indistinguishable in death, buried within the huge belly![11]

Lewis Mumford has seen in Leonardo's nightmarish vision, recorded nearly five hundred years ago, a premonition of the horrifying reality of the nuclear, biological, and chemical weapons that can now easily destroy all humankind. A closer look at Leonardo's imagery reveals another, more primitive fear: the Hero's fear of being devoured in the material matrix. This is especially clear in the last paragraph where Leonardo is haunted by visions of swimming in oceanic oblivion, all humbled with bent head, anonymously indistinguishable in death—in death of ego—buried within the huge belly of the beast, consumed in the womb of the maternal matrix transformed by fear into Leviathan, whale, Dragon, Gorgon, and witch.

In Jungian terms, visions such as Leonardo's point to the male's alienation from his anima, that is, from the feminine elements of his psyche. The repression of the anima creates fear, and fear attributes to the anima the qualities of the unconscious shadow side of the personality. Thus the anima is seen in dreams and visions as a demonic figure threatening to destroy the integrity of the ego and the persona or public personality. Since these fears, repressions, and alienations are essentially unconscious, the psyche projects them onto events and people in the outside world, which gives the conscious mind a means of targeting, acting out, and relieving its hidden anxieties. The repressed anima comes to be represented by women in general or by a particular woman with whom a man has a turbulent relationship. These projections can happen collectively as well as individually.

When the collective unconscious of a large male population is alienated from the feminine principle, women become the targets of its projected anxiety. Such was the case in Renaissance Europe.

The Renaissance had inherited the vigorous misogynistic campaign of the Christian church, fueled by the theories and dogmas of Aristotle, St. Paul, St. Augustine, and St. Thomas Aquinas. The resulting images of women variously held that they had little or no soul; were the source of all evil in the world; were simply inert nutrient matter on which men had to impose intelligence and spirit in order to beget true human beings; were not derived directly from god but only through men via Adam; were licentious in the extreme and needed to be held in check for civilization to survive; were equated with nature and the body, both of which had to be scourged if spirit was to prevail; were totally useless and helpless without male guidance and protection; were a necessary evil intended by divine providence to cater to men's needs and egos; were the very incarnation of sin; were devoid of vital force; and were incapable of rational thought. Some of these contentions still plague us today; other seem incomprehensible, though in the past they were subjects of learned discourse and widely respected as representing the highest philosophical and spiritual principles attainable by the mind of man.

While the philosophers who contributed to these views were and still are hailed as the founding fathers of modern thought, millions of women, victimized as the recipients of projected anima alienation, were burned at the stake. Although the Inquisition had been established in the Middle Ages, its original powers were quite limited—it was directed mainly against the Albigenses in the south of France, an ascetic, dualistic, suicidal sect considered heretical by the Church. It was not until the Renaissance, and the publication of the extremely misogynistic *Malleus Maleficarum*, "The Hammer of the Witches," in 1486 that the Inquisition was unleashed with hysterical frenzy all over Europe against those suspected of practicing the Old Religion. It has been estimated that at least two million and possibly as many as nine million people were executed, 80 percent of them women.[12]

All the while, the doctrine of sacerdotal celibacy was gaining momentum in the Church, so the vast multitude of men whose lives were dedicated to the Christian faith were cut off from normal personal, emotional, sexual, matrimonial, and psychological relationships with women. Many historians have pointed out that the ensuing enforced sublimation of sexual and emotional energy contributed substantially to the fervor with which the witch-hunts were carried out. The repertoire of Inquisitional tortures is notorious for its erotic sadism. The unnatural procedures of examination were themselves a perverted acting out on the part of the Inquisitors of their own repressed sexual fantasies.

Some of these practices, and the diabolical informant industry they spawned, are described in *The Spiral Dance: A Rebirth of the Ancient Religion of the Great Goddess*.

The witch-hunts were a hysterical collective exorcism of the feminine principle. Above all, women were equated with nature, and nature was to be abhorred and conquered in all its forms. Susan Griffin's *Woman and Nature* gives the most moving account of the consequences of this equation. Thus the terrible witch-burnings fired the crucible of an unnatural wisdom, a wisdom alienated from nature, from the body, from women, and ultimately from spirit. This is the dark side of the Renaissance so rarely acknowledged. While male intellectuals, artists, patrons, and clergy basked in the radiant light of the period, the female population lived a prolonged night of holy terror, never knowing when they would be carted away on bizarre charges to face unimaginably terrifying deaths. In a very real way the two interpretations of Leonardo's vision—as premonition of nuclear holocaust and as fear of the feminine—are one and the same. The run-amuck technological monster that has created the nuclear nightmare could not have been born of a natural union of masculine and feminine. It is the ultimate logical offspring of the "second birth" through the male, claimed as the superior form of begetting since the dawn of male-supremacist religion in the Four Quarters. It is the final product of centuries of thought systematically divorced from female sensibility. It is Yeats's rough beast slouching toward Bethlehem to be born.

This kind of persecution of women and alienation from the *anima* was not unique to Western civilization. Similar beliefs and behavior arose in most civilizations as they approached their materialistic, technocratic Grid phases. It happened in China and Japan, in Hellenistic Greece, throughout the Near East, and among the Aztecs. It is as if the elimination of the holistic female spirit is the beginning of the death of a civilization.

There is another important aspect of the dark side of the Renaissance: the colonization of Africa and the Americas in the late 14th and early 15th centuries. Although the sheer courage of the early explorers may have been admirable, the reasons for their voyages usually were not. Compelled by the basest, materialistic greed for gold, slaves, political position, and royal favor, the explorers and conquerors were ruthless in their treatment of indigenous peoples. Their genocidal campaigns in Africa and the Americas left millions of inhabitants dead or enslaved. In the name of Christian piety, they destroyed whole civilizations (such as the Aztec, Mayan, and Incan)—burning buildings and rare sacred books, melting down gold artifacts, looting fabulous palaces and religious centers. They justified their behavior on the grounds that the people they had conquered were subhuman heathen savages whose accomplishments were the work of the Devil, just as their brothers in Europe were burning women on the grounds that they were witches in league with Satan. Of course, both claims were projections of the Europeans' own inner derangements.

The conquests brought Europe into the imperialistic Radiant Axes archetype, which has begun to wane only in the 20th century. Since the emergence of the ego principle in the Four Quarters, women and foreigners had been perceived and persecuted as the "alien other." Only the scale was different in the Radiant Axes. Where the Four Quarters chieftains raided neighboring tribes, and the Pyramid kings conquered enough territory to form nation states, the Radiant Axes emperors sometimes subdued whole continents containing millions of inhabitants. Being of distant cultures, the conquered had beliefs, deities, and customs completely different from those of the conquerors. Some emperors, like Kublai Khan, were tolerant of the differences and interested in learning about them. The Europeans were not. Christianity bred intolerance, and intolerance demanded that the "alien other" be converted, forcing the semblance of uniformity, or killed.

But this outward enactment of intolerance also produced an inward sublimation of all that the "alien other" represented.

Anything that seemed womanly or "savage" or Indian or Black was derided and joined the shadow side of the Western character. As later conquests brought India, Indonesia, Indochina, Australia, and other parts of Asia and Oceania under the yoke of European colonialism, these areas of the world also contributed their mystique to the repressed sides of the European personality. Since Rousseau's elevation of the "noble savage" Westerners seeking to restore their lost spiritual wholeness have naturally turned to Native America, Black Africa, India, and aboriginal Australia for spiritual nourishment. They know, consciously or unconsciously, if properly tapped the shadow can release immense energy and wisdom.

The Clockwork Universe

Witch-burning reached its height in the 16th and 17th centuries, and continued into the 18th. It is no coincidence that during this time rationalism became so glorified that the 17th and 18th centuries are known as the "Age of Reason" and the "Enlightenment." Even these names suggest a worldview posited on the banishment of the darker, more irrational forces in the psyche equated at that time with the mentality of females and non-Europeans. During these two periods (which some historians use interchangeably), certain philosophers, scientists, and popularizes—Bacon, Galileo, Kepler, Descartes, Locke, Newton, Voltaire, Rousseau—outlined the powerful new mechanistic worldview that still grips the West today.

This view was radically different from the church-dominated view of the Middle Ages. It saw the universe—the celestial bodies, nature, and the material world including the human body—as a vast machine that followed regular physical laws discernible through human reason. God ceased to be the omnipotent, unknowable, mystical patriarch of the cosmos and became the Prime Mover, the master clockmaker who initially put everything into motion.

> This deist god was himself (or should one say, itself?) a highly rationalist construct—the "clockmaker god" who had to exist in order to start this Newtonian world machine' running, and guarantee that it would not run

down, but who never interfered with it, and certainly never performed miracles. Voltaire was very proud of his aphorism, "If God did not exist, it would be necessary to invent him," hardly a Christian sentiment.[15]

Voltaire's sentiment may not sound Christian, but it does sound very much like Neumann's description of the "Slaying of the Father" where "the hero ceases to be an instrument of the gods and begins to play his own independent part as a human being and ... finally becomes, in modern man, a battleground for supra-personal forces, where the human ego pits itself against the deity."[15a] Neumann is not speaking here of any ordinary revolt against religious duty and authority. We must remember that Neumann, like other Jungians, does not use terms like "deity" and "God" in the usual orthodox religious sense, but rather in the psychological sense to refer to the great, transpersonal Self. Thus, Neumann is speaking of an accelerating inner estrangement between the ego and the Self. In this light, the mechanistic worldview that leads to the Grid takes on new meaning. It becomes clear that this is a worldview based on a revolt not just against the God-figure of orthodox religion, but more importantly, against the eternal source of true spiritual wisdom: the Self.[15]

The Self can be reached only through the collective unconscious, through psychoerotic wisdom as it were. But the influential Western thinkers of the last six centuries were increasingly intent on eradicating psychoeros and promoting technelogos as can be seen in attitudes toward women and non-white people, in the elevation of reason and the eventual elimination of spirit and intuition, in the growing faith in rational science, and in the burgeoning Machine Age. In fact, the machine became the prototype for all forms of cultural expression, just as mathematics became the common language of science.

The Machine: Icon of the Grid

In *A Concise History of Mathematics*, Dirk J. Struik attributed the rapid development of mathematics during the Renaissance not only to the rise of the commercial classes but also to the "productive use and further perfection of machines." He asserts that machines would have developed more rapidly in antiquity and the Orient were it not for the use of slaves and the lack of an "economically progressive urban life." Machines came into limited use in the Middle Ages in small scale manufacturing, public works, and mining operations, but it was not until the 15th century that they really began to proliferate: In the fifteenth century mining in Central Europe developed into a completely capitalistic industry based technically on the use of pumps and hoisting machines which allowed the boring of deeper and deeper layers. The invention of firearms and printing, the construction of windmills and canals, the building of ships to sail the ocean, required engineering skill and made people technically conscious. The perfection of clocks, useful for astronomy and navigation and often installed in public places, brought admirable mechanisms before the public eye; the regularity of their motion and the possibility they offered of indicating time exactly made a deep impression upon the philosophical mind. During the Renaissance, and even centuries later, the clock was taken as a model of the universe. This was an important factor in the development of the mechanical conception of the world.[16]

The machine became the icon of Western civilization for several reasons. Firstly, every late Radiant Axes and early Grid civilization loves engineering. Think of the Roman or the Incan Empire. Indeed, the physical management of empires would be impossible without the engineering of structures and systems on an extensive scale: highways, waterworks, storage facilities, military installations, government headquarters, ships, industries, colonial capitals. Secondly, the machine gives humanity extremely powerful technological "extensions" (as McLuhan called them) that promise control over unpredictable nature. Rivers can be dammed, forests cleared, agricultural fertility ensured. Machines—and technology in general—give the illusion that it is no longer necessary to work with nature since one can control nature. Thirdly, machines themselves can be perfectly controlled. They are the absolute products and servants of the human will. They do what they are designed to do, no more, no less—until they break down. Then, although they appear to be entropically regressing to some natural state of chaos, they can, unlike nature, be repaired or replaced. This property of machines became the prototype for modem personnel management. Although human beings are more like nature than machines, managers formulated tasks and job descriptions that made human beings as interchangeable as possible, made them, in other words, replaceable like machines.[17] Finally, the machine is the product of science and mathematics, hence it is an invention with which people in Grid cultures are comfortable. It is the offspring of logic, techne, reason. Its powers of performance affirm the preeminence of these attributes. (It is important to note that the Western world is not the only Grid civilization to have exhibited an enthusiasm for the machine or engineering or both. Though their technologies were not as advanced as ours, the Roman, Incan, Greek, and Chinese civilizations under the Grid archetype displayed the same enthusiasm.)

Cartesian Dualism and the Cartesian Grid

The detailed origins of the Western mechanistic worldview have been explored in depth by other writers (Lewis Mumford, Marshall McLuhan, Fritjof Capra, and others). Here, we will simply highlight certain representative people and ideas to outline the essential building blocks of the Grid. One of the most important sires of the Grid was René Descartes, the 17th century French philosopher and mathematician. He was a rather dour figure whose life was quite devoid of feminine influence: his mother died a few days after he was born; he was educated by Jesuits, whom he greatly admired; and he never married. He was said to have had a "cold and selfish" disposition, was sickly, and had a feeble voice. Some of his contemporaries criticized him for pandering to church authority since, after the condemnation of Galileo, Descartes abandoned some of the less orthodox ideas in his own work.

On the night of November 10th, 1619, when he was twenty-three years old, he had a series of dreams that changed the course of his life, turning him from a military career to the pursuit of knowledge. After nightmares in which he was crippled by terror, prevented from reaching a church, unable to reach out to a friend, and accosted by a violent noise, Descartes dreamed that he found two books on a table: a dictionary and an anthology of poetry. The books disappeared and reappeared in altered editions, presenting various riddles, among them the recurrent question, *Quod vitae sectabor iter?* (What path of life should I follow?) He awoke feeling he had received a divine omen through the books, the dictionary representing the unified language of science, and the anthology of poetry standing for the body of wisdom and philosophy. The omen told him that he was destined to spend his life searching for a unified science of nature based on mathematics. He proceeded to write, in the course of his life, on every conceivable subject: the nature of emotions, the movements of celestial bodies, the biological workings of the human body, optics, vortices, the laws of mathematics. He is credited not only with making substantial contributions to analytical geometry and algebra, but with being a father of modem philosophy and the scientific method. The latter he set down by separating reason from feelings and stressing the need to arrive at axiomatic truths untainted by emotional deception.

In both philosophy and mathematics, Descartes contributed consistently to the Grid; two examples will make the point. Philosophically, he described in his usual engaging autobiographical style, a complete separation between body and soul. (He used "spirit" to mean the "animal spirits" or subtle nerve processes of the body.) He summarized his body/mind separation in "An Explanation of the Human Mind or Rational Soul: What it is, and what it may be," which he wrote to respond to an attack on his "Progamme." These passages reveal his thinking:

> The Human Mind is that wherein the processes of thought are first accomplished by man; and it consists of the faculty of thinking alone, and the inward principle...

> The fact that mind is in truth nothing other than a substance, or an entity really distinct from body, in actuality separable from it, and capable of existing apart and independently is revealed to us in Holy Scripture,

in many places. And thus what in the view of some, the study of nature leaves doubtful is already placed beyond all doubt for us through divine revelation in Scripture.

Nor is it any objection that we may have doubts about the body, but in nowise about the mind. For this only proves that, so long as we doubt about body, we cannot say that mind is a mode of body...

As mind is of a nature diverse from body, and from the disposition of body, and cannot arise from this disposition, therefore it is incorruptible.[18]

This mind-body dualism is not so different from the schism we saw arising first in the Four Quarters and accelerating its influence throughout the progressively more secular Pyramid and Radiant Axes archetypes. Descartes wrote this summary in 1647. Louis XIV was then four years old. Twenty years later the French king would build the same dualistic vision into the clipped gardens and rational architecture of Versailles.

In time, the "soul" half of Cartesian dualism withered and died as the leading thinkers of succeeding centuries became increasingly fascinated with discovering the mathematical laws of nature, like Louis XIV's gardeners manicuring the trees into ever more precise geometric topiaries. As W. W. Rouse Ball summarized in his 1908 *A Short Account of the History of Mathematics*:

> I have read somewhere that philosophy has always been chiefly engaged with the inter-relations of God, Nature, and Man. The earliest philosophers were Greeks who occupied themselves mainly with the relations between God and Nature, and dealt with Man separately. The Christian Church was so absorbed in the relation of God to Man as entirely to neglect Nature. Finally, modern philosophers concern themselves chiefly with the relations between Man and Nature. Whether this is a correct historical generalization of the views which have been successively prevalent I do not care to discuss here, but the statement as to the scope of modern philosophy marks the limitations of Descartes's writings.[20]

And Struik carries on from there, showing the rise of mathematics and mechanics as models for the "relations between Man and Nature:"

> In accordance with many other great thinkers of the seventeenth century, Descartes searched for a general method of thinking in order to be able to facilitate inventions and to find truth in the sciences [*techne*].
>
> Since the only known natural science with some degree of systematic coherence was mechanics, and the key to the understanding of mechanics was mathematics, mathematics became the most important means for the understanding of the universe. Moreover, mathematics with its convincing statements was itself the brilliant example that truth could be found in science. The mechanistic philosophy of this period thus came to a conclusion that was similar to that of the Platonists, but for a different reason. Platonists, believing in the harmony of the universe, and Cartesians, believing in a general method based on reason, both found in mathematics the queen of the sciences.[19]

Descartes's most important mathematical contribution to the Grid lay in what came to be known as the "Cartesian coordinates" or the "Cartesian grid." The story goes that one night while lying in bed before going to sleep, Descartes was watching a fly crawling along the ceiling. It occurred to him that the exact position of the fly could be determined if two lines were drawn at right angles to the walls adjoining the ceiling to the location of the fly. The measurements of these lines would then give the fly's precise position. These two lines became the "x" and "y" coordinates of the Cartesian grid, to which Descartes added a "z" coordinate giving the vertical dimension. This system of three lines at right angles to each other precisely pinpointing the three-dimensional location of any object in space is still used by scientists today.[20] (Descartes himself was interested mainly in the planar applications of the "x" and "y" coordinates, particularly to reduce curvilinear figures to equations of straight lines—achieving in the dry formulae of analytical geometry the last conquest of the sinuous lines of the Sensitive Chaos and the Great Round.)[21]

The Cartesian grid extended the uniformity of rational geometry infinitely in all directions. Although the "xyz" coordinates may at first sound suspiciously like the Quadrant of the Four Quarters, they were different in that rather than emanating from a central place (the Heavenly Mansion of the Lord of the Four Quarters), they formed a three-dimensional grid in which any point could be measured relative to any other point. The "observer" in other words, does not take the heroic stance of being the "center of the universe," but instead poses as a mere measurer and recorder of objective information. The observer's role is not "human" in that it has nothing to do with his or her unique personality, ego, knowledge, or place in history. The "0" point in the "xyz" coordinates is arbitrary and can be placed anywhere. The observer is simply a technocratic documenter whose task could be performed equally well by any number of interchangeable researchers, or even by a somewhat sensitive machine. It is on subtle distinctions such as this that the Grid was born in the West. Although the Cartesian grid was not intended as a metaphysical icon, it is one nevertheless. It perfectly expresses the non-centered, measurement-oriented, scientific spirit of modern Western civilization.

These two examples—Cartesian dualism and the Cartesian grid—suggest how ingrained the ideas of this complex thinker have become in Western society. After Descartes, the mechanistic, dualistic, rational worldview was applied to ever larger spheres of life. Newton's *Principia*, published in 1687, described the workings of the clockwork universe by establishing the mechanical laws of the movements of terrestrial and celestial bodies. His theories were an important affirmation of the growing idea that the physical world was not subject to the irrational whim of God, accepted for centuries on faith, but that it followed empirical physical laws that could be reasoned out by the human mind.[22]

Although Newton's inestimable contributions to physics are universally acknowledged today, his theories originally left many loose ends. Rather than solving these, Newton spent his later years studying alchemy, theology, and history. More than a century after the *Principia* was published, the obsessively tidy

French astronomer/mathematician Pierre Simon de Laplace polished off the rough edges of Newton's work, and at the same time extended the Grid mentality into several other areas. He standardized weights and measures, helped to invent the metric system, and devised a cost-effective means of census-taking. Laplace systematically went through Newton's work, neatly clearing up all errors and anomalies, until he was perfectly confident that it, together with his own probability theory, could reduce any scientific or social problem to a practical solution. Whereas Newton had suspected that the solar system was basically unstable and needed God's hand on occasion to keep it running smoothly, Laplace showed that the system's apparent variations were cyclical and regular and therefore needed no divine intervention. When Napoleon, who was one of Laplace's students at the Ecole Militaire, asked Laplace about the absence of God from his theory, he replied that he had no need of that hypothesis."[23] With this dry statement, Laplace reduced God to an expendable element in his equation. The clockwork universe could run without its clockmaker.

The Ideal State and the Tabula Rasa

By the late 17th century, Enlightenment principles were well developed in political theory, and by the late 18th century, they generated the American and French Revolutions and the writing of the Constitution of the United States. One of the most influential thinkers was John Locke, whose *Essay Concerning Human Understanding* (1690) and other writings articulated the Enlightenment ideal of the perfect state. Locke maintained that in the original state of nature, human beings were happy, tolerant, and possessed of reason. All "men" were equal and self-sufficient, and, although anarchy existed in the absence of an organized state, a natural harmony prevailed because people were inherently good. No one could infringe on another's right to "life, health, liberty, or possessions." Eventually people entered into a social contract to form an organized state based on the consent of the governed. In the state, the basic rights and liberties of the individual were preserved by natural law, but a superstructure of reciprocal obligations preserved cooperative order. These ideas formed the basis for the checks and balances in the American Constitution, but more profoundly, Locke's vision of equality and freedom eventually put an end to Western monarchy. In this, his ideas are completely consistent with the Grid's goal of distributing power equally among the people, and "power to the people" was and is the rallying cry of social revolutionaries.

Although Locke held minor governmental posts in England, he was suspected of radicalism and had to flee to Holland, where he completed his *Essay*.

Locke advocated freedom of religion (except that he favored legislation against atheism and Roman Catholicism, seeing both as threats to religion and the state), and this religious tolerance found its way into the United States' fundamental principle of separating church and state.

Much to his credit, Locke extended his egalitarian concepts to include not only the political arena but also the family. He consistently rejected the patriarchal concept of authority, whether in the guise of the divine right of kings, or the theory that Adam had been given a divine right to rule by God, or the well-established idea that the father has a natural right to rule his family. He saw the family as headed equally by mother and father, in whom is vested the responsibility of preserving the child's rights to life and liberty until it reaches the age of consent. Unfortunately, Locke's enlightened views regarding women fell by the wayside while his other ideas were enthusiastically accepted. In her book *History of Ideas on Women*, Rosemary Agonito writes:

> While Locke is often referred to as the most representative thinker in the English-American political system, his ideas on the equal rights and authority of women and men have been virtually ignored by people who adopted his other ideas wholesale. When Thomas Jefferson, who is often accused of plagiarizing [Locke's] *Second Treatise* in his Declaration of Independence, copied the phrase "all men are created equal" from Locke, he did not mean what Locke had meant—all men, male and female.[24]

The esteemed 18th century philosopher Jean Jacques Rousseau, whose ideas influenced the French Revolution and the development of French philosophy, also derived many of his ideas from Locke, especially the "noble savage" and the social contract. But unlike Locke, Rousseau did not see the logical connections between political theory and male-female relations. Agonito writes:

> One of the consistent themes of his life and works was that women are inferior and subordinate beings who should be nurtured for the sole purpose of serving men and providing them pleasure. He preached that women should be restricted to domestic chores and excluded from liberal education, urging that they be "trained to bear the yoke from the first, so that they may not feel it." In *A Discourse on Political Economy* (1755), he states that the primary function of the family is to "preserve and increase the patrimony of the father" so that he may pass it on to his heirs. He insists that the patriarchal structure of the family is natural, while denying any analogy with the state. Men govern women but not men.[25]

Thus, although Locke had enlightened views on women, those who carried his theories into action for the most part did not. If they had, perhaps the Grid would have developed differently in the West, less in the direction of a cold and sterile rationalism divorced from compassionate feelings and intuitive value judgments (the Feeling and Intuition functions in Jung's typology). Even the occasional infatuation with the "noble savage" was little more than a romantic concept. The "noble savage" represented the idyllic dream of a state of nature that never existed but was formulated in the Enlightenment as a benign foil for the development of political theories. It is true that Enlightenment thinkers revered nature inasmuch as they saw it as an uncorrupted world governed by physical laws knowable through reason. In this sense, nature was the ideal realm poised between the supernatural (the imaginary) and the unnatural (the irrational). These two poles were and still are outside the realm acceptable to the rational mind.

Locke also advanced a radical new theory of the human mind that is still as influential as his political theories. He asserted that the mind is a *tabula rasa*, a or blank slate devoid of any innate ideas, on which experience inscribes a content based on information received mechanically through the senses and interpreted through reflection. This was the beginning of the modern view that the human being is a purely conditioned animal, responsive to external stimuli. It was in direct contrast to the Church's view that human character is innate, pre-destined, God-given. It extended "mechanics" to the understanding of human nature.

The *tabula rasa* concept captured the European imagination because, in one stroke, it swept away the centuries of mental webs with which the Church had tightened its deathgrip on individual freedom and intellectual progress. Bacon, Hobbes, and Descartes had all struggled with the Church's control of thought, and, during the lifetimes of these philosophers, Galileo had faced the Inquisition and Giordano Bruno had been burned at the stake. There was not a scholar or philosopher then alive who did not deeply fear entrapment by the Inquisition's network of informers, false accusers, and trial procedures. At the same time, the explosion of scientific information since the Renaissance demanded a new kind of mind freed of fear and superstition. Only a clean sweep of repressive church dogma would enable new facts and theories to be assimilated. Locke's *tabula rasa* provided the model for such a mind.

Although the Inquisitional context of the Enlightenment eventually receded into the background, scientists have never forgotten that their freedom of inquiry is in direct enmity with the Church. How this continues to this day can be seen in the fundamentalists censorship of textbooks and in the ongoing attacks of Christian creationists against scientific evolutionists. Thus the birth of Western science, and the Grid in effect, entailed the Slaying of the Father and the pitting of the young Hero's (the scientist's) intelligence against the age-old restrictive traditions of the Church (God).

The *tabula rasa* concept of the mind eventually came to be applied in both positive and negative ways. On the one hand, it fostered more humane attitudes toward social deviants such as criminals and the insane, who had previously been seen as morally degenerate agents of Satan. The Enlightenment attitude held that such people were victims of inhumane life circumstances that had thwarted their natural gifts for reason and socially responsible behavior. (There is a third alternative, yet to be adequately explored, that combines both views and sees deviant behavior as both a moral and an "environmental" issue.) On the other hand, the *tabula rasa* concept has led to some of the more insidious manipulations of "cultural engineering" and behavioral modification. The operative assumption in these cases is that mind and brain are synonymous and both behave according to strictly mechanical, biological, chemical, and electrical patterns triggered by measurable stimuli. Alter the stimuli and you can alter behavior to any desired end.

Of course, Locke cannot be wholly indicted for this limited view of human nature. In the centuries since his death, scores of people have intervened to contribute their own theories, observations, and interpretations. But Locke is credited with being the founder of British empiricism, and as such he significantly influenced the philosophical orientation of the English-speaking world today. Empiricism (which is related to science, pragmatism, rationalism, and logical positivism) is a branch of philosophy that sees the world in extremely pragmatic terms. Based on the idea that all knowledge is gained from experience, that is, from conscious content and sense data only, empiricism denies the existence of any universal truths or instinctive inborn knowledge. In the empiricist's view, all knowledge is reducible to directly perceived data. This, of course, is the cornerstone of modern science. A real scientist would not put one whit's worth of credence in anything that did not show up measurably under the microscope, through the telescope, or in any of the multitude of instruments that have extended our sense-data collecting capacities in the Age of Science. Furthermore, one scientist's perception of data is worth nothing if other scientists do not see the same thing in replicated experiments. And so, we have come a cosmos away from the Sensitive Chaos when Universal Truths perceived by one individual in a vision quest could build a world. Whereas the people of the Sensitive Chaos, the Great Round, and to an ever decreasing extent, the succeeding archetypes sought ultimate knowledge through personal communion with the sacred, the Grid of modern science denies the very existence of ultimate knowledge and the sacred.

Progress

The idea of progress, another invention of the Enlightenment, is fundamental to Western civilization. As strange as it may seem, the notion that human civilization is progressing toward a better future did not exist in the West before the 17th century. Previously, the Church's view dominated, holding that humanity had fallen from its God-given state of grace in the Garden of Eden.

Even St. Augustine's 5th century work, *City of God*, envisioned not a better future world made on earth by mortal humans but a deliverance occasioned by the Second Coming of Christ. Before that, the Classical world had held a cyclical view of history that assumed that Golden, Silver, and Iron ages repeated themselves in endless succession, a view not unlike the one generally held in the East. Even the Renaissance humanists were nostalgic for a past glory.[26]

The clearest beginnings of a belief that the present is better than the past were stated in late 17th century arguments over whether a contemporary writer could achieve a work equal to or better than those of ancient Greek and Roman writers. Called the "quarrel of the ancients and the moderns" in France and the "battle of the books" in England, the debate was eventually decided in favor of the moderns. The belief in the superiority of the present (and the destined superiority of the future) eventually spawned the whole doctrine of progress on which industrial Western civilization is based. It bred the confidence in technological progress that led to the rampant conquest of land, nature, resources, and people known as the Industrial Revolution. The industrialists of the 19th and 20th centuries could do no wrong in the fulfillment of their destiny of realizing the full potential of Western civilization.

The imperative of progress gained momentum with the mid-19th century publications of Charles Darwin's theory of evolution. Though he was dimly understood and wildly exploited, Darwin did at one and the same time 1) deal the final scientific blow to the Church's doctrine of Creation, 2) bring the entire history of human development under the mechanistic laws of chance and change, 3) provide an empirical foundation for the principle of progress, and 4) add "scientific' affirmation to the perception that animals and less "developed" people were inferior to Western "man."

The doctrine of progress abundantly lubricated the intellectual machinery of science, since it was through science the "New God," that progress would perpetuate itself. Interestingly, faith in progress burgeoned at about the same time that Newton and Leibnitz invented the calculus, the branch of mathematics that deals with continuously changing qualities. Then as now mathematics was the rarefied, hierophantic "sacred" art that gave access to the secrets of the universe. A mind limited to dealing with static quantities and concepts cannot deal with progress. Progress implies that the world is not static, but continually changing. The calculus gave the scientific community the powerful mental tools needed to master the new worldview. (It is also interesting that one of the more recent branches of mathematics to have won the kind of excitement that the calculus met three hundred years ago is catastrophe theory, which provides a mathematical way of dealing with discontinuous phenomena. Perhaps this is another sign that the Grid is in its final death throes.)

The doctrine of progress also brought Western civilization's concept of time into conformance with the linear, rational mentality of the Grid. Time now extended in a directional line: backwards into an inferior past and forwards toward a superior future.

The Industrial Revolution

The Industrial Revolution that occurred between 1750 and 1850 in England, and somewhat later in the rest of Europe and the United States, radically transformed society, consummating all of the developments leading to the Grid that we have seen thus far. Europe's Radiant Axes empires had brought an influx of wealth and raw materials, and had greatly expanded trade and the money economy. Secularization increasingly promoted and rewarded commercial enterprise. A new class of professionals and entrepreneurs flourished on the growing infrastructures of the banking systems, public libraries, technical schools, and urbane cities. The Enlightenment's emphasis on mathematical reason and scientific progress had laid the groundwork for the technological inventions on which industrialization depended, and its ethic of individual freedom gave people the incentive to use these innovations to their own advantage. Capitalism came into its own. Europe's long history of peasant unrest made millions of people ripe for the better way of life that industrialization seemed to promise. And the general rise of the Grid archetype reworked the European mind into structures capable of achieving the vast systematization of humans and machines that industrialization required.

At first the Industrial Revolution probably did more to lower rather than raise the average person's standard of life. Before industrialization, the vast majority of people lived on farms where they not only grew their own food but also made and locally traded candles, clothing, furniture, tools, household linens, crockery, and most of the necessities of daily life. The farm was both home and place of production, and even tenant farmers enjoyed a high degree of self-sufficiency. Few institutions touched the peasant's life, aside from the local church or chapel, the elementary school if there was one, and the regional marketplace with its opportunities for learning new things and meeting new people. But money was scarce, soil-tilling chancy, toil was hard and never-ending, landlords and tax-collectors cruel. The pretty thatched cottage could be a hovel and the farm a prison. It is no wonder that after the Industrial Revolution, most families sent many of their members to work as wage laborers in mines or factories away from the household. Home and place of production were split in two, and a new dependency on the employer, money wages, and manufactured goods destroyed self-sufficiency. Industrialization also brought smoke-filled skies, new diseases, urban congestion, exploitive labor practices, social instability and family disruption, and an insufferably paternalistic employer-worker relationship. These ills plague us even today, although we now enjoy much greater affluence.

The early industrial workers, freed from the plow, were newly chained to a money economy with only the hardest won opportunities for upward mobility. They must have felt doomed to a life of inhumanly hard work with little reward. Furthermore, they were no longer "complete" people able to meet all of their own needs. Now they were obscure cogs in an incomprehensible new social machine. Rather than having mastery (tenuous and vulnerable as it was) over the production of the necessities of life, industrial workers found themselves in jobs where they produced only one item, or only one component of a product that was assembled elsewhere. This fragmentation and specialization transformed the mind as well as the workplace. Industrialization made people themselves into machines. The focus was no longer on individual creativity but on standardization, quality control, and time-motion efficiency. The entire Grid-like goal of industrialization was the mass production of thousands or even millions of identical items and even identical people.

The ability to make people perform like machines is the ultimate intelligence of the Industrial Revolution. It has enabled highly intricate products—from cars to global communications systems—to be assembled from the disparate efforts of unskilled to highly specialized workers. A television set may be assembled from metals mined in Africa, plastics made in New Jersey, electronics made in Japan and cabinetwork made in Michigan; and it may end up in the home of an Eskimo. Virtually no one in the chain has any concept of the total enterprise. Not even supervisors, managers, salespeople, and executives wholly understand the complicated interdependent system of which they are a part.

In this regard, industry works in much the same way as the ant colony. In his chapter "On Societies as Organisms" in *Lives of a Cell*, Lewis Thomas writes, "Ants are so much like human beings as to be an embarrassment. They farm fungi, raise aphids as livestock, launch armies into wars, use chemical sprays to alarm and confuse enemies, capture slaves. The families of weaver ants engage in child labor .... They exchange information ceaselessly. They do everything but watch television."[27]

What makes us uncomfortable about social insects like ants, termites, and bees is that we don't like to think that we, like they, are not only individuals but also cellular parts of collective societies that behave like organisms. Yet through this collective organization, a society of ants is capable of much more than the sum of its individual parts.

> A solitary ant, afield, cannot be considered to have much of anything on his mind; indeed, with only a few neurons strung together by fibers, he can't be imagined to have a mind at all, much less a thought. He is more like a ganglion on legs. Four ants together, or ten, encircling a dead moth on a path, begin to look more like an idea. They fumble and shove, gradually moving the food toward the Hill, but as though by blind chance. It is only when you watch the dense mass of thousands of ants, crowded together around the Hill, blackening the ground, that you begin to see the whole beast, and now you observe it thinking, planning, calculating. It is an intelligence, a kind of live computer, with crawling bits for its wits.[28]

If we apply this insight to some of our giant social institutions, we can begin to understand their power. The military, for example, is a giant Moloch, an organism whose parts are the organizational departments, its organs, serving the welfare of the whole. With its rigid hierarchical ranking, military discipline, chain of command, and emphasis on duty over individuality, the military is the most highly organized social mechanism of all, infinitely more intelligent than the ant colony. The organizational structure of the military overrides individual roles. From lowliest private to five-star general to commander-in-chief, the incumbent occupies a box in a table of organization which is, in effect, a functioning anatomy and physiology. It is the juggernaut quality of this organizational system that gives the military its might and power. And, inasmuch as industry has modeled itself on the military and shares its interests, it accrues the same might and power. By contrast, those who fight the power of the military-industrial complex—whether over an unnecessary war, nuclear bombs and power plants, toxic waste dumps, environmental issues, or consumer causes—tend to be highly individualistic. It is extremely difficult for such activists to be effective against the military-industrial complex simply because they cannot match its high-powered organizational intelligence. They are like unaffiliated individual ants against a massive, well-entrenched colony.

Even in ancient times, similar though smaller scaled organizations arose with the Grid in earlier civilizations. The Roman Empire, for instance, matured into a military-industrial Grid superstate complete with a huge bureaucracy. Perhaps one significant difference is that the Roman Empire was unified under one rule, whereas today's Grid civilization transcends national boundaries, forming an organismic reticulum that is rapidly encircling the globe.

In a very real sense, the Industrial Revolution is not over. Under Western influence, many developing countries in Central and South America, Africa, and Asia are just now going through the same transformation that England underwent between 1750 and 1850. Unfortunately, many are also experiencing the same social ills: disruption of the family, rootlessness, cultural discontinuity, and the rampant growth of slums. Values are shifting from community solidarity to individual freedom, from spiritual richness to material wealth, from cultural traditions to mass-produced status symbols. All over the world, families and cultures are disintegrating as the young, the ambitious, the impoverished, and the disenfranchised migrate to cities in hope of finding opportunity. More often than not, they find only that thousands of others have already exhausted the job market. Not able or willing to return to the soil, they fall helplessly into industrialization's universal Dickensian underworld of slum life.

The Industrial Revolution brings both the promise of the Grid—individual freedom and material progress—and its despair—anonymity and powerlessness. In dealing with this phenomenon, philosophers have waxed eloquent on existentialism, pragmatism, and Marxist ideology. But the fact remains that in the Grid, the individual is the lone ant—merely a "ganglion on legs," merely a cog in the great Machine, useless unless he or she serves its ends.

The Machine has, in fact, produced many of the benefits it promised. The generations of immigrants who labored in mines and sweatshops in the 19th and early 20th centuries were indeed able to give their children a better life than they themselves had known, and all over the world, people still seem willing to work under similar circumstances for the same reason. Industrialization also made the middle class the largest sector of society for the first time in history. For these countless millions, the Machine delivered the affluence, leisure, material comfort, upward mobility, and individual freedom it promised. And, as we saw in the last chapter, the Machine had a certain seductive glamour as an idea that made it the icon of Western civilization. It was the glamour of this idea that architects in the early 1900s began to formalize in their esthetic "programmes" for modern architecture.

The Light, the Practical, the Ephemeral, and the Swift: Manifestoes of Modern Architecture

By the early 20th century, accelerated industrialization had sparked fantastic visions in the minds of European architects. The rapid expansion of cities and industry had brought an impressive array of new technologies and structures—dams, power plants, railroads, highways, bridges, ocean liners, airplanes, cars, office towers—which fired the imagination of a new generation of architects. The 19th century's innovations in engineering and materials—cast-iron, steel and reinforced concrete, elevators, steam-heat, and the technologies and industrial infrastructure that produced the Crystal Palace and the Eiffel Tower—made it possible to realize their dreams. Architects began to envision an esthetic that would celebrate the modern psyche and the Machine Age: a pristine, hygienic architecture made of the most advanced materials. To minds swept away by this esthetic, the dated neo-classical academies and the 19th century's decorative eclecticism were steeped in decadence, and Europe's impacted medieval and Renaissance cities reeked with the mustiness of bygone eras. The stifling working class tenements and dreary factory towns that had sprung up in and around the cities added to the claustrophobia. Enraptured by the promise of progress, the early modernists advocated a physical as well as mental destruction of the past to leave a clean slate for the future. This was to architecture what Locke's *tabula rasa* had been to the mind.

For the first three decades of the 20th century, European architects issued flurries of passionate manifestoes proclaiming the principles of their futurist visions. Although the early modernists argued among themselves and formed the kinds of clubs, salons, allegiances, and adversary groups common to any artistic movement, a half century of hindsight reveals much consistency in their thinking. There were some counterrevolutionaries, but they were unable to sway the development of modern architecture to their views (which are more appreciated today now that the modern movement is in decline). Stripped of their shrill and at times sophomoric rhetoric, the pronouncements of the manifestoes have for the most part been realized. A selection of excerpts from them will convey their tone and purposes. (Unless otherwise noted, they are quoted from *Programs and Manifestoes on 20th Century Architecture*, edited by Ulrich Conrads.) One recurring theme is an opposition, colored by an almost fanatical faith in progress, of a new world to the old.

> [Futurist] architecture cannot be subject to any law of historical continuity. It must be as new as our frame of mind is new....

> The tremendous antithesis between the modem and the ancient world is the outcome of all those things that exist now and did not exist then. Elements have entered our life of whose very possibility the ancients did not even dream. Material possibilities and attitudes of mind have come into being that have had a thousand repercussions, first and foremost of which is the creation of a new ideal of beauty, still obscure and embryonic, but whose fascination is already being felt even by the masses. We have lost the sense of the monumental, of the heavy, of the static; we have enriched our sensibility by a taste for the light, the practical, the ephemeral and the swift'. We feel that we are no longer the men of the cathedrals,

the palaces, the assembly halls; but of big hotels,
railway stations, immense roads, colossal ports, covered
markets, brilliantly lit galleries, freeways, demolition and
rebuilding schemes.
  ~ Antonio Sant'Elia and Filippo Tommaso Marinetti,
    1914

In keeping with the Grid archetype, the Futurists were inspired by commercial and industrial structures. They turned their backs on the prime building types of earlier archetypal eras: the Pyramid age's cathedrals and the Radiant Axes' palaces. Sant'Elia's and Marinetti's Futurist manifesto included Sant'Elia's visionary drawings of a utopian "Citta Nuova" or "New City" which magically transformed industrial structures into robustly romantic but prophetic images of the city of the future. They showed that dams, power plants, railways, airports, multi-leveled highways, suspension bridges and the like were not merely mundane industrial necessities but the cathedrals of our age.

Some of the manifestoes describe futuristic visions in a style similar to Revelations in the Bible, as if the New Jerusalem would be manifested on earth because of new materials.

The surface of the Earth would change greatly if brick
architecture were everywhere displaced by glass
architecture.
  It would be as though the Earth clad itself in jewelry
of brilliants and enamel.

  The splendour is absolutely unimaginable. And we
should then have on the Earth more exquisite things than
the gardens of the Arabian Nights.
  We should then have a paradise on Earth and would
not need to gaze longingly at the paradise in the sky.
  ~ Paul Scheerbart, 1914

We must admit that, in a way, Scheerbart's dream has come to pass. We may not share his enthusiasm for glass architecture, but we need only walk down Sixth Avenue in midtown Manhattan or the business center of any major city to see the physical, if not the spiritual, realization of his vision.

To European modernists, the New God in the splendid world of the future, where buildings would outshine paradise, would be the Machine, master Titan of them all, and architecture would be made in its image.

> We must invent and rebuild the Futurist city; it must be like an immense, tumultuous, lively, noble, work site, dynamic in all its parts; and the Futurist house must be like an enormous machine.
> ~ Sant'Elia and Marinetti, 1914

> If we eliminate from our hearts and minds all dead concepts in regard to the house, and look at the question from a critical and objective point of view, we shall arrive at the House-Machine, the mass-production house, healthy (and morally so too) and beautiful in the same way that the working tools and instruments which accompany our existence are beautiful.
> ~ Le Corbusier, 1923

In their adoration of the Machine, and their desire to cut off the past, the modernists puritanically forbade most of the time-honored techniques for making buildings interesting and meaningful: color, historical allusion, sensual richness, ornament, symmetry, vernacular idiom, wittiness, paradox, ethnicity, social and climatic determinants, traditional iconography. Nothing was allowed that was not in strict accordance with the functional properties of the new materials. These strictures had the solemnity of Biblical moral law.

> Thou shalt comprehend the form and construction of all objects only in the sense of their strictest, elementary logic and justification for their existence.
>
> Thou shalt adapt and subordinate these forms and constructions to the essential use of the material which thou employest.
> ~ Henry van de Velde, 1907

The most puritanical architect, Adolf Loos, is famous for having equated ornament with crime.

> The evolution of culture is synonymous with the removal of ornament from utilitarian objects... not only is ornament produced by criminals but also a crime is committed through the fact that ornament inflicts serious injury on people's health, on the national budget and hence on cultural evolution .... Freedom from ornament is a sign of spiritual strength.
> ~ Adolf Loos, 1908

But the modernists were not above "ornamenting" their pristine white boxes with pipe railings, metal stair treads, glass brick, industrial lighting fixtures, and other "hi-tech" details that made their buildings look like ocean liners and factories. These details furthered the resemblance of buildings to machines and to products of industry, which, in their honest use of materials, functional design, and economy of assembly, were closer to engineering than to architecture. The early modernists bestowed upon engineers a faith and reverence formerly reserved for the priesthood. But this is not surprising since engineers, initiated in the deepest secrets of the Machine Age, constituted the new elite.

> The Engineer, inspired by the law of Economy and governed by mathematical calculation, puts us in accord with universal law. He achieves harmony.
> ~ Le Corbusier, 1923

Now the new generation of engineers is growing up! ... The new engineer does not modify, he creates afresh; that is to say, he does not improve, but provides an absolutely elemental fulfilment of every demand .... BUT THIS IS NOT THE END; Above and beyond this, an immense, far more magnificent field, whose first outlines are already emerging in science and art, will open up to the leaders among the new creators. In a decade hypotheses will develop into theories—and finally into mastered laws.

374 Spatial Archetypes

> Then the capacity to treat every fresh demand in an absolutely elemental manner will lead forward only when it has become part of man's flesh and blood.
> The new more splendid technology of tensions, of invisible movements, of remote control and speeds such as cannot even be imagined in 1922 will come into being, uninfluenced by the methods of mechanistic technology.
> The new engineer is ready and waiting. Long live elemental creativity!
> ~ Werner Graeff, 1923

Impelled by a strong social conscience, which for many was tied directly to socialism and communism, the European modernists saw the cathedrals and palaces of earlier ages as elitist symbols of the aristocracy. Their manifestoes were annunciations of a new architecture that heralded a new world freed of elitism, and even of individualism. A new "universalism" would unite all people.

> There is an old and a new consciousness of the age. The old one is directed towards the individual. The new one is directed toward the universal.... The artists of today, all over the world, impelled by one and the same consciousness, have taken part on the spiritual plane in the world war against the domination of individualism, of arbitrariness. They therefore sympathize with all who are fighting spiritually or materially for the formation of an international unity in life, art, and culture.
> ~ De Stijl, 1918

> Art and people must form a unity.
> Art shall no longer be the enjoyment of the few but the life and happiness of the masses.
> The aim is alliance of the arts under the wing of a great architecture.
> ~ Work Council for Art, 1919

> Together let us desire, conceive, and create a new structure of the future, which will embrace architecture

and sculpture and painting in one unity and which will
one day rise toward heaven from the hands of a million
workers like the crystal symbol of a new faith.
   ~ Walter Gropius, 1919

This unity would be forged in the furnace of industry. Mass production would be the great leveler bringing the spirit of the Machine Age to the masses. Le Corbusier penned the work chant:

We must create the mass-production spirit.
The spirit of constructing mass-production houses.
The spirit of living in mass-production houses.
The spirit of conceiving mass-production houses.
   ~ Le Corbusier, 1920

Finally, time itself would pivot about the Machine and the new architecture.

Architecture is breaking free from tradition. It must
perforce begin again from the beginning.
   ~ Sant'Elia and Marinetti, 1914

The machine is such a
capital event in human
history that we must ascribe
to it a major role in the
conditioning of man's
mind, a role equally as
decisive and largely more
extended than that of
the conquering hegemonies of
past ages, which through
wars replaced one people by
another. The machine
opposed not one people to
another, but a new world to
an old world, for all people.
   ~ Le Corbusier (from Cartier-Bresson 1971)

376 Spatial Archetypes

These excerpts make it clear that the early modernists wrote in anything but the dry pseudo-scientific or bureaucratic language usually associated with the Grid. The passion of their vision moved them to write in the styles of the polemical tract, the Biblical commandment, and the visionary poem. They saw modernism as a sacred sword whose strength would cleave European history in two, into "before" and "after," "past" and "future." No literary style was too extravagant or overwrought for the goal of winning converts to the Future. Meanwhile, they were stripping architecture of most of its cultural richness to make it a clean slate for the impress of the Future. The missionary zeal of the modernists captured the general optimism of the time; the belief that industrial progress would bring about a glorious new world (an optimism that did not begin to wane until the 1960s). In laying down the doctrines of the Modem Movement, the manifestoes integrated the Grid's prime motivating ideas: the romance of Progress, the wish-fulfilling potential of the Machine, the equalizing opportunities of mass-production, the mystique of engineering, and faith in the Future. But they did more. The showed how to bring the Grid into concrete realization through architecture.

Le Corbusier's Five Points

> An idealism of activity that embraces, penetrates, and unites art, science, and technology and that influences research, study, and work will construct the "art-edifice" of Man, which is but an allegory of the cosmic system Today we can do no more than ponder the total plan, lay the foundations, and prepare the building stones.
> ~ Oskar Schlemmer, 1923

> Architecture is the will of the age conceived in spatial terms.
> ~ Mies van der Rohe, 1923

Among the most important accomplishments of the manifestoes was the establishment of an esthetic for modern architecture, one which spawned rules of building that could actually be followed. The new architecture would be made of the new materials: steel, glass, and concrete. It would be clean, functional, free of anachronistic ornamentation. It would emulate the calculated products of industrial design and engineering. It would address the hygienic problems of the cities. And it would flexibly adapt to and grow out of future technology.

These were the general goals, but some manifestoes were much more specific. The "Five points towards a new architecture," published in 1926 by Le Corbusier (one of the masters of the Modern Movement) and his cousin Pierre Jeanneret, spelled out the guiding principles of modern architecture still in use today:

1. The supports. The separation of precisely calculated structural elements (columns) from non-structural walls and partitions (in contrast to traditional masonry construction where structure and enclosure were the same and were not precisely calculated); the spacing of columns at regular intervals (i.e., in a grid); and the raising of the entire building a story or two off the ground to free it from dampness, give it more light and air, and provide a garden underneath (a principle that has largely gone out of use due to its impracticality).
2. The roof garden. The provision of flat roofs with terraces and gardens (we now have flat roofs in abundance, but few roof gardens).
3. The free design of the ground-plan. Designing the floor plan with interior partitions placed wherever needed irrespective of the column grid.
4. The horizontal window. The inclusion of long horizontal "ribbon" windows running the full length of the wall between columns since the walls no longer have to support the building. (This is the origin of today's "curtain wall" office building facades).
5. The free design of the facade. Achieved by projecting the exterior wall beyond the columns (in a small cantilever) and extending windows a length of ten to two hundred meters or more, regardless of structural and interior divisions.

Concluding these principles, Le Corbusier added, "The five essential points set out above represent a fundamentally new aesthetic. Nothing is left to us of the architecture of past epochs, just as we can no longer derive any benefit from the literary and historical teaching given in schools."[29]

The Five Points were a perfect prescription for bringing architecture into conformance with the Grid. The first and third parts—the separation of structure from non-structural elements and the free design of the floor plan-separated the hard, "objective" realm of engineering from the soft, "subjective" realm of human need. The building plans of Le Corbusier and his followers scrupulously distinguished between the rigidly rectilinear column grid and the light, often curvaceous, pattern of infill partitions. In the ideal Corbusian plan, the column is not embedded in a wall. As a rule, the structural systems of important buildings reveal the underlying order and spirit of the age in which they were built; accordingly, the structure of Machine Age buildings would be laid out, as per Le Corbusier's first point, on a grid.

The second point—the principle of the flat roof—sheared off all the romantic pinnacles, spires, gables, pitches, and mansards that had traditionally helped buildings to meet the sky. Buildings became boxes, three dimensionally confined by the orthogonal Grid. The fourth and fifth points—the use of "ribbon" windows in a freely designed facade—masked the particular human activities going on in the rooms behind the facade and stretched the abstract spatial quality of the Grid over the whole exterior. Gone were the varieties of windows that in older buildings had said something about the rooms, the people, and the ambiances inside. New buildings would suppress all this specificity to accentuate the universality of modern architecture.

Le Corbusier's writings and buildings provide a richly rewarding picture of the way in which an archetype infuses a human spirit with the spirit of the time. They give us a sense of what it means to gestate the seminal energy of a time and give birth to its creations. Le Corbusier is a poet of the Grid archetype as well as one of its foremost architects. But I do not wish to give the impression that he was the only modern architect who represented the Grid or that he originated it.

The manifestoes clearly show how squarely the Grid was lodged in the mind of all the moderns, and there are other architects we could just as easily study to see how they represent the Grid: Mies van der Rohe and Walter Gropius, for instance. But Le Corbusier serves as a good case study, since only a handful of other modern architects have had as much impact (Frank Lloyd Wright, Mies van der Rohe, Louis Kahn, and possibly one or two others). During his long and prolific career before his death in 1965, Le Corbusier built his Five Points and a good many other ideas into an impressive body of work, which has influenced at least two generations of architects the world over. (Le Corbusier presents more on his notion of the Grid in his "Poem of the Right Angle." See Appendix 10.)

Le Corbusier's Existential Idea

Le Corbusier was also expressing something very modern: the existential idea that who and what we are is totally a matter of choice. Who and what we are is not dictated, in this view, by any pre-existing determinant, neither church, nor state, nor caste of birth, nor will of God. Being defined by nothing, we are absolutely free to define ourselves. "The fact. My response/my choice." This is pure Grid. It dissolves all previous centers of reference and puts in their place a void, a nothingness, as in Sartre's *Being and Nothingness*. All of the coagulating mechanisms of traditional society and culture are scattered to the winds across the endless Gridded landscape of the modern mind.

Among existential philosophers, Kierkegaard substituted ethics and an inner, subjective relationship to God for external defining forces; Husserl promoted the intentionality of consciousness as the definer of the outer world; Heidegger pondered the origins of the "sense of being," and Sartre used the term "nausea" to describe how we respond to pure freedom in a meaningless universe. Le Corbusier seems to have felt that character was an important determinant in how one would use one's freedom. In all cases, these thinkers viewed human experience as self-generated.

Although the existentialists were influenced by Hegel, they tended also to reject his positing of a "world-soul" and an inex-

380 *Spatial Archetypes*

orable "world-process" operating outside of individual will that carries civilization through predictable historical cycles. This was part of their overall rejection of any kind of "archetypal" influence on human beings, which, in turn, was part of the general despiritualization of modern thought. Spengler saw this same nihilism in the declining phase of every civilization.

> Every one of the great Cultures knows it, for it is of deep necessity inherent in the finale of these mighty organisms. Socrates was a nihilist, and Buddha. There is an Egyptian or an Arabian or a Chinese de-souling of the human being, just as there is a Western. This is a matter not of mere political and economic, nor even of religious and artistic, transformations, nor of any tangible or factual change whatsoever, but of the condition of a soul after it has actualized its possibilities in full. It is easy, but useless, to point to the bigness of Hellenistic and of modern European achievement. Mass slavery and mass machine—production, "Progress" and Ataraxia, Alexandrianism and modem Science, Pergamum and Beyreuth, social conditions as assumed in Aristotle and as assumed in Marx, are merely symptoms on the historical surface. Not external life and conduct, not institutions and customs, but deepest and last things are in question here—the inward finishedness (Fertigsein) of megalopolitan man, *and* of the provincial as well. For the Classical world this condition sets in with the Roman age; for us it will set in from about the year 2000.[30]

Spengler found in Socialism, Stoicism, and Buddhism the modes of thought that exemplified the death (or Grid archetype) of civilization in Europe, the Classical world, and India, respectively. Joseph Campbell, commenting on a Buddhist text, shows how close are the Indian and European contemplations of the great Void at the center of being:

> Here is disengagement with a vengeance. The entire mandala of the meso-micro-macrocosm is dissolved,

and the individual, having burned out of himself the so-called "impairments" (kle'sas)—or, as we might say, the "engrams" of his culturally and biologically conditioned personal character—now experiences, through complete withdrawal, the wholeness of an absolutely uncommitted consciousness in the pristine state called kaivulyam, "isolation." The universe has been rejected as a meaningless delusion, referring to nothing beyond the mirage of its own horizon, and that transcendent state has been realized which Schopenhauer celebrated at the close of his magnum opus, when he wrote that "to those in whom the will has turned and denied itself, this our world, which is so real, with all its suns and milky ways—is nothing."[31]

Here then is the ultimate alienation, which is the human condition in the Grid: free will with nothing but temporal, popular standards to follow. These, like pure willfulness, give us only apparent bearings, in the end leaving us adrift, isolated from the only reliable imperatives—those revealed by a knowledge of the Self, the identity of which is at one with all humankind and has been so since humankind began.

In this context, Le Corbusier was what all great artists have been for their time: like them, he was infused with the archetypal and reached deep into the creative unconscious as a contemporary. He arrived at the same threshold as did the existentialists, but his journey began in what the modern architect Louis Kahn called "the recessions of the mind from which comes that which is not yet said and not yet made."[32] Thus he unlocked the mansions of the mind that will remain forever closed to those who have not taken the long route through the depths of the psyche. He found truths, even in the Grid.

Modern Architecture: the Realization of the Grid

Catapulted by the lofty ideals in the manifestos and the works of Le Corbusier and other pivotal architects in the first half of the 20th century, modern architecture has proliferated in recent decades until it is now spreading mindlessly to areas of the world where it is entirely inappropriate. It has become the symbol of industrial progress and status, and also of American imperialism. It is used to create markets for Western industry and banking systems, and more insidiously, it is used, along with missionaries, to suppress and eradicate traditional cultures. Modern architecture is directly and indirectly (through mining and drilling the raw materials and producing the energy needed for buildings) destroying the last Sensitive Chaos peoples on earth.

The imperative of progress has come to mean, for Western industrialists and petty bureaucrats in developing nations alike, the building of pompous civic centers, high-rise office buildings, international airports, resort hotels, superhighways, glossy new towns, and dreary modern slum-clearance projects, whether or not these "amenities" truly alleviate the problems of the countries or raise the standard of living for people. More often than not, they merely line the pockets of multinational executives and local politicians while leaving the general populace poorer and worse off than they were before.

Witness Brazil. A few decades of vigorous industrial development have brought the country from a hard but stable and self-sufficient hunting/gathering/farming way of life to a dangerous state of economic imbalance. Furthermore, development in Brazil threatens to destroy the Amazon jungle, one of the great planetary natural resources on which we depend not only for atmospheric oxygen, but also for an incredibly rich store of genetic information in flora and fauna that future generations will need to heal, nourish, and enlighten. Also threatened are the dwindling numbers of tribal people living in the relatively untouched recesses of the Amazon forest. They are among the most "primitive" people in the world, but, like the forest itself, they store a vast amount of information about how to live naturally on the planet. Should there ever be a nuclear holocaust, they will surely be the future Adams and Eves of *homo-sapiens*. Then truly, the meek shall inherit the earth. As more and more land in Brazil is bought by industrial and agribusiness interests, the peasants and Indians who lived there lose their homes and become anonymous inhabitants of the slums and barrios swelling on the fringes of cities.

There is no more ironic symbol of this disintegrating Grid process than Brasilia, the much-touted new capital of Brazil designed in the 1950s by two of Le Corbusier's most ardent followers, Lucio Costa and Oscar Neimeyer. When it opened, Brasilia was acclaimed as the first complete realization of the Utopian city of the Future. Its pristine towers and geometric forms set ceremonially above formal reflecting pools and grand multi-lane highways seemed proof that the "New Jerusalem" of the modernists could be built on earth—and in the remote interior of the Brazilian jungle at that! But, as Robert Hughes observed in his television series and book *The Shock of the New*: "The reality of the place is markedly less noble. Brasilia was finished, or at any rate officially opened, in 1960, and ever since then it has been falling to bits at one end while being listlessly constructed at the other: a facade, a ceremonial slum of rusting metal, spalling concrete, and cracked stone veneers, put together on the cheap by contractors and bureaucrats on the take."[33]

Brasilia's multi-lane highways—the dream of Sant'Elia, the Italian Futurist of the early 20th century—are empty, save for the Volkswagens of high government officials, since few of the city's inhabitants can afford cars. The vast majority of workers must scramble across surrealistic expanses of highway on foot to work in this Futurist city built for cars where, Hughes wryly observes, "the pedestrian is an irrelevance." Surrounding the pompous but decaying civic center is a pitiful slum of shacks hastily built for the workers, servants, and unemployed pool of labor on which the city depends. Brazil's social order of haves and have-nots is enforced by a substantial military, and the country manages to maintain a facade that impresses Western investors more greedy than wise. Hughes remarks:

> Thus Brasilia, in less than twenty years, ceased to be the City of Tomorrow and turned into yesterday's science fiction. It is an expensive and ugly testimony to the fact that, when men think in terms of abstract space rather than real place, of single rather than multiple meanings, and of political aspirations instead of human needs, they tend to produce miles of jerry-built nowhere, infested

with Volkswagens. The experiment, one may hope, will not be repeated; the Utopian buck stops here.[34]

Brazil is only one example of a type of development that could be found in most other Latin American countries, as well as in those nations in Africa, Asia, the Middle East, and Oceania that have been described as "developing."

The lesson is that "development," more often than not, is a kind of economic and cultural imperialism in which the Grid of Western Civilization is glossed on countries that do not want it or are not ready for it. In one sense, the promulgation of the Grid around the world is merely an instance of a technologically superior civilization subduing less "advanced" civilizations, a process that has been at work since the first successful raids of the Iron Age chieftains. In another, it represents the lure of progress: who among us who enjoy the fruits of the Enlightenment and the freedoms of urban life can tell a peasant that he or she would be better off staying stuck on the farm. We might like to be stuck on a farm for awhile to find relief from the burdens of urban life, but can we convince someone who has known nothing else and feels trapped that their life is really better than ours? Besides, who is to know what human destiny holds in store? Perhaps we are fated—as the advocates of decentralization, no-growth, and appropriate technology declare—to exhaust the folly of progress and return to a simpler life. But, on the other hand, perhaps we are evolving through fits and starts to an omega point that will bring global civilization together in a confident new age of technological benevolence, agricultural bounty, and social maturity. Perhaps we are destined to leave our earth-womb altogether and be born among the stars.

One thing seems certain, however: our interference in other people's cultures is no longer born of confidence but of greed. We have become addicted to our industrial comforts and we are insatiable. We need our fix, our surge of energy—gas and oil, electricity, Tupperware, personal computers, Porsches, Holiday Inns, MacDonald's, Jordaches Calvin Kleins. We need them to fill the Grid's great void of being. Our corporate and political leaders work to insure that we can get these goods whenever and wherever the craving strikes. The Grid has given us leisure, affluence, and freedom, but it has stripped us of meaning in our lives. We look at other cultures, more archaic than our own, where meaning still exists, and seek to destroy them—so as not to be reminded of our own emptiness? On the mute existential Grid of being and nothingness, we erect the standards of nation, flag, God, family, *macho* masculinity and cloying femininity to convince us that we exist. We are xenophobic. People who live by other standards threaten our existence. To destroy that threat, we destroy them. We force them into concrete block houses. We make them into wage-laborers, migrant workers, illegal aliens. We confiscate their ancestral lands and their cultural heritage and make them speak English. We make them wear trousers and blouses, and convert them to Christianity. We want to see them reflect ourselves. If they do not, we obliterate them.

The greatest danger in the projection of the Grid to global scale is that it may actually homogenize the human species as it succeeds in bringing about the extinction of more and more indigenous non-Western cultures. The most fragile are the world's last remaining Sensitive Chaos people: the Amazonian Indians, Australian Aborigines, the Kung San and Pygmies of Africa, Eskimos, and a few other threatened cultures.

These people are critical to the survival of our species because they represent the outer limits of our species' adaptation to the planet. Without them, our diversity would be greatly diminished, and, as many have shown, diversity is a fundamental principle of survival. Jane Jacobs showed it to be critical to the viability of cities, and biologists have observed its importance to evolutionary survival. If we lose our last living hunter-gatherers, even though they are few in number, our species as a whole will irretrievably lose a vast store of information that could mean the difference between survival and extinction. The dilemma is compounded when we consider losing also the last of our Great Round farmers (such as the Hopi and other Pueblo Indians), nomadic herders (the Bedouin, Kirghiz, Qashqai, Tuareg, Navaho, and others), theocratic cultures (the Himalayan principalities and Tibet before the Chinese takeover, for example).

The cultural richness of human Civilization is a sacred trust and a precious commodity in the life-and-death game of evolution. It is not to be tampered with out of ignorance any more than any natural resource. The destruction of human cultures is as serious as the destruction of animal species. We cannot lose the Australian aborigines any more than we can lose the whales. Yet the richness of human civilization is being tampered with and destroyed under the great homogenizing imperative of the Grid. Homogenization is, after all, one of the defining characteristics of the Grid. To cultures not living under the archetype of the Grid, it is a puzzlement and a threat. (For more on Modern Architecture, see Appendix 11: Architecture and Chakras and Appendix 12: Modern American Architecture

SYNOPSIS OF THE GRID

World of the Bureaucrat

SPATIAL SYMBOL

Orthogonal grid

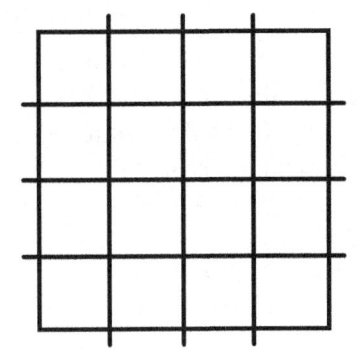

SOCIETY

Era
- Post-Imperialistic, usually following the revolutionary overthrow of an imperialistic monarchy.

Society
- International commercial-industrial network as the largest cohesive social unit.
- Marketplace dominates values.
- Economy based on mass production and trade.
- Extreme specialization and fragmentation.
- Declining peasant population as people move to industrial urban centers.
- Increasing literacy.
- Decentralization of political power—political mechanisms and ideologies ostensibly seeking to distribute

power equitably: republicanism, democracy, communism, capitalism, socialism. (The Grid also serves Radiant Axes imperial governments as a means of organizing the masses.)
- Cultural decline—empty repetition of old forms, bloating and collapse of institutions, loss of confidence, difficulties in maintaining existing systems and facilities, lack of spiritual thrust, lack of creativity.

Examples

- Hellenistic Greece; Ptolemaic Egypt to the present; declining phase of Roman Empire; Aztec and Incan empires shortly before the Conquest; communist China and Russia; Europe and America since the Industrial Revolution; contemporary Japan; any industrialized nation.

Technology

- Engineering accomplishments are most notable.
- Extreme standardization—of products, language, currency, uniforms, education, housing, recordkeeping (census), taxation, welfare, etc.
- Strongest technelogos orientation of all the archetypes; emphasis on enumeration and measurement as in census—taking, statistical surveys, empirical sciences, the "Objective" documentation of events, mathematics, reading and writing, information storage and data processing.
- Management systems involving large groups of people organized into machine-like components (industry, bureaucracy, the military, colonial governments).

Gender Roles

- Women may work for low wages in the industrial labor force, losing the greater economic power they may have had in the peasant market economy. Many roles of the family and community appropriated by large institutions.

PSYCHE

Psychology
- In adulthood, confrontation of the realities of the world and finding one's place as an ordinary person, concern with, survival of oneself and one's family.
- Sense of liberation/alienation from spirit, matter, nature, the inner Self, history, and tradition.

Stagnation
- Psychological stagnation in the Grid can produce the deflated ego overwhelmed by a sense of anonymity, purposelessness, existential malaise, and loss of contact with the inner spiritual Self.

Breakthrough
- Discovering the Inner Path to the Center.

Liberation
- Psychological liberation in the Grid can present great freedom of choice, releasing one from centralized authority and tradition. It can also contribute to the balanced perception that each individual is by turns the totemic animal, Goddess, Hero, God-King, Emperor, and commoner—in other words, that the archetypes are internalized in each of us; that we each embody the sum total of human experience and wisdom; and that we are individually capable of finding the Inner Path to illumination.

SPIRIT

Worldview
- Cosmos as a great machine knowable by the human intellect through reason and science.

Spiritual Focus
- Enlightenment consists of knowing the Inner Self as the center of the universe, container and conceiver of all that is.

390 *Spatial Archetypes*

Mythic Themes
- Mythic images and rites concerning human intelligence and the rational mind; mastery of ranked disciplines (graduations, promotions, investitures); demonstrations of human skill and character (e.g., sports as entertainment rather than as spiritual activity); closed system logics (art-for-art's-sake, the job well done), pure essences of abstract forms; existentialism; conquest of the natural world; mastery of technelogos functions; faith in progress, statistical uniformity, and predictability. Prevalence of relativism in education, eclecticism in religion, nihilism and materialism in philosophy.

CULTURE

Prime Symbol
- A mental, three-dimensional Cartesian grid extending throughout the universe on which all phenomena are perceived, conceived, mapped, and recorded.

Art
- Mass produced art, art as commodity, "Art-for-art's-sake," hermaneutics, nihilism, modernism, idiosyncratic and neurosis-driven art.

Astronomy
- The cosmos has no center and may be seen as a Grid of conceptually uniform measurable units, or as a machine, or as inert matter giving off certain appearances because of chemical and electrical interactions.

Time
- Time is linear and uniform, extending infinitely into the past and future. Progressive view of history (in some cultures).

Space
- Space is a uniform, three-dimensional Grid, which distrib-

utes everything into isolated uniform units and has no center.

Landscape
- A lifeless, inert resource meant for commercial/ industrial exploitation and divided into a grid of fields, townships, communes, etc.

Architecture
- The most dominant architectural structure is the marketplace (e.g., the agora, the 19th century factory, the World Trade Center, the shopping mall).
- Architecture and town planning reflect the Grid in orthogonal street layouts, rectilinear rooms, modular building facades (as on modern office buildings); repetitions of uniform units (suburban tract houses, workers' housing, army barracks, the office pool of desks); and grids of land divisions (agricultural fields, political provinces, counties, townships, etc.).
- Rectilinear spatial divisions such as the Cartesian coordinates, the *nomes* of ancient Egypt, the *padas* in Vedic mandalas, squares in Chinese town planning (as in Kublai Khan's plan for Peking), the *tatami* mat system of Japan.

DISSOLUTION

World of the Trickster

DISSOLUTION

World of the Trickster

[Dissolution refers to the ultimate disintegration and death of a culture. Mimi did not write this section, but here are some of her notes for it. JL]

Civilization: Breakdown of social structures and institutions, ad hoc groupings and cults, experimental communities and families, decadence, terrorism, anarchy.

Psyche: Death, survivalism, nihilism, opportunistic worldview, scavenging, recycling, sampling, eclecticism. Multidimensional time. The Inner Path.

Space: The Wasteland—charnel ground, apocalypse, chaos, shantytowns, urban decay, homelessnes, refugee camps, battlegrounds, virtual space, Home as Sacred Place.

Examples: Egypt ca. 100-700 CE, post-Hellenistic Greece, fall of the Roman Empire, any country at war, natural disasters, USA since?

CONCLUSION

By John Lobell

So, here is Mimi's book. How might we characterize her approach?

Cultures are Symbolic Entities

We are in an age of materialist interpretations of cultures which presents differences in natural resources and technologies as the sources of cultural differences. But as Mimi points out the Mayans and the ancient Egyptians were virtual twins *culturally* but very different *technologically*. Both the Egyptians and the Mayans built pyramids during their Pyramid periods. Beyond that, both were hierarchical agricultural societies with rigid cast systems. They both had theocratic states, class-stratified societies, and dynastic God-Kings at the apex of the social pyramid. Both had standing armies, public works programs, law codes, administrative bureaucracies, written records and histories, taxation systems, food storage and redistribution systems, state religious ceremonies, and urban centers. And both saw the cosmos as the World Mountain. Yet they could not have been more different *technologically*. The Egyptians had bronze, draft animals, horses, and wheeled vehicles. The Mayans had no bronze, no draft animals or horses, and didn't even have the wheel! So cultures are *symbolic* entities.

Cultures Go Through Different Periods

Cultures move from the Sensitive Chaos of hunter-gatherers to the Great Round of the Neolithic to the Four Quarters of Bronze Age warrior chieftains, to the Pyramid of theocratic nation states, to the Radiant Axes of empires, to the Grid of commercial societies, to the Dissolution at the end of cultures. Note Mimi insists that these are not stages, a subsequent one is not more advances than its predecessors, and archetypes do not change by automatic evolutionary processes. Sensitive Chaos and Great Round cultures can last indefinitely, although Four Quarter and Pyramid cultures are inherently unstable.

Cultures Have Psychologies

Each of the archetypes has a worldview, a way of seeing the relationship between people and the world. These worldviews, can be seen as cultural psychologies.

Cultures Are Different

Mimi shows the "good" and the "bad" of each culture, but definitely has favorites. She appreciates the oneness with the earth of Sensitive Chaos cultures, and the Goddess of the Great Round Cultures. She appreciates some of the heroes of Four Quarters cultures, but not their treatment of women or their war making. She finds much to dislike in Pyramid cultures, but also some things to like, but few redeeming features in the empires of the Radiant Axes. The West today is in the Grid, and while Mimi appreciates the democracy and science of our time, she deplores its loss of spirit.

Optimism or Pessimism?

For Mimi, a culture is an organism, like, for example a human being. It is born and it will die. She sees our culture today as in its late stage of its life and its death will be inevitable. So I guess that is pessimistic. If that is the case, what will come next? Materialists hold that our advances in science and technology will lead to the indefinite growth and expansion of our culture, even out into space. From Mimi's point of view, which is symbolic rather than materialistic, our end and eventually new cultures will be born.

In the meantime, do be enriched by this book.

APPENDICES

These appendices further develop some of the ideas in this book.

Appendix 1

Bits of Colored Glass: Cautions in the Use of Archetypes

We have seen strong central images of each archetype as if we were looking through a kaleidoscope with Psyche, Civilization, and Space as the three mirrors. In a kaleidoscope, we see bits of colored glass forming patterns reflected in the three mirrors. We are aware of the patterns but not of the bits of glass. Some are hidden from view; the overlapping of others changes their colors; and all appear transformed in their myriad symmetrical reflections.

Similarly, if we were to examine all the pieces of information that form an image of a spatial archetype, we would see that some of their individual characteristics have been occluded, colored, or transformed. This does not make the image invalid. It is to some degree inevitable in any conscious effort to make the world meaningful.

"Bits of Colored Glass" collects the nuances, exceptions, permutations, hidden dynamics, general observations, opinions, recommendations, and caveats that apply to all the archetypes.

1. The archetypes are not meant to be used in a reductive manner to diminish the actual complexity of cultures.

We should not force cultures to fit the archetypal profiles. For instance, it would be inappropriate to declare that if a culture appears to adhere to one archetypal worldview, it cannot exhibit characteristics of other archetypes. This would mean denying or oversimplifying the multi-layered richness of the culture in question, and consequently of civilization as a whole. Instead, we should see what characteristics a culture does exhibit, and then determine whether one spatial archetype is prevalent. Sometimes two or more co-exist, suggesting a tension between different worldviews. This can be a sign of instability or transition, or it may be that the culture consists of two or more subcultures, each of which can be considered in its own right.

The coexistence of two or more dominant archetypes may be a sign also of integration. The Dogon of Mali, for example, are marginal farmers who live by a sophisticated cosmogony that incorporates the Sensitive Chaos, the Great Round, the Four Quarters, the Pyramid, and the Grid. Although the Dogon are basically a Four Quarters culture, to define them solely in terms of one archetype is to deny the full richness of their culture.

400 *Spatial Archetypes*

2. Each spatial archetype imprints all forms of cultural expression under represents a complete worldview and way of life.

Each archetype represents a completely distinct belief pattern and way of life in its own right. Each archetypal worldview provides a complete, intricately balanced pattern of knowledge, social structures, customs, beliefs, and values. These patterns provide all that is needed for a human society to gather together, organize themselves, and live a harmonious and meaningful life.

There are no "savage," "barbaric," "backward," or even "underdeveloped" cultures. These ethnocentric terms assume that some cultures are striving to emulate the presumably more "advanced" or "developed" culture of the observer. Cultures living under the influence of "earlier" archetypes are in no way inferior to those living under "later" archetypes. Each archetype has its own coherent internal logic. Each is fundamentally different from the others, and each deserves full respect.

3. Always evaluate archetypal motifs in light of the entire cultural context. A society might use an archetypal motif in minor ways without being "in that archetype."

The meandering spiral of the Sensitive Chaos, the circle or sphere of the Great Round, the cross of the Four Quarters, the pyramidal forms of the Pyramid, the rays of the Radiant Axes, and the modular lattices of the Grid appear in many cultures. Each is dominant and has its truest archetypal meaning only within cultures adhering fully to its associated worldview. The cross, for instance, may be a decorative pattern in the pottery of late Great Round cultures, but it is not an *imago mundi* until it is fully expressed in a Four Quarters cultural context as the diagram of the caste system, the map of the cosmos, the plan of a typical walled town or palace of the Lord of the Four Quarters, and so on.

For this reason, it is important to look for the "latest" archetype in the sequence when determining the dominant archetype. The forms of "earlier" archetypes such as the Sensitive Chaos or the Great Round are often still apparent in Four Quarters, Pyramid, Radiant Axes, and Grid civilizations.

For example, domed buildings such as the Pantheon or St. Peter's in Rome, the Taj Mahal or Pearl Mosque in Agra, Beijing's Temple of Heaven, or the U.S. Capitol in Washington, D.C., might be mistaken for Great Round structures. Although these buildings are hemispherical, their overall cultural contexts do not resemble the Great Round at all. Rather, these celestialized descendents of the Great Round called "Domes of Heaven" are found in Radiant Axes cultures where they usually serve as the focus of axial systems, much in the manner of the Capitol building in Washington.

Since the Pyramid archetype subsumes and builds upon the Four Quarters archetype, the Four Quarters is frequently the ground plan of pyramids or capital cities in Pyramid cultures. The very presence of massive architectural pyramids indicates that we are dealing with a Pyramid culture rather than a Four Quarters one.

When past archetypal forms are used out of context in later cultures, the resulting anachronistic building or artifact often has the quality of a folly. One example is I. M. Pei's 1989 addition of a glass pyramid entrance to the Louvre Museum in Paris. Another is the recent completion of the Gothic Washington Cathedral in Washington, D.C. Intentional follies include Disneyworld and gambling casinos patterned after Egyptian temples, Roman palaces, and the Taj Mahal.

Some archetypal forms reappear for functional reasons, retaining fragments of the original meaning of the archetype. New York city is planned predominantly on the Grid, but for obvious reasons its airports—Kennedy, La Guardia, and Newark—are planned on Radiant Axes patterns. Maps in the airline's glossy onboard magazines reinforce the Radiant Axes vision with flight paths radiating from airports to a network of cities that laces the globe. Indeed, today's freedom to fly anywhere in the world is a legacy of the now-dismantled Radiant Axes empires.

4. All archetypes are and always have been present in every culture and individual, but some are latent and others are dominant.

When we speak of a culture or an individual as "living" or "being" in a particular archetype, we are referring to the archetype that appears to be dominant at the time under discussion. Usually one is dominant while the others are latent or subordinate. This principle explains why we often find archetypes expressed in minor ways in a culture, as mentioned above.

It explains also why it is possible for a colonized hunter-gatherer suddenly to adapt to a radically different way of life. From Australia to the Amazon there are indigenous people who have lived all their lives in the wild but adapt quickly to the Grid of their colonizers and become wage laborers, factory workers, clerks, computer programmers, and the like. They may be miserable in these jobs, but the fact that they can do them suggests that the requisite mental structures were already present, though perhaps latent, in their psyches.

5. The archetype that appears to dominate complex societies may represent only the worldview of the ruling elite.

Complex societies are made up of heterogeneous layers of subcultures, each with its own heritage, economic status, and archetypal proclivity. Often the only remains of a vanished high civilization are the palaces, tombs, and temples built by the ruling elite to solidify political power. Though these monuments may express a dominant spatial archetype, we cannot assume that the entire population understood or subscribed to the worldview represented by that archetype. More likely, the ordinary people were intimidated by such awesome symbols of power as the Egyptian or Mayan pyramids, Angkor Wat, Persepolis, or Peking's Forbidden City.

For example, the existence of a Pyramid type of nation state-indicated by the conquest and governing of a vast territory, the building of pyramids within cities or ceremonial centers, the development of a hieratic priesthood and a theocratic dynasty, the strong adherence to myths concerning a sacred mountain, the emergence of social classes, and so on—does not allow us to assume that all subjects governed by the state lived uniformly in a Pyramid culture. Many people continued to live in some or all of the previously established archetypal ways of life, especially the Great Round and the Four Quarters, while adhering-minimally and uncomfortably—to the laws and demands of the state. Radiant Axes empires and post-imperial Grid megacultures are even more multi-layered than Pyramid cultures.

Civilizations grow and change by layering, just as the earth forms new geological strata over the primeval crust. Using another natural analogy, civilizations grow like trees, expanding and adding rings each year, while the heartwood remains the same. Thus, civilizations do not change homogeneously or monolithically. Rather, new types of cultures and worldviews overlay the old. The Sensitive Chaos is the primeval stratum, the heartwood of civilization. When all the hunter-gatherers are gone, civilization will have lost its soul.

6. On the whole, there is no "natural evolution" from one archetype to the next.

The impetus to change nearly always comes from external forces. In major civilizations such as the ancient Egyptian, Greek, Western European, and Chinese, it is possible to trace the succession of archetypal worldviews over several thousand years, but the sequence represents neither evolutionary "stages of development" nor an inevitable progression toward the Grid (see also Item 12 below). Instead, each type of culture and worldview usually resists change unless under external pressure from invasions, trade contacts with other cultures, major climatic shifts, and so on.

Witness, for example, the distinctly non-Grid ways of life preserved today among Amazonian Indians, the Hopi, Australian Aborigines, the Kung San, and several nomadic pastoralist societies from the Bedouins to the Navaho—despite the tremendous pressure exerted on these cultures to "evolve" and become part of the modem world.

Although a culture may in time acquire a psychological proclivity toward change (impelled by population increases, technical innovations, or other internal changes), it rarely transforms into a completely different type of culture without external pressure. For example, the Great Round civilization of the Old World did not "evolve naturally" into the Four Quarters any more than Amerindians in the New World "evolved naturally" into modern Grid cultures. Both civilizations fiercely resisted the changes forced upon them by contact with alien cultures: the invading Indo-European tribes in the case of the Old World and the conquering European imperialists in the New.

The principle of external forces initiating change also explains why geographic thoroughfares for trade, migration, and invasion such as the Fertile Crescent saw more rapid development than did quieter outposts such as Siberia, Tierra del Fuego, Tibet, or the Mali's Bandiagara Escarpment.

7. Precise divisions between one archetype and another rarely exist.

It is seldom possible to see a precise moment when a culture passes from one archetype to another. While we can point to certain monuments, people, or events as signs of transition, the actual change is usually gradual. Even when a transition is stimulated by a dramatic event such as an invasion, the process of bringing the new archetype to full realization can take many decades or centuries.

8. A culture may live predominantly in one archetype throughout its lifetime.

In the absence of external influence, or by conscious design, a culture may remain indefinitely bound to one archetype. Sensitive Chaos cultures, in particular, can resist change for thousands of years. Most hunting-gathering societies resist the centralization of wealth and power prerequisite to forming other types of cultures. This kind of stasis is not really understood or appreciated by so-called "advanced" cultures, where even individuals can come under great pressure if they do not progress according to accepted timetables of growth, learning, and personality development. The phenomenon of cultural stasis reinforces the principle that the archetypes represent complete worldviews and ways of life, not mere way-stations on the road of progress.

The social structure becomes more complicated in each of the other five types of cultures due to increasing interaction with foreign cultures—through trade in the Great Round, pastoral nomadism and warfare in the Four Quarters, statehood in the Pyramid, colonialism in the Radiant Axes, and international economic interdependence in the Grid. Thus, these types of cultures are increasingly dynamic and even unstable, but the dynamism is mainly externally induced, as described above.

In contrast, Tibet offers an example of an extremely isolated Pyramid culture (theocratic, class-stratified, Mount Meru as the *imago mundi*, and so on). In the absence of outside influences, Tibet's traditional culture changed relatively little for over two millennia until the Chinese communists occupied and destroyed this spiritual capital of the world after 1959.

9. The sequence of archetypes is rarely reversible.

For instance, once a theocratic Pyramid culture emerges, the civilization will not revert back to the animistic Sensitive Chaos. The only exception occurs when the ruling elite of a complex culture is destroyed by invaders.

One example is the Spanish conquests of the Aztec and Incan empires. The only survivors were rural Amerindians who lived then, as they do now, by hunting, gathering, and subsistence farming. For decades scholars were baffled at how such "primitive" people could long ago have built such complex civilizations. (Unfortunately, this kind of ignorance still leads to wild but popular theories about extraterrestrial overlords who brought high-tech culture to simple natives way back when.)

10. Some cultures appear to skip archetypes.

Under colonialism and certain types of cultural contact, some societies appear to skip from one archetype to a subsequent one out of sequence. This is occurring today among many indigenous cultures-rainforest dwellers, village farmers, nomadic tribes people—who shift abruptly from the Sensitive Chaos, Great Round, or Four Quarters to the Grid as they come under the domination of industrialized countries (which produces the deceptive multi-layering of subcultures seen in Item 5 above).

An understanding of spatial archetypes could help to diagnose and prevent the severe social ills that result from such cultural discontinuity: alcoholism, depression, suicide, violence, family disintegration, welfare subsistence, and the proliferation of slums. It could help also to explain the rising resistance to Westernization among many so-called "developing" nations.

11. Every archetype has positive and negative aspects.

The paradigms generated by archetypes may be well or ill adapted to individual or social needs. For instance, the hierarchical social structure dictated by the Pyramid archetype would be appropriate for a culture that needs large-scale organization and leadership to survive, but it would be inappropriate if imposed on a hearty culture of nomadic, individualistic tribes people. Similarly, the Sensitive Chaos may seem liberating to some because it speaks to our desire to achieve a more balanced relationship with nature, but it may seem repressive to an aborigine who craves the material luxuries or individual liberties offered by the Grid.

12. An archetype usually follows a life cycle from incipience to realization to decline (apparent especially in the four archetypes from the Four Quarters through the Grid).

A new archetype appears most positive during its incipient phase, which often coincides with the declining phase of the previous archetype. Before the new archetype is realized externally, it gestates internally in the collective psyche where it forms a proclivity or readiness for change. It is purist in this form because it has not yet been tested or institutionalized. It is all promising potential. During this phase, the mythical structures of the culture are reworked to accommodate the new worldview. When sufficient pressure is brought to bear from internal and external sources, the incipient archetype comes into realization.

During the realization phase, the archetype is manifested in government, ritual, religion, art, architecture, literature, law, and social institutions. Once it becomes institutionalized, the archetype may produce several centuries of glorious cultural flowering, a Golden Age accompanied by a high degree of real or apparent social harmony. In time, however, the institutions calcify; the archetype loses its original inspiration; and decline sets in.

In the decline phase, the institutions and cultural forms generated by the archetype become empty shells, forms refined to the point of decadence surviving on inertia. Meanwhile, another incipient archetype captures the imagination, and the cycle begins anew. The transitional period, in which the decline of the old and the incipience of the new live side by side, may be marked by discontent, the dissolution of primary institutions and social structures, revolution, a failure of confidence and will, a grasping at old beliefs, underground movements, cultism, rampant experimentalism, and vulnerability to invasion.

Observing an organic life cycle in the archetypes does not imply an internal evolutionary mechanism, since it is consistent with the observation that the impetus for change is usually external (Item 6). Without sufficient external pressure, a culture can temporize indefinitely in the declining phase of its dominant archetype. Conversely, the proclivity engendered by an incipient archetype sometimes helps a culture adapt quickly and easily to externally induced change.

13. The time span of each succeeding archetype tends to be shorter than the previous one.

This time span varies enormously from archetype to archetype. If we view the archetypes as a sequence, each succeeding archetype seems to last less long than the previous one in a kind of inverse geometric progression. Even though different civilizations manifest the various worldviews at different times in history, there is often an overall pattern within each civilization that shows the Sensitive Chaos dominating for hundreds of thousands of years during the evolution from hominids to homo sapiens. The Great Round then persists for five to ten thousand years; and the Four Quarters, Pyramid, and Radiant Axes each last for successively shorter periods. The current Grid worldview of Western culture, which has flourished for only two or three centuries, is already in decline.

This shortening time effect could be an artifact of our perception— events closer to us in time appear more detailed and thus are more easily categorized into distinct periods—or it could be "real," in which case all assumptions about the "progress" of civilization, and even about our basic survival, must seriously be questioned.

14. As the archetypal periods shorten in time, they expand in space.

The main social units in the sequence of archetypes control larger and larger territories as the sequence progresses. The smallest unit is the hunting-gathering band of the Sensitive Chaos. Although the band depends on a certain amount of rangeland for food, it does not "own" the land and avoids leaving permanent territorial marks. The Great Round's social unit is larger—at least several farming compounds linked by a common marketplace or village center. Land control takes the form of homesteads and agricultural lands passed on from generation to generation. In the Near East, China, the American Southwest, and a few other areas, large urban complexes emerged during the Great Round.

The social unit of the Four Quarters is larger still—a hierarchical chieftainship that wields political control over a large region. The Pyramid's nation state is exponentially larger than the chieftainship, just as the Radiant Axes' empire is exponentially larger than the nation state. Finally, the modern Grid is throwing its commercial-industrial net over the entire globe. (Note that the political "ownership" of space is in inverse proportion to the amount of land needed to feed one person under each of the archetypes, which is greatest in the Sensitive Chaos and least in the Grid. The difference is due to growing population density coupled with increasingly efficient food production.)

There appears to be a conservation of time and space among the archetypes. The life span of an archetype seems to be inversely proportional to the size of its political territory. In other words, the larger the territory controlled by the social unit typical of the archetype, the shorter the life span of that archetype (and vice versa). It is as if a limited amount of energy is available, which can go either into longevity (time) or territoriality (space).

15. Each succeeding archetype domesticates or demonizes the driving spirit of the former archetype.

Great Round cultures domesticate the spiraling energies of the Sensitive Chaos to produce crops and livestock, and then feature the spiral as a magical/ornamental motif in pottery and stone carvings. Four Quarters cultures domesticate the powerful Goddess of the Great Round by marrying her off to the Lord of the Four Quarters, consigning her to inspire women to be dutiful wives and mothers under the nascent patriarchal system. For example, the Indo-European invaders' god Zeus raped and "married" most of the preexisting Aegean goddesses, whose myths were then refigured to support the new social order. Alternatively, the goddesses may be demonized or stripped of their powers as when Apollo slew the protective Python and stole the Delphic Oracle from the Earth Goddess Gaia. The women who resisted the Four Quarters invasions were reviled as Amazons and defeated.

The tribal Lord of the Four Quarters becomes a local subsidiary god or dutiful official in the new pantheon and politics of the Pyramid states. More negatively, Four Quarters chieftains are demonized into feudal rebels or "gangs" in the eyes of the Pyramid's orderly nation state. Under the Radiant Axes Emperor, the spiritual powers of the Pyramid's God-King are domesticated in a secularly controlled state religion. Radiant Axes monarchs are deplored as dictators by the Grid's democracies and republics, which subsume empires and emperors under their spreading webs of commercial alliances.

"Domestication" does not mean "total mastery," for there is always the threat that the former power will erupt again. The Sensitive Chaos's dragon energies can unleash natural disasters that destroy the Great Round's crops. The Great Goddess's lingering power continues to threaten patriarchal religions and values, as when Demeter withdrew life from the earth in retaliation for Hades's abduction of her daughter Persephone. Demeter further revealed her power by commanding that a temple be built in her honor where she would teach her rites, which she did even to the highest echelons of society throughout Greece's manifestly patriarchal Classic era.

Deposed tribal chieftains can become rebel leaders who raise armies to overthrow the nation state as occurred in Egypt when petty princes caused the Old Kingdom to collapse into feudalism. A nation state can rise to imperial power and, like the Roman Empire, be perpetually at war with surrounding nation states. And the empires subsumed in the Grid continue to create tension around the "balance of power" and "balance of payments."

All of these dynamic tensions charge the sequence of archetypes with a subtle alternating current that courses through historical events, animates the character of different nationalities, and scrambles our attempts to predict the future.

16. All archetypes are culturally represented in the world today. Archetypes exist outside of time. They are all always present in every culture and individual.

Although the world is becoming homogenized into a global industrialized grid, there are still living societies of Paleolithic hunter-gatherers (Kung San, Mbuti Pygmies, Australian Aborigines), Neolithic farmers (the Pueblo Indians), nomadic pastoralists (Bedouin, Navaho), hierarchical chieftainships (many traditional African and Polynesian cultures), and theocracies (Tibet before Chinese rule, Himalayan principalities).

It is important that we protect these endangered societies, not just to be humanitarian, but because they keep alive ways of life that have proved successful over thousands and even millions of years. It is a matter of evolutionary survival that we preserve the cultural diversity remaining in the world, especially since our own way of life has not yet passed the test of time.

17. All archetypes are alive in each of our psyches.

If spatial archetypes existed only "out there"—in culture, in history, in the world somewhere—they could be a dry subject indeed. But they thrive vibrantly "in here"—inside of us, in our dreams, sensibilities, personalities, beliefs, opinions, likes, dislikes, emotions, and everyday moods. In a single day we may awake trailing filaments of the Sensitive Chaos, unleash the Four Quarters warrior hero in our chariot-cars on the way to work, truss ourselves up in the Grid to face the working day, feel a surge of Radiant Axes power animate a business meeting, and return to the security and warmth of the Great Round at night.

We know people whose personalities reflect each archetypal orientation. The nomadic hippies of the 1960s who sought liberation from material possessions and boundaries were, in effect, struggling to return to an idealized Sensitive Chaos. We have all encountered-whether in world leaders, street gangs, or Archie Bunkeresque TV characters—the braggadocio of a type of contemporary Four Quarters warlord obsessed with protecting and enhancing his territories and the racial purity of his tribe. The stereotypical, empire-building, corporate executive is the modern equivalent of the solar-identified Radiant Axes monarch. Jim Jones and David Koresh are pathological examples of the Radiant Axes' inflated ego that knows no bounds in its deadly God-identification.

Archetypes empower the contemporary mythology of movies, television, and advertising, molding us whether we know it or not. But how much more interesting our lives can be, and how much more purposeful, when our relationship to myths and archetypes is more conscious.

18. Through understanding archetypes we can achieve a sense of unity with all other human beings while at the same time preserving and enjoying cultural diversity.

This is the most important benefit of learning to sense the archetypal level of our own consciousness. It gives us access to the primal stratum in our psyche where we store the latent archetypal imagery that can make us whole. Furthermore, when we understand the archetypal stratum of our psyches and are conversant with its imagery, we can begin to understand that same imagery, formerly alien to us, in the traditional art and customs of people in other cultures. Thus we sense the human unity of the collective unconscious and know that people in "foreign" cultures are actually living out a latent part of us, and vice versa.

Everyone is aware that we are increasingly in contact with and interdependently tied to other cultures. The American business community tries to learn the mysterious customs of the Japanese, the Nigerians, the Brazilians, the Chinese. A graduating college student is as likely to work in or have clients in Africa or Asia or South America as in the United States and Europe. Our belongings are manufactured in China, Taiwan, Guatemala, India, Kenya, Mexico, and Japan. A tribal New Guinean gold-panner now knows the morning's London gold standard, and when he wants to buy a Mercedes with his gold, he knows the going price.

Tourists are traveling in ever greater numbers to the age-old attractions as well as to newly popular exotic outposts—New Guinea, Bali, Mali, the Amazon, the Australian outback, Point Barrow, Tibet. Adventure vacations have become a major tourist industry, bringing people of vastly different cultural backgrounds into everyday contact with one another.

We have the terrifying responsibility of getting along internationally so that we don't blow each other up. For all of these reasons, we are in an era of international culture shock, and it is more important than ever that we learn to tolerate and respect our fellow human beings throughout the world even if their customs and beliefs seem strange.

Reaching the archetypal level of consciousness helps us to see that rather than having a paranoid, xenophobic reaction to people in other cultures, we can celebrate their differences from us because we know that deep down they represent a part of us. This revelation can be the basis for real peace and understanding in the world. And it does not depend upon—and in fact, is strongly against—homogenizing everyone into a uniform "world culture."

It is a view of humanity, embracing both unity and diversity, that is right for our time and urgently needed. It is especially important to the enlightened preservation of extant aboriginal hunting—gathering, farming, and pastoralist cultures currently endangered by the spread of the Grid. Without these cultures living and breathing and flourishing in the world today, we are all deeply incomplete, like an individual who has lost her whole family and has to make it alone in a cold world.

Appendix 2

Neumann's Archetypal Stages

The description of individual psychology that offers the most fertile analogies to the psychology of culture is presented by Erich Neumann in *The Origins and History of Consciousness*. (All Neumann quotes not ednoted are from *Origins*.) Neumann's observations are based on his extensive clinical experience as a Jungian psychoanalyst and on his knowledge of art and mythology. In keeping with Western psychoanalytic tradition, he sees the development of the psyche as a gradual emergence of ego, the principle that permits the formation of individual identity and consciousness. (In direct contrast, most Eastern spiritual traditions seek the transcendence of ego.[1])

With a Germanic flair for drama, Neumann describes this emergence as a transformative process that equates the ego, always a masculine principle, with the Hero. During the process, the ego/Hero encounters compelling archetypal figures: the Uroborus, the Great Goddess, the Divine Child, the World Parents, the Father God, the Dragon, the Terrible Mother, and the Terrible Male. Just as the Hero must pass tests to complete his quest, so must the ego confront, assimilate, or conquer these internal spectres to proceed on its path to liberation. "Ego consciousness" Neumann writes, "evolves by passing through a series of 'eternal images' and the ego, transformed in the passage, is constantly experiencing a new relation to the archetypes." Not only do these images arise in the dreams and fantasies of individuals, but, as archetypes speaking the same symbolic language, they arise also in world art and myth.

Apart from Neumann's dated equation of consciousness with masculinity and the ego, his penetrating observations have greatly influenced this book. For this reason, his archetypal stages in the evolution of the psyche are outlined below. Neumann uses the term "stages" to mean structural layers, not chronological time periods: "In individual development and perhaps also in that of the collective, these layers do not lie on top of one another in an orderly arrangement, but, as in the geological stratification of the earth, early layers may be pushed to the top and late layers to the bottom."

The Uroborus

Neumann first describes the preconsciousness state of absorbtion in uroboric oneness with the world. The oroborus is "the circular snake, the primal dragon of the beginning that bites its own tail, the self-begetting ...." Among its myriad meanings, "it is the time of existence in paradise where the psyche has her pre-worldly abode, the time before the birth of the ego, the time of unconscious envelopment, of swimming in the ocean of the unborn." This embryonic state describes the child in the womb and any experience of primordial origins (symbolized by the En-soph of the Kabbalah, the *muladhara chakra* in Kundalini yoga, and the *wu chi* of Chinese philosophy). In this time before the coming of opposites.

> Everything is still in the "now and for ever" of eternal being;
> sun, moon, and stars, these symbols of time and therefore of
> mortality, have not yet been created; and day and night, yesterday
> and tomorrow, genesis and decay, the flux of life and birth and death,
> have not yet entered into the world. This prehistoric state of being is
> not time, but eternity, just as the time before the coming of man and
> before birth and begetting is eternity. And just as there is no time
> before the birth of man and ego, only eternity, so there is no space,
> only infinity.[2]

Since there is as yet no ego to mark a central reference point and set up boundaries between self and other, uroboric existence is graced with the participation mystique—an oceanic oneness in which all things animate and inanimate are imbued with vitality, consciousness, and volition. In this world, all of being is linked in a magical continuum that transcends the laws of space and time. It is the "animalistic" world of primitive societies and young children. Its egoless quality makes the uroborus the source of wisdom as well as of creation. As the creative principle, it is associated first with the womb, but also with such elemental creative forces as the "breath of life," the "Word of God," and the self-incubating "inner heat" or tapas. As the principle of wisdom, Neumann likens it to the "ocean of wisdom" in which, according to *The Tibetan Book of the Dead*, "Thine own consciousness, shining, void, and inseparable from the Great Body of Radiance, hath no birth, nor death, and is the Immutable Light—Buddha Amitabha."[3]

> The uroboric realm, both *preworldly* and *otherworldly*, is revealed
> before birth and after death. It is the knowledge of the unformed
> attributable to young children.

The Great Mother

The whole uroboric mindset is contained in the womb and the nurturing maternal matrix, symbolized in prehistoric art by the "Venus figurine" that is all breasts and belly. As the child is born from the womb, the nascent ego emerges from uroboric paradise. It is born, in Neumann's words, into the "lower world of reality, full of dangers and discomforts .... Consequently the world becomes ambivalent."

Since the mother is the first person with whom the awakening ego has a relationship, the ego now experiences the world archetypally as the matriarchate of the Great Goddess. More personal and complex than the uroborus, the Great Goddess reflects the ego's ambivalence and increasing capacity to differentiate pleasure and pain. She is, by turns the good mother (like Isis and Demeter in classical mythology) and the devouring mother (like Hecate or Kali). As the ego develops, her guises multiply: sorceress, virgin, seductress, maenad, dragon of chaos, ocean of life, teacher, healer, goddess of fate, etc.

In the mythos of the matriarchate, the emerging ego is the Divine Child:

the miraculous male seed generated by the female, symbol of the self-fructifying cycle of life. The Mother, like the earth, is eternal: the child, like the seed that is born, reaped, and replanted to be born anew, is mortal. "The female is primary, the male is only what comes out of her. He is part of the visible but ever-changing created world. He exists only in perishable form. Woman exists from ever-lasting self-subsistent, immutable; man, evolving, is subject to continual decay."[4]

As the ego becomes conscious of itself as an entity separate from its mother, it outgrows the role of Divine Child and identifies with the more mature role of the Son/Lover of the Goddess (seen in consorts of the Goddess such as Attis, Adonis, and Tammuz). This dual role, still wholly defined by the matriarchate, expresses the ego's transition from unconsciousness (the dependent son) to consciousness (the fructifying lover). That the ego functions as a procreative partner with the Mother principle is a sign of its growing independence and equality. However, the Son/Lover, like the Divine Child, is ultimately sacrificed. Understandably, it is not long before the ego desires to break free of the matriarchate altogether.

The Separation of the World Parents

The next archetypal experience, the Separation of the World Parents, is dominated by the mythic image of the ego exerting its newfound presence by creating space. "Space only came into being when, as the Egyptian myth puts it, the god of the air, Shu, parted the sky from the earth by stepping between them. Only then, as a result of his light-creating and space-creating intervention, was there heaven above and earth below, back and front, left and right—in other words, *only then was space organized with reference to an ego*."[5]

The theme is universal. In the Bible, God creates heaven and earth by dividing light from darkness and the waters above from the waters below. In Greek myth, the Titans rend apart their parents, the Earth Goddess Gaia and the Sky God Uranus. The most heroic Titan is Cronos, the God of Time (thus our word "chronology"). Time as well as space is created by the Separation of the World Parents.[6] The splitting of the original uroboric oneness tears the world into primal dualities: eternity/temporality, inside/outside, I/you, mine/thine, male/female, body/mind, sacred/profane, order/chaos, good/evil, friend/enemy, etc.

As psychic agents, the World Parents are not simply symbolic stand-ins for the individual's own mother and father. They are personifications of the inner self—rent apart by the emancipation of ego. The ego defines itself by saying "I am this, I am not that." Fundamentally a point of reference that organizes the world in relation to itself, the ego isolates itself and sets up barriers that reinforce its identity by asserting its "differentness." It stands in opposition to the participation mystique. Its discriminations destroy the psyche's original unity, creating in effect a "self-division" that can be healed only by becoming "in-dividuated" again.

In Neumann's view, the Separation of the World parents marks the beginning of consciousness, of becoming conscious of oneself, which "begins with saying 'no' to the uroborus, to the Great Mother, to the unconscious." He observes that this separation "is not experienced only as passive suffering and loss, but also as an actively destructive deed. It is symbolically identical with killing, sacrifice, dismemberment, and castration. (Cronus castrated Uranus with a flint sickle, dual symbol of reaper and castrator.)

This psychic violence induces the feeling of original sin or guilt, which is the psychological origin of the mythic Expulsion from Paradise (from uroboric oneness). Expulsion myths (such as the Expulsion from the Garden of Eden) encode the psyche's archetypal loss of wholeness, of the participation mystique, of the inner Self, and of uroboric innocence—all sacrificed under the discriminating sickle of the emerging ego. From all this psychic carnage the adolescent Hero is born, which, according to Neumann, is the masculinity that lies at the root of consciousness.

The Birth of the Hero

In the violent passion of its struggle for autonomy, the ego splits apart not only the World Parent but also the Mother. Once the whole of existence—the unity before duality—she is now perceived only in her negative aspect as the Devouring Mother. As the ego/Hero gains independence, it identifies with the Father to consolidate its forces against the matriarchate. This archetypal psychological experience (especially for males), which Neumann calls "the Birth of the Hero," entails the ego/Hero's initiation into the secret male societies that arise compensatorily in matriarchal cultures. Thus the Hero seeks the collective wisdom that the fathers garnered in dealing with the same problem he now faces.

Neumann writes, "The male collective is the source of all the taboos, laws, and institutions that are destined to break the dominance of the uroborus and the Great Mother. Heaven, the father, and the spirit go hand in hand with masculinity and represent the victory of the patriarchate over the matriarchate."[7]

Male society represents "a world system which we may call, symbolically, 'heaven,' because it stands at the opposite pole of the feminine earth. The system embraces the whole sacrosanct and magical world order, down to the law and the reality of the state."[x] Initiation into this society constitutes the "second birth" of the Hero, this time through the Father, whereby he ascends to a higher masculinity (synonymous in Neumann's mind with consciousness) symbolized by the light, the sun, the head, and the eye. "Not until the hero identifies himself with what we have called the masculine 'heaven' can he enter upon his iight with the dragon. The identification culminates in the feeling that he is the son of God, embodying in himself the whole mightiness of heaven."[8] To the developing ego, the spiritual Self appears in the form of the archetypal Father. The sacred formula "I and my Father are one," as Christ said of God, captures the essence of this experience.

The Slaying of the Mother

After his initiation into male society, the ego/Hero must test his newly gained "higher masculinity" against the uroboric dragon that threatens to swallow him back into the "maternal unconscious." Neumann calls this scenario "the Slaying of the Mother. " Replete with incest and castration anxieties, it plays out the Hero's fear of the female. "For the ego and the male, the female is synonymous with the unconscious and the nonego, hence with darkness, nothingness, the void, the bottomless pit. In Jung's words: '... it should be remarked that emptiness is a great feminine secret. It is something absolutely alien to man; the chasm, the unplumbed depths, the yin.'"[9]

Battling the uroboric unconscious in the cavernous depths of the underworld, the Hero, always the champion of the light, faces the supreme test. He rises to the dragon fight as "a transfiguration, a glorification, indeed an apotheosis, the central feature of which is the birth of a higher mode of personality."[10] The glorified, deified Hero is often represented as the Sun God, hence one of the most common versions of the dragon fight is the sun myth where the Hero battles the nocturnal serpent, dragon, or sea monster that swallows him up every evening. In Egypt, for example, the Sun God spears and scorches the giant serpent Apophis before rising victoriously at dawn.

Sometimes the Slaying of the Mother is acted out more explicitly. Citing the mother-murder themes in the Oresteia, Hamlet, and the Indian myths of Rama, Neumann says, "Here, identification with the father is so complete that the maternal principle can be killed even when it appears, not in the symbolic form of a dragon, but as the real mother—and killed precisely because this principle has sinned against the father principle."[11]

The Slaying of the Father

There comes a time when the ego/Hero must rebel also against the Father. The fathers and elders of male society represent law and order, the established values of the culture. To Neumann, the maternal authority, which guards life and nature, is absolute. The paternal authority is relative, changing as the culture changes. The agent of change is the Hero. Thus, he must slay the archetypal Father in order to listen to the "inner voice" that will show him how "'to give the world a new and better face.'"

This archetypal experience involves a complex psychological restructuring of the Hero's relationship with his four parents—the personal mother and father and the archetypal Mother and Father—in their positive and negative aspects. The climax is an "archetypal war of the gods," seen in mythic history in "the patriarchal gods struggle against the Great Mother, the invaders' gods against the indigenous gods, Jehovah against the gods of the heathen." Ultimately, according to Neumann, "the hero ceases to be an instrument of the gods and begins to play his own independent part as a human being; and ... finally becomes, in modern man, a battleground for suprapersonal forces, where the human ego pits itself against the deity."[12]

Also important is the Promethean Theft of Fire theme. The archetypal Father is now to be subdued and robbed of his powers. In resisting, he becomes the Terrible Male, just as the archetypal Mother became the Devouring Mother to the ego struggling for independence. So begins "an intensified rivalry among the male groups:" the conflicts between son and father, youth and age, new world and old world. "So begins man's political life, which is almost always identical with the rise of the patriarchate."

Neumann continues with a lengthy analysis of how the ego eventually reunites with the self to achieve wholeness. (In a second part of *Origins and History*, he reviews the sequence in more specific psychoanalytical applications.) Few analogies between the psychology of the individual and the psychology of culture can be drawn beyond this point. Neumann himself laments that civilization as a whole has not yet achieved individuation. He looks forward to a time when it will heal its "differentiation into races, tribes, and groups ... and will then realize the center, which the individual personality today experiences as his own self-center, to be one with humanity's very self ..."

Appendix 3

Piaget and the Worldviews of Children

The late Swiss biologist-turned-child-psychologist Jean Piaget has a somewhat different view of child development. Nonetheless, his conclusions are as necessary to our understanding of the psyche as are Neumann's. Where Neumann saw the evolution of consciousness as a Wagnerian struggle against the dark, primitive, matriarchal demon of the unconscious who threatens at every turn to devour the nascent ego back into her maw, Piaget, who studied children for more than fifty years, calmly concluded that consciousness, or rather, intelligence and reason, are present from the beginning of life.

He concentrated on penetrating the charming, magical worlds that children construct during different stages in their development. Unlike Neumann, Piaget always worked directly with children, especially his own and his grandchildren, interviewing them about the way they saw the world and giving them structured games and tasks that revealed their inner thoughts. To read his interviews is to walk with him into the secret world of the child's mind and to see again through a child's eyes.

In this interview, Piaget questions Hub, a six-and-a-half year old boy, about the sun.

"What does the sun do when you are out for a walk?" asks Piaget.
"It moves," recalls Hub.
"How?"
"It goes with me."
"To make it light, so that you can see clearly."
"How does it go with you?"
"Because I look at it."
"What makes it move when it goes with you?"
"The wind."
"Does the wind know where you are going?"
"Yes."[1]

From his answers, we see that Hub is delightfully unaware of the abstract scientific concepts that would deny his subjective experience and tell him that the sun does not follow him but only appears to do so because of its great distance from the earth, or that the sun and wind are inert natural phenomena that take no account of his person, let alone of his movements or his need for light.

Through interviews such as this, Piaget made the momentous discovery, for which he is most famous, that children of different ages operate from different worldviews. In *The Quest for Mind*, Howard Gardner writes: "He found that children at certain ages not only gave wrong answers to questions but also exhibited qualitatively different ways of reasoning. The young child was neither 'dumber' nor just a few steps behind the older one; rather, he thought about things in a wholly different way, possessing a distinctive conception of the world that was manifested in every application of his reasoning power ...."[2] In other words, although Hub's answers are "wrong" in the eyes of contemporary science, they are "right" within the logic of Hub's pre-scientific, intuitive worldview.

Hub's perceptions echo a more "primitive" awareness of the "unity of all existence" which Eric Holm describes as a characteristic of the worldview expressed in the myths and rock art of the Kung San (Bushmen) of South Africa. Holm writes: "The finest picture of this unity of all existence is given in the fable of the origin of the Milky Way: A girl threw glowing ashes from the evening camp-fire—which was an offence—up into heaven to enable the distant hunters to find their way home in the darkness. These ashes form, as it were, a link between the terrestrial and celestial path."[3] The milky way shows the hunters their way in the darkness just as the sun followed Hub to light his way. The link between the terrestrial and celestial path mentioned in the myth recalls the *axis mundi*, the archetypal link between consciousness and the unconscious, which is severed with the socialization of growing up.

To Piaget, Hub's answers express a state of mind that he consistently observes in young children: *egocentrism*. By egocentrism, Piaget does not mean that the ego is central, but that there is no separation of the child's inner self from his surroundings, "The egocentric child," Gardner says, "is unable to differentiate himself from the rest of the world; he has not separated himself out from others or from objects. Thus he feels that others share his pain or pleasure, that his mumblings will inevitably be understood, that his perspective is shared by all persons, that even animals and plants partake of his consciousness?[4]

Egocentrism is equivalent to Neumann's uroboric oneness in the participation *mystique*, a term derived from the "law of participation" that Lucien Levy-Bruhl, a philosopher-anthropologist and contemporary of Jung, observed among primitive peoples. Ernst Cassirer also spoke of it in his book *Essay on Man* as a kind of sympathetic identification, and Holm writes, "In the primitive state there was apparently no differentiation, and no special significance was attached to the individual living being or material object: a man can be a stone, just as a stone can become a picture, a spirit, everything can take place in heaven as well as on earth."[5]

The beliefs expressed by children in Piaget's interviews suggest other parallels with the beliefs of primitive peoples and ancient cultures. At a certain stage, for instance, children exhibit a belief in "nominal realism," the view that the name or word for something is not merely a linguistic convention, interchangeable from language to language, but an absolute term embodying the essence of the thing itself. This is almost identical to the belief held in many cultures, including the Hindu, Native American, and ancient Egyptian, that names are magical entities and sources of power. A similar view is expressed in the opening verse of The Gospel According to St. John: "In the beginning was the Word, and the Word was with God, and the Word was God."[6]

Piaget found that three broad trends characterized mental development in children. Gardner summarizes these as 1) "the decline of egocentrism whereby the child gradually distinguishes between itself and the surrounding world," 2) the "internalization or interiorization of thought," which allows the child to begin to solve problems through formal mental operations rather than through physical actions; and 3) the growing reliance upon "various kinds of symbols—words, pictures, mathematical or artistic concepts" through which the child learns to "replace overt actions with symbolic representations of them" and thus becomes capable of abstract thought and logical analysis.[7] In this we see the emergence of the logos principle, which increasing dominates each succeeding archetype from the Sensitive Chaos to the Grid.

Appendix 4

The Question of Stages

In general, evolutionary views of civilization are currently out of favor among social scientists. This is traceable in part to a reaction led by Franz Boas against the evolutionists, whose theories had deteriorated by the early 20th century into "Social Darwinism." He urged anthropologists to forget generalizations and get detailed information about specific cultures by working directly with them. Thanks to the diligent work of archaeologists and anthropologists, the 20th century has seen a vast expansion of knowledge of the world's prehistoric and primitive cultures. Improved techniques of field research generated a proliferation of findings that invalidated the evolutionists' naive generalizations. The anti-evolutionary sentiment is due also in part to the increasing fragmentation of academic disciplines, which renders nearly inconceivable even the most valid cross-cultural generalization. Anthropology and archaeology are as prey to fashion as any field involving human thought, and several modes are currently distinguishable: logical positivism, systems theory, ecological or technological determinism (or a combination of the two), cultural geography, semiology, structuralism, post-structuralist deconstructionism, and several varieties of Marxism.

There are even more ideas about what constitute important indicators of cultural change: social complexity, class structure, technological innovations, artistic expression, pottery styles, settlement types, geographical distribution, gender relations, racial mix, spiritual orientation, types of languages and writing systems, ecological adaptation, degree of centralized leadership, material wealth, ability to acquire territory, and so forth. Furthermore, most theorists use some combination of these indicators to hypothesize syndromes or causal sequences. In the latter half of the 20th century a modified evolutionary theory emerged in anthropology. Its proponents, such as Marshall Sahlins and Elman Service, avoided the generalizations of the earlier theories and took into account recently accumulated data showing the great variety and complexity of human cultures. Without claiming the existence of universal stages or motivating forces, they recognized different types of societies, distinguished by their degree of social complexity and their technological adaptation to the environment.

Types of Society

The distinctions between types of societies indicate what a group of people is capable of achieving and how much control it can muster over natural and human adversity. A society that has managed to organize an army, an irrigation system, and a system of food storage and distribution is obviously more powerful than one whose members must fend for themselves. To determine the degree of social complexity, some important questions are: Is the society egalitarian or does it have some sort of leader? Is everybody equal or are there classes or castes? Does everybody do much the same thing, like hunting or farming, or do some people have specialized skills, perhaps ones that give them status? Are all people buried in the same way, indicating equality, or are some people honored by being buried in larger, richer, or better located graves? And what about dwellings? Are they all the same or do some show signs of wealth and prestige? Despite the variety of approaches among different scholars, Robert J. Wenke provided a useful synopsis of current theories in his book Patterns of Prehistory. Wenke's summary of the "ethnographic taxonomies" of Morton Fried, Elman Service, Kent Flannery, and other anthropologists, divides societies into bands, tribes, chiefdoms, states, and empires. Since these distinctions dovetail well with the first five spatial archetypes, Wenke's summary is quoted here almost in full with the analogous spatial archetypes noted in brackets:

Bands [The Sensitive Chaos]: The Copper Eskimo, Kalahari Bushman, Australian aborigines, and most other contemporary hunting and gathering societies are examples of this type of social organization. Based on archaeological evidence, it appears that prior to the appearance of agriculture almost all people lived in bands, which are very simply organized. There are minor differences among members of the group in terms of prestige, but no one has any greater claim to material resources than anyone else .... Band members spend most of their lives in groups of fifteen to forty people, moving often as they exploit wild plants and animals. Territoriality, ceremonialism, and descent reckoning are usually very weakly developed. Division of labor is along basic age and sex lines and exchange usually takes place between people who consider themselves friends or relatives. This gift giving is usually done very casually and relationships are frequently cemented by offers of reciprocal hospitality .... One of the most impressive things about bands is their stability and long-term success. For millions of years they were the only ... cultural organization.

Tribes [The Great Round, with modifications]: Tribes are seen as differing from bands in several respects, the most obvious of which is size. People living in tribes are often subsistence farmers, such as the Pueblo Indians of the American Southwest, or the New Guinea highlanders. Tribes often have a nominal leader who acts to redistribute food and perform a few minor ceremonial activities, but, as in band societies, he has no privileged access to wealth or power. He can lead only by example, and serves at the pleasure of the tribe. Exchange in such societies is still usually accomplished through reciprocal trading within a kinship structure. Typically, tribal societies are larger, more territorial, have more elaborate ceremonialism and kinship systems, and make more distinctions in terms of prestige than band societies ....

Chiefdoms [The Four Quarters]: While in many cases tribes seem little more than large bands, chiefdoms represent a quantum change in social organization. Chiefdoms are based on the concept of hereditary inequality: different status is ascribed at birth, and members of the society are classed as "chiefly" or as "common" regardless of their individual abilities .... These differences in prestige usually correlate with preferential access to material resources, so . that chiefs and their families can claim the best farmlands or fishing places, as well as more food and more exotic and expensive items than "commoners." They are often regarded as divine and typically marry only within noble families. The economies of these societies typically show a greater degree of specialization and diversification than those of tribes or bands. Craftsmen exist, but they are usually also farmers, and there is no permanent class of artisans as there is in states. Chiefdoms are much larger than tribes, often involving thousands of people. Examples of chiefdoms include the precontact Nootka of British Columbia, early Hawaiian societies, and the Tonga of Africa.

States [The Pyramid]: States typically have centralized governments composed of political and religious elites who exercise economic and political control. In addition to being larger in population and territory than other societal forms, states are characterized by having full-time craftsmen and other specialists, and residence within a settlement is often determined more by occupational specialization than by kinship ties…. The state codifies and enforces laws, drafts soldiers, levies taxes, and exacts tributes. States have powerful economic structures, often centered upon market systems, and they typically have a diversity of settlement sizes, such as villages, hamlets, towns, and sometimes, cities. Early states formed essentially independently in at least six areas of the ancient world: Mesopotamia, Egypt, the Indus Valley, China, Mesoamerica, and Peru.

Empires [The Radiant Axes]: A still more complex societal division is the empire, which has more people, controls more territory, exploits more environments, and has more levels of social, economic, and political stratification than early states ... Many of the early states seem to have been involved in competitive relationships with adjacent states, and for long periods this factor apparently limited their size and power. Eventually, however, in all the . early centers of state formation these competitive relationships broke down and one state was able to increase its size and influence drastically—usually so rapidly that it had few competitors. In fact, its ultimate size seems to have been limited only by the level of its communications technology and its administrative efficiency. Empires of this type first appeared in Mesopotamia toward the end of the second millennium B.C., and within 1,000 years thereafter in Egypt, the Indus Valley, and China. The Inca state of Peru and the Aztec state of Mexico also seem to have achieved imperial dimensions just before the arrival of the Europeans, in the sixteenth century A.D.

Wenke does not offer a category of society that corresponds to the Grid, but one called Techno-Bureaucracies or Post-Imperialistic Military-Industrial Complexes might be suggested. In the past, technocracies and bureaucracies were usually substructures of empires—the managerial and industrial networks that supported imperialistic control. Today, however, they have transcended the boundaries of empires to become a globally interlocked superstructure, the most complex form of human organization yet devised. The Progressive Sequence versus the Psychological Metaphor Even though human societies can be roughly classified into a number of types, we must resist the temptation to interpret the different types of cultures as a developmental sequence. Consider two basic types of sequences: the progressive and the psychological. In the progressive sequence, the "simple, primitive" hunting-gathering culture represents the beginning of a line of evolutionary progress that inevitably culminates in the "complex, advanced" international commercial-industrial culture. This may sometimes be true, however, there are four main problems with the concept of progressive stages of cultural development or evolution: First, it assumes a Eurocentric value system, which holds that earlier, more "primitive" stages were merely savage groupings toward later, more "advanced" stages, culminating in modern Western civilization as the pinnacle of human achievement. Second, as we will see when we look at the spatial archetypes individually, each archetype actually constitutes a distinctly different and independent world view fully developed in its own right. Each is a complete cultural system with its own way of knowing the world, its own means of insuring survival and expressing the human spirit, and its own methods of organizing people to promote the common good.

Third, the progressive evolutionary view implies that cultures will naturally change from one type to the next through an inborn, organic process. (Actually, biological evolution is not based on this. Species change and evolve mostly in response to changes in their environment such as pressures from decreasing food resources, climatic changes, and competing species, which induce them to adapt to new evolutionary niches,) In fact, most traditional human societies actively resist change. Hunter-gatherers have means of sharing wealth and power designed precisely to prevent the kinds of social inequities that would cause them to "evolve to the next level." When egalitarian farming cultures in Europe learned metallurgy, they used it to make ritual objects and farming tools rather than weapons.2 They often were conquered by iron-age warrior chiefdoms, but they did not "evolve naturally" into this type of culture. Fourth, most human societies are multi-layered. An empire, for example, may contain conquered chiefdoms and states, and the people living in these social structures would probably adhere to a different world view ... from that of their overlords. To see the types of societies as developmentally sequential often means greatly oversimplifying the actual complexity of human cultures, especially after the advent of states. Such simplification may at times be useful to isolate and analyze one aspect of a culture, but the enveloping complexity should never be forgotten. In the psychological sequence, the "primitive" culture is analogous to civilization's infancy; the "advanced" one, to its old age. In this view, the observation that "ontogeny recapitulates phylogeny"—the evolution of the species is repeated in the development of the individual—is carried beyond the biological realm, its usual meaning, to apply to the psychological and cultural realms as well.

To some extent, the psychological sequence reverses the Eurocentric values of the progressive sequence. Some proponents idealize the hunting-gathering way of life as representing humanity's innocence and primeval oneness with nature. They view the development of civilization as a fall from this state of grace, with the "advanced" industrial stage progressing ultimately into rigor mortis. The appeal of the evolutionary concepts is that they make the whole of human history comprehensible in terms we all familiar with: beginning, middle, end; or childhood, adolescence, maturity, old age. The psychological sequence is especially appealing because each of us goes through these stages in our own lives. It can be a convenient framework, and is even quite accurate in a general way, however, like the progressive sequence, it can foster stereotypes and oversimplifications. The psychological sequence is most useful as a metaphor.

Appendix 5

Architecture as Worldview: Houses of the Mind

One of the primary ways in which we deal with the world is by organizing and symbolizing it in spatial terms. All spatial forms made by the human hand or mind—architectural, artistic, mythic, or scientific—began as configurations in the psyche. The psyche conceives even of itself in spatial terms. Its inner territories appear in myths and dreams as architectural spaces that are journeyed through, named, circumambulated, built, and destroyed. The Cretan Labyrinth is perhaps the most famous metaphor for the threatening birth passages of the unconscious; by successfully penetrating the Labyrinth and vanquishing its demonic guardian, the Minotaur, Theseus emerges a hero. Of course, it is in the nature of mythic images such as this to be readable on many levels. The Minotaur, for instance, personifies the terrors lurking in the depths of the unconscious, but he symbolizes also the culture that preceded the Greeks. (As they migrated into the Aegean, the Indo-European tribes who became the Greeks mythically transformed the earlier cultures' sacred beasts, such as the bull, and priestesses, such as the Gorgons, into demons whom Theseus, Perseus, Heracles, and other Greek heroes slew to aid in establishing the new social order.[1]

In our dream journeys through the houses of the mind, we react strongly to being pent in a dark cellar, climbing a winding staircase toward an unseen source of light, exploring a dusty attic, being in a sunlit walled garden, or slowly opening a creaking door. Our emotions can range from dread to delight to horror as we encounter the strange rooms in the psyche closed to our conscious minds. How the houses of the mind test and influence people has been a subject of world mythology and literature from earliest times. Houses of planetary influence have been important in the symbol system of astrology since ancient Babylon. In the *Popul Vuh*, the sacred book of the Quiché Mayas, the twins Hunaphu and Zbalanqué are subjected to trials in the various houses of the underworld. The most elaborate house symbolism appears in *The Egyptian Book of the Dead* where the deceased (the initiate) must pass through the Hall of judgment, the Hall of Maati (naming the bolts, lintels, threshold, fastenings, socket, door-leaves, and door-posts), the seven halls of Osiris, and the twenty-one hidden pylons of the House of Osiris in the Elysian Fields. *The Egyptian Book of the Dead* places great emphasis on the deceased's ability to name all of the architectural elements of the Land of the Gods (the psyche). Naming something is a way of mastering it by becoming conscious of it.

Another way of mastering something is by circumambulating or encircling it. The symbolic circumambulation of the Four Quarters of the universe is acted out around Medicine Wheels by the Plains Indians, with the sacred pipe in Native American ceremonies, around stupas and chortens by Buddhist pilgrims in Asia, in coronation ceremonies by village chieftains in Africa, in European cloisters by

Christian monks, in certain nuptial rites by brides and grooms, around Egyptian fertility temples by women wishing to bear children, and in countless other rituals the world over. In all cases, the circumambulation of the Four Quarters is an attempt to seal the ritual in accord with the laws of the universe. It is an extension of human will to the boundaries of space, and at the same time, a respectful appropriation of the powers of nature, which under ordinary circumstances lie beyond human reach.

Building and destroying sacred cities and temples has long served as a metaphor for building and destroying whole worldviews. The Bible ends with the vision of the New Jerusalem, the apotheosis of redeemed Christians. This City of Revelation is destined to be made manifest only after the "pagan fortune-tellers and idolaters" have, like the Minotaur, been annihilated (or converted) and their sacred groves and idols destroyed. Believing that the destruction of the old Pagan groves and idols represented the destruction of the pre-Christian, Goddess-centered way of life, the neo-pagan Z. Budapest wrote in 1976, "Today, there is a new dawn. We are welcoming new witches into our coven as we strive to replant the Goddess' groves. We, the wimmin [sic], are the grove; through us the return of the Goddess is evident."[2]

Sacred Place

Sacred places in nature such as groves, springs, caves, and special rocks and trees are not outside the province of architecture. On the contrary, *the identification of sacred places in nature is the beginning of architecture.* Through this act of identification, the psyche begins to differentiate between space and place and seeks place as a home of the Self. The emergence of a sense of place marks the beginning of an architectural sensibility. When the sacred place inside the psyche meets a magical place in nature, a sanctuary is born. The place may be special because it is the site of a healing spring, a place where medicinal or hallucinogenic herbs grow, where animals seek shelter from storms or go to give birth, where there are meteorological anomalies, where the genius loci is particularly strong, or where magical events have left their mark. The place may be sacred to one person only, to a group of people, or, as in the case of places like Jerusalem or Mecca, to whole civilizations.

As psyche and civilization change, so do sacred places. They begin as simple, natural sites, perhaps marked only in the minds of those who frequent them. As millennia pass and different cultures inhabit the same landscape, this simple veneration of nature may give way to increasingly formalized religions, culminating perhaps in a highly ceremonial state religion. As this occurs, primitive natural sanctuaries give way first to simple shrines, then to temples, and finally to vast temple complexes and sacred cities. Attitudes about these places change also as the psychology of the parent culture changes. In "primitive" cultures, a sacred place may be considered a powerful living aspect of the spirits in nature. For instance, during rituals Australian Aborigines embellish certain sacred places in nature with blood and feather mandalas to mark places where legendary ancestors and spirits came into the world. In ancient high civilizations, temples were considered the actual abodes of gods and goddesses who were fully independent external beings having power over human life. For example, the Sumerians erected great ziggurats or temple-mountains to entice the all-powerful sky deities to earth so that they could attend to human needs. Today, many think of gods and goddesses rather as symbolic projections of the psyche. The spaces identified with them—their temples and sanctuaries—have become internalized structures. For instance, when Z. Budapest wrote, "We, the wimmin, are the grove; through us the return of the Goddess is evident," she was saying that the Goddess's grove is within us by replanting the grove—that is, by becoming conscious of this neglected inner place and rebuilding it—we give the Goddess alive within us a home, thereby strengthening the feminine principle in our lives.

We can use meditation and other techniques to gain access to the sacred places in the unconscious. In guided imagination sessions, I have led people into their inner sanctuaries and have had them draw what they saw. I then took their drawings and made slides of similar images in world architecture. People were amazed to find they had drawn buildings they had never seen before: Coptic rock-cut churches, Islamic mosques, Buddhist stupas, Chinese palaces, Neolithic beehive dwellings and tholoi, Pueblo kivas, Indian cave-temples, and so on. These sessions showed that all the archetypal forms of world architecture are alive in each of our psyches and can be generated with no prior knowledge. Even if these drawings were of structures the subjects had seen, in pictures or otherwise, and thought they had forgotten, the conclusion is the same: it is no accident that they selected from the vast storehouses of their buried impressions the archetypal forms to reflect their inner sanctuaries.

Using another technique, I have asked my architecture students to describe their design projects in the first person singular. One student said of his building, "I have many welcoming entrances." Like his building, this student was friendly, open, and uncomplicated. Another described his building saying, "I am meticulously organized and very well structured, but I guess I am forbidding to people." This student was indeed rigid and inhibited. Practicing architects also project their personalities into their work (as does anyone in any field). We have all felt depressed in buildings that we subliminally sensed were designed by callous and neurotic architects, and elated in buildings that made us feel good about their designers. Frank Lloyd Wright may have been alluding to psychological as well as physical space when he said of his design for Unity Temple: "You will find the sense of a great room coming through—space not walled in now but more or less free to appear. In Unity Temple you will find the walls actually disappearing; you will find the interior space coming to the outside and see the outside coming in."[3] Wright was saying as much about himself here as about Unity Temple.

The Celestial Mansion

Spatial form can mirror the character of a civilization as well as the character of an individual. Every village and city reflects the nature of the society that built it. Every idea and value system has spatial connotations. A civilization shapes its environs to conform to its image of the cosmos—as above so below—and we can learn to read its art, architecture, and town planning to discern its worldview. In the West, for instance, the ancient Greeks saw the universe as a great mandala with all the heavenly bodies locked into perfectly concentric spheres that moved majestically about the earth center. This statically symmetrical conception of space held until Copernicus's heliocentric theory was accepted, and even then the sun simply replaced the earth as the center of the spherical universe. Western architecture remained a play of static symmetries until Johannes Kepler's early 17th century discovery of the dynamic, non-uniform speed and elliptical paths of planetary orbits. At about the same time Western architecture exploded into a Baroque vocabulary of ellipses, distorted axes, and optical illusions.

To the Maya, the universe was an octahedron, or double pyramid, with thirteen steps of heaven above and nine steps of hell below, a concept clearly modeled in the Mayan pyramid. The Himalayan Buddhist stupa or chorten, is simultaneously a model of Mount Meru (the World Mountain), the human body as microcosm, the life and teachings of the Buddha, and the spiritual journey between the multiplicity of daily life and the unity of the Buddha-mind. Similarly, an Islamic mosque is a model of the Islamic cosmos; a Dogon granary, of the Dogon cosmos; and the Medicine Wheel, of the cosmos of the Plains Indians. Each of these structures acts as a mediator between the microcosm of the psyche and the macrocosm of the universe. Each reflects back upon the other until the symbolic resonances are so rich that a kind of a continuous harmonic alignment is established. One who is familiar with the symbolism and open to its power can be transported to a realm of consciousness that transcends the dualities of microcosm and macrocosm, matter and energy, time and space, and even life and death.

Often massive, seemingly superhuman resources were harnessed in the construction of sacred cosmological architecture. What could have inspired such efforts? One is compelled to believe that it was the knowledge that certain configurations of architectural form and topographical siting could not only mirror human consciousness but also profoundly alter it. Like a magnet, the undying power of sacred sites to alter consciousness has, over the centuries, attracted pilgrims, explorers, archaeologists, and tourists to architectural monuments around the world. Even today, beneath the surface of jet-age tourism runs an undercurrent of fascinated anticipation, as if the travelers secretly hope, by visiting Stonehenge or the Great Pyramid, to recover some long lost power to enter non-ordinary states of reality. The body of world architecture harbors immensely exciting secrets. It is a code, a symbolic language like myths and dreams. With the patience of geological time, it silently awaits deciphering as it struggles against the forces of humanity and nature to preserve its precious stone and mortar records.

Two Million Years of Daily Life

Architecture does more than alter consciousness and mirror worldviews. On a more mundane level, it accommodates daily life. It is this functional level that renders works of architecture most human and most immediately understandable. A building or a city is the product of many human hands and minds working in concert to create appropriate settings for ordinary human activities. The layout of a building such as a house can reveal how many people are in the family, what their relationships are, what kind of work they do in the home, how they cook and what they eat, whether they are set up to accommodate guests or extended family members on a temporary or permanent basis, and so on. Similarly, buildings housing institutions such as schools, churches, prisons, hospitals, and government centers tell us much about the nature of those institutions. Towns and cities are like great houses revealing the complex interactions among their inhabitants.

Because of its ability to reveal the patterns of daily life as well as the cosmological models on which civilizations are based, architecture provides one of the most complete and extensive records of human life. It provides also one of the oldest. Remains of rudimentary stone windbreaks have been found in Olduvai Gorge that were built by Australopithecines over two million years ago! Naturally, like "animal architecture" such early structures lack the intentionality and symbolic meaning that distinguish true architecture from mere construction. However, the picture begins to change with fragments of a thatched roof house that have been excavated at Terra Amata in Nice, France, dating from 300,000 B.C. This inconceivably ancient dwelling—built more than 200,000 years before the presumed appearance of such hallmarks of humanity of burial, art, and religion—already contained the archetypal signs of "house:" a oval structure with a stone foundation, a pitched roof probably with ridge beam and rafters, and a central hearth around which the whole house had been built!

Spatial Archetypes

It is surprising how often people from different cultures widely separated in space and time built in strikingly similar ways. Seventeen thousand years ago, hunters in Mal'ta, Siberia, built skin tents nearly identical with the tipis used until recently by Plains Indians in the midwestern United States. The longhouses of Europe's Danubian culture, built around 5000 B.C., were much like those built by the Iroquois in New York State until 1700 A.D. Stepped pyramids in Mesopotamia, Cambodia, Polynesia, and Mexico bear many resemblances to each other even though the cultures that built them were separated in time by as much as 4500 years and in space by half the earth's circumference.

There are obvious reasons for some of these similarities. For instance, both the Siberian and the Plains Indian tent-builders were nomadic hunters in need of portable shelter in cold climates where animal hides were the most readily available building material. Thus, the two cultures developed similar dwellings. But practical considerations do not explain why several complex cultures built massive stepped pyramids—structures that served little or no practical purpose and yet consumed vast quantities of labor and materials. Some archaeologists assert that such structures served a social function by contributing to the formation of state societies through channeling surplus wealth and helping to organize administrative structures and class systems. While these explanations may be plausible as far as they go, they can only be part of the picture.

Monumental structures such as stepped-pyramids were built because their symbolic meaning powerfully reinforced the archetypal image of the state—not just in its social and political aspects, but in its full mythic, spiritual, and cosmological grandeur. Furthermore, it was not necessary to be educated in this symbolism. Being archetypal, it was innate in every person; every person could immediately grasp its message and meaning, at least on a subconscious level.

Similarities of architectural form and meaning from one region of the world to another that cannot be accounted for by climate and use usually stem from culture. There are countless examples of architectural forms used worldwide whose symbolic meanings transcend purely practical considerations: the central tent pole as the "Axis of the World," the vaulted ceiling as the "Dome of Heaven," the pyramid as the "World Mountain," the road from town to temple as the "Sacred Way," the walled garden as an image of Paradise, and so on. These are architectural archetypes. An architectural archetype is a form that 1) recurs in different cultures in different parts of the world at different times, 2) is associated always with essentially the same meaning, and 3) is not generated by purely practical considerations.

One cannot begin to comprehend what a city is, as a human product, without reference to the archetype that inspired its builders. Within the great ambit of the archetype, there are no irrelevant factors, no determinants of form that fall outside its limits. Even the ways in which builders respond to terrain and climate fall within the imperatives of the archetype, because it preselects the range of possible responses. As a result, a city's character and aura are as real as those of any product of an individual—even though its structures and spaces are conceived and built by many hands over centuries. This is not to suggest that everything emanates from and is absolutely determined by archetypes as if they were teleological forces. They probably do operate a dialectic with external circumstances. For instance, environmental and climatic changes may activate an archetype that was formerly latent, stimulating a different worldview to come to the fore.

Above and beyond the myriad architectural archetypes shaping individual buildings and towns, there are a few "mega-archetypes" so powerful that they shape whole patterns of civilization for centuries and even millennia. These "mega-archetypes" are the subject of this book: the Sensitive Chaos of hunter-gatherers, the Great Round of Neolithic farmers, the Four Quarters of Bronze and Iron Age chieftainships, the Pyramid of the nation state, the Radiant Axes of empires, and the Grid of post-imperialistic commercial-industrial networks.

Appendix 6
The World of the Shaman

Terms for Shamanic Consciousness:

- Shamanic State of Consciousness (Hamer's SSC)
- Non-Ordinary Reality (Castaneda)
- shamanic reality
- shamanic consciousness
- magico-religious experience
- peak experience
- visionary state ecstasy
- second sight
- magic flight
- trance
- ESP
- Contrasted with: Ordinary Reality (Castaneda)
- Ordinary State of Consciousness (Harnefs OSC)
- mundane experience
- everyday life
- waking consciousness

Access to Shamanic Reality is gained through:

- Drums, rattles, and other percussion instruments
- Chants, songs, dances, whirling and spinning
- Meditation, vision quests, dreams, yoga
- Art, concentrated creative "flow"
- Possession
- Psychoactive plants and drugs
- Sensory deprivation, fatigue, illness, fever
- Psychosis, visionary states
- Sexual ecstacy, childbirth
- Near death experiences, death

Shamanic Initiation

- Ego transcendence, often experienced as death, dismemberment, and resurrection

A Shaman's Skills

- The Shamanic Journey
- Seeing Healing
- X-Ray vision
- Divination
- Soul retrieval
- Shamanic extraction
- Sacrifices
- Breaking through obstacles
- Transformative powers
- Sorcery/ Black Magic (universally disapproved)

The Three Worlds of Shamanic Reality

- Upper/Middle/lower
  Or
- Sky/Earth/Underworld

The Difficult Passage from Ordinary to Shamanic Reality

- Precarious Bridge
- Paradoxical Passage
- Strait Gate
- Clashing Rocks
- Scylla and Charybdis
- "Between a rock and a hard place"
- Ominously closing doors or walls

Spirit Paths to Shamanic Reality

- Stairway Path or road
- Vine, plant, or tree
- Underground passage, hole in the ground
- Smoke, fire, lightning, volcano, tornado
- Rainbow, sunbeam
- Shooting star, meteor

Shamanic Vehicles

- The Drum
- Spirit canoes and boats
- Horses and other animals

- Birds and flying creatures
- Dolphins, whales, and fish
- Rainbows

Spirit Guides and Allies

- Animal Allies (Lower World)
- Nature spirits, devas, genii loci, the "little people," fairies, sprites, etc. (Middle World, Earth)
- Spirits, deities, teachers, mentors, guides, sages, wizards, alchemisls, etc. (Upper World, usually)
- Ancestors (Upper World)

The Center of the World

- Navel of the World
- Cave of Emergence
- Shamanic Tunnel
- Open Center
- Eternal Spring
- Mandala/*nierika*
- "Point existing here and everywhere, new and always"
- Pole Star and the Pleiades (as sky holes) corpus callosum
- Vagina

The Axis Mundi (World Axis)

- World Tree, Tree of Life
- Cosmic Mountain
- Volcano Ladder/ stairs Rope or vine
- Tent pole Pole Star (as tent pole)
- World Pillar
- Spinal Column
- Phallus

The World Pillar (a type of axis mundi)

- Pole Star
- "Pillar of the Sky"
- "Sky Nail"
- "Golden Pillar"
- "Powerful Posts of the Center of the City"
- Stake to which Star-Horses are tethered
- "Man-Pillar of Iron"
- Man
- Father

The Serpent

- Apparition
- Kundalini energy
- Earth energies
- Milky Way
- Rainbow Totem or guide

The Cardinal Directions
(prevalent in Four Quarters cultures)

North , South , East , West , Heaven , Earth , Center

The Elements

Most common: • Earth • Water • Fire Air • Space or Ether
Chinese: • Earth • Water • Fire • Wood • Metal

Other Motifs

- Drum Cosmology
- The Celestial Ceiling
- The Sky House
- The Celestial Throne
- Summit of the Axis Mundi
- Colors of the Celestial Regions, Light
- Alchemical Transformation, Gold, Crystals, Metallurgy
- Masks
- Membrane between the Worlds
- Doors of Perception
- *Imago Mundi*
- Horns of Consecration
- The Dreamtime

Some Shamanic Cultures
(includes many non-Sensitive Chaos Cultures)

- Eurasia: Tungus, Chukchee, Samoyed, Yakut Buryat, Kirgiz Tatar, Sami Korean, Japanese
- Oceania and Southeast Asia: Australian aborigines Dyak, Andamanese
- Africa: Pygmy !Kung, Dogon
- South America: Desana, Barasana, Bororo, Yanomami, Iivaro, Amahuaca
- North America: Eskimo Satish, Tlingit, Sioux, Huichol

Note: These characteristics of shamanism were gleaned mainly from Eliade 1964, Harner 1980 and 1978, and Halifax 1982.

Appendix 7

Sites and Cultures of the Great Round

[One of Mimi's points in this book is that the cultures of the archetypes are widespread. When we think of Bronze Age warrior chieftains, we may think first of the Greeks of the *Iliad*, but Mimi shows that there were dozens of similar Four Quarter cultures. The same goes for the Neolithic cultures of the Great Round. Below is an incomplete list of such cultures. – JL]

Within the limitations of regional differences (climate, topography, flora and fauna, raw materials), the cultures outlined generally display the typical features of the Great Round listed below, so only their outstanding features and architectural characteristics are given, along with a few sites. All dates are B.C. unless noted as A.D.

Typical Features of Great Round Cultures:

- Agriculture (farming of wheat, rye, barley, oats, millet, maize, gourds, rice, legumes, roots, vegetables, etc.).
- Domestication of animals (cattle, sheep, goats, pigs, donkeys, fowl, llama, alpaca).
- Pottery, usually in a variety of shapes and decorated with the spirals, meanders, whirls, snake coils, chevrons, lozenges, triangles, zigugs, eggs, and linear designs that make up *The language of the Goddess*. 97 Female figurines are also nearly universal, suggesting some form of Goddess-worship.
- Permanent buildings and villages.
- Collective or egalitarian communal burial Woven textiles, looms.
- Tools of flint, bone, stone, antler, obsidian.
- Trade in flint, obsidian, shells, alabaster, marble, dyes, salt, fibre staples, and so on.
- No signs of warfare or weapons.

NEAR EAST
Mesopotamia to the Udaid period

Anatolia (Turkey)
Çatal Hüyük and Hacilar (ca. 7000-5500)

EUROPE AND THE MEDITERRANEAN
Central and Eastern Europe

Starcevo Cutlure. Yugoslavia, Hungary (Koriis culture), and Romania (Cris culture), 6300-5300. Major core culture. Develops into the Vinca, Butrnir, Tisza, and Lengyel cultures from 5400-5200 B.C.

Features: Spiral pottery motifs. Bull's head on gable of clay model house or temple. Stylized multi-colored Bird Goddess vase with chevrons, meanders, zigzags, red triangles. Footed and bird-shaped pots.

Architecture: Rectangular timber one-room houses on stone foundations, with clay floors and round hearths. Two-roomed stone-paved temples with horseshoe hearths and ceremonial vessels. Over fifty trapezioidal temples in Lepenski Vir, with vulviform stone floor layouts, containing red-ochre covered vulva stones, fish goddesses, and other symbols of regeneration.

Sites: Obre I, Anza, Divostin, Lepenski Vir, Let, Porodin, Gradesnica.

Karanovo Culture. Central Bulgaria, phases I-IV, ca. 6300-5000. Related to Sesklo and Starcevo cultures.

Features: Many goddess figurines including terracotta Bird Goddesses, pregnant hand-on- belly goddesses, white marble "stiff nudes" with supernatural pubic triangles. Architecture: Massive tells with well-planned villages with log-paved streets, housing about 300 people in single-room, clay-coated wood-framed dwellings with beehive ovens. Painted interiors in some houses suggest temples.

Sites: Azmak, Cevdar, Karanovo, Muldava.

Linearbandkeramik (LBK) Culture. Eastern France to Romania, 5500-4900. Similar to late Starcevo (Koros) culture. Fuses with the Bug-Dniester culture after 5000, and with the Lengyel after 4300.

Features: Pottery motifs: snakes, spirals, meanders, triangles, V's, chevrons, and concentric squares; relief images of horns, breasts.

Architecture: Villages of up to 500 inhabitants, most with five to eight occupied timber longhouses up to 150 feet long (45 m). No defensive features (until after invasions begin ca. 4000). Sites: Elsloo, Bylany, Brno area, Seehausen, Nitra, River Aisne.

Bükk Culture. Hungary, eastern Slovakia, northern Romania, ca. 5500-5000. Also called Eastern Linearbandkeramik.

Architecture: Underground and semi-subterranean pit-houses (early phase). Aboveground houses (later phase) with adjacent obsidian and flint workshops. Cave sanctuaries with wooden entrance structures with graves underneath. Cave walls and abstract figurines decorated with meanders, zig-zags, chevrons, and other geometric motifs.
Sites: Oros II, Domica, Ardovo, Aggtelek.

Danilo-Hvar Culture. Adriatic Coast in Dalmatia, 5500-4000.
Features: Ring-handled, four-footed zoomorphic offering vessels with spiral and zig-zag engravings. Sailboats on pottery suggest a seafaring culture. Architecture: Open villages surrounded by one or two ditches. Cave sanctuaries with fine painted pottery.

Sites: Smilcic, Danilo, Grapceva spilja.

Butmir Culture. Bosnia, 5300-4200. Site: Obre II. Starcevo and Danilo-Hvar influences.

Features: Vases with elegant painted and relief running spirals, geometric motifs, and stylized serpent heads. Hundreds of terracotta figurines including bird masks and female heads, probably dedicated to a Bird Goddess.

Architecture: Two-room houses with one room containing a beehive bread oven, grinding stones, loom, and flint-and-bone work area. Storage pits sunk over six feet (2 m) in the ground could have served as refrigerators. Long, peaceful occupation of sites (nearly 1000 years).

Sites: Obre II, Sarajevo, Butmir, Nebo.

Vinca Culture. Central Balkans, 5400-4300. Major descendant of Starcevo culture covering roughly the same area.

Features: Thousands of clay sculptures and vessels, most showing the Bird Goddess, the primary deity, or Snake Goddesses or Madonnas. About twenty percent of figurines (some carved in marble and alabaster) show snakes, fish, frogs, and other animals, and males with ram or he-goat masks. Several bucrania (bull or ox skulls coated with clay and painted) were attached to clay columns or walls in temples. One double goddess statue was found with a bucranium. Copper was mined from 5000 on.

Architecture: Large number of known sites (650), including many settlements near waters considered sacred today. Tells with up to ten habitation strata, with well-planned villages ranging in size from under 200 to 2,500 residents (larger than Early Dynastic Near Eastern towns). One and two room early houses; later houses up to sixty-five feet long (20 m) with two to five rooms. Temples similar to houses, but painted inside and out with red, blue, and white chevrons and meanders.
Sites: Vinca, Anza IV, Banjica, Crnokalacka Bara, Gradesnica, Rast, Valac, Selevac, Divostin, Gomolava.

Tisza Culture. Hungary, northern Yugoslavia, 5400-3700. Descendant of Starcevo/Kiiros culture. Probably ended with the Kurgan invasions.

Features: Enthroned small-breasted goddess vases richly ornamented with panels of geometric symbols. Some male gods (e.g., the "Sickle God"). Rich ritual

paraphernalia: portable altars, kemoi, amphoras, foot-high pedestaled bowls, large bird-headed lids, goddess faced vases; many decorated with meanders, chevrons, and other motifs—"elements of a symbolic language associated with the sphere of the Life-giving Goddess." Four Quarters type design in one pedestal bowl. Burial in wooden coffins built for carrying. Architecture: Multi-roomed, two-story, timber-framed, richly equipped houses and house-temples, with red-painted and incised meander designs on the walls, ovens in each room, and clay animal heads on the gables. Ornamental bulls heads on wall of one house-temple. Various settlement sizes clustered together.
Sites: Gorzsa, Herpaly, Kokenydomb, Veszto.

Lengyal Culture. Middle Danube basin and north-central Europe (western Hungary, northwestern Yugoslavia, eastern Austria, Moravia, western Slovakia, southern Poland), ca. 5000-4000. Descended from the Starcevo culture, influenced by the Danilo-Hvar culture, and supplanted the LBK.

Features: Female figurines with abstract heads (some bird-beaked), small breasts, upraised abbreviated arms, thin waists, and large buttocks (e.g., "Lady of Sé). Offering vessels shaped like a foot, a leg, a bear. Spiral pottery in many shapes.

Architecture: Settlement at Svodin had over 1000 houses. Clay house-temple model with ram or bull head on gable. Trapezoidal longhouses 45 to 132 feet long (15 to 40 m). Three settlement types: large with multiple longhouses, single longhouse, and temporary.

Sites: Zengovarkony, Lengyal, Streelice, Svodin, Luzianky, Aszod, Brzesc Kujawski.

Hamangia Culture. Black Sea coast of Romania and Bulgaria, 5500- 4700.

Features: Noted for a female and male pair of seated, nude, masked, terra cotta figurines less than five inches high, from the Cernavoda cemetery. (The male is called "The Thinker" after Rodin's sculpture.) Other terracottas and marbles include flat-backed White Goddesses of Death and Stiff Nude types from both female and male graves, hand-on-belly pregnant goddesses on village temple walls, and corpulent seated and standing females with columnar heads.

Architecture: Early semi-subterranean pit-houses, hundreds of graves, and later aboveground settlements. No long houses in either the Hamangia or the neighboring Boian culture of the lower Danube basin.

Sites: Dourankulak, Cernavoda, Golovita.

Karanovo-Gumelnita Culture. Western Black Sea and Aegean coasts (Romania, Bulgaria, Turkey, northeastern Greece), 5500-4200. A southward expansion of the Karanovo culture. Features: Magnificent ceramics (including gold-painted pottery) are a focus of aesthetic and technological development. Many spiral designs; also meanders, whirls, crescents, eggs, chevrons, triangles, shell impressions, checkerboards, and four-cornered and linear motifs. Sculptures include several masterpieces such as the enthroned "Lady of Pazardzik," whose vulva is marked with a double spiral. Other figures: Stiff Nudes 100; women with death masks carrying vases; hundreds of tiny, schematic figures with Goddess symbols; birds' heads; and animal heads, masks, and figurines.

Architecture: Massive tells with early well-planned villages with log-paved streets, housing about 300 people in single—room, clay-coated wood-framed dwellings with beehive ovens. Painted interiors in some houses suggest temples. A square village at Poljanica (4800- 4600) has a triple palisade 101 with entrances on all four sides, two main cross-streets, and multi-room timber-framed houses in a rectilinear layout. Villages have two-story central buildings with a worship area on the second floor and workshop underneath. The largest of several painted clay models shows four temples on the upper floor, 103 and some show round windows on the stereobates (lower floor as temple base). Few of the 6000 tells have been excavated, but some in central Bulgaria had as many as 5000 inhabitants.

Sites: Azmak, Karanovo, Vama, Gumelnita, Poljanica, Vinica, Ovcarovo, Radingrad.

Cucuteni (Trpolye) Culture. Northeastern Romania (Moldavia) and western Ukraine, 4800-3500.

Features: Schematic goddess figurines—some with pronounced pubic triangles and buttocks, some heavily incised with chevrons and lozenges—representing the Bird and Snake Goddesses, the Pregnant Goddess, and Stiff Nudes. A few male figurines, one a youthful attendant of the Pregnant Goddess. About thirty percent of figurines and vases represent animals (bears, deer, dogs, pigs, bulls, frogs, and birds). Fine polychrome (white, red, and black) ceramics with S-shapes, chevrons, spirals, meanders, eggs, four-comer designs. Unusual shapes include footed vases, tall (I m) vases, and double-bodied ritual vessels that resemble binoculars. Late Cucuteni vases have pictorial friezes rich with mythic imagery.

Architecture: Due to increasing population density, the largest Late Cucuteni towns were circular or oval, covered 1000 acres (400 hectares), had 2000 buildings arranged in ten to twelve concentric rings, and housed as many as ten thousand people. They had no protective ditches or ramparts. One-story, multi-room houses, twenty-five to one hundred feet long (8-30 m). Two-story, temple buildings with ground floor workshops for making fine ritual ceramics.

Sites: Cucuteni, Tripolye, Habasesti, Trusesti, Petreni, Maydanets'ke, Dobrovody, Tallyanky, Frumusica, Izvoare.

WESTERN AND NORTHERN EUROPE

Funnel-Necked Beaker Culture; (also called TRB, an acronym for the German and Danish names for the culture). 4300-2500. Formed as the Lengyal, Late LBK, and other agriculturalists migrated northward from the Danube basin after the first invasions of the Kurgans (an Indo-European Four Quarters culture from the eastern steppes). Mixing with local mesolithic (between Paleo- and Neo-lithic) populations, they subdivided into regional groups from Holland to Poland and from Bohemia to northern Scandinavia. Features: Various shapes of beakers, amphorae, bowls, and other pottery. Pottery in megalithic graves is named "Tiefstich" for their deep incisions. Pottery rams and ram head handles on ceremonial vases.

Architecture: Earthen long-barrows, megalithic dolmens and passage graves.

Sites: Megaliths and earthworks: Silbury, Avebury, West Kennet Long Barrow, Stonehenge (phase I, ca. 3000) Carnac, Newgrange, Knowth, Dowth, Maes Howe.

SOUTHEASTERN EUROPE

Sesklo Culture. Thessalian and Macedonian plains of northern Greece, 6500-5500.

Sites: Sesklo, Nea Nikomedeia.

Dimini Culture. (Late Neolithic continuation of the Sesklo culture), 5500-4000

Aegean
Cycladic culture, Cyclades Islands, ca. 5200-4600
Cyprus: Khirokitea
Crete: Knossos (7000-
Malta: Hypogeum at Hal Saflieni (4000-2500); megalithic temples at Mnajdra, Hagar Qim, Tarxien, Ggantija (ca. 3500-2500)
Sardinia: Anghelu Ruju hypogea

AFRICA
Egypt
Amratian culture

East Africa
Neolithic Zimbabwe

North Africa
Tassili n'Ajjer

Features: Abundant rock art, pottery, grinding stones, hearths,

ASIA
Northern Asia

Amur Culture. Lower Amur and Ussuri river basins, Far Eastern Russia (Siberian taiga), ca. 4000-2000. Neolithic era ends with advent of the Bronze Age at the end of the second millennium B.C. and the Iron Age in the first millennium.

Features: Fired and burnished clay female figurines found in Neolithic pit dwellings. Pottery vessels, effigies, and balls decorated with spirals, meanders, triangles, zigzags, serpents, and nets. Petroglyphs of animals (bears, elk, tigers), birds, serpents, spirals, concentric rings, and shamanic themes (ape-like masks, rayed masks, x-ray art, spirit images). Mother Goddess worship and abundant spiral ornamentation and survive today among the modern Amur (the Nanai, Olcha, and Nivkh).106

Sites: Kondon, Suchu Island, Nahodka, Takhta, Silkachi-Alian (x-ray animal perroglyphs)

China
Yang Shao Culture

Japan
Jomnn Culture

India
lndus Valley (Harappan) civilization

SOUTH AMERICA

Valdivia Culture. Ecuador, ca. 3550-1600.

Features: Maize cultivated by 4000. Earliest known Andean pottery already displays advanced techniques (no potters' wheels in the New World until the Conquest): red-slips, maize-impressions, incising, engraving, and a variety of shapes including footed bowls, head-rests, and figurines, some of which are hollow. Decorations include lozenges, triangles, crosses, and faces. A bowl dated 2100 has schematic faces and designs that resemble simplified early Chinese masks and I Ching markings (eyes are broken yin lines, mouth is an unbroken yang line). The influential Valdivia style diffused over a wide area. Standing, terracotta, Goddess figurines, up to six inches (15 cm) high, with pronounced breasts, simplified but expressive features, and heavy fringed hair. At least one, dated 2300, is two-headed. A tiny but monumentally styled, geometrically schematized statuette (2400) of grey volcanic rock looks like a prototype of later pre-Columbian hieratic statues such as the Ponce Tela at Tiahuanaco.

Architecture: The town of Real Alto had 120 to 150 large, post and wattle-and-daub, oval huts, about 26 by 33 feet (8 by 12 m) each, aligned around two sunken plans. Since each hut could hold 25 to 30 people, the town had at least 3000 residents. A festival house and a funerary hut stood on mounds near the plazas were. The thatched-roof, funerary hut, 36 feet (1 lm) long, had an undulating oval plan (like Borromini's San Carlo), with a front door and exterior columns in the four indentations around the perimeter. At its entrance was a stone- lined grave of a woman, accompanied by other human remains. 107 (Real Alto's plan resembles contemporary villages of the Brazilian Ge tribe.)

Sites: Valdivia, Real Alto, Loma Alta

Northern Columbia, 3500-
Sites: Puerto Hormiga (Reichel-Dolmatoff has found pottery dating to 3500-3000 B.C.).

MEXICO AND CENTRAL AMERICA
Tehuacan Valley

Features: Maize cultivation arrives sometime between 4000 and 3000 B.C.
Architecture: Permanent villages by 2500. 108
Sites: Tlatilco, Anasazi, Pueblo

EASTERN UNITED STATES

Adena Culture. Ohio River valley,

Features: Seated female figurines, some holding infants, spiral pottery Architecture:

Hopewell Culture. Ohio River valley, south central Ohio, 100 B.C.-A.D. 400.
Features: Spiral pottery, mica effigies (snake, hand, etc.),
Architecture: Small farming settlements clustered around ceremonial centers. Earthen embankments in geometric forms: circles, octagons, squares, some astronomically aligned. Earthen mounds containing burials.

Sites: Newark, Mound City, Serpent Mound

SOUTHWESTERN UNITED STATES

Mogollan Culture. Highlands of Arizona, New Mexico, and northern Mexico, A.D. 750-1250. Name means "Mountain People." Descendants of the Cochise. Considered the earliest agriculturalists, house-builders, and potters in the Southwest. Eventually absorbed by the Anasazi.

Features: Mimbres pottery with elegant stylized geometric and figurative designs. Basketry, weavings, and artifacts of stone, wood, bone, and shell.

Architecture: Early pit-houses and kivas, later above ground structures influenced by Anasazi pueblos.

Sites: Mimbres, Wupatki

Hohokam Culture. Arizona, 300 B.C. ? -A.D. 1450. Name means "Vanished Ones." Decline probably due to drought or salinization of the soil. The modern O'Odham (Pima and Papago) people may be descendants.

Features: Hundreds of miles of irrigations canals. Etching by A.D. 1000.

Architecture: Hall courts,.

Sites: Phoenix, Wupatki, Tuzigoot, Casa Grande

Sinagua Culture, Arizona. Name means 'Without Water"—the Sinagua raised crips without irrigation.

Architecture: Early pit-houses, then stone apartment complexes.

Sites: Montezuma Castle, Wupatki, Tuzigoot, Walnut Canyon

Anasazi Culture. Colorado Plateau and the "Four Comers" area (where Colorado, Utah, Arizona, and New Mexico meet), A.D. 700-. Name means "Ancient Ones." Features: Pottery with abundant spiral designs, petroglyphs

Architecture: Early pit-houses later evolved into aboveground multi-story pueblos and round subterranean kivas topped with plazas. Astronomical alignments and observatories.

Sites: Mesa Verde, Chaco Canyon, Canyon de Chelly, Aztec Ruins, Betatakin, Bandelier, Frijoles, Wupatki, Kayenta.

Pueblo Culture. Western Arizona and New Mexico, ca. A.D. 1100 to present.

Sites: Acoma, San Ildefonso

Appendix 8

Torture of Accused Witches

Some of the practices of the torture of accused witches, and the diabolical informant industry they spawned, are described by Starhawk in her book, *The Spiral Dance: A Rebirth of the Ancient Religion of the Goddess*.

> The terror was indescribable. Once denounced, by anyone from a spiteful neighbor to a fretful child, a suspected Witch was arrested suddenly, without warning and not allowed to return home again. She was considered guilty until proven innocent. Common practice was to strip the suspect naked, shave her completely in hopes of finding the Devil's "marks," which might be moles or freckles. Often the accused were pricked all over their bodies with long, sharp needles, spots the Devil had touched were said to feel no pain. In England, "legal torture" was not allowed, but suspects were deprived of sleep and subjected to slow starvation, before hanging. On the continent, every imaginable atrocity was practiced—the rack, the thumbscrew, "boots" that broke the bones in the legs, vicious beatings—the full roster of the Inquisition's horrors. The accused were tortured until they signed confessions prepared by the Inquisitors, until they admitted to consorting with Satan, to dark and obscene practices that were never part of true Witchcraft ...
>
> Witch hunters and informers were paid for convictions, and many found it a profitable career. The rising male medical establishment welcomed the chance to stamp out midwives and village herbalists, their major economic competitors. For others, the Witch trials offered opportunities to rid themselves of "uppity women," and disliked neighbors. Witches themselves say that few of those tried during the Burning Times actually belonged to covens or were members of the Craft. The victims were the elderly, the senile, the mentally ill, women whose looks weren't pleasing or who suffered from some handicap, village beauties who bruised the wrong egos by rejecting advances, or who had roused lust in a celibate priest or married man. Homosexuals and free thinkers were caught in the same net. At times, hundreds of victims were put to death in a day. In the Bishropic of Trier, in Germany, two villages were left with only a single female inhabitant apiece after the trials of 1585.[1]

Appendix 9
Europe's Radiant Axes Timeline

- First portolan atlas
- 1473 Copernicusbom
- Vasco de Gama's voyage
- 1492 Columbus first voyage to America
- Magellan
- Andre Le Notre designs the Tuileries Gardens for Catherine de Medici
- 1506 Bramante designs St. Peters, Rome
- 1543 Copernicus dies after publishing his heliocentric theory
- 1545 French portolan atlas
- 1545 Michelangelo's Campidoglio, Rome
- 1546-64 Michelangelo's St. Peter's, Rome
- 1546 Tycho Brahe born
- 1564 Galileo born
- 1571 Johannes Kepler born
- 1585-90 Reign of Pope Sixtus V
- 1593 Scamozzi designs Palmanova, Italy
- 1596 Descartes born
- 1601 Tycho Brahe dies
- 1630 Johannes Kepler dies
- 1638-41 Borromini's San Carlo alle Quattro Fontane, Rome
- 1642 Galileo dies, Newton born
- 1643 Louis XIV becomes king
- 1650 Descartes dies
- 1656 Bernini designs St. Peter's Piazza
- 1669 Louis XIV begins to build palace at Versailles outside Paris
- 1727 Newton dies
- 1783 Montgolfier Brother's hot air balloon lifts off at Versailles
- L'Enfant designs Washington, D.C.
- Burnham designs Chicago
- Lutyens designs New Delhi
- Mussolini's axis at St. Peter's

Appendix 10
Le Corbusier's Poem of the Right Angle

Le Corbusier's writings and buildings provide a richly rewarding picture of the way in which an archetype infuses a human spirit with the spirit of the time. They give us a sense of what it means to gestate the seminal energy of a time and give birth to its creations. Le Corbusier is a poet of the Grid archetype as well as one of its foremost architects. (However, I do not wish to give the impression that he was the only modern architect who represented the Grid or that he originated it in some way.)

The manifestoes clearly show how squarely the Grid was lodged in the mind of all the modems, and there are other architects we could just as easily study to see how they represent the Grid: Mies van der Rohe and Walter Gropius, for instance. But Le Corbusier serves as a good case study, since only a handful of other modern architects have had as much impact (Frank Lloyd Wright, Mies van der Rohe, Louis Kahn, and possibly one or two others). During his long and prolific career before his death in 1965, Le Corbusier built his Five Points and a good many other ideas into an impressive body of work, which has influenced at least two generations of architects the world over.

As is often the case with innovators, Le Corbusier was a man of much richer understanding than most of his followers. Many were (and still are) content to copy the outer forms of his esthetic without understanding how they originated or adapting them to changing times as Le Corbusier himself surely would have done. Although the Five Points dealt specifically with how modern buildings should be designed and laid down the principles of the Grid in architecture, this was only their exoteric or overt purpose. Their hidden meaning tapped Le Corbusier's lifelong search for the universal laws of human nature and the phenomenal world, a search that drew him not only to the classical world of Greece and the brassy new world of America, but also into the inner worlds of alchemical metaphor and the collective unconscious. In this he was aided by the work of his Swiss compatriot Carl Jung, which was being published in Europe at the same time that Le Corbusier was formulating his ideas.

Le Corbusier left many records of his inner exploration in his writings and buildings, but the most explicit is in his long "Poem to the Right Angle," which he began in 1947 and completed in 1953. The poem deserves inclusion here, at least in abbreviated form, because it illustrates not only Le Corbusier's spiritual richness, but also the existential basis for modern architecture. It is facile to assume that modern architecture was merely the calculated brain-child of a civilization in its death-throes, although the sterile modern buildings around us may seem to warrant that assumption.

In its incipience, modern architecture was as spiritually exuberant in its expression of the worldview of modern culture as the Egyptian pyramid was in the expression of its culture. From our perspective, living in the decline of the Grid—with its dehumanizing lack of centeredness; its repetitive glass boxes; its industrial environmental destruction; its effect of alienating people from their jobs and from each other; its anonymity, fragmentation, and over-specialization; and its materialistic mechanization of life—we may find it hard to imagine that the Grid was born in the same spirit of wonder and awe as any other archetype. It is in this spirit that Le Corbusier wrote the "Poem of the Right Angle," drawing on the same "visionariness" we have seen inspiring other archetypal eras.

The poem has been analyzed by Richard A. Moore in his catalog to the 1977 Georgia State University exhibition Le Corbusier: Myth and Meta Architecture. Some of the comments that follow are based on the thesis developed in this book-the recurrence of archetypal themes in myth and architecture; some are based on Moore's interpretations; others on those of Ann Koll to whom I am indebted for bringing the catalog and the poem to my attention.

The poem is arranged in seven parts, which Le Corbusier illustrated with a painting he called the *iconostase*, a seven-tiered mural named for the screen of icons in a Russian Orthodox church that separates the altar from the nave. The screen, says Moore, "serves both to veil those elements of the eucharist ritual which only the priests, or initiates, can witness, and to reveal the liturgical promise of salvation in a visual form accessible to the congregation." Presumably Le Corbusier saw his poem and its accompanying mural as serving a similar purpose.

The poem opens with introductory lines setting forth the Sensitive Chaos-like idea that the language of animals and plants can also be spoken by humans:

> Some men can hold
> such discourse as
> well as beasts
> and even perhaps the plants
> And only on this earth
> which is ours

This seems to be a hint that we are entering the universal language of the collective unconscious. The first of the poem's seven parts—and the highest level of the *iconostase*—is called "milieu." It invokes the "sun master of our lives...."

> Exact machine timing
> from time immemorial gives
> birth at each instant of the
> twenty four hours the gradation
> nuance and imperceptibility
> almost giving them
> measure. But he breaks it
> brutally twice the
> morning and the evening (x) The perpetual
> belongs to him while he
> imposes on us the alternative—
> night and day - The two rhythms

which regulate our destiny
> A sun rises
> A sun sets
> A sun rises again

The exact machine—the master timepiece of the Age of Reason's clockwork universe—falls short of giving true measure. Instead, it gives us the alternating rhythms of night and day, which, for Le Corbusier as for countless others throughout history, were the prime symbols of life's dualism between the roiling netherworld of the unconscious and the radiant purity of consciousness.

The next section of "milieu" shows this dualism in another guise as the primordial separation of the waters. Taking the form of a creation myth, it contains the first statement of the *niveau*, the "level" or horizontal plane visualized in archetypal female form as water flowing back to its original level, back to the primordial sea. The active agent that divides this uroboric potentiality is the sun. Like a Titan, the sun causes the "mobility" that overrides the "amorphous." As a result the waters are cleaved, the horizon is established, and being stands upright. Thus, the horizon—the second statement of the *niveau*—makes possible the uprightness of human acts:

> The level establishes where
> stops the descent of the waters
> > to the seas
>
> the sea daughter of droplettes
> and mother of vapors (x) And
> the horizontal defines the
> liquid content.
> Sun streaks ground mist
> condensation squalls clouds
> unstable weights one rises
> and the other sinks sliding
> one on the other rubbing the one
> pushing against the other
> vertically horizontally
> (x) The mobility has over ridden
> the amorphous
> > And from the equator planetary boiler
>
> the buoyant clouds
> departed, grouped,
> regimented, rose
> met and collided
> The storm broke loose.
> > They have cleaved the water
>
> has fallen it streams
> gathers flows
> stretched
> The Universe of our eyes rests
> on a plateau bordered by the horizon

> The fact turned toward the sky
> Consider the space ineffable
> until new beyond grasp.
> To rest to lie down to sleep
> —to die
>   The back to the soil ...
> But I put myself upright!
>   Because you are upright
> here you are up to right acts.
> upright on the terrestrial plateau
> of things perceptible you
> contract with nature an
> act of solidarity: it is the right angle

The separation of the waters is the archetypal Separation of the World Parents. It releases "the space ineffable" where being splits into separate entities brought face to face with each other: "I put myself upright! Because you are upright." This self-versus-other duality extends to nature and a contract is made. The opposition *is* the right angle.

The poem proceeds with awesome images of the hero's classical struggle to emerge fully from the uroboric matrix. There is a tumultuous slipping and sliding back to the worms and serpents and the "potential of carrion" (the nightmare of the nascent ego), all reflected in the meandering courses of rivers and streams as they swarm together into deltas seeking the oblivion of the sea. These are but metaphors for the confusion of emerging consciousness:

> ... The idea
> also fumbles searches bumps into all
> going to extremes asking
> the boundaries of the left and of the
> right. It touches one of the shores
> and then the other. It fixes there
> beached! The truth is there
> only in some place within the stream
> always searching its bed ....

One is reminded of Rainer Maria Rilke's 1904 poem "Tombs of the Hetaerae" in which he, too, likened men's search for self to a buffeting against the boundaries of primordial feminine river beds. Amidst the turmoil, Le Corbusier encounters two paths: the meander, the inexorable movement of nature over the millennia, and the trajectory, the will of life to cut through the vicissitudes of nature:

> The law of meander is active
> in the ideas, thoughts and
> enterprises of men forming their
> ever renewing avatars

But the trajectory gushes out
from the mind and is projected by
the clairvoyants beyond
confusion.

The trajectory cutting through confusion brings polar tension, at first irreconcilable, then resolved in the image of joined hands:

I have thought that two hands
and their interlocking fingers
express this right and
this left unrelentingly
unified and so necessary
to reconciliation.
The only possibility of survival
offered to life.

In this image Le Corbusier suggests the quest for a union of opposites that tests the Hero's fitness to receive the world-enriching gift. The second part of the poem, called "spirit," shows this gift to be tools and inventions that will clear the "route of thorns" and bring liberty. It is a gift of the gods.

To put at the tip of the fingers
and finally in the hand an
agile tool capable of increasing
The harvest of invention
clearing the route of thorns
and cleaning up will give
liberty to your liberty.
Flames borrowed from the tripod
which the gods fed to
insure the games of the world ...
    Mathematical!

And with this gift comes the realization that what the sun could not measure can be measured through the miracle of numbers, with the human body as the proportional standard.

The value is in
this: the human body
chosen as admissible
support of numbers ...
    ... Here is proportion which places
order in our
relation with
our environment

Tools in hand, Le Corbusier now conceives of the primordial house;

> cleared of shackles better
> that before the house of
> men mistress of his form
> takes up its abode in nature.
>   Complete in herself
> making her case on all grounds
> Open to the four horizons
>   it lends its roof
> to the frequentation of the clouds
> or of the sky or of the stars

This is a third statement of the *niveau*, now in the form of a flat roof "open to the four horizons," a fitting stage on which the human figure may stand under the sky to witness space. In this "house of men mistress of his form" the human figure is the *aplomb* or "plumb line," the vertical axis of will and action. This axis is like the gnomen of the sundial that registers the sun's shadows and, therefore, its movement. It is, in other words, the *perceiver*. The next section of the "spirit" part of the poem brings the sun and architecture together in a cosmic epiphany.

> dance the Earth and the sun
>   the dance of the four seasons
>   the dance of the year
>   the dance of the days of
>   twenty-four hours
> The summit and the abyss of the
> solstices
> the plain of equinoxes
> The clock and the sundial
> brought to
> architecture the 'sun breaker'
> installed in front of the windows of
> modern buildings. An
> architectural symphony
> gets ready under this title:
> "The House Daughter of the Sun'
> and Vignola finally is had
>   Merci!
>   Victory!

(The jibe at the Renaissance architect Vignola is a jibe at neo-classical architecture.) Following this vigorous proclamation of victory, Le Corbusier relaxes in the third part of the poem called "flesh," where he leaves the brilliance of the sun for another kind of warmth in the realm of the senses. After musing on various visceral animal instincts in us, he surrenders himself to reflections on love.

> The woman always somewhere
> at the crossroads is meaningful to us

> that love is a game of destiny
> of numbers and of luck
> at the crossing as accidental
> as it is inexorable of two particular
> roads suddenly marked by a surprising happiness!
> > One could be two and of two
> and not combine the two.

The world of flesh subsumes the miracles of numbers into love's game of chance at the crossroads of destiny, sublimely recalling the more primitive crossing of the meander and the trajectory. Le Corbusier now relaxes the trajectory and luxuriates in the natural feminine law of the meander, which, further on in the poem, leads him to the unconscious through "the profound refuge...in the great cavern of sleep that other side of life in the night." He muses on harmony and tenderness. He dallies in caressing a seashell ("The hand and the shell love one another"), and he meanders into the realization that the abandonment of reason may bring truth nearer.

> finally subtracted
> from control
> of
> reason
> carried beyond
> daily
> realities
> admitted
> to the heart
> of an
> illumination
> God
> incarnated
> in
> the illusion
> the perception
> of truth
> maybe
> well

But Le Corbusier's affair with the senses also has a grounding effect, bringing him to earth, to daily life, and to his mortal body.

> But he must be on
> the earth and
> present
> in order to
> attend
> his own
> wedding

> to be
> at home
> in the sack of his skin
> to do his affairs for himself and say thank you to the creator

The mention of a wedding brings to "flesh" the hint of *hieros gamos* and the possibility of fusion as an alternative to the earlier formulation, "one could be two and of two and not combine the two." Le Corbusier's romance with the feminine, colored with the rosiness of his projected *anima* (his idealized feminine side), is also tinged with the blues of an ordinary love-weary adult male.

> The men speak
> of women in their poems
> and their music
> They carry on their side an
> eternal laceration from top
> to bottom They are but
> half, giving
> to life only one half
>   and the second part comes
> to them and fuses
> And good or bad comes to them
> the two
> who met

That Le Corbusier was indeed building up to a *hieros gamos* union is revealed in the title of the fourth section: "fusion." Here he refers directly to the powerful alchemical symbol of the fusion of metals, which in turn evokes Jung's *coniunctio* or union of opposites. Like one who has glimpsed the potential fullness of being, he couches his revelation in a plea for tolerance of the risk-taker, of the one who is actively engaged in life.

> sitting on too many mediating causes
> seated at the side of our lives
> and the others there
> and everywhere is the: "No."
> And always more against
> than for
> Do not overwhelm then he
> who wants to take his part of the
> risks of life. Let
> the metals fuse
> tolerate the alchemists who
> besides leave you outside
> the cause
>   It is by the door of the
> open pupils that glances
> meeting could lend to

> the terrifying act of communion
> 'The unfolding the grand
> silences'...
>   The sea has recoiled
> to low tide in order
> to be able to come back on time.
> A new time opens up
> a stage a delay an interruption
> Then let us not be
> at rest sitting at the side of our lives.

The fourth section, on "fusion" quoted above in its entirety, is the centerpiece of the whole poem around which the first and last three parts revolve. The "terrifying act of communion: 'The unfolding the grand silences'" consummates the inner journey, which, in the first half of the poem, has taken us from primal creation through all the archetypal stages of the Hero's quest. The last half brings the seeds of that journey to fruition in the world. The fifth part of the poem, on "character" establishes Le Corbusier's identity as an active participant in life. To set the theme of action, it begins with images of horses, battles, amazons, soldiers, (and fish) and then goes on to define character in terms of the right angle.

> ...
> Categorical
> right angle of the character
> of the spirit of the heart
> I mirrored myself in this character
> and found myself there
> found at home
> found
> Horizontal vision in front,
> of the spires

There follows another invocation of Le Corbusier's anima. This time her grounding effect appears as the conscience that tempers arrogance with the humility of the child, the heart, and the earth.

> It is she who rightly reigns
> she detains the arrogance
> and does not know it
> Who has made it thus where
> she comes from
> She is the rectitude of the child of the
> limpid heart present on the earth
> near me. Humble acts
> and daily are guaranteed
>   by her grandeur.

Finally, Le Corbusier knows who he is.

> I am a constructor
> of houses and of palaces
> I live among men
> among their entangled skins
> to create architecture is to make a creature.
> To be filled to fill oneself to have
> been filled to burst to rejoice
> ice cold at the heart of
> complexity. To become a game
> happy pup
> To become order,
> The modern cathedrals
> will be constructed on this
> alignment of fish
> of horses of amazons
> The constancy the uprightness the
> patience the wait the desire
> and the vigilance
> will appear l sense it
> The splendor of brute concrete
> and the grandeur which it will
> have had to think the marriage
> of lines
> to weight the forms
> to weight ...

The fullness of his being is fused into the making of architecture. There is no separation between who he is and what he creates. He is the constructor of houses and palaces. Bringing archetypal patterns into concrete realization, he *weights the forms*. He is the master of *techne*.

The original gift of tools and inventions received from the gods (from the collective unconscious) has been worked and shaped and processed through the character of a singular human being to create works that, recalling their origin in the universal Self, are in the nature of an offering symbolized by the open hand. The sixth part of the poem, titled "offer" describes this hand.

> It is open since
> all is present available
> seizable
> Open to receive
> Open also in order that each
> comes there to take
> > The waters stream
> > The sun illumines
> > The complexities have woven
> > their web
> > the fluids are everywhere
> The tools in the hand

> The caresses of the hand
> The life that they tasted by
> the kneading of the hands
> The view from which is in the touch.
> ....
> Full hand I received
> Full hand I give

The seventh and last part of the poem, called "tool," is a simple expression of the ultimate meaning of the right angle: existential choice.

> One traced
> with a piece of coal
> the right angle
>   the sign
> It is simple and naked
> but perceptible
> The savants discuss
> the relativity of its precision
> But awareness
> has made it a sign
> It is the response and the guide
> The fact.
> my response
> my choice.

The "Poem of the Right Angle" unlocks the deepest meaning of the Grid in modern architecture and the contemporary psyche, shedding new light on the Five Points. The column grid and the free plan dance with each other like the trajectory and the meander. The flat roof is the *niveau*, the horizontal plane of being on which the human figure stands upright before the cosmos, The horizontal windows open the eye to the epiphany of sun and space.

In seeing the human body as the "proportion which places order in our relation with our environment" Le Corbusier echoed the Renaissance idea, taken from the 5th century B.C, Greek sophist Protagoras: "Man is the measure of all things." Expressing this idea architecturally with his "Modular," a system that used the age-old Golden Section to multiply the proportions of the body to the scale of buildings and ultimately to the scale of the universe, Le Corbusier sought to make his architecture a mediator between the Self and the Cosmos, just as the Greeks and Egyptians before him had used the Golden Section in their temples and pyramids. Vincent Scully, Charles Jencks, and others have noted that, in his glorification of the individual standing erect, heroic, and free, Le Corbusier was essentially a Hellenic architect. His buildings stand apart from nature, just as Greek temples glisten pure against their surroundings, and just as the perfect human form in Greek statues stands free in space.

But Le Corbusier was also expressing something very modern: the existential idea that who and what we are is totally a matter of choice. Who and what we are is not dictated, in this view, by any pre-existing determinant, neither church, nor state, nor caste of birth, nor will of God. Being defined by nothing, we are absolutely free to define ourselves. "The fact. My response/my choice." This is pure Grid. It dissolves all previous centers of reference and puts in their place a void, a nothingness, as in Sartre's *Being and Nothingness*. All of the coagulating mechanisms of traditional society and culture are scattered to the winds across the endless Gridded landscape of the modern mind.

456 Spatial Archetypes

Appendix 11

Architecture and Chakras

Modern architecture's complicity in the homogenization of the world under Western standards goes back to the visions of the manifesto writers. They proclaimed that the modern esthetic was appropriate not only for the West, but for the entire world. They were certain that it would beneficently sweep away the cobwebs of old cultures everywhere on earth, uniting all people in the brilliance of the Machine Age. This vision produced one of their most devastating assumptions: that modern architecture is "culture-free" or culturally neutral. This assumption betrays the ethnocentric bias of the modernists. They did not realize that modem architecture is as culturally specific to the industrialized West as Japanese architecture is to Japanese culture or Islamic architecture is to Islamic culture. They either did not realize or did not care that different cultures express and celebrate their different worldviews through their architecture.

Intoxicated by the illusion of progress, the modernists assumed that every un-industrialized (better than the biased term "pre-industrialized") country was implicitly backward and naturally longed to be brought into the Machine Age. They were ignorant of the archetypal stratum of human civilization, which ensures a natural unity that makes superficial uniformity (of architectural style, for instance) superfluous and degrading. Yet, because of its assumed cultural neutrality and its economic advantages to the military-industrial Grid, modern architecture has been promoted with great missionary zeal.

Not only has the "International Style" (as Philip Johnson and Henry Russell Hitchcock dubbed modern architecture in 1932) mushroomed in the large cities of every nation; it is also spreading in the form of crude prefab housing or concrete-block and tin-roofed hovels being exported to "developing" nations in fruitless attempts to clear the burgeoning slums that industrialization brings. This housing, which is much like the slum-clearance projects in the U.S., is the Grid at its worst, reducing people to the lowest common denominator of biological functioning. The first criterion in the minds of its designers is hygiene. If the housing provides running water and toilets (along with basic shelter from the elements, of course), then it is considered to have done its job. Only very recently have a few critics ventured to suggest that people need more than hygiene if they are to be housed like human beings.

One can test the *humanness* of architecture against five criteria based on the chakras of Kundalini yoga:

1. FUNCTIONAL: Muladhara Chakra

Is the work structurally sound? Does it foster the health of all life forms, human and animal alike? Is it ecologically sound? (This criterion needs to be applied to the entire making of a work, from raw materials to finished product.)

2. INDIVIDUAL: Svadisthana Chakra

Does it satisfy the individual's capacity for sensual delight, fantasy, humor, and self-expression?

3. SOCIAL: Manipura Chakra

Does it contribute to the health of social structures, customs, institutions, economies, and communications?

4. CULTURAL: Anahata Chakra

Does it preserve and embody living cultural heritage, myths, history, and traditions? Does it speak a meaningful cultural language?

5. SPIRITUAL: Vishuddi, Ajrna, and Svadisthana Chakras

Is it in harmony with the order of the universe? Is it a mediator between the Self and the Cosmos?

These five sets of questions never fail to reveal the extent to which a work of architecture, whether house or city, fulfills human needs and aspirations. By these criteria, much of modern architecture fails. It addresses only the first or functional questions, and does not solve even them very well.

In contrast, most indigenous "architecture without architects" addresses these issues with a sensitivity deepened by hundreds of years of being built in the same locale by the same society. Functional needs arising from the local climate and ecology are usually met with ease and grace. Individual expression and sensual delight abound in folk-art decorations, texturally rich assemblages, and brightly colored paints. The social structure of families and communities is finely woven into the very fabric of houses and villages. Cultural heritage flourishes everywhere in painted and carved religious symbols and historical scenes, in special shrines for the ancestors, in the overall look and feeling and layout of a town. The spiritual is never very far away. Even the humblest abode—a yurt, a tipi, a mud hut—is a model of the cosmos.

No matter how poor people are by material measures, when left to their own devices, they surround themselves with an architecture that expresses the full spectrum of their humanity. Poverty is not due to the indigenous poverty of their culture, but rather to the disruption brought about by Westernization. To assume that this sensitive spectrum can be replaced by a concrete block house with a toilet (the latter being a 1596 European invention that people managed to live without for millennia) is the height of arrogance. This well-intended but architecturally and culturally degrading type of home is foisted upon millions of "Third World" people (both at home and abroad) under the technological juggernaut of the West's Grid civilization.

The mentality that produced such an impoverished idea of what constitutes adequate architecture is summed up by Spengler's observation of the prevailing role of science in declining civilizations:

> Scientific worlds are superficial worlds, practical, soulless and purely extensive worlds .... Life is no longer to be lived as something self-evident—hardly a matter of consciousness, let alone choice—or to be accepted as God-willed destiny, but is to be treated as a problem, presented as the intellect sees it, judged by "utilitarian" or "rational" criteria .... The brain rules because the soul abdicates.[1]

For the most part, people with vested interests in the military-industrial Grid are willing to subject others to the degradations of slum-clearance housing because they themselves do not have the depth of being that would tell them that something is missing. The warming ties they might have had to fantasy, sensual delight, social involvement, cultural heritage, The spiritual wonder has been cut by the cold utilitarian Grid. People in whom these ties are dead cannot perceive them at work in the lives of others.

The reduction of architecture to a utilitarian, problem-solving, pseudo-science is most clearly seen in the Bauhaus, a German school that flourished prior to World War II, where artists and architects tried to fulfill the goals of the modern movement by designing prototypes for industry. The Bauhaus attempted to integrate high design into mass-production to bring modernism to the masses. In this it was only partly successful, but its method of education was extremely influential and completely transformed the way architects saw themselves and the way they designed buildings.

The Bauhaus curriculum was based on the revolutionary idea that what an architect does is *solve problems*, working from a program of stated objectives like an engineer or an industrial designer. In effect, this made the architect into a calculator instead of an *artist*. The previously prevailing approach of the École des Beaux Arts and other academies was founded on an altogether different tradition. Drawing on history, it recognized that what an architect did essentially was to express something meaningful—the nature of the state, the spirit of the church, the essence of an institution. Problems arose and were solved along the way, but they were not the focus and *raison d'etre* of the work. This kind of design required immense inner resources. It demanded that the architect be not only technically competent but also a master of the symbolic power of architecture. The important question to the artist-architect was "What does it mean?" The problem-solving architect asks only "Does it work?"

Appendix 12

Modern American Architecture

Until shortly before World War II, American architects were living in an historical environment different from that of the European architects. Compared to the age-weary countries of Europe, America was still young and ripe with opportunity, unexplored territory, growth potential, and an innocent faith in democracy. While Europe's mainstream architects slogged through centuries-old philosophical and social conundrums, advancing carefully positioned attitudes in their works and writings, America's architects simply rolled up their sleeves and built! Unselfconsciously, they started on the East coast with the townhouses and plantations of the rich, and then moved with the Great American Westward Expansion toward California, dotting the eastern woodlands and mid-western plains with middle-class houses, banks, office buildings, department stores, libraries, colleges—whatever needed to be built. Chicago, the steel-conscious center of the country, spawned a school of skyscraper-builders who left Europe in awe. Robert Hughes writes:

> The skyscraper, like other things American, intrigued the European public; it seemed to be the American equivalent of the Eiffel Tower, and the *Wolkenkratzer* (or "cloud-scratcher," as the Germans called it) became an object of romance and fantasy. It was identified with Promethean democracy *all' Americana* and in this [Louis] Sullivan himself heartily concurred: "With me," he remarked, "architecture is not an art, but a religion, and that religion is but a part of Democracy." The modular grid was the face of equality.[1]

Although Sullivan (Frank Lloyd Wright's mentor) heartily exploited the steel frame grid in his skyscrapers, and although he is the source of the much misunderstood dictum "form follows function" he never let his buildings stand stark naked. Instead, he swathed their cornices and spandrels in the most sensuously beautiful terra cotta arabesques and floral ornaments. To him, these were a revealed part of the religion of architecture—the part that evoked recognition and the possibility of human kinship with the structure. He also proportioned his skyscrapers in harmony with the human form, and because of this Vincent Scully calls him "the great, perhaps the only, humanist architect of the late nineteenth century."[2]

While the European architects were infatuated with the machine and idealized it in their esthetic to the point of fanatic sterility, American architects took the machine for granted and were not in awe of it. Industrialization came earlier in Europe than in America, but always had to accommodate itself to already congested social and physical conditions. America gave industry a clean slate. Industrialization was the Manifest Destiny of the nation. It was a practical fact of life, a tool to be used to further human comfort, not to be worshipped for its own sake.

In *The Architecture of the Well-Tempered Environment*, Reyner Banham illustrates the contrast between European and American attitudes toward the machine with two houses, one by Le Corbusier and the other by Frank Lloyd Wright. The Villa Cook by Le Corbusier (1926) exemplifies the stark, sterile machine esthetic; but its actual use of technology is so crude that its living room has only a single exposed radiator under its long ribbon window—hardly adequate to fight the profuse downdrafts that such windows cause. Furthermore, in the geometrical center of the ceiling hangs a bare light bulb so bright and glaring that it burned a hole in the emulsion of the photograph of the room taken for Le Corbusier's *Complete Works*. Wright's Robie House (1910), on the other hand, has a brick-and-wood warmth far removed from the machine esthetic, but its use of technology is much more sophisticated and innovative than Villa Cook's. As a "Prairie House," born of the American plains, it has long horizontal lines molded by gently sloping overhanging roofs, which shield the interior from the glare of the sun in a way that is impossible in the boxy, flat-roofed Le Corbusier house. Then, to mediate the cold that does seep in through its bands of casement windows, it has wooden grilles masking a series of radiators extensive enough to adequately fight downdraft. Wright also made provisions for small radiators to be sunk into the floor under brass grilles in front of French windows. He put hot pipes in cupboards, slotted so that warm air could circulate. Instead of a bare bulb as the single source of light, the house has dimmer-controlled ceiling lighting recessed above oaken slats, as well as frosted globes set in "Japonaiserie frames" that provide soft illumination. Finally, Wright designed the house in such a way that any excess heat from the sun, the radiators, or the lights would be vented through a circulating air space under the sloping roof. Thus, where Le Corbusier and the European modernists in general emulated the look of the machine but failed to master its use, Frank Lloyd Wright and other American architects mastered the use of technology, but subordinated it to the creation of humane architecture.

In consequence, modern architecture was proceeding along two different paths: the European, toward a stripped-down machine esthetic that reduced everyone to a common level; the American, toward a technologically advanced but robustly individualistic tradition. Unfortunately, the American path dead-ended when some of the most famous European architects came to America to escape Hitler's Germany in the 1930s. America has always had an inferiority complex about Europe, and the refugee architects immediately found high positions in American Schools. Mies van der Rohe (the designer of New York's Seagram Building) went to head the school that became IIT in Chicago. In the same city, Lazlo Moholy-Nagy turned the Institute of Design into an American Bauhaus. Walter Gropius, the guiding spirit of the original Bauhaus, became chairman of Harvard's School of Architecture. By 1938, the winning submissions to the major design competitions were in the European style, and by the early 1950s the last Beaux-Arts types of schools shifted to the Bauhaus model. The conversion was so complete that in many schools the name of Frank Lloyd Wright was an anathema.

Once the European takeover was complete in the intellectual arena—in the schools, competitions, journals, and in institutions like the Museum of Modern Art (which played a major role in proselytizing the new esthetic)—it was only a matter of time before it would hit the streets and transform the built environment. The big boost came after World War II, both in Europe and America. Europe needed to rebuild its decimated cities, and America needed housing for the post-war baby-boom families, as well as facilities for its new industrial prosperity. European modernism allowed cheap, easily constructed, mass producible buildings, and the manufacture of their component parts was itself a lucrative industrial enterprise. Furthermore, it was an easy style for architects with limited talent and skill.

The moral and social issues the Europeans thought they were dealing with had become irrelevant by this time. Although the public never really liked modern architecture, there was no choice but to accept it—not because it was uniting them in a wondrous world of the future, but because it was the most commercially expedient way to build. Thus, today we find ourselves constrained to live in rectangular cubicles with eight foot ceilings; to work in factories and offices that surround us with only what is needed to maintain proper body temperatures and illumination levels for the tasks at hand; to send our children to school in fluorescent-lit "jerry-built nowhere"; to park in *Alphaville* garages and shop in muzak-architecture malls.

Several years ago at a conference on "Women and Minorities in Architecture," a black professor spoke about the differences between the slave quarters and the big house in Southern plantations. He showed how the plantation owner's dwelling in the big house enjoyed a stunning architectural richness that articulated their every activity in grand spaces—domed entranceways, winding processional staircases, bay windows for reading on a sunny day, elegantly symmetrical libraries, perfectly oval dining rooms, suites of bedrooms and sitting rooms. In contrast, the slaves were confined to mean little rectangular, flat-roofed low-ceilinged quarters. One could not avoid reflecting on the similarity to European modern architecture, which houses everyone as the plantation owners housed the slaves.

Many American architects wanted to bring the full richness of architecture to every individual—witness Burnham's plan for Chicago, Wright's Usonian houses, Olmstead's Central Park, the Chicago World's Fair, L'Enfant's plan for Washington, D.C., the Beaux-Arts scheme for Jones Beach in New York, and the innumerable monumental public libraries, museums, courthouses, banks and train stations throughout the country. Tragically, the American vision was mowed under by the European.

The contrast between these two views is much deeper than the surface esthetics of architecture. They represent two very different interpretations of Enlightenment ideals. Both rejected monarchical elitism. Both attempted to design for equality. But the Europeans, who were deeply influenced by socialism, said, "Everyone is a worker. We will put everyone in worker's housing." The Americans looked out over the horizon of the New World and said, "Everyone is a worthy idividual. We will put everyone in a special home."

The European view defined human beings in social terms, and, in the social community of the Grid, people tend to act as organizational creatures. They bureaucratize. They test alternatives by utilitarian rationales. They see the individual as a cog in the machinery of civilization. The American view struggled for a definition of human beings in individual terms. How profound the difference!

In the lonely individuality of the Grid we can discover a spiritual quality. We can discover a private wholeness within each of us. We can each see ourselves as worthy idividual, a Hero, and an embodiment of the great transpersonal Self. We can discover in ourselves a residue of all that has gone before and is yet to be. The American view is, I think, closer to the coming understanding of humanity. It recognizes that the archetypes we have been projecting throughout recorded history into goddesses and gods, chieftains and rulers, heroes and demons, friends and enemies, savages and savants, are in reality united and ever-present within each of us. Each human being carries the sum total of human experience and potential. This is the "Promethean democracy *all' Americana*" that so baffles and intrigues the European.

It is a uniquely American sense born of our nation's rootlessness and lack of history, and of the great plains in which so many of us grew up—and whose impress we carry wherever we go. It is a restless searching for roots and heritage that can never be satisfied by anything American since we are essentially a nation of immigrants and land-robbers. Thus our eyes can rise to the big sky above the great plains, across the distant horizon to foreign lands where our genes had their biological ancestors, where our humanness searches for archaic strength, where our soul can quicken to the echoes of previous lives, where our ideologies find social models, where the mythic part of our minds can find strangely familiar resonances. This part of us is the best of what America can have given us. It is the part that can transcend the specificities of tribe, village, and culture because our interconnections are so tenuous and mobile. There is pain in this. There is also a reward: the possibility of an expanse of understanding not open to those whom we may secretly envy for their innocent embeddedness in the certainties and specificities of traditional life. Perhaps this is the positive side of the alienated, existential Grid of individual freedom that has been taken to an extreme in America more than anywhere else.

Perhaps this is what even the European modernists envisioned bequeathing to the citizens of the New World. That we have all been defined as workers, drones, and slaves by the execution of the Grid need not be the final expression of the archetype.

ENDNOTES

ENDNOTES FOR INTRODUCTION

1. Louis Kahn 1979: 54.
2. Archetypes (Heaven, Earth, World Mountain, Dragon-Slayer, Great Goddess, and so on) are capitalized. In some cases, the same word can signify the archetype itself or its local, specific, or generic manifestation. "Pyramid" is one such word. "Pyramid" (capitalized) refers to the Pyramid archetype, while "pyramid" (lower case) might refer to a generic shape or to specific architectural pyramids. During the Old Kingdom in Egypt, the Pyramid archetype inspired the building of numerous, massive, stone pyramids that survive to this day.
3. For example, here were a few of the New York Open Center's offerings in Fall 1992: Taoist Qi Gong, A Day with a Russian Healer, the Egyptian Healing Mysteries, A Walking Tour of China Town's Herb Markets, Little India Walk, Intermediate Shiatsu, T'ai Chi Chuan, Afrocize, Tibetan Yantra Yoga, Dream Work Within a Sufi Tradition, Kundalini Awakening, The Tea Ceremony, The Spirit of Aloha, Astrology and the Kabbalah, the Sacramental Gnosis of Jesus, Judaism as a Sacred Path, Lakota Sioux Worldview, the Viking Runes, The Way of the Shaman, I Ching, Buddhist Spirituality and American Democracy, Aboriginal Life and the Didjeridu, Middle Eastern Dance, Flamenco, Language of the Drums, Hot Gospel, the Sacred Stone Art of Scotland, Divine Horsemen Video, Huichol Arts & Culture trip, and A Los Incas Concert.
4. Jaynes 1976: 59-61.
5. I suspect that this spatialization occurs whether we are visually, orally, or tactilely oriented. For Instance, where visually oriented people see spatial patterns and structures in their minds, orally oriented people conceptualize similar structures when they hear music or receive auditory clues from the environment. I would enjoy hearing from anyone who has scientifically researched this or conducted laboratory experiments on it.
6. Mies van der Rohe 1986: 74.
7. The name of this archetype comes from *The Sensitive Chaos*, a book by Theodor Schwenk on the spiraling currents of air, water, and other natural forces.
8. Cassirer 1944.
9. Neumann 1970. See Appendix 2. (Drawing parallels between Sensitive Chaos people and children emphatically does not suggest that Sensitive Chaos people are "childish" or that children are "little savages." In fact, I fervently hope that this book can help to eradicate such backward views. Sensitive Chaos people have complete, fully mature, social systems. For practical and spiritual reasons, they choose to adhere to the Uroboric worldview even though they are capable of the same skills as industrialized peo-

ple—as shown when contemporary hunter-gatherers are assimilated into the modern world and become wage laborers or computer programmers.
10. The Great Round archetype's name is taken from an aspect of the feminine principle described by Erich Neumann in *The Great Mother: Analysis of the Archetype*.
11. Neumann 1970. See Appendix 1.
12. The Bronze and Iron Ages are time frames of the Old World. The same sequence of archetypes occurs in the New World, though the names of the periods are not standardized and do not easily lend themselves to a brief listing. (The "Old World" is the Eastern Hemisphere—roughly Europe and the Mediterranean, the Middle East, Africa, Asia, and possibly Australia and part of Oceania. The "New World" is the Western Hemisphere—the Americas and possibly part of Oceania. Since some cultures in the so-called "New World" are as old as some cultures in the so-called "Old World," the terms can be misleading, but they are in common usage. "Eastern" and "Western" Hemispheres can be confusing, too, since Europe is considered to be in the Eastern Hemisphere, but we commonly refer to it as part of the 'West.")
13. Neumann 1970. See Appendix 1.
14. The Four Quarters archetype takes its name from John Weir Perry's book *The Four Quarters: Myths of the Royal Father*.
15. Even when the two realms are presented as being ostensibly complementary or harmoniously balanced, as in China's yin-yang philosophy, in practice the "masculine" realm is the more highly valued or socially powerful or both, while the "feminine" is enjoined to maintain harmony by being submissive to this greater power.
16. Neumann 1970. See Appendix 1.
17. Neumann 1970. See Appendix 1.

ENDNOTES FOR THE SENSITIVE CHAOS

1. Theodor Schwenk 1965: 9; quoting Novalis, Fragments, 1909.
2. We need to rescue the word "primitive" from the negative connotations of "backward" and "savage" that it gained when social Darwinism dominated scholarship. Throughout this book, the word "primitive" means "primal" or "original," indicating our earliest roots, through which we can tap into the deepest wisdom in our being.
3. According to child psychologist Piaget, very young children have not yet developed egos. (Piaget 1975 and Gardner 1974). This is another seeming correspondence between young children and hunter-gatherers.
4. It is important to remember that we are seeing models of major types of cultures and worldviews generated by the spatial archetypes. No specific culture will exhibit all the characteristic of the model it most closely resembles. See "Bits of Colored Glass."
5. Cassirer 1944: 81.

6. Farb 1978: 89.
7. Some scholars are replacing the term "hunter-gatherers" with "gatherer-hunters," recognition that the food gathered by women provides more of the diet than the meat hunted by men. I use the two terms interchangeably. See Dahlberg 1981 for discussions of women's roles in hunting-gathering cultures.
8. A Dutch archaeologist claims to have evidence of animal carvings and female figurines produced over 200,000 years ago—170,000 years earlier than any other art ever found. See Musch 1985.
9. Stewart 1988: 24.
10. Some of the most beautiful art of Egypt's Pyramid and Radiant Axes cultures (the Old and New Kingdoms, respectively) celebrates gods and goddesses in their animal forms—the celestial cow-goddess Hathor, one of the earliest Egyptian deities; the lion-headed sun-goddess Sekhmet, whose sphinxes lined avenues to monumental New Kingdom sun temples; Horus, the solar falcon, symbol of the living pharaoh; the ibis-headed magician-scribe Thoth and the jackal-god Anubis, who officiated at funerals; Buto, the cobra-goddess who ruled Lower Egypt, and her counterpart in Upper Egypt, the vulture-goddess Nekhbet. In Egypt, some sacred animals were mummified when they died, and, like pharaohs, were accorded elaborate burials. Much Indian art also illustrates the animal incarnations and vehicles of Hindu deities.
11. Giedion 1964: 99.
12. The stele reveals also the glorification of ego that typically accompanies the development of hierarchical societies: Ningirsu, presumably the patron who commissioned the stele, is portrayed much larger and mightier than his enemies.
13. Giedion 1964: 61.
14. "Non-literate" is more accurate than "pre-literate"; "non-agricultural" better than "pre-agricultural"; "non-industrial" better than "preindustrial"; "non-historic" better than "pre-historic"; and so on. "Pre" implies that the culture will progress inexorably from "pre-literate" to "literate," "pre-industrial" to "industrial" etc., fulfilling its natural destiny to become like "us." Replacing "pre-" with "non-" recognizes that these cultures make choices and are complete in their own right, rather than stuck in some backward stage in an inevitable line of progress.
15. Lonsdale 1981: 12.
16. Blurton Jones and Konner 1976: 328.
17. Biesele 1976: 309.
18. Campbell 1983: 90-101; also Katz 1976: 282-301.
19. Described by Marshall McLuhan in *Understanding Media*
20. See Feininger 1975, and Schwenk 1965.
21. Particularly the weak currents blanketing the earth's surface that NASA scientists have found in maps made by the Magsat satellite of "magnetic anomalies" in the earth's crust, Bartusiak 1981. [And since Mimi wrote this, it has been discovered that some birds detect magnetic currents and use them to navigate. JL]
22. Gleick 1987: 228-29.

466 *Spatial Archetypes*

23. Katz 1976: 286.
24. Katz 1976
25. Eliade 1964: 99.
26. Tibetan Buddhists—one of the few cultures living today in the Pyramid archetype—know this heat as *Tummo*, which they cultivate through yogic practices partly as a spiritual exercise and partly to survive the cold climate.
27. Krishna 1971: 107.
28. Griaule 1970: 19-20.
29. Lao Tsu: 1972.
30. Cognition: the prefix co- (together with) + the Indo-European root gno-(to know, as in gnosis), meaning "together with knowledge" or "to learn."
31. I myself had this experience occasionally in the late 1960s and early 1970s
32. Lamb 1971: 88.
33. Lamb 1971: 90-91.
34. Kensinger 1978: 12.
35. Harner 1978: 15-16.
36. It can take apprentice shamans a year or more of diligent study to learn their chants and songs, and without them, they may see only terrifying visions of snakes (Siskind 1978: 32).
37. Note the similarity to the !Kung dancers remark, "But when you get into !kia, you're looking around because *you see everything*, because you see what's troubling everybody…" [My italics.].
38. Because shamanic healing acts on a mythological level, it has psychological effects that can supplement Western medical treatment. It does not have to be an "either-or" choice. The systems within which the two forms of healing operate are different—the one, psychological; the other, physical—thus, they are inherently complementary and mutually reinforcing.
39. Krishna 1971: 213, my italics.
40. Eliade 1964: 482-486.
41. Elkin 1964: 211-212.
42. Maria Reiche, a German schoolteacher, dedicated about fifty years to surveying, studying, recording, and preserving the Nazca lines and figures, mostly without financial support. For her work, see Kunstraum München 1974. For more on her, see Hadingham 1987: 60-89.
43. Hawkins 1973: 141.
44. Hadingham 1987: 141.
45. Zuidema 19W.
46. Jung 1965: 20-21.
47. Holm 1961: 187.
48. Castaneda is a reclusive person, and his inaccessibility has given rise to questions about how literal his accounts really are, but anthropologists generally accept the accuracy of his descriptions of shamanistic activity.
49. The Yaqui are not a Sensitive Chaos culture. They are closer to the Four Quarters, another archetype in which shamanism is quite common.
50. Castaneda 1972: 187-189.
51. Fraser 1968: 13.
52. Fraser 1968: 13.
53. Yellen 1976: 54.

54. Yellen 1976: 65.
55. England 1968.
56. Though some anthropologists report evidence of "headmen" in certain Bushman groups, the power of these men is very limited and does not alter their basic equality with other band members Other archaeologists have found no evidence of headmen in !Kung groups.
57. Yellen observed that most of a !Kung family's possessions can be carried by one adult.
58. Lonsdale 1981: 187-188.
59. In his lectures, Joseph Campbell often commented that Jung said to James Joyce, in reference to the writer's schizophrenic daughter, "She is drowning in the same ocean you are swimming in." The shaman's visions come from the same realm as the madman's delusions.
60. Argüelles 1975.
61. Marshack 1972.

ENDNOTES FOR THE GREAT ROUND

1. Neumann 1972: 211.
2. In this book, "civilization" can refer to a loose grouping of cultures characteristic of the archetype under discussion (e.g., the Great Round civilization), as well as to a unified, contiguous, single civilization in the usual sense (e.g., Chinese civilization). This seems appropriate, since even though the cultures of the Great Round, for example, flourished in widely differing parts of the world, millennia apart from each other, they nonetheless shared a significant number of characteristics (see "Synopsis of the Great Round"). The same is true of all the archetypes.
3. Garraty 1972: 47.
4. Stierlin 1984: 27.
5. Majno 1975: 112-115.
6. Many scholars reject the idea that there ever were matriarchal cultures in ancient times, let alone that there was a "Golden Age of Matriarchy" They assume that a matriarchy would be the mirror image of a patriarchy. Not finding cultures with the same kinds of social structures, values, and institutions that we have today but with women in dominant positions instead of men—in other words, not finding evidence of strong queens, women warriors, and oppressed men—they decide that matriarchies never existed. Their assumptions eliminate the possibility of finding an altogether different kind of society. For more on this problem see Lobell 1986b.

   Both the terms matriarchal and patriarchal have become "buzzwords" with a "charge" that renders them less useful as generic designations, at least for now. The terms matrilineal and matrilocal are problematic because they have specific anthropological meanings. (Matrilineal means that geneologies and inheritance are traced through the mother's bloodline; matrifocal means that the family lives at the house of the mother or her clan. In Western culture, families are predominantly patrilineal, tracing descent through the father's line; and patrilocral, dwelling in the house of the husband or his family.) Therefore, in this book the terms matrifocal, gynocentric (or gynaecocentric), and female-oriented are used interchangeably to denote female-centered cultures; and patrifocal, androcentric, and male-oriented are used to denote male-centered cultures.

7. Extensive trading is not an exclusive characteristic of the Great Round. In fact, trading becomes more extensive as succeeding cultures become more complex and vaster in their domains. Sometimes a characteristic is credited to a particular archetype because that is the first time the characteristic appears on a significant scale. The Great Round civilization was about trading almost as much as it was about agriculture. It traded instead of hunting, waging war, and acquiring colonies—the activities that motivated other types of cultures to venture beyond their homelands.

8. Campbell 1970: 70.

    I do not mean to pass lightly over the question of innate psychological similarities and differences between women and men. Certainly it remains one of the most debated issues in contemporary thought—whether in literary circles, art salons, psychology labs, feminist caucuses, or academic conferences. To give the issue the in-depth consideration it deserves, especially if I wished to prove to the skeptic that there are gender differences, would involve such a lengthy discussion of the ever-growing body of research and literature on the question that it would skew the focus of this chapter. Even though I assume throughout the book that there are innate psychological gender differences, actual individual women and men vary all over the lot. And there are even other genders (see "The Five Sexes: Why Male and Female Are Not Enough" by Brown University professor of medical science Anne Fausto-Sterling, *The Sciences*, March/April 1993). Thus it is most important that intimations of gender differences not be translated into rigid sex roles or behavioral expectations, and that they not be used to limit individual expression or opportunity. Finally, I hope that this book can make a contribution to the discussion, since many of the current discussants do not draw on history in depth.

9. In *The Origin of Consciousness in the Breakdown of the Bicameral Mind*, Julian Jaynes argued that cultural changes in the Old World paralleling the shift from the Great Round to the Four Quarters and Pyramid worldviews resulted from evolutionary changes in the human brain which divided the functions of the left and right cerebral hemispheres. This theory unrealistically depends on a major evolutionary change in the brain in the much too recent past. Although theories in left-right brain research are changing rapidly, as of this writing, a better explanation might be that ancient civilization moved away from the holistic feminine principle and toward the dualistic masculine principle as it moved from the worship of goddesses to gods and from matrilineal to patrilineal social structures. Thus, the female-centered cultures of the Neolithic era reflect the more holistic functioning of the female cerebral hemispheres that researchers have been finding in left-right brain experiments. In contrast, the later cultures reflect the somewhat different functioning of the male brain, in which the two hemisphere are more specialized and divided. Reasons for the cultural shift from female-centeredness to male-centeredness are considered in the next chapter.

10. These little goddesses can be found near the beginning of chronological displays in archeological museums throughout the world, just after the arrowheads.
11. The distinction gives us a greater accuracy in describing and evaluating the character of various goddesses and their "cults." This is especially important to women who look to goddess lore to find the elemental feminine archetype beneath the characteristics acquired within and defined by male—dominated cultures. Many secondary goddesses are little more than male anima projections. These are almost unrecognizable as archetypal female figures in the purest sense. There are now many books on "The Goddess," but the ones that understand this basic distinction (such as Erich Neumann's, Marija Gimbutas's and Cristina Biaggi's, for example) are most helpful in this search. For more discussion of primary and secondary goddess-worship, see my essays entitled "The Buried Treasure: Women's Ancient Architectural Heritage" (Lobell 1989) and "Male-Biased Paradigms in Archaeology" (Lobell 1986b).
12. For an in-depth discussion of the mythic, physical, political, and geographical dimensions of the world-body of the Goddess, see Rachel Pollack's book *The Body of the Goddess*.
13. Campbell 1986: 38-39.
14. Flannery 1973: 28,
15. Ironically, in this post-industrial electronic era, we are again growing sensitive to these elusive Telluric forces. Witness, for example, how wary we are becoming of low-level magnetic fields that threaten to erase our burgeoning electronic libraries on which we are increasingly dependent.
16. Charpentier 1972: 20-21.Both John Michell's *The View Over Atlantis* and Chapter 2 of Louis Charpentier's *The Mysteries of Chartres Cathedral* introduced many of the terms, imagery, and symbols through which I came to understand Telluric currents in my earliest inquiries into the subject. A number of these influences find their way into this chapter, and even without further reference to either author, I am indebted to them (but see caveat in note 23).
17. Harner 1978.
A familiar literary apparition is the hookah-puffing caterpillar—representing the larval stage of the butterfly that symbolized the flight of the spirit—enthroned on the magic mushroom in *Alice's Adventures in Wonderland*. "Wonderland" can be seen as Carroll's Victorian euphemism for the irrational, psychoerotic realm of the mind; and the magic mushroom, the means to enter it.
18. 18. Schafer 1967: 80.
19. In Jungian psychology, women can also achieve wholeness by reuniting with their animus or masculine principle. This is not based so much on ancient archetypes and mythology as on Jung's somewhat arbitrary adoption of the law of symmetry—if a man has an anima or inner feminine archetype, then a woman must have an animus or inner masculine archetype. Lauter 1985: 8.

However he happened on it, this mirror image of the *hieros gamos* may help modern women to regain wholeness by regaining the so-called "masculine" traits that have been increasingly repressed in women since the

dawn of the Four Quarters. For an in-depth discussion of this and other gender issues in Jungian psychology, see Lauter and Rupprecht's *Feminist Archetypal Theory: Interdisciplinary Re-Visions of Jungian Thought.*
20. Feuchtwang 1974: 1.
21. Feuchtwang 1974: 2.
22. As practiced today—and judging by the books being published on it, it seems to be flourishing—Chinese geomancy seems to be an amalgam of ecology, esthetics, folklore, superstition, and hucksterism. Undoubtedly there is much to it, but the claims are nearly always anecdotal. We need serious research to retrieve and develop that which is genuinely useful in Eastern and Western geomancy.
23. Feuchtwang 1974: 11.
24. Research into European geomancy is highly controversial, and most of it is not taken seriously by academia. The evidence of astronomical alignments in megalithic structures once met the same skepticism but is now more widely accepted, perhaps because our logos oriented culture still prefers to turn its eyes to the stars instead of to the earth Certainly the methods of the "ley-hunters" journalists, and dowsers researching European geomancy can and should be scrutinized. Nonetheless, many discoveries pioneered by amateurs in the past have later been substantiated by rigorous scientists. Perhaps future archaeologists and anthropologists will consider the subject worth exploring. In the meantime, the amateurs' theories deserve a look.
25. Briggs 1971, vol. 1: 215.
26. Katherine Briggs' voluminous two-volume *Dictionary of British Folktales* offers dozens of stories featuring the motif of "work of day magically overthrown at night." The many varieties of magical agents include fairies (Langton House, vol 1: 215, and the New Church at Marske, vol. 2: 277-78), giants (St. Chads, Rochdale, vol. 2: 173-74), invisible agents (Callaly Castle, vol. 2: 175), the Devil (Biddeford Bridge, vol. 1: 52, and Cowthally Castle, vol. 2: 184), supernatural agencies (North Otterington Church, vol. 2: 281), a spirit in the form of a cat (Church at Whittle-le-Woods, pp. 361-62) and a spirit in the form of a pig (Winwick Church, vol. 2: 398). See also Evans Wentz 1978. 27. Some British researchers such as Keith Critchlow and John Michell, while contributing valuable insights and information to the study of ancient sacred architecture, have explored Telluric currents (or ley lines) and megalithic structures in terms of their relation to Egyptian sacred geometry, Biblical systems of measurement, mystical Near Eastern numerology, and Neoplatonic cosmology. Not only are these explorations culturally mismatched and historically inaccurate; they also seem motivated by a logos-oriented masculine mystique far removed from the sensibilities that moved the matrifocal cultures of the Great Round. Certainly, systematic means of measurement (such as the megalithic yard identified by Alexander Thom) and astronomical alignments were integral to the making of stone circles and other megalithic monuments. These structures do show the beginnings of rational architectural design, but this nascent rationalism is tempered by the subtle intelligence of psychoeros.
27. Chapman 1967: 6-7, my italics.
28. Gauquelin 1973.

29. For eight months in 1979 and 1980, a magnetic field satellite named Magsat orbited the Earth taking more than a billion readings of Earth's magnetic field. The largest component of the field is generated by the Earth's molten core. Added to this are important but faint fields called "magnetic anomalies" caused by rocks deep within the Earth's crust. In March 1981, *Discover* magazine published colorful maps NASA had made of these magnetic anomalies. The colors show "highs" (reddish-brown) and "lows" (blue-green) in the field. "Each bright color tells the scientists how rocks beneath the surface are being magnetized by the main field—much the way a needle is magnetized by being rubbed on a magnet." See Bartusiak 1981: 41.
30. Eliade 1978: 41.
31. When Tiamat was threatened by the rebel Babylonian gods, she gave birth to eleven serpents and dragons to aid her in the contest but lost, nonetheless, to the conquering hero-god Marduk in a classic battle between the besieged Goddess of the Great Round and the conquering Lord of the Four Quarters.
32. Gimbutas 1974, 1989, 1991.
33. Anton 1973:28.
34. National Geographic Society 1989: 135-205.
35. Price 1979: 29-30.
36. Joan Price, phone conversation, October 17th, 1992
37. "...At one Russian spa scientists have found a total ion count of 100,000 per cubic centimeter, with neg-ions being in the majority. A few hundred yards away the count drops abruptly to a normal 1,030 to 2,000 ions per cubic centimeter" (Soyka 1978: 24).
38. Like Native Americans in the region, Ms. Price is concerned about the destruction of the Colorado Plateau due to the mining of its radioactive uranium deposits and protective layers of coal, and the depletion of its aquifers for mining processes.

    "The weather of the Colorado Plateau affects an ocean region called the Southern Oscillation, birthplace of the El Nino, the great serpentine current which influences the weather all along the Pacific coast of the Western Hemisphere. The Southern Oscillation has been shown to be in phase with the moisture cycles of the Colorado Plateau and the Tibetan Plateau. These are vibration points or pulse points for meteorology. To the Hopi, they are spiritual centers. They are 'breath" or "wind."' Price, phone conversation, October 17th, 1992.
39. For a related view see Lovelock 1979.
40. See note 8.
41. Dames 1976: 110-114.
42. This hierophany would work today just as well as it did 5000 years ago were it not for the silting up of the moat.
43. Dames 1976: 174-175.
44. A symbol has a metaphorical one-to-many relationship to its referents, in contrast to a sign, which has a literal one-to-one or one-to-few relationship. Take the example of Pegasus, the winged horse who sprang from Medusa when she was beheaded by the Greek hero Perseus. Pegasus' connotations as a symbol include:

472 *Spatial Archetypes*

1. Conveyor of divine power. Pegasus carries thunder and lightning for Zeus and is his thundering horse.
2. Gift of the Warrior Goddess Athena, the co-opted goddess who empowers the Indo-European invaders, and gives Pegasus to Bellerophon.
3. Reward and champion of heroes (Perseus and Bellerophon).
4. Destroyer of Telluric energies. Pegasus enables Bellerophon to destroy the demonized, female, fire-breathing Chimaera, mother of the Sphinx and geomantic symbol of "the volcanic character of the Lycian soil" (Peck 1963: 328). Also Pegasus himself is born of the destruction of another Telluric force: the demonized serpent-goddess Medusa.
5. The Cosmic Horse that mystically gives the new Indo-European patriarchate supremacy over the old Neolithic matriarchate, with its sacred cows and bulls. After the destruction of the Chimaera, Pegasus helps Bellerophon conquer the Lycians and the Amazons.
6. Punisher of hubris. Pegasus throws Bellerophon when the inflated hero wants to ride him up to the heavens. Instead, Bellerophon suffers a miserable end.
7. A vehicle of inspiration. With his hoof, Pegasus produces the inspirational fountain Hippocrené and becomes associated with the Muses.
8. A shamanic vehicle to the upper heavens.
9. A constellation.
10. The spiritualization of libidinous energy born of the ocean and ascending to the sky.
11. Intelligence and "the swiftness of thought" (Cooper 1978: 85).
12. An embodiment of masculine intelligence and virility.
13. An *animus* figure for women.
14. As a sign, Pegasus denotes Mobil Oil. (Signs, however, can lead to symbols. As a child growing up in the cornfields of Illinois, I used to sit on top of my slide to see over the hedge to a Mobil gas station across the street. l was fascinated by is sign: Pegasus, the Flying Horse. It was my first introduction to the wondrous world of mythology.)

45. Chippindale 1983: 265.
The term "causewayed camp" misleadingly suggests military fortifications, but as Chippindale indicates, they were just circular enclosures. We are not certain of their purpose, but they probably were marketplaces, fairgrounds, or dwelling compounds. Their protective ditches and banks must have kept wild animals out and domestic animals in. The multiple burials in the long barrows are consistent with the egalitarian social structure of the Great Round: everyone received essentially the same type of burial.
46. Believing that Stonehenge was a Roman ruin, the English Renaissance architect Inigo Jones contrived drawings of its "original" state that distorted the monument's geometry into Vitruvius's plan for a Roman theater (Chippindale 1983: 58-59). The romantic attribution of Stonehenge to the Druids, first tentatively suggested by John Aubrey in 1666, was avidly promoted by William Stukeley in his 1740 publication, *Stonehenge, a Temple restor'd to the British Druids*. By the Victorian era, tourists were eager to see the "Slaughter Stone" where "Druid sacrifices" had occurred (Chippindale

1983: 216). Stukeley's Druidic Revival continues even today in annual summer solstice sunrise neo-Druidic rituals at Stonehenge. At the dawn of the 20th century, Norman Lockyer opened the subject of Stonehenge's astronomical alignments, initiating what was to become the Space Age mystique advanced most energetically by Gerald Hawkins. In his 1963 article "Stonehenge Decoded," Hawkins boldly declared that the monument was an astronomical observatory and computer. (Nature, October 26, 1963, reprinted in Hawkins 1965: 169-173). In effect, Hawkins had announced that we had ventured not only into the Space Age but into the electronic era as well.
47. The complexities of the monument's astronomical alignments have been covered by Gerald Hawkins, Fred Hoyle, and others.
48. Renfrew 1979.
49. See Lobell 1986b.
50. Brennan 1983.
51. In the Loughcrew Mountains, not far from the remains of the Celtic stronghold at Tara and the medieval monastery at Kells, Brennan found a similar pattern of alignments in a sister group of megalithic chambers hugging the barrerc sheep-grazed hills called Slieve na Calliagh, "Mountain of the Sorceress." Brennan 1983: 48.
52. Eddy 1979, 1977, 1974.
53. See Aveni 1977; Krupp 1983, 1977; and Williamson 1984.
54. Fajada Butte was dubbed "An American Stonehenge" in *Science 80*, Frazier 1979. See also Sofaer 1983 for the documentary film, The Anasazi Sun Dagger (narrated by Robert Redford), in which she describes her findings.
55. Neumann 1972: 56.
56. Marshack 1972. According to anthropologist Alexander Marshack, the first heavenly body to be observed systematically was the moon, not the sun. After careful study, he concluded that certain enigmatic engravings on Upper Paleolithic artifacts could have been daily records of the waxing and waning moon.
57. Hawkins 1965.
58. Krupp 1977: 70-80.
59. Aveni 1980: 75.
60. Aveni 1980: 27.
61. A Washington state epidemiologist, Samuel Milham, found that workers exposed to strong electrical or magnetic fields had a much higher than normal rate of deaths from leukemia (*Science News*, 8/21/82).
62. Michel and Francoise Gauquelin caused a stir in scientific circles through their research on birth. Their data led them to assert that under natural childbirth conditions, infants actually choose their time of birth according to certain planetary configurations. They said also that the choice of configurations may be hereditary. In *The Cosmic Clocks*, Gauquelin states: "We took our sample of birth dates and compared, day by day, the effect of planetary heredity with geomagnetic disturbances—which, as we know, are due to solar activity. The results of this study were presented at 1966 at the Fourth International Congress of Biometeorology. They show a clear, direct relationship between magnetic variations and the effects of planetary

heredity; if a child is born on a disturbed day, the number of hereditary similarities is twice as high as on quiet days. This suggests that the moon and the planets do affect life through the solar field." Gauquelin 1973: 168.

There is also a relationship between the sun, the moon, and human blood. In *The Cosmic Clocks*, Michel Gauquelin describes the work of Maki Takata, an eminent Japanese physician who has shown that the flocculation index of human blood (the tendency of albumin to curdle in the blood) is directly related to the sun—the index is low at night and rises just before dawn. Takata also found that the index declines sharply during solar eclipses when the moon cuts off the sun's rays. But it is not simply light that affects the index. Takata could not duplicate the eclipse effect in houses or thick concrete battlements. Only by placing subjects in a 600 foot deep mine shaft was he able to replicate the blocking power of the moon, indicating that some solar power other than light was involved. Takata became interested in this effect in 1938 when hospitals reported abnormal rises in the flocculation index of their patients. That was a year of markedly increased solar activity, and intense solar activity always has a disturbing influence on the Earth's magnetic field.

63. To distinguish between primary and secondary goddess-worship, see my paper entitled "Male-Biased Paradigms in Archæology" (Lobell 1986b). In brief, primary goddess-worship is found sometimes in the Sensitive Chaos but mainly in the female-centered cultural context of Great Round (egalitarian, peaceful, matrifocal, and matrilineal, with art and architecture primarily featuring female imagery). Secondary goddess worship is found in the patriarchal cultural contexts characteristic of the other archetypes. Thus the Venus of Laussel and the Neolithic Maltese goddesses are objects of primary goddess worship. Athena in Classical Greece, Isis in pharaonic Egypt, Innana in Sumer, Ix Chel among the Maya, Amaterasu in Japan, and the Virgin Mary in Medieval Europe are foci of secondary goddess worship. This distinction avoids confusing the primal goddess, as defined in female-centered cultures, with the later goddesses, as defined in male-dominated cultures. This is especially important to women who look to goddess lore to find the elemental, self-defined or female-defined, feminine archetype beneath the characteristics acquired in and defined by male-dominated cultures. There are now many books on "'The Goddess" but the ones that understand this basic distinction (such as Marija Gimbutas's books, for example) are most helpful in this search.
64. Watanabe 1974.
65. Eliade 1974: 16, my italics.
66. Kramer 1969: 165.
67. Stone 1976: 40.
68. Lao Tsu 1972: Verse Six.
69. Athene Parthenos is a Self-creating Virgin within a secondary goddess worshipping context, the extremely male-oriented culture of Classical Greece. Her name means the parthenogenetic or Self-generating one. Her earthly home, the Parthenon in Athens, is named for her. In primary goddess-centered cultures, this female autonomy, rather than sexual innocence, is the primary meaning of virginity. For a discussion of this

interpretation of "Virgin," see Harding 1973a: 115-137, and Campbell 1949: 297-314.
70. Lao Tsu 1972: Verse One.
71. Crim 1981: 499.
72. The original womb-granary contrasts sharply with modern phallic silos, which show that the male is now considered the prime carrier of the seed, reinforcing the ideology of patrilineal descent.
73. The expression that a pregnant woman has "something in the oven" is still in use today.
74. Gimbutas 1991: 261.
75. Waters 1963: 22-24.
76. See Waters 1969 (*Pumpkin Seed Point*) for an especially moving account of this observation.
77. Graves 1960 l: 75.
78. Stone 1976: 199-214.
79. Wasson 1978: 37.
80. Wasson 1978: 81.
81. Giving direct access to the collective unconscious, hallucinogens were ideally suited to the egalitarian communities of the Sensitive Chaos and the Great Round, which revered the psychoerotic state of mind. But they were a threat to the elite priesthoods of later hierarchical cultures alienated from psychoeros and intent on developing technelogos. Centuries of efforts to suppress and outlaw hallucinogens and the entire culture surrounding them finally succeeded, in the West, at least. In Europe, the church fathers killed millions of women, fearing the power of their mysterious practices involving herbs, flowers, fungi, animal "familiars" (shamanic allies), and "flying ointments" (preparations that induced shamanic journeys into the deeper realms of the psyche).

    Today, it is both revealing and tragic that what was once a sacrament of immense spiritual power, one that originated many of our ideas of the sacred, has become so degraded. Its meaning and rituals lost, it has been reduced to a recreational but highly destructive ravaging of the psyche.
82. Persephone's hallucinogenic flowers are symbolized today in the bridal bouquets carried by women as they, too, are abducted metaphorically by their grooms. Also, the sentimental gesture of sending flowers to women, particularly on Mother's Day, carries traces of powerful Great Round traditions.
83. Spretnak 1978: 98-111.
84. Graves 1966: 28.
85. Graves 1960 1:75.
86. Krishna 1971: 63-65.
87. Krishna 1971: 59-60.
88. This may explain why people are occasionally consumed by spontaneous combustion, although the phenomenon might not be real or might have other causes.
89. Waters 1969.
90. Bradley Smith: 15-19.
91. Houston 1967: 38-39.

476 Spatial Archetypes

92. Shinell 1980.
93. The converse would be to sum up the whole of Christianity—with its preoccupation with crucifixion, martyrdom, celibacy, renunciation, penance, mortification of the flesh, control of nature, and final judgment—as a "death cult."
94. Eliade 1978: 80.
95. Jerusalem Bible, quoted in Argüelles 1977: 130.
96. For a full exposition of how these motifs form a visual vocabulary descriptive of the Great Goddess, see Marija Gimbutas's *The language of the Goddess* (Gimbutas 1989).
97. The list of European and Mediterranean cultures draws heavily on Marija Gimbutas's indispensable book *The Civilization of the Goddess* (Gimbutas 1991), which describes and illustrates the available evidence on the cultures, has a Glossary of Cultures and Major Sites, an extensive bibliography, and a detailed chronology.
98. Gimbutas 1991: 75.
99. "These [Stiff Nudes] have huge pubic triangles and masks with perforations for the attachment of earrings. The masks have the round eyes of a snake and a long mouth with dots underneath it for teeth." Gimbutas 1991: 101.
100. Gimbutas says the three palisades served "perhaps as protection from wild animals" and "are not to be confused with hill-fort fortifications of the Indo European type." Gimbutas 1991: 93.
101. 102. Clearly, in this village's palisades, square plan, cross-axial entrances, crossing main streets, and important central building we are seeing the beginnings of the Four Quarters.
102. "As it is now known from actual temples and their models" Gimbutas writes, "the two-story buildings were not houses of chieftains or village elders, as was presumed by excavators, but communal temples and centers of arts and crafts.... Poljanica, Ovcharovo, and other totally excavated settlement tells are excellent examples of well-organized small towns. According to the excavator H. Todorova, people must have lived there in tightly knit egalitarian communities, their lives revolving around temple activities." Gimbutas 1991: 94.
103. These tells—sites mounded by many layers of undisturbed successive habitations, some over forty feet high (13 m)—suggest long, peaceful habitation, sometimes lasting a millennium or more.
104. Gimbutas 1991: 111.
105. Okladnikov 1981: 17, 92.
106. Stierlin asserts that these accompanying remains are evidence of human sacrifice and even of cannibalism. He extrapolates this assumption from evidence from later Four Quarters cultures, such as the brutal reliefs at Serro Sechin (Stierlin 1984: 42). Many scholars and writers make this mistake. They do not differentiate between the Great Round (Neolithic and Chalcolithic cultures) and the Four Quarters (Bronze and Iron Age cultures), despite the overwhelming evidence that they are entirely different. Thus, they blithely but wrongly ascribe various Four Quarters rites of human sacrifice (agricultural, religious, and funereal) to the cultures of the Great Round, even to the point of characterizing the Goddess

civilization itself as one of rampant, blood-thirsty sacrifice (as has Joseph Campbell and Christopher Whitmont, for example).

In The Man-Eating Myth (Arens 1979), W. Arens documents how common it is for people to ascribe human sacrifice, baby-killing, cannibalism, and "blood-sucking" to their enemies or to people they hold in low regard (as Europeans and Americans generally hold people of other cultures and earlier times). The vast majority of these accusations prove exaggerated, misinterpreted, or outright false—demonizing projections of intertribal rivalry, whether the "tribes" are the New Guinean Arapesh versus the Mundugumors, Christian missionaries versus the Congolese, inquisitors versus heretics, Cambridge archaeologists versus prehistoric Goddess-worshipping farmers, or American "Right-to-Lifers" versus "Reproductive Freedom" advocates.

Hence, it is important to look very closely at assertions of human sacrifice and cannibalism, especially in prehistoric societies (Sensitive Chaos and Great Round). Such practices could have existed, but we must be scrupulous about separating fact from projection and evidence from assumption.

In the case of Real Alto, we need to know if the dates of all the remains are the same, or were some placed later. Are there other explanations, such as communal burial commonly practiced in Great Round cultures? Or was Real Alto a transitional site already displaying Four Quarters characteristics? Is there any corroboration of human sacrifice in the abundant record of Valdivia art as there is in the later cultures? If there was human sacrifice, even in a Great Round context, was it stimulated by native hallucinogens, as Stierlin suggests?

107. Burenhult 1993: 66-67.
108. Waldman 1985: 16.
109. Burenhult 1993: 178.

ENDNOTES FOR THE FOUR QUARTERS

1. Perry 1970.
2. Neumann 1955: 62-63.
3. See Appendix 1:Bits of Colored Glass
4. Harding 1973.
5. The typical Roman plan, derived from the sundial, was quartered by cross-axial avenues the cardo and decumanus. An early version can be seen in Cosa, Italy, which the Romans rebuilt in the third century B.C. after expelling the Etruscans. The towns of Eburacum (York), England; Thamugadi (Timgad), Algeria; Avendcum (Avanche), Switzerland; and Ravenna, Italy, represent the later, more perfected, walled and squared *castrum* plan (Moholy-Nagy 1968: 180-181; Finlay 1977: 34-35, 73-75, 100-103).
6. Campbell 1974: 77.
7. Neumann 1954: 102-103.

478 *Spatial Archetypes*

8. Many have noted that the standard "missionary position" in sex, with the man on top, originated from this mythic image.
9. Graves 1960 l: 27-28.
10. Tarnas 1980.
11. Graves 1960 l: 18-19.
12. Neumann 1970: 109.
13. Neumann 1970: 110.
14. Stone 1976.
15. According to Graves, the name Yahweh (or Jehovah) is derived from the Sumerian Juhu.
16. The Separation of the World Parents as a living archetype was brought home to me by one of my students a few years ago. I had asked my design class to do drawings that illustrated the most moving experience they had ever had in their lives. I wanted to help them connect with their most basic, personal sources for understanding the meaning of space. All of the students' drawings revealed amazingly archetypal material, but the one that lingered most in my memory was a series of three rather ineptly drawn sketches by one of the weaker students in the class. His first sketch showed a simple rectangular block of blue on top of a matching block of green. The second showed the same two blocks parting but not fully separated, as if they were hinged at their rear edges. The third showed the block of blue lifted above the block of green so that some of the white paper showed between them. Lying on the top face of the lower green block was a stick figure of a boy. I asked the student what the drawings meant. He said that they illustrated an experience he'd had when he was about six years old. One lazy afternoon during a last timeless summer of his childhood before beginning school, he was lying in a green meadow looking up at the blue sky. He was simply musing. He had nowhere to go and nothing to do, and it was a beautiful sunny day. Suddenly he was overwhelmed with the feeling that he existed. He was a presence in the world. As he realized this, the sky seemed to lift off the earth to make room for his being. It was as if he had "moved heaven and earth." At the same time he felt a new sense of responsibility for his life and for the state of the world in which he lived. In his drawings, the blue block represented the sky, which at first adhered to the green block of meadowed earth, but as he felt himself come into being, the two parted. Clearly, this was a spontaneous, contemporary example of the Separation of the World Parents. Of course, the student had no idea that he had reenacted the feats of Shu, Enlil, Cronos, Tane, and Jehovah, but in my mind these mythic precedents illuminated the archetypal nature of his experience and I was delighted to share them with him.
17. Kinsella 1970.
18. Kinsella 1970: 150-153.
19. Kinsella 1970: 153-155.
20. Kinsella 1970: 253.
21. Hapgood 1979: 5.
22. Hapgood 1979: 41.
23. Hapgoocl 1979: 62.
24. In *The Intelligence Agents*, Timothy Leary wittily captures how such "mam-

malian politics" have imprinted international affairs (Leary 1979: 39-42).
25. Wenke 1980: 390.
26. Wenke 1980: 399.
27. Wenke 1980: 366-367.
28. It is too early to rely on the research demonstrating these differences, but future developments bear watching to see if they affirm or rule out this possible insight into the ancient cultural shift.
29. Many scholars believe that Thera or Crete or both were the mythical Atlantis, exquisite font of benevolent high civilization—one of the most enduring mythic realms in the Western mind, second only to the Garden of Eden as an image of ideal life. Actually, the prevailing classical and modem views of Atlantis correspond more to an urbane, hierarchical, logos-driven Pyramid culture than to the Great Round culture manifested in Thera and Crete.
30. Some scholars believe the civilizations of the Americas may have been influenced by travelers from across the seas, who brought ideas if not technology, and there is some evidence to support this,
31. Renfrew 1979: 137.
32. Renfrew 1979: 215.
33. Richard l. C. Atkinson quoted in Renfrew 1979: 227.
34. Biel 1980: 435-436.
35. Coudert 1980: 18.
36. Eliade 1978: 56-57.
37. Eliade 1978: 20.
38. Eliade continues with a discussion of sexual symbolism: "... the thunderbolt became the sign of the sacred union between the God of the Hurricane and the Goddess Earth. This may account for the large number of double-axes discovered in this period in the clefts and caves of Crete. These axes, like the thunderbolt and the meteorites, "cleaved" the earth [ref.: W.F. Jackson Knight, Cumaean Gates, (Oxford, 1936), p. 101]; they symbolized, in other words, the union between heaven and earth. Delphi, the most famous of the clefts of ancient Greece, owed its name to this mythical image; "Delphi" signified in fact the female generative organ .... Many other symbols and appellations liken the earth to a woman."
39. he male meteorite and thunderbolt, then, were phallic symbols that "cleaved" the female earth. Eliade 1978: 20-21.
40. Eliade 1978: 67.
41. Quoted in Jaffe 1979: 229.
42. Henderson 1964: 120-121.
43. This is why, on a personal level, the lessons that we learn when we regard our enemies as teachers can have such a healing effect. We say, "What is it about them that I don't like, and how am I like that? I can't change them, but can l change myself." At this point, we are acknowledging an abandoned, rejected, or hated part of ourselves. Consciously taking responsibility for it cleanses us and helps us to become whole.
44. Graves 1960 l: 244.
45. In lectures given at the Foundation for the Open Eye in New York City between the early '70s and the mid-'80s.

46. Neumann 1954: 195.
47. Neumann 1954: 213.
48. Neumann 1954: 199.
49. Pennick 1979: 44-46.
50. This observation was first brought to my attention by Joan Price in about 1978.
51. Pennick 1979: 44.
52. Radhakrishnan 1971: 110.
53. Campbell 1972: 144.
54. The myth of Amma and the Earth Mother "justifies" the widespread, brutal practice of cutting out girls' clitorises, which are considered the "male" in the female—symbolically, they become scorpions after excision. The "female" in the male is the foreskin, which is circumcised, symbolically becoming a lizard. This practice highlights the dualistic nature of the Four Quarters. It is as if in the Chinese yin/yang symbol, the little circle of yin in the yang (the anima, the feminine element in the masculine) and the little circle of yang in the yin (the animus, the masculine element in the feminine) were cut out, polarizing the two principles and eliminating any possibility of mutual understanding. This leads Dogon society into an obsession with healing, balancing, and transcending duality, as seen for example in its reverence for twins and androgyny.
55. Griaule writes in his Preface to *Conversations with Ogotemmeli*, "The teaching on these subjects was imparted to the author by a venerable individual, Ogotemmeli, of Lower Ogol. This man, a hunter who had lost his sight by accident, was able, as a result of his infirmity, to devote long and careful study to these things. Endowed with exceptional intelligence, a physical capacity that was still apparent in spite of his affliction, and a wisdom, the fame of which has spread throughout his country, he had quickly appreciated the interest attaching to the ethnological work of the Europeans, and had been waiting fifteen years for an opportunity to impart his knowledge to them. He was anxious, no doubt, that they should be acquainted with the most important institutions, customs, and rituals of his own people. "In October 1946 he summoned the author to his house, and on thirty-three successive days, in a series of unforgettable conversations, he laid bare the framework of a world system, the knowledge of which will revolutionize all accepted ideas about the mentality of Africans and of primitive peoples in general" Griaule 1970: 2.
56. Griaule 1970: 31-32.
57. After doing some mental mathematical calculations, Griaule asked Ogotemmeli how all these things could fit on the steps. The old wise man patiently explained that "everything on the steps is a symbol, symbolic antelopes, symbolic vultures, symbolic hyenas .... Any number of symbols could find room on a one-cubit step." Griaule 1970: 37.
58. Griaule 1970: 37.
59. Griaule 1970: 38-40.
60. Radhakrishnan 1971: 19-20.
61. Kramrisch 1976: 7.
62. Volwahsen 196% 44.

63. Volwahsen 1969: 45, my italics.
64. Kramrisch 1976: 133.
65. Volwahsen 1969: 48.
66. Volwahsen 1969: 46.
67. Volwahsen 1969: 49-50.
68. Storm 1972: 6.
69. ung also saw the whole person as an integration of four psychological functions: thinking, feeling, sensation, and intuition.
70. Suomi 1972: 24.
71. Campbell 1970, Or.Myth.: 15-17.
72. Campbell 1970, Or.Myth.: 17.
73. Eliade 1978.
74. Neumann 1954.

ENDNOTES FOR THE PYRAMID

1. Egyptian Pyramid Inscription, 24th c. B.C. (Prichard 1969: 3)
2. The eastem half of the United States was once dotted with thousands of earth mounds and pyramidal earthen platforms; the few surviving ones are well worth visiting—see Folsom 1983 for locations and infomiation.
3. M. Klein 1970.
4. Graves 1960 1: 15-20.
5. See Appendix 2.
6. Adapted from Prichard 1969: 43. The text continues with an account of the Flood that predates the Biblical account by several centuries.
7. Lao Tsu 1972: Verse 18.
8. Stutley 1977: 165.
9. Coe 1980: 61.
10. Giedion 1964: 206.
11. Frankfort 1978: 3.
12. Edinger 1972: 5.
13. Edinger 1972:4.
14. Frankfort 1978: 3.
15. Campbell 1974:
16. Eliade 1964: xii.
17. Eliade 1964: 6.
18. Eliade 1964: 363n.
19. Halifax 1979: 14.
20. Eliade 1964: 76.
21. For a discussion of the meaning of "aesthetic arrest," see Campbell 1986: 117-148.
22. Eliade 1964: 266-267.
23. Campbell 1972: 157-158.
24. Campbell 1970: 238-239.
25. Stutley 1977: 125. Note the similarity to Plato's account of the concentrically-ringed continents of Atlantis.

26. Monier-Williams 1976: 833.
27. Campbell 1970, Or. Myth: 224.
28. Rawson 1973: 139.
29. Rawson 1973: 139.
30. C. Klein 1982.
31. Thompson 1970: 195.
32. Among the nine-stepped Mayan pyramids are the Pyramid of the Inscriptions at Palenque. Temple I at Tikal (not counting the temple on top, which is set back), the Great Pyramid at Uxmal (also called the "Pyramid of the Magician"), the Pyramid of Kukulcan in Chichen Itza (also called the "Castillo"), and the "Castillo" in Coba. Perhaps these "inverted underworlds"—if that is what the pyramids signified—expressed the Maya's anxiety over their relationship with the Lords of Death. Their pyramids may have been a form of appeasement or an attempt to provide a proper setting in which to negotiate with netherworld masters.
33. East was red; South, yellow; West, black; and North, white.
34. Thompson 1970: 196
35. Roys 1967.
36. This concept is not unlike one we will see later in the cooperation of the gods and demons in the Churning of the Sea of Milk. It is also reminiscent of the Hopi myth of the twin brothers made by Spider Woman at the beginning of creation. They controlled the North and South Poles of the World Axis to keep the earth properly spinning. One brother had the "power to keep the earth in a stable form of solidness" (Waters 1963: 5), perhaps like Heart of Earth. The other, possibly like Heart of Heaven, could send out his call along the vibratory centers of the earth's axis (the earth's chakra system) to keep the universe harmonically attuned.
37. Thompson 1970: 198-199.
38. Campbell 1974: 172.
39. The planet Venus has a 584 day cycle relative to Earth, Spending 263 days as a morning star and 263 days as an evening star. These periods of visibility are separated by Venus's two disappearances: for eight days when it is in front of the sun and for fifty days when it is behind the sun. In Mesopotamia, the goddess Ishtar (Inanna) represented the planet Venus, and her mythology, like Quetzalcoatl's, features a Descent into the Underworld paralleling the invisible periods of the planet.
40. Diaz-Bolio 1964.
41. Lhalungpa 1983: 8.
42. Prichard 1969: 3.
43. Prichard 1969: 4.
44. Scholars vary slightly in their dating of the periods of Egyptian history.
45. Upper Egypt is upstream on the Nile and therefore to the south since the Nile is one of the few major rivers in the world that flows north. Conversely, Lower Egypt is downstream and therefore to the north where the Nile Delta empties into the Mediterranean. Thus, on the map, Lower Egypt is confusingly north of Upper Egypt
46. Quoting C. G. Seligman's *The Races of Africa*, Frankfort writes, "Within such a conglomerate of small communities, larger political units may orig-

inate: 'It is in some such loose organization .... that in this part of Africa paramount chiefs may arise, when a strong man or war leader begins to extend his power beyond his own group, thus originating loose confederacies, which in the face of a hostile attack are welded into something approaching a small nation.'" (Frankfort 1978: 17). This is reminiscent of Homer's Iliad, which tells the story of the loose alliance of Greek chieftains under Agamemnon, formed to lay siege to Troy.
47. It should be noted that Menes was the legendary unifier of Egypt and founder of the First Dynasty. Narmer was the *historical* king shown on the Narmer Palette, which credits him with unifying Egypt and founding the First Dynasty. Some historians believe that Menes and Narmer were the same person. Since for our purposes it makes little difference, we will assume for simplicity's sake that Menes and Narmer were the same.
48. Frankfort 1978: 18.
49. We can see this same dissolution after the fall of a state occurring over and over again in history. One example is the Four Quarters type of tribal warfare, rape, brutality, and chaos that tore Yugoslavia apart after the breakup of the Soviet Union.
50. Atum and his creations: the air god Shu and the moisture goddess Tefnut; their children, the earth god Geb and the sky goddess Nut; and their offspring, Isis and Osiris, Nephthys and Seth.
51. Prichard 1969: 4-5.
52. Prichard 1969: 5.
53. Frankfort 1978: 31.
54. There are some signs in the West of renewed interest in the relationship between healing and architecture: the banning and removal of asbestoses; the discovery of people's need for year round full-spectrum lighting; the growing concern with eliminating toxic building materials; the attention to energy-conservation through better insulation and other means; increasing sensitivity to the impact that the whole construction industry and its insatiable appetite for building materials and energy resources has on endangered habitats such as rainforests; the renewed interest in geomancy as an ecological science, and so on.
55. American presidential candidates echo this rite when they diligently perform their morning jogs for the TV cameras, and their wives fulfill the role of the Goddesses when they hold the Bibles on which their winning husbands are sworn into office. The frequency with which the king's sovereignty is symbolized and bestowed by female figures suggests the lasting hold of the goddesses of the Great Round on later cultures. In Egypt the throne was the goddess Isis. Besides demonstrating their physical vitality and fabricating new myths, another way that Egyptian Pharaohs confined their authority to Nile was to have themselves depicted being crowned, created, or advised by the gods and goddesses. Rulers were frequently shown suckling the udders of the celestial cow—goddess Hathor, implying that she was their mother and that they have drunk her sacred milk of the stars. Frankfort noted that the king's mythical predecessors traced through semidivine spirits and the gods to the creator Re, making monarchical rule coeval with the universe, and marking the end of prehistoric times and the

beginning of history..
56. Giedion 1964: 312.
57. Giedion 1964: 89-94, 277-292.
58. Hoffman 1979: 322.
59. Frankfort 1978: 76.
60. Frankfort 1978: 75.
61. Frankfort 1978: 108.
62. Scully 1969.
63. Giedion 1964: 78.
64. Giedion 1964: 129.
65. Giedion 1964: 343.
66. Gcvinda 1976: 8.
67. Govinda 1976: 5.
68. Burns 1974.
69. Rowland 1970: 54.
70. Volwahsen 1969: 90, my italics.
71. Volwahsen 1969: 90, my italics.
72. Booz 1986: 48.
73. See Allione 1986.
74. Willson 1986.
75. Booz 1986: 66-67.
76. In a lecture on the Silk Route (New York Open Center, March 27, 1987), Edwin Bernbaum pointed out that in the East, West is the direction of spiritual discovery; just as in the West, corresponding quests lead to the East
77. Adams 1959.
78. Spengler 1937.
79. Angkor and Mayan architecture share uncanny resemblances, both in form—stepped pyramids with temples on top—and in ornaments such as stone-carved meanders and serpents.
80. Rowland 1970: 393.
81. Rowland 1970: 401405.
82. *Apsaras* are celestial nymphs—their gestures are a complete language related to that still preserved in Thai and Balinese dancing.
83. Rowland 1970: 401-402.
84. The myth of the Churning of the Sea of Milk, of which there are several versions, was beautifully interpreted from a psychological point of view in an anonymous article in an obscure publication called *Material for Thought* (Far West Institute 1974), on which this summary is mainly based.
85. Coomaraswamy 1967: 316.
86. Zimmer 1972: 202-203.
87. Cohen 1975: 78.
88. See Kramer 1969. Kramer maintains that this highly erotic Sumerian poetry was the prototype for Solomon's Sang of Songs in the Bible.
89. Eliade 1978: 39 (see the Rig Veda, III, 29, 2 sq.; V, 11, 6; V1, 48, 5).
90. Eliade 1978: 121.

ENDNOTES FOR THE RADIANT AXES

1. Hawkins 1973: 208.
2. Ego-inflated people are the ones who claim to be God, uttering fantastic revelations. Psychologists sometimes comment that if Christ were alive today, he would probably be locked up as an incurable psychotic. Such cases have been described in *The Three Christs of Ypsilanti* reference. The Jungian analyst views ego-inflation as a pathological—danger on the road to individuation. It prevents people from becoming whole, actualized, fulfilled human beings. Analysts try to bring afflicted people back to their senses and ground them in their humanness so they can function in the world.
3. We see this behavior of the Hindu moth in fanatical cult members whose own individual integrity and critical judgment have been extinguished by their zealous identification with and trust in a charismatic cult-leader such as Jim Jones or David Koresh.
4. Although small residual pyramids continued to be built even in the New Kingdom (Egypt's Radiant Axes period), they had lost their meaning and function as tombs and had become merely decorative adjuncts to rock-cut tombs They were so poorly constructed, they are now in complete ruin.
5. It is worth noting that from the more than eighty pyramids built during Egyptian history, only one pyramidion survives. A pyramidion is a specially carved, inscribed block, which forms very peak of a pyramid. The surviving one, made of grey basalt, the material of eternity, is the peak of the pyramid of Amenemhat III, a middle Kingdom Pharaoh. Its beautiful inscriptions show hieroglyphics surrounding its base and an elegant winged sun-disk at its peak.

    In the Old Kingdom, the pyramidion was the abode of the deity and the magical point where the *ka* entered matter to channel its energy into earthly life. It was also the point where heaven and earth met, where matter diminished into nothingness and the mystical fusion of matter and spirit could be effected. With its solar disk, the pyramidion was also an icon of the sun, intended to evoke the constancy, light, and consciousness that the sun symbolized. It is one of those oddly significant feats of chance that the only surviving pyramidion is from the Middle Kingdom. It is like a beacon announcing the solar-oriented Radiant Axes era to come, which is to be symbolized by what the pyramid—and the pyramidion—evolve into: the obelisk.
6. Ironically, though the obelisk is manifestly phallic, the tallest Egyptian obelisk was built by a woman: Queen Hatshepsut. The New Kingdom's only female Pharaoh, this remarkable queen wore a false beard and masqueraded as a man when she appeared on state occasions. In general, however, she saw her role somewhat differently from her male counterparts. Often cited as a peace-loving Pharaoh, she preferred to extend her empire through trade and building programs rather than through war.
7. Bacon 1974.
8. One of my most exciting professors at the University of Pennsylvania, Ed Bacon strongly influenced my perception of the Radiant Axis. At that time,

he headed Philadelphia's City Planning Commission. Part of the thrill of his course was that he would arrive breathless from City Planning meetings with high-powered architects and developers with whom he was putting the historical principles he discussed in class into direct use in the redesign of Philadelphia. The course, on which his book *Design of Cities* is based, was a true "living laboratory" of historical ideas made fresh by Bacon's imaginative, forceful and very contemporary application. He is widely admired for the success of his urban design vision for Philadelphia.

9. The Aswan Dam, sponsored by the former USSR, is one of the great technological follies of the 20th century. It virtually destroyed the agriculture base of Egypt that had worked perfectly well for thousands of years on the silt deposited by the natural annual flooding of the Nile. So in the past, the Nile would flood every year and bring needed nitrogen fertilizer. Now this nitrogen is no longer provided by the flooding Nile. Instead electricity is generated by the hydroelectric generators at the dam, and is used to make nitrogen fertilizer.

10. Imagine an American president commissioning a colossal sculpture along the lines of Mount Rushmore, showing his face alongside those of God, Christ, and the Virgin Mary. This gives an idea of the audacity Ramses II shows at Abu Simbel.

11. Billard 1978: 240.

12. The spiritual universe does have a way of compensating for human folly and frailty: a few years ago, a group of women goddess-worshippers went on a pilgrimage to Philae and ritually invited the healing spirits of the old site to relocate to the new.

13. The astrological Age of Aries the Ram from approximately 2000 B.C. to 0 A.D., following the Age of Taurus the Bull from about 4000 to 2000 B.C., coincides with the historical period of the most intense cultural change from the Great Round to the Four Quarters.

    The enmity between cattle-farmers and sheepherders is legendary— from the Biblical tale of Cain and Abel, to Inanna's choice of a shepherd as consort in Sumerian mythology, to the conflicts between cattle-ranchers and sheepherders in Westerns. There are practical reasons for this enmity: grazing cattle chew only the tops of grasses, while sheep crop so close as to make the land susceptible to erosion, which necessitates frequent moves to fresh pastures. Cattle-raising is therefore compatible with farming, while sheepherding is not.

14. Billard 1978: 168.

15. Hawkins 1973: 208, my italics.

16. Hawkins 1973: 209.

17. Kublai Khan used firearms and cannons to subdue the Song. These axially projected explosives are another manifestation of the Radiant Axes.

18. Moholy-Nagy 1968: 53.

19. The "Xanadu" of Coleridge's poem.

    Coleridge darkly alluded to this privilege when he warned:
    Weave a circle round him thrice,
    Arid close your eyes with holy dread,
    For he an honeydew hath fed,
    And drunk the milk of Paradise.

Endnotes 487

20. Polo 1961: 157.
21. Argüelles 1975: 43-61.
22. Hibbert 1972: 58.
23. Bacon 1974.
24. Hibbert 1972: 35.
25. As my former teacher, the landscape architect Ian McHarg, used to say in his hearty Scottish brogue, dramatically lavished with rolled "r's," "The avenues converged in his very crotch!"
26. Aerial views of Chan Chan resemble the multiple palace compounds at Persepolis, the capital of the Radiant Axes Persian Empire.
27. von Hagen 1976: 167.
28. Cavendish 1980: 255.
29. Cavendish 198Ck 7.55.
30. Mama Huaco hiding Manco Capac in a cave to protect him is similar to Zeus's mother Rhea hiding her son in the Diktaean cave on Crete to protect him from his father.
31. Poma 1978: 33.
32. Zuidema points out that 328 = 12 x 271/3 = 8 x 41. 12 is the number of solar months. 27 1/3 is the number of days in the sidereal lunar month, the time it takes for the moon to reappear against the same stars. This month was the basis for the Andean calendar. Stated simply, 12 solar months x 27 1/3 days in the month = 328 days in a year divided into 41 weeks of 8 days each. Zuidema 1975.
33. von Hagen 1976: 145-146.
34. Garcilaso de la Vega, for instance.
35. The same thing happened, for example, at Delphi when the invading Apollo worshippers, a Four Quarters culture, took the Oracle away from the Earth-Mother Gaia and her devotees, a Great Round culture.

ENDNOTES FOR THE GRID

1. Yeats 1959:
2. Hubble 1965:
3. Scientistic" endeavors value numerical measurement and categorization above creative discovery, usually as result of pretentiously mimicking scientific rationality without understanding the creative and artistic aspects of science. The social sciences, which are essentially humanistic in nature, are especially prey to "scientistic" pretensions.

    While truly scientific endeavors value observation, measurement, objectivity, and empirical knowledge, they respect also the value of wonder, insight, and the unknown. Many scientific discoveries have come from dreams; the benzine ring is one example. Many brilliant scientists—Einstein being the most famous—have poetic natures.
4. That the Grid often fails to give everyone "a place in the sun" has less to do with the Grid itself than with human frailty and with the natural life cycles of archetypes. What an archetype promises in the beginning inevitably

sours as the archetype become realized, institutionalized, and finally corrupted (see Bits of Colored Glass, #12). When this happens, a new archetype emerges to offer deliverance, but it, too, is destined ultimately to follow the same pattern of promise, realization, and dissolution.

5. The ideal term for this sphere is really "Western European" rather than "Celtic," but for our purposes in this chapter, this is too broad and too easily confused with the "West" or with "Western civilization" in general. For instance, "Celtic Christianity" is much more specific than "Western Christianity" which could include the Byzantine Empire and the Eastern Orthodox Church. Although the term "Celtic" may seem inaccurate when used to encompass such a wide variety of peoples, it is more suitable than the biased terms favored by Christian scholars: "Tribal" or "Barbaric" Europe. At least "Celtic" evokes in its full dignity one of a number of cultures whose widespread influence on modern Europe has not been fully parsed.

The separation of Celtic Europe from Graeco-Roman Europe and the East is consistent with the radio carbon dating methods that were revised in the 1970s to be far more accurate. The new chronology shifted European prehistory several hundred years back, placing such achievements as Brittany's passage graves, Newgrange, and Stonehenge well before the cultures of Crete, Egypt, Greece, and the Near East that were formerly thought to have diffused Westward and influenced Europe. History books and commentaries written before the late 1970s, and many written since, are marred by ignorance of this revision in prehistoric chronology. See Renfrew 1979.

6. Gimbutas 1974.
7. The hottest argument among Renaissance architects was whether the altar should be placed at the center of the church or against one of its walls. See Wittkower 1971.
8. This rather provisional nave is easy to spot in a plan of St. Peter's. Its walls are not as thick as those in Michelangelo's design for the main church. With its weak poché (the black ink infill on walls in architectural drawings), the nave looks like an afterthought compared to the rest of the cathedral. Of course, when you are there in person, surrounded by the glory of St. Peter's full effect, you don't notice this.
9. The same suppression later led to the trial of Galileo, the execution of Giordano Bruno, and the intimidation of Copernicus. Out of fear of the Church's persecution, Copernicus waited until he was near death to publish his unorthodox heliocentric theory of the solar system.
10. Marco Polo's descriptions of his journeys (albeit at second hand) indicate that the vast territories between Europe and the East saw a similar flowering.
11. Quoted in Mumford 1979: 313-314.
12. Starhawk 1979: 6. [The scholarship that Mimi used at the time she wrote this book referred to as many as nine million people, mostly wome, being executed as witches. More recent scholarship referenced in various articles on Wikipedia put the numbers in the tens, and at most hundreds, of thousands. ~ John Lobell.]
13. Susan Griffin's *Woman and Nature* gives the most moving account of the

consequences of this equation.
14. Brinton 1967: 522.
15. Neumann 1970:
16. Struik 1967: 99.
17. Even today's training seminars on everything from assertiveness to alcoholism and fitness are founded on the principle that machinelike personnel and be tuned up or repaired to work properly.
18. Lewis Mumford, Marshall McLuhan, Fritjof Capra, and others.
19. Struik 1967: 102.
20. Ball 1960: 272.
21. Descartes himself was interested mainly in the planar applications of the "x" and "y" coordinates, especially to reduce curvilinear figures to equations of straight lines- achieving in the dry formulae of analytical geometry the last conquest of the sinuous lines of the Sensitive Chaos and the Great Round.
22. Newton's laws are still the backbone of the ordinary branch of physics called "mechanics;" the revolutionary ideas of Einstein apply mainly to micro- and macrocosmic phenomena.
23. Harré 1967: 392.
24. Agonito 1977: 104
25. Agonito 1977: 115-116
26. Brinton 1967: 520-521
27. Thomas 1974
28. Thomas 1974: 12
29. Conrads 1986: 99-100
30. Spengler 1939: 1:352
31. Campbell 1972: 177
32. Kahn
33. Hughes 1981: 209
34. Hughes 1981: 211
35. The term, "The International Style" comes from an exhibition organized at New Yorks Museum of Modern Art by Philip Johnson and Henry Russell Hitchcock, and from a book accompanying the exhibition that they coauthored.
36. Spengler 1939: 353
37. Hughes 1981: 175
38. Scully 1974: 19

ENDNOTES FOR CONCLUSION

No notes.

490 *Spatial Archetypes*

ENDNOTES FOR APPENDICES

Appendix 1: Bits of Colored Glass

No notes.

Appendix 2: Neumann's Archetypal Stages

1. For a further discussion of this, see Alan Watts's *Psychotherapy East and West* and Fromm, Suzuki, and De Martino's *Zen Buddhism and Psychoanalysis*.
2. Neumann 1970: 12.
3. Evans-Wentz 1927: 96.
4. Neumann 1970: 47.
5. Neumann 1970: 108, (my italics).
6. Tarnas 1980.
7. Neumann 1970: 147.
8. Neumann 1970: 148.
9. Neumann 1970: 157-158.
10. Neumann 1970: 149.
11. Neumann 1970:168.
12. Neumann 1970: 177.

Appendix 3: Piaget and the Worldviews of Children

1. Piaget 1975: 216.
2. Gardner 1974: 56.
3. Holm 1961: 187.
4. Gardner 1974: 63.
5. Holm 1961: 187.
6. John 1:1.
7. Gardner 1974: 63-61.

Appendix 4: The Question of Stages

1. Wenke 1980: 342-344.
2. Renfrew 1973: 187-191.

Appendix 5: Architecture as Worldview

1. Graves 1960: 1:17
2. Budapest 1976
3. Wright 1960

Appendix 6: The World of the Shaman

1. These characteristics of shamanism were gleaned mainly from Eliade 1964, Harner 1980 and 1978, and Halifax 1982.

Appendix 7: Sites and Cultures of the Great Round

No notes.

Appendix 8: Torture of Accused Witches

1. Starhawk 1979: 6.

Appendix 9: Europe's Radiant Axes Timeline

No notes.

Appendix 10: Le Corbusier's Poem of the Right Angle

No notes.

Appendix 11: Architecture and Chakras

No notes.

Appendix 12: Modern American Architecture

1. Hughes 1981: 175.
2. Scully 1974: 19.

BIBLIOGRAPHY

Note: In addition to listing books quoted in the text or used for basic research, this bibliography cites many books used for visual material (paintings, sculpture, pottery, textiles, buildings, gardens, town plans, maps, symbolic motifs, book illuminations, cosmological diagrams, and so forth) in the cross-cultural research for this book.

ADAMS, Barbara
1974 Ancient Hierakonpolis: Supplement. Warminster, Wiltshire: Aris and Phillips Ltd.

ADAMS, Henry
1959 Mont-Saint-Michel and Chartres. Garden City, NY: Doubleday & Cc., Inc./ Anchor Books. (First published by the American Institute of Architects, 1913.)

AGONITO, Rosemary
1977 History of Ideas on Women. New York: G. P. Putnam's Sons/Capricorn Books.

ALBARN, Keith, et al.
1974 The Language of Pattern. New York: Harper & Row/Icon Editions.

ALBERS, Anni
1970 Pre-Columbian Mexican Miniatures. New York: Praeger Publishers, Inc.

ALBUQUERQUE MUSEUM
1985 Maya: Treasure of an Ancient Civilization. New York: Harry N. Abrams, Inc, with the Albuquerque Museum.

ALLEN, Judy, and Jeanne Griffiths
1979 The Book of the Dragon. Secaucus, NJ: Chartwell Books, Inc.

ALLIONE, Tsultrim
1986 Women of Wisdom, London, Boston, and Henley: Arkana.

ANDERSON, Douglas and Barbara
1976 Chaco Canyon. Globe, AZ: Southwest Parks and Monuments Association.

ANDRONICOS, Manolis
1976 Delphi. Athens: Ekdotike Athencn, S. A.

ANTON, Ferdinand
1973 Woman in Pre-Columbian America. New York: Abner Schram, The Image of Woman series.

ARDALAN, Nader, and Laleh Bakhtiar
1973 The Sense of Unity: The Sufi Tradition in Persian Architecture. Chicago: University of Chicago.

ARGUELLES, José A.
1975 The Transformative Vision: Reflections on the Nature and History of Human Expression. Boston: Shambhala Publications, Inc.

ARGUELLES, José and Miriam
1977 The Feminine, Spacious as the Sky. Boston: Shambhala Publications, Inc.
1972 Mandala. Boston: Shambhala Publications, Inc.

AROCHI, Luis
1981 La Piramide de Kukalcan. Mexico City: Editorial Orion.

ARTHUR, Marylin
1977 "Liberated" Women: The Classical Era. Becoming Visible: Women in European History, Renate Bridenthal and Claudia Koonz, editors. Boston: Houghton Mifflin Co.

ASIAN ART MUSEUM OF SAN FRANCISCO
1979 5000 Years of Korean Art.

ATTENBOROUGH, David
1976 The Tribal Eye. New York: W. W. Norton and Co., Inc.

AVALON, Arthur (Sir john Woodroffe)
1974 The Serpent Power. New York: Dover Publications, Inc. (First edition London: Luzac & Co., 1919.)

AVENI, Anthony F.
1980 Skywatchers of Ancient Mexico. Austin, TX: University of Texas Press.
1979 Old and New World Naked-Eye Astronomy. Astronomy of the Ancients, Kenneth Brecher and Michael Feirtag, editors. Cambridge, MA: MIT Press.
1977 Editor, *Native American Astronomy*. Austin, TX: University of Texas Press.

AVENI, Anthony F., and Horst Hartung
1982 Precision in the Layout of Maya Architecture. Ethnoastronomy and Archaeoastronorny in the American Tropics, Anthony F. Aveni and Gary Urton, editors. Annals of the New York Academy of Sciences, Volume 385.

BACON. Edmund
1974 The Design of Cities, revised edition. New York: Viking Press.

BALL, W. W. Rouse
1960 A Short Account of the History of Mathematics. New York: Dover Publications, Inc. (fourth edition, originally published in 1908).

BAMBERGER, Joan
1974 The Myth of Matriarchy. Woman, Culture and Society, Michelle Zimbalist Rosaldo and Louise Lamphere, editors. Stanford, CA: Stanford University Press.

BANDI, Hans-Georg, et al.
1961 The Art of the Stone Age. New York: Crown Publishers, Inc.

BANHAM, Reyner
1969 The Architecture of the Well-Tempered Environment. London: The Architectural Press, and Chicago: University of Chicago Press.

BARBER, Richard
1979 The Arthurian Legends: An Illustrated Anthology. Totowa, NJ: Littlefield Adams and Co.

BARNATT, John
1982 Prehistoric Cornwall: The Ceremonial Monuments. Wellingborough, Northamptonshire: Turnstone Press Ltd.

EARNET, Lincoln
1957 The Universe and Dr. Einstein. New York: Bantam Books. (First edition: New York: Harper and Row, 1948.)

BARRACLOUGH, Geoffrey
1979 The Times Atlas of World History. Maplewood, NJ: Hammond, Inc.

BARTUSIAK, Marcia
1981 Maps of Magnetism: New satellite maps of magnetic features in the earth's crust may reveal geological secrets. Discover, March. New York: Time, Inc.

BAZIN, Germain
1968 The History of World Sculpture. Boston: New York Graphic Society.

BELLWOOD, Peter
1979 Man's Conquest of the Pacific: The Prehistory of Southeast Asia and Oceania. London, Oxford, and New York: Oxford University Press.

BENSON, Elizabeth
1981 Editor, Mesoamerican Sites and Worldviews. Washington, D. C.: Dumbartan Oaks.
1972 The Mochica: A Culture of Peru. New York: Praeger Publishers.

BERNAL, Ignacio
1976 The Olmec World. (Doris Hayden and Femando Horcasitas, translators). Berkeley: University of California Press. (First published, 1969.)

BERNBAUM, Edwin
1990 Sacred Mountains of the World San Francisco: Sierra Club Books.
1987 The Silk Route. Lecture given at the New York Open Center, March 27. The Way to Shambhala.

BERRIN, Kathleen
1978 Art of the Huichol Indians. New York: Harry N. Abrams, Inc., for the Fine Arts Museums of San Francisco.

BIEL, Jorg
1980 Celtic Tomb. National Geographic, March. Washington, D. C: The National Geographic Society.

BIESELE, Megan
1976 Aspects of !Kung Folklore. Kalahari Hunter-Gatherers: Studies of the !Kung San and Their Neighbors. Richard B. Lee and Irven DeVore, editors. Cambridge, MA: Harvard University Press.

BILLARD, Jules B.
1978 Editor, Ancient Egypt. Washington, D. C: The National Geographic Society.

BINFORD, Lewis R.
1983 In Pursuit of the Past: Decoding the Archaeological Record. London: Thames and Hudson Ltd.

BLOCK, Raymond
1965 Etruscan Art. Boston: New York Graphic Society.

BLURTON JONES, Nicholas, and Melvin J. Konner
1976 !Kung Knowledge of Animal Behavior: or: The Proper Study of Mankind is Animals. Kalahari Hunter-Gatherers: Studies of the !Kung San and Their Neighbors. Richard B. Lee and Irven DeVore, editors. Cambridge, MA: Harvard University Press.

BOER, Charles, translator
1979 The Homeric Hymns, second edition, revised. Zurich: Spring Publications. (First published, 1970.)

BOOZ, Elizabeth B.
1986 Tibet: A Fascinating Look at the Roof of the World, Its People and Culture. Lincolnwood, IL: Passport Books.

BORD, Janet
1975 Mazes and Labyrinths of the World. New York: E.P. Dutton.

BORST, L. B. and B. M.
1975 Megalithic Software. Williamsville, NY: Twin Bridge Press.

BOULANGER, Robert
1965 Egyptian and Near Eastern Painting. New York: Funk and Wagnalls.

BRENNAN, Martin
1983 The Stars and the Stones: Ancient Art and Astronomy in Ireland. London: Thames and Hudson Ltd.

BRESSON, Cartier
1971 Man and Machine.

BRIGGS, Katherine
1971 A Dictionary of British Folktales, Volumes 1 and 2. Bloomington: Indiana University Press.

BRINTON, Crane
1967 Enlightenment. Encyclopedia of Philosophy, Vol. 2. New York: MacMillan Publishing Co., Inc.

BROOKS, Robert R. R., and Vishnu S. Wakankar
1976 Stone Age Painting in Indra. New Haven and London: Yale University Press.

BROWN, Frank A., Jr.
1973 Introduction. The Cosmic Clocks, Michel Gauquelin. St. Albans: Paladin.

BUDAPEST, Z.
1976 My Salem in L.A. Moon, Moon, Anne Kent Rush, editor. New York: Random House/Moon Books

BUDGE, E.A. Wallis
1971 Egyptian Magic. New York: Dover Publications, Inc. (First published, 1901.)
1967 Egyptian Book of the Dead. New York: Dover Publications Inc. (First published, 1895, by order of the Trustees of the British Museum.)

BURL, Aubrey
1985 Megalithic Brittany: A Guide to over 350 Ancient Sites and Monuments. London: Thames and Hudson Ltd.
1980 Rings of Stone: The Prehistoric Stone Circles of Britain and Ireland. New Haven and New York: Ticknor and Helds.
1979 Prehistoric Avebury. New Haven and London: Yale University Press.

BURLAND, C. A., and Werner Forman
1975 Feathered Serpent and Smoking Mirror. New York: G. P. Putnam's Sons.

BURNS, Edward McNall, and Philip Lee Ralph
1974 World Civilizations, fifth edition, volume 1. New York: W. W. Norton and Co., Inc. (First published, 1955)

CALDWELL, Joseph R., and Robert L. Hall, editors
1964 Hopewellian Studies. Springfield, IL: Illinois State Museum Scientific Papers Volume XII.

CAMPBELL, J. F., and George Henderson
1981 The Celtic Dragon Myth. North Hollywood, CA: Newcastle Publishing Co.

CAMPBELL, Joseph
1986 The Inner Reaches of Outer Space: Metaphor as Myth and as Religion. New York: Alfred van der Marck Editions.
1983 The Way of the Animal Powers, Volume 1, Historical Atlas of World Mythology. San Francisco: Harper & Row/Alfred van der Marck Editions.
1974 The Mythic Image. Princeton: Princeton University Press/Bollingen Series C.
1972 The Flight of the Wild Gander. Chicago: Henry Regnery/ Gateway Edition.
1970 The Masks of God: Primitive Mythology, Oriental Mythology, Occidental Mythology, Creative Mythology (four volumes). New York: Viking Press. (Originally published 1959-1968.)
1949 The Hero with a Thousand Faces. Princeton: Princeton University Press, Bollingen Series XVII.

CARLSON, John B.
1982 The Double-Headed Dragon and the Sky. Ethnoastronomy & Archaeoastronomy in the American Tropics, Anthony F. Aveni and Gary Urton, editors. Annals of the New York Academy of Sciences, Volume 385.

CASSIRER, Ernst
1944 An Essay on Man. New Haven and London: Yale University Press.

CASTAGNOLI, Ferdinando
1971 Orthogonal Town Planning in Antiquity. Cambridge, MA: MIT Press.

CASTANEDA, Carlos
1972 Journey to Ixtlan. New York: Simon & Schuster.

CAVENDISH, Richard
1980 Mythology: An Illustrated History New York: Rizzoli International Publications, Inc.

CHADWICK, Nora
1970 The Celts. New York: Penguin Books.

CHAN, Wing-Tsit
1969 A Sourcebook in Chinese Philosophy. Princeton: Princeton University Press. (First published, 1963.)

CHANG, Kwang-Chih
1977 The Archaeology of Ancient China, third edition. New Haven and London: Yale University Press. (First published 1963.)

CHAPMAN, Sidney
1967 Solar Emissions and Magnetic-Auroral Storms on the Earth. Magnetism and the Casinos. New York: American Elsevier Publishing Co., Inc.CHARON, Jean
1970 Cosmology: Theories of the Universe. New York: McGraw-Hill Book Co./World University Library.

CHARPENTIER, Louis
1972 The Mysteries of Chartres Cathedral. London: Research Into Lost Knowledge Organization. (Originally published, Paris: Robert Laffont, 1966.)

CHIPPINDALE, Christopher
1983 Stonehenge Complete. Ithaca, NY: Cornell University Press.

CRIM, Keith
1981 General editor. The Perennial Dictionary of World Religions. San Francisco: Harper & Row.

CHRISTIE, Anthony
1968 Chinese Mythology. London: Hamlyn Publishing Group Ltd.

CLAIBORNE, Robert, and the editors of Time-Life Books
1973 The First Americans. New York: Time-Life Books, Emergence of Man series.

CLARK, R. T. Rundle
1978 Myth and Symbol in Ancient Egypt. London: Thames and Hudson Ltd. (First published 1959.)

COARELLI, Fillipo
1975 General editor, Etruscan Cities. New York: G. P. Putnam's Sons.

COE, Michael D.
1980 The Maya, revised edition. London: Thames and Hudson Ltd. (First edition published, 1966.)

COFFEY, George
1977 New Grange and Other Incised Tumuli in Ireland. Poole, Dorset: Dolphin Press. (First published, 1912.)

COGGINS, Clemency
1982 The Zenith, the Mountain, the Center, and the Sea. Ethnoastronomy & Archaeoastronomy in the American Tropics, Anthony F. Aveni and Gary Urton, editors. Annals of the New York Academy of Sciences. Volume 385.

COHEN, Joan L.
1975 Angkor: Monuments of the God-Kings. New York: Harry N. Abrams, Inc.

COLERIDCE, Samuel Taylor
1959 Kubla Khan (ca. 1797-1800). Major British Writers, enlarged edition. New York: HBJ Press. (First published, 1954.)

CONTI, Flavio
1978 Shrines of Power. New York: HBJ Press, The Grand Tour series.

CONRADS, Ulrich
1986 Editor, Programs ami Manifzstaes on 20th-cmlury Architecture. Cambridge, MA: MIT Press. (First English edition, 1970.)

COOK, Roger
1974 The Tree of Life: Image for the Cosmos. New York: Avon Books, Art and Cosmos series.

COOMARASWAMY, Ananda K., and Sister Nivedita
1967 Myths of the Hindus and Buddhists. New York: Dover Publications, Inc. (First published by George G. Harrap and C0., 1913.)

COOPER, J. C.
1978 An Illustrated Encyclopaedia of Traditional Symbols. London: Thames and Hudson.

COPPLESTONE, Trewin
1972 General editor, World Architecture. London: Hamlyn Publishing Group Ltd. (First edition, 1963.)

COTTERELL, Arthur
1981 The First Emperor of Chinn. New York: Holt, Rinehart and Winston.
1980 Editor, The Encyclopedia of Ancient Civilizations. New York: Mayflower Books.

COUDERT, Allison
1980 Alchemy: The Philosopher's Stone. Boston: Shambhala Publications, Inc.

COXHEAD, David, and Susan Hiller
1975 Drums: Visions of the Night. New York: Avon Books, Art and Cosmos series.

CRISTOFANI, Mauro
1979 The Etruscans: A New Investigation. New York: Galahad Books.

DAHLBERG, Frances
1981 Editor, Woman the Gatherer. New Haven and London: Yale University Press.

DAMES, Michael
1977 The Avebury Cycle. London: Thames and Hudson Ltd.
1976 The Silbury Treasure: The Great Goddess Rediscovered. London: Thames and Hudson Ltd.

DAVID, A. Rosalie
1975 The Egyptian Kingdoms. Oxford and Lausanne: Elsevier Phaidon, The Making of the Past series.

DAVID-NEEL, Alexandra
1971 Magic and Mystery in Tibet. New York: Dover Publications, Inc. (Originally published in France, 1929.)

DE LEON, Piedro de Ciem (see von Hagen)

DE STIJL
1918 Manifesto 1. Programs and Manifestoes on 20th Century Architecture. Ulrich Conrads, editor. Cambridge, MA: MIT Press, 1986. (First English edition, 1970.)

DEARBORN, D, S., and R.E. White
1982 Archaeoastronomy at Machu Picchu, Ethnoastronomy and Archaeoastronomy in the American Tropics, Anthony F. Aveni and Gary Urton, editors. Annals of the New York Academy of Sciences, Volume 385.

DENNY, Norman, and Josephine Filmer-Sankey
1985 The Bayeux Tapestry: The Story of the Norman Conquest. London: Collins. (First published, 1966.)

DESCARTES, René
1967 The Philosophical Works of Descartes, Vol. I., Elizabeth S. Haldane and G. R. T. Ross, translators. London: Cambridge University Press. (First edition, 1911.)

DIAZ-BOLIO, José
1964 la Serpiente Emplumada eje de Cultura, third edition. Mérida: Registro de Cultura Yucateca.

DIXON, Philip
1976 Barbarian Europe. Oxford and Lausanne: Elsevier Phaidon, The Making of the Past series.

DORNER, Alexander
1958 The Way Beyond Art. New York: New York University.

DOUMAS, Christos
1979 Cycladic Art: Ancient Sculpture and Ceramics of the Aegean from the N. P. Goulandris Collection. Washington, D. C.: National Gallery of Art.

DRAPER, Patricia
1975 !Kung Women: Contrasts in Sexual Egalitarianism in Foraging and Sedentary Contexts. Toward an Anthropology of Women, Rayna R. Reiter, editor. New York: Monthly Review Press.

DROSCHER, Vitus B.
1971 The Magic of the Senses. New York: Harper & Row/ Harper Colophon. (First published in Germany as Magie Der Sinne Im Tierreich, Munich: Paul List Verlag KG, 1966.)

DUDLEY, Rosemary J.
1978 She Who Bleeds, Yet Does Not Die. Heraies 5: The Great Goddess, Spring. New York.

DRURY, Carel J.
1969 Art of the Ancient Near and Middle East. New York: Harry N. Abrams, Inc.

DYER, lames
1982 The Penguin Guide to Prehistoric England and Wales. New York: Penguin Books.
1973 Southern England: An Archaeological Guide. Park Ridge, NJ; Noyes Press.

EDDY, John A.
1979 Medicine Wheels and Plains Indian Astronomy. Astronomy of the Ancients, Kenneth Brecher and Michael Feirtag, editors. Cambridge, MA: MIT Press.
1977 Medicine Wheels and Plains Indian Astronomy. Native American Astronomy, Anthony F. Aveni, editor. Austin, TX: University of Texas Press.
1974 Astronomical Alignment of the Big Hom Medicine Wheel. Science 184.

EDEY, Maitland A., and the editors of Time-Life Books
1976 Lost World of the Aegean. New York: Time-Life Books, Emergence of Man series.

EDINGER, Edward F.
1972 Ego and Archetype. New York: G.P. Putnam's Sons.

EGAMI, Namio
1973 The Beginnings of Japanese Art. Weatherhill/Heibonsha, Survey of Japanese Art Series.

ELIADE, Mircea
1978 The Forge and the Crucible. Chicago: University ot Chicago Press.
1974 Gods, Goddesses, and Myths of Creation. New York: Harper & Row.
1964 Shamanism: Archaic Techniques of Ecstasy. Princeton: Princeton University Press, Bollingen Series LXXVI.

ELIOT, Alexander.
1975 Myths. New York: McGraw-Hill Book Co.

ELKIN, A. P.
1964 The Australian Aborigines. Garden City, NY: Doubleday and Co., Inc./ Natural History Library. (Originally published by Angus and Robertson Ltd., 1938.)

ENCYCLOPEDIA BRITANNICA
1985 Various entries. The New Encyclopedia Britannica, fifteenth edition. Chicago: Encyclopaedia Britannica, Inc.

ENGLAND, Nicholas
1968 Music Among the Zhu/wa-si of South Africa, unpublished doctoral dissertation, Harvard University. Cited in Fraser 1968: Illustration 16, Plan of Bushman werf.

EVANS, J. D.
1971 The Prehistoric Antiquities of the Maltese Islands. London: Athlone Press, University of London.

EVANS WENTZ, W. Y.
1978 The Fairy Faith in Celtic Countries. Atlantic Highlands, NJ: Humanities Press. (Originally published in 1911.)
1960 Editor, The Tibetan Book of the Dead. London: Oxford University Press. (Originally published in 1927.)

EYO, Ekpo, and Frank Willett
1982 Treasures of Ancient Nigeria. New York: Alfred A. Knopf/ Detroit Institute of the Arts.

FAEGRE, Torvald
1979 Tents: Architecture of the Nomads. Garden City: Doubleday and Co., Inc./ Anchor Books.

FAGAN, Brian
1974 Men of the Earth. Boston: Little, Brown A: C0. (later edition retitled People of the Earth).

FAIRSERVIS, Walter A., Jr.
1975 The Roots of Ancient India. Chicago: University of Chicago Press. (First published, 1971.)

FAR WEST INSTITUTE
1974 The Temples of Angkor Wat and the Search for Meaning in Life. Material for Thought. San Francisco: Far West Undertakings.

FARE, Peter
1978 Hiunankind. Boston: Houghton Mifflin Company.

FAUSTO-STERLING, Anne
1993 The Five Sexes: Why Male and Female Are Not Enough. The Sciences, March/April. New York: New York Academy of Sciences.

FEININGER, Andreas
1975 Roots of Art: The Sketchbook of a Photographer. New York: Viking Press.

FERGUSON, William M., and John Q. Royce
1977 Maya Ruins of Mexico in Color. Norman, OK: University of Oklahoma Press.

FEUCHTWANG, Stephan D. R.
1974 An Anthropological Analysis of Chinese Geomancy. Laos: Editions Vithagna.

FINCHER, Jack
1984 New machines may soon replace the doctor's black bag: Modem medical technology uses radiation, sound, magnetic fields and computers to see inside the human body as never before. Smithsonian, January. Washington, D. C.: The Smithsonian Institution.

FINLEY, M. I.
1977 Editor, Atlas of Classical Archaeology. New York: McGraw-Hill Book Company.

FLANNERY, Kent
1973 The Origins of the Village as a Settlement Type in Mesoamerica and the Near East: A Comparative Study. Territoriality and Proxemics: Archaeological and Ethnographic Evidence for the Use of Organization of Space, Ruth Tringham, editor. Andover, MA; Warner Modular Publications.

FLETCHER, Sir Banister
1954 A History of Architecture on the Comparative Method, sixteenth edition. New York: Charles Scribner's Sons. (First published, 1896.)

FOLSOM, Franklin, and Mary Elting Folsom
1983 America's Ancient Treasures, third revised and enlarged edition. Albuquerque, NM: University of New Mexico Press.

FONTENROSE, Joseph
1981 The Delphic Oracle: Its Responses and Operations With a Catalogue of Responses. Berkeley and Los Angeles: University of California Press. (First published, 1978.)
1980 Python: A Study of Delphic Myth and Its Origins. Berkeley and Los Angeles: University of California Press. (First published, 1959.)

FORD, Patrick K.
1977 Translator and editor, The Maginogi and Other Medieval Welsh Tales. Berkeley and Los Angeles: University of California Press.

FORDE-JOHNSTON, J.
1976 Prehistoric Britain and Ireland. New York: W. W. Norton & Co., Inc.

FORMAN, Bedrich
1980 Borobudur, the Buddhist Legend in Stone, London: Octopus Books Ltd.

FORRESTER-BROWN, James S.
1974 The Two Creation Stories in Genesis. Boston: Shambhala Publications, Inc. (First published, London: Johh M. Watkins, 1920.)

FRANKFORT, Henri
1978 Kingship and the Gods. Chicago: University of Chicago Press/Phoenix Edition.
1970 The Art and Architecture of the Ancient Orient. New York: Penguin, Pelican History of Art series. (First published, 1954.)
1949 Before Philosophy. New York: Penguin. (Original edition: The Intellectual Adventure of Ancient Man. Chicago: University of Chicago, 1946).

FRASER, Douglas
1974 African Art as Philosophy. New York: Interbook.
1968 Village Planning in the Primitive World. New York: George Braziller, Inc.

FRAZIER, Kendrick
1979 The Anasazi Sun Dagger. Science 80, Volume 1, No. 1. Washington, D. C.: American Association for the Advancement of Science.

FROMM, Erich, D.T. Suzuki, and Richard De Martino
1970 Zen Buddhism and Psychoanalysis. New York: Harper and Row/ Harper Colophon. (First published, 1960.)

GARDINER, Patrick
1972 Vico, Giambattista. Encyclopedia of Philosophy. New York: MacMillan Publishing Co., Inc. (First edition, 1967.)

GARDNER, Howard Z.
1974 The Quest For Mind. New York: Random House/ Vintage.

GARLAKE, Peter S.
1990 The Making of the Past: The Kingdoms of Africa, second edition. New York: Peter Bedrick Books/Equinox. (First edition: Oxford and Lausanne: Elsevier Phaidon, The Making of the Past series, 1978.)
1973 Great Zimbabwe. New York: Stein and Day.

GARMONSWAY, G. N.
1975 Translator and editor, The Anglo-Saxon Chronicle. New York: E. P. Dutton.

GARRATY, John A., and Peter Gay, editors
1972 The Columbia History of the World. New York: Harper lr Row.

GASTER, Theodor H.
1958 The Oldest Stories in the World. Boston: Beacon Press. (First published, New York: The Viking Press, 1952.)

GATHERCOLE, Peter, Adrienne L. Kaeppler, and Douglas Newton
1979 The Art of the Pacific Islands. Washington, D. C.: National Gallery of Art.

GAUQUELIN, Michel
1973 The Cosmic Clocks. St. Albans: Paladin. (First published in Great Britain by Peter Owen Ltd., 1969.)

GIEDION, Sigfried
1964 The Eternal Present: The Beginnings of Architecture. New York: Pantheon, Bollingen Series XXXV. 6. II.
1962 The Eternal Present: The Beginnings of Art. New York: Pantheon, Bollingen Series XXXV. 6. I.

GIMBUTAS, Marija
1991 The Civilization of the Goddess. San Francisco: HarperCollins.
1989 The language of the Goddess. San Francisco: Harper & Row.
1974 The Gods and Goddesses of Old Europe: 7000 to 3500 B.C.: Myths, Legends and Cult Images. Berkeley and Los Angeles: University of Califomia Press. (Later edition retitled The Goddesses and Gods of Old Europe ...)

GIMPEL, Jean
1961 The Cathedral Builders. New York: Grove Press.

GLEICK, James
1987 Chaos: Making a New Science. New York 6: Middlesex: Penguin Books.

GODWIN, Joscelyn
1979 Robert Fludd: Hermetic Philosopher and Surveyor of Two Worlds. Boston: Shambhala Publications, Inc., Art and Imagination series.
1979a Athanasius Kircher: A Renaissance Man and the Quest for Lost Knowledge. London: Thames and Hudson Ltd., Art and Imagination series.

GOUGH, Kathleen
1975 The Origin of the Family. Toward an Anthropology of Women, Rayna R. Reiter, editor. New York: Monthly Review Press.

GOVINDA, Lama Anagarika
1976 The Psycho-Cosmic Symbolism of the Buddhist Stupa. Emeryville, CA: Dharma Publishing.

GRAEF, Werner
1923 The New Engineer is Coming. Programs and Manifestoes on 20th Century Architecture. Ulrich Conrads, editor. Cambridge, MA: MIT Press, 1986. (First English edition, 1970..)

GRAHAM-CAMPBELL, James
1980 The Viking World New Haven and New York: Ticknor and Fields.

GRANT, Campbell
1967 Rock Art of the American Indian. New York: Promontory Press.

GRAVES, Robert
1966 The White Goddess, amended and enlarged edition. New York: Farrar, Straus and Giroux. (First published, 1948.)
1960 The Greek Myths: 1 8 Z. New York: Pengiin Books.

GRIAULE, Marcel
1970 Conversations with Ogotemmeli: An Introduction to Dogon Religious Ideas. London, Oxford, and New York: Oxford University Press for the International African Institute. (Originally published in 1948 as Dieu d'Eau.)

GRIFFIN, Susan
1978 Woman and Nature: The Roaring Inside Her. New York: Harper and Row, Inc.

GROF, Stanislav and Christina
1980 Beyond Death: The Gates of Consciousness. London: Thames and Hudson Ltd., Art and Imagination series.

GROPIUS, Walter
1919 Programme of the Staatliches Bauhaus in Weimar. Programs and Manifestoes on 20th Century Architecture. Ulrich Conrads, editor. Cambridge, MA: MIT Press, 1986. (First English edition, 1970.)

GUIDONI, Enrico
1978 Primitive Architecture. New York: Harry N. Abrams, Inc.

GUIDONI, Enrico, and Roberto Magni
1977 Monuments of Civilization: The Andes. New York: G. P. Putnam's Sons/ Grosset & Dunlap. (First published in Italian, 1972.)

HACKIN, J., et al.
Asiatic Mythology: A Detailed Description and Explanation of the Mythologies of All the Great Nations of Asia. New York: Crescent Books. (Reprint of an earlier edition.)

HADINGHAM, Evan
1987 Lines to the Mountain Gods: Nazca and the Mysteries of Peril. New York: Random House.
1984 Early Man and the Cosmos. New York: Walker Co.
1976 Circles and Standing Stones: An Illustrated Exploration of the Megalith Mysteries of Great Britain. Garden City, NY: Doubleday and Co., Inc./ Anchor Press.

HAFNER, German
1968 Art of Crete, Mycenae, and Greece. New York: Harry N. Abrams, Inc.

HALEVI, Z'ev ben Shimon
1979 Kabbalah: Tradition of Hidden Knowledge. London: Thames and Hudson Ltd., Art and Imagination series.

HALIFAX, Joan
1982 Shaman: The Wounded Healer. New York: Crossroads, The illustrated Library of Sacred Imagination series.
1979 Shamanic: Voices: A Survey of Visionary Narratives. New York: E. P. Dutton.

HALLIDAY, W. R.
1967 Greek Divination: A Study of Its Methods and Principles. Chicago: Argonaut, Inc. (Reprint of 1913 edition.)

HAMBLIN, Dora lane, and the editors of Time-Life Books
1973 The First Cities. New York: Time-Life Books, Emergence of Man series.

HAMMOND, Norman
1980 The Earliest Maya. Pre-Columbian Archaeology. San Francisco: W. H. Freeman and Co. (Reprinted from Scientific American, March, 1977.)

HAPGOOD, Fred
1979 Why Males Exist: An Inquiry into the Evolution of Sex. New York: New American Library/ Mentor. (Originally publisher: William Morrow and Co., Inc.)

HARDING, Dennis. W.
1978 Prehistoric Europe. Oxford and Lausanne: Elsevier Phaidon, The Making of the Past series.
1974 The Iron Age in Lowland Britain. London: Routledge and Kegan Paul.

HARDING, M. Esther
1973 The "I" and the "Not-I": A Study in the Development of Consciousness. Princeton: Princeton University Press/Bollingen.
1973a Wornarfs Mysteries, Ancient and Modern. New York; Bantam Books. (First published, New York: G. P. Putnam's Sons for the C. G. lung Foundation lor Analytical Psychology, 1971.)

HARDOY, Jorge
1968 Urban Planning in Pre-Columbian America. New York: George Braziller.

HARNER, Michael
1980 The Way of the Shaman: A Guide to Power and Healing. San Francisco: Harper & Row.
1978 Editor, Hallucinogens and Shamanism. London: Oxford University Press. (First published, 1973.)

HARRE, R.
1967 Laplace, Pierre Simon De. Encyclopedia of Philosophy, Vol. 4. New York: MacMillan Publishing Co., Inc.

HAWKES, Jacquetta
1976 The Atlas of Early Man. New York: St. Martin's Press.
1974 Atlas of Ancient Archaeology. New York: McGraw-Hill Book Co.

HAWKINS. Gerald S.
1973 Beyond Stonehenge. New York: Harper & Row.
1965 in collaboration with John B. White. Stonehenge Decoded. Garden City, NY: Doubleday and Co., Inc.
1963 Stonehenge Decoded. Nature, October 26. London: Macmillan (Journals) Limited.

HAY, John
1973 Ancient China. New York: Henry Z. Walck.

HEIDEL, Alexander
1963 The Gilgamesh Epic and Old Testament Parallels. Chicago: University of Chicago Press, Phoenix Edition. (First published 1946.)
1963a The Babylonian Genesis. Chicago: University of Chicago Press, Phoenix Edition. (First published 1942.)

HEIZER, Robert F., and Martin A. Baumhoff
1962 Prehistoric Rack Art of Nevada and Eastern California. Berkeley and Los Angeles: University of California Press.

HEMMING, John
1981 Machu Picchu. New York: Newsweek Book Division, Wonders of Man series.

HENDERSON, George
1968 Chartres. New York: Penguin Books.

HENDERSON, Joseph L.
1964 Ancient Myths and Modern Man. Man and His Symbols. Garden City, NY: Doubleday & Co., Inc.

HENINGER, S. K., Jr.
1977 The Cosmographical Glass: Renaissance Diagrams of the Universe San Marino, CA: The Huntington Library.
1974 Touches of Sweet Harmony. Pythagorean Cosmology and Renaissance Poetics. San Marino, CA: The Huntington Library.

HERITY, Michael, and George Eogan
1977 Ireland in Prehistory. London: Routledge Gt Kegan Paul.

HERODOTUS
1972 The Histories, Aubrey de Sélincourt, translator. New York: Penguin Books. (First published in this translation, 1954.)

HESIOD
1979 Theogony, Norman O. Brown, translator. Indianapolis: Bobbs-Merrill Educational Publishing. (First published in this translation, 1953.)

HEYDEN, Doris
1981 Caves, Gods, and Myths: World-View and Flaming in Teotihuacan. Mesoamerican Sites and Worldviews, Elizabeth P. Benson, editor. Washington, D. C.: Dumbartan Oaks.

HIBBERT, Christopher, and the editors of Newsweek Book Division
1972 Versailles. New York: Newsweek.

HIGGINS, Reynold
1967 Minoan and Mycenaeen Art. London: Thames and Hudson Ltd.

HINDMARSH, W. R. et al.
1967 Magnetism and the Cosmos. New York: American Elsevier Publishing Co., Inc.

HIRAI, Kiyoshi
1973 Feudal Architecture of Japan. New York: Weatherhill/Heibonsha, Survey of Japanese Art Series.

HOFFMAN, Michael A.
1979 Egypt Before the Pharaohs: The Prehistoric Foundations of Egyptian Civilization. New York: Alfred A. Knopf.

HOLM, Eric
1961 The Rock Art of South Africa. The Art of the Stone Age. New York: Crown Publishers, Inc.

HORI, Ichiro
1968 Folk Religion in Japan. Chicago: University of Chicago Press.

HOULDER, Christopher
1975 Wales: An Archaeological Guide. Park Ridge, NJ: Noyes Press.

HOUSTON, James A.
1967 Eskimo Prints. Barre, MA: Barre Publishing Co., Inc. -

HUBBLE, Edwin P.
1965 The Exploration of Space. Theories of the Universe, Milton K. Munitz, editor. New York: Macmillan Co./The Free Press.(Reprinted from Edwin Hubble, The Realm of the Nebula. New Haven and London: Yale University Press, 1936.)

HUGHES, Robert
1981 The Shock of the New. New York; Alfred A. Knopf.

HUGH-JONES, Stephen
1985 The Maloca: a world in a house. The Hidden Peoples of the Amazon. London: British Museum, Museum of Mankind.
1982 The Pleiades and Scorpius in Barasana Cosmology. Ethno astronomy and Archasoastronomy in the American Tropics, Anthony F. Aveni and Gary Urton, editors. Annals of the New York Academy of Sciences, Volume 385.

HUXLEY, Francis
1979 The Dragon: Nature of Spirit, Spirit of Nature. London: Thames and Hudson, Inc., Art and Imagination series.

IONS, Veronica
1990 Egyptian Mythology. New York: Peter Bedrich Books, Library of the World's Myths and Legends series. (First published, Landon and New York: Hamlyn, 1968..)

JAFFE, Aniela
1979 Editor, C. G. Jung: Ward and Image. Princeton: Princeton University Press/ Bollingen Series XCVII: 2.
1975 The Myth of Meaning: Jung and the Expansion of Consciousness. New York: Penguin Books. (First published in the U.S. by G.P. Putnam's Son, New York, for the C. G. Jung Foundation for Analytical Psychology, 1971.)

JAMES, John
1985 Chartres: The Masons Who Built a Legend. London: Routledge and Kegan Paul. (First published, 1982..)

JAYNE, Walter Addison
1962 The Healing Gods of Ancient Civilizations. New Hyde Park, NY: University Books, Inc. (First published, New Haven: Yale University Press, 1915.)

JAYNES, Julian
1982 The Origin of Consciousness in the Breakdown of the Bicumzrul Mind. Boston: Houghton Mifflin Co. (First published, 1976..)

JELINIK, J.
1975 The Pictorial Encyclopedia of the Evolution of Man. London: Hamlyn Publishing Group Ltd.

JELLICOE, Geoffrey and Susan
1975 The Landscape of Man. New York: Viking Press.

JETTMAR, K.
1967 Art of the Steppes. New York: Crown Publishers, Inc., Art of the World series. (First published in 1964.)

JOHNSON, Buffy, and Tracy Boyd
1978 The Eternal Weaver. Heresies 5: The Great Goddess, Spring. New York.

JOHNSTON, Alan
1976 The Emergence of Greece. Oxford and Lausanne: Elsevier Phaidon, The Making of the Past series.

JUNG, C [arl] G [ustav]
1972 Mandala Symbolism: Princeton: Princeton University Press/Bollingen Series. (First published, 1959..)
1968 Psychology and Alchemy, second edition; Volume 12: The Collected Works of C. G. Jung. Princeton: Princeton University Press/Bollingen Series XX. (Originally published, Zurich: Rascher Verlag, 1944; second edition revised, 1952.)
1967 Symbols of Transformation, second edition; Volume 5: The Collected Works of C. G. Jung. Princeton: Princeton University Press/Bollingen Series XX. (Originally published, Zurich: Rascher Verlag, 1952.)
1965 Memories, Dreams, Reflections. New York: Vintage Books.
1964 Man and His Symbols. Garden City, NY: Doubleday & Co., Inc.

JUNG, C. G., and C. Kerényi
1969 Essays on a Science of Mythology: The Myth of the Divine Child and the Mysteries of Eleusis. Princeton: Princeton University Press/Bollingen Series XXII. (First published, 1949.)

JUNG, Emma
1978 Animus and Anima. Zurich: Spring Publications. (First published by The Analytical Psychology Club of New York, 1957.)

KAHN, Louis
1979 Quoted in Between Silence and Light, Spirit in the Architecture of Louis I. Kahn by John Lobell. Boston: Shambhala Publications, Inc.

KARAGEORGHIS, Vassos
1976 The Civilization of Prehistoric Cyprus. Athens: Ekdotike Athenon S. A.

KATZ, Richard
1976 Education for Transcendence: !Kia Healing with the Kalahari !Kung. Kalahari Hunter-Gatherers: Studies of the !Kung San and Their Neighbors. Cambridge, MA: Harvard University Press.

KAUFMANN, Edgar, and Ben Raeburn, editors
1960 Frank Lloyd Wright: Writings and Buildings. New York: World Publishing Co./ Meridian Books.

KENSINGER, Kenneth M.
1978 Banisteriopsis Usage Among the Peruvian Cashinahua. Hallucinogens and Shamanism, Michael Harner, editor. London, Oxford, and New York: Oxford University Press.

KENTON, Warren
1974 Astrology: The Celestial Minor. New York: Avon Books, Art and Cosmos series.

KERENYI, C.
1977 Eleusis: Archetypal Image of Mother and Daughter. New York: Schocken Books. (First published, Princeton: Princeton University Press/Bollingen Series, 1967.)

KHANNA, Madhu
1979 Yantra, The Tantric Symbol of Cosmic Unity. London: Thames and Hudson Ltd.

KING, Francis
1975 Magic: The Western Tradition. New York: Avon Books, Art and Cosmos series.

KING, Patrick
1975 Pueblo Indian Religious Architecture. Salt Lake City: Patrick King.

KISCHKEWITZ, Hannelore
1972 Egyptian Drawings. London: Octopus Books Ltd.

KINSELLA, Thomas, translator
1970 The Tain (8th century). London. Oxford, and New York: Oxford University Press.

KLEIN, Cecelia F.
1982 Woven Heaven, Tangled Earth: A Weaver's Paradigm of the Mesoamerican Cosmos. Ethnoastronomy and Archaeoastronomy in the American Tropics, Anthony F. Aveni and Gary Urton, editors. Annals of the New York Academy of Sciences, Volume 385.

KLEIN, Mina C. and H. Arthur
1970 Temple Beyond Time. New York: van Nostrand Reinhold.

KNAUTH, Percy, and the editors of Time-Life Books
1974 The Metalsmiths. New York: Time-Life Books, Emergence of Man series.

KNAPPERT, Jan
1990 The Aquarian Guide to African Mythology. Wellingborough Aquarian Press (or San Francisco: HarperCollins).

KONNER, Melvin J.
1976 Maternal Care, Infant Behavior and Development among the !Kung. Kalahari Hunter-Gatherers: Studies of the !Kung San and Their Neighbors. Richard B. Lee and Irven DeVore, editors. Cambridge, MA: Harvard University Press.

KRAMER, Samuel Noah
1972 Sumerian Mythology. Philadelphia: University of Pennsylvania. (First published: Philadelphia: American Philosophical Society, 1944.)
1969 The Sacred Marriage Rite. Bloomington, IN: Indiana University Press.

KRAMRISCH, Stella
1981 Manifestations of Shiva. Philadelphia: Philadelphia Museum of Art.
1976 The Hindu Temple, 2 volumes. Delhi: Motilal Banarsidass. (First published, Calcutta: University of Calcutta, 1946.)

KRISHINA, Gopi
1971 Kundalini: The Evolutionary Energy in Man. Boston: Shambhala Publications, Inc.

KRUPP, E. C.
1983 Echoes of the Ancient Sinks: The Astronomy of Lost Civilizations. New York: Harper & Row.
1977 Editor, In Search of Ancient Astronomers. Garden City: Doubleday and Co., Inc.

KUBLER, George
1962 The Art und Architecture of Ancient America. New York: Penguin, Pelican History of Art series.

KUNSTRAUM MUNCHEN in collaboration with Maria Reiche
1974 Paranische Erdzeichen/Peruvian Ground Drawings. Munich: Kunstraum München.

LAUTER, Estella, and Carol Schreier Rupprecht
1985 Feminist Archetypal Theory: Interdisciplinary Re-Visions of Jungian Thought. Knoxville: University of Tennessee Press.

LAMB, F. Bruce
1971 Wizard of the Upper Amazon: The Story of Manuel Cordova-Rios. Boston: Houghton Mifflin Co.

LAMPL, Paul
1968 Cities and Planning in the Ancient Near East. New York: George Braziller.

LANDA, Friar Diego de
1978 Yucatan: Before and After the Conquest (translation of the 1566 manuscript titled Ralacrion de las cosas de Yucatan). New York: Dover Publications, Inc.

LANNING, Edward P.
1967 Peru Before the Incas. Englewood Cliffs, NJ: Prentice-Hall, Inc.

LAO TSU
1972 Tao Te Ching (6th century B.C.), Gia-Fu Feng and Jane English, translators. New York: Vintage.

LAROUSSE
1971 New Larousse Encyclopedia of Mythology, new edition. London: Hamlyn Publishing Group Ltd./Prometheus Press. (First published 1959.)

LAUBIN, Reginald and Gladys
1971 The Indian Tipi: Its History, Construction, and Use. New York: Ballantine Books, Inc. (First published by the University of Oklahoma Press, 1957.)

LAUDE, Jean
1973 African Art of the Dogon. Brooklyn, NY: Brooklyn Museum/Viking Press.

LAUER, Jean-Philippe
1976 Saqqara: The Royal Cemetery of Memphis: Excavations and Discoveries since 1850. New York: Charles Scribner's Sons.

LAUF, Detlef Ingo
1976 Tibetan Sacred Art, The Heritage of Tantra. Boston: Shambhala Publications Inc. (Originally published in German, 1979 C.)

LE CORBUSIER
1920 Towards a New Architecture: Guiding Principles. Programs and Manifestoes on 20th Century Architecture. Ulrich Conrads, editor.
Cambridge, MA: MIT Press, 1986. (First English edition, 1970.)
1977 Poem of the Right Angle (written, 1947-1953). English translation from Le Corbusier: Myth and Meta Architecture by Richard A. Moore. Atlanta, GA: Georgia State University.
1946 Towards a New Architecture. London: The Architectural Press; and New York: Praeger Publishers, Inc. (First published in England, 1927.)

LE CORBUSIER, and Pierre Jeanneret
1926 Five Points Towards a New Architecture. Programs and Manifestos an 20th Century Architecture. Ulrich Conrads, editor. Cambridge, MA: MIT Press, 1986. (First English edition, 1970.)

LEACOCK, Eleanor
1977 Women in Egalitarian Societies. Becoming Visible: Women in European History, Renata Bridenthal and Claudia Koonz, editors. Boston: Houghton Mifflin Co.

LEAHY, A. H.
1974 Heroic Romances of Ireland, 2 volumes. New York: Lemma Publishing Corporation. (Originally published, 1905-06.)LEARY, Timothy
1979 The Intelligence Agents. Culver City, CA: Peace Press.

LEE, Richard B.
1976 !Kung Spatial Organization: An Ecological and Historical Perspective. Kalahari Hunter-Gatherers: Studies of the !Kung San and Their Neighbors. Richard B. Lee and Irven DeVore, editors. Cambridge, MA: Harvard University Press.

LEGEZA, Laszlo
1975 Tao Magic: The Chinese Art of the Occult. New York: Random House/ Pantheon Books.

LEONARD, Jonathan Norton, and the editors of Time-Life Books
1973 The First Farmers. New York: Time-Life Books, Emergence of Man series.
1968 Early Japan. New York: Time-Life Books, Great Ages of Man series.

LETHABY, William
1975 Architecture, Mysticism and Myth. New York: George Braziller, Inc. (First published, 1891.)

LEFVIN, Jerome Y.
1979 The Gorgon's Eye. Astronomy of the Ancients, Kenneth Brecher and Michael Feirtag, editors. Cambridge, MA: MIT Press.

LEVY, Gertrude Rachel
1963 The Gate of Horn. London: Faber.

LHALUNGPA, lobsang P.
1983 Tibet The Sacred Realm: Photographs 1880-1950. New York: Aperture/ Viking Penguin.

LING, Roger
1976 The Greek World. Oxford and Lausanne: Elsevier Phaidon, The Making of the Past series.

LINKLATER, Eric
1934 Robert the Bruce. New York: D. Appleton-Century Co.

LIPSIUS, Frank
1974 Alexander the Great. New York: Saturday Review Press.

LLOYD, Seton, Hans Wolfgang Miiller, and Roland Martin
1974 Ancient Architecture: Mesopotamia, Egypt, Crete, Greece. New York: Harry N. Abrams, Inc.

LOBELL, Mimi
1989 The Buried Treasure: Women's Ancient Architectural Heritage. Architecture: A Place for Women, Ellen Perry Berkeley, editor; Matilda McQuaid, associate editor. Washington, D.C.: Smithsonian Institution Press, pp. 139-57. (Reprinted in condensed form in Woman of Power magazine, Issue 23, pp, 36-41.)
1986a Archetypal Worldviews in the Development of Complex Societies. Comparative Studies in the Development of Cumplar Societies, Vol. 2. London: Allen and Unwin, for the World Archaeological Congress.
1986b: Male-Biased Paradigms in Archaeology. Paper presented at the World Archaeological Congress, Southampton, England.
1986c Ancient Religions in the Context of Cultural Types. Archaeology and

Fertility Cult in the Ancient Mediterranean: Papers Presented at the First International Conference on "Archaeology of the Ancient Mediterranean" Anthony Bonanno, editor. Amsterdam: B. R. Grüner Publishing Co.
1986 Spatial Archetypes. ReVISION, Volume 6, Number 2.
1978 Temples of the Great Goddess. Heresies 5: The Great Goddess, Spring. New York.
1977 Spatial Archetypes Quadrant, Volume 10, Number 2. New York: C.G. Jung Foundation.

LONSDALE, Steven
1981 Animals and the Origins of Dance, London: Thames and Hudson Ltd.

LOOS, Adolf
1908 Ornament and Crime. Programs and Manifestoes an 20th Century Architecture. Ulrich Conrads, editor. Cambridge, MA: MIT Press, 1986. (First English edition, 1970.)

LOVELOCK, J. E.
1979 Gaia: A New lock at Life an Earth. London, Oxford, and New York: Oxford University Press.

LUMBRERAS, Luis G.
1974 The Peoples and Cultures uf Ancient Peru (translated by Betty J. Meggers). Washington, D. C.: The Smithsonian institution Press. (First published, 1969.)

MACALISTER, R. A. S.
1931 Tara: A Pagan Sanctuary of Ancient Ireland. New York: Charles Scribner's Sons.

MacCANA, Proinsias
1970 Celtic Mythology. London: Hamlyn Publishing Group Ltd.

MACKLE, Euan W.
1977 The Megalith Builders. Oxford: Phaidcn Press Ltd.
1975 Scotland: An Archaeological Guide. Park Ridge, NJ: Noyes Press.

MACLAGAN, David
1977 Creation Myths: Man's Introduction to the World. London: Thames and Hudson Ltd., Art and Imagination series.

MACQUEEN, J. G.
1975 The Hittites and Their Contemporaries in Asia Minor. Boulder, CO: Westview Press.

MACQUITTY, William
1976 Island of Isis: Philae, Temple of the Nile. New York: Charles Scribner's Sons.

MAJNO, Guido
1975 The Healing Hand: Man and Wound in the Ancient World. Cambridge, MA: Harvard University Press.

MALE, Emile.
1983 Chartres. New York: Harper St Row (First U. S. edition).
1958 The Gothic Image. New York Harper S: Row. (Originally published in English as A Study in Mediaeval Iconography and its Sources of Inspiration. New York: E. P. Dutton, 1913.)

MARSHACK, Alexander
1972 The Roots of Civilization: The Cognitive Beginnings of Man's First Art, Symbol and Notation. London: Weidenfeld and Nicolson.

MARSHALL, George N.
1978 Buddha: The Quest for Serenity. Boston: Beacon Press.

MARSHALL, Lorna
1976 Sharing, Talking, and Giving: Relief of Social Tensions Among the !Kung. Kalahari Hunter-Gatherers: Studies of the !Kung San and Their Neighbors. Richard B. Lee and Irven DeVore, editors. Cambridge, MA: Harvard University Press.
1960 !Kung Bushman Bands. Africa 30: 325-355.

MARTEN, Michael, John Chesterman, John May, and John Trux
1977 Worlds Within Worlds. New York: Holt, Rinehart and Winston.

MASCARO, Juan
1962 The Bhagavad Gita. New York: Penguin Books.

MASUDA, Tomoya
1970 Living Architecture Japanese. G. P. Putnam's Sons/Grosset & Dunlap.

MATTHEWS, John
1981 The Grail: Quest for the Eternal. New York: Crossroads, The Illustrated Library of Sacred Imagination series.

MAZER, Benjamin
1975 The Mountain of the Lord. Garden City, NY: Doubleday and Co., Inc.

McINTYRE, Loren
1975 The Incredible Incas and Their Timeless Land. Washington, D. C.: National Geographic Society.

McLUHAN, Marshall
1965 Understanding Media, the Extensions of Man. New York: McGraw-Hill Book Co.

McMANN, Iean
1980 Riddles of the Stone Age: Rock Carvings of Ancient Europe. London: Thames and Hudson Ltd.

MEGAW, I. V. S., and D. D. A. Simpson
1979 Introduction to British Prehistory. Leicester: Leicester University Press.

MELLAART, James
1978 The Archaeology of Ancient Turkey, London: The Bodley Head.
1975 The Neolithic of the Near East, New York; Charles Scribner's Sons.
1965 Earliest Civilizations of the Near East. New York: McGraw-Hill Book Co.

MERCER, Henry C.
1975 Hill Caves of Yucatan. Norman, OK: University of Oklahoma Press. (First published, Philadelphia: J. B. Lippincott Co., 1896.)

METROPOLITAN MUSEUM OF ART
1986 Treasures of the Holy land: Ancient Art from the Israel Museum. New York.
1984 The Flame and the Lotus: Indian and Southeast Asian Art from the Kronos Collection, Martin Lerner, curator. New York: MMA/Harry N. Abrams, Inc.
1980 Treasures from the Bronze Age of China. New York: MMA/Ballantine Books.
1979 Greek Art of the Aegean Islands. New York.
1977 Treasures of Early Irish Art: 1500 B.C. to 1500 A.D. New York.
1976 Treasures of Tutankhamun. New York.

MICHELL, George
1978 Architecture of the Islamic World. New York: William Morrow 6: Co.

MICHELL, John
1975 The Earth Spirit: Its Ways, Shrines, and Mysteries. New York: Avon Books, Art and Cosmos series
1972 The View Over Atlantis. New York: Ballantine Books.
(For revised edition, see the New View Over Atlantis, San Francisco: Harper 6: Row, 1983. First published as The View Over Atlantis in 1969.)

MIES VAN DER ROHE, Ludwig
1923 Working Theses. Programs and Manifestos on 20th-century Architecture. Ulrich Conrads, editor. Cambridge, MA: MIT Press 1986. (First English edition, 1970.)

MILLON, Henry A., editor, and Alfred Frazer
1965 Key Monuments of the History of Architecture. New York: Harry N. Abrams, Inc.

MILLON, René
1980 Teotihuacan. Pre-Columbian Archaeology. San Francisco: W. H. Freeman and Co. (Reprinted from Scientific American, June, 1967.)

MOCTEZUMA, Eduardo Matos
1988 The Great Temple of the Aztecs: Treasures of Tenochtitlan. London: Thames and Hudson Ltd.

MOHOLY-NAGY, Sibyl
1968 Matrix of Man. New York: Praeger Publishers. Inc.

MONAGHAN, Patricia
1990 The Book of Goddesses and Heroines, revised and enlarged edition. St. Paul: Llewellyn Publications.

MONIER-WILLIAMS, Sir Monier
1976 Sanskrit-English Dictionary. New Delhi: Munshiram Manoharlal. (First published, 1899.)

MOOKERJEE, Ajit
1983 Kundalini: The Arousal of Inner Energy. New York: Destiny Books.
1975 Yugu Art. Boston: New York Graphic Society.
1971 Tantra Asanu. Basel, Paris, New Delhi: Ravi Kumar.

MOOKERJEE, Ajit, and Madhu Khanna
1977 The Tanfri: Way. Boston: New York Graphic Society.

MOORE, Richard A.
1977 Le Corbusier: Myth and Meta Architecture. Atlanta: Georgia State University.

MOOREY, P. R. S.
1975 Biblical Lands. Oxford and Lausanne: Elsevier Phaidon, The Making of the Past series.

MORRIS, A. E. J.
1979 History of Urban Form: Before the Industrial Revolution. London: George Godwin Ltd.

MORRIS, Ronald W. B.
1977 The Prehistoric Rock Art of Argyll. Poole, Dorset: Dolphin Press.

MUMFORD, Lewis
1979 Interpretations and Forecasts: 1922-1972. New York: HBJ Press/ Harvest.

MURPHY, Joseph M.
1988 Santeria: An African Religion in America. Boston: Beacon Press.

MURRAY, Jocelyn
1981 Editor. Cultural Atlas of Africa. New York: Facts-on-File/ Equinox.

MUSCH, J. E.
1985 Animal Farm: Paleolithic Sculptures from the Northwest European Plains. Paper distributed at the World Archeological Congress, University of Southampton, England, 1986.

MUSER, Curt
1978 Facts and Artifacts of Ancient Middle America. New York: E. P. Dutton.

MYLONAS, George E.
1969 Eleusis and the Eleusinihn Mysteries. Princeton: Princeton University Press. (First published, 1961).

NATIONAL GEOGRAPHIC SOCIETY
1989 National Geographic's Guide to the National Parks of the United States. Washington, D.C.
1983 People and Places of the Past: the Natibnal Geographic Illustrated Cultural Atlas of the Ancient World. Washington, D.C.
1982 lost Empires: Living Tribes. Washington, D.C.
1978 Ancient Egypt: Discovering its Splendors, Washington, D.C.
1974 World of the American Indian. Washington, D.C.
1971 Primitive Worlds: People Lost in Time. Washington, D.C.
1971 Nomads of the World. Washington, D.C.
1968 Vanishing Peoples of the Earth. Washington, D.C.

NEGEV, Avraham
1980 Editor, Archaeological Encyclopedia of the Holly land. Englewood, NY: SBS Publishing Inc.

NEUMANN, Erich
1972 The Great Mother: An Analysis of the Archetype. Princeton: Princeton University Press, Bollingen Series XLVII. (First published, 1955.)
1970 The Origins and History of Consciousness. Princeton: Princeton University Press, Bollingen Series XLII. (First published, 1954.)

NEWSWEEK
1980 Museums of Egypt, text by Robert S. Bianchi. New York: Newsweek, Great Museums of the World series.
1979 National Archaeological Museum: Athens, text by Licia Collobi Ragghianti. New York: Newsweek, Great Museums of the World series.

NORTON-TAYLOR, Duncan, and the editors of Time-Life Books
1976 The Celts. New York; Time-Life Books, Emergence of Man series.

NUTTALL, Zelia
1975 Editor, The Codex Nuttall: A Picture Manuscript from Ancient Mexico. New York: Dover Publications, Inc.

OATES, David, and Joan Oates
1976 The Rise of Civilization. Oxford and Lausanne: Elsevier Phaidon, The Making of the Past series.

OKAKURA, Kakuzo
1964 The Book of Tea. New York: Dover Publications, Inc. (First published by Fox, Duffield and Co., 1906.)

O'KELLY, Michael
1982 Newgrange Archaeology, Art and Legend. London: Thames and Hudson Ltd.

OLIVER, Paul
1971 Editor, Shelter in Africa, New York: Praeger Publishers.

ORTNER, Sherry B.
1974 Is Female to Male as Nature Is to Culture? Woman, Culture, and Society, Michelle Zimbalist Rosaldo and Louise Lamphere, editors. Stanford, CA: Stanford University Press.

OTTO, Martha Potter
1980 Ohio's Prehistoric Peoples. Columbus, OH: Ohio Historical Society.

PAGELS, Elaine
1981 The Gnostic Gospels. New York: Vintage Books. (First edition: New York: Random House, 1979.)

PAINE, Robert Treat, and Alexander Soper.
1975 The Art and Architecture of Iapan. New Yorlc Penguin Books, Pelican History of Art series. (First published 1955.)

PAL, Pratapaditya
1978 The Sensuous Immortals. Los Angeles: Los Angeles County Museum of Art.

PARRHQDER, Geoffrey
1971 Editor, World Religions from Ancient History to the Present. New York: Facts on File.

PECK, Harry Thurston
1963 Editor, Harper's Dictionary of Classical Literature and Antiquities. New York: Cooper Square Publishers, Inc.

PENNICK, Nigel
1979 The Ancient Science of Geomancy. London: Thames and Hudson Ltd.

PERERA, Sylvia Brinton
1981 Descent to the Goddess: A Way of Initiation for Women. Toronto: Inner City Books,

PERRY, John Weir
1970 Lord of the Four Quarters. New York: Collier Books. (First published, New York: George Braziller, Inc., 1966.)

PETERSON, Ivars
1984 Super Problems for Supercomputers. Science News, Vol. 126, September 29. Washington, D. C.: Science Service, Inc.

PIAGET, Jean
1975 The Child's Conception of the World. Totowa, NJ: Littlefield, Adams A: Co. (First published in English by Routledge and Kegan Paul, London, 1929.)

PIAGET, Jean and Barbel Inhelder
1967 The Child's Conception of Space. New York: W.W. Norton & Co., Inc. (First published in France, 1948.)

PIGGOT, Suart
1974 The Druids. New York: Penguin Books. (First published, London: Thames and Hudson, 1968).
1961 Editor, The Dawn of Civilization. New York: McGraw-Hill Book Co.

PIKE, Donald G.
1974 Anasazi: Ancient People of the Rock. Palo Alto, CA: American West Publishing Co.

PISCHEL, Gina
1975 A World History of Art, revised edition. New York: Simon and Schuster. (First edition: Milan: Arnoldo Mondadori Editore, 1966.)

POIGNANT, Roslyn
1967 Oceanic Mythology: The Myths of Polynesia, Micronesia, Melanesia, Australia. London: Hamlyn Publishing Group Ltd.

POLO, Marco
1961 The Travels of Marco Polo (ca. A.D. 1298), Milton Rugoff, editor. New York: New American Library/Signet.

POMA, Huaman
1978 Letter to a King: A Picture History of Inca Civilization (late 16th or early 17th century), Christopher Dilke, editor. London: George Allen & Unwin.

POWELL, T. G. E.
1980 The Celts, new edition. London: Thames and Hudson Ltd. (First published, 1958).

PRICE, Joan
1988 The Sacred Landscape, Frederick Lehrman, ed.
1979 The Earth is Alive and Running Out of Breath. East West Journal, September, pages 29-30. Boston.

PRICHARD, James B.
1969 Ancient Near Eastern Texts, third edition with supplement. Princeton: Princeton University Press.
1969a The Ancient Near East in Pictures. Princeton: Princeton University Press.

PRIDEAUX, Tom, and the editors of Time-Life Books
1973 Cro-Magnon Man. New York: Time-Life Books, Emergence of Man series.

PURCE, Jill
1974 The Mystic Spiral: Journey of the Soul. New York: Avon Books, Art and Cosmos series.

QUISPEL, Gilles
1979 The Secret Book of Revelation. New York: McGraw-Hill Book Co.

QUONG, Rose
1968 Chinese Written Characters, Their Wit and Wisdom. Boston: Beacon Press.

RADHAKRISHNAN, Sarvepalli, and Charles A. Moore
1971 A Sourcebook in Indian Philosophy. Princeton: Princeton University Press. (First published, 1957.)

RAFFEL, Burton, translator
1963 Beowulf. New York: New American Library/Mentor.

RAFTERY, Joseph
1951 Prehistoric Ireland. London: B. T. Bahsford Ltd.

RAPOPORT, Amos
1969 House Form and Culture. Englewood Cliffs, NJ: Prentice-Hall.

RAWSON, Philip
1973 The Art of Tantra. Boston: New York Graphic Society.
1973a Tantra: The Indian Cult of Ecstasy. New York: Avon Books, Art and Cosmos series.

RAWSON, Philip, and Laszlo Legeza
1973 Tao: The Eastern Philosophy of Time and Change. New York: Avon Books, Art and Cosmos series.

READER'S DIGEST, editors
1978 The World's Last Mysteries. Pleasantville, NY: Reader's Digest Association.

RECINOS, Adrian, translator.
1950 Popul Vuh: The Sacred Book of the Quiché Maya. English version by Delia Goetz and Sylvanus G. Morley. Norman, OK: University of Oklahoma Press.

REES, Alwyn, and Brinley Rees
1961 Celtic Heritage: Ancient Tradition in Ireland and Wales. London: Thames and Hudson Ltd.

REICHE, Maria, see KUNSTRAUM MUNCHEN

REICHEL-DOLMATOFF, Gerardo
1971 Amazonian Cosmos: The Sexual and Religious Symbolism of the Tukano Indians. Chicago: University of Chicago, 1971.
1982 Astronomical Models of Social Behavior Among Some Indians of Columbia. Ethnoastronomy and Archaeoastronorny in the American Tropics, Anthony F. Aveni and Gary Urton, editors. Annals of the New York Academy of Sciences, Volume 385.

RENFREW, Colin
1985 Editor, The Prehistory of Orkney: BC 4000-1000 AD. Edinburgh: Edinburgh University Press.
1984 Approaches to Social Archaeology. Cambridge, MA: Harvard University Press.
1981 Editor, The Megalithic Monuments of Western Europe. London: Thames and Hudson Ltd.
1979 Before Civilization: The Radiocarbon Revolution and Prehistoric Europe. London: Cambridge University Press. (First edition: London: Jonathan Cape, Ltd., 1973.)

REYMOND, E. A. E.
1969 The Mythical Origin of the Egyptian Temple. Manchester: Manchester University Press.

RIDLEY, Michael
1976 The Megalithic Art of the Maltese Islands, revised and enlarged edition. Poole, Dorset: Dolphin Press. (First edition, 1971.)

ROBINSON, James M.
1977 General editor, The Nag Hammadi Library: in English. New York: Harper and Row.

ROGERS, Michael
1976 The Spread of Islam. Oxford and Lausanne: Elsevier Phaidon, The Making of the Past series.

ROHRLICH-LEAVITT, Ruby
1977 Women in Transition: Crete and Sumer. Becoming Visible: Women in European History, Renate Bridenthal and Claudia Koonz, editors. Boston: Houghton Mifflin Co.

ROHRLICH-LEAVITT, Ruby; Barbara Sykes; and Elizabeth Weatherford
1975 Aboriginal Woman: Male and Female Anthropological Perspectives. Toward an Anthropology of Women, Rayna R. Reiter, editor. New York: Monthly Review Press.

ROLA, Stanislas Klossowski de
1973 Alchemy: The Secret Art. New York: Avon Books, Art and Cosmos series.

ROSS, Anne
1967 Pagan Celtic Britain. London: Routledge and Kegan Paul.

ROSS, Kurt, commentator
1978 The Codex Mendoza: Aztec Manuscript (16th century). Fribourg: Productions Liber S. A. Miller Graphics.

ROWLAND, Benjamin
1970 The Art and Architecture of India. New York; Penguin.

ROYS, Ralph
1967 The Book of Cilam Balam of Chumayel. Norman, OK: University of Oklahoma Press, The Civilization of the American Indian Series. (First published, Washington, D. C.: The Carnegie institution, 1933.)

SABLOFF, Jeremy A., and William L. Rathje
1980 The Rise of a Maya Merchant Class. Pre-Columbian Archaeology. San Francisco: W. H. Freeman and Co. (Reprinted from Scientific American, October, 1975.)

SANT'ELIA, Antonio, and Filippo Tommaso Marinetti
1914 Futurist Architecture. Programs and Manifestoes on 20th Century Architecture. Ulrich Conrads, editor. Cambridge, MA: MIT Press, 1936. (First English edition, 1970.)

SAUER, Carl O.
1969 Agricultural Origins and Dispersals: The Domestication of Animals and Foodstuffs. Cambridge, MA: MIT Press.

SAVAGE, Anne
1983 The Anglo-Saxon Chronicles. New York: St. Martin's/ Marek.

SCHAFER, Edward H.
1980 The Divine Woman: Dragon ladies and Rain Maidens. San Francisco: North Point Press.
1967 Ancient China. New York: Time-Life Books, Great Ages of Man series.

SCHLEMMER, Oskar
1923 Manifesto for the First Bauhaus Exhibition. Programs and Manifestoes on 20th Century Architecture. Ulrich Conrads, editor. Cambridge, MA: MIT Press, 1986. (First English edition, 1970.)

SCHODER, Raymond V., S. J.
1974 Ancient Greece from the Air. London: Thames and Hudson Ltd.

SCHULTES, Richard Evans, and Albert Hofmann.
1979 Plants of the Gods. New York: McGraw-Hill Book Co.

SCHWENK, Theodor
1965 Sensitive Chaos. London: Rudolf Steiner Press.

SCIENCE NEWS
1982 Environment: Leukemia and Magnetic or Electronic Fields. Science News, Volume 122, No. 8, August 21, p 123. Washington, D.C

SCULLY, Vincent, Jr.
1974 Modern Architecture, the Architecture of Democracy. New York: George Braziller, Great Ages of World Architecture series.
1969 The Earth, the Temple, and the Gods: Greek Sacred Architecture, revised edition. New York: Praeger Publishers, Inc. (First edition: New Haven and London: Yale University Press, 1962.)

SEIBERT, Ilse
1974 Women in the Ancient Near East. New York: Abner Schram.

SEJOURNE, Laurette
1976 Burning Water: Thought and Religion in Ancient Mexico. Boston: Shambhala Publications, Inc.

SERVICE, Elman R.
1975 Origins of the State and Civilization. New York: W. W. Norton & Co.

SHARKEY, John
1975 Celtic Mysteries: The Ancient Religion. New York: Avon Books, Art and Cosmos series.

SHARMA, R. K.
1978 The Temple of Chaunsatha-yogini at Bheraghat. Delhi: Agam Kala Prakashan.

SHEERBART, Paul
1914 Glass Architecture. Programs and Manifestoes on 20th Century Architecture. Ulrich Conrads, editor. Cambridge, MA: MIT Press, 1986. (First English edition, 1970.)

SHERRAT, Andrew
1980 Editor, The Cambridge Encyclopedia of Archaeology. New York: Crown Publishers, Inc./University of Cambridge.

SHINELL, Grace
1980 Toward a Feminist Metaphysics: To Hell and Back Again. Womanspirit, Volume 6, No. 23. Wolf Creek, OR.

SICKMAN, Laurence, and Alexander Soper
1971 The Art and Architecture of China. New York: Penguin Books, Pelican History of Art series. (First published 1956).

SILVERBERG, Robert
1968 Mound Builders of Ancient America: The Archaeology of a Myth. Boston: New York Graphic Society.

SIMON, Cheryl
1983 Inner Geography. Science News, Vol. 123, April 30. Washington, D.C.: Science Service, Inc.

SISKIND, Janet
1978 Visions and Cures among the Sharanahua. Hallucinogens and Shamanism, Michael Harner, editor. London, Oxford, and New York: Oxford University Press.

SLOCUM, Sally
1975 Woman the Gatherer: Male Bias in Anthropology. Toward an Anthropology of Women, Rayna R. Reiter, editor. New York: Monthly Review Press.

SMITH, Bradley, and Wang-go Weng
China: A History in Art. Garden City, NY: Doubleday and Co., Inc./Gemini Smith, Inc.

SMITH, E. Baldwin
1971 The Dome: A Study in the History of Ideas. Princeton: Princeton University Press. (First edition 1950.)

SOFAER, Anna and Albert Ihde, producers
1983 The Anasazi Sun Dagger. The Solstice Project, distributed by Atlas Video, Inc., Bethesda, MD.

SOYKA, Fred, with Alan Edmonds
1978 The Ion Effect. New York: Bantam Books.

SPENGLER, Oswald
1937 The Decline of the West, 2 vols. in one. New York: Alfred A. Knopf. (Volumes 1 and 2 originally published in Germany, 1918 and 1922 respectively.)

SPRETNAK, Charlene
1978 Lost Goddesses of Early Greece: A Collection of Pre-Hellenic Mythology. Berkeley: Moon Books.

SREJOVIC, Dragnslav
1972 Europe's First Monumental Sculpture: New Discoveries at Lepenski Vir. New York: Stein and Day.

STARHAWK (Miriam Simos)
1979 The Spiral Dance: A Rebirth of the Ancrenl Religion of the Great Goddess. San Francisco: Harper & Row.

STEIN, R. A.
1972 Tibetan Civilization. Stanford: Stanford University Press. (Originally published, Paris: 1962.)

STEWART, David
1988 Editor, Burnan Burnum's Aboriginal Australia. North Ryde, NSW, Australia: Angus & Robertson Publishers.

STIERLIN, Henri
1984 Art of the Incas: And Its Origins. New York: Rizzoli International Publications, Inc.
1983 Encyclopedia of World Architecture. New York: van Nostrand Reinhold.
1981 Art of the Maya: From the Olmecs to the Toltec-Maya. New York: Rizzoli International Publications, Inc.

STONE, Merlin
1976 When God Was a Woman. New York: The Dial Press. (First published in Great Britain as The Paradise Papers.)

STORM, Hyemeyohsts
1972 Seven Arrows. New York: Ballantine Books.

STRUIK, Dirk J.
1967 A Concise History of Mathematics. New York: Dover Publications, Inc. (Originally published, 1948).

STUART, George, and Gene S. Smart
1969 Discovering Man's Past in the Americas. Washington, D, C.: National Geographic Society.

STUTLEY, Margaret and James
1977 Harper's Dictionary of Hinduism: Its Mythology, Folklore, Philosophy, Literature and History, New York: Harper and Row.

SWANSON, Earl H., Warwick Bray, and Ian Farrington
1975 The New World. Oxford and Lausanne: Elsevier Phaidon, Making of the Past series.

TANSLEY, David V.
1977 Subtle Body: Essence and Shadow. London: Thames and Hudson Ltd., Art and Imagination series.

TARNAS, Rick
1980 Astrology vs Astronomy, Esalen Tuesday Night Forum, March 18, (Tape cassette). Big Sur, CA: Workshop Cassettes.

TERRELL, John Upton, and Donna M. Terrell
1976 Indian Women of the Western Morning, Garden City, NY: Doubleday and Co., Inc./Anchor Books. (First published, 1974.)

THOM, Alexander
1967 Megalithic Sites in Britain. London, Oxford, and New York: Oxford University Press.

THOMAS, Lewis
1974 Lives of a Cell: Notes of a Biology Watcher. New York: Viking Press.

THOMPSEN, Dietrick E.
1983 Medicine's New Magnetic Field. Science News, Vol. 123, June 25. Washington, D.C.: Science Service, Inc.

THOMPSON, J. Eric S.
1970 Maya History and Religion. Norman: University of Oklahoma Press.

TORBRUGGE, Walter
1968 Prehistoric European Art. New York: Harry N, Abrams.

TOWNSEND, Richard Fraser
1982 Pyramid and Sacred Mountain. Ethnoastronomy and Archaeoastronorny in the American Tropics, Anthony F. Aveni and Gary Urton, editors. Annals of the New York Academy of Sciences, Volume 385.

TREISTMAN, Judith M.
1972 The Prehistory of China: An Archeological Exploration, Garden City, NY: Doubleday and Co., Inc./Natural History Press,

TRIPPETT, Frank, and the editors of Time-Life Books
1976 The First Horsemen. New York: Time-Life Books, Emergence of Man series.

TRUMP, D. H.
1980 The Prehistory of the Mediterranean. New Haven and London: Yale University Press.

TRUNGPA, Chogyam
1973 Cutting Through Spiritual Materialism, Boston: Shambhala Publications Inc.

TRUPP, Fritz
1981 The Last Indians: South America's Cultural Heritage. Wörgl, Austria: Perlinger.

TUAN, Yi-Fu
1977 Space and Place: The Perspective of Experience. Minneapolis, MN: University of Minnesota Press.
1974 Topophilia: A Study of Environmental Perception, Attitudes, and Values, Englewood Cliffs, NJ: Prentice Hall, Inc.

TUCCI, Giuseppe
1970 The Theory and Practice of the Mandala. New York: Samuel Weiser, Inc. (English translation, Rider A: Co., 1961.)

TURNBULL, Colin
1962 The Forest People: A Study of the Pygmies of the Congo. New York: Simon and Schuster/Touchstone.

TYNG, Anne Griswold
1969 Geometric Extensions of Consciousness, Zodiac 19. Milan, Italy.

URTON, Gary
1982 Astronomy and Calendrics on the Coast oi Peru. Ethnoastronomy and Archaeoastronorny in the American Tropics in the American Tropics, Anthony F. Aveni and Gary Urton, editors. Annals of the New York Academy of Sciences, Volume 385.
1981 At the Crossroads of the Earth and the Sky: An Andean Cosmology. Austin: University of Texas,

VAN DE VELDE, Henry
1907 Credo, Programs and Manifestoes on 20th Century Architecture. Ulrich Conrads, editor. Cambridge, MA: MIT Press, 1986. (First English edition, 1970.)

VAN DER ROHE, Ludwig Mies
1923 Working Theses. Programs and Manifestoes on 20th Century Architecture. Ulrich Conrads, editor. Cambridge, MA: MIT Press, 1986. (First English edition, 1970.)

VAZQUEZ, Pedro Ramirez et al.
1968 The National Museum of Anthropology, Mexico: Art, Architecture, Archaeology, Anthropology. New York: Alexis Gregory, Publishers.

VENTURI, Robert
1966 Complexity and Contradiction in Architecture. New York: Museum of Modern Art.

VICO, Giambattista
1961 The New Science of Giambattista Vico, translated from the third edition, 1744, by Thomas G. Bergin and Max H, Fisch. Garden City, NY: Anchor Books/Doubleday and Co., Inc. (First edition: Ithaca, NY: Cornell University, 1948.)

VIVIAN, Gordon, and Paul Reiter
1975 The Great Kivas uf Chaco Canyon and Their Relationships, Monograph No. 22, The School of American Research. Albuquerque, NM: University of New Mexico Press. (First published, 1965.)

VOLWAHSEN, Andreas
1969 Living Architecture: Indian. New York: G.P. Putnam's Sons/Grosset & Dunlap.

VON CLES-REDON, Sibylle
1961 The Realm of the Great Goddess: The Story of the Megalith Builders. London: Thames and Hudson Ltd.

VON FRANZ, Marie-Louise
1978 Time: Rhythm and Repose. London: Thames and Hudson Ltd., Art and Imagination series.

VON HAGEN
1976 The Incas of Pedro de Cieza de Leon. Norman, OK: University of Oklahoma Press. (First edition, 1959.)

WAECHTER, John
1976 Man before History. Oxford and Lausanne: Elsevier Phaidon, The Making of the Past series.

WALEY, Arthur
1958 The Way and Its Power: A Study of the Tao Te Ching and Its Place in Chinese Thought. New York: Grove Press.

WARREN. Peter
1975 The Aegan Civilization. Oxford and Lausanne: Elsevier Phaidon, The Making of the Past series.

WASSON, R. Gordon, Carl A. P. Ruck, and Albert Hofmann
1978 The Road to Eleusis: Unveiling the Secret of the Mysteries. New York: HBJ Press.

WATANABE, Yasutada
1974 Shinto Art: Ise and Izumo Shrine. New York: Weatherhill/Heibonsha, Survey of Japanese Art Series.

WATERS, Frank
1969 Pumpkin Seed Point. Chicago: The Swallow Press, Inc./Sage Books.
1963 Book of the Hopi. Chicago: The Swallow Press, Inc./Sage Books.

WATTS, Alan
1971 Erotic Spirituality. New York: MacMillan Publishing Co., Inc./Collier Books
Psychotherapy East and West
WEBB, William S., and Raymond S. Baby
1973 The Adena People – No. 2. Columbus, OH: The Ohio Historical Society. (First published, 1957).

WEBSTER, Paula
1975 Matriarchy: A Vision of Power. Toward an Anthropology of Women, Rayna R. Reiter, editor. New York: Monthly Review Press.

WEDEL, Waldo R.
1977 Native Astronomy and the Plains Caddoans. Native American Astronomy, Anthony F. Aveni, editor. Austin, TX: University of Texas Press.

WELCH, Holmes
1966 Taoism, The Parting of the Way. Boston: Beacon Press. (First published, 1957.)

WELLARD, James
1973 The Search for the Etruscans. London: Sphere Books Ltd./Cardinal.

WENKE, R. J.
1980 Patterns in Prehistory: Mankind's First Three Million Years. London, Oxford, and New York: Oxford University Press.

WENIG, Steffen
1978 Africa in Antiquity: The Arts of Ancient Nubia and the Sudan, 2 volumes, Brooklyn, NY: The Brooklyn Museum.

WERNICK, Robert, and the editors of Time-Life Books
1973 The Monument Builders. New York: Time-Life Books, Emergence of Man series.

WESTON, Jessie L.
1957 From Ritual to Romance. Garden City, NY: Doubleday 6: Co.! Anchor Books. (First published by Cambridge University Press, 1920.)

WHEELER, Sir Mortimer
1968 The Indus Civilization, third edition. London: Cambridge University Press. (First edition, 1953).
1966 Civilizations of the Indus Valley and Beyond. London: Thames & Hudson/McGraw-Hill Book Co.

WHITEHOUSE, David and Ruth
1975 Archaeological Atlas of the World. San Francisco: W. H. Freeman and Co.

WHTTEHOUSE, Ruth D.
1983 The Facts on File Dictionary of Archaeology. New York: Facts on File Publications.

WIEGER, S. I.
1965 Chinue Characters. New York: Dover Publications, Inc., and Paragon Book Reprint Corp., Inc. (First edition, 1915.)

WILLETS, William
1958 Chinese Art, 2 volumes. New York: Penguin Books.

WILLIAMSON, Ray A.
1984 Living the Sky: The Cosmos of the American Indian. Boston: Houghton Mifflin Company.
1977 Anasazi Solar Observatories. Native American Astronomy, Anthony F. Aveni, editor. Austin, TX: University of Texas Press.

WILSON, David M.
1980 Editor, The Northern World: The History and Heritage of Northern Europe, AD 400-1100. New York: Harry N. Abrams, Inc.

WITTKOWER, Rudolf
1971 Architectural Principles in the Age of Humanism. New York: W. W. Norton and Co., Inc. (First published, 1962.)

WORK COUNCIL FOR ART
1919 Under the Wing of a Great Architecture. Programs and Manifestos on 20th Century Architecture. Ulrich Conrads, editor. Cambridge, MA: MIT Press, 1986. (First English edition, 1970.)

WORTH, R. Hansford
1981 Worth's Dartmoor, edited posthumously by G. M. Spooner and F. S. Russell. North Pomfret, VT: David and Charles.

WOSIEN, Maria-Gabriele
1974 Sacred Dance: Encounter with the Gods. New York: Avon Books, Art and Cosmos series.

WRIGHT, Frank Lloyd
1957 A Testament. New York: Horizon Press.

WYMAN, Leland C.
1967 The Sacred Mountains of the Navajo. Flagstaff, AZ: Northland Press.

YEATS, William Butler
1959 The Second Coming (1919). Mayor British Writers, enlarged edition. New York: HBJ Press. (First published, 1954.)

YELLEN, John E.
1976 Settlement Patterns of the !Kung: An Archeological Perspective. Kalahari Hunter-Gatherers: Studies of the !Kung San and Their Neighbors. Richard B. Lee and Irven DeVore, editors. Cambridge, MA: Harvard University Press.

ZIMMER, Heinrich
1972 Myths and Symbols in Indian Art and Civilization, edited posthumously by Joseph Campbell. Princeton: Princeton University Press/Bollingen Series VI.
1969 Philosophies of India, edited posthumously by Joseph Campbell. Princeton: Princeton University Press/Bollingen Series XXVI.

ZUIDEMA, R. T.
1977 The Inca Calendar. Native American Astronomy, Anthony F. Aveni, editor. Austin, TX: University of Texas Press.

Detailed Table Of Contents

PREFACE BY JOHN LOBELL i
   A Remarkable Book i
   Mimi's Approach i
   Spiritual Feminism iii
   For Whom is this Book? v
   About Mimi Lobell v
   About This Manuscript vii

PREFACE BY CRISTINA BIAGGI ix

INTRODUCTION 1
   Volume Zero 1
   The Sensitive Chaos 5
   The Great Round 7
   The Four Quarters 8
   The Pyramid 10
   The Radiant Axes.. 11
   The Grid 12
   The Dissolution 14
   Bits of Colored Glass 14

THE SENSITIVE CHAOS: World of the Animal Powers 17
    Origins... 21
    The Animal World.. 24
   Animal Dancing 27
   Sympathetic Identification 28
   Psychoerotic Extensions 30
   The Cosmic Continuum 31
   Ego and Transcendence 33
   Mythical Time... 36
   Serpent Energy 37
   Order and Chaos 39
   The Nummo's First Word 39
   Language... 41
   Hallucinogens, Shamanism, and Psychoerotic Perception .. 42

Spirit Centers: "The Point Existing Here
   and Everywhere, Now and Always" 47
Jung's Stone 51
A Place of Predilection 53
The Architecture of the Sensitive Chaos 55
The !Kung: A Sensitive Chaos Culture 57
The Invisible Architecture of Shamanism 58
SYNOPSIS OF EACH ARCHETYPE 61
SYNOPSIS OF THE SENSITIVE CHAOS 63

THE GREAT ROUND: World of the Great Goddess 67
Origins of the Great Round 71
Life in the Great Round 73
Female-Centered Civilizations 75
The Great Goddess 77
Primary and Secondary Goddesses 78
Telluric Currents 80
Geomancy 84
Spirals 87
Springs 90
The Colorado Plateau 92
Silbury Hill 94
Cyclical Time 97
Stonehenge 98
Newgrange and the Boyne Valley Calendar 101
The Anasazi Sun Dagger 102
Lunar Eclipses 103
The Queen of Heaven 105
The Womb-Cavern 109
The Kiva 112
The Pueblo Indians: A Great Round Culture 114
Soma, Ambrosia, and the Witch's Brew 116
The Fire of Immortality 119
Serpent Energy Revisited 121
SYNOPSIS OF THE GREAT ROUND 127

THE FOUR QUARTERS: World of the Hero 133
    The Divine Child 137
    The Separation of the World Parents 141
    Ego and War.. 146
    Cuchulainn's Battle Frenzy 148
    Why Males Exist 151
    From the Great Round to the Four Quarters:
        The Social Scientist's View 153
    From the Great Round to the Four Quarters:
        Other Theories 156
    Indo-Europeans on the Move 158
    The Birth of the Hero from the Burial Mound 161
    Metallurgy and the Violation of the Earth Mother 165
    The Dragon-Slayer 168
    Navel of the World 174
    The Mandala of Reintegration 176
    The Granary of the Master of Pure Earth 178
    The Hindu Temple and the Union of Opposites................................... 182
    The Medicine Wheel: Journey to the Self 188
    Under The Bodhi Tree 190
    SYNOPSIS OF THE FOUR QUARTERS 193

THE PYRAMID: World of the God-King 201
    From the Four Quarters to the Pyramid 205
    The Rise of the Pyramid in the Nation State 208
    The Social Pyramid 210
    The Spiritual Pyramid 212
    Morality and Individual Will 214
    The Emergence of Technelogos 215
    The Hermetization of the Sacred 218
    The Mountain Arising from the Sea of Chaos 221
    The World Mountain of the Shaman 223
    The World Mountain of the Priest 227
    Mount Meru and the Mayan Imago Mundi 230
    The Ben-Stone: The Primeval Hillock Arises 236
    The Narmer Palette and The Egyptian Union of Opposites ... 238
    Mythology Rewritten: The Memphite Theology 239
    The Egyptian Pyramid.. 241

The Ka 243
Fire, the Feminine, and the Sun 244
The Horns of Consecration: Gateway to the Great Mystery ... 247
The Buddhist Stupa 251
Borobudur.. 256
The Potala in Lhasa 258
The Gothic Cathedral: Pyramid of the West 261
Angkor 264
The Churning of the Sea of Milk 267
The Hieros Gamos 270
Patterning Energy... 274
SYNOPSIS OF THE PYRAMID 277

THE RADIANT AXES: World of the Emperor 281
The Empire and the Inflated Ego 285
Decadence 287
Secularism and the State Religion 288
Palaces and Radiating Roads 289
Obelisks and Colossi 290
Abu Simbel 292
The Solar Temples of the New Kingdom 294
The High Room of the Sun... 297
The Forbidden City 298
Versailles: Palace of the Sun-King... 301
Copernicus, Kepler, and the Baroque Radiant Axes 304
The Radiant Axes in the Americas 305
South America Before the Incas 306
The Incas: Children of the Sun 308
The Ceque System of Cuzco 314
The Temple of the Sun 316
SYNOPSIS OF THE RADIANT AXES 319

THE GRID: World of the Bureaucrat 325
The Rise of the Grid 329
The Grid in Western Civilization 332
The Celtic Sphere 334
The Celtic Individual... 335
The Graeco-Roman Sphere 335

The Eastern or Christian Sphere 335
Humanism 340
The Dark Side of the Renaissance 344
The Clockwork Universe 350
The Machine: Icon of the Grid 351
Cartesian Dualism and the Cartesian Grid 353
The Ideal State and the Tabula Rasa 358
Progress 363
The Industrial Revolution 364
The Light, the Practical, the Ephemeral, and the Swift:
   Manifestoes of Modern Architecture 369
Le Corbusier's Five Points 376
Le Corbusier's Existential Idea... 379
Modern Architecture: the Realization of the Grid 381
SYNOPSIS OF THE GRID 387

THE DISSOLUTION: World of the Trickster................................. 393

CONCLUSION 397
   Cultures are Symbolic Entities 397
   Cultures Go Through Different Periods................................ 397
   Cultures Have Psychologies... 398
   Cultures Are Different.. 398
   Optimism or Pessimism?.. 398

APPENDICES 399
   1. Bits of Colored Glass 399
   2. Neumann's Archetypal Stages 409
   3. Piaget and the Worldviews of Children 415
   4. The Question of Stages... 418
   5. Architecture as Worldview... 422
   6. The World of the Shaman 428
   7. Sites and Cultures of the Great Round 433
   8. Torture of Accused Witches.. 442
   9. Europe's Radiant Axes Timeline.. 443
   10. Le Corbusier's Poem of the Right Angle........................ 444
   11. Architecture and Chakras 456
   12. Modern American Architecture 459

ENDNOTES 463
   Endnotes for Introduction 463
   Endnotes for The Sensitive Chaos 464
   Endnotes for The Great Round 467
   Endnotes for The Four Quarters 477
   Endnotes for The Pyramid 481
   Endnotes for The Radiant Axes 485
   Endnotes for The Grid 487
   Endnotes for Appendices 490

BIBLIOGRAPHY 493

DETAILED CONTENTS 537

ACKNOWLEDGMENTS 543

ABOUT MIMI LOBELL 547

ACKNOWLEDGMENTS

Quotations

Quotations from Joseph Campbell's *The Inner Reaches of Outer Space* Copyright © Joseph Campbell Foundation (jcf.org) 2002. Used with permission.

Quotations from Joseph Campbell's *Flight of the Wild Gander* Copyright © Joseph Campbell Foundation (jcf.org) 2002. Used with permission.

Illustration Credits

Cover photo: Jonathan Beacom

The Sensitive Chaos

1a. Wikimedia Commons contributors, "File:Swirling cloud at sea.jpg," Wikimedia Commons, the free media repository, https://commons.wikimedia.org/w/index.php?title=File:Swirling_cloud_at_sea.jpg&oldid=247317864 (accessed January 4, 2018).

1c. Wikimedia Commons contributors, "File:ShabanoYanomami.jpg," Wikimedia Commons, the free media repository, https://commons.wikimedia.org/w/index.php?title=File:ShabanoYanomami.jpg&oldid=121358639 (accessed November 26, 2017).

1d. From the Alberto Manuel Cheung Gallery in New York City.

The Great Round

2a. Wikimedia Commons contributors, "File:Evolution du plan des temples copie.jpg," Wikimedia Commons, the free media repository, https://commons.wikimedia.org/w/index.php?title=File:Evolution_du_plan_des_temples_copie.jpg&oldid=262161777 (accessed November 26, 2017).

2d. Wikimedia Commons contributors, "File:DSC 5961-w.jpg," Wikimedia Commons, the free media repository, https://commons.wikimedia.org/w/index.php?title=File:DSC_5961-w.jpg&oldid=147024772 (accessed November 25, 2017).

544 *Spatial Archetypes*

The Four Quarters

3a. Museum number1848,0801.1

3b. Wikimedia Commons contributors, "File:Saint george raphael.jpg," Wikimedia Commons, the free media repository, https://commons.wikimedia.org/w/index.php?title=File:Saint_george_raphael.jpg&oldid=191414176 (accessed November 25, 2017).

3c. Wikipedia contributors, "Medicine wheel," Wikipedia, The Free Encyclopedia, https://en.wikipedia.org/w/index.php?title=Medicine_wheel&oldid=791543246 (accessed November 25, 2017).

3d. Wikimedia Commons contributors, "File:IE expansion.png," Wikimedia Commons, the free media repository, https://commons.wikimedia.org/w/index.php?title=File:IE_expansion.png&oldid=268425866 (accessed January 4, 2018).

The Pyramid

4a. Wikimedia Commons contributors, "File:Kheops-Pyramid.jpg," Wikimedia Commons, the free media repository, https://commons.wikimedia.org/w/index.php?title=File:Kheops-Pyramid.jpg&oldid=191100215 (accessed November 26, 2017).

4c. Wikimedia Commons contributors, "File:Borobudur Temple.jpg," Wikimedia Commons, the free media repository, https://commons.wikimedia.org/w/index.php?title=File:Borobudur_Temple.jpg&oldid=218790683 (accessed November 26, 2017).

4d. Wikipedia contributors, "Chartres Cathedral," Wikipedia, The Free Encyclopedia, https://en.wikipedia.org/w/index.php?title=Chartres_Cathedral&oldid=811740369 (accessed November 25, 2017).

The Radiant Axes

5b. Wikimedia Commons contributors, "File:McMillan Plan.jpg," Wikimedia Commons, the free media repository, https://commons.wikimedia.org/w/index.php?title=File:McMillan_Plan.jpg&oldid=256524832 (accessed November 25, 2017).

The Grid

6c. Wikimedia Commons contributors, "File:NYC-GRID-1811.png," Wikimedia Commons, the free media repository, https://commons.wikimedia.org/w/index.php?title=File:NYC-GRID-1811.png&oldid=207112965 (accessed November 25, 2017).

6d. Wikimedia Commons contributors, "File:NewYorkSeagram 04.30.2008.JPG," Wikimedia Commons, the free media repository, https://commons.wikimedia.org/w/index.php?title=File:NewYorkSeagram_04.30.2008.JPG&oldid=105408015 (accessed November 25, 2017).

About Mimi Lobell

Mimi studied architecture at the University of Pennsylvania with some of the leading architects of her time, worked in the offices of prominent architects, and was a professor of architecture at Pratt Institute in Brooklyn, New York.

She was born Miriam Louise Comings in the Midwest on July 18, 1942 and died on April 7, 2001 in New York after a brief illness. She grew up in farm country in Illinois and Indiana. Her father was a professor of chemical engineering, and later a department chair and then a dean. Her mother was college-educated and a-stay-at-home housewife, although she sold real estate, taught speed-reading, and at one point started a home day-care center so that Mimi would have playmates. Mimi had two brothers, seven and nine years older.

During WW II Mimi's parents had a large victory garden and they were surrounded by cornfields. As a child Mimi would sit on the top of her slide (built by her father, since such things could not be bought during the war), look over the hedge at the Pegasus on the sign of a nearby Mobil gas station, and imagine stories of mythology and travels to far away places. Her life became rich with both. Her parents took her on car trips throughout the U.S. and sent her off to a school in Switzerland during her junior year of high school. She traveled all over the world, usually to present papers and attend conferences or to look at architecture and archaeological sites, including to Austria, Belgium, Brussels, Canada, Costa Rica, Denmark, England, France, Germany, India, Indonesia, Ireland, Italy, Malta, Mexico, the Netherlands, Norway, Russia, Scotland, Spain, Sweden, Switzerland, and throughout the United States. And she studied the world's cultures and mythologies and their impacts on architecture.

Mimi's high school junior year in Europe came about because her father was on a Fulbright and she and her parents traveled in Europe the summer before her father's teaching job started, with her mother seeing to it that they visited museums and cathedrals. When the summer ended her parents put Mimi on a train to Switzerland for school. Traveling alone for the first time, and then finding herself in a school full of older army brats gave Mimi a sense of confidence that lasted the rest of her life.

Mimi attended Middlebury College (choosing it in part because she could stay in a French speaking dorm) where she majored in art history and philosophy and transferred to the University of Pennsylvania to study architecture. Her professors at Penn included Edmund Bacon, Denise Scott Brown, Robert Geddes, Romaldo Giurgola, Ian McHarg, G. Holmes Perkins, and Robert Venturi. Louis Kahn was at Penn and she watched many of his juries. While at Penn, she married John Lobell, a fellow student.

Mimi and John moved to New York where she worked in several architectural offices. At Kahn and Jacobs she worked on an airport for Buffalo and the Minskoff office building in Manhattan, among other projects. In Marcel Breuer's office she worked on the Grand Coulee Dam Third Power Plant among other projects. (At the time very few architects were women. Occasionally, upon telling someone that she was an architect, she would be asked, "Oh, do you do houses?" She would reply, "No, I am working on the Grand Coulee Dam Third Power Plant.") At John Johansen's office she worked on Roosevelt Island Housing, designing a complex skip-corridor scheme. She became a registered architect in 1974 at a time when less than two percent of registered architects were women. She passed all of the exams in one sitting, which very few people do.

In the late 1960s she became involved in the New York art scene in projects challenging social norms, and in the women's movement in architecture. She was one of the originators of an exhibit at the Brooklyn Museum in 1977 titled "Women in American Architecture." She co-founded the Alliance of Women in Architecture and The Archive of Women in Architecture and briefly explored with several colleagues creating an office of women architects.

In the 1960s she also began various spiritual studies including Tai Chi with Professor Cheng Man-ch'ing, and Buddhism at the New York study center of Chogyam Trungpa. She pursued other Buddhist studies and also studied Shamanism with Michael Harner.

She attended dozens of lectures by Joseph Campbell, read the works of Carl Jung and attended various lectures at the New York Jung Foundation, and pursued on her own studies in the history of the Goddess, particularly in Neolithic and ancient cultures. She became a member of a Goddess study group, she associated with Marija Gimbutas, Cristina Biaggi, and other scholars interested in the

Goddess, and she attended conferences and presented papers with them.

Thus Mimi became heavily involved in architecture, art, women's issues, social norms, and spirituality. Not wanting to live schizophrenically, she sought to bring all of these together in one synthesis, which she began with the design of a contemporary Goddess Temple in 1975 that was extensively published, and contributions to a Goddess Mound by Cristina Biaggi. All of this led her to a mythological and symbolic approach to architecture that informed her teaching and led to numerous articles and to this book, *Spatial Archetypes*.

Encountering glass ceilings in the offices in which she worked and realizing that despite being one of the most competent people in these offices she was not going to be made an associate, Mimi started teaching at the School of Architecture at Pratt Institute in 1972, becoming full time in 1976, only the second women at the School to receive a full time appointment and tenure. She taught there until her death in April 2001.

Mimi's contributions to Pratt were extensive. She served on many committees and was Chair of Curriculum in the School of Architecture (equivalent to a departmental chair). She taught Architectural History and various electives including Architectural Alternatives, Non-Western Architecture, and Myth and Symbol in Architecture. For a brief time she taught Life Support Systems, an engineering course. The Architectural History sequence was team-taught, and Mimi typically gave the lectures on Paleolithic, Neolithic, Egypt, Mesopotamia, India, Buddhism, China, Japan, Pre-Columbian American, and Gothic architecture.

She also taught First Year Design and Advanced Design (advance design at Pratt for most of the time Mimi was teaching combined third, fourth, and fifth year students) with various themes. In the years before her death, students in her Advanced Design studio designed "a place of a creative person." "A place" might mean anything from a studio for that person in their time to a park today in their honor. The "person" might be anyone in whom the student was interested, from a basketball star to a reggae singer to a science fiction writer. Her studios used various techniques, including guided imaginations, to access the students' unconscious creativity, that produced remarkable results, in part because of Mimi's abilities as a teacher and in part due to the students' enthusiasm because they were dealing with things that interested them. And because Mimi herself was an excellent designer. Occasionally she would set up a drafting table and say to her students, "Ok, chose a building." (They might arrive at a library.) Then she would ask, "How large? For what kind of community? What is the site like?" She would then work for several hours, explaining to the students what she was doing as she proceeded, and produce preliminary designs for a building.

Mimi never stopped exploring. Outside of Pratt, she pursued interests in astronomy (she owned a good telescope, collected astronomy books and star charts, and studied the impact of cosmologies on architecture and astronomical alignments of ancient architecture), needlework (she sewed her own clothes when she was younger and mastered various forms of knitting and crocheting), and playing the harp among many others things. She lived a rich life in which she was able to study, travel, and teach. Many of her students remember her to this day as an important influence in their lives.

John Lobell

Résumé of Mimi Lobell, Architect

[This résumé is from 2000, the year before Mimi died, so "present" here refers to 2000. Mimi took great pride in her résumé and formatted it carefully. That formatting is lost here. You can see much of the work referred to in this résumé in the Archive for Mimi Lobell, The Architectural Archives of the University of Pennsylvania, Meyerson Hall, 102, Philadelphia, PA 19104-6311. Telephone: 215-898-8323. ~ John Lobell.]

Address
New York, NY 00000 USA
Tel 212-000-0000 • Cell 917-000-0000
Fax 212-000-0000

Pratt Institute School of Architecture
200 Willoughby Avenue
Brooklyn, NY 11205
E-mail: MimiLobell@aol.com

2000 Résumé

EDUCATION

1966
Master of Architecture. University of Pennsylvania, Graduate School of Fine Arts. Professors included Edmund Bacon, Denise Scott Brown, Robert Geddes, Romaldo Giurgola, Ian McHarg, G. Holmes Perkins, and Robert Venturi.

1963
Bachelor of Arts, major in architecture. University of Pennsylvania.

1959–61
Middlebury College, Middlebury, VT.
Majors in art history and philosophy.

1966–present
Supplementary Studies: See below.

ARCHITECTURE LICENSE REGISTRATION

1974
New York State

552 *Spatial Archetypes*

TEACHING EXPERIENCE

Pratt Institute, School of Architecture
Brooklyn, New York

Professor with tenure since 1986.
Establishing the Myth & Symbol in Architecture Study Center, 1995-present.
Chairperson of Curriculum (equivalent to departmental chairperson), 1977–80.
Full-time since 1976.
Visiting and adjunct, 1972–76.

REQUIRED COURSES
1972–present
Architectural Design Studio
1st through 5th years. Themes and projects have included a Place for a Creative Person, Cosmological Architecture, Archæoastronomy Center in Uxmal, Tibet House in New York, United Nations Planetary Forum, the New York Open Center, an Ideal School, and Transforming the Villa Rotunda for the Third Millennium.

1984–present
History of Architecture
Team-taught required sequence. Developed and give lectures on Palæolithic, Neolithic, African, Egyptian, Near Eastern, Islamic, Gothic, Pre-Columbian, Indian, Chinese, and Japanese architecture from historical, cultural, and symbolic perspectives. Also taught sections 1984-1992.

1976–78
Life Support Systems
Lectures and sections in team-taught course on mechanical equipment, energy conservation, etc.

ELECTIVE COURSES
1984–present
Myth & Symbol in Architecture
Slide lecture/seminar course based on my cross-cultural research on spatial archetypes in world architecture from prehistory to the present. Covers the worldviews, art, and architecture of palæolihtic hunter-gatherers (Sensitive Chaos); Neolithic farming cultures (Great Round); warlike hierarchical chieftainships (Four Quarters); nation and city-states (Pyramid); empires (Radiant Axes); international, post-imperialistic, commercial-industrial networks (Grid); and the death of cultures (Dissolution).

1976–84
History of Non-Western Art & Architecture
Precursor to the Myth & Symbol in Architecture course.

1972–77
Architectural Alternatives
Course I developed to visit and interview architects practicing in non-traditional ways. Guests included Peter Eisenman, François D'Allegret, Haus Rucher, Arthur Drexler, Jaquelin Robertson, Rem Koolhaus, Juan Downey, Ron Shiffman, Romaldo Giurgola, and many others. Cited in Design & Environment, Spring '74.

COMMITTEES
1993–95
Board of Trustees Committee on Honorary Degrees and Awards

1991–92
Peer Evaluation Committee, School of Architecture

1984–89
Pratt Journal of Architecture Advisory Board (Volumes 1 and 2 published by Rizzoli, 1985, 1989)

1982–83
Faculty Council (all-Institute)

1987–88
Presidential Task Force on the Long Range Plan for Pratt Institute
School of Architecture Curriculum Committee

1984–85
Search Committee for department chair

1981–82
Faculty Profiles Editorial Advisor

1980–81
Board of Trustees Nominating Committee

1978–80
Committee on the Liberal Arts and Professional Education

1975–76
School of Architecture Advisory Board Selection Committee
School of Architecture Student/Faculty Council
NAAB Accreditation Planning Committee

1974–75
School of Architecture Committee on Women in Architecture

Teaching at the C. G. Jung Foundation of New York
1985
Spatial Archetypes, an eight week course

1983
Myth, Symbol, and Architecture, an eight week course

Architectural Design Juries

1976–present
Pratt Institute: Studios of Livio Dimitriu, Juan Downey, and others

1983
Yale University: Studio of Alec Purves

1978
New Jersey Institute of Technology: Studio of Susana Torre and Leslie Weisman

1977
Columbia University: Master's Thesis Studio of Alex Kouzmanoff

University of Pennsylvania: Master's Studio of Anne Tyng

GRANTS, FELLOWSHIPS, SABBATICALS

1997
Ligurian Study Center for the Arts & Humanities, Bogliasco, Italy.
Invited by the sponsoring Bogliasco Foundation as Artist-in-Residence, March 1997.

1996
Pratt Institute, grant of $2000 for the Myth & Symbol in Architecture Study Center

1993, 1986
Pratt Institute, Sabbaticals

1992
Graham Foundation, grant of $5000 toward illustrations for my book on Spatial Archetypes

1964–66
Augustus Trask Ashton Fellowship, for graduate studies at the University of Pennsylvania

PUBLICATIONS

BOOK-IN-PROGRESS

1976–present
Spatial Archetypes: The Hidden Patterns of Psyche and Civilization (working title) Manuscript substantially completed. [This refers to this book.]

Contributions to Books

1997
Gender-Biased Paradigms in Archæology. From the Realm of the Ancestors, Essays in Honor of Marija Gimbutas. Joan Marler, editor. Manchester, CT: Knowledge, Ideas & Trends, Inc.

1989
The Buried Treasure: Women's Ancient Architectural Heritage. Architecture: A Place for Women. Ellen Perry Berkeley, editor; Matilda McQuaid, associate editor. Washington, D.C.: Smithsonian Institution Press, pp. 139–57.

1986
The Philadelphia School: An Architectural Philosophy. Louis I. Kahn, l'uomo, il maestro, Alessandra Latour, editor. Rome: Edizioni Kappa, pp. 381–397. Excerpts from *The Philadelphia School*, a manuscript co-authored with John Lobell.

1975
Architecture and the Body Cosmos. Catalog of Sexual Consciousness, Saul Braun, editor. New York: Grove Press, pp. 264–65.

The Goddess. *Catalog of Sexual Consciousness*, pp. 266–67.

1974
Pickin' Up the Pieces: Of Universal Order and Architecture. *On Site On Energy*, SITE, Inc., pp. 118–123.

The future of women in architecture. Essay in *Women in the Year 2000*, Maggie Tripp, editor. New York: Arbor House.

Published Articles and Essays

1994
The Buried Treasure. Woman of Power magazine, Issue 23, pp. 36–41.
Adapted from article originally published in *Architecture: A Place for Women*, see above.

1986
Ancient Religions in the Context of Cultural Types. Archæology and Fertility Cult in the Ancient Mediterranean, Anthony Bonanno, editor. Amsterdam: B.R. Grüner, pp. 43–54.

Archetypal Worldviews in the Development of Complex Societies. World Archæological Congress, Peter Ucko, National Secretary; H.R.H. The Prince of Wales, Patron. London: Allen & Unwin.

Male-Biased Paradigms in Archæology. World Archæological Congress. London: Allen & Unwin. Invited paper for the Special Session on The History of Pre- and Proto-Historic Archæology arranged by Dr. Colin Renfrew.

1985
Ancient Solstice Sites and Rites. Sun Times, June 21. New Wilderness Foundation.

1985
A Conversation with John Hejduk. Pratt Journal of Architecture: Architecture and Abstraction, Vol. 1. New York: Rizzoli, pp. 46–49. Co-authored interview.

1983
Spatial Archetypes. Revision, Vol. 6, No. 2, pp. 69–82.

Vastu Purusha House. Ear Magazine, Vol. 8, No. 3, p. 5.

1978
Temples of the Great Goddess. Heresies, Issue 5, pp. 32–39.

The Goddess Temple. Chrysalis, No. 6.

1977
Spatial Archetypes. Quadrant: Journal of the C.G. Jung Foundation for Analytical Psychology, Vol. 10, No. 2, pp. 5–44.

1976
Kahn, Penn, and the Philadelphia School. Oppositions 4, Institute for Architecture and Urban Studies, pp. 63–64.

Architecture for the Poor. East West Journal, June, pp. 52–53. Review of Hassan Fathy's book of the same title.

Building the Goddess Temple. East West Journal, June, pp. 34–35.

1975
The Goddess Temple. Journal of Architectural Education, Vol. XXIX, No. 1, Humanist Issues in Architecture, Kent Bloomer, editor. Association of Collegiate Schools of Architecture (ACSA), pp. 20–23.

The Feminine Principle in the History of Architecture. ACSA Teachers' Seminar Catalog.

Pickin' Up the Pieces: Of Universal Order and Architecture. East West Journal, February, pp. 14–17. (Reprinted from On Site On Energy, see Contributions to Books above.)

1974
Symbol, Myth, and Meaning in Architecture. JAE Pedagogical Catalog 2, ACSA.

Publication/Discussions Of My Work

2000
In The Footsteps of the Goddess. Cristina Biaggi, editor. Manchester, CT: Knowledge, Ideas & Trends, Inc. Interview on Oracular Architecture and my design studio at Pratt.

Architecture Inside Out. Karen Frank, Bianca Lepori, et al., editors. New York: John Wiley & Son.

1996
Ecopsychology Newsletter, Christopher Castle, editor. Fall/Winter, Ecopsychology Institute (Theodore Roszak), California State University. My "Riding the Tiger" Design Studio at Pratt.

1994
The Power of Feminist Art. New York: Harry N. Abrams, Inc., pp. 128, 177.
The Goddess Temple.

1989
The Once and Future Goddess. Elinor W. Gadon. San Francisco: Harper & Row, pp. 345–46.
The Goddess Mound project.

1987
Antiquity Journal. Christopher Chippindale, editor. Vol. 61, No. 231, March, pp. 7–9. Review of the Goddess Mound proposal.

1986
Myth, Symbolism and Rubber. Karen Dean. Rubberstampmadness, April, pp. 3–5.
My rubberstamp art based on archæological, architectural, and mythic images.

1981
Alliance of Women in Architecture. Built by Women.
Roosevelt Island Housing for which I was senior designer in the office of John Johansen, FAIA.

1980
La Réemergence de la Grande Déesse. Gloria Feman Orenstein. Sorcières, Issue 20. Translation of Heresies essay below.

1978
The Reemergence of the Archetype of the Great Goddess in Art by Contemporary Women. Gloria Feman Orenstein. Heresies 5, Issue 5, pp. 74–84.
The Goddess Temple.

1977
Progressive Architecture, April.
The Vastu Purusha House.

Women in American Architecture. Susana Torre, editor. New York: Watson-Guptill/Whitney Library of Design.
The Goddess Temple.

1976
Unbuilt America. Alison Sky and Michelle Stone, editors. SITE, Inc., New York: McGraw-Hill, p. 167.
The Goddess Temple.

Living in one Room. Jon Naar and Molly Siple. New York: Vintage Books, pp. 117, 134–135. Interiors of my former New York apartment.

1975
Architectural Awards: What Aren't They Telling Us? Regina Baraban. Designer Magazine, July, pp. 12–13.
Interview.

1974
The Middle-Class Minority. Neil Kleinman. Design & Environment Magazine, Spring.
The Architectural Alternatives elective course I developed at Pratt.

1965
Progressive Architecture. The Psychological Dimension of Architectural Space. April, pp. 158–167. Prototypical mental hospital I designed at Penn in Robert Geddes' studio with guest critic Dr. Humphrey Osmond.

Citations Of My Work In Works By Others
(partial list)

1995
Mann, Nicolas. *His Story: Masculinity in the Post-Patriarchal World.* St Paul, MN: Llewellyn, pp. 126, 141, 228, 243, 293.

1992
Arrien, Angeles. *Signs of Life*. Sonoma: Arcus, pp. 85, 90.
1989
Wilshire, Donna. Gender Stereotypes and Spatial Archetypes. Anima: The Journal of Human Experience, Vol. 15, No. 2, 1989; pp. 77–86.
1983Lippard, Lucy R. Overlay: Contemporary Art and the Art of Prehistory. New York: Pantheon.

1981
Waters, Frank. *Mountain Dialogues*. Athens, OH: Sage/Swallow Press, 1981; p. 91.

LECTURES, CONFERENCES AND SYMPOSIA

Lectures
All are slide-illustrated lectures unless otherwise noted

1996
Dallas Institute for the Humanities & Culture, Dallas, TX
Feminine Architecture lecture/workshop

1995
Esalen Institute, Big Sur, CA
A Mythological Toolbox, March 26-31. The Joseph Campbell Foundation's annual six-day workshop commemorating Campbell's birthday, when he traditionally gave talks at Esalen.

Riding the Tiger: Creativity by Design
Mandalas (slide presentation)
Animal Powers (slide presentation)

Pacific Graduate Institute, Santa Barbara, CA
Spatial Archetypes

1994
Mythos Institute, Frontenac, MN
Joseph Campbell and the Tarot

Esalen Institute, Big Sur, CA
A Mythological Toolbox, March 20–25. Joseph Campbell Foundation.
Joseph Campbell and the Tarot
Mandalas (slide presentation)
Archetypal Imagery (slide presentation)
Animal Powers (slide presentation)
Masks (slide presentation)

1993
Tibetan Buddhist Center of Philadelphia, Philadelphia, PA
Center established by friends and students of the Venerable Lobsang Samten.
The Buddhist Stupa

The World Parliament on Religion, Chicago, IL
Conference celebrating the 100th anniversary of the first World Parliament on Religion held during the 1893 Chicago World's Fair.

Mandalas (slide presentation)
Archetypal Imagery (slide presentation)

Esalen Institute, Big Sur, CA
A Mythological Toolbox, March 21-26. Joseph Campbell Foundation.

Spatial Archetypes and the Emergence of the Heroic Monomyth
The Chakra System
Archetypal Imagery (slide presentation)
Mandalas (slide presentation)

1992
Namgyal Monastic University, Dharamsala, India
Monastery of the Dalai Lama.
The Buddhist Stupa

Joseph Campbell Foundation Inauguration, Smithsonian Museum of Natural History, Washington, D.C.
Archetypal Imagery (slide presentation)

1991-92
New York Open Center, New York
Slide lectures in my ongoing Secrets of World Architecture series

The Invisible Architecture of Shamanism
Spatial Archetypes: The Worldviews of Psyche & Civilization
Borobudur: Mount Meru in the Ring of Fire

1991
Long Island AIA Chapter, New York Institute of Technology, Old Westbury, NY
Lecture accompanying the opening of an exhibition of work by Long Island women architects organized by Christine Friello.

The Buried Treasure: Women's Ancient Architectural Heritage

Himalayan Institute, Honesdale, PA
Spatial Archetypes

1989–90
New York Open Center
Slide lectures in my Secrets of World Architecture series
Ancient Egypt
The Dogon of Mali
The Cosmic Mountain of Sumer & Shamanism
The Hindu Temple
The Buddhist Stupa
Pueblos and Moundbuilders
Land of the Feathered Serpent
The Inca and Their Ancestors
Sacred Places of the Great Goddess

1989
Dallas Institute for the Humanities, Dallas, TX
Spatial Archetypes

Royal Ontario Museum, Toronto, Canada
Goddess Festival

Sacred Places of the Great Goddess

Spotted Fawn's West Coast Moot, Sonoma, CA
Explorations of Sacred Architecture: Spatial Archetypes
Goddess Temples

1988
New York Open Center
The Chakras of Architecture
Goddesses, Stars, and Megaliths
Spatial Archetypes (all-day workshop)
Spirit in Architecture (all-day workshop with John Lobell)

1988
Jacques Marchais Center of Tibetan Art, Staten Island, NY
Symbolism of Buddhist Architecture
University of North Carolina, Department of Interior Design, Greensboro, NC
Spatial Archetypes
The Five Levels of Architecture

1986
Cooper-Hewitt Museum, New York, NY
Saturday Symposium on Archæoastronomy
Spatial Archetypes

University of Illinois, Department of Architecture, Champaign, IL
Spatial Archetypes

562 *Spatial Archetypes*

1985
New Wilderness Foundation, New York, NY
Archæoastronomy

1983
Yale University, School of Architecture, New Haven, CT
Spatial Archetypes

1980
Esalen Institute, Big Sur, CA
Spatial Archetypes

1978
University of Pennsylvania, Graduate School of Fine Arts, Philadelphia, PA
Spatial Archetypes

1976
University of Kansas, Department of Architecture, Lawrence, KS
The Gains and Losses of the Modern Movement

Western Michigan University, Kalamazoo, MI
Lecture and workshop introducing architecture to non-architects

A.I.R. Gallery, New York, NY
Goddess Temples (lecture and workshop)

1975
Columbia University, Graduate School of Architecture and Planning, New York, NY
Wednesday Night Lecture Series
Archetypal Architecture's Celebrations of the Feminine

Columbia University, Graduate School of Architecture and Planning
Dark Side of the Moon Lecture Series
Architecture as Astronomical Observatory

Carleton University, Department of Architecture, Ottawa, Canada
Architecture as a Spiritual Path

Lindisfarne Association, Southampton, NY
Three Lectures on the Feminine Principle

1974
Architectural League of New York
Young Architects Series

The Vastu Purusha House (see Design Projects below)

Conferences and Symposia

2000
Blacklines, Brooklyn, NY
Bridging the Gap between Education, Theory and Practice Conference. Session on History and the Perspectives from Design fields: African Architecture and Its Global Connections
Panel member

1997
Woman and Earth, St. Petersburg, Russia
International conference.
The Buried Treasure: The Goddess in Archæology

New York Open Center, New York
In the Realm of the Ancestors, panel on the influence of the late archæologist Marija Gimbutas, with Joan Marler (moderator), Cristina Biaggi, and myself.
The Buried Treasure: Women's Ancient Architectural Heritage

1989
Rutgers University, Brunswick, NJ
The Artist as Mystic—The Mystic as Artist, panel organized by Rafael Montanez Ortiz in Rutger's International Symposium on Art and the Invisible Reality USA
1989
The Chakras & the Creative Process

1988
Children's Museum of Manhattan, New York
Advisory panel on the opening exhibition in the museum's new quarters on Amsterdam Avenue
Spatial Archetypes

St. John the Divine, New York
Architecture for a Global Community Symposium sponsored by the Center for Peace Through Culture
Keynote Speech

1986
World Archæological Congress, Southampton, England
Dr. Peter Ucko, National Secretary; held at the University of Southampton
Archetypal Worldviews in the Development of Complex Societies, paper
Male-Biased Paradigms in Archæology, paper invited by Dr. Colin Renfrew for a special session on The History of Pre-and Proto-Historic Archæology

Urban Center, New York
Panel in conjunction with an exhibition celebrating the Tenth Anniversary of the Alliance of Women in Architecture, which I co-founded (see Professional Affiliations)
Women in Architectural Education

A.I.R. Gallery, New York
All-day seminar that I organized, with guest speakers Martin Brennan and Cristina Biaggi, Ph.D.
Megaliths, Stars, and Goddesses

1985
University of Malta, Valletta, Malta
International Conference on Archæology and Fertility Cult in the Ancient Mediterranean
Ancient Religions in the Context of Cultural Types

Women's Caucus for Art, New York
Symposium on The Great Goddess: Archaic Images and as She Appears in the Art of Contemporary Women Artists, held at Soho 20 Gallery
The Goddess Mound

1984
University of Berlin, Berlin, Germany
Congress of the Union Internationale des Femmes Architectes
Spatial Archetypes

A.I.R. Gallery, New York
Panel on Consciousness: The Artist and the Shaman, moderated by Alan Gussow
Shamanic Origins of Architectural Archetypes

1983
University of Pennsylvania, Graduate School of Fine Arts, Philadelphia, PA
Symposium on The Design of Fitting Environments

The Philadelphia School (with John Lobell)

1980
Interiors Magazine, New York
Panel on Energy
Energy East & West

Women's Caucus for Art, New York
Panel in the Third Annual Symposium, held at Marymount Manhattan College
20 Years Before the Millennium: The Responsibility of Women in Art

Association for Humanistic Psychology, Philadelphia, PA
Annual Eastern Regional Conference
Transpersonal Consciousness Workshop

1979
World Symposium on Humanity, Toronto, Canada
Architecture
Spatial Archetypes

1978
Networks: Women in Architecture Conference, New York
Held at Columbia University's School of Architecture & Planning
Curricular Issues Workshop

1977
Brooklyn Museum, Brooklyn, NY
Symposium in conjunction with the Women in American Architecture exhibit based on the Archive of Women in Architecture, which I co-founded
Panel member

College Art Association Annual Meeting, Los Angeles
Panel that I organized and moderated in the Women's Caucus for Art Program, with guest speakers Gloria Feman Orenstein, José Argüelles, Z. Budapest, and Mary Beth Edelson.
The Goddess in Art

1976
United Nations Conference on Human Settlements/Habitat Forum, Vancouver, BC
The Spiritual Dimensions of World Architecture

1975
Boston Architectural Center, Boston, MA
Conference on Women in Architecture and Planning
Workshop leader

1975
ACSA Annual Teachers' Seminar, Lincoln, NE
Held at the University of Nebraska
Delegate from Pratt Institute, lecturer, and workshop leader

International Business Design Seminars, New York
Panel on Futurism with Bill Katavolos and others
The Importance of the Past

1974
Washington University, St. Louis, MO
Women in Architecture Conference
Panel member and workshop leader

Radio and Television Interviews

2000
WBAI/FM, New York
Interviewed by Carletta Joy Walker on Oracular Architecture and my design studio at Pratt.

1985
WBAI/FM, New York
Co-interviewed Joseph Campbell

1975–88
WBAI/FM, New York
Interviewed by Margo Adler, Patricia Hunt Perry, Gary Null, and others.

1985
CBC, Canada
Interviewed by Merlin Stone for series on the Great Goddess

1979
PBS Television, PBS and WOSU of Columbus, OH
Interviewed by Patricia Hunt Perry in five part series "Prospects for Humanity"

1974
WOR/TV, New York
Interviewed by Eleanor Guggenheimer and Gloria Rojas on "Straight Talk" with other founders of the Alliance of Women in Architecture

PROFESSIONAL EXPERIENCE
(Construction completed on all works except those designated as projects)

Architecture License Registration
1974
New York State

1972–73
Donald Cromley, Architect, New York
Associate
Madsen residence, Roxbury, CT, and other projects.

1970–72
John M. Johansen, FAIA, New York
Senior Designer
Roosevelt Island Housing, New York, sponsored by the Urban Development Corporation. Design and coordination of 900 apartments, two schools, a day-care center, recreational facilities, and retail space.

1968–70
Marcel Breuer & Associates, New York
Architectural Designer. Member of design and production teams for:
Cleveland Museum of Art
Grand Coulee Dam Third Power Plant
Health & Human Services Office Building, the Mall, Washington, DC
High School project, Roxbury, MA

IBM Headquarters project, Armonk, NY

1966–68
Kahn & Jacobs, Architects, New York
Architectural Designer (design department headed by Der Scutt). Work included:
Barlow School buildings, Amenia, NY (partially completed)
Buffalo International Airport project
Minskoff Office Building and Theaters, New York
Office buildings in New York, Cleveland, and Puerto Rico
Pennsylvania Avenue Commission Feasibility Studies, Washington, DC

1963–65
Richard Phillips Fox, A.I.A., Newark, DE
Architectural Designer, summers.
Richard Phillips Fox Residence
Housing for the Elderly and Low-Income Housing
Newark Cinema
University of Delaware Stadium

DESIGN PROJECTS
(All are conceptual projects)

1985
The Goddess Mound
In collaboration with and at the invitation of artist Cristina Biaggi, Ph.D.
Published in Antiquity and The Once and Future Goddess. Exhibited at SOHO 20 Gallery and Thorpe Intermedia Gallery.

1978
Waterside Labyrinth, New York
Proposal for a full scale replica of the Chartres Labyrinth in the plaza at Waterside.
Presented to and accepted by Doris Friedman and Davis & Brody, Architects.

1977
Arcosanti Labyrinth, Arcosanti, AZ
Proposal invited by Karin Bacon for a participatory art event to recreate a stone Cretan-style labyrinth.

1975
The Goddess Temple, Rocky Mountains, CO
An architectural celebration of the feminine principle. In collaboration with Jan Clanton.
Published in Women in American Architecture, Unbuilt America, Heresies, Chrysalis, Sorciéres, East West Journal. Exhibited at the Brooklyn Museum, SOHO 20 Gallery, and other shows.

1974
The Vastu Purusha House, East coast seashore, USA
Design for a retreat based on Kundalini yoga.
Published in Progressive Architecture, Ear Magazine, and The Catalog of Sexual Consciousness. Exhibited at the Urban Center in New York and Pratt Institute.

EXHIBITIONS

1975–present
Pratt Institute, Brooklyn, NY, faculty exhibits
Various design projects and buildings

1986
SOHO 20 Gallery, New York , Public Vision/Public Monuments exhibit
The Goddess Temple
The Goddess Mound

1984
Thorpe Intermedia Gallery, Sparkill, NY, Architecture/Sculpture, Sculpture/Architecture The Goddess Temple

1982
The Urban Center, New York, Alliance of Women in Architecture Tenth Anniversary Exhibition
The Vastu Purusha House

1977
The Brooklyn Museum, Brooklyn, NY, (also toured other U.S. museums for two years) Women in American Architecture exhibit, Susana Torre, curator.
The Goddess Temple

1970
Architectural League of New York, Your Worst Work show, Les Levine, curator
Theoretical Project

PROFESSIONAL AFFILIATIONS

1998-present
Blacklines
Advisory Board member

1989–1994
Joseph Campbell Foundation
Member
Presenter at annual "Mythological Toolbox" at Esalen Institute (see Lectures)

Prepared slide presentations for various events
1988–present
New York Open Center
Member
Faculty member: Secrets of World Architecture Series and other lectures & workshops
Sponsored Tibetan Buddhist monk, the Venerable Lobsang Samten, as Scholar-in-Residence, Fall 1990

1990–present
Sacred Sites International
Advisory Board member

1980–present
Center for Myth & Symbol in Architecture
Founder and director. Maintain an 8,000 volume private library, a collection of 60,000 slides, a 1000 name mailing list, and various research materials.

1967–1992
Architectural League of New York
Member, 1967–1992
Officer, 1970–73
Board Member, 1970–76
Co-founded the Alliance of Women in Architecture and the Archive of Women in Architecture (see below)

1984–85
New Wilderness Foundation
Advisory Committee on 1985 Summer Solstice Celebration in Central Park

1984
A.I.R Gallery
Board of Advisors for exhibit on women in architecture titled Detail: The Special Task

1973
Archive of Women in Architecture
Co-founded through the Architectural League of New York during my tenure as an officer and board member.
The archive collected work from a thousand American women architects, and, with Susana Torre as curator, produced the exhibit Women in American Architecture, which opened at the Brooklyn Museum in 1977 and toured U.S. museums for two years. The book Women in American Architecture, edited by Torre (Watson-Guptill/Whitney Library of Design, 1977), is based on the exhibit and archive.

570 *Spatial Archetypes*

1972–85
Alliance of Women in Architecture
Co-founded through the Architectural League.
Membership organization for women in architecture and related design fields. Offered registration courses and business seminars; sponsored publications, tours, exhibits; etc.

1970–73
Fine Arts Federation of New York
Delegate from the Architectural League

1980–present
Other Memberships
Tibet House
Foundation for Shamanic Studies
Survival International
C.G. Jung Foundation
Archæological Institute of America
Various museums

RESEARCH TRAVEL

(highlights, not including contemporary architecture in Europe & North America)

1997
Russia
The Hermitage and other palaces, museums, and architecture in St. Petersburg and Novgorod

1992
India
Moghul and Hindu art, architecture, and observatories in Delhi, Agra, Jaipur, and Amber
British colonial city planning (Lutyens' New Delhi)
Tibetan Buddhist temples, monasteries, nunneries, stupas, and cultural centers in Dharamsala

Scotland
Ancestral family castles throughout the Central Highlands
Clava Cairns megalithic ruins

1990
Indonesia
Bali: arts, crafts, and architecture in Ubud, Singaraja, Besakih, and elsewhere
Java: Borobudur Buddhist Stupa, Yogyakarta, and Hindu temples in the area

1986
England
Stonehenge, Avebury, Silbury, West Kennett Long Barrow, Wayland's Smithy, Maiden Castle, and many other megalithic sites throughout Southwestern England from London to Land's End.
Oxford University, Ashmolean Museum
Lutyens' Drogo Castle, Dartmoor
Bath: Roman architecture
English Gothic architecture at Salisbury, Wells, Glastonbury, etc.

1985
Malta & Gozo
Neolithic Goddess temples and tombs
Walled medieval towns & cities

Italy
Rome: Roman, Renaissance, and Baroque architecture
Cumae: Cave of the Cumaean Sibyl, Apollo Temple

1984
Ireland
Boyne Valley: Newgrange, Knowth, and Dowth Passage Mounds and other megalithic sites
Loughcrew Mountains: Slieve na Cuiligne and other megalithic sites
Tara and surroundings: seat of sovereignty, Maeve's Mound, and other Bronze and Iron Age Celtic sites
Kells: early medieval Christian Monastery
Dublin: Book of Kells at Trinity College Library

1981
Mexico
Chichen Itza, Uxmal, and other Mayan sites in the Yucatan

1976
Teotihuacan
Museum of Anthropology, Mexico City

United States
Hopewell and Adena Earth Mounds in Ohio, West Virginia, Indiana, and Illinois
Anasazi, Mogollan, Hohokam, and Sinaqua cliff-dwellings and pueblos in the Southwest

Costa Rica
San José: Pre-Columbian museums
Guanacaste Province: Pre-Columbian burial sites and nature preserves

1972
Canada

Studied and collected Eskimo art in Toronto
1967
Canada
Montreal: Expo 67

1957–58
Europe
Cathedrals, churches, palaces, castles, villas, gardens, ruins, etc. throughout Norway, Sweden, Denmark, Belgium, Brussels, the Netherlands, Germany, Austria, Switzerland, France, Italy, Spain, England, and Southern Scotland

Chesieres-sur-Ollon, Switzerland, attended Institute La Villan International School for one year

SUPPLEMENTARY STUDIES

BUDDHISM AND BUDDHIST EMPOWERMENTS

1992
Namgyal Monastic University
Member of an invited delegation led by the Venerable Lobsang Samten to the Dalai Lama's Namgyal Monastery, Dharamsala, India, for Tibetan New Year's celebrations at the end of 1991–The Year of Tibet.

1991
Kalachakra initiation, five day ceremony with His Holiness the Dalai Lama, New York City.

1990
Mandala of the Five Dakinis with Tsultrim Allione. A three-week retreat in Bali, Indonesia, which included the Simhamukha Dakini initiation and practice.

1989
Kalachakra initiation, two week course & empowerment ceremony with H.H. the Dalai Lama, Los Angeles.
1989–94
Other Empowerments: Green Tara, Red Tara, White Tara, Amatayus, and other initiations by Tibetan lamas.

COURSES & TEACHINGS ATTENDED

1988–94
Robert Thurman, Ph.D. Courses and lectures on Buddhist art and philosophy at the NY Open Center.

1988–92
Ven. Lobsang Samten of Namgyal Monastery. Courses on the Kalachakra Mandala

and Initiation, Lam Rim, Buddhist Meditation, and Tibetan Ritual Dance.
1989
H.H. the Dalai Lama. Preparatory Bodhisattva teachings for the Kalachakra Initiation in Los Angeles.

1970–72
Chögyam Trungpa Rinpoche and his senior students. Buddhist studies at the New York Dharmadhatu.

MYTHOLOGY

1972–87
Joseph Campbell Lectures
Attended 15 years of Campbell's quarterly 3-day lecture marathons at the Foundation for the Open Eye

FEMALE SPIRITUALITY

1975–present
Co-founder and member of an ongoing study group on the Great Goddess and female-centered civilizations that has included Cristina Biaggi (Habitations of the Goddess), Marija Gimbutas (Language of the Goddess, Civilization of the Goddess), Buffie Johnson (Lady of the Beasts),Vicki Noble (Motherpeace Tarot), Merlin Stone (When God was a Woman), Barbara Walker (The Women's Book of Myths & Secrets), Donna Wilshire (Maiden, Mother, Crone), and artists Mary Beth Edelson, Donna Henes, and Carolee Schneemann. The group formed the core of the Heresies Collective for the Great Goddess Issue #5.

ARCHÆOASTRONOMY

Conferences attended

1985
Ethnoastronomy Conference, Smithsonian Institution, Washington, DC. Organized by Dr. Anthony F. Aveni and colleagues.

1982
Ethnoastronomy and Archæoastronomy in the American Tropics conference, New York Academy of Sciences. Organized by Anthony F. Aveni and Gary Urton.

TAI CHI CHUAN

1970–72
Courses taken
Professor Cheng Man-ch'ing and his senior students in New York plus refresher courses and workshops with other teachers over the years.

SHAMANISM

Foundation for Shamanic Studies

1991–96
Experiment participant for Sandra Harner's Ph.D. dissertation research.

1987
Five-day Professional Training Course in Shamanic Counseling with Sandra Harner.

1982
Basic Course on Shamanic Journeying with Dr. Michael Harner.

1979–present
Others
Various lectures and workshops with Joan Halifax, Joseph Campbell, NY Open Center faculty, etc.

Made in the USA
Columbia, SC
30 October 2018

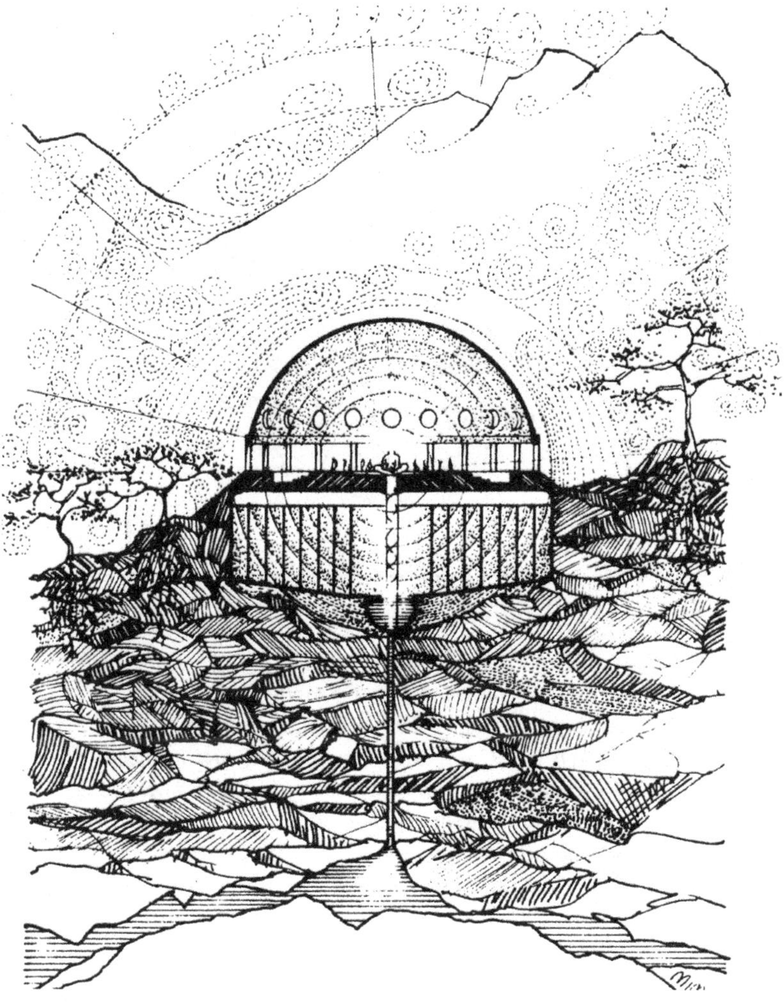

Labyrinth

Above and previous page: The Goddess Temple. Designed by Mimi Lobell in collaboration with Jan Clanton in 1975. It was intended for a site in the Rocky Mountains near Aspen Colorado. It is rich with symbols and presents a contemporary manifestation of traditional feminine rituals. The project was widely published and exhibited. This shows a plan of a labyrinth in the lower level of the Temple, while the previous page shows a section.

Cover image: View of the Ġgantija Temples on the island of Malta. Built in the form of the body of the Goddess, these temples were erected between 3600 and 2500 BC in the Neolithic Great Round period. Photo: Jonathan Beacom.

SPATIAL ARCHETYPES
The Hidden Patterns of Psyche and Civilization

Mimi Lobell

JXJ Publications